New Perspectives on Leadership

The International Library of Leadership

Editors: J. Thomas Wren
Associate Professor of Leadership Studies
Jepson School of Leadership Studies, University of Richmond, USA

Douglas A. Hicks
Associate Professor of Leadership Studies and Religion
Jepson School of Leadership Studies, University of Richmond, USA

Terry L. Price
Associate Professor of Leadership Studies
Jepson School of Leadership Studies, University of Richmond, USA

1. Traditional Classics on Leadership
2. Modern Classics on Leadership
3. New Perspectives on Leadership

For a list of all Edward Elgar published titles visit our site on the World Wide Web at
www.e-elgar.com

New Perspectives on Leadership

Edited by

J. Thomas Wren
Associate Professor of Leadership Studies
Jepson School of Leadership Studies, University of Richmond, USA

Douglas A. Hicks
Associate Professor of Leadership Studies and Religion
Jepson School of Leadership Studies, University of Richmond, USA

and

Terry L. Price
Associate Professor of Leadership Studies
Jepson School of Leadership Studies, University of Richmond, USA

THE INTERNATIONAL LIBRARY OF LEADERSHIP

An Elgar Reference Collection
Cheltenham, UK • Northampton, MA, USA

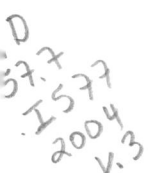

Paul and Rosemary Trible Library
Christopher Newport University
Newport News, VA

© J. Thomas Wren, Douglas A. Hicks and Terry L. Price 2004. For copyright of individual articles, please refer to the Acknowledgements.

All rights reserved. No part of this publication may be reproduced, stored in a retrieval system, or transmitted in any form or by any means, electronic, mechanical, photocopying, recording, or otherwise without the prior permission of the publisher.

Published by
Edward Elgar Publishing Limited
Glensanda House
Montpellier Parade
Cheltenham
Glos GL50 1UA
UK

Edward Elgar Publishing, Inc.
136 West Street
Suite 202
Northampton
Massachusetts 01060
USA

A catalogue record for this book is available from the British Library.

Library of Congress Cataloguing in Publication Data

The international library of leadership / editors, J. Thomas Wren, Douglas A. Hicks, Terry
  L. Price.
      p. cm. — (Elgar mini series)
   Includes index
   1. Leadership. I. Wren, J. Thomas, 1950- II. Hicks, Douglas A. III. Price, Terry L.,
1966- IV. Series.

HD57.7.I577 2004
303.3'4—dc22
                                                                              2004043429

ISBN   1 84376 403 2
       1 84064 747 7 (3 volume set)

Printed and bound in Great Britain by MPG Books Ltd, Bodmin, Cornwall

Contents

Acknowledgements	ix
Preface J. Thomas Wren, Douglas A. Hicks and Terry L. Price	xiii
Introduction J. Thomas Wren, Douglas A. Hicks and Terry L. Price	xv

PART I   CONCEPTUALIZING LEADERSHIP

1. James MacGregor Burns (1978), 'Toward a General Theory', in *Leadership*, Chapter 16, New York: Harper and Row, 422–43, 505–6   **3**
2. Joseph C. Rost (1991), 'The Nature of Leadership', in *Leadership for the Twenty-first Century*, Chapter 5, New York: Praeger, 97–128, references   **27**
3. Howard Gardner with Emma Laskin (1995), 'Lessons from the Past, Implications for the Future', in *Leading Minds: An Anatomy of Leadership*, Chapter 15, New York: BasicBooks, 285–306, 365, references, 308–25   **60**
4. Robert K. Greenleaf (1970/1991), excerpt from *The Servant as Leader*, Indianapolis, IN: The Robert K. Greenleaf Center, re-set   **102**
5. Peter M. Senge (1990), '"Give Me a Lever Long Enough... and Single-Handed I Can Move the World"', in *The Fifth Discipline: The Art and Practice of the Learning Organization*, Chapter 1, New York: Currency Doubleday, 3–16, notes   **107**

PART II   POWER, AUTHORITY AND LEADERSHIP

6. Hannah Arendt (1951), 'The Totalitarian Movement', in *The Origins of Totalitarianism*, Chapter Eleven, New York: Harcourt, Brace and Company, 333–75   **123**
7. Bertrand Russell (1962), 'Leaders and Followers', in *Power: A New Social Analysis*, Chapter II, London: George Allen and Unwin Ltd and New York: Barnes and Noble, Inc., 12–24   **166**
8. Michel Foucault (1975/1979), excerpt from 'Panopticism', in *Discipline and Punish: The Birth of the Prison*, Chapter 3, New York: Vintage Books, 195–209   **179**
9. Jane Mansbridge (1996), 'Using Power/Fighting Power: The Polity', in Seyla Benhabib (ed.), *Democracy and Difference: Contesting the Boundaries of the Political*, Chapter Three, Princeton, NJ: Princeton University Press, 46–66   **195**

PART III   ETHICS, VALUES AND LEADERSHIP

10. Isaiah Berlin (1959/1990), 'The Pursuit of the Ideal', in Henry Hardy (ed.), *The Crooked Timber of Humanity: Chapters in the History of Ideas*, Princeton, NJ: Princeton University Press, 1–19   **219**

11. James MacGregor Burns (1978), 'The Structure of Moral Leadership', in *Leadership*, Chapter 2, New York: Harper and Row, 29–46, 469–71 — 238
12. Michael Walzer (1973), 'Political Action: The Problem of Dirty Hands', *Philosophy and Public Affairs*, **2** (2), Winter, 160–80 — 259
13. Thomas E. Hill, Jr. (1991), 'Servility and Self-Respect', in *Autonomy and Self-Respect*, Chapter I, Cambridge: Cambridge University Press, 4–18 — 280
14. Norman Bowie (2000), 'A Kantian Theory of Leadership', *Leadership and Organization Development Journal*, **21** (4), 185–93 — 295
15. Joanne B. Ciulla (1998), 'Leadership Ethics: Mapping the Territory', in Joanne B. Ciulla (ed.), *Ethics, the Heart of Leadership*, Chapter 1, Westport, CT: Quorum Books, 3–25 — 304

PART IV LEADERSHIP AND SOCIAL CHANGE

16. Martin Luther King, Jr. (1986), 'Letter from Birmingham City Jail', in James Melvin Washington (ed.), *A Testament of Hope: The Essential Writings of Martin Luther King, Jr.*, Chapter 46, San Francisco, CA: Harper and Row, a division of HarperCollins Publishers, 289–302 — 329
17. Clayborne Carson (1987), 'Martin Luther King, Jr.: Charismatic Leadership in a Mass Struggle', *Journal of American History*, **74** (2), September, 448–54 — 343
18. Paulo Freire (1970/2000), Chapter 1 from *Pedagogy of the Oppressed*, 30th Anniversary Edition, Translated by Myra Bergman Ramos, New York: Continuum, 43–69 — 350
19. Richard A. Couto (1993), 'Narrative, Free Space, and Political Leadership in Social Movements', *Journal of Politics*, **55** (1), February, 57–79 — 377

PART V INCLUSION AND DEMOCRATIC LEADERSHIP

20. Benjamin R. Barber (1984), 'Strong Democracy: Politics as a Way of Living', in *Strong Democracy: Participatory Politics for a New Age*, Chapter Six, Berkeley, CA: University of California Press, 117–38 — 403
21. Ronald A. Heifetz (1994), 'On a Razor's Edge', in *Leadership Without Easy Answers*, Chapter 6, Cambridge, MA: Belknap Press of Harvard University Press, 125–49, 312–17 — 425
22. Cornel West (1993), 'The New Cultural Politics of Difference', in *Keeping Faith: Philosophy and Race in America*, Chapter 1, New York: Routledge, 3–32 — 456
23. Anne Phillips (1993), 'Must Feminists Give up on Liberal Democracy?', in *Democracy and Difference*, Chapter 6, University Park, PA: Pennsylvania State University Press, 103–22 — 486

| | 24. | Jean Lipman-Blumen (1992), 'Connective Leadership: Female Leadership Styles in the 21st-Century Workplace', *Sociological Perspectives*, **35** (1), Spring, 183–203 | 506 |

PART VI   INTERNATIONAL LEADERSHIP

	25.	Geert Hofstede (1980), 'Motivation, Leadership, and Organization: Do American Theories Apply Abroad?', *Organizational Dynamics*, **9** (1), Summer, 42–63	529
	26.	Nancy J. Adler (1996), 'Global Women Political Leaders: An Invisible History, An Increasingly Important Future', *Leadership Quarterly*, **7** (1), Spring, 133–61	551
	27.	Robert J. House, Paul J. Hanges, S. Antonio Ruiz-Quintanilla, Peter W. Dorfman, Mansour Javidan, Marcus W. Dickson, Vipin Gupta et al. (1999), 'Cultural Influences on Leadership and Organizations: Project GLOBE', in William H. Mobley, M. Jocelyne Gessner and Val Arnold (eds), *Advances in Global Leadership*, Volume 1, Stamford, CT: JAI Press, Inc., 171–233	580
	28.	Martha C. Nussbaum (2003), 'Compassion and Terror', *Daedalus*, Winter, 10–26	643

Name Index   661

Acknowledgements

The editors and publishers wish to thank the authors and the following publishers who have kindly given permission for the use of copyright material.

Basic Books, a member of Perseus Books, LLC, for excerpt: Howard Gardner with Emma Laskin (1995), 'Lessons from the Past, Implications for the Future', in *Leading Minds: An Anatomy of Leadership*, Chapter 15, 285–306, 365, references, 308–25.

Belknap Press of Harvard University Press and the President and Fellows of Harvard College for excerpt: Ronald A. Heifetz (1994), 'On a Razor's Edge', in *Leadership Without Easy Answers*, Chapter 6, 125–49, 312–17.

Blackwell Publishing Ltd for article and excerpt: Richard A. Couto (1993), 'Narrative, Free Space, and Political Leadership in Social Movements', *Journal of Politics*, **55** (1), February, 57–79; Anne Phillips (1993), 'Must Feminists Give up on Liberal Democracy?', in *Democracy and Difference*, Chapter 6, 103–22.

Cambridge University Press for excerpt: Thomas E. Hill, Jr. (1991), 'Servility and Self-Respect', in *Autonomy and Self-Respect*, Chapter I, 4–18.

Continuum International Publishing Group, Inc. and Penguin Books Ltd for excerpt: Paulo Freire (1970/2000), Chapter 1 from *Pedagogy of the Oppressed*, 30th Anniversary Edition, Translated by Myra Bergman Ramos, 43–69.

Daedalus, Journal of the American Academy of Arts and Sciences for article: Martha C. Nussbaum (2003), 'Compassion and Terror', *Daedalus*, Winter, 10–26.

Doubleday, a division of Random House, Inc., for excerpt: Peter M. Senge (1990), '"Give Me a Lever Long Enough… and Single-Handed I Can Move the World"', in *The Fifth Discipline: The Art and Practice of the Learning Organization*, Chapter 1, 3–16, notes.

Elsevier for article and excerpt: Nancy J. Adler (1996), 'Global Women Political Leaders: An Invisible History, An Increasingly Important Future', *Leadership Quarterly*, **7** (1), Spring, 133–61; Robert J. House, Paul J. Hanges, S. Antonio Ruiz-Quintanilla, Peter W. Dorfman, Mansour Javidan, Marcus W. Dickson, Vipin Gupta et al. (1999), 'Cultural Influences on Leadership and Organizations: Project GLOBE', in William H. Mobley, M. Jocelyne Gessner and Val Arnold (eds), *Advances in Global Leadership*, Volume 1, 171–233.

Emerald MCB University Press Ltd for article: Norman Bowie (2000), 'A Kantian Theory of Leadership', *Leadership and Organization Development Journal*, **21** (4), 185–93.

Greenleaf Center for Servant-Leadership for excerpt: Robert K. Greenleaf (1970/1991), excerpt from *The Servant as Leader*, re-set.

Greenwood Publishing Group, Inc. for excerpts: Joseph C. Rost (1991), 'The Nature of Leadership', in *Leadership for the Twenty-first Century*, Chapter 5, 97–128, references; Joanne B. Ciulla (1998), 'Leadership Ethics: Mapping the Territory', in Joanne B. Ciulla (ed.), *Ethics, the Heart of Leadership*, Chapter 1, 3–25.

Harcourt, Inc. for excerpt: Hannah Arendt (1951), 'The Totalitarian Movement', in *The Origins of Totalitarianism*, Chapter Eleven, 333–75.

HarperCollins Publishers, Inc. for excerpts: James MacGregor Burns (1978), 'The Structure of Moral Leadership', in *Leadership*, Chapter 2, 29–46, 469–71; James MacGregor Burns (1978), 'Toward a General Theory', in *Leadership*, Chapter 16, 422–43, 505–6.

Geert Hofstede for his own article: (1980), 'Motivation, Leadership, and Organization: Do American Theories Apply Abroad?', *Organizational Dynamics*, **9** (1), Summer, 42–63.

Johns Hopkins University Press for article: Michael Walzer (1973), 'Political Action: The Problem of Dirty Hands', *Philosophy and Public Affairs*, **2** (2), Winter, 160–80.

Organization of American Historians for article: Clayborne Carson (1987), 'Martin Luther King, Jr.: Charismatic Leadership in a Mass Struggle', *Journal of American History*, **74** (2), September, 448–54.

Penguin Books Ltd and Georges Borchardt, Inc. for excerpt: Michel Foucault (1975/1979), excerpt from 'Panopticism', in *Discipline and Punish: The Birth of the Prison*, Chapter 3, 195–209.

Princeton University Press for excerpts: Isaiah Berlin (1959/1990), 'The Pursuit of the Ideal', in Henry Hardy (ed.), *The Crooked Timber of Humanity: Chapters in the History of Ideas*, 1–19; Jane Mansbridge (1996), 'Using Power/Fighting Power: The Polity', in Seyla Benhabib (ed.), *Democracy and Difference: Contesting the Boundaries of the Political*, Chapter Three, 46–66.

Routledge/Taylor and Francis Books, Inc. for excerpt: Cornel West (1993), 'The New Cultural Politics of Difference', in *Keeping Faith: Philosophy and Race in America*, Chapter 1, 3–32.

University of California Press for excerpt: Benjamin R. Barber (1984), 'Strong Democracy: Politics as a Way of Living', in *Strong Democracy: Participatory Politics for a New Age*, Chapter Six, 117–38.

University of California Press Journals and the Pacific Sociological Association for article: Jean Lipman-Blumen (1992), 'Connective Leadership: Female Leadership Styles in the 21st-Century Workplace', *Sociological Perspectives*, **35** (1), Spring, 183–203.

Unwin Hyman (Taylor and Francis Books) and the Bertrand Russell Peace Foundation Ltd for excerpt: Bertrand Russell (1962), 'Leaders and Followers', in *Power: A New Social Analysis*, Chapter II, 12–24.

Writers House LLC for excerpt: Martin Luther King, Jr. (1986), 'Letter from Birmingham City Jail', in James Melvin Washington (ed.), *A Testament of Hope: The Essential Writings of Martin Luther King, Jr.*, Chapter 46, 289–302.

Every effort has been made to trace all the copyright holders but if any have been inadvertently overlooked the publishers will be pleased to make the necessary arrangement at the first opportunity.

In addition the publishers wish to thank the Library of the University of Warwick and the Library of Indiana University at Bloomington, USA for their assistance in obtaining these articles.

Authors' Acknowledgements

Completing a collection of this sort requires many hands and minds, and the editors are deeply grateful to a number of people who made it possible. Noreen Cullen and Nancy Vick in the interlibrary loan office at Boatwright Memorial Library at the University of Richmond processed literally hundreds of requests with unfailing good humor. Eric Wilson, Christopher Griffin, John Armstrong, Jonathan Wight, Dean Simpson, and Juliette Landphair provided guidance by suggesting readings for the collection, helping with translations, and offering interpretations of selections that bettered those of the editors. Gill Hickman, Richard Couto, and Elizabeth Faier, faculty colleagues at the Jepson School of Leadership Studies at the University of Richmond, were constant sources of ideas and inspiration. Fred Jablin as Acting Dean of the Jepson School provided considerable institutional support and personal encouragement. Joanne Ciulla, another faculty colleague, and Bruce Avolio read all or parts of the results of our efforts and offered useful advice and criticism along the way.

In the actual production of the work we were fortunate to enjoy superb editorial and administrative assistance. Nicola Mills at Edward Elgar Publishing spearheaded this project from the beginning and graciously accommodated the whims of her sometimes cranky editors. Edward Elgar himself never failed to respond quickly and creatively to our occasionally unorthodox requests. We also thank Caroline McLin and Clare Arnold at Edward Elgar for their fine work in the production phase. At the University of Richmond, Kathy Bradley, Judy Mable, Sue Murphy, Jackie Duresky, Melissa Foster, Michael Frankston, Emily Latshaw, and Kristina Lam provided helpful administrative and technological support.

Our research assistant, Cassie King, deserves special mention and appreciation. She devoted untold hours to this project. Not only did she do the bulk of the legwork, but it is safe to say that nary a word or a comma in this entire collection has escaped her meticulous attention. This work is as much hers as it is our own.

Of course, our families contributed to this endeavor in the way that the families of academics always contribute: in the missed opportunities for shared time together, and in their toleration of distracted spouses and fathers. For that we thank, with love, Catherine, Lori, Noah, Harper, Suzanne, and Jack.

Preface

J. Thomas Wren, Douglas A. Hicks and Terry L. Price

This book is one of a three-volume set devoted to bringing together in one place the most significant writings and scholarship on leadership. When Edward Elgar Publishing first contacted the editors about creating a reference collection pertaining to leadership, an opportunity presented itself to reshape the traditional formulation of leadership studies and to suggest a deeper and more fundamental understanding of the phenomenon. In scholarly circles, the term *leadership studies* has often been used to connote a rather narrow corpus of social science analyses, chiefly from the fields of social psychology and management science. Such studies have contributed mightily to our understanding of leadership, yet they are limited in scope and purpose. On the other hand, the recent popularity of 'leadership' has spurred an outpouring of publications in the trade press. These popular treatments are almost invariably simplistic and shallow.

The premise underlying this collection is that the phenomenon of leadership is too important and too complex to leave the field to these champions alone. Our view of leadership is that it is a universal component of the human condition. It is the process by which and through which groups, organizations, and societies seek to achieve their perceived needs and objectives. As such, leadership has occupied center stage throughout human history. It embraces far more than the mere running of modern formal organizations, and it is much too complex to summarize neatly in a short paperback. Fortunately, because leadership has played such a central role in the human endeavor, it has not lacked for study and analysis. Indeed, the greatest minds in history have considered its implications, probed its dilemmas, and prescribed solutions for its problems.

The goal of this collection is to make readily available to the serious student of leadership a compilation of sources the editors think are representative of the best insights into this important phenomenon. The selections contained in these volumes, it should be noted, come solely from Western traditions. Many works from other cultural traditions are obviously relevant, but constraints of space would limit our inclusion of them to anecdotal status. Such works deserve fuller treatment, perhaps in a future Edward Elgar collection.

Volume I, *Traditional Classics on Leadership*, contains our version of the most insightful and important writings on leadership from ancient times to the dawn of the twentieth century. Moreover, the selections are arranged according to what we believe have been the key leadership issues in the preindustrial age. The volume begins with the central question of the moral purpose of leadership. The selections in this section – from Plato, Aristotle, Rousseau, Kant, Madison, and Nietzsche – suggest the sort of intellectual capital that has been brought to bear upon our topics. Other issues that the volume addresses include: What is the nature of ideal leadership? What constitutes legitimate authority? What is the role of followers? How might one go about challenging authority? We have taken care to include voices that have traditionally been out of the mainstream: women such as Christine de Pizan, Mary Wollstonecraft, Elizabeth Cady Stanton, and Virginia Woolf, and men of color such as David Walker and W.E.B. Du Bois. Taken together, the selections in this volume provide a rich and textured reference collection for an initial understanding of some of the central issues of leadership.

Volume II we have labeled *Modern Classics on Leadership*. It is here that we collect for the reader the seminal articles and chapters that have shaped what is commonly known as the modern field of leadership studies. With the rise of the modern business corporation (and other precedent-shattering developments such as modern warfare), there was an increasing perception that the role of leadership needed closer study. Concurrent with this was the rise of professional academic disciplines in the social sciences. Thus began a fortuitous pairing of leadership with serious academic scholarship that has spawned enormous insights. This volume seeks to bring together the best of that work. Beginning with the paradigm-shaping work of Frederick Winslow Taylor early in the twentieth century, this volume traces the field of leadership studies as it evolved throughout the twentieth century and became a sophisticated scholarship of considerable influence. We place at the reader's disposal the path-breaking studies that led to trait theory, behavior theory, contingency theories of leadership, transformational leadership, charismatic leadership, cognitive approaches to leadership, and studies of power. We also trace the insights that social scientists have brought to the study of followers, organizational culture, and such specific leadership issues as the role of gender. Thus, this volume provides in one place the 'giants' of modern social science leadership literature.

Volume III we call *New Perspectives on Leadership*. Here we seek to demonstrate how the insights of many intellectual approaches contribute to an understanding of current leadership issues. In this volume you will find writings by contemporary philosophers, management scientists, political scientists, social and political activists, and others. We have sought to organize these writings around the questions and themes that we believe most pertain to the study of leadership in the postmodern age. The questions include how leadership should be conceptualized; the role of power and authority; and questions of values, morality, and ethics. The themes that this volume explores reflect what we believe are the most important for our contemporary society: leadership and service, social change, democratic leadership and inclusion, and international leadership. Volume III of the Edward Elgar collection, then, should provide an important intellectual foundation for anyone interested in the current challenges of leadership.

If one were to take a step back and look at the Edward Elgar *International Library of Leadership* collection as a whole, it is our hope that the view thus gained would be one of coherence. It has been our goal in this editing project to do more than just collate good writings on leadership. Our aim has been one of integration. The challenges of our modern world make an understanding of leadership too important to leave to happenstance or haphazard experience. We have sought to make it possible for those serious about leadership to have easy access to the best thinking of the great minds of past and present. Moreover, we have arranged these selections around what we believe are the central issues that modern leaders continue to confront. Many of the selections in these volumes are not an easy read. But they represent what the editors believe to be the most important collection of sources on leadership now available. The 'unity' we have sought is the unity of a common subject matter that has, through the ages, occupied the attention of the brightest luminaries. We hope that this collection may serve as the steppingstone toward a better understanding of the subject of leadership and, in the process, a better world.

Introduction

J. Thomas Wren, Douglas A. Hicks and Terry L. Price

The initial two volumes of this Edward Elgar *International Library of Leadership* series represent reference collections of historic leadership texts (Volume I) and the seminal works in twentieth-century scholarship of leadership studies (Volume II). In this, the third of the series, we bring you the most innovative and important contemporary writings on leadership.

This collection, entitled *New Perspectives on Leadership*, makes available in one volume the works on leadership that are likely to shape the field in the new century. Not all of the included works are recent; that is to say, some date back to the middle years of the twentieth century. Nonetheless, each has been chosen because of its central place in framing the issues that will occupy the study and understanding of leadership in the twenty-first century. Readers of Volume I of this series will recognize that many of the issues that occupy contemporary writers are remarkably similar to those that have drawn the attention of commentators since the beginning. This should not be surprising; some leadership challenges are indeed perennial. At the same time, our present circumstances also pose novel challenges unknown to earlier eras. This introduction, then, and the volume itself should serve as a guide to the key leadership issues of our contemporary world.

Conceptualizing Leadership

It may be recalled that a central focus of Volume I involved various conceptions of the ideal form of leadership. Similarly, one of the most important recent developments in leadership studies has been a spate of new ways of conceptualizing the phenomenon. One of these paradigm-shattering moments occurred when James MacGregor Burns published his classic book *Leadership* in 1978. In the selection included, Burns demonstrates the sophistication of his conceptualizations of leadership in his definition: 'Leadership is the reciprocal process of mobilizing, by persons with certain motives and values, various economic, political, and other resources, in a context of competition and conflict, in order to realize goals independently or mutually held by both leaders and followers.' Burns proceeds to suggest the necessary components of a general theory of leadership and spins out some of his most notable contributions to the field: the distinction between transactional and transformational leadership, the role of modal and end values, and the intermingling of power and collective purpose. Burns's work is substantially more sophisticated than much of what preceded him in twentieth-century work on leadership. It could be argued that his insights signaled a rebirth of the field of leadership studies.

Leadership scholar Joseph Rost explicitly builds upon the foundations of Burns's work when he constructs a definition of leadership designed for a post-industrial world. He adds specificity to some of Burns's points and formalizes others. 'Leadership,' says Rost, 'is an influence relationship among leaders and followers who intend real changes that reflect their mutual purposes.' The focus of Rost's work is upon a leadership process that is multidirectional and noncoercive. In positing such a view of the leadership process, Rost rejects the premises of the old 'industrial paradigm' that viewed leadership as hierarchical and leader-centric.

Yet another path-breaking discourse on leadership is Howard Gardner's *Leading Minds: An Anatomy of Leadership*. Through a series of case studies, Gardner distills what he believes are the central tenets of leadership. In his conclusion, included here, Gardner makes a signal contribution to our understanding of the phenomenon: he identifies the importance of the cognitive role of narrative in leadership. A leader, suggests Gardner, must be able to relate relevant stories to his or her constituents. Such stories should provide a sense of background for followers, as well as a sense of identity. They should help group members to address essential questions and frame future options. The key insight for Gardner is the relationship between leader and followers – the audience, if you will. The relationship is complex; the leader must appreciate the nature of his/her audience, develop a story that relates to it, and then embody that story. Gardner's work opens up important new possibilities. He asks us to consider cognitive dimensions of leader–follower relations not traversed before.

Gardner is not the only recent author to introduce a radical new conceptualization of leader–follower relations. In a classic piece, Robert Greenleaf introduces us to the notion of 'The Servant as Leader.' In it, he characterizes appropriate leadership as serving the interests of the followers, helping them to 'become healthier, wiser, freer, more autonomous, more likely to become servants themselves.' Such a view is consistent with the emphasis of many of the selections in this volume: the wants and needs of followers take on a high moral priority. Although other pieces are more systematic, Greenleaf makes a compelling case for the leaders' need to serve their followers. His work articulates a normative conceptualization of leadership that has had a large impact upon the field.

In the final selection, Peter Senge opens yet another new leadership horizon when he focuses upon how people and processes interrelate. Senge discusses the application of systems thinking to organizations in his book *The Fifth Discipline*. Systems thinking represents an entirely new way of approaching the dynamics of an organization. 'Business and other human endeavors,' says Senge, 'are ... systems.' One can only understand a system by contemplating the whole, not any individual part of the pattern. 'Systems thinking is a conceptual framework [that helps] ... to make the full patterns clearer, and to help us see how to change them effectively.' What is needed, in Senge's terms, is a 'learning organization,' where 'people continually expand their capacity to create results they truly desire, where new and expansive patterns of thinking are nurtured, where collective aspiration is set free, and where people are continually learning how to learn together.' In his book, Senge turns to the implications for leadership. Leadership is needed to create such an organization, but it must be leadership newly conceived. Instead of the traditional view of leader-as-hero, leaders should be designers, stewards, and teachers. Such a new approach has a focus upon purpose and learning and is an appropriate model for leadership in a postmodern world.

In sum, each of these readings helps us to perceive leadership in a new light. Taken together, the selections depict leadership as a complex set of relationships, involving leaders, followers, and contextual factors. The next section delves into some of the important issues that emerge from that complex dynamic.

Power, Authority and Leadership

Just as the classical writers in Volume I of this series addressed issues of legitimate authority, the unprecedented challenges of the mid-to-late twentieth century have evoked important new thinking about the relationship of power and authority in the leadership relation. The selections in this section suggest some of the insights that have resulted and some of the new questions for leadership when followers have significant power and leaders sometimes lack authority.

Hannah Arendt's classic book *The Origins of Totalitarianism* helped define the postwar discussion of power, especially as it was exercised in Stalinism and Nazism. In the selection included in this volume, Arendt traces how the exercise of power shifts from the use of raw force, which motivates people by fear, to the more effective use of propaganda, which transforms beliefs by indoctrination. The effective control of – indeed the crafting of – information was the key to maintaining total control. The totalitarian structure, with its various organizational layers separating party leaders, party members, supporters, and citizens, isolated the totalitarian worldview in a way that protected it from criticism. Although some aspects of the analysis are dated and specific to the historical period, Arendt's insight into the potential for technology to be employed 'scientifically' toward oppressive ends – she compares it to the effective use of advertising techniques – is a caution even for modern, democratic societies. Her convincing example of the ability of leaders to build a system in which citizens could be convinced of what seems absurd from our perspective calls us to understand the important ways in which ethical leadership depends upon correct belief.

While Arendt looks to the abuse of power by leaders, Bertrand Russell argues that followers, too, share in the desire for power. Russell suggests that the power impulse is explicit in leaders and implicit in followers. People follow, he thinks, 'with a view to the acquisition of power by the group.' In contrast to the 'slave morality' of Nietzsche, Russell argues that 'in every genuinely co-operative enterprise, the follower is psychologically no more a slave than the leader.' For Russell, followers as much as leaders, then, have a desire for power; they merely take a different tack to obtain it. Russell concludes with an introduction to the notion of 'mechanical' (technological) power. He writes: 'The man who has vast mechanical power at his command is likely, if uncontrolled, to feel himself a god – not a Christian God of Love, but a pagan Thor or Vulcan.' Like Arendt before him and Foucault after him, Russell focuses our attention on the potential of technology to contribute to power, which could be used for good or bad ends.

Michel Foucault explores other potential evils that can emerge when modern technology merges with the authority of leadership. Foucault imagines a technologically perfect system designed to control a group of people. Using Jeremy Bentham's famous model of the Panopticon (a kind of prison-in-the-round), Foucault suggests that a system can be created that operates directly upon both subjects and supervisors and assures proper behavior and functioning. Power within the system, once it is set up, does not even require a supervisor's presence; the fear of a supervisor is enough to enforce the system. This model of power relies not upon the individual functioning of political leaders, but rather envisions a system of discipline diffused throughout society and, ultimately, overseen by it. Foucault thus offers a method of maintaining order in society that echoes 'Big Brother.' Although frightening in some respects, Foucault's analysis suggests the sort of thinking that results from the modern world's confrontation with the evils of power in the leadership relation. He calls the reader to confront the reality of the potential power that technology can exercise over people. It is up to properly wary leaders and followers not to allow technological power to dominate its subjects, even in times of national and international crisis.

In the next selection, Jane Mansbridge offers a brilliant essay concerning the role of power, which she defines in this selection as 'coercion,' in democratic societies. Far from decrying or attempting to eliminate coercion in a democracy, Mansbridge says that coercion is a necessary aspect of such a polity. Anytime a decision is made that is less than unanimous, coercion (of the losing side) is present. Realistically, then, democracies cannot avoid it. Of course, coercion has its risks. Mansbridge accepts the obvious protections against abuses provided by constitutional rights and the rule of law. But she also suggests that democracies must 'fight that coercion at the same time as using it.' Specifically, there must be informal deliberative enclaves in civil society that foster interactions among the coerced, in order that they might 'decide ... in a more protected space in what way or whether to continue the battle.' In that way 'conflicting accounts of self-interest as well as conflicting accounts of the common good ... must supplement both mainstream discourse about the common good and formal deliberations that take place in local and national governments.' This 'affirmative pluralism' holds the best hope of avoiding 'illegitimate coercion and substantive injustice.' Although neither Foucault nor Mansbridge focuses upon leadership *per se*, the implications should be obvious. As we continue to face down the challenges of power in democratic societies, our preeminent leadership task is how to create structures that recognize the realities of power while at the same time preserving the ability of those most affected by it to maintain lives of freedom and dignity.

Ethics, Values and Leadership

Volume I of this collection began with a series of classical authors addressing the moral purposes of leadership. Just as the challenges of the modern world occasioned a revisiting of notions of power, so too have they caused modern commentators to rethink values, morality, and ethics related to leadership in the contemporary era. This section presents some of the best of such recent contributions.

An appropriate place to begin is Isaiah Berlin's essay on 'The Pursuit of the Ideal.' Berlin looks back upon 'the great ideological storms' of the twentieth century and seeks their lessons. In particular, he looks to their implications for ethics, which he defines as 'the systematic examination of the relations of human beings to each other.' This involves the study of the source of these ideals and the systems of value upon which they are based. Looking far back into history, Berlin finds that many sources – e.g., Plato, Rousseau, Christian writings, and, more recently, scientific rationalism – assume that there is one single, unitary solution to the central problems. Other writers, such as Machiavelli and Vico, suggest otherwise. Vico, for example, holds that all cultures have their own version of reality, each incommensurable with the others. This, argues Berlin, is not relativism so much as pluralism. Values such as liberty and equality can clash. These clashes, argues Berlin, are the essence of what we are. The fact that there is no ultimate resolution does not mean that we should abandon the field or thoughtful debate about how society should be organized. Rather, we must engage in trade-offs – even in the face of imperfect knowledge – and seek a 'precarious equilibrium.' This is the precondition for decent societies and morally acceptable behavior. With this essay, Berlin provides the leadership challenge of the postmodern world: how to achieve group, organizational, and societal goals in the face of conflicting and pluralistic values.

James MacGregor Burns was among the first modern leadership writers to address explicitly the role of values and morality in leadership. In 'The Structure of Moral Leadership,' Burns articulates his normative conception of leadership by appeal to the ways in which needs and values can be used to raise leaders and followers to higher levels of morality. Burns suggests that leadership is a process of morality to the extent that leaders engage with followers on the basis of shared values, motives, and goals. Leaders can help followers choose among appropriate alternatives based upon the followers' true needs. Conflict is at the heart of this process. Leaders act as catalytic agents; they shape as well as express and mediate conflict. The essential strategy of leadership is mobilizing power to articulate and realize the motives and goals of followers. The work of Burns in this area has proven to be catalytic in its own right. His focus upon the central place of values in leadership has transformed the field.

The next two selections in this section represent important essays by contemporary thinkers addressing specific ethical issues pertaining to leadership. Michael Walzer explores the dilemma of 'dirty hands.' He begins with the premise that politics forces leaders to do immoral things, often in the pursuit of an admirable end. The challenge to Walzer is how to restrain this tendency within reasonable bounds. He draws upon the insights of several of the writers from Volumes I and II – e.g., Plato, Machiavelli, Weber, and Thoreau – to craft an answer. Although a politician is forced to do bad, concludes Walzer, we want someone who is a good enough person to feel guilty about it. Moreover, a leader's suffering should involve more than his inner conscience; it must be socially expressed as well, perhaps even in the form of punishment. This confirms that certain acts are wrong and limits their use. Walzer's work, then, identifies and confronts one of the key challenges to modern political leadership. His solutions seek to accept an unpleasant reality of leadership while retaining moral boundaries.

In the next selection, Thomas Hill returns to the ideal of leadership as service, as articulated by Greenleaf, and posits a potential moral pitfall. Although he does not address servant leadership specifically, Hill objects to any individual who allows himself or herself to become servile or who would literally place his/her own interests or rights below those of others. A servile person is one who tends to disavow his or her moral rights. Drawing upon Kant, Hill argues that a person has a duty to him- or herself to respect his or her own moral rights. He or she has a 'right to some minimum degree of respect from others .... To the extent that a person gives even tacit consent to humiliations incompatible with this respect, he will be acting as if he waives a right which he cannot in fact give up.' Thus, to the extent that a servant leader sacrifices his or her own moral interests to those of his or her followers, servant leadership results in an unacceptable undertaking.

The final selections for this section return to broader moral and ethical leadership themes. Norman Bowie, in his 'A Kantian Theory of Leadership,' employs the principles of Immanuel Kant's moral philosophy both to critique existing leadership theory and to posit a theory of leadership that promises to realize Kant's commitment to individual dignity and autonomy, as well as his 'categorical imperative.' The formulation of the categorical imperative that Bowie draws upon is that of the 'kingdom of ends,' in which 'the members are all equally subject and sovereign' and will thereby act according to rules that all can accept. Such egalitarian premises pose problems for many conceptualizations of leadership. Bowie utilizes these criteria to reject instrumental theories of leadership, charismatic leadership, and even servant leadership, to the extent that it falls prey to Hill's pitfall of servility. Burns's transformational leadership holds more promise, but it, too, can fall short of Kant's theoretical demands. In its place, Bowie posits his own approach to leadership that fulfills Kant's requirements. His theory stresses participation and enhancement of followers' autonomy by teaching followers to be leaders themselves.

Our section ends with an important contribution to the field of leadership by Joanne Ciulla. In her 'Leadership Ethics: Mapping the Territory,' Ciulla assesses the status of research in the ethics of leadership and finds it wanting. The predominant research in leadership studies derives from the social sciences. From an ethical standpoint, it is disappointing. Rather than concern oneself with the question, What is leadership?, the question investigated should be, What is good leadership? This question lies at the heart of public debate about leadership. 'No matter how much empirical information we get from the "scientific" study of leadership,' says Ciulla, 'it will always be inadequate if we neglect the moral implications.' Ciulla also explores two of the putative 'normative' approaches to leadership, James MacGregor Burns's transformational leadership and Robert Greenleaf's servant leadership. Both hold promise, but they are not well developed in terms of ethical theory. In sum, Ciulla finds that much work remains to be done in the field of leadership ethics. Her call to action is an appropriate end to this segment on new directions in leadership research in this area.

Leadership and Social Change

The dizzying social, economic, political, and intellectual changes that have swept the world since the middle of the twentieth century have generated an important literature related to the role of leadership and social change. This section draws upon some of the most insightful pieces of this literature to suggest the role leadership can play in effecting such change.

The initial selection comes not from a scholar, but from a deeply reflective practitioner, Martin Luther King, Jr. Following in the tradition of Thoreau's tract on civil disobedience contained in Volume I, King's 'Letter from Birmingham City Jail' has become one of the truly classic pieces of literature devoted to the role of leadership and social change. In defending his activism in the civil rights movement from criticism by local white ministers, King offers a manifesto of the role of leaders in fostering social change through nonviolent action. Such action, King says, is necessary in order to feed tensions so that the social problems will be addressed; further delay merely plays into the hands of the oppressors. King embraces civil disobedience: it is right to resist unjust laws. Indeed, he embraces 'extremism,' if that means refusing to compromise with evil. In defending the timing, tactics, and morality of his actions, King's missive has become an inspiration to social activists.

In our second selection, Clayborne Carson offers a scholarly assessment of the role of Martin Luther King, Jr., as a leader of social change. Carson argues that King should not be raised to the level of a legend. His myth both overstates and understates his importance. It overstates it in assuming that only through King's charismatic leadership could the civil rights movement be successful. This is not true; there were many able leaders, effective local organizations, and irresistible social forces that would have led to the movement's success. At the same time, King was more than an emotional motivator. He was both an intellectual and an able tactician. He had the ability to create a unique message and could conciliate disparate factions. Carson concludes that King's role as a leader was important to the movement but that social change ultimately requires multiple leaders in a complex mobilization effort at local and national levels.

The third selection represents a more radical strand of the literature dealing with the leadership of social change. Paulo Freire takes a neo-Marxist approach in his classic *Pedagogy of the Oppressed*. Hearkening back to Hegel (*see* Volume I of this series), Freire begins from the premise that oppression exists and asserts that it is the great humanistic and historical task of the oppressed to liberate themselves and their oppressors too. This can only be achieved by a 'pedagogy of the oppressed,' wherein both oppressed and oppressors regain their humanity. The oppressed must first realize – through the process of 'conscientization' – that they are oppressed and then act to free themselves. These actions, however, must be accompanied by dialogue and reflection. Once the reality of oppression has been transformed, the pedagogy ceases to belong to the oppressed and becomes a pedagogy of all the people in the process of permanent liberation. The result will be a 'new man,' neither oppressor nor oppressed, but one who is becoming fully human. There is a role for leadership in this process, but it is not of a traditional kind. Freire is skeptical of leaders who try to 'help' or 'serve' the people without giving up their privileged position. Not even the best intentioned leadership can bestow independence as a gift; people must discover their own agency. The correct method of revolutionary leadership is not libertarian propaganda but action and dialogue about what it takes to be human.

In our final selection of this segment, Richard Couto effectively draws upon social-movements literature to illuminate various dimensions of leadership for positive change. Couto writes of 'Narrative, Free Space, and Political Leadership in Social Movements.' He begins where Freire does – with the oppressed. Social movements, argues Couto, should be viewed as the politics of oppressed people. 'Free spaces' and 'narrative' are the engines of change in such movements. 'Free spaces' are areas in which it is safe for groups of people to mobilize. Such spaces include schools, neighborhood groups, and churches. In the most repressive regimes, such spaces may be confined to the family – or even only to the human memory and imagination. When leadership for social change is successful, the free spaces expand and become a part of the public sphere, as happened in the March on Washington in March 1963. In these free spaces, leaders help construct narratives that allow seemingly powerless people to preserve the ability to resist oppression. Narratives preserve an understanding of why such movements are necessary. They provide a sense of virtue for the oppressed and a sense of group identity and worth. Moreover, narratives enshrine precedents for resistance and can inspire groups to attempt change. Such narratives, for the most part, are the work of less visible tiers of leadership. It is through such invisible (to outsiders) leaders that great social movements emerge.

If social change has been a characteristic of the modern world that has demanded a leadership response, so too have been the waves of democracy and diversity that have swept us into the twenty-first century. Our next section details some of the most important writings relating to these developments.

Inclusion and Democratic Leadership

The challenges of leadership in societies characterized by egalitarian democracy and diversity are neither small nor trivial. The achievement of public ends and public goods is a formidable task when there is conflict over means and ends and no independent grounds for adjudicating this conflict. The selections below represent some of the best contemporary work in this field.

Benjamin Barber introduces us to the concept of 'strong democracy.' He advocates 'the creation of a political community capable of transforming dependent, private individuals into free citizens and partial and private interests into public goods.' This, according to Barber, can be achieved by active citizens engaged in common deliberation. Through public scrutiny and debate, individual values can be transformed into public norms.

Barber anticipates the important contributions of Ronald Heifetz to our understanding of the leadership process in a world characterized by conflict and a commitment to recognizing the interests of all. Heifetz discusses leadership in terms of what he calls 'adaptive challenges.' An adaptive challenge – and hence a need for leadership – occurs when people confront contradictions in their lives or communities or when existing values come into conflict with new realities. The leadership response is anything but traditional. 'Rather than fulfilling the expectation for answers, one provides questions; rather than protecting people from outside threat, one lets people feel the threat in order to stimulate adaptation; instead of orienting people to their current roles, one disorients people so that new role relationships develop; rather than quelling conflict, one generates it; instead of maintaining norms, one challenges them.' A leader, according to Heifetz, has a very important role to play, but it is one that turns the 'work' of leadership back to the constituents. A leader is expected to identify the adaptive challenge; keep the level of distress within a tolerable range for doing adaptive work; focus attention on ripening issues and not on stress-reducing distractions; give work back to the people but at a rate they can stand; and protect voices of leadership without authority. Through such innovative methods, Heifetz opens up new possibilities for a new leadership for a new age.

One specific leadership challenge of enormous consequence in our modern world is the issue of race. In the next selection, Cornel West critically analyzes a plethora of disparate cultural critics, suggesting ways in which leadership can become a part of the societal solution to race-based and other forms of exclusion. According to West, we need to establish a new framework, a 'new cultural politics of difference,' that acknowledges our basic humanity without reducing important aspects of identity to sameness. To do this, we need to generate new leadership – leaders who respond to the intellectual, existential, and political challenges created by a history of social structures that marginalize African Americans and other persons of color. This leadership must take on a 'critical,' 'prophetic,' and 'catalytic' orientation towards mainstream cultural and social systems, appropriating elements that promote justice but rejecting forms that dehumanize or objectify persons. The leader – whether an artist, an intellectual critic, or a politician – must learn to improvise and to collaborate with diverse persons and groups in order to engineer fundamental social change.

In her essay 'Must Feminists Give up on Liberal Democracy?' Anne Phillips engages feminist and liberal theorists over the ways in which liberal democracy has tended, historically and conceptually, to marginalize women. Phillips takes seriously the critique of feminists who discount any hope of reforming liberal democracy in a way that would establish genuine gender equality, but she argues that a 'richer and more equal democracy may still be possible within the broad framework liberal democracy implies.' For such an expanded form of 'strong democracy' to be possible, however, liberal theorists will need to respond to trenchant criticisms of liberal democracy, especially feminist perspectives on citizenship, participation, and – most challenging for liberalism – group heterogeneity and difference. Gender-based perspectives on leadership call for equal participation of men and women at the group level as well as gender-equal laws and institutions at the societal level.

Jean Lipman-Blumen utilizes conceptions of gender in her discussion of leadership styles in the contemporary workplace. Lipman-Blumen suggests a model of 'connective leadership' that draws upon, and ultimately transcends, traditional masculine models. She argues that two kinds of behaviors often associated with women – relational and instrumental styles – are increasingly important in a time of unavoidable interdependence at personal, corporate, and national levels. Thus, Lipman-Blumen suggests that women's creative appropriation of traditional roles and responsibilities places them in a good position to be effective leaders in the present moment. This is not to say, however, that relational and instrumental styles are not available to men. If organizations are adapted to transform exclusively competitive structures into cooperative ones, men and women alike can develop their own competencies to practice connective leadership.

If race and gender represent challenges on the current leadership horizon, the new reality of leadership in an internationalizing world represents both a challenge and an opportunity. It is to this subject that we now turn.

International Leadership

It is appropriate that international leadership be the final topic in a volume devoted to new perspectives on leadership thought. The impact of globalization has transformed the reality of individuals, organizations, and societies. As a result, the need for appropriate leadership responses to the new challenges has risen apace. The selections in this concluding section represent some of the best recent scholarship concerning leadership within an international context.

Perhaps the most important article in the field of international leadership studies is Geert Hofstede's study of cultural constraints in leadership theories. Hofstede asks the question, To what extent do theories developed in one country (here, the United States) simply reflect the cultural boundaries of that country and, so, fail to apply to other countries? He classifies national cultures according to four dimensions: power distance, uncertainty avoidance, individualism–collectivism, and masculinity–femininity. National cultures, he finds, vary greatly around these dimensions. Moreover, leadership theories almost inevitably imbibe the assumptions of the culture of their birth. This calls into question the universal validity of such theories. The cultural particularity of leadership theories poses serious problems for both the theory and practice of leadership.

Nancy Adler's article explores how women take on global leadership roles from different backgrounds and in different contexts. Adler maps the twenty-five women who have served either as president or prime minister in the modern era. In an impressively wide analysis, she demonstrates that these women come from diverse socioeconomic and religious backgrounds but almost all have a strong (often international) education. Many are part of political families. She demonstrates that they differ in their leadership styles and issues of principal attention. They share some common elements, however, including being able to employ their identity as women to say that change is possible and to leverage visibility from being 'different.' Many are able to use a consensus-building process for change. Yet they often face doubts from the electorate. This article encourages thought about gender and leadership in the international context and also raises important questions about doing an analysis of leadership of any kind across national boundaries.

The article by Robert J. House et al. is an overview and early report by the chief investigator of the largest, and arguably the most significant, contemporary exploration into global leadership: the GLOBE project, or the Global Leadership and Organizational Behavior Effectiveness research program. The GLOBE project has drawn together 150 scholars and examines data from over 50 countries. This social scientific approach to leadership is a legacy of the approaches contained in Volume II of this series. As Geert Hofstede helped shape the field of cross-cultural management theories a few decades ago, Robert House and his colleagues are making defining contributions to that field in the current moment. This essay outlines the phases of the projects and the kind of research being conducted and analyzed in three industries in countries in every region of the world. Thus, it introduces the reader to the GLOBE project and how the best contemporary social scientific scholarship is considering the ways that cultural factors shape leadership practices around the world.

The final essay in the volume returns to a humanities perspective – offered by a philosopher who is also informed by social science approaches to economic development. Martha Nussbaum proposes a moral framework by which persons should consider themselves, above all, to be 'citizens of the world.' In a period of anxiety about terrorism and underdevelopment, such a thesis can help us reflect on what good leadership entails. Nussbaum argues that, in the light of the events of September 11, 2001, persons can draw upon compassion as a fundamental part of forming a cosmopolitan vision. The moral imagination can spark compassion, but compassion must be 'educated' in order to avoid expressing concern only for some in-group and not for all human beings. This essay thus acknowledges the dangers of jingoism or exclusivity that can be raised at times such as ours, when political and other leaders 'circle the wagons' against enemies. Nussbaum's moral argument would have us extend our circle to include all human beings (and she would have us reach out in compassion to all other beings as well). The article thus builds upon themes raised in this volume about ethics, democratic inclusion, and social change. In so doing, Nussbaum raises a host of issues that currently face students and scholars of leadership studies in a globalizing world with a wide array of opportunities as well as critical challenges.

In the Preface to this three-volume Edward Elgar collection, the editors suggest that it is our ambition to make available to those serious about the study of leadership a corpus of the best thinking and writing about leadership from the past and the present. With the completion of this volume, it is our sincere hope that we have made progress toward accomplishing that objective. The stakes are not low. As we state in the Preface, 'The challenges of our modern world make an understanding of leadership too important to leave to happenstance or haphazard experience.' If the selections in this and the other two volumes come to provide the intellectual capital for others to mold a better world, then this collection will be a success.

Part I
Conceptualizing Leadership

[1]
TOWARD A GENERAL THEORY

Late in the winter of 1968, in response to my request that I interview President Johnson about his memories of Franklin Roosevelt, I received an invitation from the President and Mrs. Johnson to an informal family dinner. Making my way across Lafayette Park toward the White House a few days later, I was struck by the appearance of the imposing old building. The place now seemed dark, cold, diminished. Was it my imagination that it appeared to be under siege?

After close inspection of my credentials by guards at the gate, I was escorted into the mansion, taken in the little elevator to the second floor, and ushered into the family living room. In addition to the President and First Lady only a staff member and an ex-governor of Texas and their wives were present. The conversation was guarded and subdued, with everyone avoiding the subject that lay over the White House like a shroud, until one of the President's daughters flounced into the room in a housecoat, sat in her father's lap, then beside him on the floor, and suddenly started talking about Vietnam. Most of her friends and those of her husband were military men, she said, but she understood the feelings of young people who hated the war. She then presented those feelings, as simply and eloquently as I could remember having heard. The President listened, saying nothing.

During a lull I turned to my host and inquired about a meeting between Johnson and Franklin Roosevelt during the war years. The President dealt briefly and uninterestedly with the query, then began to reminisce about his boyhood years in Texas. He talked until dinner—about his parents, his mother's expectations of him, his father's discipline, his brothers and sisters. He talked during dinner, hardly bothering to eat, about his life and troubles growing up. He talked on and on after dinner, while his wife and friends listened with apparent interest to stories they must have heard many times. Finally, exhausted by the flow of words and overcome with a feeling of guilt over the presidential time I was monopolizing, I managed to rise to my feet and murmur my apologies. The President accompanied me halfway to the elevator, then announced and conducted a tour of the family living quarters, including a look at the presidential bedside piled with memoranda and reports.

Next day I happened to be standing outside the office of a presidential aide when the tall figure loomed again. The President led me to a tiny room off the oval office, where he produced a bound collection of the messages exchanged between Washington and Moscow during the Arab-Israeli hostilities of 1967. A large finger pointed to an ominous message from the Kremlin that virtually threatened war, then pointed proudly to the President's de-escalating response. Once again I made my escape. I left with no illusions as to the role I was expected to serve. Deserted by large portions of the constituencies that had given him his landslide victory of 1964, the President was seeking a final victory before the bar of history. Even this academic might have a vote to cast in the ultimate verdict. Every juror would count.

I reflected on the vagaries of power and leadership. Here was a President who had his hand on all the alleged levers of influence. The party he headed enjoyed majorities in both houses of Congress. After five years in the White House he had the constitutional right to run for four more. He had billions to budget and spend. He commanded a huge staff, talent, presidential attention, television screens, planes, cars. Only his finger could pull the nuclear trigger. Yet the man was almost impotent. He could not run again, for reasons of both bodily and political health. His congressional majorities were no longer dependable. He could not win in Southeast Asia with conventional war tactics and dared not employ nuclear strategy. Looking at him, especially from afar, people saw a man of vast power; looking out at the people, he felt lonely and powerless.

At night, I learned later, Johnson dreamed a recurring dream of impotence. He dreamed that he was lying in bed in the Red Room of the White House, paralyzed from the neck down, listening to his aides in the next room quarreling over the division of power. He could hear them but could not speak to them. Waking from his sleep after such a dream, the President would make his way through the empty corridors of the White House to the place where Woodrow Wilson's portrait hung. It soothed him to touch Wilson's portrait, for Wilson had been paralyzed and now was dead but Johnson was still alive and active. In the morning the fears would return—of paralysis of the body, paralysis of his presidency. And soon he would quit.

He would do so with a wrenching sense of damaged self-esteem. He felt that he had been, above all, a leader—of the poor, the blacks, the sick, the alienated. Perhaps he did not comprehend that the people he had led—as a result in part of the impact of his leadership—had created their own fresh leadership, which was now in some ways outrunning his. In sensing black wants, recognizing black needs, arousing black aspirations, legitimating black expectations, meeting black demands, Johnson had not only helped focus the effort and reinvigorate the organization of the old Negro groups like the NAACP. He had mobilized in the South and in the ghettos a new breed of militant black who was brassy, noisy, assertive, and moving far beyond the reach of that long presidential arm. Leadership had begat leadership and hardly recognized its offspring. Vietnam was more than perplexing to him, it was sickening. He had followed the responsible, the moderate strategy of Truman, Eisenhower, and Kennedy; he had learned from earlier wars that if you clung to your course and persevered, victory would come. But victory would not come in Vietnam; and now young men were resisting the draft, religious leaders were demonstrating at the White House gates, college students were so hostile that there was hardly a campus he could visit. And a brash young rival, Bobby Kennedy, and others waited offstage. Political leadership had simply passed out of the President's hands, and with it had gone political power. Followers had become leaders.

On the face of it, there was nothing unusual about Johnson's loss of power. Winston Churchill, Chiang Kai-shek, Nikita Khrushchev, Sukarno, and later Richard Nixon, de Gaulle, Indira Gandhi all suddenly slid—or were pushed—down the "greasy pole." But Johnson's plight was especially poignant and significant. On the one hand, in meeting to some degree the economic needs of blacks and others he had unwittingly aroused higher needs and values that he could neither comprehend fully nor gratify. On the other hand, in *not* meeting the demands of the anti-Vietnam militants he had generated new dimensions and intensities of conflict, thereby producing a whirlwind he could not control. His "abdication" a few weeks after I visited him was simple recognition of that fact.

If leaders who seemed to wield power often lacked it, followers who seemed impotent might unexpectedly exert influence. The Maoist demand that leaders struggle against self-advancement and privilege has been traced to the Taoist insistence that the sage must make himself lower than the people in order not to offend them. Few would seem more powerless and passive than slaves, but in the American antebellum South slaves were not mere recipients of power; the masters' paternalism aroused expectations other than those intended. "By developing a sense of moral worth and by asserting rights,"

Eugene Genovese concluded, "the slaves transformed their acquiescence in paternalism into a rejection of slavery itself."

We need not look so far back to glimpse the interlocking of leadership and followership, of power-wielding and power-receiving. The programs of private television are mainly financed by advertisers who make a massive effort to gauge the wants and needs of buyers, whose buying habits in turn are closely influenced by the messages on the tube. Politicians organizing revolutionary movements or planning to run for office take soundings in the villages or through opinion polls to see what the people want—but what the people want is mightily affected by the promises and preachings of politicians. Next to me as I write hangs a cartoon published in London in 1830 showing a frock-coated John Bull reading *The Times,* with a chain running from the *Times* masthead to his nose. The cartoon is captioned, "The man wot is easily led by the nose." But the editors of the newspaper, ever needful of readers, faced the threat of competing papers.

So again the paradox: Who are the leaders and who the led? Who is leading whom to where? For what purposes? With what results?

Leadership and Collective Purpose

To answer such questions we must proceed to the formidable task of seeing the role of leadership, as we have defined it, in historical causation. Let us take stock of the definition. Leadership is the reciprocal process of mobilizing, by persons with certain motives and values, various economic, political, and other resources, in a context of competition and conflict, in order to realize goals independently or mutually held by both leaders and followers. The nature of those goals is crucial. They could be separate but related; that is, two persons may exchange goods or services or other things in order to realize independent objectives. Thus Dutchmen (colonists in America) give beads to Indians in exchange for real estate, and French legislators trade votes in the Assembly on unrelated pieces of legislation. This is *transactional* leadership. The object in these cases is not a joint effort for persons with common aims acting for the collective interests of followers but a bargain to aid the individual interests of persons or groups going their separate ways.

Leaders can also shape and alter and elevate the motives and values and goals of followers through the vital *teaching* role of leadership. This is *transforming* leadership. The premise of this leadership is that, whatever the separate interests persons might hold, they are presently or potentially united in the pursuit of "higher" goals, the realization of which is tested by the achievement of significant change that represents the collective or pooled interests of leaders and followers.

Both forms of leadership can contribute to human purpose. If the *transactions* between leaders and followers result in realizing the individual goals of each, followers may satisfy certain wants, such as food or drink, in order to realize goals higher in the hierarchy of values, such as aesthetic needs. The chief monitors of transactional leadership are *modal values,* that is, values of means—honesty, responsibility, fairness, the honoring of commitments—without which transactional leadership could not work. Transformational leadership is more concerned with *end-values,* such as liberty, justice, equality. Transforming leaders "raise" their followers up through levels of morality, though insufficient attention to means can corrupt the ends.

Thus both kinds of leadership have moral implications. How can we define that morality? Summoned before the "bar of history," Adolf Hitler would argue that he spoke the true values of the German people, summoned them to a higher destiny, evoked the noblest sacrifice from them. The most crass, favor-swapping politician can point to the followers he helps or satisfies. Three criteria must be used to evaluate these claims. Both Hitler and the politician would have to be tested by modal values of honor and integrity—by the extent to which they advanced or thwarted fundamental standards of good conduct in humankind. They would have to be judged by the end-values of equality and justice. Finally, in a context of free communication and open criticism and evaluation, they would be judged in the balance sheet of history by their impact on the well-being of the persons whose lives they touched.

Because our emphasis is on collective purpose and change we stress the factors that unite leaders and followers as well as those that differentiate them. This distinction may be elusive to an observer who sees leaders leading followers but does not understand that leaders may modify their leadership in recognition of followers' preferences, or in order to anticipate followers' responses, or in order to harmonize the actions of both leader and follower with their common motives, values, and goals. Leaders and followers are engaged in a common enterprise; they are dependent on each other, their fortunes rise and fall together, they share the results of planned change together.

So defined, leadership—especially transforming leadership—is far more pervasive, widespread—indeed, common—than we generally recognize; it is also much more bounded, limited, and uncommon. *Common,* because acts of leadership occur not simply in presidential mansions and parliamentary assemblies but far more widely and powerfully in the day-to-day pursuit of collective goals through the mutual tapping of leaders' and followers' motive bases and in the achievement of intended change. It is an affair of parents, teachers, and peers as well as of preachers and politicians. *Uncommon,* because many acts heralded or bemoaned as instances of leadership—acts of oratory, manipulation, sheer self-advancement, brute coercion—are not such. Much of what commonly passes as leadership—conspicuous position-taking without followers or follow-through, posturing on various public stages, manipulation without general purpose, authoritarianism—is no more leadership than the behavior of small boys marching in front of a parade, who continue to strut along Main Street after the procession has turned down a side street toward the fairgrounds. Also, many apparent leaders will be only partial leaders. They may tap followers' motives or power bases; or they may take value-laden positions; or they may sharpen conflict; or they may operate at the final policy-making or implementation stages; or they may do some or all of these. The test of their leadership function is their contribution to change, measured by purpose drawn from collective motives and values.

Even if we exclude acts of nonleadership from our analysis, we must include an enormous variety and range of actions that in themselves constitute complete leadership acts—that is, the process and achievement of intended change—or that consciously make up significant links in the total process of achieving intended change. Not only the building of a new political party aimed at mobilizing tribal groups for the sake of social change, or a campaign against illiteracy, or a community development program, but a mother consciously acting in such a way that her small son's sensitivity to others will be improved, a taxi driver deliberately setting an example of considerate driving, a Red Guard leader making sure that food and drink are equally shared on a work project in the country—all these are parts of the totality of the leadership process. Leadership begins earlier, operates more widely, takes more forms, pervades more sectors of society, and lasts longer in the lives of most persons than has been generally recognized.

In the billions of acts that comprise the leadership process, or parts of it, a pattern can be discerned that makes possible generalizations about leadership, generalizations that in turn would underlie an effective general theory and serve as a guide to the successful practice of leadership. The answer will not be found in conventional wisdom and the hoary adages about leadership—that leaders are born and not made, or made and not born, that they must be trained, or cannot be trained, that they have to exhibit certain physical qualities like imposing height or unusual endurance or commanding voice, or mental qualities like memory for faces and names or unusual intelligence, or magical qualities. We have seen that leadership, as we have defined it, is a function of complex biological, social, cognitive, and affective processes, that it is closely influenced by the structures of opportunity and closure around it, that it may emerge

IMPLICATIONS: THEORY AND PRACTICE

at different stages in different peoples' lives, that it manifests itself in a variety of processes and arenas—in short, we have seen that the usual generalizations are without foundation (or at best apply only to highly specific subcultures). Can we *generalize* about leadership across polities and over time?

We of this generation can so generalize because of the concepts and data now available from those working in the field of moral development. These scholars have concluded that all persons in all cultures are not mere internalizers of specific values and beliefs and opinions that surround them, nor are they simply passive inheritors of parental ideology or reflectors of situationist ethics. These scholars believe that they "have rather firmly established a culturally universal invariant sequence of stages of moral judgment." This is a bold claim, and it awaits further systematic examination and verification. But one need not accept the claims of absolute invariance and irreversibility and universality to see the vital implications of these findings for a general theory of leadership. The emphasis on the developmental nature of human values and behavior is in accord with the work of Adler, Maslow, Piaget (especially the development of intelligence), Erikson, Rokeach, Kohlberg, and others who see the powerful role of growth and change in humankind.

The hierarchy of needs, the structure of values, the stages of moral development have been presented in earlier pages; we now need to analyze these developmental processes more closely and to see their implications for a general theory of leadership. The main question concerns the role of leaders in helping to move followers up through the levels of need and the stages of moral development. Just as leadership processes convert Maslow's "static" model into a dynamic one of ever-evolving deprivations and satisfactions, so these processes convert the structure of moral behavior into a structure of change and development. The central process involved, as we have emphasized, is one of *conflict* and *choice*. As children move through the stages of moral development they are caught between "natural" wants and needs and the necessity of obeying rules in order to avoid punishment; between idiosyncratic impulses and desires and the incentive to conform in order to receive awards, the return of favors, and the approval of others; between the desire to explore deviant kinds of behavior and the avoidance of unacceptable behavior because of guilt instigated by censure from legitimate authorities; between conflicting sets of personal values; and ultimately between condemnation by others and self-condemnation. Such conflicts are the main "motor" or condition for "upward" movement. They are worked out and movement is spurred not simply by reasoning about higher modes of thinking but by day-to-day exposure to concrete choices that reflect moral conflicts. Often the conflicts can be resolved not in the circumstances of a particular moral stage but in the reorganized perspective of the next stage above, in role-taking, or in the resort to leadership.

Dominating and personifying these alternatives are grass-roots leaders: parents, teachers, peers, priests, gang leaders, party officials, village elders. The sharper the conflict, the larger the role of leaders will tend to be. Children move through stages of moral development only in part as a result of the teachings of parents, preachers, teachers, and others; they are influenced by what the teachers *are* as well as by what they teach. Children may internalize the values of parents, school, and culture—the social matrix—and move to "higher" stages only as they see the linkages between those values and the widening social environment through which they proceed. Their growth is a continuous process of stages of response. Assuming new roles as they deal with new social pressures, children gain perspectives on themselves by imaginatively taking the view of their own actions held by their partners in role relationships. Role-taking demands an appreciation of others' situations and perspectives, empathy for others' needs and goals. Children, parents, teachers, and others variously and transiently become leaders and followers. Those with stronger and clearer motivations and purposes as "legitimate" teachers have the greater influence. In most cultures those teachers are parents.

We find two powerful leadership forces operating. Leaders and followers are locked into relationships that are closely influenced by particular local, parochial, regional, and cultural forces. In the progression of both leaders and followers through stages of needs, values, and morality, leaders find a broadening and deepening base from which they can reach out to widening social collectivities to establish and embrace "higher" values and principles. This broader, more principled kind of leadership—the kind of leadership that tends to be visible, formal, and legitimate—is usually expressed at the higher stages of moral development. Gandhi and Wilson and Tito and Franklin Roosevelt are prime examples in this century.

The process is not a simple or smooth one, nor is it predetermined. Leaders constantly come up against the intense, highly structured "situationist ethics" of particular groups and localities. What may seem to some principled leaders to be parochialism, inertia, perversity, or apathy may be, in fact, highly charged leader-follower relationships with their own tradition, structure, logic, and morality. Only with time, determination, conviction, and skill—and with the indispensable element of conflict—can followers be drawn out of these narrower collectivities and into "higher" purpose and principle validated by the most enduring criteria of justice and humanity and forged in an open and continuing conflict of values.

These higher principles and purposes comprise values that earlier we termed *modal values* and *end-values*. Typical modal values, such as honesty, responsibility, courage, and simple fairness, in the sequence of moral stages take on increasingly the qualities of more broadly and socially defined morality. At preconventional levels modal values are defined by rewards and penalties. Avoidance of punishment is a value in its own right. Fairness is valued, but only on the basis of reciprocity or mutual back-scratching, not on the higher level of fidelity or justice, at which level modal values become end-values. At conventional levels valued behavior is viewed as that which helps or pleases others and meets their approval. Good intentions—"meaning well"—are esteemed. Conformity to dominant opinion, to established rules, authority, and the demands of the social order is necessary and desirable within limits. The postconventional levels put greater emphasis on adhering to standards that conform to the agreed-on principles of the whole society and to the fundamental constitutional arrangements of its political system. Law is emphasized on the condition that law can be changed. *At the highest level* modal values are rights defined on the basis of a conscience that expresses the broadest, most comprehensive, and universal principles; hence they merge with the end-values of justice, equity, and human rights.

The fact that modal values involve individual *conduct* more than change, *style* more than *substantive results* (real change), does not diminish their significance. Fairness, civility, tolerance, openness, and respect for the dignity of others undergird and legitimate the elaborate system of due process that characterizes decent relations among human beings and informs constitutional democracies at their best. However, while these qualities have important implications for political and governmental systems, they are largely shaped in environments such as school and family that are not *overtly* political. While they are affected by conflicts and dilemmas within and between persons, moreover, they are not especially controversial. Indeed, investigators have found considerable similarity as well as differences in the manner in which persons in different cultures adhere to modal values. The dynamics of such values are dynamics chiefly of *personal* leadership.

Personal leadership becomes heavily politicized—becomes *political* leadership—as it relates to purposes issuing from and addressed to end-values such as security and order, liberty and equality, freedom and justice. If differences over modal values in personal conduct persist in some respects among persons and localities, among regions and cultures, one might expect that conflict on a truly grand scale dominates people's attachment to end-values. Within nations liberals and conservatives, leftists and rightists, socialists and Tories, struggle with one another over the essential purposes and goals of government; violent differences over explicit substantive ends feed the ideological battles that in turn embitter relations among nations. Often the conflict pits not value against value but *definitions* of values against one another. Both Roosevelt and Hitler made the symbol "freedom" the great object for which their nations fought during World War II; it was conflict over the *substance* of freedom that radically separated the two men and their ideologies.

Just as investigators have identified a "culturally universal" sequence of stages of moral judgment about personal conduct, there is considerable evidence of a large degree of commonality across cultures of consensus and conflict over end-values held by both leaders and followers. In a massive investigation of popular attitudes in more than a dozen countries, Hadley Cantril found a strong pattern across cultures of human concerns and aspirations; he found also common sequences of intensifying responses to deprivation that proceeded in developmental steps from acquiescence in miserable conditions (as in India) to an awakening of potentialities, to a grasping of means of realizing goals, and finally to self-reliance and self-assertion leading to action. A more common aspect of diverse cultures was the evident desire of large numbers of people for the freedom to exercise choice, to assert their own identity, to achieve personal respect and dignity. Milton Rokeach found a pattern in the development of values that responded to human need and correlated with Maslow's and Erikson's developmental sequences in a method of investigation that, he concluded, could be employed cross-culturally. The four-nation study concluded that relationships among leaders' values in different countries were highly comparable and that leaders differed more among themselves within the same community than they did from country to country.

These are preliminary findings; much more data must be collected and analyzed. If the findings hold up, however, a profoundly important hope may begin to be justified—that principles can be identified that to a marked degree transcend national and cultural borders, that these principles constitute both modal values and end-values, that political leaders and followers can mutually shape their purposes on the sustaining basis of these values, and that—because of the sequential and developmental forces at work—political leadership will elevate followership as followers sustain their leaders. This is not to minimize the force of conflict that divides persons over values. Yet much depends on the *alignment* of conflict—that is, on whether conflict isolates people in their nations, regions, or localities or whether conflict *cuts through* these entities and arrays human beings by purpose and principle rather than by geography or ethnocentricity. Conflict over purpose and principle compels political leadership to divide forcibly and responsibly over the most significant values in terms of potential for change—that is, over end-values that emerge directly out of the wants and needs, aspirations and expectations, of humankind.

Dare we speculate about these end-values and ultimate purposes? Only to a degree. Probably the worldwide debate over principle and purpose will focus even more directly, over the decades ahead, on the mutually competing and supporting values, the paradoxical trade-offs, of *liberty* and *equality*. Conflict over freedom of political and literary and artistic expression will probably sharpen within the Communist nations and the developing nations, just as it will continue to be a central political issue in the Western democracies. The claim of unfulfilled egalitarian promises will be asserted in "bourgeois" democracies and will continue and perhaps escalate in Communist societies that make equality their central tenet. How these values will be defined; how they will relate to one another in hierarchies of principles or priorities of purposes; how "subvalues"—liberty as privacy, for example, or equality as opportunity—will support or contradict related subvalues; how idiosyncratic talent and freedom of innovation will be protected under the doctrine of liberty of expression—these and many other questions can only be roughly answered. Fortunately, analysts can proceed on the basis of reason and logic as well as empirical data collection and analysis. One of the remarkable intellectual developments of recent years has been the rise in the quality and quantity of the investigation across national borders of peoples' needs, aspirations, and values at the same time that scholars have been reanalyzing concepts of equality in terms of the principles of "justice."

The debate over liberty and equality and related values, in the contemporary worldwide arena of discourse, is a debate not over the Good and the Bad but over concepts and priorities. Some—John Rawls, for example, and this author—would grant priority to *liberty* over any other social good, assuming it be equal liberty. (The only value, I believe, that might be elevated over liberty is security, but security would decline in desirability if it guaranteed only survival and not the values such as liberty that make life worth living.) Others would make *equality* the archstone of their hierarchy of values. We can see the implications for leadership in the process of choice and priority-making. Leaders who appeal to followers with simplistic slogans such as Equality, Progress, Liberty, Justice, Order are neither offering a guide to followers on where leaders really stand nor mobilizing followers to seek explicit objectives; they are seeking the widest possible consensus on the basis of the thinnest—or least thoughtful—consensus. They are not acting as leaders as we have defined leadership. Leaders who act under conditions of conflict within hierarchies of needs and values, however, must act under the necessity of choosing between certain *kinds* of liberties, equalities, and other end-values. They both exploit purpose and are guided by it.

Out of the varying motives of persons, out of the combat and competition between groups and between persons, out of the making of countless choices and the sharpening and steeling of purpose, arise the elevating forces of leadership and the achievement of intended change.

Leadership as Causation

To define leadership in terms of motivation, value, and purpose is to glimpse its central role in the processes of historical causation. That definition may help us to right certain imbalances and to sort out certain misplaced priorities that have plagued the search for causal explanations.

The definition allows us to make crucial distinctions between historical events without purpose and human acts that have purpose, between intended and unintended acts of persons, and between acts of *power* and acts of *leadership*. By starting with a totally inclusive concept of historical causation, we can successively narrow the scope of our definition of causal influence so as to identify and isolate the role of leadership. Each succeeding concept will serve as a subset of the preceding, more generalized concept.

1. *Historical causation* is the totality of forces, human and nonhuman, affecting the behavior of persons directly or indirectly. It includes *all* causal interrelations: the effects on human beings of physical environment, biological evolution, climate, natural disasters, insect and animal life, epidemics, and famine, as well as persons' decisions and actions. Historical causation includes the phenomena of both the spread of a disease like typhus and the reactions of human beings to it. Personal and impersonal forces together produce combinations of intended and unintended change.

2. *Social causation* embraces those processes and effects of historical causation that are produced by the decisions and nondecisions, the intended and unintended efforts of *persons*. Wars, migrations, technological inventions, decisions to run for office, and planning to counter the effects of anticipated catastrophe such as drought are examples of social causation, as is a decision *not* to act. Decisions of human beings do not always produce intended effects or planned change, of course; they may even produce intended effects that in turn produce unintended and undesired effects. Thus rulers take purposeful action (e.g., to win a battle) that helps set off chains of intended and unintended interactions (e.g., to lose the war and succumb to revolution). Social causation is that part of history that is caused by human action.

3. *Power* consists of those processes and effects of social causation that are produced by the intended, purposeful efforts of persons with power resources (power base)—the efforts stemming from the motives of the power wielder *regardless of whether or not the motives of power wielders are congruent with those of power recipients*. The actual extent of the exercise of power is measured by the extent that intended results are realized. Power is *intended* social causation.

IMPLICATIONS: THEORY AND PRACTICE

4. *Political power* comprises those processes and effects of power that relate to the "authoritative allocation of values"—that are considered legitimate uses of power under existing conventions, traditions, understandings, or constitutional processes. This legitimacy is usually linked to formal authority and the established government, but it need not be. Revolutionary leaders too are seen as legitimate by their supporters; theirs is a different kind of legitimacy, one stemming from their perceived recognition and satisfaction of popular wants, needs, and aspirations, either in a context—unless and until the new revolutionary regime cracks down—or in a relatively free and spontaneous expression of opinion.

5. *Political leadership* is those processes and effects of political power in which a number of actors, varying in their composition and roles from situation to situation, spurred by aspirations, goals, and other motivations, appeal to and respond to the needs and other motives of would-be followers with acts for reciprocal betterment or, in the case of transforming leaders, the achievement of real change in the direction of "higher" values. Political leadership is tested by the extent of real and intended change achieved by leaders' interactions with followers through the use of their power bases. Political leadership is *broadly intended "real change."* It is *collectively purposeful causation.*

These definitions are designed to enlarge the usefulness of the concept of political leadership in the analysis of collectively motivated political acts. They will also aid us in dealing with the age-old analytic "dichotomy" between behavioral and structural factors. The dichotomy takes many forms, but typically the structuralist approach emphasizes systemic, institutional, "functional" aggregations, such as class alignments, legal systems, educational bureaucracies, political organizations (parties, interest groups, electoral machinery), and other "external" forces. The behavioralist focuses on "internal" influences, such as motivations, perceptions, and understanding and knowledge as reflected in behavior, some of which can be measured by polls, surveys, and election results. This dichotomy, which has been simplistically but usefully described as the difference between pressures "on" persons and pressures "in" persons, this dialectical interplay between the socially derived "me" and a biologically based "I" (as Robert Friedrichs has termed it in a different context) can be resolved if we see the leader as empowered or constrained not by some cloudy or ephemeral entity such as class support or party opposition but by an estimate (accurate or not) of the political resources (votes, money) the leader can find in that entity, *as modified by leaders' and supporters' motivations.* The "structure" (a union, corporation, regional party, politicized church) is judged by its potential for constraining or blocking possible alternative courses by the leader.

The leader is dealing with persons—potential followers—who have their own power bases, however small, and their own hierarchies of motives.

In this process *both* behavioral and structural variables are converted into two sets: (1) the *motive bases*—hierarchies of want, need, aspiration, etc.—that can be mobilized by competing leaders and (2) the *actual power* that can be mustered through these motive bases—power that rests in economic, social, and other resources centered in institutions, technology, coalitions, constitutions, rules, traditions, ballots, money, information, intelligence, genius, skills. The leader eternally must deal with the double and interrelated question: what *can* these persons do for (or against) me in a pursuit of collective goals and what *will* these persons do for (or against) me? Hence leaders must assess collective motivation—the hierarchies of motivations in both leaders and followers—as studiously as they analyze the power bases of potential followers and rival leaders. Thus the power of a big corporation, which may appear to the casual observer (or to the ideologue) to wield massive political power because of its financial, skill, and organizational resources, must be tested by the acts and decisions of corporation leaders relevant to their own motives, to the motives of others that relate to available choices, to the power bases of specific persons inside and outside the corporation as they relate to those choices, to the convertibility of the corporation's economic power into political power (requiring recomputation of leaders' and followers' power bases), and to the degree to which preferred choices can be acted on. The largest restriction on the corporate leader in this regard may not be the difficulty of mobilizing the power bases of leaders and followers within the corporation but that of identifying and aligning commonalities between leader and follower hierarchies of motivations, especially in the transfer of those motivations to the *political* sphere.

All this can also be said about the "powerful" labor union. The relations between the New Deal and the United Mine Workers, between Franklin Roosevelt and mine workers chief John L. Lewis, illustrate the fascinating connections and degree of convertibility of respective sets of motive and power bases. In 1933 the New Deal administration proposed and Congress passed the National Recovery Act with the prime goal of putting people back to work, not of aiding and abetting unionism. Lewis, exploiting Roosevelt's popularity in the pits, plastered posters throughout the mining areas proclaiming, PRESIDENT ROOSEVELT WANTS YOU TO JOIN THE UNION. Roosevelt belatedly supported the Wagner Act in 1935, which also boosted labor's power to organize, especially in industrial unions. In 1936 Lewis and his newly formed Committee for Industrial Organization supported Roosevelt's re-election bid. Lewis walked into Roosevelt's office with a check for $250,000 and a photographer to put the donation on record. Roosevelt, aware of the possible impact of this transaction on some of his own followers' motivations, genially waved away the check. "No, John," he said. "Just keep it, and I'll call on you if and when any small need arises." In the following weeks campaign requests quietly extracted almost half a million dollars from Lewis' treasury. During Roosevelt's second term, however, Lewis broke with him over labor, political, and foreign policy. The union leader called the President weak, tricky, and lacking in conviction. In 1940 Lewis announced that he would resign as CIO president if Roosevelt won a third term. It was a test of Roosevelt's and of Lewis' political power in coal mining areas, and Roosevelt won. Later, during the war years, mine workers "voted" for Lewis when the President appealed to miners not to strike or to return to work if they had struck. Exploiting the motive bases and power bases of their followers to the hilt, the rival leaders failed or succeeded in varying degrees in transferring their support into a common battleground. Certainly neither the New Deal nor the mine workers union was "monolithic."

Another advantage of this view of leadership is that it enables us to sort out, at least in a preliminary way, the multiple forces at work and to shun explanations that turn on such a multitude of causes and so many different kinds of causes as to end up as nonexplanations. At the same time it avoids further search for *the* single cause. Certain causal factors can be converted into common, comparable, and potentially measurable and quantifiable scales. It is impossible to compare the political effect on persons of their unemployment, affiliation with a noneconomic interest group, general interest in public affairs, Oedipal tendencies, ethnic attitude, and late socialization experiences unless factors can be converted into common elements of power and motivational bases that permit identification and possible measurement. A single factor that might superficially be seen as crucial—membership in the "working class," for example, or possession of a million pounds—can be discounted until converted into power and motive bases relevant to leaders' choices and decisions.

Possessing a million pounds *may* be a crucial fact, but only if it is congruent with other power-base elements in a situation relevant to leadership. Possessing the right to hire and fire *may* be a crucial fact, but only in relation to employees' desires to keep their jobs, the interest of others in getting jobs, attitudes within the corporation and within the community as to the proper exercise of the right to hire and fire, union rules and attitudes, local or national newspaper reporters looking for "issues," legal rights and the ease and difficulty of invoking them, and—always—employees' and bosses' hierarchies of motivations relevant to the issue. In numerous situations "naked power" *is* exercised. An oligarchic corporation boss in a company-controlled town with no competing centers of power such as a newspaper or an independent church, with considerable control over company funds for paternalistic uses in meeting employees' wants and needs, with a plant "security" unit and perhaps a vigilante group among the citizenry, and with the capacity to appeal to the "nigger issue" in helping influence employee solidarity—such an oligarch is a power wielder, not a leader. A jail keeper may control the persons in his cells, but his would be acts of coercive power, not of leadership, for leadership always assumes some commonality of hierarchies of motives between leader and follower, and some degree of choice in a context of conflict or competition.

To perceive the working of leadership in social causation as motivational and volitional rather than simply as "economic" or "ideological" or "institutional" is to perceive not a lineal sequence of stimulus-response "sets" or "stages," nor even a network of sequential and cross-cutting forces, but a rich and pulsating *stream* of leadership-followership forces flowing through the whole social process. The living tissue is unimaginably complex. Much that is causal must be inferred, as apparent "leaders" react to anticipated motivations of apparent "followers" before initial action is taken and as followers react in advance to expected leadership actions. The actual interplay and conflict of countless and infinitely varied motive and power bases produce a density of relationships beyond full comprehension, although the hierarchical and developmental organization of motives, values, and purposes imparts some order and direction.

To handle this complexity analytically we may follow heuristically a "clean sheet" device of observing the leadership-followership process at a starting point where a Moses or a Joseph Smith has led his flock to a new life in a promised land, or a politician has mobilized a new popular movement, or a bureaucrat has set up a new agency in a city remote from the capital. The clean sheet is hypothetical, of course, since the leaders will carry with them socializing experiences and sets of motives and values acquired in previous habitats, and a rough leadership structure will have developed before or during the "exodus." But the new home will at least provide a more isolated context, one with fewer influences to track.

The signal aspect of the new situation will be the creation of new leadership as "exodus" leaders infuse their flock with heightened motivations, purpose, and missionary spirit. Followers become proselytizers who act on their own raised consciousness and arouse motivations in others. "Whatever the source of the leader's ideas," David McClelland says, "he cannot inspire his people unless he expresses vivid goals which in some sense they want. Of course, the more closely he meets their needs, the less 'persuasive' he has to be; but in no case does it make sense to speak as if his role is to force submission. Rather it is to strengthen and uplift, to make people feel that they are the origins, not the pawns, of the socio-political system." Such proselytizing will not assume consensus. Establishment of goals will be surer and firmer in a context of conflict, which at first may lie between the exodus group and hostile forces (in both its former and new environments) and later will develop within the exodus group.

As the new movement or organization expands and stabilizes, its structure takes on institutional and bureaucratic form, generating new motives and behaviors associated with careerism, professional recognition, organizational status, financial betterment. In the process original purpose may become blurred. The influence of the movement or organization on leaders and followers and on the wider public will be largely determined, however, by the thrust and appeal of the purpose established by the leadership at all levels within it. To maintain discipline, militance, and purpose and to counter the diffusion of energy, leadership will use psychological and institutional resources. The movement or organization will be separated from former environments insofar as possible, as in the exodus; hierarchical relationships will be developed; communication will be centralized; discipline will be maintained. Military forces, with their physical and geographical autonomy, separate identification achieved through distinctive uniforms and other symbols, and internal reward and discipline systems, are extreme examples of the attempted coordination of purpose, organization, and operation, in part through isolation. Such leadership structures are designed for maximum causal effect.

If concert of purpose provides direction for leadership-followership, then power bases of leaders and followers are social energies forceful enough to bring about real change. In the competition among leaders and in the mobilization of followers by leaders, the parties will seek to exploit their power bases so as to realize particular goals. The nature of these power resources will vary enormously: economic, ideological, military, political (personal popularity, access to voters, control of communication), skills, traditions, rules, friendship networks, access to decision-making centers, ability to appeal to wider publics through the press, certain persons' desire for publicity and others' fear of it. Would-be leaders ascertain the distribution of power resources *relevant to the purpose at hand*. Crucial in this process is accurate judgment of the capacity and willingness of various power holders using specific resources for specific purposes. *Purpose and power are commingled.* And in this process motive is, or should be, central. Power bases of followers that leaders hope to mobilize on behalf of their own purposes may be used by followers *against* the leaders. There is a time dimension too: leaders and followers may hoard power resources in order to fight different battles at later times.

To catalogue the power bases in one polity or even in one political organization of some size would be impossible, both because of the variety of the types and locations of resources and because those resources would need to be inventoried not for their abstract or reputed significance but for their causal influence *in specific situations relevant to the motivational and power bases of other specific actors involved*. To propose this concept, we must again insist, is not to assume a radically pluralistic distribution of power; it is not to contend that power bases and motive hierarchies are so varied, intransitive, and noncomparable that concentrated power is a myth. It is only to repeat that such power must be *analyzed* rather than assumed, viewed in its specific motivational contexts rather than hypothesized in advance. In some cases it will be found that countervailing motivation tendencies on the part of would-be followers are so weak, the motivations of power holders are so strong and congruent, their power resources are so ample and assured and relevant to the goal at hand, and the followers have so few avenues of appeal to public opinion, escape, defiance, sabotage, counterorganization (as in unions), legal assistance, judicial intervention, support from guerrilla or revolutionary groups, resort to tradition, "rights," constitutional guarantees—that in the light of the absence or presence of such factors a "power elite" may exist. If certain "leaders" held such power, however, the situation would be coercive and hence outside the bounds of our definition of leadership.

Paradoxically, it is the exercise of *leadership* rather than that of "naked power" that can have the most comprehensive and lasting causal influence as measured by real change. This is so because leaders engaging with the motivations of followers and of other leaders at all levels of movements and organizations are able to exploit the massed social energies of all the persons consciously involved in a joint effort. There is nothing so power-full, nothing so effective, nothing so causal as common purpose if that purpose informs all levels of a political system. Leadership *mobilizes,* naked power *coerces*. To be sure, leaders, unlike power holders, will have to adjust their purposes in advance to the motive bases of followers, but this still leaves a wide field for leadership, innovation, and action. Moreover, unity of purpose and congruence of motivation foster causal influence far down the line. Nothing can substitute for common purpose, focused by competition and combat, and aided by *time*.

Leadership and Change

The ultimate causal impact of leadership can be understood only in the flow of specific leadership-followership interactions emerging from the clash and congruence of hierarchies of motivations. In some theories of historical causation the movement of causal forces is pictured as a series of discrete acts or thrusts or stages, giving the impression that history resembles—to return to our earlier metaphor—a group of croquet players swinging mallets that knock croquet balls through a succession of wickets. But even if we hypothesize that causal influences are set in motion when leaders take the initiative in linking themselves with followers to fulfill mutual purposes, we cannot identify discrete steps in the process. We always find a stream of evolving interrelationships in which leaders are continuously evoking motivational responses from followers and modifying their behavior as they meet responsiveness or resistance, in a ceaseless process of flow and counterflow.

Consider a common Third World experience of this century. A left-wing, anti-colonial party, with strong and purposeful leadership, responding to mass wants and needs and aspirations as articulated by party leaders, throws out the old colonial regime and sets up a nationalist and socialist one. Nationalizing industry is a top priority. The new regime puts a bill through parliament to take over the mines, sets up a new coal board, dispossesses the colonial owners, establishes new management, and assumes "control" of the enterprise. Mobilization of mass needs and aspirations has thus created a power base for the new regime in a series of "steps." Responses, however, vary. Native managers and foremen, who had actually run the mines under the colonial masters, object to the new dispensation and perhaps turn to the courts, which have retained a measure of independence. Technical problems require consultation with the former colonial owners or managers. Adjoining "new nations" cut official imports in order to develop their own resources. Mine development requires more capital from domestic and foreign sources, and not every source may be motivated to cooperate. Life in the mines, set in the molds of routine, rules, tradition, long-established expectations and personal relationships, managerial rights and obligations, technical and technological imperatives, hardly changes. Production fails to increase and perhaps falters.

Little change has in fact been accomplished. But the process does not end there. Conflict over the situation is engendered among national leaders, new managers, management and employees, party and revolutionary organizations, national and local government officials, the employed and the jobless. Out of these conflicts new purposes are fashioned, new goals set, new procedures and institutions established. But the extent of real change in the working lives of the miners, in the rules they live under, in the distribution of power around them, in their lives at home, *must be investigated, not assumed.*

Processes such as these can be treated with some sophistication by the "field theoretical approach," which rejects the "genetic" conception of causality in favor of emphasis on the cause and effect of closely related events; "the field at the present moment is seen as a product of the field in the immediate neighborhood at a time just past." Attention is concentrated on measuring behavior at points close to succeeding and dependent behavior. The difficulty is that long-term psychological and social forces are embedded in the motive bases, and often in the power bases, of the actors in the field. The field theory encourages attention to movement among multilateral sequences of causal action; for example, voters may be affected by a number of simultaneous events, such as a depression, the advent of a new regime, and guerrilla action; voters may simultaneously be exposed to different channels of communication; voters may react in terms of affiliations held at the same time, such as union membership, party allegiance, religious choice, sex, and age; resulting acts may include voting in a certain way or not voting, turning to direct action or deciding on individual betterment as against taking part in a collective effort. Even these multilateral factors, however, will have a certain mechanical quality—will be like mallets hitting croquet balls—unless attention is paid to the interplay among both sequential and simultaneous forces, and that interplay cannot but draw into account the effects of needs, expectations, goals, and other motivational factors.

So causal influences as finally concretized in visible, tangible social change will be a product of the motivational interactions as they in turn mobilize leaders' and followers' power bases. This is a continuous, seamless set of processes as policy is made in party congresses, interest-group headquarters, legislative chambers, and executive offices and as policy is executed at the final action end of collective effort. Politicians will be tapping power bases—mobilizing interest groups, calling in credits, appealing to traditions and rules that help their cause, evoking party platforms or the farewell addresses of founding fathers as legitimations, calling on talent and expertise relevant to the policy issue. At the "final stage" of implementation the tapping of power bases will continue, but here the resources to be used may be more tangible: funds from treasuries and budget officers, personnel taken from other agencies or freshly recruited authority to issue rules and regulations, bureaucratic facilities such as communication and transportation. These entities do not sit around ready for the taking; bureaucrats have their own motivations and power bases.

We speak of final stages, but of course there are no final stages. The combinations of means and instrumental ends constantly open up new possibilities as others are foreclosed. Real change means the creation of new conditions that will generate their own changes in motivations, new goals, and continuing change.

Leadership analysis, with its emphasis on motivation, improves explanation by enabling the analyst to identify *purpose* among all the eddies and crosscurrents of the many forces at work—purpose that can be measured in itself to some degree and compared to intended results (real change). Consider a simple example: (a) Jones dies from arsenic; (b) he drank it in a glass of port; (c) Smith put the arsenic into the glass of port; (d) Smith wanted to kill Jones; (e) Smith wanted to do so because he would benefit from Jones' will. All these are causal, but as a factor of significance in both common sense and theory, Smith's *motivation* for wanting to kill Jones towers over causal relations a, b, and c. The motive is the paramount object of the police investigation; it is the factor that gives us food for thought as to whether we can prevent such murders; the other factors are matters of mere personal or technical interest (Jones likes port; arsenic kills). We might even conclude that arsenic should be made harder to procure and yet recognize that the dominant cause lies in human motivation, in this case greed. It is persons' *intent*, along with skill in exploiting power bases, that signalizes the most *human* factor in all the economic, social, military, and other "deterministic" forces that are said to make history. It is purpose that puts man into history.

Restoring the role of purposeful leadership to theories of history moves us from the world of abstraction to the world of day-to-day relationships, to what Peter Berger and Thomas Luckmann have called the "reality of everyday life" in discussing the "social construction of reality," the commonsense knowledge that people share with other people. It enables us, in the fashion of modern historians, to look at history from the bottom up and not merely at the "great men" and from the top down. It enables us to see history, in Isaiah Berlin's words, as "the sum of the actual experience of actual men and women *in their relation to one another* and to an actual, three-dimensional, empirically experienced, physical environment."

Traditional conceptions of leadership tend to be so dominated by images of presidents and prime ministers speaking to the masses from on high that we may forget that the vast preponderance of personal influence is exerted quietly and subtly in everyday relationships. The Indian shopkeeper who reads the newspaper, the uncle who travels, the local party zealot returned from a gathering of the faithful, the newspaper editor who transmits messages from far-off leaders (or suppresses them or garbles them), the village scrivener, the itinerant preacher, the bartender, the elevator operator, the most articulate of the women washing clothes in the nearby stream—these are the people who, with their more or less independent sets of hopes and goals, pass on to the "masses" the messages from on high—but at a price. Local, unofficial, unrecognized leaders of opinion, themselves motivated by needs such as self-esteem and esteem from others, they understand what motivates the people they see face to face, day after day, to a degree and with an accuracy that the leaders outside cannot match.

The role of the "great man" need not be diminished in this analytical process; he is only de-mythicized and de-mystified. That role is all the more legitimate and powerful if top leaders help make their followers into leaders. Only by standing on *their* shoulders can true greatness in leadership be achieved.

SOURCES: *Pages 417–431*

16. TOWARD A GENERAL THEORY

Lyndon Johnson's dream: Doris Kearns, *Lyndon Johnson and the American Dream* (New York: Harper & Row, 1976), p. 342.

Taoist and Maoist emphasis on self-expression by the masses: Robert Jungk et al., *China and the West: Mankind Evolving* (New York: Humanities Press, 1971).

Slaves' resistance: Eugene D. Genovese, *Roll, Jordan, Roll* (New York: Pantheon Books, 1974).

Leadership and Collective Purpose

Transactions between leaders and followers: note discussion in Bernard M. Bass, *Leadership, Psychology, and Organization Behavior* (New York: Harper & Brothers, 1960), pp. 94ff.

Quotation on the establishment of "a culturally invariant sequence of stages of moral judgment": Lawrence Kohlberg, "The Claim to Moral Adequacy of a Highest Stage of Moral Judgment," *Journal of Philosophy*, Vol. 70, No. 18 (October 25, 1973), 630–631; see also Elizabeth Léonie Simpson, "A Holistic Approach to Moral Development and Behavior," ch. 9 in T. Lickona, ed., *Moral Development and Behavior* (New York: Holt, Rinehart and Winston, 1976), pp. 159–170.

Other sources of development theory: Lawrence Kohlberg, "Moral Development and Identification," ch. 7, in Harold W. Stevenson, ed., *Child Psychology* (62nd Yearbook of the National Society for the Study of Education), Part I (Chicago: University of Chicago Press, 1963), pp. 277–332; Kohlberg, "Development of Moral Character and Moral Ideology," in Martin L. Hoffman and Lois Wladis Hoffman, eds., *Review of Child Development Research*, Vol. 1 (New York: Russell Sage Foundation, 1964), pp. 383–431; Kohlberg, "Stage and Sequence: The Cognitive-Developmental Approach to Socialization," in David A. Goslin, *Handbook of Socialization Theory and Research* (Chicago: Rand McNally, 1969), pp. 347–480; and other apposite articles in these collections.

See generally Theodore Mischel, ed., *Cognitive Development and Epistemology* (New York: Academic Press, 1971).

Roosevelt's and Hitler's definitions of freedom: James MacGregor Burns, "Hitler, Roosevelt, and the Battle of Symbols," *Antioch Review*, Vol. 2 (1942), 407–421; see also Ralph K. White, "Hitler, Roosevelt and the Nature of War Propaganda," *Journal of Abnormal and Social Psychology*, Vol. 44 (1949), 157.

Cantril: Hadley Cantril, *The Pattern of Human Concerns* (New Brunswick: Rutgers University Press, 1965), pp. 14–16, 327–328.

Four-nation study of differences among leaders: International Studies of Values in Politics, *Values and the Active Community* (New York: Free Press, 1971), esp. pp. 10, 149ff; see also Florence Rockwood Kluckhohn and Fred L. Strodtbeck, *Variations in Value Orientations* (Evanston, Ill.: Row, Peterson, 1961).

506   SOURCES: *Pages 432–447*

Rawls on justice: John Rawls, *A Theory of Justice* (Cambridge, Mass.: Harvard University Press, 1971); Norman Daniels, ed., *Reading Rawls* (New York: Basic Books, 1974).

Leadership as Causation

"Dichotomy" between structural and behavioral variables: McFarland, pp. 125–128.

Friedrichs on the interplay between the socially derived "me" and biologically based "I": Robert W. Friedrichs, *A Sociology of Sociology* (New York: Free Press, 1970), p. 227.

Transferability of power between Roosevelt and Lewis: James MacGregor Burns, *Roosevelt: The Lion and the Fox* (New York: Harcourt, Brace, 1956), pp. 216–217, 286–287, 449–450.

McClelland on leaders' arousing motivations of followers: David C. McClelland, *Power: The Inner Experience* (New York: Irvington, 1975), p. 260.

I have found useful on aspects of historical causation: R. M. MacIver, *Social Causation* (Boston: Ginn, 1942); Erich Kahler, *The Meaning of History* (Cleveland: World Publishing, 1964); Edward Hallett Carr, *What Is History?* (New York: Knopf, 1962); Hans Meyerhoff, ed., *The Philosophy of History in Our Time* (Garden City, N.Y.: Doubleday, 1959).

Leadership and Change

Field theory analysis: Kurt Lewin, *Field Theory in Social Science* (New York: Harper & Brothers, 1951).

My example of Jones and Smith was suggested by a somewhat similar example in Morton White, *Foundations of Historical Knowledge* (New York: Harper & Row, 1965), pp. 144–145.

Berger and Luckmann on the reality of everyday life: Peter L. Berger and Thomas Luckmann, *The Social Construction of Reality* (Garden City, N.Y.: Doubleday, 1967), pp. 21–28; see also the work of Erving Goffman.

Berlin on the actual experience of men and women: Isaiah Berlin, *The Hedgehog and the Fox* (New York: Simon and Schuster, 1970), p. 11 (emphasis added).

[2]
The Nature of Leadership

DEFINING LEADERSHIP

Beyond all the difficulties scholars have had with definitions of leadership that were expressed in the two previous chapters, we have the constant misuse of the term in the daily press, on television, and in advertisements. Leadership has become a "hot" word, and there is no better proof of that than its use in advertisements.

In San Diego, people can see a magazine advertisement or a mailer proclaiming "LEADERSHIP, COMMITMENT, AND VISION." Under that banner, they read: "For more than a hundred years, Great American First Savings Bank has been helping the West grow. We're proud of all the communities we serve. And our leadership role in their continuing success."

In the *San Diego Union* and on the local television Channel 10, there is a picture of three men and two women with the words "LEADERSHIP: 10 NEWS" printed across the picture.

In *Fortune* magazine there is a full page ad about "ASTRA Leadership... by design."

In the *Chronicle of Higher Education* there is an advertisement recruiting for a "Director of Leadership Gifts Development & Alumni Affairs" by Skidmore College.

I decided to go to one of my favorite fish restaurants in San Diego, and when I sat down at the table, there were place mats on the table proclaiming "SEA-FOOD LEADERSHIP, ANTHONY'S FISH GROTTOS."

The usage in these advertisements reflects the excellence theory of leadership. Leadership is being number one, leadership is producing excellence.

A second use of the word *leadership* is as a substitute for "the collective leaders who are in office" or "the leaders in an administration." Headline writers for daily newspapers constantly use the word this way. Some examples from the *New York Times* in 1989 will give the flavor. (The same kind of usage of the word *leadership* can be found in major daily newspapers throughout the country.) "Interim Rumanian Leadership Is Named"; "Where Mayors Lead With the Left: The leadership is new, but the agenda is much the same"; "Leadership: An Aristocrat Among the Revolutionaries"; "Worried Chinese Leadership Says Gorbachev Subverts Communism." This usage is much beyond the century-old meaning of the word commonly found in dictionaries: "The office or position of a leader."

A third popular notion of leadership is that of one person directing other people. Thus, a conductor exerts leadership over an orchestra, a director over a choir, a coach over a sports team, a captain over a platoon, a chairperson over a committee, a manager over a business firm, a principal over a school, and so on. Leadership is equated with what one person *does to* a group of people who make up an organization. This is the Pied Piper of Hamlin idea of leadership. An updated version would be the John Wayne or the Patton view of leadership. This notion of leadership has been very popular since the 1930s. It was more popular in the 1980s than in the 1960s and 1970s, so its currency is on the rise, not suffering.

All three of these meanings of leadership—being number one, the collectivity of leaders in an organization, and one person in charge of a group of people— are legitimate uses of the term because they reflect the dominant characteristics of the industrial paradigm as people have experienced it for the past century or more. These notions of leadership do not come out of thin air; they come out of the lived experience of the people in the United States and other Western societies. They are part of our mythology, the folklore that people use to make sense out of life. Being number one, putting top officials into a collective unit, and having one person in charge are how people have made sense of the world in the industrial era. These notions of leadership are simplistic, but the nature of mythology is to reduce complex realities to simple explanations.

However, if scholars want to study leadership, a more sophisticated definition of leadership is needed to make sense of the data that scholars gather both to generate and to prove theories of human behavior. The same is true for practitioners of leadership. Leaders and followers who use mythological understandings of leadership are at a distinct disadvantage in practicing leadership. The reality that leaders and followers face in their organizations and societies is much more complex than the simplistic notions of leadership handed down in the mythology would have us believe.

In an effort to capture some of that complexity, leadership scholars and practitioners since about 1910 (perhaps longer) have tried to develop a reality-based understanding of leadership in groups, organizations, and societies. There has been a great deal of fumbling, as the detailed story of defining leadership presented in the last two chapters has made abundantly clear. On the surface, these attempts to define leadership have been confusing, varied, disorganized, idiosyncratic, muddled, and, according to conventional wisdom, quite unrewarding. These scholars have not provided a definition of leadership that is (1) clear, (2) concise, (3) understandable by scholars and practitioners, (4) researchable, (5) practically relevant, and (6) persuasive. Most, if not all, analysts have concluded that the leadership literature since about 1910 has not generated a school of leadership. We have had, according to this view, no consensus on the meaning of leadership, no generally accepted understanding of what leadership is.

I have presented an alternative view. A more penetrating analysis—one that looks under the surface for background assumptions and takes a more holistic view of the literature over the long haul—suggests that despite all the apparent confusion of the hundreds of definitions and dozens of models, leadership has consistently been understood since the 1930s as good management. In a culture that has been managerial at its core, the scholars and practitioners in that culture could do no less than give the coveted and new concept of leadership a definition that equated it not with just management but with good management.

If that analysis is at all accurate, we have to reject the conclusion that there has been no school of leadership in the twentieth century. On the contrary, there has been a pervasive and powerful school of leadership, one that I believe should be called the industrial school of leadership. This school of leadership helped people imbued with the industrial paradigm make sense out of the concept because they already had a more or less sophisticated sense of what good management was. And the mythology of leadership—being number one, putting top officials into a collective unit, and having one person take charge—makes sense when leadership is understood as good management.

The problem today is that this school of leadership is no longer accepted by some scholars and practitioners of leadership. The consensus that leadership is good management has, to some degree, broken down. In an effort to make sense of the world they see, some leadership scholars and practitioners have defined leadership in a way that significantly challenges the dominant school of leadership. Many of these scholars and practitioners no longer see leadership and good management as the same. In issuing such challenges, these people are calling for a new school of leadership. They are involved in a paradigm shift which changes our understanding of leadership so that it makes sense in a postindustrial world.

LEADERSHIP AND THE LARGER TRANSFORMATION OF SOCIETY

Futurists and other commentators are virtually unanimous in their belief that a new era is rapidly approaching and that the Western world (and perhaps the whole world) is presently going through a radical transformation which is changing the basic values upon which the present, industrial era has been used. Futurists have not settled on a name for this new era, but many have called it *postindustrial*. The word *postindustrial* doesn't tell us much about the central beliefs of the new era and paradigm. It does tell us, however, that it will not be like the industrial era, since *postindustrial* denotes that the new era is beyond, or more than, or different from the present, industrial era.

The message that futurists keep sending over and over again is that the Western world is at present in a state of transition, a fundamental or paradigmatic transition wherein the values of the industrial paradigm are being transmuted in ways that eventually will produce a new paradigm, a postindustrial paradigm. This new paradigm will presumably become the mainstream paradigm sometime in the twenty-first century, and at that point the new era and paradigm will be firmly entrenched. Some people argue that the new paradigm and era are already upon us, and what we have now is a cultural lag—a period in which the mainstream culture catches up with the new reality that is already present. (I do not accept that view, but that is another issue.) Whether we are in transition or are already in a new era, there is a pervasive sense that our values are changing radically, and that the values built into the industrial paradigm are not going to be the ones that support a transformed Western civilization in the postindustrial world.

Leadership is one such value, and it, too, is being transformed. However, the definitions of leadership from the 1980s analyzed in Chapter 4 clearly show that the mainstream leadership literature is overwhelmingly industrial in its concept of leadership, demonstrating that the transformation of leadership thought to a postindustrial framework has barely begun.

If this analysis is accurate—if our thought and practice about leadership in the 1990 still express the dominant values of the industrial era—then a profound transformation of leadership thought and practice must take place in the 1990s if the needs of the people living in this decade and the twenty-first century are to be well served. Indeed, it could be argued that during this time of transition, the crisis in leadership is not that we in the United States and the Western world lack good leaders or that the leaders lack a vision of what is needed in the 1990s, but that our school of leadership is still caught up in the industrial paradigm while much of our thought and practice in other aspects of life have undergone considerable transformation to a postindustrial paradigm. We will not resolve that crisis in leadership until scholars and practitioners begin to think radically new thoughts about leadership, until they begin to make quantum leaps in leadership theory, until they develop a new school of leadership that is serviceable to the coming era. When that happens, the new school of leadership can be used to train and develop the thousands—indeed, hundreds of thousands—of local, regional, national, and international leaders who will help propel Western societies into the postindustrial era and who will help shape the future of our civilization and the quality of life of future generations.

In short, if a transformation to a postindustrial era is to happen in the 1990s, we need leaders who are imbued with a postindustrial model of leadership that guides the choices, behaviors, and thoughts of leaders and followers—which, in turn, molds their relationships with other followers and leaders. The crisis of leadership which people in the Western world are facing today is that they have not developed such a postindustrial school of leadership and that the leaders and followers—with rare exception—are still acting, choosing, and thinking on the basis of an industrialized leadership paradigm. While the industrialized model of leadership has served the people of the United States well since the late 1800s, it increasingly ill serves our needs as we approach the twenty-first century. While I know less about other Western nations, I would guess that the same statement could be made for them. Certainly, the events in Eastern Europe dramatically suggest that the old paradigms of change (and thus of leadership) ill served the needs of those people. Perhaps the revolutions of Eastern Europe are the cataclysmic events that were needed to help leadership scholars and practitioners understand the importance of dealing explicitly with the need for a paradigm shift in leadership studies.

WHAT IS LEADERSHIP?

The purpose of this chapter is to explicate a postindustrial definition of leadership. Before developing this definition of leadership, I had been using Burns's definition (1978, p. 18 or p. 425). Over a period of five years and with the help of many of the doctoral candidates in leadership studies at the University of San Diego, I found several significant inconsistencies between the reality that I researched and knew from daily experience and Burns's definition of leadership. For instance, there is an inconsistency between his definition of leadership and the concept of transformational leadership that he favored (rightly, I believe) in the final three chapters of his book. That inconsistency posed the question: What is Burns's *real* definition of leadership? Many scholars and practitioners who have read Burns's book think that his *real* definition of leadership is his definition of transformational leadership.

As a result of this and other conceptual problems, I set about trying to construct a definition that dealt with these inconsistencies and yet remained somewhat faithful to Burns's thought, which is much more forward-looking than the traditional conceptual frameworks of leadership. Thus, I view this definition as a development of Burns's thought. This definition of leadership could not have been constructed without repeatedly and thoroughly studying his concept of leadership as developed in his 1978 book. I read and reread, discussed and rediscussed, that book, often with doctoral candidates and graduates of the leadership program at USD, more than I have done with any other book. Studying Burns's book is like having scales fall off your eyes; you can never view leadership as you did before.

As a development of Burns's model of leadership, however, it is important to understand from the beginning that this definition and the conceptual framework embedded therein are significantly different from his concept of leadership in ways that will be very clear as the definition is analyzed in this chapter. It is an attempt to begin a new school of leadership that consistently and consciously accepts postindustrial assumptions and values. There is considerable textual evidence in Burns's book that in 1978 he was still under the influence of the industrial paradigm. In 1990, I have the advantage of twelve years' further experience that includes the 1980s with all its Yuppie characteristics, the new ideas about leadership, and the momentous events of 1989–1990. And I have the advantage of being only a decade away from the twenty-first century. Even more, it is hard to ignore the paradigm-shattering events and in Eastern Europe during the fall and winter of 1989–1990. As suggested earlier, the industrial leadership paradigm doesn't explain the history-making events of 1989–1990. A new school of leadership that articulates a postindustrial concept of leadership is more and more imperative. While this definition may not be the last word on the subject, it may be the first, and that is where both scholars and practitioners have to start when paradigm leaps are in the making.

The definition of leadership is this: *Leadership is an influence relationship among leaders and followers who intend real changes that reflect their mutual purposes.* Every word in that definition was carefully selected to convey very specific meanings that contain certain assumptions and values which are necessary to a transformed, postindustrial model of leadership.

What follows in the remainder of this chapter is, first, an outline of the four essential elements of leadership and their various parts; second, a listing of the four essential elements of leadership that are contained in the definition and a short discussion of what a definition means and how it is useful to scholars and practitioners alike; and, third, an extended discussion of each of the four elements and the various parts of each element. The chapter ends with some concluding comments on the definition as a powerful expression of the postindustrial paradigm.

A DEFINITION OF LEADERSHIP: AN OUTLINE

Leadership is an influence relationship among leaders and followers who intend real changes that reflect their mutual purposes.

From this definition, there are four essential elements that must be present if leadership exists or is occurring:

1. The relationship is based on influence.

    a. The influence relationship is multidirectional.

    b. The influence behaviors are noncoercive.

2. Leaders and followers are the people in this relationship.

a. The followers are active.

b. There must be more than one follower, and there is typically more than one leader in the relationship.

c. The relationship is inherently unequal because the influence patterns are unequal.

3. Leaders and followers intend real changes.

   a. *Intend* means that the leaders and followers purposefully desire certain changes.

   b. *Real* means that the changes the leaders and followers intend must be substantive and transforming.

   c. Leaders and followers do not have to produce changes in order for leadership to occur. They intend changes in the present; the changes take place in the future if they take place at all.

   d. Leaders and followers intend several changes at once.

4. Leaders and followers develop mutual purposes.

   a. The mutuality of these purposes is forged in the noncoercive influence relationship.

   b. Leaders and followers develop purposes, not goals.

   c. The intended changes reflect, not realize, their purposes.

   d. The mutual purposes become common purposes.

THE ESSENTIAL ELEMENTS OF LEADERSHIP

Definitions have been problematic in the behavioral and social sciences. And, generally speaking, the definitions themselves have not been well served (if I could be excused an anthropomorphic reference in this instance) because the scholars in these disciplines, in contradistinction to those in the hard sciences, have not paid enough attention to them in the form of serious, prolonged thought, nor have they reaped the rewards that accurate definitions would bring to their disciplines. The kinds of sloppy definitions of leadership that were documented in the last two chapters could be repeated in every behavioral and social science concerning very important words in those sciences. So leadership studies is hardly alone in this problem.

Definitions should have several properties in order to be useful to scholars and practitioners. Without going into an extended discussion on this subject, those properties will be explained. Then the readers can evaluate whether I have fulfilled my own criteria in constructing the postindustrial definition of leadership.

A definition must be clearly worded to communicate very specific messages as to what constitutes the reality being defined.

A definition must state specific criteria for people to use in separating one reality from similar realities. In other words, for a definition to be serviceable, it must say that these criteria must be fulfilled for this phenomenon to be called what is being defined. These criteria take the form of essential elements. A phenomenon must include all the essential elements if it is to be called the reality that is being defined.

A definition must be usable by practitioners as well as by scholars. If the definition is unusable in the real world by people who live and work in that world, it is useless in any research that scholars may want to conduct to understand that world.

A definition must be usable now, giving the user the power to do an analysis of a particular phenomenon immediately after gathering data. How much data must be gathered of course depends on the complexity of the phenomenon. Good definitions limit the data gathering necessary and shorten the analysis needed; poor definitions do the opposite. For example, any definition of leadership that requires the user to wait a month or a year to find out if such and such resulted from a phenomenon is unacceptable. People in the real world will not wait for extended periods, suspending judgment of people and events, to determine what that phenomenon was. Ordinarily, definitions must give people the ability to make decisions about determining the nature of something in a matter of minutes, if not seconds. There are exceptions, of course. Many scholarly definitions require that scholars and practitioners take long periods of time to gather and analyze data to determine the nature of some phenomenon. And some definitions make such a determination impossible, no matter the amount of data collected and analyzed and the amount of time elapsed.

The definition of leadership given above includes four essential elements:

1. The relationship is based on influence.
2. Leaders and followers are the people in this relationship.
3. Leaders and followers intend real changes.
4. Leaders and followers develop mutual purposes.

All four of these elements must be present if any relationship is to be called leadership. Three out of four are not sufficient. All that people need to do to establish if leadership is happening is to determine if these four essential elements are present. If they are present, the phenomenon is leadership.

Scholars and practitioners should be able to use these four elements to distinguish leadership from other relationships they have as human beings, and to do so in a matter of several seconds or a minute, not hours or days or months or years. Once a person understands these four elements, they are easily used as criteria in analyses of whether some phenomenon is leadership. The elements are clear and simple, they are expressed in words that people use in everyday English, and they are very easy to remember. Judgments that these four criteria require are well within the scope of the thousands of similar assessments people make daily in their professional and personal lives.

A discussion of these elements will clarify the exact meaning of each element and give some rationale for why each, and all four together, are essential in defining leadership from a postindustrial perspective. Each element has several parts, which are delineated by a subheading. Under each subheading there is explication of the element as a whole, followed by an extended analysis of each part of the element, and then a summary.

This kind of discussion is necessary at this time because (1) these essential elements are significantly different from those contained in other definitions, so they have to be justified or rationalized in order to persuade other people that they are necessary, and (2) people need help to understand this new definition of leadership because it is so radically different from previous definitions. Once they understand it, it will be part of their thinking patterns.

Influence Relationship

The relationship that is leadership must be based on influence. Influence is defined with Bell (1975) as the process of using persuasion to have an impact on other people in a relationship.

Persuasion, as Neustadt (1980) has so cogently reminded us, "amounts to more than the charm of reasoned argument" (p. 27). Along with rational discourse, influence as persuasion involves reputation, prestige, personality, purpose, status, content of the message, interpersonal and group skills, give-and-take behaviors, authority or lack of it, symbolic interaction, perception, motivation, gender, race, religion, and choices, among countless other things. I call these things *power resources*. Influence does not come out of thin air. It comes from people using these power resources to persuade.

If we conceive of leadership as an influence relationship and influence is persuasion, then two consequences follow.

Multidirectional Relationship

First, the leadership relationship is multidirectional. The relationship involves interactions that are vertical, horizontal, diagonal, and circular. This means that (1) anyone can be a leader and/or a follower; (2) followers persuade leaders and other followers, as do leaders; (3) leaders and followers may change places (I do not like the word *roles* because it has heavy industrial paradigm connotations) in the relationship; and (4) there are many different relationships that can make up the overall relationship that is leadership. These relationships can be small and large groups, departmental, organizational, societal, or global, and can be based on race, gender, ethnicity, family relations, clubs, political parties, and friendships, among other things. These relationships are often subsumed under or component parts of a leadership relationship. If a relationship is one-sided, unidirectional, and one-on-one, those are clear signs that the relationship is not leadership.

Noncoercive Relationship

Second, leadership as an influence relationship means that the behaviors used to persuade other people must be noncoercive. If the behaviors are coercive, the relationship becomes one of authority or power, or one that is dictatorial.

Authority is a contractual (written, spoken, or implied) relationship wherein people accept superordinate or subordinate responsibilities in an organization. Power is a relationship wherein certain people control other people by rewards and/or punishments. Both authority and power relationships can be coercive, although they need not be. In such relationships, people can be forced to behave in certain ways if they want to remain in the relationship. Coercion is not only an acceptable behavior in authority and power relationships, it is often essential if the relationship is going to be productive or effective. For instance, our system of highways and streets is fundamentally based on coercive authority relationships. Obey the traffic laws or get caught and be punished. Freedom is not essential in authority or power relationships, although a limited notion of freedom is often a part of authority and power relationships as they are practiced today in many business organizations. Freedom can also be used to get out of some authority and power relationships. People are free to change jobs, for example, in order to get out of an authority relationship. Or people can move to rural areas to avoid having to obey so many traffic laws. Other such relationships are practically impossible to get out of, short of total isolation from society or death or significant risk to one's personal welfare.

Dictatorial relationships are what Burns (1978) termed *power wielding*, though again his use of the term is inconsistent. Such relationships rely on physical and psychological abuse that one person or several persons use to control other people absolutely. Dictatorial relationships use people as objects, not as persons; keep people in subservient roles, not just subordinate ones; and are often life threatening in the extent of the abusive actions taken to control people. Obviously, dictatorial relationships are coercive at their core. Ceausescu in Romania, Noriega in Panama, and the drug lords in Colombia and other countries are obvious cases. Examples closer to home may be street gangs, godfathers in organized crime, party bosses, church officials, and employers or labor union officers who are abusive of their employees or members.

Coercion is antithetical to influence relationships. People in influence relationships can refuse to behave in prescribed ways and still remain on good terms with other people in the relationship. Freedom is essential to influence relationships. Of course, one can exercise so much freedom that one loses much of the influence one could have. Freedom is never absolute, and in influence relationships people can lose influence by exercising freedom of thought and action. The point is that people are free to influence or not influence, to drop out of one influence relationship and join another, or to drop out of all influence relationships. Passivity is not ruled out of the postindustrial paradigm.

There are more descriptions of coercive and noncoercive behaviors in Chapter 7. Coercion and noncoercion have implications for the essential nature of leadership (which is the topic here) and for the ethics of leadership. Deciding what is coercive or not coercive is a bit more tricky than deciding whether the relationship is multidirectional. The key word is *influence*, so concentrate on a clear understanding of influence as the basis for a relationship. If influence is what makes the relationship tick, then it is leadership. If not, some other relationship is happening.

Summary

To summarize the first essential element of leadership, it is a relationship based on influence, which is defined as using persuasion to have an impact on other people in a relationship. Leadership as an influence relationship has two characteristics: (1) it is multidirectional, in that influence flows in all directions and not just from the top down; and (2) it is noncoercive, meaning that it is not based on authority, power, or dictatorial actions but is based on persuasive behaviors, thus allowing anyone in the relationship to freely agree or disagree and ultimately to drop into or out of the relationship.

Leaders and Followers Are the People in This Relationship

The second essential element flowing from the definition of leadership is that the people involved in this relationship are leaders and followers. This sounds rather innocuous, but there are several important points to be gained from examining this element, especially the meaning of the word *followers*.

Active Followers

I have no trouble with the word *followers*, but it does bother a number of other scholars and practitioners, who view the word as condescending. Gardner (1986, 1990), for instance, has rejected the word in favor of *constituents*. That word is problematic, however, because it has strong political connotations. People don't speak about constituents in small groups or clubs, business or religious organizations, and the like. The word is mostly used in political organizations and as a result is unsatisfactory for a model of leadership that applies to all organizations and groups. Ford (1990) used the word *participants*, which has much more generalizability to different organizations. Gardner and Ford are two of quite a number of leadership scholars who want to get rid of the word *followers* for mostly egalitarian reasons.

My view is that the problem is not with the word, but with the passive meaning given to the concept of followers by people who lived and worked and wrote in the industrial era. Followers, as a concept, connoted a group of people who were (1) part of the sweaty masses and therefore separated from the elites, (2) not able to act intelligently without the guidance and control of other, (3) willing to let other people (elites) take control of their lives, and (4) unproductive unless directed by others. In the leadership literature since the 1930s, therefore, followers were considered to be subordinates who were submissive and passive, and leaders were considered to be managers who were directive and active. Since leaders were managers, followers had to be the subordinate people in an organization. There is no other logical equation.

In a postindustrial frame, leaders are not equated with managers, so followers are not equated with subordinates. Since leaders can be anyone, followers can be anyone. That does not mean that leaders and followers are equal. No amount of egalitarian idealism will change the fact that there will be followers as long as human beings inhabit this planet. Only the meaning of the word *followers* will change, not the existence of human beings who are followers.

A distinction between leaders and followers remains crucial to the concept of leadership. Since leadership is a relationship, leaders must interact with other people. If all the people with whom leaders interacted were other leaders, leadership as a meaningful construct would not make much sense.

For one thing, leadership would be quite an elitist or exclusive group of people, since there are and will be many people who are not motivated to be leaders, who do not have the personal development needed to be leaders in a sophisticated and complex society, or who are not willing to use the power resources at their command to exercise significant influence through persuasion. I think we need to reject any elitist notion of leadership in spelling out who can participate in the relationship that is leadership.

One could argue that if all people were leaders, the notion of leadership would not be elitist. I agree. But everyone being leader is not consistent with what we know of human nature, even if we do not equate leadership with good management. Our human nature is not going to change all that much in the postindustrial era.

A second difficulty with the notion that we are all leaders is the complexity of our times and that of the postindustrial era. Active people may be involved in a dozen or more leadership relationships at any one time, and it is conceptually impossible to conceive of them being leaders in all of these influence relationships. Scholars tend to think of people being in only one leadership relationship, but that is not the way people live their lives. Even people who are less active may have several leadership relationships going on at any one time. The only possible way for people to cope with such multiple relationships is for them to be leaders in some relationships and followers in others. If one examines the many other relationships in which these active people are involved (love, friendship, professional, work, religious, etc.), the complexity of their lives becomes clear. Time restraints alone require that people be followers in some leadership relationships.

Realistically, we know from past experience that some people choose to be followers all the time and that many other people choose not be involved in any leadership relationships. The complexity of life and our understanding of human nature based on centuries of experience would suggest that these two groups of people will continue to exist in the postindustrial era.

Thus, followers are part of the leadership relationship in a new paradigm of leadership. What is different about the emerging view of followers is the substantive meaning attached to the word and the clarity given to that understanding. The following five points give the concept of followers substance and clarity.

First, only people who are active in the leadership process are followers.

Passive people are not in a relationship. They have chosen not to be involved. They cannot have influence. Passive people are not followers.

Second, active people can fall anywhere on a continuum of activity from highly active to minimally active, and their influence in the leadership process is, in large part, based on their activity, their willingness to get involved, their use of the power resources they have at their command to influence other people. Some followers are very active; others are not so active. Some followers are very active at certain times and not so active at other times.

Third, followers can become leaders and leaders can become followers in any one leadership relationship. People are not stuck in one or the other for the whole time the relationship exists. Followers may be leaders for a while, and leaders may be followers for a while. Followers do not have to be managers to be leaders. This ability to change places without changing organizational positions gives followers considerable influence and mobility.

Fourth, in one group or organization people can be leaders. In other groups and organizations they can be followers. Followers are not always followers in all leadership relationships.

Fifth, and most important, followers do not do followership, they do leadership. Both leaders and followers form one relationship that is leadership. There is no such thing as followership in the new school of leadership. Followership makes sense only in the industrial leadership paradigm, where leadership is good management. Since followers who are subordinates could not do management (since they were not managers), they had to do followership. No wonder followership connoted subordination, submissiveness, and passivity. *In the new paradigm, followers and leaders do leadership.* They are in the leadership relationship together. They are the ones who intend real changes that reflect their mutual purposes. Metaphorically, their activities are two sides of the same coin, the two it takes to tango, the composer and musicians making music, the female and male generating new life, the yin and the yang. Followers and leaders develop a relationship wherein they influence one another as well as the organization and society, and that is leadership. They do not do the same things in the relationship, just as the composers and musicians do not do the same thing in making music, but they are both essential to leadership.

Numbers of Leaders and Followers in the Relationship

The next point to be made concerning the people involved in the leadership relationship has to do with the number of people in the relationship. The question boils down to this: Can dyadic relationships be leadership? Typical dyadic relationships are wife-husband, parent-child, employee-employer, teacher-student, client-therapist, doctor-patient, buyer-seller, and so on.

Industrial era models of leadership have been unanimous in viewing dyadic relationships as leadership. Such models show how much humanistic psychology had been infused into the leadership paradigm. The human relations movement in organizational behavior has had a large impact on leadership thought and practice. The apex of such thought is Hersey and Blanchard's (1988) situational leadership theory, which reduces leadership to one manager and one employee fitting into one of four style boxes based on the maturity of the employee. Blanchard et al.'s (1985) one-minute manager and leadership model reduces situational theory to one manager and one employee spending one minute together practicing leadership. The *Blanchard Training and Development Catalog* for the winter/spring of 1990 proclaims that "Situational Leadership II is the cutting edge of leadership training."

Despite the popularity of reducing leadership to pop psychology and equating leadership with styles of human relations, leadership scholars and practitioners would do well to exclude dyadic relationships from their concept of leadership. Those relationships are much better categorized as parental, educational, love, friendship, therapeutic, counseling, or management relationships. Leadership is better thought of as larger, more complex, and less intimate than a dyadic relationship typically is. The changes that leaders and followers intend are usually more involved than changing one or two persons. The mutual purposes that feed leadership relationships rarely, if ever, are limited to two people.

Many people feel they have to ennoble relationships by calling them leadership. A more natural view is that these relationships are already exalted in the very essence of what they are. The teacher-student relationship is a wonderful, highly elevated relationship on its own. Teachers do not have to lead their students to ennoble their calling; teachers educating their students are noble enough. The same can be said of other dyadic relationships: parent-child, wife-husband, counselor-client, doctor-patient, and so on. Why do people think they have to infuse these inherently exalted relationships with leadership in order to make them more appealing, more workable, more developmental, and/or more interesting and exciting?

From the point of view of a leadership expert, such practices only add confusion to our already confused understanding of the nature of leadership. There is no other way of getting a handle on the meaning of leadership except by limiting the concept to some restricted describable phenomena. Eliminating dyadic relationships from our notion of what leadership is would help greatly.

Eliminating dyadic relationships from the definition of leadership means that people do not call a single husband and wife relationship *leadership*. That does not mean, of course, that a wife and husband may not be part of a leadership relationship. They may, but the operative words are that they are *part of* that relationship, not the whole relationship. The husband and wife may be part of an environmental movement to save the ocean from pollution. The teacher and student may be part of a movement to reform education by emphasizing critical thinking. The doctor and patient may be part of a movement to stop the medical practitioners in a certain hospital from keeping terminally ill people alive by artificial means. The manager and subordinate may be part of a movement to upgrade the quality of product made in their department. And so on. Notice that the leadership relationship adds a new dimension to the nature of the dyadic relationship. The wife and husband do not just want to love one another and raise children (the very noble and exalted purposes of the husband-wife relationship); they want to help save the ocean environment, and to achieve that purpose they join with other people in a leadership relationship. Saving the ocean environment is not inherently necessary to a loving wife-husband relationship, but it is absolutely necessary to the leadership relationship in this instance.

These one-on-one relationships are important within the overall leadership relationship because, for one thing, they are the source of tremendous power resources that people use to persuade others of the righteousness of their cause and to form coalitions and other types of connections. However, these dyadic relationships individually considered are not the relationship that is leadership. Leadership is the sum total of all the interactions among all the leaders and followers in that relationship, not the individual interactions between one leader and one follower in that relationship.

With considerable enlightenment and cogency, Foster (1989) stated:

The idea that leadership occurs within a community suggests that ultimately leadership resides in the community itself. To further differentiate leadership from management, we could suggest that leadership is a communal relationship, that is, one that occurs within a community of believers. Leadership, then, is not a function of position but rather represents a conjunction of ideas where leadership is shared and transferred between leaders and followers, each only a temporary designation. Indeed, history will identify an individual as the leader, but in reality the job is one in which various members of the community contribute. Leaders and followers become interchangeable. (p. 49)

This view of leadership as community is a larger notion than is being developed here, but Foster's point is very well taken. We must learn to think of leadership as a "communal relationship," as a "community of believers," which is something larger than one leader and one follower, and even more than a number of loosely connected dyadic relationships.

For a leadership relationship to exist, there must be more than one follower, and there typically is more than one leader. I say *typically* because the norm in the postindustrial era will be for leadership relationships to have more than one leader. However, more than one leader is not absolutely essential. Much depends on the size of the community of believers, to use Foster's phrase. Think of a small group organized to change something. Is it possible to conceive of a small group with only one leader? I think it is, and such small group leadership relationships will continue to exist in the postindustrial era. Of course, a small group organized to change something, a leadership relationship, also can have more than one leader.

The conclusion is that one leader is possible in a leadership relationship. The trend, however, is quite clearly toward shared or collaborative leadership. As the postindustrial paradigm becomes more and more accepted in mainstream thought and practice, leadership will lose its Lone Ranger or Pied Piper of Hamlin image—the idea that there is one person who is out in front taking charge, and everyone else is following, more or less blindly, toward leader-initiated goals. As the new school of leadership takes hold, we will be less willing to agree that Lee Iacocca single-handedly turned Chrysler around or that Peter Ueberroth single-handedly took charge of the summer Olympic Games in Los Angeles and made them the rousing success that they were. Such leadership relationships—those involving one leader and numerous followers—become less and less possible and more and more improbable as we move to a postindustrial era.

Unequal Relationship

The third and final point that flows from leaders and followers being the people in the leadership relationship is this: The relationship is inherently unequal because the influence patterns are unequal. Typically, leaders have more influence because they are willing to commit more of the power resources they possess to the relationship, and they are more skilled at putting those power resources to work to influence others in the relationship.

However, there are times when followers may exert more influence than leaders, times when they seize the initiative, and times when their purposes drive the relationship. If one or a few followers cause this influence pattern to develop, the followers then become leaders. If this influence pattern develops from a larger number of people, I think analysts should see this as followers being more active in the relationship but still being followers. These fluctuating patterns of influence are normal and developmental, as viewed from a postindustrial school of leadership. The industrial paradigm of leadership saw/sees these fluctuations as abnormal, an aberration of the real leadership process, and counterproductive to the attainment of goals—which is the purpose of leadership. Such a view is no longer acceptable as followers take an increasingly active part in the leadership process. Again, followers do leadership, not followership. And, while followers sometimes change places and become leaders, they do not have to be leaders to exert influence, to use power resources to persuade others of their position. In sum, followers are active agents in the leadership relationship, not passive recipients of the leader's influence. That is the new meaning of the word *followers* in a postindustrial model of leadership.

Summary

Leaders and followers are the people in the influence relationship called leadership. A distinction between leaders and followers is crucial in the new school of leadership, but the concept of followers takes on new meaning as we move to the postindustrial era. Followers are active, not passive, in the relationship. They do leadership, not followership. There is typically more than one leader, and there must be more than one follower. And, finally, the influence patterns in the relationship are inherently unequal because leaders typically exert more influence than do followers.

Leaders and Followers Intend Real Changes

The third essential ingredient of leadership that flows from the definition of leadership is the notion that leaders and followers intend real changes. This concept comes from Burns's (1978) model of transformational leadership, but a postindustrial school of leadership would take the concept much further than Burns took it.

Burns did not include the concept of real, intended change in his definition of leadership on page 18 or page 425. His definition is different from his concept of transformational leadership, which he defines on page 20 and elsewhere. The centrality of real, intended change was never prominent in Burns's model of leadership, which he explicated in the first five chapters of his book. Real, intended change was rather like an afterthought that he emphasized in the last three chapters of his book, wherein he discarded transactional leadership (for the most part) and wrote eloquently and persuasively about transformational leadership.

On pages 413–461, Burns stated and reiterated that the test of leadership is real, intended change. "The leadership process," he wrote, "must be defined, in short, as carrying through from decision-making stages to the point of concrete changes in people's lives, attitudes, behaviors, institutions.... Leadership brings about real change that leaders intend, under our definition" (p. 414). In the end, Burns stated that "the test [of leadership] is purpose and intent, drawn from values and goals, of leaders, high and low, resulting in policy decisions and real, intended change" (p. 415). On the next-to-last page of his book, Burns concluded with considerable force: "*The ultimate test of practical leadership is the realization of intended, real change that meets people's enduring needs*" (p. 461).

Beyond the problem of having to wade through 400-plus pages to come to the conclusion that leadership is intended, real change, the fact is that the conclusion is not consistent with Burns's definition of leadership that he reiterates as late as page 425: "Leadership is the reciprocal process of mobilizing, by persons with certain motives and values, various economic, political and other resources, in a context of competition and conflict, in order to realize goals independently or mutually held by both leaders and followers." (The notion of "independently...held" also contradicts his definition on page 18, but that is another issue.) In the definition just quoted, there is no requirement for intended, real change. The "goals independently or mutually held by both leaders and followers" in Burns's definition could be status quo goals that change nothing. Much of his concept of transactional leadership can be interpreted in that fashion. Transactional leadership is an exchange of valued things, and as we know from real life, such bargains often promote the status quo. In summary, Burns's notion of real, intended change is consistent only with his transformational model of leadership, not with his overarching definition of leadership.

The way out of this conceptual confusion is both easy and clear. The way out is to put the concept of intended, real change into the definition of leadership and make it essential for any human relationship to be called leadership. That is what I have done. The definition articulated in this book states that leadership is a relationship wherein leaders and followers intend real changes. Thus, a relationship wherein leaders and followers do not intend real changes is not leadership.

Leaders and Followers Intend Changes

The word *intend* means that the leaders and followers purposefully desire certain changes in an organization and/or in the society. The desire is not accidental or developed by chance. The intention is deliberate and initiated on purpose.

Since the leaders and followers intend the changes *now*, while they are in a relationship with one another, the intention is in the present and is part of the leadership relationship. The changes, if they take place, are in the future, defined as any time beyond the present, and are not necessarily part of the leadership relationship. They may result from the leadership relationship, or they may result from other factors beyond the leadership relationship. Establishing cause and effect in situations where leadership and change are the variables is very difficult to do, and this definition of leadership frees us as practitioners and scholars from getting caught up in that problem.

This view points up a major difference between Burns's model of leadership and this postindustrial school of leadership. Burns's test of leadership (real, intended change) is in the past tense. It is primarily a test for analysts (leadership researchers and practitioners) who want to look back on a series of events and decide whether leadership took place. To reiterate, Burns did not place this requirement in his definition of leadership. Since it is now an essential element in the postindustrial definition of leadership, the criterion must be framed in the present tense: "leaders and followers who intend real changes." The present tense allows leaders and followers to recognize leadership as it is happening—to distinguish leadership from other human relationships in the here and now—and it allows leadership scholars and commentators (as well as leadership watchers) to do the same. This definition also allows analysts to look back on a process of change to evaluate whether it was a leadership relationship. Thus, this definition allows people to assess leadership relationships as they are happening, but it still allows analysts to evaluate situations that happened in the past.

Intention must be demonstrated by action. People cannot analyze the minds of leaders and followers to determine what they are intending. Persons typically evaluate the intentions of others by their words and actions. The same is true with the leaders and followers in a leadership relationship. They cannot interact and influence one another unless they show their intentions by communicating through speaking, writing, and doing. To make the leadership process work, the followers and leaders must show their intentions—that they intend certain changes—through their words and actions. They must try to influence others in the relationship by using power resources to persuade others. In their acts of persuading, leaders and followers reveal their intentions.

Real Changes

The word *real* means that the changes the leaders and followers intend must be substantive and transforming. *Real* means that leaders and followers intend changes in people's lives, attitudes, behaviors, and basic assumptions, as well as in the groups, organizations, societies, and civilizations they are trying to lead.

How does one decide if the changes the leaders and followers intend are real or if they are spurious or pseudo changes? The problem is quite difficult, and I do not have a good answer. One answer may be that in the beginning people will take the words and actions of the leaders and followers at face value. As the relationship continues, people make judgments concerning the intentions of the leaders and followers. Some of those judgments have to do with whether the intentions of the leaders and followers are perceived as serious after they have had some time to work on the proposed changes, or whether the leaders and followers show that they mean what they say by backing up their words with actions, or whether their intentions are sham and posturing because the leaders and followers do not follow through when crucial decisions about the changes they intend are made.

These judgments are made by people in and out of the leadership relationship. Followers make judgments about the leaders and other followers; leaders make judgments about the followers and other leaders; people in other leadership relationships that, for instance, might be opposed to the changes the leaders and followers intend, make judgments about the leaders and followers; and leadership watchers and commentators make judgments about the leaders and followers.

Even though the analysis is difficult, a definition of leadership must include the concept of *real* change in it. That concept must be included to be both logical and consistent with the other elements of the definition. If the definition allowed leaders and followers to intend pseudo changes, it would sink into the morass of confusion for which other definitions of leadership have been justly criticized. Change is the most distinguishing element of leadership, and if the integrity of that word is not preserved, people cannot possibly distinguish leadership from other social processes. Preserving the integrity of the word *change* is accomplished in this definition by modifying it with the word *real*. Intending pseudo changes will not qualify Make-believe, sham, fakery, pretense, posturing, masquerading, hypocrisy, simulation, and other dishonest behaviors that suggest the leaders and followers are not serious about intending real changes are unacceptable in applying this definition. Only when leaders and followers actually intend real changes is a leadership relationship possible.

Do Leaders and Followers Have to Produce Changes?

Another difference between the postindustrial definition of leadership and Burns's leadership model is that this definition eliminates the notion that leadership has to result in a product—a change that is real and was intended. Burns's view is quite product-oriented, and to that extent his model still articulates an industrial concept of leadership. "By social change, I mean here *real change—* that is, a transformation to a marked degree in the attitudes, norms, institutions, and behaviors that structure our daily lives" (Burns, 1978, p. 414). On the same page Burns wrote: "The leadership process, in short, must be defined as carrying through from the decision stages to a point of concrete changes in people's lives, attitudes, behaviors and institutions." On page 461, he stated: "Political leadership, however, can be defined only in terms of, and to the extent of the realization of, purposeful, substantive change in the conditions of people's lives." Note the emphasis on "transformation to a marked degree," "carrying through . . . of concrete change," and "realization of [,] purposeful, substantive change." All these statements define leadership in terms of intended change that has been achieved—a product. Leadership can be leadership only when the relationship is effective, that is, when it produces what it intended to produce.

In the 1980s, a new group of leadership scholars took their cue from Burns, as well as from a long tradition of leadership researchers of the industrial paradigm who predated Burns, and developed a new twist on the effectiveness orientation to leadership. In earlier chapters I have labeled this conceptual framework the "excellence theory of leadership" because these scholars define leadership as people achieving excellence in outcomes.

The fundamental concept of the excellence leadership framework can be stated very concisely. Leadership is that which is done by excellent managers, and management is that which is done by average managers. Leadership delivers excellent organizations, excellent products and services, and excellent people in the organization. The major result, of course, is an excellent bottom line. In sum, leadership is excellent management. People (leaders, followers, leadership watchers and commentators) evaluate whether leadership happened by the excellent results, by the effectiveness of the leader's behavior on the organization and on the employees of the organization in terms of excellence. If the results add up to excellence, leadership happened. If not, leadership did not happen.

The postindustrial school of leadership proposed here is process oriented. The definition states: "Leadership is an influence relationship among leaders and followers who intend real changes that reflect their mutual purposes." Leadership is not limited to relationships that achieve results, the real changes that the leaders intended. Leadership happens when leaders and followers enter into a relationship that intends real changes. Effectiveness or whatever synonym is used—achievement, results, excellence, products, success, peak performance— is not an essential element of leadership. A relationship wherein leaders and followers intend real changes but are unsuccessful or ineffective, or achieve only minimum changes, is still leadership. Leaders and followers can fail to achieve real changes and still be in a relationship called leadership.

As indicated earlier, this definition puts the intention to change in the present and makes it an essential element in a leadership relationship. The changes that may result from the leadership relationship are in the future (defined as any time beyond the present), and the changes themselves are not essential elements of the relationship that is leadership. One obvious reason for this distinction is that the leadership relationship may (and often does) dissolve before the intended changes are actually achieved. To make achieving changes part of the definition means that people could not decide whether a leadership relationship existed until after the changes were in place. As a result, leadership is always a process that was in the past; it can never be taking place in the present. Such a criterion is unacceptable because it makes leadership analysis and practice unattainable in the here and now.

Changes

A third difference from Burns's model of leadership is that the word *change* has been pluralized in this definition, in contrast with the singular form that Burns used. Leaders and followers rarely, if ever, intend one change; ordinarily they intend several changes at any one time. The plural allows for several important ideas to be included in the new, postindustrial framework. First, *changes* means that different people in the relationship can emphasize different but related purposes. Second, *changes* indicates that most leadership relationships have a long-term focus; when one change is actually accomplished, the relationship need not break up, because those involved in the relationship ordinarily have other changes they intend. Third, *changes* suggests that leaders and followers can rarely focus on only one change if they seriously intend real change; real change rarely comes in the singular. Fourth, *changes* connotes that the intentions regarding one or several changes may themselves change—develop maturity, be reassessed, undergo revision, even disappear—as time passes. Events impact on the relationship, words and actions take on new meanings, different networks or coalitions are formed, and the people in the relationship grow and develop. As a result, the people in the relationship reformulate their intentions.

Summary

The third essential element of leadership is that the leaders and followers intend real changes. *Intend* means that the changes are purposeful and are in the future. The intention is in the present, and the leaders and followers give solid evidence of their intention by their words and actions. The intention is part of the glue that holds the relationship together. *Real* means that the changes the leaders and followers intend are substantive and transforming, not pseudo changes or sham. To be leadership, the intention to change is all that is required. Leadership does not require the leaders and followers actually to accomplish the changes. Finally, leaders and followers ordinarily intend more than one change at any one time, so the word is pluralized in the definition to *changes*.

From all of these statements, it is clear that the third element of this definition of leadership places the postindustrial school of leadership squarely against the notion prominent in the industrial paradigm of leadership: that leadership must be effective to be leadership; that leadership must produce excellence, achievement, success, or results; that leadership is good management. Leadership is a relationship of leaders and followers who *intend* real changes, not who *produce* real changes. Changes may, indeed, be produced as a result of a leadership relationship, but they are not essential to it. Leadership can still be leadership when the relationship fails to produce results.

Leaders and Followers Develop Mutual Purposes

The fourth essential element of leadership that flows from the definition of leadership is the concept of mutual purposes. The changes the leaders and followers intend reflect their mutual purposes.

Mutual Purposes

If the purposes are mutual, the changes cannot reflect only what the leaders want or only what the followers want. They must reflect what the leaders and followers have come to understand from numerous interactions as the mutual purposes of the leaders and followers. Notice that I did not say the mutual purposes of all the leaders and followers. That is too high a standard, and it is unrealistic from any point of view. How would the leaders or followers know if the mutual purposes encompassed every single person in the relationship? How would analysts know? One of the reasons the word *purposes* is pluralized is to alleviate this problem. When leaders and followers have several purposes, the likelihood of mutuality is enhanced because different leaders and followers can emphasize related purposes and still achieve some mutuality. It also means that there are several purposes around which different followers and leaders can build a common vision or mission.

Purposes, Not Goals

The concept of mutual goals is very strong in Burns's model of leadership (1978, pp. 18–20). He used the word *goals*, which reflects the influence that the industrial model of leadership had on him and the obsession that leadership scholars before him had with the products and results of leadership. The goal concept of leadership has had a long and illustrious history among leadership scholars of the industrial era, as even a short perusal of *Stogdill's Handbook on Leadership* (Stogdill, 1974; Bass, 1981) makes abundantly clear.

Burns did not seem to make a distinction between goals and purposes. At times he suggested that leaders initiate a purpose to which the followers respond on the basis of their individual, personal goals. At other times he treated the words as synonyms. "*Leadership is morally purposeful.* All leadership is goal-oriented. The failure to set goals is a sign of faltering leadership. . . . Both leaders and followers are drawn into the shaping of purpose" (p. 455; the first sentence is a heading, not an emphasis).

There may not be any difference between purposes and goals, but I tend to think there is. Purposes are broader, more holistic or integrated, more oriented to what people ordinarily think of as a vision or mission. Purposes are often stated in qualitative terms. Goals, on the other hand, are usually quite specific, more segmental and often prioritized, and more oriented to what people ordinarily think of as objectives. Goals are often stated in quantitative terms.

Be that as it may, I deliberately chose the word *purposes* in this definition rather than the word *goals* to get away from the industrial and managerial perspective of leadership and to shift to a postindustrial one; to suggest a long-range frame of reference instead of a short-range one; to indicate that leadership has more to do with who we are than with what we do, with the culture of the organization than with its effectiveness, and with how leaders and followers integrate into the community or society than with how they get their needs and wants met as individuals or a group.

Foster (1989) reflected the same idea in what he called a critical practice of leadership:

It is an enduring feature of human life to search for community; to attempt to establish patterns of living based on mutual need and affection, development and protection. But this communitarian impulse is never 'accomplished'; rather it is an ongoing and creative enterprise in which actors or agents continually re-create social structure, and it is this which allows us to identify "communities"....

Certain agents can engage in transformative practices which change social structures and forms of community, and it is this that we label leadership. But for leadership to exist in this capacity requires that it be critical of current social arrangements and that this critique be aimed at more emancipatory types of relationships; any other type of "leadership" is basically oriented toward the accumulation of power and, while this is certainly a feature of all relationships within social structures, such accumulation indicates a personal rather than communitarian impulse. Emancipation, it should be stressed, does not mean total freedom; rather, the concept as it is used here means the gradual development of freedoms, from economic problems, racial oppression, ethnic domination, the oppression of women and so on. (pp. 48–49)

Reflect, Not Realize

Burns used the word *realize* in his definition: "... in order to realize goals mutually held by both leaders and followers" (p. 18). Realizing goals is a necessary element of leadership if one conceives of leadership as producing results. The concept of realizing goals is—as indicated above—embedded in the industrial paradigm of leadership as good management. Under that framework, it is very logical to expect the manager–subordinate relationship to produce good results and then call it leadership. With that theme so dominant in the literature, it is little wonder that Burns wanted the leadership process to "realize goals mutually held by both leaders and followers."

In constructing a postindustrial school of leadership, the notion of realizing goals has to go. It is essential that it be eliminated if we define leadership as an influence relationship among leaders and followers who intend real changes that reflect their mutual purposes. A concept of leadership so defined cannot include the notion of realizing goals.

I chose the word *reflect* not only to eliminate the results and effectiveness dimensions of the industrial approach to leadership but also to soften the linear and exchange notions built into the idea of "realizing goals mutually held by both leaders and followers." *Reflecting* the mutual purposes suggests that there is no 2 + 2 = 4 view of the changes that the leaders and followers intend. *Reflects* suggests ambiguity and fluidity in the intentions; it suggests development (progressive change) in the purposes of the leaders and followers rather than fixed, stable positions on what often are complicated and rapidly changing issues.

Reflects is meant to eliminate the hierarchical notions built into the industrial leadership paradigm: the background assumptions (1) that leaders and followers resemble a hierarchical chain of command; (2) that leaders announce the goals they have for a group or organization and followers more or less automatically accept those goals and then set about achieving them; (3) that leadership is primarily a one-way communication process which involves telling and selling when ordering is not feasible; (4) that leaders have the right answers and thus lead the parade of followers. A postindustrial school of leadership must put aside such linear views of leadership. These notions were acceptable when leadership was equated with good management. They are unacceptable when leadership is distinguished from management.

Mutual Purposes Are Common Purposes

Neither do we want to think of leadership as exchange theorists would have us view it. Purposes are not mutual just because exchanges are made, because leaders and followers have bargained one thing for another or traded valued objects. This kind of cost-benefit, interest group approach to leadership may "realize goals independently or mutually held by both leaders and followers" (Burns, 1978, p. 425), but it does not *reflect* the mutual purposes of leaders and followers.

To reflect their mutual purposes, leaders and followers must come to some agreement about their purposes. That agreement must be consciously achieved by the interaction of leaders and followers. It must be developed using noncoercive methods. It must be forged in the relationship that leaders and followers have, one which allows followers to influence leaders (and other followers) as well as leaders to influence followers (and other leaders).

The concept of mutuality has been deeply eroded by two of the central strands of American culture called utilitarian individualism and expressive individualism. These, along with the biblical and republican strands, were eloquently described by Bellah et al. (1985) in their perceptive and popular book, *Habits of the Heart*.

Utilitarian individualism applies "a basically economic understanding of human existence" to a society wherein human life is seen as "an effort by individuals to maximize their self-interest" relative to the basic goals of life (p. 336).

Expressive individualism holds that each person has a unique core of feelings and intuition that should unfold or be expressed if individuality is to be realized. This core, though unique, is not necessarily alien to other persons or to nature. Under certain conditions, the expressive individualist may find it possible through intuitive feelings to "merge" with other persons, with nature, or with the cosmos as a whole. (pp. 333–334)

Burns reflected both of the individualistic strands of the United States culture in his definition of leadership: " . . . in order to realize goals independently or mutually held by both leaders and followers" (p. 425). The word *independently* speaks for the utilitarian individualists and the word *mutually* speaks for the expressive individualists.

Burns's transactional leadership model is made to order for both kinds of individualists. This conclusion is easily documented in his descriptions of transactional leadership. There are many examples of cost-benefit analyses, exchange processes, what's-in-it-for-me, and self-interest politics (all of which articulate utilitarian individualism) in his model of transactional leadership. There are also many examples of Maslovian self-actualization, personal fulfillment by getting one's wants and needs met, interpersonal and group dynamics, and therapeutic psychology (all of which represent expressive individualism) in Burns's thought on transactional leadership.

It is not until Burns finally settles on his transformational model of leadership in the last three chapters of his book that his readers gain a view of leadership that speaks to the biblical and republican strands of the United States culture.

The biblical tradition "originates in biblical religion and, though widely diffused in American culture, is carried primarily by Jewish and Christian religious communities" (Bellah et al., 1985, p. 333). The core of this tradition is a belief in God and in human redemption.

The republican tradition originated in Greece and Rome, was expressed in medieval and modern Europe, and contributed to the development of modern Western democracies. "It presumes that the citizens of a republic are motivated by civic virtue as well as self-interest. It views public participation as a form of moral education and sees its purposes as the attainment of *justice and the public good*" (Bellah et al., 1985, p. 335).

Burns, in describing transformational leadership, consistently developed the notions that leaders "shape and alter and elevate the motives and values and goals of followers through the vital teaching role of leadership" (p. 425); that "transformational leadership is more concerned with end-values such as liberty, justice, equality" (p. 425); and that "transforming leaders 'raise' their followers up through levels of morality" (p. 425). "Leaders and followers," he wrote, "are engaged in a common enterprise; they are dependent on each other, their fortunes rise and fall together" (p. 426). Or, again, "There is nothing so powerfull [*sic*], nothing so effective, nothing so causal as common purpose if that purpose informs all levels of a political system. Leadership *mobilizes*, naked power *coerces*. . . . Moreover, unity of purpose and congruence of motivation foster causal influence far down the line. Nothing can substitute for common purpose, focused by competition and combat, and aided by time" (p. 439). And on the next-to-last page of his book, he summed up his concept of leadership: "The function of leadership is to *engage* followers, not merely to activate them, to commingle needs and aspirations and goals in a common enterprise, and in the process make better citizens of both leaders and followers" (p. 461). He concluded his book with this sentence: "That people can be lifted *into* their better selves is the secret of transforming leadership and the moral and practical theme of this work" (p. 462).

Such grand and eloquent statements (and others that could be cited) are Burns's finest hour, making it abundantly clear that the biblical and republican strands of the United States culture dominate Burns's view of transformational leadership. This basic thrust probably accounts for the widely popular and enthusiastic reception accorded the book by academics and practitioners alike. I love and respect the book immensely for the same reason. It was, as they say, a breath of fresh air in the polluted libraries of leadership books. It is this theme from Burns's transformational leadership that I want to pick up and infuse into this postindustrial school of leadership by insisting on a proper understanding of the words *mutual purposes*.

The changes that leaders and followers intend must reflect their mutual purposes. Mutual purposes are common purposes, not only because they are forged from the influence relationship, which is inherently noncoercive, not only because they develop over time from the multidirectional nature of the relationship, *but because the followers and leaders together do leadership*. Leadership is their common enterprise, the essence of the relationship, the process by which they exert influence. If leadership is the common enterprise of the leaders and followers, it cannot be done without commonality of purposes. Independent goals mutually held, a concept pervasive in Burns's overarching model of leadership that includes transactional as well as transformational leadership, are not enough because they are not common purposes.

The mutual purposes have an impact on the changes that the leaders and followers intend. The intention changes when the mutual purposes grow and develop. The changes that are intended themselves change when the mutual purposes grow and develop. When the mutual purposes become more common among the leaders and followers, leadership takes on new meaning as a communal relationship, a community of believers (Foster, 1989). At that point, leaders and followers can articulate the second language about which Bellah and his associates (1985) wrote: a mode of public, moral discourse that springs out of the biblical and republican traditions, a language that speaks to the habits of the heart because it deals with public virtue and the common good. At that point, leaders and followers will have come to the understanding that putting their own good as individuals, groups, or organizations ahead of the common good of the community or society is not leadership, because that kind of understanding does not reflect mutual purposes, only independent goals mutually held. In leadership writ large, the mutual purposes are the common good.

Using the second language, mutual purposes go to the heart of what Burns called *end values*: liberty and equality, freedom and justice, equity and care, peace and security. These are the values that serve as standards, representing the most comprehensive and highest of universal human goods. When leaders and followers reflect true mutual purposes, leadership expresses the common good: (1) a common striving for a community wherein public discourse about end values is commonplace, (2) a common commitment to a social ecology wherein public discourse addresses the issue of how living things, including human beings, can exist in relationship with one another in their common habitat, (3) a common mission to transform our culture and our society so as to reconstitute the social world (Bellah et al., 1985, pp. 283-290).

Summary

Leaders and followers develop mutual purposes.

1. The mutuality of these purposes is forged through the noncoercive, influence relationship.
2. These are purposes, not goals. Purposes are more overarching and holistic than goals, and they are less oriented to quantification. Purposes allow for the development of more mutuality; goals tend to be more fixed and rigid.
3. The leaders and followers reflect, not realize, their purposes.
4. Mutual purposes become common purposes because followers and leaders engage in leadership together. Independent goals mutually held do not qualify for what is meant here as mutual purposes. Mutual purposes are common purposes held by a community of believers.

TRANSFORMATION AND LEADERSHIP

Leadership is about transformation. Burns said it, but he failed to follow through as well as he could have throughout his penetrating book. In this attempt at a new paradigm of leadership for the postindustrial age, I want to say it, and I want transformation to be the cornerstone of the postindustrial school of leadership. Real transformation involves active people, engaging in influence relationships based on persuasion, intending real changes to happen, and insisting that those changes reflect their mutual purposes. The definition of leadership offered herein includes all four of those essential elements.

Transformation is done by active people. A definition of leadership that states only active people are able to do leadership and a definition that insists the followers—as well as the leaders—be active is a concept of leadership that engenders transformation. Passive people are rarely transformed by ordinary human processes. Calamities may transform them, but not leadership. Leadership helps to transform people in organizations who engage themselves in the relationship that is leadership. In the process, organizations and societies may also be transformed.

Transformation is about influence relationships based on persuasion, not coercion. A definition that states that leadership is a multidirectional influence relationship of people who use persuasion to make an impact is a paradigm that articulates what transformation is all about. People, groups, and organizations that are persuaded to change may be transformed; those that are coerced to change are rarely transformed.

Transformation is about people intending real changes to happen. A definition of leadership that encompasses only those relationships of people who intend real changes and that excludes those relationships of people who intend the status quo or pseudochanges, is a conceptual framework that takes transformation seriously. When real, substantive changes are intended, transformation is possible and even likely. When pseudochanges are intended, transformation is quite unlikely.

Transformation is insisting that the changes reflect the mutual purposes of the people engaged in the transformation. A definition of leadership which requires that the changes the leaders and followers intend reflect their mutual purposes is a model of leadership which explicates the nature of transformation. Changes that realize mutually held independent goals may have some impact, but they will not often engender transformation. Transformation happens in groups, organizations, and societies when people develop common purposes. In leadership writ large, mutual purposes help people work for the common good, help people build community.

A second point that should be made about leadership and transformation is this: Including a moral requirement in either the definition of leadership or an understanding of transformation is too limiting, and thus unacceptable.

There are no moral criteria in the postindustrial definition of leadership. An influence relationship among leaders and followers who intend real changes that reflect their mutual purposes can be moral or immoral. While there is a requirement that the process of leadership be ethical (noncoercive, multidirectional, influence-oriented, real, and mutual), the changes that the leaders and followers intend can fall along a continuum of morality. Thus, it is possible to have an influence relationship among leaders and followers who intend abortion upon demand as a public policy in the United States, as that position reflects their mutual purposes, and to have another influence relationship among leaders and followers who intend a public policy centered on the right to life, as that position reflects their mutual purposes. Some people believe that the pro-abortion position is immoral; other people believe that the anti-abortion position is immoral. If morality is a requirement for leadership, neither of these influence relationships could be labeled leadership, since each of them is considered immoral by a large portion of the population.

The same can be said about the concept of transformation. To limit the notion of transformation to those changes that take the higher moral ground (to use Jesse Jackson's phrase) is unacceptable because in many situations and for many issues there is no consensus as to what the higher moral ground is. Capital punishment is a good example. Many people passionately insist that capital punishment is the higher moral ground and that they want our society (and the world) transformed to punish convicted murderers so that other people will not be murderers. Other people just as vehemently say that life in prison without parole is the higher moral ground and that they want our society (and the world) transformed so as to eliminate the possibility of states (nations) killing prisoners as a punishment for their crime. If morality is a requirement for transformation, neither of these changes could be labeled a transformation because each of them is immoral according to a large portion of the population.

Burns's notion of transformational leadership is that "leaders and followers raise one another to higher levels of motivation and morality" (p. 20). Toward the end of his work, he is even stronger. "*Transforming leadership is elevating.* It is moral but not moralistic. Leaders engage with followers, but from higher levels of morality; in the enmeshing of goals and values both leaders and followers are raised to more principled levels of judgment" (p. 455; the first sentence is a heading, not an emphasis).

Burns based his concept of transformational leadership on *only* the moral development of the leaders and followers. This requirement means that the real intended changes inherent in transformational leadership must be of the kind that raise leaders and followers to higher levels of morality. The raising of groups, organizations, societies to higher levels of morality was not emphasized by Burns, although the idea could be implied from his model of transformational leadership. One could make the argument that if leaders and followers raised their levels of morality, the morality of the groups, organizations, and societies to which they belonged would also be raised. There is considerable controversy concerning that view of moral development. Moreover, the question of what critical mass of morally raised individuals it takes to have an impact on a group, organization, or society is, at this point, unanswerable. That an organization or society is better because of individuals who raise their morality is unquestioned. Whether that organization or society is itself raised to a higher level of morality by such individual actions is an issue about which we do not have a clear understanding or a satisfactory answer.

Having a moral requirement for transformational leadership may be acceptable if the overall definition of leadership does not include that moral requirement (which Burns's definition does not) and there is another kind of leadership that allows for what some people would consider immoral changes (as Burns does in his model of transactional leadership). But the problem is that the large majority of people reading Burns's book have not paid attention to the overall definition of leadership and have deliberately ignored or rejected transactional leadership as leadership; thus they are left with the inevitable conclusion that Burns's concept of leadership is transformational with the moral requirement included. Such an understanding of leadership is scientifically impossible to accept because it does not account for many human relationships that practically everyone labels leadership. The facts do not support such a definition. Such an understanding of leadership is conceptually unacceptable because it does not make sense. It makes it impossible for analysts to agree on what leadership is, since that is dependent upon what they believe is moral. We have more than enough trouble untangling the confusion about what leadership is without linking the concept of leadership to some notion of moral development.

Since two forms of leadership that allow for one form of leadership to be immoral and the other to be moral, have not been included in the postindustrial paradigm of leadership, and since the purpose here is to focus on a single definition that takes into account all possible situations with extremely diverse phenomena involved, a moral requirement cannot be included in the postindustrial definition of leadership.

The same is true of the concept of transformation. Stated bluntly, there are more transformations that people and organizations go through than those which raise them to higher levels of morality. In my view, transformation can take place in many aspects of our personal, professional, and moral lives as well as in many aspects of the groups, organizations, communities, and societies in which we live and work. These transformations can be physical, intellectual, aesthetic, psychological, social, civic, ecological, transcendental, moral, spiritual, and holistic. A leadership paradigm that is serious about transformation must take into account all of these transformations, not exclude all of them except one. A definition of leadership that requires leaders and followers to intend real changes must take the notion of transformation seriously, not limit it to certain kinds of changes. Changes come in all shapes, sizes, qualities, and moral perspectives; so do transformations. The facts of life are that some transformations are good and others are bad; some may be good for a while and not so good after some time elapses; some are considered good by one portion of the people and mediocre or bad by another portion. Leadership and transformation, properly conceived, must deal with the reality of human existence as it is lived, wherein changes are variously evaluated and desired. Leadership, properly defined, is about transformation, all kinds of transformations.

CONCLUSION

I have tried to put together a consistent, coherent, workable, and accurate model of leadership that is easily understood by both academics and practitioners. This new model is not more of the same; it is an attempt to start a new school of leadership, a school that is radically different from the industrial school of leadership, which articulates an understanding of leadership as good management. This new school of leadership presents a substantial paradigm shift toward a model of leadership that is postindustrial in its basic background assumptions and in its definition. That this paradigm shift is massive is immediately evident from the complete separation of leadership from management inherent in the definition and the seriousness with which that distinction is taken. Other telltale signs are in the four essential elements of leadership that flow from the definition: (1) a relationship based on influence, (2) leaders and followers develop that relationship, (3) they intend real changes, and (4) they have mutual purposes. These four elements are radically different from any set of essential elements which are presently found in the industrial paradigm of leadership that does not distinguish leadership from good management. These elements are, as we have seen, quite different from Burns's definition of leadership, which is viewed as a transitional model from the industrial to the postindustrial paradigms of leadership.

While a moral definition of leadership has been rejected, I have insisted that the ethics of leadership be included in the definition. The ethics of leadership has to do with the process of leadership—the relationship that is leadership—and not with the content of leadership, not with the question of whether such and such changes that certain leaders and followers intend are morally uplifting. While such questions are obviously very important to the people who do leadership—and I am one of those people—they do not deal with the nature of leadership, which is what this chapter is all about.

The ethics of leadership is a subject just now taking hold. Leadership scholars and practitioners must pay increasing attention to the subject. Professional development workshops and seminars must be developed to deal with the subject. But leaders and followers should not confuse the nature of leadership with what they think good leadership is. The two are not the same. What leaders and followers, as well as leadership watchers and commentators, need to know about the ethics of leadership is the centrality of influence in the leadership process and the essentiality of mutual purposes as common purposes. When they have learned that, they can then talk about and encourage good leadership—that which will, according to their moral standards, generate people, groups, organizations, and societies that exude a higher moral purpose.

There are exciting times ahead. Change is so rapid that the people living today are the first generation who can participate in a massive paradigm shift and know that they are going through it. The shift to a postindustrial paradigm certainly involves many significant changes in our lives and in our background assumptions. Ferguson (1980) and others have already documented the extensive changes many people have experienced in this monumental swing to the twenty-first century, and these authors have also predicted some of the transformations the postindustrial era has in store for us in practically every aspect of life. Leadership is one of the concepts and practices that will be transformed as Western societies move from an industrial to a postindustrial paradigm. Indeed, leadership may be crucial to a peaceful and orderly process as people individually and collectively struggle with that paradigm shift. But leaders and followers are not up to that job unless leadership scholars and practitioners begin now to move toward model of leadership that is more attuned to the postindustrial era. What our organizations and communities need are leadership relationships based on a postindustrial model of leadership. Such relationships will facilitate the transition to the postindustrial era. But they will not become widespread until scholars and practitioners build a new school of leadership.

References

Bass, B. M. (1981). *Stogdill's handbook of leadership* (rev. ed.). New York: The Free Press.

Bell, D. J. (1975). *Power, influence, and authority.* New York: Oxford University Press.

Bellah, R. N., Madsen, R., Sullivan, W. M., Swidler, A., & Tipton, S. M. (1985). *Habits of the heart.* New York: Harper & Row.

Blanchard, K., Zigarmi, P., & Zigarmi, D. (1985). *Leadership and the one minute manager.* New York: Morrow.

Burns, J. M. (1978). *Leadership.* New York: Harper & Row.

Ferguson, M. (1980). *The Aquarian conspiracy.* Los Angeles: Tarcher.

Ford, J. F. (1990). *Education for Christian leadership.* Doctoral dissertation, University of San Diego.

Foster, W. F. (1989). Toward a critical practice of leadership. In J. Smyth (Ed.), *Critical perspectives on educational leadership* (pp. 39–62). London: Falmer.

Gardner, J. W. (1986). *The nature of leadership.* Washington, DC: Independent Sector.

Gardner, J. W. (1990). *On leadership.* New York: The Free Press.

Hersey, P., & Blanchard, K. (1988). *Management of organizational behavior: Utilizing human resources* (5th ed.). Englewood Cliffs, NJ: Prentice-Hall.

Neustadt, R. (1960/1980). *Presidential power* (2nd ed.). New York: Wiley. (Original published in 1960.)

Stogdill, R. M. (1974). *Handbook of leadership.* New York: The Free Press.

[3]
Lessons from the Past, Implications for the Future

> We are shaping the world faster than we can change ourselves, and we are applying to the present the habits of the past.
>
> —*Winston Churchill*

My survey completed, I can reflect on the overall enterprise. In doing so, I abandon the thematic approach of the preceding chapters and revert to a more systematic method. My stocktaking begins with a sketch of the life of a hypothetical leader—an "ideal-type" description that captures patterns evident from the study.* Next, I review the principal findings with respect to six features imminent in all forms of leadership. For greater perspective, I contrast the eleven leaders on whom I have focused with six "creators" of my earlier study and with the ten leaders of the Second World War. This comparative perspective should illuminate the steps across the Einstein-Eureka continuum that I introduced at the beginning of this book.

In the final pages I focus on a number of issues that remain open. I consider three key questions raised by the study; identify six trends that will affect the shape of leadership in the foreseeable future; and, in conclusion, recommend the courses of action that may facilitate leaders' work in the future.

Introducing an Exemplary Leader

As a youth, the exemplary leader (whom I have dubbed E.L.) displays special gifts in two areas: she is a skilled speaker, and she displays a keen interest in, and an understanding of, other people. Unless she displays a particular strength in schoolwork, she is unlikely to consider a career as a teacher,

---

*An ideal type does not purport to apply in equal measure to every member of a class; rather it seeks to highlight those features that recur prominently in most members of a group and that help others to understand the nature of that group.

researcher, or other highly trained professional. Individuals who observe E.L. comment on her general energy and resourcefulness, rather than on her specific talents: there is consensus that she will accomplish something, but it is not yet apparent in which spheres that accomplishment will occur.

The primary exception to this picture comes from the youth with a strong academic bent. That person—one such as Mead, Oppenheimer, or Lenin—is likely initially to pursue some kind of scholarly or professional career. Only gradually does such a person come to realize that he is more likely to achieve his personal goals or to satisfy his community if he addresses a wider audience than if he remains completely within a specific domain.

Among the early markers of the leader's personality, the most telling indication is a willingness to confront individuals in authority. Sometimes this confrontation is abrasive, but it need not be so. Rather, E.L. stands out in that she identifies with and feels herself to be a peer of an individual in a position of authority. To E.L. it therefore feels natural—or at least possible—to address that person directly. Moreover, E.L. has pondered the issues involved in a specific position of leadership and believes that her own insights are at least as well motivated and perhaps more likely to be effective than those of the person currently at the helm. Perhaps this feeling of confidence stems from the fact that E.L.'s proposed solutions to problems grow out of her own life circumstances and thus are more appropriate than solutions conceived in earlier times or in other places. E.L., like many other future leaders, lost her father when she was young. Perhaps this loss empowers her to speak up, whereas another person might allow his or her literal or surrogate father to exercise authority in the public sphere.

This feeling of entitlement, this willingness to challenge, entails risk. Many individuals who, as young adults, have challenged those in power have been slapped down, jailed, or even killed. But future leaders like E.L. are risk takers and do not easily withdraw from the fray. (The principal exceptions to this pattern would be individuals who belong to a highly bureaucratized organization, such as the military, the church, or a large corporation. Here, the future leader must sometimes hold her tongue and wait her turn. Yet, despite their lower profiles, individuals such as George Marshall, Pope John XXIII, and Alfred Sloan, Jr., were all prepared to speak their mind when this proved necessary.) Those individuals who sometimes became ambivalent about asserting themselves, such as J. Robert Oppenheimer, were at risk for attack by those who did not lack such compunctions.

Some other early markers are worth noting. E.L. stands out because of her concern with moral issues. She also tends to be competitive and to enjoy achieving a position of control. Sometimes, power is intoxicating in itself, but most of the leaders on whom I focus in this book sought power in order to attain certain goals.

Lessons from the Past, Implications for the Future

Whatever her ultimate aspirations are, E.L. begins by working out personal relations with individuals in her own orbit—her family, her neighbors, and other residents of her community. It is the mark of a future leader that the size of these circles increases rapidly, and that the aspiring leader is dealing with hundreds of individuals, rather than a dozen or a score, by the time she has reached her majority. These individuals might be other practitioners in E.L.'s domain, or they might be heterogeneously drawn from a range of domains. Typically, the future leader maintains these heterogeneous contacts. In this respect, she differs from the prototypical creator, who characteristically abandons contacts when they no longer prove relevant to the next project. E.L. readily identifies with individuals who occupy leadership positions; she sometimes imitates them and sometimes challenges them. While interactions with others take varied forms, E.L. exhibits a talent for coming up with explanations or solutions that satisfy the parties in a dispute.

As a young woman, E.L expands her experiences and viewpoints by traveling outside of her homeland. This choice contrasts with the pattern common among future tyrants, who generally elect not to venture far from their homelands, perhaps because they fear that their well-worked scheme of things may be unduly complexified or uncomfortably challenged by experiences of living in a radically different environment.

In studying creators, I noted that these individuals take at least a decade to master the domain in which each ultimately effects a breakthrough. Many direct leaders do not operate in traditional scholarly or artistic domains and so do not require the daily application that undergirds ultimate mastery. However, no leader is born with the knowledge that she needs to operate effectively in the public sphere. And so, E.L. needs to complete the necessary apprenticeships—whether to gain knowledge of domains, skill in communicating, or mastery of organizational politics. Such training periods may well stretch out for a decade or longer.

Successful leadership requires much more than personal gifts and vaulting ambition. The aspiring leader like E.L.—or an individual, like Martin Luther King, Jr., or Eleanor Roosevelt, who is propelled by circumstances—must be attuned to an audience that is posing basic questions and searching for guidance, particularly regarding issues of identity. E.L. may find that audience either in her professional domain or in a wider or less readily identifiable constituency. At this time, provided that she herself has worked out answers to these basic questions, can express them eloquently, and can embody them in her way of life, E.L. is poised to occupy a position of leadership.

The less well defined the domain, the institution, or the constituency, the more necessary it is for E.L. to invent a life for herself, to reflect on its implications, and then to share the resultant stories with others. The stories that prove effective will differ from circumstance to circumstance, and E.L. must

Leading Minds

be prepared to revise her story, to combat counterstories, to anticipate future stories (and counterstories), or even to create wholly new ones. She has to develop a position on the extent to which a story is inclusive or exclusive, traditional or innovative, and related chiefly through words or conveyed through some other kind of symbolic system or embodiment. When monitoring the effectiveness of the story, E.L. needs to bear in mind the contours and the limits of the unschooled mind.

Among the stories created by leaders, stories that deal with identity are at a particular premium. Typically, these identity stories have their roots in the personal experiences of the leader in the course of her own development. But it is characteristic of the effective leader that her stories can be transplanted to a larger canvas—that they make sense not only to members of her family and her close circle, but to increasingly large entities, including institutions and, at an extreme, heterogeneously constituted political entities.

Leadership is never guaranteed; it must always be renewed. E.L. witnesses a constant interplay among her favored stories, the audience's reactions, and the often unpredictable events in the society. Leaders succeed, fail, return, and recover, often many times in the course of a career. What operates effectively at one time or in one situation may not be effective in other circumstances, and E.L. must be flexible, though not so flexible that she ceases to stand for anything. At a special premium are the capacities to adjust stories in light of changing circumstances while still adhering to basic principles and remaining—and appearing to remain—an individual of conviction. (President Bill Clinton has had trouble living up to this requirement.)

Leaders cannot create and control their charisma (though image makers certainly strive toward that end). There is little question, however, that from an early age, certain individuals stand out among others for their personal attractiveness, as is true of E.L. Most often, the traits are physical—leaders are often tall, good-looking, and graceful. If they lack these physical characteristics, they may at least have strong defining facial features or piercing eyes. Different traits—such as the power of Oppenheimer's mind, the spirituality surrounding Pope John XXIII, or even the reassuring ordinariness of Eleanor Roosevelt—may captivate different audiences. Invariably, though, leaders find a way to exercise a strong hold over an audience. Leaders must be aware of these charismatic capacities and avoid actions or stories that undermine such power. De Gaulle, for example, conveyed charisma partly through his remoteness from others, and he carefully maintained a studied distance from the fray.

One of the other factors that will affect the course of E.L's career is her relationship to institutions and organizations. Such entities serve as the basis for power and support. Indeed, those who find themselves at the helm of well-entrenched organizations have a guaranteed authorized platform from which to issue stories and at least some reason to expect that they will be listened to attentively; the president of any institution commands attention. The maintenance and renewal of organizations is a special kind of skill. If E.L. does not wish to tend this matter herself, if she prefers to focus on her storytelling mission, she must ensure that others maintain and nurture her organizational base. And, of course, if E.L. does not begin with an organizational base, she must either establish one (as did Gandhi and King) or run the risk that her chief messages will quickly disappear in the welter of competing counterstories.

Another feature is the opportunity for reflection. While creators spend most of their time alone and feel the need to mix with other people only occasionally, E.L. confronts the opposite situation. Often the demands for personal attention are so great that she loses the opportunity to reflect, to step back, and to take stock. Yet, in the absence of such time for reflection, the leader risks losing her sense of agency: she may become the tool of other individuals or of forces beyond her control.

The major reason that reflection is so important is that a leader like E.L. must be able to perceive the big picture—its constant features, its changes. No matter how skilled her associates, it is not reasonable to expect that they will have the vantage point of the exemplary leader, who has presumably attained her privileged status because of her special understanding of the situation and her special ties to the audience. The noted political leader and student of leadership John Gardner speaks about the desirability of an "uncluttered mind"—a perspective that is not distracted by the transitory events of the day. The uncluttered mind must constantly remove those obstacles that block vision and scan to identify those issues and trends that are truly important.

Whatever our successes, we must all ultimately face our frailty and our limitations. Perhaps because she aims so high and carries such burdens, E.L. is especially at risk for failure. In many cases, the failure of the leader is not within her control. Opponents may rise, other stories may gain favor, supporters may shield the leader from uncomfortable but vital information, or the particular conditions of popularity or authority may change unpredictably. Indeed, the greater the accomplishment of the leader, the greater the strain on her milieu; strong accomplishments breed strong reactions, and by and large, only those effective leaders who die at a young age are spared the disheartening sight of their accomplishments being severely challenged, if not wholly undone.

It is important to note that E.L., by and large, is not thrown by apparent failures. Tough and robust, she expects that there will be downs as well as ups. Sometimes, indeed, she is energized by setbacks and returns to the fray with new vigor. While some withdraw after defeats or failure, E.L. is likely to follow Jean Monnet's practice of construing every defeat as an opportunity. And indeed, this capacity to place a positive spin on apparently unproductive experiences sends a very important and reassuring message to one's followers.

Yet, despite this capacity to discern the silver lining in a cloud, E.L. often is seen as having failed in her primary mission. And, in a way reminiscent of tragic heroines, E.L. often contributes to her own ultimate downfall. Fiercely ambitious and capable of risk taking, she aims too high, makes overly harsh demands on others, and pays too little attention to those whom she is supposed to nurture. Paradoxically, even those creators with relatively little interest in posterity may continue to exert impact for centuries after their death; conversely, the very leaders with the greatest ambition may end up undermining their own achievements within their lifetime.

Thus, failure may result from a number of different sources: changing conditions, unexpected historical upheavals, a story that proves too inclusionary or too exclusionary, excessive demands by the leader on others, or excessive demands by the leader on herself. Each of the leaders in this study experienced signal successes that make them worthy of study. Yet, in one way or another, all experienced failure: thwarting of their mission, loss of their position, or both. Perhaps only the ordinary leader-manager can reasonably expect to appear successful to her immediate successors, but this success comes at the cost of little significant change. In contrast, the exemplary leader may well appear to have been ineffective immediately after the end of her term; but there remains the chance that she will ultimately prove to have set into operation a series of events that have long-term consequences. Should this prove to be the case, the optimism that characterizes such leaders will have been vindicated.

Six Constants of Leadership

In the introductory chapters I introduced six key features that have guided my study of effective twentieth-century leadership. I now return to review some of the principal findings that have emerged.

THE STORY

A leader must have a central story or message. The story is more likely to be effective in a large and heterogeneous group if it can speak directly to the untutored mind—the mind that develops naturally in the early lives of children without the need for formal tutelage. Stories ought to address the sense of individual and group identity, the "we" and the "they," though that sense may actually be expanded or restricted by the story. They should not only provide background, but should help group members to frame future options.

In rare cases, a more novel or transformational story can succeed in persuasiveness even if the group membership extends beyond a single domain. Chances for success are greater if that story becomes the central mission for a leader, if it can be promulgated for a long time, and if it has the opportunity to take hold in a noncrisis situation. Crises (such as a war or an economic depression) demand rapid clarification and typically result in simplification. Leaders benefit from the ability to build on stories that are already known—for example, those drawn from religion or history or those that have already been circulated within an institution—and to synthesize them in new ways, as Martin Luther King, Jr., was able to do.

Most of the leaders in this study put forth stories that were inclusionary, that encouraged individuals to think of themselves as part of a broader community. Among the eleven leaders profiled in-depth, the chief exceptions to this generalization are Robert Maynard Hutchins and Margaret Thatcher, both of whom gained influence—and perhaps pleasure—by encouraging an "in-group/out-group" perspective. Also, the leaders of the Second World War found themselves in a situation where exclusion was as crucial as inclusion.

At first blush, an inclusionary story may seem wholly preferable. More people will feel included, and the leader may feel that she is being a generous, morally praiseworthy individual. The actual situation is more complex, however. To the extent that a story is inclusionary, it denies special status to groups that may have felt so entitled. These groups will eventually come to oppose the leader and her inclusionary story—a story that to them may seem all *too* inclusionary. Thus, Hindus resented Gandhi's efforts to include Muslims in his vision of India. Moreover, when any leader's course is examined at closer range, one can see that there are always inclusionary and exclusionary forces vying with one another. Even Gandhi needed to have opponents; he stood out in his effort to include British imperialists constructively within the stories that he was relating.

The various kinds of stories that leaders tell have many parallels. Yet, each leader is distinguished by the particular stories that, typically on the basis of her own experience, she has created—stories of identity, stories that address other essential questions, stories that obtain within and/or across domains. The stories told by the leaders profiled earlier are summarized in Appendix I.

THE AUDIENCE

Even the most eloquent story is stillborn in the absence of an audience ready to hear it; even mediocre stories unimpressively related will achieve some effectiveness for an audience that is poised to respond. The relationship between leader and audience is complex and interactive; perhaps especially in the case of leaders of nondominant groups, a dynamic interplay exists between the needs and desires of the audience, on the one hand, and the contours of the leader's story, on the other. Moreover, in the case of leadership of nondominant groups, the leader generally has to create her story afresh and to revise it in accordance with often rapidly changing conditions. Conversely, those authorized to lead an organization with a preexisting hierarchy have a relatively unproblematic time in guiding the audience, so long as they do not require its members to move in new and unexpected directions.

A leader can effect small changes in a large audience fairly easily and sometimes effect larger changes in an already dedicated and knowledgeable group, such as other members of her domain, without overwhelming effort. The greatest challenge the leader faces is to bring about significant and lasting changes in a large and heterogeneous group. A leader must not only develop messages in a number of nuanced languages but, in the absence of specialized knowledge, begin by addressing an unschooled mind. The examples of Gandhi and Monnet suggest that the best chances for success lie in a steadfast concentration on the same core message, along with flexibility in how it is presented, and openness to the message being apprehended at a number of levels of sophistication.

Note, in contrast, that the traditional creator has an easier task. While he is creating a breakthrough work, he need pay only scant attention to his audience. Once the work has been completed, it may speak for itself, or it can be promoted by other individuals. The cross-domain leader has no such luxury. The story cannot be conceived in isolation; and while others can help disseminate the story, the leader will be expected to embody the story personally, at least to some degree.

THE ORGANIZATION

While a leader can sometimes speak directly to a large audience and achieve initial success via the perceived bond between himself and his auditors, enduring leadership ultimately demands some kind of institutional or organizational basis. If the leader already belongs to an organization, such as the church, a corporation, or a political party, it is his job to bring the organization along. While the ascribed leader of an organization can demand initial attention, simply by virtue of his position, there is no guarantee that he will remain a viable vessel of authority if he makes significant demands on his membership. And if, as is typically the case with leaders of nondominant groups, no organization is at hand, such an organization must be created and guided. The achievements of twentieth-century totalitarian leaders would have been inconceivable in the absence of the powerful political organizations that they helped to build up and then carefully policed; and nontotalitarian leaders like de Gaulle and Churchill discovered the tenuousness of their command after the abatement of the crises that had brought them to the fore.

Lessons from the Past, Implications for the Future

Leaders of traditional domains such as scholarly disciplines are less dependent on a highly differentiated organization. On the one hand, these domains often organize themselves without the need for much intervention; on the other hand, the actual power of ideas and the existence of seminal work can exert effects independent of the current shape of the domain. Yet, once the leader wishes to guide the fate of her creations, direct forms of leadership become necessary. From the academic examples in chapters 4 and 5, one can see how difficult it is to provide continuing direct leadership to independent scholars. When Robert Maynard Hutchins, as an aspiring direct leader, tried to create new and enduring organizations, he was ineffective; Margaret Mead's decision to avoid organizational commitments may have been personally judicious, but it also assured that there would be no "school of Mead" after her death.

THE EMBODIMENT

The creator must in some sense embody his story, although he need not be saintly. Indeed, the credibility of some leaders may actually be enhanced if they have had—and have come to terms with—a rocky or even a counterstory past (as did Saint Augustine). But if the leader seems to contradict the story by the facts of his existence, if he appears hypocritical, the story probably will not remain convincing over the long run.

The story may grow out of the leader's personal experiences and may well have been embodied in his or her daily living before being expressed overtly. Indeed, in selected cases, the actual embodiment by the leader serves as the principal story. George C. Marshall and Pope John XXIII spoke about the kinds of lives they believed in, but their actions "spoke" even more eloquently than their voices.

The issue of embodiment raises the question of authenticity. Just as one can ask whether a story is true, one can ask whether an individual truly embodies what she speaks about. Short of foolproof polygraph examination, it is not possible to determine whether an individual's embodiment is genuine. After all, phonies are never in short supply. Moreover, in the current climate, many individuals are well compensated for helping the leader look credible and convincing. Lacking any magical solution to this enigma, I am content to believe, along with Abraham Lincoln, that one cannot fool all of the people all of the time. The individual who does not embody her messages will eventually be found out, even as the inarticulate individual who leads the exemplary life may eventually come to be appreciated.

DIRECT AND INDIRECT LEADERSHIP

Most creative leaders exert their influence indirectly through the symbolic products that they create; most political leaders relate their stories directly to their audiences. But leaders do have the option of pursuing the alternative course. Some indirect leaders, like Mead and Oppenheimer, attempt to provide direct leadership within their domains; and some direct leaders, like Vaclav Havel of the Czech Republic and Léopold Sédar Senghor of Senegal, have created political or artistic works that influence other people.

Direct leadership is more tumultuous and risky, but in the short run, it can be more efficient and more effective. However, those leaders whose time for considered reflection has vanished—who can no longer "retreat to the mountaintop" to discern "the big picture"—are often in an unfavorable position for making judicious decisions. Indirect leaders have the advantage of more time for reflection and revision; and often their impact proves more enduring, if slower to emerge. It is possible to have a "mixed model"; Jean Monnet, for example, achieved political ends by working through the existing political leadership, rather than by erecting or seizing a direct platform himself.

If there is voluntary movement between these forms, it is almost always from indirect to direct forms of leadership. In general, my study indicates that the transition is most easily effected when the direct and indirect stories and embodiments are relatively similar. Thus, Mead and Sloan were adept at making the transition from leading within their domains to leading a more heterogeneous group, presumably because the content of their stories required relatively little transformation. In contrast, individuals like Oppenheimer and Hutchins, whose initial stories were more specialized, found it more difficult to succeed with a completely nonacademic audience.

Even when the stretch is modest, however, leaders must make a choice. It is almost impossible to meet the quickly changing needs and demands of a specialized domain, on the one hand, and the far less rigorous (though often equally fickle) demands of a heterogeneous unschooled audience on the other. In the end, leaders must cast their primary lot either with a domain or with a wider society. The individual may continue to have some effectiveness in the rejected terrain, but this glory is likely to be reflected, at most.

THE ISSUE OF EXPERTISE

In nearly every domain of experience today, there will be important technical knowledge unavailable to most leaders or to most members of an audience. Only those individuals who actually began as domain experts—such as Mead and Oppenheimer—even have the option of continuing to access such knowledge directly. They may call on that knowledge as needed, so long as they can adapt it to the demands of particular situations.

Within a domain, an individual is unlikely to achieve any credibility unless her work is seen as being of high quality. Mead and Oppenheimer could not have become direct leaders within their domains if their colleagues had not esteemed their work. And Hutchins was always considered something of an outsider at faculty meetings because he did not have advanced training in one of the traditional scholarly disciplines.

The more that such individuals become involved in direct leadership, the more difficult it will be for them to retain their technical expertise; and they may well become spurned as popularizers or ex-specialists by the more strict constructionists among their expert colleagues. Most career politicians, of course, lack expertise in any traditional domain, though they may certainly have acquired sophisticated knowledge about political processes and organizations. Thus, a paradox: Direct leaders typically lack direct knowledge, while indirect leaders often can proceed on the basis of direct knowledge. How to attain and maintain expertise is an acute problem for anyone who aspires to direct leadership, and particularly for those who wish to direct a heterogeneous group on the basis of the best current information drawn from the most relevant domains.

Questions Raised by This Study

In a study of this scope, numerous questions can be posed; and if I did not raise them, readers certainly would—and appropriately so. Of the many issues that have given me pause, I restrict myself here to a discussion of three principal topics.

CONCEPTION OF LEADERSHIP

While my conception of leadership is not unique, I have definitely emphasized certain features and minimized others. From one perspective, the present view might be thought of as traditional. I focus on the single leader—generally recognized as such—and on the considerable agency that that person may gain because of his authoritative position and/or powers of persuasion. I readily acknowledge my belief that individuals matter, and that a few individuals matter a great deal.

Note that I do not question the validity of other views of leadership—views that focus on power, policies, the public, or the personality of the leader (see chapter 1). I have not concerned myself with contemporary revisionist critiques of leadership—leadership as collective; leadership as instigated by the audience, rather than by the nominal leader; leadership on the part of those who have been relatively "without voice" or "without a place at the table"; or a deconstructionist or postmodern critique that would question the entire legitimacy of talk about leadership. I have little sympathy for those who challenge the "great person" theory of leadership but then invoke unspecified "forces of history" in its place. Any serious study of history must take into account human as well as social and economic factors, and the most convincing studies illuminate their continuing interactions.

295

Leading Minds

My study has focused on individuals generally seen as leaders by their contemporaries and, for the most part, on individuals who have had available the customary levers of leadership or who have created effective substitutes. It remains an open question whether leaders defined in a radically different way can still satisfy my criterion of "affecting thoughts, feelings, and behaviors of a significant number of individuals."

While traditional in some respects, however, my conception is iconoclastic in others. In particular, my emphasis on leadership as a cognitive enterprise, as a process occurring and recurring within—and between—the minds of leaders and followers, has few antecedents. The notion of leaders as presenting messages is certainly familiar, but the assertions about various kinds of stories and counterstories, competing with one another in Darwinian fashion, explore new and somewhat controversial ground. The distinction between indirect leadership, through the creation of symbolic products, and direct leadership, through storytelling and embodying, is also novel: I have sought to build bridges between the influence exerted by a creative individual and the influence wielded by a traditional organizational or national leader. Finally, the emphasis throughout on the power of the five-year-old mind, as well as the limits that the unschooled mind imposes on forms of leadership that transcend traditional domain boundaries, also represents a contribution to contemporary considerations of leadership.

THE REPRESENTATIVENESS OF FINDINGS

It is a point of logic that, given any finite number of examples, one can find an infinite number of generalizations that obtain across them. It is also a point of logic that any generalization may be undone by the first counterexample. Given these formidable constraints, what faith can one place in the profile of leadership that is presented here—in my prototype of the exemplary leader and in the various generalizations about the six constants of leadership?

Let me stress once again that the enterprise I have undertaken is not scientific in a strict sense. As I described in *Creating Minds*, I am trying to forge a link between idiographic case studies undertaken by scholars like Howard Gruber and the nomothetic, quantitative studies undertaken by scholars like Dean Keith Simonton. In my earlier study of creativity, I sought generalizations based on seven creators of the modern era; in the present study, my generalizations (and contrasts) are based on studies of eleven leaders. I have provided a modest "test" of these generalizations by noting the ways in which they are modified by a brief examination of the ten "world leaders," and also by occasional contrasts with the profiles of the previously studied creators.

Without doubt, my "sample" is skewed in certain directions. I am aware of some biases—for example, toward voluntary, inclusionary, and innovative leaders—but no doubt unaware of others. Equally, I recognize that each of my leaders operated in a limited set of contexts and that other leaders, operating in other contexts, might well differ in unpredictable ways. And it is worth underscoring that my leaders are all drawn from the modern era, and largely from America and Western Europe. A different kind of inquiry would have to be launched, were one in search of generalizations about leadership in other eras, or from other cultural traditions.

I fully expect that studies of other leaders—direct, indirect, or a Monnet-like amalgam of these two species—will undermine certain generalizations and give rise to others. Thus scholarship advances. Rather than fearing such refutations or modifications, I welcome them. (Indeed, I have been greatly stimulated by exchanges with other scholars who have found my generalizations about extraordinary individuals to be provocative—in both senses of that term!) I hope that the methods developed here and the set of criteria I have applied will prove useful in further comparisons of this sort. Robust characterizations can emerge only if the same set of lenses is applied to additional members of the class of leaders, broadly defined.

THE MORAL DIMENSION OF LEADERSHIP

It has been observed that the word *leader* is often applied in a positive sense, as we praise someone for being a leader, or as we ask, plaintively, "What has become of our leaders?" I should state, then, that my approach to leadership does *not* presuppose a positive view of leadership. Indeed, the stories that leaders tell, the ways in which they embody these stories, and the ways in which they affect others turn out to be as characteristic of reprehensible leaders—the Hitlers and the Stalins—as of leaders whom we might wish to praise.

But while my schematization is meant to be value neutral, I do not deny my own interest in the moral aspects of leadership. It is no accident that, as noted, I have focused in this book on "leaders of choice"—individuals who operate in democratic societies. Nor is it mere coincidence that most of the eleven leaders chose to put forth an inclusionary story, one that enlarged, rather than splintered, the primary human group to which it was addressed. In at least some ways, I admire each of the eleven leaders portrayed in this book.

Leaders who have used their power and their pulpit to turn individuals against one another have wrought incalculable damage. I see this study as one modest effort to examine individuals who have essentially adopted a prosocial perspective—to see what they have accomplished and where they have encountered obstacles. I believe that we are more likely to secure responsible leadership in the future if we can demystify its constituent processes. In that sense, enhanced knowledge about leadership may go hand-in-hand with more morally desirable forms of leadership. However, before uncritically embracing this essentially optimistic point, one should not forget that Machiavelli and Hitler wrote two of the most influential tracts about leadership.

Six Trends Affecting Twentieth-Century Leadership

At least provisionally, one may assume that the six features identified earlier are enduring properties of leadership. But in any consideration of the future, one should take into account a number of additional factors that might influence or even change the ways in which leadership—and leaders—achieve success. I have identified six major trends, each discernible from the beginning of the twentieth century, if not before, and none showing any signs of lessening in recent years. These trends will be familiar to all readers; however, their implications for leadership in the future merit concentrated attention.

THE POTENTIAL FOR GLOBAL DESTRUCTION

Warfare achieved unprecedentedly destructive proportions during the two world wars. And the construction of nuclear weapons now makes it conceivable that, for the first time in recorded history, the entire planet could be effectively destroyed in a matter of days. National leaders must take this possibility into account. They can either use weapons as a threat or implement policies that will help limit or control the spread of these weapons. What they cannot afford to do is ignore the possibility of widespread destruction. The prospect of nuclear annihilation influences not only political leaders but also any other leaders who presume to address the major dimensions of human experience. And while less immediately catastrophic, the possibility of the destruction of the world as we know it—whether through ecological disasters or through uncontrolled population growth—will increasingly affect leaders as well. The possibility of quick or gradual planetary destruction is the often tacit leitmotif of any serious identity story related today.

INSTANT—OFTEN SIMPLISTIC—COMMUNICATION

With every passing year, it becomes easier for individuals not only to learn almost instantaneously what is happening around the world but also to participate in the "global information super-highway." The broadening and democratizing implications of such flexible transmission of information have often been emphasized. However, an increase in quantity of information and an increase in quality of information are not synonymous. Indeed, more channels often mean more low-grade, spurious, and specious information; and the ubiquitous temptation to transmit easily digested sound bites will come as no surprise to anyone who has explored the powers of the unschooled mind. Such a barrage of undigested and often simplistic information may make it even more difficult to have an uncluttered mind that can discern the big picture.

ABSENCE OF PRIVACY

Hand-in-glove with the ease of information transmission is an ebbing of any sense of privacy. Not only is it easier for governmental (and nongovernmental) agencies to collect detailed information about the lives of all individuals, but traditional respect for the distinction between public and private lives has already been eroded with public figures and is increasingly ignored with private citizens as well.

Ready global communication and the disappearance of privileged information influence the lives of leaders and audiences. Far more individuals have the opportunity to convey their messages quickly and directly—though the din of competing messages may make it more difficult for any specific message to become prevalent. Charges and countercharges, stories and counterstories abound. The speedy revelation of even the most intimate details of the lives of individuals—sometimes with their cooperation, more often against their wishes—means that leaders have increasing difficulty retaining any mystique. It is intriguing—but also alarming—to ponder what would have happened to the leaders of the Second World War if they had had to deal with the kind of public scrutiny of their foibles that has become routine in American (and, increasingly, in all nontotalitarian) political life.

The disappearance of privacy entails another, so far incalculable cost. Disabused of heroes, audiences come to have less respect for their leaders in general, and many capable individuals no longer consider a career or even a brief stint in public service.

It is worth noting, however, that current or aspiring leaders do not need to accept without protest the increasing invasions of privacy. Individuals retain the right to refuse to reveal information and, in the extreme, to seek legal redress from those who libel them. In my own view, current political leadership in America is far too accepting of impertinent queries—a polite "that is really none of your business" might constitute a promising beginning to an effective new counterstory.

THE RISE OF ENTITIES THAT TRANSCEND NATIONAL BOUNDARIES

At least in many respects, the heyday of the nation-state may have passed. The multinational corporation has been a prominent fact of life for at least a generation. So many issues—aviation, ecology, contagious illnesses, growth and movement of populations, human rights, nuclear inspection and fallout, fuel, disarmament, and trade, just to name a few of the more visible ones—do not neatly respect national boundaries. Consequently, thousands of organizations—some national, some international, many nongovernmental—have arisen in the past few decades, and a number of these have attained a surprising amount of influence. Joining such mainstays as the Red Cross and the World Bank are numerous less well known and less traditionally configured international scientific organizations, computer bulletin boards, commercial entities, and institutions concerned with population control, resource deployment, disease control, preservation of the environment, and human rights.

Newly configured agencies, arising in response to fresh kinds of threats and hitherto-unavailable opportunities, are unlikely to attract leaders of the usual stripe. Some have a much flatter, more heterarchical structure, and others may have no discernible leadership whatsoever. Whether the more established forms of governance will fall into their familiar place over time or whether nonnational entities will evolve new forms of group leadership or audience membership is by no means clear. The political consultant Max Kampelman reflects on the current unsettled situation: "Everything is becoming interconnected and yet in the world of politics, we are still in the Middle Ages."

NATIONALISTIC AND FUNDAMENTALIST REACTIONS

Quite possibly in response to the apparent lessening of power of long-standing national organizations, equally powerful pockets of opposition have arisen. The Monnet-inspired movement toward a single Europe has been countered by strong nationalistic currents in nearly all European countries, and by an unexpectedly virulent form of ethnic pride—sometimes leading to calls for "ethnic purity"—in Eastern Europe. Within the United States, nearly all of the aforementioned international tendencies—from nuclear disarmament to human rights to ecological control—are vociferously opposed by individuals who either disdain these themes on principle or feel that they should be handled only by the sovereign state or by an organized religious entity.

Just as a call for nontraditional institutional forms requires a new and flexible viewpoint about identity, the reactions against these innovative organizations exploit the most elemental reservoirs of group identity. In their call for literal embracing of long-standing religious, political, and social verities, fundamentalist leaders speak directly to the least-modulated minds. Given the power of the unschooled mind, it is no easy matter to counter these entrenched beliefs.

EVER MORE TECHNICAL EXPERTISE

In nearly every domain, knowledge continues to accumulate at a spectacular rate, and technical experts are expected to be on top of this accruing knowledge. Nowhere is this trend more evident than in government. Most leaders 150 years ago went about their business with a small staff and could often themselves grasp the details of issues; today the "governmental affairs" wings of even modest-sized entities (ranging from universities to hospitals to municipalities) require a large body of experts, technicians, consultants, and other authorities. Even political figures, expert in politics if in nothing else, depend on teams of consultants who are more expert in the various specializations of politics, from fund-raising to focus groups. Most everyone agrees that one cannot get along without experts; yet recalling George Bernard Shaw's quip that "professions are a conspiracy against the public," experts are often the target of abuse.

Knowing how to take such expert knowledge, judge its importance, and convey it to nonspecialist leaders and then to the more general public is a daunting challenge. The tensions are plain. On the one hand, one wants the best information, and one hopes to base decisions on that information after it has been thoroughly digested and judiciously weighed. On the other hand, neither leaders nor their audiences really have the expertise to master the information. And even if they could achieve such command, there is tremendous pressure to present the information in a simplified way, so that such information can be readily comprehended and readily transmitted to others. The result is often a distortion of the issues. Reflecting on recent political life in America, the sociologist Daniel Bell commented:

> Leadership is a sense of judgment. It is judgment as to what is relevant and how to do things. The result is either people oversimplify, as Reagan did, or you try to lean the other way, become as Dukakis [George Bush's opponent in the 1988 presidential election] did, rather technocratic. So the person who can strike the right balance between the sense of complexity and the sense of judgment is increasingly rare, and that is a problem it seems to me in every society.

Concomitant with the increasing need for technical expertise is an attenuation of the specialists' bonds to the rest of society. Experts must spend so much time focusing on their specialties that they have very little time to devote to issues of the more general good. Many experts have a lessened sense of obligation to the wider society, or even to a wider profession, apart from their own specific area of technical knowledge. The sense of identity of contemporary experts is less frequently rooted in their community or the nation, let alone in the wider world; nor is it, as seems to have been the case a century ago, linked to a morally tinged calling such as the law, medicine, the academy, or the clergy. Particularly because experts are so mobile and the institutions for which they work are so fluid, their bonds are chiefly to the few individuals who know what they know (an exceedingly circumscribed domain) and, equally, to themselves (an exceedingly selfish constituency).

Leading Minds

Dating back to Greek times, this tension can be noted. As the historian H. D. F. Kitto has pointed out, "The highly trained expert, the specialist, finds no natural place in the polis, and when he appears, as he did in so many departments of life in the fifth century, the cohesion is weakened or the natural bounds of the polis are overpassed." Confucius, a historical contemporary of the ancient Athenians, noted the problem in another mode: "While the advisers of a great leader should be as cold as ice, the leader himself should have fire, a spark of divine madness." How to harmonize the mind of the specialist with the mind of the five-year-old is a challenge that grows more acute with every passing year. Yet, in my view, unless we can find or form leaders who retain some links to expert knowledge, on the one hand, and some ability to communicate to non-experts on the other, our world is likely to spin ever further out of control. Far from becoming anachronistic, competent leaders promise to become more crucial than ever before.

Guidelines for Effective Leadership

In this concluding account, I have identified six enduring themes of leadership and singled out six recent trends that have certainly changed—and in all likelihood have complexified—the tasks of leadership for the twentieth century and, more than likely, for succeeding eras. Were this book a systematic sociological treatise on the training of new leaders, or perhaps a Machiavellian version of the same enterprise, I might examine each of the six constants, in terms of the six trends, coming up with thirty-six points to ponder. It is more in the spirit of this book (and of its author), however, to conclude this study with three lessons that are relevant for the proper training of leaders and for the successful prosecution of their enterprises.

APPRECIATE ENDURING FEATURES OF LEADERSHIP

Any leader who wishes to be effective must acknowledge, and attempt to deal realistically with, the enduring features of leadership. While leaders will differ from one another in the extent of their ambition, the size of their audiences, and the uniqueness of their message, all of them must confront the six enduring features. A leader is likely to achieve success only if she can construct and convincingly communicate a clear and persuasive story; appreciate the nature of the audience(s), including its changeable features; invest her own (or channel others') energy in the building and maintenance of an organization; embody in her own life the principal contours of the story; either provide direct leadership or find a way to achieve influence through indirect means; and, finally, find a way to understand and make use of, without being overwhelmed by, increasingly technical expertise.

These considerations should constitute part of the training of leaders.

They should be monitored by the leader and her associates over the course of a leader's incumbency.

ANTICIPATE AND DEAL WITH NEW TRENDS

Those who would lead in the world of the future must be aware of, and find ways of coping with, new and often complexifying trends. The trends that affect leadership will of course vary across time, place, and situation. I have suggested that leaders today must directly confront the possibilities of immediate or gradual world destruction; new forms of instant, copious, and often overly simplified forms of communication; the virtual demise of any sense of privacy; the proliferation of entities and concerns that transcend national boundaries; the perhaps predictable reaction to these unsettling trends, in the form of heightened nationalism and fundamentalism; the ever-increasing amount of hermetic knowledge; the unsettling lack of wider commitment that seems to accompany the frenetic and uncertain life of the expert; and, as a result, the leader's greatly complexified task of sifting through what must be communicated to a decidedly non-expert audience.

While these trends will be reflected in particular domains in distinctive ways, all aspiring leaders need to recognize them. Indeed, in precollegiate education—the domain that I know best—leaders have to consider each of these factors, though they will weigh them in ways different from a business or military leader. For example, a precollegiate educator probably will be particularly affected by the pressure to decide *what* of an increasingly expanded knowledge base merits study and by the temptations of constructing curriculum and pedagogy around instant, but often superficial, forms of communication. In contrast, a businessperson must direct special attention to the proliferation of organizations around the world and the explosion of technical knowledge. And a military leader will probably be preoccupied with the possibilities for world destruction, the dissolution of many national entities, and the correlative rise of vociferous ethnic sects. In any event, any program that educates leaders needs to consider these six facets in light of the domain's dimensions and audiences.

ENCOURAGE RECOGNITION OF THE PROBLEMS, PARADOXES, AND POSSIBILITIES OF LEADERSHIP

Those concerned with the quality of future leadership must design ways of educating citizens—audiences as well as leaders. Such education must consider not only the constants and the variables of leadership but also the tensions that complicate the leader's role, without in any way rendering that role less essential. An enhanced cadre of future leaders can materialize only if we engender widespread appreciation of the principal issues that surround effective leadership.

Leading Minds

Certainly, our society has not ignored the education of leaders. Many institutions, such as professional schools or the military, have as their stated goal cultivating leaders. The seemingly endless stream of books, articles, seminars, workshops, and broadcast programs on political leadership, business leadership, and community leadership testifies to the widespread belief that leadership is important and that we need to prepare potential leaders more effectively.

Yet, despite specific regimens of leadership in specific domains, most of the larger society remains ignorant about leadership—not only about its importance but also about the ways in which it can be effective. To some, leadership is an added ingredient—somewhat like a clever remark that someone can use to spice up an already drafted speech—rather than an essential way of thinking about the thoughts, behaviors, and feelings of human beings. To others, leaders are mysteriously charismatic heroes who operate according to rules of their own devising (or flouting). The very fact that many of the ideas in this book are not (to my knowledge) widely known—and that even when they are known, there exist few avenues for familiarizing individuals with their consequences—testifies to the continuing orphan status of leadership knowledge in our broader society.

The American predilections for egalitarianism and for laissez-faire education exacerbate the situation. Dating back to ancient times, many civilizations have considered it part of their responsibility to provide milieus in which leadership can be identified and fostered. The European and Asian high-prestige professional training schools and long-entrenched civil service have been tried-and-true means of achieving a cadre acquainted with the demands and subtleties of leadership. Margaret Mead used to point out that Americans do not want leaders. By pretending that leadership will happen naturally or that leadership can be inculcated incidentally, we ensure that there will be an unacceptably low number of individuals who can fill the essential desiderata of leadership. And we make it less likely that leaders will emerge from less-dominant groups and less-privileged institutions in the society.

Indeed, if I can be permitted to caricature a bit, it seems that leadership is too often seen as one of two polarities: as unproblematic ("you too can be a leader") or as unreachable ("the born leader" or "the charismatic leader"). Instead, we need to begin to think of leadership as a subject that can be mastered and a role that can be achieved, should one be willing to invest heavily in such enterprises.

But if we desire a leadership that is responsible as well as effective, we must do more than simply train a body of "legitimated" leaders. The "best" leadership training *for* potential leaders, I submit, should be the best training *about* leadership for all—not in a sense of training everyone to be a designated leader of a designated organization, but rather in the sense of familiarizing the population with what is entailed in being a leader, and what can go wrong, as well as what can go right.

I term this knowledge *consciousness about the issues and paradoxes of leadership*. Those close to the phenomena of leadership—and I hope that readers of this book now consider themselves as belonging to those ranks—become intimately aware of a number of issues and paradoxes:

- The tension between the need for technical expertise—which requires sophisticated thinking—and the necessity for broad-based communication skills, so that one can reach the "unschooled mind"
- The need for stories that can speak to many individuals and help them achieve a more satisfying individual and group identity
- The potential of such stories either to broaden or to fragment a sense of community
- The realization that more comprehensive knowledge may well be distributed across members of a group, but that it is much easier to deal with a single authorized leader
- The knowledge that all leaders are limited in what they can accomplish, that all leaders experience failure as well as triumph, and that nearly all leaders eventually encounter obstacles that they cannot overcome
- The alternative possibilities of an audience that is manipulated by a leader, an audience that influences the leader, and an audience that cooperatively molds a message in conjunction with the leader
- The need to aid leaders, or to share their burdens, rather than try to exploit or undermine their authority
- The choice between leadership that is direct (a leader speaking to her audiences) or indirect (a leader achieving effects either through symbolic products or through the education of political leaders), and the possibility of combining both direct and indirect strands in a synergistically effective manner
- The tension between a rational approach and one that is founded on spiritual dimensions, and the desirability of synthesizing these complementary stories

There are other issues and other paradoxes, some contained in this book and others that remain to be identified. No one can be expected to understand and master all of them, but familiarity with some can help individuals appreciate the *possible* and the *probable*, as well as the *problematic* and the *paradoxical* facets of leadership.

Such knowledge can be brought to bear when one considers the leadership that most of us deal with regularly: the leaders of one's workplace, school, and community. But it is equally relevant when one turns one's attention to the broader political scene. As I write in early 1995, we have just witnessed in the United States some of the most vicious political campaigning in recorded history. To characterize the rhetoric as "unschooled" would be to compliment it. While knowledge about leadership cannot be seen as a panacea, I feel confident in asserting that mindless negative campaigning is far more likely to be seen for what it is, if the audience has been educated to understand the aforementioned issues and paradoxes. Within a remarkably short time, American citizens have become more aware of how to enhance their physical health. There is no reason in principle why they cannot become more aware of how to promote (or thwart) their political well-being.

A tension will always exist between those who use their knowledge to manipulate and those who use their knowledge to empower. Political "spinmasters" remind us of this unsettling reality. Yet I believe that the more widely these issues are understood, the less likely it is that irresponsible leadership can rise and prevail in the long run. Moreover, I hope that those who come to appreciate these issues, and who design means of articulating them to a wider audience, will help to usher in a world in which leadership is less coercive, more empowering of the broad citizenry, and better able to achieve constructive ends.

Chapter 15. Lessons from the Past, Implications for the Future

285 Churchill, "We are shaping the world . . . " is quoted in Walsh, 1993, p. 21.
289 For more on leaders losing opportunities for reflection, see Sutton and Galunic, 1994.
289 Gardner, "uncluttered mind," is from J. Gardner, 1995.
296 For more information on idiographic and nomothetic studies, see Gruber, 1981, and Simonton, 1984.
300 For more on the types of influential, international organizations that have arisen in the past few decades, see Simmons, 1994.
300 Kampelman, "Everything is becoming interconnected . . . " is quoted in Walsh, 1993, p. 155.
301 Bell, "Leadership is a sense of judgment . . . " is from Bell, 1992, p. 6.
302 Kitto, "The highly trained expert . . . " is from Kitto, 1951, p. 169.
302 Confucius, "While the advisors of a great leader . . . " is quoted by Korda, 1984, p. 63.

References

Bell, D. "A Conversation with Daniel Bell." *Harvard Gazette*, October 28, 1992, pp. 5–6.

Gardner, J. Personal communication, March 15, 1995.

Gruber, H. *Darwin on Man*. Chicago: University of Chicago Press, 1981.

Kitto, H. D. F. *The Greeks*. London: Penguin, 1951.

Korda, M. "How to Be a Leader." In W. E. Rosenbach and R. L. Taylor, eds., *Contemporary Issues in Leadership*. Boulder, Colo.: Westview Press, 1984, p. 61.

Simmons, A. "President's Essay: Citizen Groups Are Essential Partners in the New Global Governance." *1993 Report on Activities of the MacArthur Foundation*. Chicago: The MacArthur Foundation, 1994, pp. 2–6.

Simonton, D. K. *Genius, Creativity, and Leadership: Historiometric Inquiries*. Cambridge, Mass.: Harvard University Press, 1984.

Sutton, R., and D. C. Galunic. "Consequences of Public Scrutiny for Leaders and Their Organizations." Unpublished paper, Stanford University, 1994.

Walsh, J. "Where Have All the Leaders Gone?" *Time*, July 12, 1993, pp. 17–21.

Appendix I: The Eleven Leaders viewed along the Principal Dimension of Leadership.

	Initial Domain	Stance within Domain	Identity Story within Domain
Margaret Mead, 1901–1978	Anthropology	Inclusionary	We anthropologists have the privilege of chronicling the cultures of the world, demonstrating that none is superior. We bring back the insights and convey them in plain language to our compatriots.
J. Robert Oppenheimer, 1904–1967	Physics (expert and leader of laboratory)	Inclusionary (all should participate in Manhattan Project)	We scientists have the skills to play a major role in prosecution of the all-important war effort. We must bury all differences and be able to work in secrecy.
Robert Maynard Hutchins, 1899–1977	Institutional leader (law dean, college president)	Initially inclusionary, became more exclusionary	We educators must reconstruct the university so that we can produce a liberally educated population rather than gadabouts or narrow specialists. We must avoid frills, progressivism, mindless pluralism, and the worship of science.
Alfred P. Sloan, Jr., 1875–1966	Automotive corporation	Inclusive within corporation; competitive externally	We in business are doing God's work. General Motors knows the best way to conduct business and has produced the most effective corporate family. We in the corporation are willing to help others.
George C. Marshall, 1880–1959	U.S. Army	Inclusionary, but with high standards	We in the military must be disinterested professionals. We must avoid politicization, be ready for any contingency, and inspire others by our exemplary actions.

Pope John XXIII, 1881–1963	Catholic Church	Inclusionary	Catholics and Christians must return to the simple teachings of Christ. We must avoid bureaucratic and political infighting. The spiritual life is all-important.
Eleanor Roosevelt, 1884–1962	Recently enfranchised American women	Inclusionary	We women can and should be full participants in the political life of the nation, and we should stand up for what we believe is right.
Martin Luther King, Jr., 1929–1968	Black Americans, particularly those in the church and those involved in civil rights causes	Inclusionary	We blacks must stand up for our rights and do so non-violently.
Margaret Thatcher, 1925–	Politics, which is inherently a heterogeneous domain	N.A.	N.A.
Jean Monnet, 1888–1979	Politics, which is inherently a heterogeneous domain	N.A.	N.A.
Mahatma Gandhi, 1869–1948	Politics, which is inherently a heterogeneous domain	N.A.	N.A.

continued overleaf

	Counterstories within Domain	Nonidentity Stories within Domain
Margaret Mead, 1901–1978	Certain cultures are superior to others. It is not possible to compare cultures. We should beware of popularization.	1. Racist, evolutionary, and tumultuous portraits of adolescence are wrong. 2. Interdisciplinary work is crucial. 3. We should study families and children. 4. Cultures can be organized according to patterns, such as those found in temperament-and-sex combinations. 5. Samoans have a pleasant adolescence, and Americans can learn from their example.
J. Robert Oppenheimer, 1904–1967	Scientists should stay out of any political or military endeavors. Scientists should serve as a counterweight to the government, and all work should be totally open.	1. Quantum mechanics, relativity, and other features of the new physics are important. 2. We physicists have known sin by unleashing nuclear power.
Robert Maynard Hutchins, 1899–1977	There is no "best way " to educate. We must be open to many electives and a variety of educational philosophies. Beware of a new scholasticism or a new orthodoxy.	1. Be prepared to accept sacrifices such as reductions in salary. 2. American education has lost its way.
Alfred P. Sloan, Jr., 1875–1966	There are many ways to run a business. General Motors is paternalistic and monopolistic, or at least no different from any other large corporation.	1. One can create an organizational chart that combines centralization and decentralization. 2. New ideas about marketing, collaboration, research, and planning are best generated by skilled teams of analysts.
George C. Marshall, 1880–1959	The military is privy to special knowledge and deserves special attention and privileges. Military personnel, however, need not be held to markedly higher standards of behavior than other people are.	The military must be strengthened and modernized, and deadwood must be removed.

Pope John XXIII, 1881–1963	Catholics cannot afford to risk interacting with other religious groups. We should trust our hierarchy. Spirituality is an ideal that cannot be achieved by all.	1. Power should reside with the bishops and the people, not the curia. 2. Learn from history, but do not be bound to it. 3. Rethink traditional dogma in terms of contemporary conditions. 4. One can be a good Catholic and a good human being even if one sins.
Eleanor Roosevelt, 1884–1962	Women are better off staying in the background, helping and supporting men.	1. All can participate regardless of rank and background. 2. A president's wife can provide leadership.
Martin Luther King, Jr., 1929–1968	It is hopeless to try to achieve equality in American society. We must be prepared to be violent.	1. It is important to know and to attempt to fuse church traditions, American history, and Gandhian tactics. 2. The Southern Christian Leadership Conference provides a new stance toward racial issues. 3. The time for gradualism is over.
Margaret Thatcher, 1925–	N.A.	N.A.
Jean Monnet, 1888–1979	N.A.	N.A.
Mahatma Gandhi, 1869–1948	N.A.	N.A.

continued overleaf

	Other Counterstories within Domain	Direct/Indirect Leadership within Domain
Margaret Mead, 1901–1978	1. The more traditional stories of racial difference, evolution of cultures, and a turbulent adolescence have merit. 2. Interdisciplinary work is perilous. 3. The study of family life and child development should be left to other academic specialties. 4. Beware of generalizations about patterns of culture. 5. Mead's observations in Samoa are suspect.	Both forms
J. Robert Oppenheimer, 1904–1967	1. These new ideas are not yet established truths. 2. We should not dramatize our role in developing the nuclear weapons.	Began as indirect leader; with Manhattan Project, became direct leader
Robert Maynard Hutchins, 1899–1977	1. Do not fiddle with faculty members' prerogatives. 2. American education is in decent shape and should not be fundamentally reoriented.	Both forms: effective speaker and writer
Alfred P. Sloan, Jr., 1875–1966	1. Henry Ford's antipathy toward organizational charts, variety of markets, and careful planning and analysis. 2. Durant's laissez-faire attitude. 3. Skilled analysts create more trouble than they are worth.	Began as indirect leader through his organizational plan; became effective direct leader
George C. Marshall, 1880–1959	1. Beware of changes in traditional military practice. 2. Seniority must be honored.	Mostly direct leadership, though could write excellent summaries

Pope John XXIII, 1881–1963	1. It is better to leave power to the Vatican. 2. Tradition should govern all. 3. Catholicism is all-important; punish those who deviate.	Direct
Eleanor Roosevelt, 1884–1962	1. Only certain privileged women can participate fully in American life. 2. A president's wife should stay in the background and support her husband.	Direct, primarily
Martin Luther King, Jr., 1929–1968	1. It is not possible to draw together church, American history, and Gandhian traditions in fashioning a viable approach to effecting change. 2. Blacks should use traditional organizations such as the National Association for the Advancement of Colored People and established strategies such as litigation. 3. Blacks must be prepared to take violent actions.	More direct than indirect
Margaret Thatcher, 1925–	N.A.	N.A.
Jean Monnet, 1888–1979	N.A.	N.A.
Mahatma Gandhi, 1869–1948	N.A.	N.A.

continued overleaf

	Embodiment within Domain	Ultimate Domain	Stance across Domains
Margaret Mead, 1901–1978	Considerable	American public, especially middle class	Inclusionary
J. Robert Oppenheimer, 1904–1967	Excellent laboratory and institutional leader; not as great a scientist as might have been expected; somewhat intimidating on the personal level	America's educated public, including policy makers	Inclusionary, though with personal remoteness
Robert Maynard Hutchins, 1899–1977	Embodied his educational philosophy at a superficial level, but not clear whether he really favored debate, had strong enduring positions, or was a good listener; may have wanted to stimulate his own interests	American educated public	Some inclusionary, some exclusionary aspects
Alfred P. Sloan, Jr., 1875–1966	Effective model of desired behaviors for his staff and dealers	American public, citizens of other industrialized nations	Inclusionary, but competitive
George C. Marshall, 1880–1959	Exemplary—his life actions constituted a major story	U.S. and world public	Inclusionary, though things became murkier after the Second World War

Pope John XXIII, 1881–1963	Excellent	Citizens of the world	Inclusionary; perhaps appreciated more outside the church
Eleanor Roosevelt, 1884–1962	Increasingly excellent; did not stand on rank or ceremony	The nation and beyond, especially the disadvantaged and those who can help them	Inclusionary
Martin Luther King, Jr., 1929–1968	Excellent	The American nation	Inclusionary
Margaret Thatcher, 1925–	N.A.	British nation and its allies	Exclusionary, for the most part
Jean Monnet, 1888–1979	N.A.	European leaders and others involved in decision making	Inclusionary
Mahatma Gandhi, 1869–1948	N.A.	Indian nation, Great Britain, and the rest of the world	Inclusionary

continued overleaf

	Identity Story	Counterstories
Margaret Mead, 1901–1978	As human beings, we can make wise decisions about our own lives by studying options that many other cultures pursue.	We Americans are special, and we have little to learn and much to fear from the examples of other cultures.
J. Robert Oppenheimer, 1904–1967	All of us—scientists, policy makers, laypersons—must work together in a new nuclear world. Working as much as possible in tandem with our adversaries, we must voluntarily control weapons of destruction and put nuclear energy to positive use.	Scientists should stay out of politics. The Soviet Union is our mortal enemy, and we must oppose the Soviets at all costs. The cold war will continue indefinitely.
Robert Maynard Hutchins, 1899–1977	We educated Americans are the bulwark of a democracy. A certain intellectual heritage, represented by Great Books, is the best way toward such an education.	Great Books are parochial and middle brow.
Alfred P. Sloan, Jr., 1875–1966	Business holds the key to the best life for all of us, and it deserves to be at the center of America's life as a nation.	There is more to life than markets and profits. Life has a spiritual dimension. While business can bring about a more prosperous life, it also leads to market cycles and to a materialistic concern that can be destructive.
George C. Marshall, 1880–1959	We Americans must defend our values, through battle if necessary, but we must also try to share them with the wider world. We must prepare to aid the victims of global war.	Americans must win at all costs. We are special and cannot be compared with other lands. We owe no support to those who have committed aggressive acts against us.

New Perspectives on Leadership

Pope John XXIII, 1881–1963	We are human beings first, religious persons second. We must work together to save the world from disaster and to build a lasting peace.	Religious divisions cannot be mediated. The cold war is inevitable and must be pursued.
Eleanor Roosevelt, 1884–1962	Everybody must work together to help the dispossessed, especially women, blacks, and the citizens of third world countries. We have to be prepared to be confrontational, though not too much so.	This is a social Darwinian world, and there is not much that one can do about it.
Martin Luther King, Jr., 1929–1968	We must be color-blind.	Racial differences will always exist and cannot be ignored or minimized; perhaps some day they can be reduced, but the time is not at hand.
Margaret Thatcher, 1925–	Britain has lost its way in defeatism and socialism. We must reclaim the leadership from "them" (socialists, union troublemakers, and the "wets") and restore earlier grandeur.	Imperial Britain was a mistake and certainly should not be reinstituted. Despite its flaws, the socialist/labor way is still the best way.
Jean Monnet, 1888–1979	Europe must become one society, with close links to America.	The European nations have a long and glorious past and cannot simply jettison this past for a risky and uncertain future.
Mahatma Gandhi, 1869–1948	We in India are equal in status and worth to all other human beings. We should work cooperatively with our antagonists if possible, but be prepared to be confrontational if necessary.	There is inherent inequality between colonizer and colonist. Might is right. If one is going to be confrontational, one must be prepared to be violent.

continued overleaf

Other Stories

Margaret Mead,
1901–1978

1. Cultures assume patterns, and one can recognize the pattern of American culture. Human nature is accessible to us, in its unity and its variety.
2. Americans should be prepared to experiment with different lifestyles.

J. Robert
Oppenheimer,
1904–1967

1. The world of knowledge and practice is rife with paradoxes (about secrecy, power, knowledge, and science), and we must revel in them.
2. Human knowledge is still frail and limited.

Robert Maynard
Hutchins,
1899–1977

1. Wise men and women should reflect on the great issues and report the results of their reflections.
2. Civil liberties are important.
3. America should be careful about getting involved in international conflicts (before the Second World War).

Alfred P.
Sloan, Jr.,
1875–1966

1. Cars are central to life.
2. Anything that opposes business is bad.

George C.
Marshall,
1880–1959

1. The cold war should not be allowed to dominate all our actions.
2. It is premature to recognize the State of Israel.

318

Pope John XXIII, 1881–1963
1. It is possible to lead a spiritual life and to ennoble others.
2. We should work to aid the poor.

Eleanor Roosevelt, 1884–1962
1. The ideas of the New Deal must continue within American society and be transported to the rest of the world.
2. An ordinary-appearing and -acting woman can accomplish extraordinary things.

Martin Luther King, Jr., 1929–1968
1. The sources of disadvantage are economic, and a reallocation of resources is needed.
2. The dispossessed of the world must join forces, and America's belligerent foreign policy stands in the way.
3. Reformers must turn their attention to the northern ghettos.

Margaret Thatcher, 1925–
1. Nationalism is better than internationalism.
2. Privatize as many industries and functions as possible.
3. Maintain the cold war, be firm against all aggressors, but try to do business with the Soviet Union's Mikhail Gorbachev.

Jean Monnet, 1888–1979
1. Reconciliation begins with economics. Place one's faith in reason.
2. One should work with leaders and give them the limelight and the credit.
3. One should pursue a single goal steadfastly.

Mahatma Gandhi, 1869–1948
1. The industrial revolution is inherently destructive; one should go back to a village life. One should follow a certain hygiene.
2. Conflict can strengthen both parties.
3. The dispossessed everywhere should unite.
4. Reform work should be fully public.
5. The spiritual dimension of life is the most important one.

continued overleaf

Other Counterstories

Margaret Mead, 1901–1978
1. All cultures can be ranked, or, alternatively, all cultural comparisons are futile.
2. Beware of scientists attempting to tell us about how to lead our lives.
3. Experiments with family and personal lives are dangerous.

J. Robert Oppenheimer, 1904–1967
1. Avoid paradoxes and look for clarity, direction, and solutions.

Robert Maynard Hutchins, 1899–1977
1. Centers and foundations are inherently elitist and unreliable.
2. We as a society need more conservative thinkers and ideologies, not liberals, who have gotten us into trouble.
3. America needs an activist foreign policy.

Alfred P. Sloan, Jr., 1875–1966
1. We must be prepared for industries very different from the automobile industry, and for competitors very different from the Big Three auto makers.
2. The union's viewpoint is very different from the management's.
3. Marxism harbors deeper insights than the classical economic analysis.

George C. Marshall, 1880–1959
1. The cold war dwarfs all other issues.
2. Israel merits recognition now.

Pope John XXIII, 1881–1963	1. Religious leaders should stay out of the political arena. 2. Cynicism about genuine spirituality is merited. 3. The poor should accept their lot.
Eleanor Roosevelt, 1884–1962	1. The New Deal is and should be finished. 2. Only a superperson can accomplish extraordinary things.
Martin Luther King, Jr., 1929–1968	1. The search for economic causes signals that one is a Marxist, and that is dangerous. 2. America is special and has to police the rest of the world. 3. Southerners should stay away from northern urban situations that they cannot understand.
Margaret Thatcher, 1925–	1. Nationalism is anachronistic and dangerous. 2. Many functions are better run by the government. 3. Abandon the cold war, and be wary of Gorbachev.
Jean Monnet, 1888–1979	1. Reconciliation begins with social issues. Spiritual considerations are more important than rational ones. 2. It is bad to work behind the scenes. 3. It is unrealistic to stick to only one goal, especially an international one, given changing conditions and priorities.
Mahatma Gandhi, 1869–1948	1. One cannot turn back the clock. Learn from science. 2. Conflict is a zero-sum undertaking. 3. It is unrealistic for the dispossessed from different societies to feel part of the same population. 4. Do not air your dirty linen publicly; work behind the scenes. 5. Trust reason and analysis, not spirituality.

continued overleaf

	Direct/Indirect Leadership	Embodiment across Domains	Consonance of Within- and Across-Domain Stories
Margaret Mead, 1901–1978	Both forms	Considerable	Considerable
J. Robert Oppenheimer, 1904–1967	Both forms, more problems with direct leadership	Ambivalent, could not defend himself adequately against charges of disloyalty; hauteur was troubling to many	Stretch of domain stories proves problematic, when one deals with a fickle and fearful public
Robert Maynard Hutchins, 1899–1977	Tried both forms, but neither was very effective in later life	Seemed to be all over the map and was not convincing; difficult for ordinary persons to identify with him	Fair degree of consonance at first, but education issues became less important as he addressed the full range of global issues
Alfred P. Sloan, Jr., 1875–1966	Direct leadership	Effective during lifetime, but would rapidly have become anachronistic after 1960	Considerable
George C. Marshall, 1880–1959	Direct leadership	Excellent; more important than story	Considerable

Pope John XXIII, 1881–1963	Direct	Excellent	High consonance
Eleanor Roosevelt, 1884–1962	Direct	Quite convincing, despite her unusual background and position	High
Martin Luther King, Jr., 1929–1968	Direct	Not as effective as within domains	Initially very high; as stories changed, consonance was reduced
Margaret Thatcher, 1925–	Direct	Very convincing	Personally consonant from first days of political life, though she did not reveal her full agenda until she gained high office
Jean Monnet, 1888–1979	Indirect, using leaders as one's vehicle; but primarily direct, in working with leaders	First-rate; cosmopolitan and not parochial; tenacious long-term focus on one issue	N.A.
Mahatma Gandhi, 1869–1948	Both forms	Very convincing	Amazing consistency in long-term goal, flexibility in stories

continued overleaf

Areas of Failure

Margaret Mead, 1901–1978	Never set up an enduring organization or a viable program; analysis of Samoa may have been flawed; her progressive ideas lost currency when the society took a more conservative turn in the 1970s and 1980s; her personal life became fragmented
J. Robert Oppenheimer, 1904–1967	Could not convince policy makers to rein in their desire for weapons; judged a security risk during the anti-Communist witch-hunt and forced to withdraw from public life; his experiences suggested the limits of scientists' participation in the hurly-burly world of politics
Robert Maynard Hutchins, 1899–1977	Could not convince his faculty of many of his programs; never succeeded in launching an effective institution or program after leaving the University of Chicago; general public and many faculty members had difficulty in identifying with Hutchins; not clear that he welcomed debate, except on his terms; toward the end, his messages were not distinguishable from those of other pooh-bahs
Alfred P. Sloan, Jr., 1875–1966	Never anticipated the success of Japan or the rise of the information society; erroneously discerned little difference among General Motors, American society, and the rest of the industrialized world
George C. Marshall, 1880–1959	Not selected to lead Operation Overlord; foreign policy after the Second World War was much more vexed than during the war; attacked by Senator Joseph McCarthy and received little support from President Eisenhower; the military that he built up was rapidly demobilized

Pope John XXIII, 1881–1963	Negative reactions within the Catholic Church; successive leaders did not carry forth John's program within the church; most links forged between Khrushchev and Kennedy did not survive their departures from office
Eleanor Roosevelt, 1884–1962	Much of her domestic agenda had to be muted during the Second World War; became seen as increasingly partisan after the war; leadership of the disadvantaged populations shifted to younger and more representative figures; felt herself an unsuccessful mother and had an extremely strained marriage; led a secret life that was never successfully worked through
Martin Luther King, Jr., 1929–1968	Overtaken by militants within the civil rights movement; under personal attack by the FBI; efforts to attack problems in the urban North were frustrated; core constituency was not interested in the problems of faraway nations and peoples; evidence of his plagiarism and sexual promiscuity
Margaret Thatcher, 1925–	Eventually followed her own dictates without even taking into account the views of others; at the end of her tenure in office, political failures were largely self-inflicted; did not achieve many of her goals for Britain, though she did change the nature of the debate
Jean Monnet, 1888–1979	Had difficulty getting support from leaders of many nations; faced great institutional resistance to change; even today, relevant treaties have not yet been ratified, the spirit of "one Europe" seems remote, tribalism has reemerged
Mahatma Gandhi, 1869–1948	India was and remains wracked with conflict; to some extent, more successful outside of India; family life was not harmonious; Gandhiism is more of an ideal than a reality

[4]
The Servant as Leader*

Robert K. Greenleaf

Servant and leader. Can these two roles be fused in one real person, in all levels of status or calling? If so, can that person live and be productive in the real world of the present? My sense of the present leads me to say yes to both questions. This paper is an attempt to explain why and to suggest how.

The idea of *The Servant as Leader* came out of reading Herman Hesse's *Journey to the East.* In this story we see a band of men on a mythical journey, probably also Hesse's own journey. The central figure of the story is Leo who accompanies the party as the *servant* who does their menial chores, but who also sustains them with his spirit and his song. He is a person of extraordinary presence. All goes well until Leo disappears. Then the group falls into disarray and the journey is abandoned. They cannot make it without the servant Leo. The narrator, one of the party, after some years of wandering finds Leo and is taken into the Order that had sponsored the journey. There he discovers that Leo, whom he had known first as *servant,* was in fact the titular head of the Order, its guiding spirit, a great and noble *leader.*

One can muse on what Hesse was trying to say when he wrote this story. We know that most of his fiction was autobiographical, that he led a tortured life, and that *Journey to the East* suggests a turn toward the serenity he achieved in his old age. There has been much speculation by critics on Hesse's life and work, some of it centering on this story which they find the most puzzling. But to me, this story clearly says — *the great leader is seen as servant first,* and that simple fact is the key to his greatness. Leo was actually the leader all of the time, but he was servant first because that was what he was, *deep down inside.* Leadership was bestowed upon a man who was by nature a servant. It was something given, or assumed, that could be taken away. His servant nature was the real man, not bestowed, not assumed, and not to be taken away. He was servant first.

I mention Hesse and *Journey to the East* for two reasons: first to acknowledge the source of the idea of *The Servant as Leader.* Then I want to use this reference as an

---

* Robert K. Greenleaf first published this essay in 1970. This particular selection was excerpted from Robert K. Greenleaf, *The Servant as Leader* (Indianapolis, IN: The Robert K. Greenleaf Center, 1991), 1-8.

introduction to a brief discussion of prophecy.

Fifteen years ago when I first read about Leo, if I had been listening to contemporary prophecy as intently as I do now, the first draft of this piece might have been written then. As it was, the idea lay dormant for eleven years until, four years ago, I concluded that we in this country were in a leadership crisis and that I should do what I could about it. I became painfully aware of how dull my sense of contemporary prophecy had been. And I have reflected much on why we do not hear and heed the prophetic voices in our midst (not a new question in our times, nor more critical than heretofore).

I now embrace the theory of prophecy which holds that prophetic voices of great clarity, and with a quality of insight equal to that of any age, are speaking cogently all of the time. Men and women of a stature equal to the greatest of the past are with us now addressing the problems of the day and pointing to a better way and to a personeity better able to live fully and serenely in these times.

The variable that marks some periods as barren and some as rich in prophetic vision is in the interest, the level of seeking, the responsiveness of the hearers. The variable is not in the presence or absence or the relative quality and force of the prophetic voices. The prophet grows in stature as people respond to his message. If his early attempts are ignored or spurned, his talent may wither away.

It is *seekers,* then, who make the prophet; and the initiative of any one of us in searching for and responding to the voice of a contemporary prophet may mark the turning point in his growth and service. But since we are the product of our own history, we see current prophecy within the context of past wisdom. We listen to as wide a range of contemporary thought as we can attend to. Then we *choose* those we elect to heed as prophets — *both old and new* — and meld their advice with our own leadings. This we test in real-life experiences to establish our own position....

One does not, of course, ignore the great voices of the past. One does not awake each morning with the compulsion to reinvent the wheel. But if one is *servant,* either leader or follower, one is always searching, listening, expecting that a better wheel for these times is in the making. It may emerge any day. Any one of us may find it out of his own experience. I am hopeful.

I am hopeful for these times, despite the tension and conflict, because more natural servants are trying to see clearly the world as it is and are listening carefully to prophetic voices that are speaking *now*. They are challenging the pervasive injustice with greater force and they are taking sharper issue with the wide disparity between the quality of society they know is reasonable and possible with available resources, and, on the other hand, the actual performance of the whole range of institutions that exist to serve society.

A fresh critical look is being taken at the issues of power and authority, and people are beginning to learn, however haltingly, to relate to one another in less coercive and more creatively supporting ways. A new moral principle is emerging which holds that the only authority deserving one's allegiance is that which is freely and knowingly granted by the led to the leader in response to, and in proportion to, the clearly evident servant stature of the leader. Those who choose to follow this principle will not casually accept the authority of existing institutions. *Rather, they will freely respond only to individuals who are chosen as leaders because they are proven and trusted as servants.* To the extent that this principle prevails in the future, the only truly viable institutions will be those that are predominantly servant-led.

I am mindful of the long road ahead before these trends, which I see so clearly, become a major society-shaping force. We are not there yet. But I see encouraging movement on the horizon.

What direction will the movement take? Much depends on whether those who stir the ferment will come to grips with the age-old problem of how to live in a human society. I say this because so many, having made their awesome decision for autonomy and independence from tradition, and having taken their firm stand against injustice and hypocrisy, find it hard to convert themselves into *affirmative builders* of a better society. How many of them will seek their personal fulfillment by making the hard choices, and by undertaking the rigorous preparation that building a better society requires? It all depends on what kind of leaders emerge and how they — we — respond to them.

My thesis, that more servants should emerge as leaders, or should follow only servant-leaders, is not a popular one. It is much more comfortable to go with a less demanding point of view about what is expected of one now. There are several undemanding, plausibly-argued alternatives to choose. One, since society seems corrupt, is to seek to avoid the center of it by retreating to an idyllic existence that minimizes involvement with the "system" (with the "system" that makes such withdrawal possible). Then there is the assumption that since the effort to reform existing institutions has not brought instant perfection, the remedy is to destroy them completely so that fresh new perfect ones can grow. Not much thought seems to be given to the problem of where the new seed will come from or who the gardener to tend them will be. The concept of the servant-leader stands in sharp contrast to this kind of thinking.

Yet it is understandable that the easier alternatives would be chosen, especially by young people. By extending education for so many so far into the adult years, the normal participation in society is effectively denied when young people are ready for it. With education that is preponderantly abstract and analytical it is no wonder that there is a preoccupation with criticism and that not much thought is given to "what can *I* do about it?"

Criticism has its place; but as a total preoccupation it is sterile. In a time of crisis, like the leadership crisis we are now in, if too many potential builders are taken in by a complete absorption with dissecting the wrong and by a zeal for instant perfection, then the movement so many of us want to see will be set back. The danger, perhaps, is to hear the analyst too much and the artist too little.

Albert Camus stands apart from other great artists of his time, in my view, and deserves the title of *prophet,* because of his unrelenting demand that each of us confront the exacting terms of his own existence, and, like Sisyphus, *accept his rock and find his happiness in dealing with it.* Camus sums up the relevance of his position to our concern for the servant as leader in the last paragraph of his last published lecture, entitled *Create Dangerously.*

> One may long, as I do, for a gentler flame, a respite, a pause for musing. But perhaps there is no other peace for the artist than what he finds in the heat of combat. "Every wall is a door," Emerson correctly said. Let us not look for the door, and the way out, anywhere but in the

wall against which we are living. Instead, let us seek the respite where it is — in the very thick of battle. For in my opinion, and this is where I shall close, it *is* there. Great ideas, it has been said, come into the world as gently as doves. Perhaps, then, if we listen attentively, we shall hear, amid the uproar of empires and nations, a faint flutter of wings, the gentle stirring of life and hope. Some will say that this hope lies in a nation, others, in a man. I believe rather that it is awakened, revived, nourished by millions of solitary individuals whose deeds and works every day negate frontiers and the crudest implications of history. As a result, there shines forth fleetingly the ever-threatened truth that each and every man, on the foundations of his own sufferings and joys, builds for them all.

One is asked, then, to accept the human condition, its sufferings and its joys, and to work with its imperfections as the foundation upon which the individual will build his wholeness through adventurous creative achievement. For the person with creative potential there is no wholeness except in using it. And, as Camus explained, the going is rough and the respite is brief. It is significant that he would title his last university lecture *Create Dangerously*. And as I ponder the fusing of servant and leader it seems a dangerous creation: dangerous for the natural servant to become a leader, dangerous for the leader to be servant first, and dangerous for a follower to insist that he be led by a servant. There are safer and easier alternatives available to all three. But why take them?...

Who is the Servant-Leader?

The servant-leader *is* servant first — as Leo was portrayed. It begins with the natural feeling that one wants to serve, to serve *first*. Then conscious choice brings one to aspire to lead. He is sharply different from the person who is *leader* first, perhaps because of the need to assuage an unusual power drive or to acquire material possessions. For such it will be a later choice to serve — after leadership is established. The leader-first and the servant-first are two extreme types. Between them there are shadings and blends that are part of the infinite variety of human nature.

The difference manifests itself in the care taken by the servant-first to make sure that other people's highest priority needs are being served. The best test, and difficult to administer, is: do those served grow as persons; do they, *while being served,* become healthier, wiser, freer, more autonomous, more likely themselves to become servants? *And,* what is the effect on the least privileged in society; will he benefit, or, at least, will he not be further deprived?

As one sets out to serve, how can one know that this will be the result? This is part of the human dilemma; one cannot know for sure. One must, after some study and experience, hypothesize — but leave the hypothesis under a shadow of doubt. Then one acts on the hypothesis and examines the result. One continues to study and learn and periodically one re-examines the hypothesis itself.

Finally, one chooses again. Perhaps one chooses the same hypothesis again and again. But it is always a fresh open choice. And it is always an hypothesis under a shadow of doubt. "Faith is the choice of the nobler hypothesis." Not the *noblest,* one never knows what that is. But the *nobler,* the best one can see when the choice is made. Since the test of results of one's actions is usually long delayed, the faith that sustains the choice of the nobler hypothesis is psychological self-insight. This is the most dependable part of the true servant.

The natural servant, the person who is *servant first,* is more likely to persevere and refine his hypothesis on what serves another's highest priority needs than is the person who is *leader first* and who later serves out of promptings of conscience or in conformity with normative expectations.

My hope for the future rests in part on my belief that among the legions of deprived and unsophisticated people are many true servants who will lead, and that most of them can learn to discriminate among those who presume to serve them and identify the true servants....

[5]
"GIVE ME A LEVER LONG ENOUGH... AND SINGLE-HANDED I CAN MOVE THE WORLD"

From a very early age, we are taught to break apart problems, to fragment the world. This apparently makes complex tasks and subjects more manageable, but we pay a hidden, enormous price. We can no longer see the consequences of our actions; we lose our intrinsic sense of connection to a larger whole. When we then try to "see the big picture," we try to reassemble the fragments in our minds, to list and organize all the pieces. But, as physicist David Bohm says, the task is futile—similar to trying to reassemble the fragments of a broken mirror to see a true reflection. Thus, after a while we give up trying to see the whole altogether.

The tools and ideas presented in this book are for destroying the illusion that the world is created of separate, unrelated forces. When we give up this illusion—we can then build "learning organizations," organizations where people continually expand their capacity to create the results they truly desire, where new and expansive patterns of thinking are nurtured, where collective aspiration is set free, and where people are continually learning how to learn together.

4 THE FIFTH DISCIPLINE

As *Fortune* magazine recently said, "Forget your tired old ideas about leadership. The most successful corporation of the 1990s will be something called a learning organization." "The ability to learn faster than your competitors," said Arie De Geus, head of planning for Royal Dutch/Shell, "may be the only sustainable competitive advantage." As the world becomes more interconnected and business becomes more complex and dynamic, work must become more "learningful." It is no longer sufficient to have one person learning for the organization, a Ford or a Sloan or a Watson. It's just not possible any longer to "figure it out" from the top, and have everyone else following the orders of the "grand strategist." The organizations that will truly excel in the future will be the organizations that discover how to tap people's commitment and capacity to learn at *all* levels in an organization.

Learning organizations are possible because, deep down, we are all learners. No one has to teach an infant to learn. In fact, no one has to teach infants anything. They are intrinsically inquisitive, masterful learners who learn to walk, speak, and pretty much run their households all on their own. Learning organizations are possible because not only is it our nature to learn but we love to learn. Most of us at one time or another have been part of a great "team," a group of people who functioned together in an extraordinary way—who trusted one another, who complemented each others' strengths and compensated for each others' limitations, who had common goals that were larger than individual goals, and who produced extraordinary results. I have met many people who have experienced this sort of profound teamwork—in sports, or in the performing arts, or in business. Many say that they have spent much of their life looking for that experience again. What they experienced was a learning organization. The team that became great didn't start off great—it *learned* how to produce extraordinary results.

One could argue that the entire global business community is learning to learn together, becoming a learning community. Whereas once many industries were dominated by a single, undisputed leader—one IBM, one Kodak, one Procter & Gamble, one Xerox—today industries, especially in manufacturing, have dozens of excellent companies. American and European corporations are pulled forward by the example of the Japanese; the Japanese, in turn, are pulled by the Koreans and Europeans. Dramatic improvements take place in corporations in Italy, Australia, Singapore—and quickly become influential around the world.

There is also another, in some ways deeper, movement toward learning organizations, part of the evolution of industrial society. Material affluence for the majority has gradually shifted people's orientation toward work—from what Daniel Yankelovich called an "instrumental" view of work, where work was a means to an end, to a more "sacred" view, where people seek the "intrinsic" benefits of work.[1] "Our grandfathers worked six days a week to earn what most of us now earn by Tuesday afternoon," says Bill O'Brien, CEO of Hanover Insurance. "The ferment in management will continue until we build organizations that are more consistent with man's higher aspirations beyond food, shelter and belonging."

Moreover, many who share these values are now in leadership positions. I find a growing number of organizational leaders who, while still a minority, feel they are part of a profound evolution in the nature of work as a social institution. "Why can't we do good works at work?" asked Edward Simon, president of Herman Miller, recently. "Business is the only institution that has a chance, as far as I can see, to fundamentally improve the injustice that exists in the world. But first, we will have to move through the barriers that are keeping us from being truly vision-led and capable of learning."

Perhaps the most salient reason for building learning organizations is that we are only now starting to understand the capabilities such organizations must possess. For a long time, efforts to build learning organizations were like groping in the dark until the skills, areas of knowledge, and paths for development of such organizations became known. What fundamentally will distinguish learning organizations from traditional authoritarian "controlling organizations" will be the mastery of certain basic disciplines. That is why the "disciplines of the learning organization" are vital.

DISCIPLINES OF THE LEARNING ORGANIZATION

On a cold, clear morning in December 1903, at Kitty Hawk, North Carolina, the fragile aircraft of Wilbur and Orville Wright proved that powered flight was possible. Thus was the airplane invented; but it would take more than thirty years before commercial aviation could serve the general public.

Engineers say that a new idea has been "invented" when it is proven to work in the laboratory. The idea becomes an "innovation"

THE FIFTH DISCIPLINE

only when it can be replicated reliably on a meaningful scale at practical costs. If the idea is sufficiently important, such as the telephone, the digital computer, or commercial aircraft, it is called a "basic innovation," and it creates a new industry or transforms an existing industry. In these terms, learning organizations have been invented, but they have not yet been innovated.

In engineering, when an idea moves from an invention to an innovation, diverse "component technologies" come together. Emerging from isolated developments in separate fields of research, these components gradually form an "ensemble of technologies that are critical to each others' success. Until this ensemble forms, the idea, though possible in the laboratory, does not achieve its potential in practice.[2]

The Wright Brothers proved that powered flight was possible, but the McDonnell Douglas DC-3, introduced in 1935, ushered in the era of commercial air travel. The DC-3 was the first plane that supported itself economically as well as aerodynamically. During those intervening thirty years (a typical time period for incubating basic innovations), myriad experiments with commercial flight had failed. Like early experiments with learning organizations, the early planes were not reliable and cost effective on an appropriate scale.

The DC-3, for the first time, brought together five critical component technologies that formed a successful ensemble. They were: the variable-pitch propeller, retractable landing gear, a type of lightweight molded body construction called "monocque," radial air-cooled engine, and wing flaps. To succeed, the DC-3 needed all five; four were not enough. One year earlier, the Boeing 247 was introduced with all of them except wing flaps. Lacking wing flaps, Boeing's engineers found that the plane was unstable on take-off and landing and had to downsize the engine.

Today, I believe, five new "component technologies" are gradually converging to innovate learning organizations. Though developed separately, each will, I believe, prove critical to the others' success, just as occurs with any ensemble. Each provides a vital dimension in building organizations that can truly "learn," that can continually enhance their capacity to realize their highest aspirations:

> *Systems Thinking.* A cloud masses, the sky darkens, leaves twist upward, and we know that it will rain. We also know that after the storm, the runoff will feed into groundwater miles away, and the sky will grow clear by tomorrow. All these events are distant in

time and space, and yet they are all connected within the same pattern. Each has an influence on the rest, an influence that is usually hidden from view. You can only understand the system of a rainstorm by contemplating the whole, not any individual part of the pattern.

Business and other human endeavors are also systems. They, too, are bound by invisible fabrics of interrelated actions, which often take years to fully play out their effects on each other. Since we are part of that lacework ourselves, it's doubly hard to see the whole pattern of change. Instead, we tend to focus on snapshots of isolated parts of the system, and wonder why our deepest problems never seem to get solved. Systems thinking is a conceptual framework, a body of knowledge and tools that has been developed over the past fifty years, to make the full patterns clearer, and to help us see how to change them effectively.

Though the tools are new, the underlying worldview is extremely intuitive; experiments with young children show that they learn systems thinking very quickly.

Personal Mastery. Mastery might suggest gaining dominance over people or things. But mastery can also mean a special level of proficiency. A master craftsman doesn't dominate pottery or weaving. People with a high level of personal mastery are able to consistently realize the results that matter most deeply to them— in effect, they approach their life as an artist would approach a work of art. They do that by becoming committed to their own lifelong learning.

Personal mastery is the discipline of continually clarifying and deepening our personal vision, of focusing our energies, of developing patience, and of seeing reality objectively. As such, it is an essential cornerstone of the learning organization—the learning organization's spiritual foundation. An organization's commitment to and capacity for learning can be no greater than that of its members. The roots of this discipline lie in both Eastern and Western spiritual traditions, and in secular traditions as well.

But surprisingly few organizations encourage the growth of their people in this manner. This results in vast untapped resources: "People enter business as bright, well-educated, high-energy people, full of energy and desire to make a difference," says Hanover's O'Brien. "By the time they are 30, a few are on the "fast track" and the rest 'put in their time' to do what matters to them on the weekend. They lose the commitment, the sense of mission, and the excitement with which they started their careers. We get damn little of their energy and almost none of their spirit."

And surprisingly few adults work to rigorously develop their own personal mastery. When you ask most adults what they want from their lives, they often talk first about what they'd like to get rid of: "I'd like my mother-in-law to move out," they say, or "I'd like my back problems to clear up." The discipline of personal mastery, by contrast, starts with clarifying the things that really matter to us, of living our lives in the service of our highest aspirations.

Here, I am most interested in the connections between personal learning and organizational learning, in the reciprocal commitments between individual and organization, and in the special spirit of an enterprise made up of learners.

Mental Models. "Mental models" are deeply ingrained assumptions, generalizations, or even pictures or images that influence how we understand the world and how we take action. Very often, we are not consciously aware of our mental models or the effects they have on our behavior. For example, we may notice that a coworker dresses elegantly, and say to ourselves, "She's a country club person." About someone who dresses shabbily, we may feel, "He doesn't care about what others think." Mental models of what can or cannot be done in different management settings are no less deeply entrenched. Many insights into new markets or outmoded organizational practices fail to get put into practice because they conflict with powerful, tacit mental models.

Royal Dutch/Shell, one of the first large organizations to understand the advantages of accelerating organizational learning came to this realization when they discovered how pervasive was the influence of hidden mental models, especially those that become widely shared. Shell's extraordinary success in managing through the dramatic changes and unpredictability of the world oil business in the 1970s and 1980s came in large measure from learning how to surface and challenge manager's mental models. (In the early 1970s Shell was the weakest of the big seven oil companies; by the late 1980s it was the strongest.) Arie de Geus, Shell's recently retired Coordinator of Group Planning, says that continuous adaptation and growth in a changing business environment depends on "institutional learning, which is the process whereby management teams change their shared mental models of the company, their markets, and their competitors. For this reason, we think of planning as learning and of corporate planning as institutional learning."[3]

The discipline of working with mental models starts with turning the mirror inward; learning to unearth our internal pictures of the world, to bring them to the surface and hold them rigorously to scrutiny. It also includes the ability to carry on "learningful" conversations that balance inquiry and advocacy, where people expose their own thinking effectively and make that thinking open to the influence of others.

Building Shared Vision. If any one idea about leadership has inspired organizations for thousands of years, it's the capacity to hold a shared picture of the future we seek to create. One is hard pressed to think of any organization that has sustained some measure of greatness in the absence of goals, values, and missions that become deeply shared throughout the organization. IBM had "service"; Polaroid had instant photography; Ford had public transportation for the masses and Apple had computing power for the masses. Though radically different in content and kind, all these organizations managed to bind people together around a common identity and sense of destiny.

When there is a genuine vision (as opposed to the all-too-familiar "vision statement"), people excel and learn, not because they are told told to, but because they want to. But many leaders have personal visions that never get translated into shared visions that galvanize an organization. All too often, a company's shared vision has revolved around the charisma of a leader, or around a crisis that galvanizes everyone temporarily. But, given a choice, most people opt for pursuing a lofty goal, not only in times of crisis but at all times. What has been lacking is a discipline for translating individual vision into shared vision—not a "cookbook" but a set of principles and guiding practices.

The practice of shared vision involves the skills of unearthing shared "pictures of the future" that foster genuine commitment and enrollment rather than compliance. In mastering this discipline, leaders learn the counterproductiveness of trying to dictate a vision, no matter how heartfelt.

Team Learning. How can a team of committed managers with individual IQs above 120 have a collective IQ of 63? The discipline

THE FIFTH DISCIPLINE

of team learning confronts this paradox. We know that teams can learn; in sports, in the performing arts, in science, and even, occasionally, in business, there are striking examples where the intelligence of the team exceeds the intelligence of the individuals in the team, and where teams develop extraordinary capacities for coordinated action. When teams are truly learning, not only are they producing extraordinary results but the individual members are growing more rapidly than could have occurred otherwise.

The discipline of team learning starts with "dialogue," the capacity of members of a team to suspend assumptions and enter into a genuine "thinking together." To the Greeks *dia-logos* meant a free-flowing of meaning through a group, allowing the group to discover insights not attainable individually. Interestingly, the practice of dialogue has been preserved in many "primitive" cultures, such as that of the American Indian, but it has been almost completely lost to modern society. Today, the principles and practices of dialogue are being rediscovered and put into a contemporary context. (Dialogue differs from the more common "discussion," which has its roots with "percussion" and "concussion," literally a heaving of ideas back and forth in a winner-takes-all competition.)

The discipline of dialogue also involves learning how to recognize the patterns of interaction in teams that undermine learning. The patterns of defensiveness are often deeply engrained in how a team operates. If unrecognized, they undermine learning. If recognized and surfaced creatively, they can actually accelerate learning.

Team learning is vital because teams, not individuals, are the fundamental learning unit in modern organizations. This where "the rubber meets the road"; unless teams can learn, the organization cannot learn.

If a learning organization were an engineering innovation, such as the airplane or the personal computer, the components would be called "technologies." For an innovation in human behavior, the components need to be seen as *disciplines*. By "discipline," I do not mean an "enforced order" or "means of punishment," but a body of theory and technique that must be studied and mastered to be put into practice. A discipline is a developmental path for acquiring certain skills or competencies. As with any discipline, from playing the piano to electrical engineering, some people have an innate "gift," but anyone can develop proficiency through practice.

To practice a discipline is to be a lifelong learner. You "never arrive"; you spend your life mastering disciplines. You can never say, "We are a learning organization," any more than you can say, "I am an enlightened person." The more you learn, the more acutely aware you become of your ignorance. Thus, a corporation cannot be "excellent" in the sense of having arrived at a permanent excellence; it is always in the state of practicing the disciplines of learning, of becoming better or worse.

That organizations can benefit from disciplines is not a totally new idea. After all, management disciplines such as accounting have been around for a long time. But the five learning disciplines differ from more familiar management disciplines in that they are "personal" disciplines. Each has to do with how we think, what we truly want, and how we interact and learn with one another. In this sense, they are more like artistic disciplines than traditional management disciplines. Moreover, while accounting is good for "keeping score," we have never approached the subtler tasks of building organizations, of enhancing their capabilities for innovation and creativity, of crafting strategy and designing policy and structure through assimilating new disciplines. Perhaps this is why, all too often, great organizations are fleeting, enjoying their moment in the sun, then passing quietly back to the ranks of the mediocre.

Practicing a discipline is different from emulating "a model." All too often, new management innovations are described in terms of the "best practices" of so-called leading firms. While interesting, I believe such descriptions can often do more harm than good, leading to piecemeal copying and playing catch-up. I do not believe great organizations have ever been built by trying to emulate another, any more than individual greatness is achieved by trying to copy another "great person."

When the five component technologies converged to create the DC-3 the commercial airline industry began. But the DC-3 was not the end of the process. Rather, it was the precursor of a new industry. Similarly, as the five component learning disciplines converge they will not create *the* learning organization but rather a new wave of experimentation and advancement.

12   THE FIFTH DISCIPLINE

THE FIFTH DISCIPLINE

It is vital that the five disciplines develop as an ensemble. This is challenging because it is much harder to integrate new tools than simply apply them separately. But the payoffs are immense.

This is why systems thinking is the fifth discipline. It is the discipline that integrates the disciplines, fusing them into a coherent body of theory and practice. It keeps them from being separate gimmicks or the latest organization change fads. Without a systemic orientation, there is no motivation to look at how the disciplines interrelate. By enhancing each of the other disciplines, it continually reminds us that the whole can exceed the sum of its parts.

For example, vision without systems thinking ends up painting lovely pictures of the future with no deep understanding of the forces that must be mastered to move from here to there. This is one of the reasons why many firms that have jumped on the "vision bandwagon" in recent years have found that lofty vision alone fails to turn around a firm's fortunes. Without systems thinking, the seed of vision falls on harsh soil. If nonsystemic thinking predominates, the first condition for nurturing vision is not met: a genuine belief that we can make our vision real in the future. We may say "We can achieve our vision" (most American managers are conditioned to this belief), but our tacit view of current reality as a set of conditions created by somebody else betrays us.

But systems thinking also needs the disciplines of building shared vision, mental models, team learning, and personal mastery to realize its potential. Building shared vision fosters a commitment to the long term. Mental models focus on the openness needed to unearth shortcomings in our present ways of seeing the world. Team learning develops the skills of groups of people to look for the larger picture that lies beyond individual perspectives. And personal mastery fosters the personal motivation to continually learn how our actions affect our world. Without personal mastery, people are so steeped in the reactive mindset ("someone/something else is creating my problems") that they are deeply threatened by the systems perspective.

Lastly, systems thinking makes understandable the subtlest aspect of the learning organization—the new way individuals perceive themselves and their world. At the heart of a learning organization is a shift of mind—from seeing ourselves as separate from the world to connected to the world, from seeing problems as caused by someone or something "out there" to seeing how our own actions create the problems we experience. A learning organization is a place where people are continually discovering how they create their reality. And how they can change it. As Archimedes has said, "Give me a lever long enough . . . and single-handed I can move the world."

METANOIA—A SHIFT OF MIND

When you ask people about what it is like being part of a great team, what is most striking is the meaningfulness of the experience. People talk about being part of something larger than themselves, of being connected, of being generative. It becomes quite clear that, for many, their experiences as part of truly great teams stand out as singular periods of life lived to the fullest. Some spend the rest of their lives looking for ways to recapture that spirit.

The most accurate word in Western culture to describe what happens in a learning organization is one that hasn't had much currency for the past several hundred years. It is a word we have used in our work with organizations for some ten years, but we always caution them, and ourselves, to use it sparingly in public. The word is "metanoia" and it means a shift of mind. The word has a rich history. For the Greeks, it meant a fundamental shift or change, or more literally transcendence (*"meta"*—above or beyond, as in "metaphysics") of mind ("noia," from the root *"nous,"* of mind). In the early (Gnostic) Christian tradition, it took on a special meaning of awakening shared intuition and direct knowing of the highest, of God. "Metanoia" was probably the key term of such early Christians as John the Baptist. In the Catholic corpus the word metanoia was eventually translated as "repent."

To grasp the meaning of "metanoia" is to grasp the deeper meaning of "learning," for learning also involves a fundamental shift or movement of mind. The problem with talking about "learning organizations" is that the "learning" has lost its central meaning in contemporary usage. Most people's eyes glaze over if you talk to them about "learning" or "learning organizations." Little wonder—for, in everyday use, learning has come to be synonymous with "taking in information." "Yes, I learned all about that at the course yesterday." Yet, taking in information is only distantly related to real learning. It would be nonsensical to say, "I just read a great book about bicycle riding—I've now learned that."

14   THE FIFTH DISCIPLINE

Real learning gets to the heart of what it means to be human. Through learning we re-create ourselves. Through learning we become able to do something we never were able to do. Through learning we reperceive the world and our relationship to it. Through learning we extend our capacity to create, to be part of the generative process of life. There is within each of us a deep hunger for this type of learning. It is, as Bill O'Brien of Hanover Insurance says, "as fundamental to human beings as the sex drive."

This, then, is the basic meaning of a "learning organization"—an organization that is continually expanding its capacity to create its future. For such an organization, it is not enough merely to survive. "Survival learning" or what is more often termed "adaptive learning" is important—indeed it is necessary. But for a learning organization, "adaptive learning" must be joined by "generative learning," learning that enhances our capacity to create.

A few brave organizational pioneers are pointing the way, but the territory of building learning organizations is still largely unexplored. It is my fondest hope that this book can accelerate that exploration.

PUTTING THE IDEAS INTO PRACTICE

I take no credit for inventing the five major disciplines of this book. The five disciplines described below represent the experimentation, research, writing, and invention of hundreds of people. But I have worked with all of the disciplines for years, refining ideas about them, collaborating on research, and introducing them to organizations throughout the world.

When I entered graduate school at the Massachusetts Institute of Technology in 1970, I was already convinced that most of the problems faced by humankind concerned our inability to grasp and manage the increasingly complex systems of our world. Little has happened since to change my view. Today, the arms race, the environmental crisis, the international drug trade, the stagnation in the Third World, and the persisting U.S. budget and trade deficits all attest to a world where problems are becoming increasingly complex and interconnected. From the start at MIT I was drawn to the work of Jay Forrester, a computer pioneer who had shifted fields to develop what he called "system dynamics." Jay maintained that the causes of many pressing public issues, from urban decay to global ecological threat, lay in the very well-intentioned policies designed to alleviate them. These problems were "actually systems" that lured policymakers into interventions that focused on obvious symptoms not underlying causes, which produced short-term benefit but long-term malaise, and fostered the need for still more symptomatic interventions.

As I began my doctoral work, I had little interest in business management. I felt that the solutions to the Big Issues lay in the public sector. But I began to meet business leaders who came to visit our MIT group to learn about systems thinking. These were thoughtful people, deeply aware of the inadequacies of prevailing ways of managing. They were engaged in building new types of organizations —decentralized, nonhierarchical organizations dedicated to the well-being and growth of employees as well as to success. Some had crafted radical corporate philosophies based on core values of freedom and responsibility. Others had developed innovative organization designs. All shared a commitment and a capacity to innovate that was lacking in the public sector. Gradually, I came to realize why business is the locus of innovation in an open society. Despite whatever hold past thinking may have on the business mind, business has a freedom to experiment missing in the public sector and, often, in nonprofit organizations. It also has a clear "bottom line," so that experiments can be evaluated, at least in principle, by objective criteria.

By why were they interested in systems thinking? Too often, the most daring organizational experiments were foundering. Local autonomy produced business decisions that were disastrous for the organization as a whole. "Team building" exercises sent colleagues white-water rafting together, but when they returned home they still disagreed fundamentally about business problems. Companies pulled together during crises, and then lost all their inspiration when business improved. Organizations which started out as booming successes, with the best possible intentions toward customers and employees, found themselves trapped in downward spirals that got worse the harder they tried to fix them.

Then, we all believed that the tools of systems thinking could make a difference in these companies. As I worked with different companies, I came to see why systems thinking was not enough by itself. It needed a new type of management practitioner to really make the most of it. At that time, in the mid-1970s, there was a nascent sense of what such a management practitioner could be. But

16 THE FIFTH DISCIPLINE

it had not yet crystallized. It is crystallizing now with leaders of our MIT group: William O'Brien of Hanover Insurance; Edward Simon from Herman Miller, and Ray Stata, CEO of Analog Devices. All three of these men are involved in innovative, influential companies. All three have been involved in our research program for several years, along with leaders from Apple, Ford, Polaroid, Royal Dutch/Shell, and Trammell Crow.

For eleven years I have also been involved in developing and conducting Innovation Associates' Leadership and Mastery workshops, which have introduced people from all walks of life to the fifth discipline ideas that have grown out of our work at MIT, combined with IA's path-breaking work on building shared vision and personal mastery. Over four thousand managers have attended. We started out with a particular focus on corporate senior executives, but soon found that the basic disciplines such as systems thinking, personal mastery, and shared vision were relevant for teachers, public administrators and elected officials, students, and parents. All were in leadership positions of importance. All were in "organizations" that had still untapped potential for creating their future. All felt that to tap that potential required developing their own capacities, that is, learning.

So, this book is for the learners, especially those of us interested in the art and practice of collective learning.

For managers, this book should help in identifying the specific practices, skills, and disciplines that can make building learning organizations less of an occult art (though an art nonetheless).

For parents, this book should help in letting our children be our teachers, as well as we theirs—for they have much to teach us about learning as a way of life.

For citizens, the dialogue about why contemporary organizations are not especially good learners and about what is required to build learning organizations reveals some of the tools needed by communities and societies if they are to become more adept learners.

Notes

1. Daniel Yankelovich, *New Rules: Searching for Self-fulfillment in a World Turned Upside Down* (New York: Random House). 1981.
2. I am indebted to my MIT colleague Alan Graham for the insight that basic innovation occurs through the integration of diverse technologies into a new ensemble. See A. K. Graham, "Software Design: Breaking the Bottleneck," *IEEE Spectrum* (March 1982): 43–50; A. K. Graham and P. Senge, "A Long-Wave Hypothesis of Innovation," *Technological Forecasting and Social Change* (1980): 283–311.
3. Arie de Geus, "Planning as Learning," *Harvard Business Review* (March/April 1988): 70–74.

Part II
Power, Authority and Leadership

[6]
The Totalitarian Movement

I: *Totalitarian Propaganda*

ONLY THE MOB and the elite can be attracted by the momentum of totalitarianism itself; the masses have to be won by propaganda. Under conditions of constitutional government and freedom of opinion, totalitarian movements struggling for power can use terror to a limited extent only and share with other parties the necessity of winning adherents and of appearing plausible to a public which is not yet rigorously isolated from all other sources of information.

It was recognized early and has frequently been asserted that in totalitarian countries propaganda and terror present two sides of the same coin.[1] This, however, is only partly true. Wherever totalitarianism possesses absolute control, it replaces propaganda with indoctrination and uses violence not so much to frighten people (this is done only in the initial stages when political opposition still exists) as to realize constantly its ideological doctrines and its practical lies. Totalitarianism will not be satisfied to assert, in the face of contrary facts, that unemployment does not exist; it will abolish unemployment benefits as part of its propaganda.[2] Equally important is the fact that the refusal to acknowledge unemployment realized—albeit in a rather unexpected way—the old socialist doctrine: He who does not work shall not eat. Or when, to take another instance, Stalin decided to rewrite the history of the Russian Revolution, the propaganda of his new version consisted in destroying, together with the older books and documents, their authors and readers: the publication in 1938 of a new official history of the Communist Party was the signal that the superpurge which had decimated

---

[1] See for instance E. Kohn-Bramstedt, *Dictatorship and Political Police. The Technique of Control by Fear*, London, 1945, pp. 164 ff. The explanation is that "terror without propaganda would lose most of its psychological effect, whereas propaganda without terror does not contain its full punch" (p. 175).

The same opinion is expressed by the Nazi theorist, Eugen Hadamovsky, *Propaganda und nationale Macht*, 1933: "Propaganda and violence are never contradictions. Use of violence can be part of the propaganda" (p. 22).

[2] "At that time, it was officially announced that unemployment was 'liquidated' in Soviet Russia. The result of the announcement was that all unemployment benefits were equally 'liquidated'" (Anton Ciliga, *The Russian Enigma*, London, 1940, p. 109).

a whole generation of Soviet intellectuals had come to an end.[3] Similarly, the Nazis in the Eastern occupied territories at first used chiefly antisemitic propaganda to win firmer control of the population. They neither needed nor used terror to support this propaganda. When they liquidated the greater part of the Polish intelligentsia, they did it not because of its opposition, but because according to their doctrine Poles had no intellect, and when they planned to kidnap blue-eyed and blond-haired children, they did not intend to frighten the population but simply thought these children were superior to all other Poles.[4]

Totalitarian propaganda is fully developed before the movements seize power, and its services are retained later only insofar as totalitarian regimes continue to have dealings with the external, nontotalitarian world where totalitarian movements either exist or are being created. Whenever indoctrination at home comes into conflict with the propaganda line for consumption abroad (which happened in Russia during the war, not when Stalin had concluded his alliance with Hitler, but when the war with Hitler brought him into the camp of the democracies), the propaganda is explained as a "temporary tactical maneuver."[5] As far as possible, this distinction between the doctrine for the initiated and propaganda for the outside world is already realized in the prepower existence of the movements. The relationship between propaganda and indoctrination usually depends upon the size of the

[3] Victor Kravchenko, *I Chose Freedom. The Personal and Political Life of a Soviet Official*, New York, 1946, p. 304: "It was the wind-up of this long war [*i.e.*, from 1936-1938] that was signalized by the appearance of a new history [of the Communist Party]. It proved to be a document probably without precedent. . . . It revised half a century of Russian history. I don't mean simply that it falsified some facts or gave a new interpretation of events. I mean that it deliberately stood history on its head, expunging events and inventing facts."

[4] For authentic reports on these plans of Himmler which apparently could not be carried out in time, see *Nazi Conspiracy and Aggression*. Office of the United States Chief of Counsel for the Prosecution of Axis Criminality. U. S. Government, Washington, 1946, III, 640, which refers to a speech delivered by Himmler in Cracow on March 13 and 14, 1942, and the speech made at Bad Schachen in 1943, extracts of which are published in Kohn-Bramstedt, *op. cit.*, p. 244.

[5] For Stalin's confidence that Hitler would not attack Russia, see Isaac Deutscher, *Stalin: A Political Biography*, New York and London, 1949, pp. 454 ff., and especially the footnote on p. 458: "It was only in 1948, that the chief of the State Planning Commission, Vice-Premier N. Voznesensky, disclosed that the economic plans for the third quarter of 1941 had been based on the assumption of peace and that a new plan, suited for war, had been drafted only after the outbreak of hostilities."

Kravchenko adds more significant indications for the correctness of the hypothesis that "Stalin entered into his compact with Hitler in earnest": First, anti-Fascist propaganda was completely abandoned in favor of anti-imperialist propaganda, and this line was carried into the cadres of high party officials; second, the USSR kept its economic agreements with Germany and, consequently, was drained of necessary war materials and had to decrease its own war production. *Op. cit.*, p. 335.

In contrast to the attitude taken during the Hitler-Stalin alliance, democratic and nationalist propaganda during the war never penetrated the higher ranks of the party, where "the retreat from Leninism was simply a temporary tactical maneuver" (*ibid.*, p. 422).

THE TOTALITARIAN MOVEMENT

movements on one hand, and outside pressure on the other. The smaller the movement is, the more energy it will expend in mere propaganda; the greater the pressure on totalitarian regimes from the outside world, which even behind iron curtains cannot be ignored entirely, the more actively will the totalitarian dictators engage in propaganda. Conversely indoctrination, together with terror, increases with the strength of the movements or the totalitarian governments' isolation and security from outside interference.

Propaganda is indeed part and parcel of "psychological warfare"; but terror is more. Terror continues to be used by totalitarian regimes even when its psychological aims are achieved; its real horror is that it reigns over a completely subdued population. Where the rule of terror is brought to perfection, as in concentration camps, propaganda disappears entirely; it was even expressly prohibited in Nazi Germany.[6] Propaganda, in other words, is one and possibly the most important instrument of totalitarianism for dealing with the nontotalitarian world; terror, on the contrary, is the very essence of its form of government. Its existence depends as little on psychological or other subjective factors as the existence of laws in a constitutionally governed country depends upon the number of people who transgress them.

Terror as the counterpart of propaganda played a greater role in Nazism than in Communism. The Nazis did not strike at prominent figures as had been done in the earlier wave of political crimes in Germany (the murder of Rathenau and Erzberger); instead, by killing small socialist functionaries or influential members of opposing parties, they attempted to prove to the population the dangers involved in mere membership. This kind of mass terror, which still operated on a comparatively small scale, increased steadily because neither the police nor the courts seriously prosecuted political offenders on the so-called Right.[7] It was valuable as what a Nazi publicist has aptly called "power propaganda"[8]: it made clear to the population at large that the power of the Nazis was greater than that of the authorities and that it was safer to be a member of a Nazi paramilitary organization than a loyal Republican. This impression was greatly strengthened by the specific use the Nazis made of their political crimes. They always admitted them

---

[6] "Education [in the concentration camps] consists of discipline, never of any kind of instruction on an ideological basis, for the prisoners have for the most part slave-like souls" (Heinrich Himmler, *Nazi Conspiracy*, IV, 616 ff.).

[7] David Riesman, "Democracy and Defamation," in *Columbia Law Review*, 1942, pp. 1092 ff., analyzes Nazi propaganda as systematic defamation and shows how they succeeded in weakening the authority of officials simply by slandering them while, at the same time, they could enhance their own prestige and authority by literally and publicly "getting away with murder."

[8] Eugen Hadamovsky, *op. cit.*, is outstanding in the literature on totalitarian propaganda. Without explicitly stating it, Hadamovsky offers an intelligent and revealing pro-Nazi interpretation of Hitler's own exposition on the subject in "Propaganda and Organization," in Book II, chapter xi of *Mein Kampf* (2 vols., 1st German edition, 1925 and 1927 respectively. Unexpurgated translation, New York, 1939).—See also F. A. Six, *Die politische Propaganda der NSDAP im Kampf um die Macht*, 1936, pp. 21 ff.

publicly, never apologized for "excesses of the lower ranks"—such apologies were used only by Nazi sympathizers—and impressed the population as being very different from the "idle talkers" of other parties.

The similarities between this kind of terror and plain gangsterism are too obvious to be pointed out. This does not mean that Nazism was gangsterism, as has sometimes been concluded, but only that the Nazis, without admitting it, learned as much from American gangster organizations as their propaganda, admittedly, learned from American business publicity.

More specific in totalitarian propaganda, however, than direct threats and crimes against individuals is the use of indirect, veiled, and menacing hints against all who will not heed its teachings and, later, mass murder perpetrated on "guilty" and "innocent" alike. People are threatened by Communist propaganda with missing the train of history, with remaining hopelessly behind their time, with spending their lives uselessly, just as they were threatened by the Nazis with living against the eternal laws of nature and life, with an irreparable and mysterious deterioration of their blood. The strong emphasis of totalitarian propaganda on the "scientific" nature of its assertions has been compared to certain advertising techniques which also address themselves to masses. And it is true that the advertising columns of every newspaper show this "scientificality," by which a manufacturer proves with facts and figures and the help of a "research" department that his is the "best soap in the world." [9] It is also true that there is a certain element of violence in the imaginative exaggerations of publicity men, that behind the assertion that girls who do not use this particular brand of soap may go through life with pimples and without a husband, lies the wild dream of monopoly, the dream that one day the manufacturer of the "only soap that prevents pimples" may have the power to deprive of husbands all girls who don't use his soap. Science in the instances of both business publicity and totalitarian propaganda is obviously only a surrogate for power. The obsession of totalitarian movements with "scientific" proofs ceases once they are in power. The Nazis dismissed even those scholars who were willing to serve them, and the Bolsheviks use the reputation of their scientists for entirely unscientific purposes and force them into the role of charlatans.

But there is nothing more to the frequently overrated similarities between mass advertisement and mass propaganda. Businessmen usually do not pose as prophets and they do not constantly demonstrate the correctness of their predictions. The scientificality of totalitarian propaganda is characterized by its almost exclusive insistence on scientific prophecy as distinguished from the more old-fashioned appeal to the past. Nowhere does the ideological origin, of socialism in one instance and racism in the other, show more clearly than when their spokesmen pretend that they have discovered the hidden forces that will bring them good fortune in the chain of fatality.

[9] Hitler's analysis of "War Propaganda" (*Mein Kampf*, Book I, chapter vi) stresses the business angle of propaganda and uses the example of publicity for soap. Its importance has been generally overestimated, while his later positive ideas on "Propaganda and Organization" were neglected.

THE TOTALITARIAN MOVEMENT

There is of course a great appeal to the masses in "absolutist systems which represent all the events of history as depending upon the great first causes linked by the chain of fatality, and which, as it were, suppress men from the history of the human race" (in the words of Tocqueville). But it cannot be doubted either that the Nazi leadership actually believed in, and did not merely use as propaganda, such doctrines as the following: "The more accurately we recognize and observe the laws of nature and life, . . . so much the more do we conform to the will of the Almighty. The more insight we have into the will of the Almighty, the greater will be our successes." [10] It is quite apparent that very few changes are needed to express Stalin's creed in two sentences which might run as follows: "The more accurately we recognize and observe the laws of history and class struggle, so much the more do we conform to dialectic materialism. The more insight we have into dialectic materialism, the greater will be our success." Stalin's notion of "correct leadership," [11] at any rate, could hardly be better illustrated.

Totalitarian propaganda raised ideological scientificality and its technique of making statements in the form of predictions to a height of efficiency of method and absurdity of content because, demagogically speaking, there is hardly a better way to avoid discussion than by releasing an argument from the control of the present and by saying that only the future can reveal its merits. However, totalitarian ideologies did not invent this procedure, and were not the only ones to use it. Scientificality of mass propaganda has indeed been so universally employed in modern politics that it has been interpreted as a more general sign of that obsession with science which has characterized the Western world since the rise of mathematics and physics in the sixteenth century; thus totalitarianism appears to be only the last stage in a process during which "science [has become] an idol that will magically cure the evils of existence and transform the nature of man." [12] And there was, indeed, an early connection between scientificality and the rise of the masses. The "collectivism" of masses was welcomed by those who hoped for the appearance of "natural laws of historical development" which would eliminate the unpredictability of the individual's actions and behavior.[13] There has been cited the example of Enfantin who could already "see the time approaching when the 'art of moving the masses' will be so perfectly developed that the painter, the musician, and the poet will possess the power to please and to move with the same certainty as the mathematician solves a geometrical problem or the chemist analyses any substance," and it has been concluded that modern propaganda was born then and there.[14]

---

[10] See Martin Bormann's important memorandum on the "Relationship of National Socialism and Christianity" in *Nazi Conspiracy*, VI, 1036 ff.

[11] J. Stalin, *Leninism* (1933), Vol. II, chapter iii.

[12] Eric Voegelin, "The Origins of Scientism," in *Social Research*, December, 1948.

[13] See F. A. v. Hayek, "The Counter-Revolution of Science," in *Economica*, Vol. VIII (February, May, August, 1941), p. 13.

[14] *Ibid.*, p. 137. The quotation is from the Saint-Simonist magazine *Producteur*, I, 399.

Yet whatever the shortcomings of positivism, pragmatism, and behaviorism, and however great their influence on the formation of the nineteenth-century brand of common sense, it is not at all "the cancerous growth of the utilitarian segment of existence" [15] which characterizes the masses to whom totalitarian propaganda and scientificality appeal. The positivists' conviction, as we know it from Comte, that the future is eventually scientifically predictable, rests on the evaluation of interest as an all-pervasive force in history and the assumption that objective laws of power can be discovered. Rohan's political theory that "the kings command the peoples and the interest commands the king," that objective interest is the rule "that alone can never fail," that "rightly or wrongly understood, the interest makes governments live or die" is the traditional core of modern utilitarianism, positivist or socialist, but none of these theories assumes that it is possible "to transform the nature of man" as totalitarianism indeed tries to do. On the contrary, they all implicitly or explicitly assume that human nature is always the same, that history is the story of changing objective circumstances and the human reactions to them, and that interest, rightly understood, may lead to a change of circumstances, but not to a change of human reactions as such. "Scientism" in politics still presupposes that human welfare is its object, a concept which is utterly alien to totalitarianism.[16]

It is precisely because the utilitarian core of ideologies was taken for granted that the anti-utilitarian behavior of totalitarian governments, their complete indifference to mass interest, has been such a shock. This introduced into contemporary politics an element of unheard-of unpredictability. Totalitarian propaganda, however—although in the form of shifted emphasis—indicated even before totalitarianism could seize power how far the masses had drifted from mere concern with interest. The truth is that interest as a collective force can be felt only where stable social bodies provide the necessary transmission belts between the individual and the group; no effective propaganda based on mere interest can be carried on among masses whose chief characteristic is that they belong to no social or political body, and who therefore present a veritable chaos of individual interests. The fanaticism of members of totalitarian movements, so clearly different in quality from the greatest loyalty of members of ordinary parties, is produced by the lack of self-interest of masses who are quite prepared to sacrifice themselves. The Nazis have proved that one can lead a whole people into war with the slogan "or else we shall go down" (something which the war propaganda of 1914 would have avoided carefully), and this not in times of misery, unemployment, or frustrated national ambitions. The same spirit

[15] Voegelin, op. cit.
[16] William Ebenstein, *The Nazi State,* New York, 1943, in discussing the "Permanent War Economy" of the Nazi state is almost the only critic who has realized that "the endless discussion . . . as to the socialist or capitalist nature of the German economy under the Nazi regime is largely artificial . . . [because it] tends to overlook the vital fact that capitalism and socialism are categories which relate to Western welfare economics" (p. 239).

THE TOTALITARIAN MOVEMENT

showed itself during the last months of a war that was obviously lost, when Nazi propaganda consoled an already badly frightened population with the promise that the Fuehrer "in his wisdom had prepared an easy death for the German people by gassing them in case of defeat." [17]

Totalitarian movements use socialism and racism by emptying them of their utilitarian content, the interests of a class or nation. The form of infallible prediction in which these concepts were presented has become more important than their content.[18] The chief qualification of a mass leader has become unending infallibility; he can never admit an error.[19] The assumption of infallibility, moreover, is based not so much on superior intelligence as on the correct interpretation of the essentially reliable forces in history or nature, forces which neither defeat nor ruin can prove wrong because they are bound to assert themselves in the long run.[20] Mass leaders in power have one concern which overrules all utilitarian considerations: to make their predictions come true. The Nazis did not hesitate to use, at the end of the war, the concentrated force of their still intact organization to bring about as complete a destruction of Germany as possible, in order to make true their prediction that the German people would be ruined in case of defeat.

The propaganda effect of infallibility, the striking success of posing as a mere interpreting agent of predictable forces, has encouraged in totalitarian dictators the habit of announcing their political intentions in the form of prophecy. The most famous example is Hitler's announcement to the German Reichstag in January, 1939: "I want today once again to make a prophecy: In case the Jewish financiers . . . succeed once more in hurling the peoples into a world war, the result will be . . . the annihilation of the Jewish race in Europe." [21] Translated into nontotalitarian language, this

---

[17] See Friedrich Percyval Reck-Malleczewen, *Tagebuch eines Verzweifelten*, Stuttgart, 1947, p. 190.

[18] Hitler based the superiority of ideological movements over political parties on the fact that ideologies (*Weltanschauungen*) always "proclaim their infallibility" (*Mein Kampf*, Book II, chapter v, "*Weltanschauung* and Organization").—The first pages of the official handbook for the Hitler Youth, *The Nazi Primer*, New York, 1938, consequently emphasize that all questions of *Weltanschauung*, formerly deemed "unrealistic" and "ununderstandable," "have become so clear, simple and *definite* [my italics] that every comrade can understand them and co-operate in their solution."

[19] The initiation ceremony in every formation of the Nazi movement contained as the first or one of the first watchwords the principle: "The Fuehrer is always right." See *Organisationsbuch der NSDAP; Nazi Primer*, etc.

"Their claim to be infallible, [that] neither of them has ever sincerely admitted an error" is in this respect the decisive difference between Stalin and Trotsky on one hand, and Lenin on the other. See Boris Souvarine, *Stalin. A Critical Survey of Bolshevism*, New York, 1939, p. 583.

[20] That Hegelian dialectics should provide a wonderful instrument for always being right, because they permit the interpretation of all defeats as the beginning of victory, is obvious. One of the most beautiful examples of this kind of sophistry occurred when, after 1933, the German Communists for nearly two years refused to recognize that Hitler's victory had been a defeat for the German Communist Party.

[21] Quoted from Goebbels: *The Goebbels Diaries (1942-1943)*, ed. by Louis Lochmer, New York, 1948, p. 148.

meant: I intend to make a war and I intend to kill the Jews of Europe. Similarly Stalin, in the great speech before the Central Committee of the Communist Party in 1930 in which he prepared the physical liquidation of intraparty right and left deviationists, described them as representatives of "dying classes." [22] This expression gave his whole argument its particular force; it fitted the liquidation into a historical process in which man does only what would have happened in any event, according to its law. The Nazis likewise fitted their crimes—against the Republican constitution, against the Jews, against Eastern European peoples, against mentally ill persons—into the laws of nature which would not let those live who "did not seem fit to live." [23]

This method, like other totalitarian propaganda methods, is foolproof only after the movements have seized power. Then all debate about the truth or falsity of a totalitarian dictator's prediction is as weird as arguing with a potential murderer about whether his future victim is dead or alive—since by killing the person in question the murderer can promptly provide proof of the correctness of his statement. The only valid argument under such conditions is promptly to rescue the person whose death is predicted. Before mass leaders seize the power to fit reality to their lies, their propaganda is marked by its extreme contempt for facts as such,[24] for in their opinion fact depends entirely on the power of man who can fabricate it. The assertion that the Moscow subway is the only one in the world is a lie only so long as the Bolsheviks have not the power to destroy all the others. In other words the method of infallible prediction, more than any other totalitarian propaganda device, betrays its ultimate goal of world conquest, since only in a world completely under his control could the totalitarian ruler possibly realize all his lies and make true all his prophecies.

The language of prophetic scientificality corresponded to the needs of masses who had lost their home in the world and now were prepared to be reintegrated into eternal, all-dominating forces which by themselves would bear man, the swimmer on the waves of adversity, to the shores of safety. "We shape the life of our people and our legislation according to the verdicts of genetics," [25] said the Nazis, just as the Bolsheviks assure their followers that economic forces have the power of a verdict of history. They thereby promise a victory which is independent of "temporary" defeats and failures in specific enterprises. For masses, in contrast to classes, want vic-

---

[22] Stalin, *op. cit., loc. cit.*

[23] Gunter d'Alquen, *Die SS.* Schriften der Hochschule für Politik, 1939. "We had to carry the revolution, the vivaciousness of an extensive movement . . . with all means, with and against the law. We had to overthrow that which did not seem fit to live." Translation quoted from *Nazi Conspiracy*, IV, 973 ff.

[24] Konrad Heiden, *Der Fuehrer. Hitler's Rise to Power,* Boston, 1944, underlines Hitler's "phenomenal untruthfulness," "the lack of demonstrable reality in nearly all his utterances," his "indifference to facts which he does not regard as vitally important" (pp. 368, 374).—Stalin's attitude to facts is best expressed in his periodic revision of Russian history.

[25] *Nazi Primer.*

THE TOTALITARIAN MOVEMENT

tory and success as such, in their most abstract form; they are not bound together by those special collective interests which they feel to be essential to their survival as a group and which they therefore may assert even in the face of overwhelming odds. More important to them than the cause that may be victorious, or the particular enterprise that may be a success, is the victory of no matter what cause, and success in no matter what enterprise.

Totalitarian propaganda perfects the techniques of mass propaganda, but it neither invents them nor originates their themes. These were prepared for them by fifty years of the rise of imperialism and disintegration of the nation-state, when the mob entered the scene of European politics. Like the earlier mob leaders, the spokesmen for totalitarian movements possessed an unerring instinct for anything that ordinary party propaganda or public opinion did not care or dare to touch. Everything hidden, everything passed over in silence became of major significance, regardless of its own intrinsic importance. The mob really believed that truth was whatever respectable society had hypocritically passed over, or covered up with corruption.

Mysteriousness as such became the first criterion for the choice of topics. The origin of mystery did not matter; it could lie in a reasonable, politically comprehensible desire for secrecy, as in the case of the British Secret Services or the French Deuxième Bureau; or in the conspiratory need of revolutionary groups, as in the case of anarchist and other terrorist sects; or in the structure of societies whose original secret content had long since become well known and where only the formal ritual still retained the former mystery, as in the case of the Freemasons; or in age-old superstitions which had woven legends around certain groups, as in the case of the Jesuits and the Jews. The Nazis were undoubtedly superior in the selection of such topics for mass propaganda; but the Bolsheviks have gradually learned the trick, although they rely less on traditionally accepted mysteries and prefer their own inventions—since the middle thirties, one mysterious world conspiracy has followed another in Bolshevik propaganda, starting with the plot of the Trotskyites, followed by the rule of the 300 families, to the sinister imperialist (*i.e.,* global) machinations of the British or American Secret Services.[26]

The effectiveness of this kind of propaganda demonstrates one of the chief characteristics of modern masses. They do not believe in anything visible, in the reality of their own experience; they do not trust their eyes and ears but only their imaginations, which may be caught by anything that is at once universal and consistent in itself. What convinces masses are not facts, and not even invented facts, but only the consistency of the system of which

---

[26] It is interesting to note that the Bolsheviks somehow accumulate conspiracies, that the discovery of a new one does not mean they will discard the former. The Trotskyite conspiracy started around 1930, the 300 families were added during the Popular Front period, from 1935 onward, British imperialism became an actual conspiracy during the Stalin-Hitler alliance, the "American Secret Service" followed soon after the close of the war (for information on Russian press and magazine publicity see Edmund Demai in the New York *Times,* February 13, 1949, p. 32); the newest, Jewish cosmopolitanism, has an obvious and disquieting resemblance to Nazi propaganda.

they are presumably part. Repetition, somewhat overrated in importance because of the common belief in the masses' inferior capacity to grasp and remember, is important only because it convinces them of consistency in time.

What the masses refuse to recognize is the fortuitousness that pervades reality. They are predisposed to all ideologies because they explain facts as mere examples of laws and eliminate coincidences by inventing an all-embracing omnipotence which is supposed to be at the root of every accident. Totalitarian propaganda thrives on this escape from reality into fiction, from coincidence into consistency.

The chief disability of totalitarian propaganda is that it cannot fulfill this longing of the masses for a completely consistent, comprehensible, and predictable world without seriously conflicting with common sense. If, for instance, all the "confessions" of political opponents in the Soviet Union are phrased in the same language and admit the same motives, the consistency-hungry masses will accept the fiction as supreme proof of their truthfulness; whereas common sense tells us that it is precisely their consistency which is out of this world and proves that they are a fabrication. Figuratively speaking, it is as though the masses demand a constant repetition of the miracle of the Septuagint, when, according to ancient legend, seventy isolated translators produced an identical Greek version of the Old Testament. Common sense can accept this tale only as a legend or a miracle; yet it could also be adduced as proof of the absolute faithfulness of every single word in the translated text.

In other words, while it is true that the masses are obsessed by a desire to escape from reality because in their essential homelessness they can no longer bear its accidental, incomprehensible aspects, it is also true that their longing for fiction has some connection with those capacities of the human mind whose structural consistency is superior to mere occurrence. The masses' escape from reality is a verdict against the world in which they are forced to live and in which they cannot exist, since coincidence has become its supreme master and human beings need the constant transformation of chaotic and accidental conditions into a man-made pattern of relative consistency. The revolt of the masses against "realism," common sense, and all "the plausibilities of the world" (Burke) was the result of their atomization, of their loss of social status along with which they lost the whole sector of communal relationships in whose framework common sense makes sense. In their situation of spiritual and social homelessness, a measured insight into the interdependence of the arbitrary and the planned, the accidental and the necessary, could no longer operate. Totalitarian propaganda can outrageously insult common sense only where common sense has lost its validity. Before the alternative of facing the anarchic growth and total arbitrariness of decay or bowing down before the most rigid, fantastically fictitious consistency of an ideology, the masses probably will always choose the latter and be ready to pay for it with individual sacrifices—and this not because they are stupid or wicked, but because in the general disaster this escape grants them a minimum of self-respect.

THE TOTALITARIAN MOVEMENT

While it has been the specialty of Nazi propaganda to profit from the longing of the masses for consistency, Bolshevik methods have demonstrated, as though in a laboratory, its impact on the isolated mass man. The Soviet secret police, so eager to convince its victims of their guilt for crimes they never committed, and in many instances were in no position to commit,[27] completely isolates and eliminates all real factors, so that the very logic, the very consistency of "the story" contained in the prepared confession [28] becomes overwhelming. In a situation where the dividing line between fiction and reality is blurred by the monstrosity and the inner consistency of the accusation, not only the strength of character to resist constant threats but great confidence in the existence of fellow human beings—relatives or friends or neighbors—who will never believe "the story," are required to resist the temptation to yield to the mere abstract possibility of guilt.

To be sure, this extreme of an artificially fabricated insanity can be achieved only in a totalitarian world. Then, however, it is part of the propaganda apparatus of the totalitarian regimes to which confessions are not indispensable for punishment. "Confessions" are as much a specialty of Bolshevik propaganda as the curious pedantry of legalizing crimes by retrospective and retroactive legislation was a specialty of Nazi propaganda. The aim in both cases is consistency.

Before they seize power and establish a world according to their doctrines, totalitarian movements conjure up a lying world of consistency which is more adequate to the needs of the human mind than reality itself; in which, through sheer imagination, uprooted masses can feel at home and are spared the never-ending shocks which real life and real experiences deal to human beings and their expectations. The force possessed by totalitarian propaganda—before the movements have the power to drop iron curtains to prevent anyone's disturbing, by the slightest reality, the gruesome quiet of an entirely imaginary world—lies in its ability to shut the masses off from the real world. The only signs which the real world still offers to the understanding of the unintegrated and disintegrating masses—whom every new stroke of ill luck makes more gullible—are, so to speak, its lacunae, the questions it does not care to discuss publicly, or the rumors it does not dare to contradict because they hit, although in an exaggerated and deformed way, some sore spot.

From these sore spots the lies of totalitarian propaganda derive the element of truthfulness and real experience they need to bridge the gulf between reality and fiction. Only terror could rely on mere fiction, and even the terror-sustained lying fictions of totalitarian regimes have not yet become

---

[27] Since the Moscow Trials, defendants in Soviet Russia have insisted on confessing meetings with foreigners at nonexisting hotels in countries which neither they nor the foreigners ever visited.

[28] Kravchenko, *op. cit.*, p. 263, describes the impression which the very consistency of the story in a prepared confession makes on the defendant under these peculiar circumstances.

entirely arbitrary, although they are usually cruder, more impudent, and, so to speak, more original than those of the movements. (It takes power, not propaganda skill, to circulate a revised history of the Russian Revolution in which no man by the name of Trotsky was ever commander-in-chief of the Red Army.) The lies of the movements, on the other hand, are much subtler. They attach themselves to every aspect of social and political life that is hidden from the public eye. They succeed best where the official authorities have surrounded themselves with an atmosphere of secrecy. In the eyes of the masses, they then acquire the reputation of superior "realism" because they touch upon real conditions whose existence is being hidden. Revelations of scandals in high society, of corruption of politicians, everything that belongs to yellow journalism, becomes in their hands a weapon of more than sensational importance.

The most efficient fiction of Nazi propaganda was the story of a Jewish world conspiracy. Concentration on antisemitic propaganda had been a common device of demagogues ever since the end of the nineteenth century, and was widespread in the Germany and Austria of the twenties. The more consistently a discussion of the Jewish question was avoided by all parties and organs of public opinion, the more convinced the mob became that Jews were the true representatives of the powers that be, and that the Jewish issue was the symbol for the hypocrisy and dishonesty of the whole system.

The actual content of postwar antisemitic propaganda was neither a monopoly of the Nazis nor particularly new and original. Lies about a Jewish world conspiracy had been current since the Dreyfus Affair and based themselves on the existing international interrelationship and interdependence of a Jewish people dispersed all over the world. Exaggerated notions of Jewish world power are even older; they can be traced back to the end of the eighteenth century, when the intimate connection between Jewish business and the nation-states had become visible. The representation of *the* Jew as the incarnation of evil is usually blamed on remnants and superstitious memories from the Middle Ages, but is actually closely connected with the more recent ambiguous role which Jews played in European society since their emancipation. (Cf. chapter iii.) One thing was undeniable: in the postwar period Jews had become more prominent than ever before.

The point about the Jews themselves is that they grew prominent and conspicuous in inverse proportion to their real influence and position of power. Every decrease in the stability and force of the nation-states was a direct blow to Jewish positions. The partially successful conquest of the state by the nation made it impossible for the government machine to maintain its position above all classes and parties, and thereby nullified the value of alliances with the Jewish sector of the population, which was supposed also to stay outside the ranks of society and to be indifferent to party politics. The growing concern with foreign policy of the imperialist-minded bourgeoisie and its growing influence on the state machinery was accompanied by the steadfast refusal of the largest segment of Jewish wealth to engage itself in industrial enterprises and to leave the tradition of capital trading. All this taken together almost ended the economic usefulness to the state of the Jews as a group, and the advantages to themselves of social separation. After the first World War, Central European Jewries became as assimilated and nationalized as French Jewry had become during the first decades of the Third Republic.

How conscious the concerned states were of the changed situation came to light when, in 1917, the German government, following a long-established tradition, tried to use its Jews for tentative peace negotiations with the Allies. Instead of addressing itself to the established leaders of German Jewry, it went to the small and comparatively uninfluential Zionist minority which were still trusted in the old way precisely because they insisted on the existence of a Jewish people independent of citizenship, and could therefore be expected to render services which depended upon international connections and an international point of view. The step, however, turned out to have been a mistake for the German government. The Zionists did something that no Jewish banker had ever done before; they set their own conditions and told the government that they would only negotiate a peace without annexations and reparations.[29] The old Jewish indifference to political issues was gone; the majority could no longer be used, since it was no longer aloof from the nation, and the Zionist minority was useless because it had political ideas of its own.

The replacement of monarchical governments by republics in Central Europe completed the disintegration of Central European Jewries, just as the establishment of the Third Republic had done it in France some fifty years ago. (Cf. chapter iv.) The Jews had already lost much of their influence when the new governments established themselves under conditions in which they lacked the power as well as the interest to protect their Jews. During the peace negotiations in Versailles, Jews were used chiefly as experts, and even antisemites admitted that the petty Jewish swindlers in the postwar era, mostly new arrivals (behind whose fraudulent activities, which distinguished them sharply from their native coreligionists, lay an attitude which oddly resembled the old indifference to the standards of their environment), had no connections with the representatives of a supposed Jewish international.[30]

Among a host of competing antisemitic groups and in an atmosphere ripe with antisemitism, Nazi propaganda developed a method of treating this subject which was different from and superior to all others. Still, not one Nazi slogan was new—not even Hitler's shrewd picture of a class struggle caused by the Jewish businessman who exploits his workers, while at the same

[29] See Chaim Weizmann's autobiography, *Trial and Error*, New York, 1949, p. 185.
[30] See, for instance, Otto Bonhard, *Juedische Geld- und Weltherrschaft?*, 1926, p. 57.

time his brother in the factory courtyard incites them to strike.[81] The only new element was that the Nazi party demanded proof of non-Jewish descent for membership and that it remained, the Feder program notwithstanding, extremely vague about the actual measures to be taken against Jews once it came to power.[32] The Nazis placed the Jewish issue at the center of their propaganda in the sense that antisemitism was no longer a question of opinions about people different from the majority, or a concern of national politics,[33] but the intimate concern of every individual in his personal existence; no one could be a member whose "family tree" was not in order, and the higher the rank in the Nazi hierarchy, the farther back the family tree had to be traced.[34] By the same token, though less consistently, Bolshevism changed the Marxist doctrine of the inevitable final victory of the proletariat by organizing its members as "born proletarians" and making other class origins shameful and scandalous.

Nazi propaganda was ingenious enough to transform antisemitism into a principle of self-definition, and thus to eliminate it from the fluctuations of mere opinion. It used the persuasion of mass demagogy only as a preparatory step and never overestimated its lasting influence, whether in oratory or in print.[35] This gave the masses of atomized, undefinable, unstable and futile individuals a means of self-definition and identification which not only restored some of the self-respect they had formerly derived from their function in society, but also created a kind of spurious stability which made them better candidates for an organization. Through this kind of propaganda, the

---

[81] Hitler used this picture for the first time in 1922: "Moses Kohn on the one side encourages his association to refuse the workers' demands, while his brother Isaac in the factory invites the masses . . ." to strike. *Hitler's Speeches. 1922-1939*, ed. Baynes, London, 1942, p. 29.

[32] Feder's 25 points contain only standard measures demanded by all antisemitic groups: expulsion of naturalized Jews, and treatment of native Jews as aliens. Nazi antisemitic oratory was always much more radical than its program.

Waldemar Gurian, "Antisemitism in Modern Germany," in *Essays on Antisemitism*, ed. by Koppel S. Pinson, New York, 1946, p. 243, stresses the lack of originality in Nazi antisemitism: "All these demands and views were not remarkable for their originality—they were self-evident in all nationalistic circles; what was remarkable was the demagogic and oratorical skill with which they were presented."

[33] A typical example of mere nationalistic antisemitism within the Nazi movement itself is Roehm who writes: "And here again, my opinion differs from that of the national philistine. Not: the Jew is to be blamed for everything! We are to be blamed for the fact that the Jew can rule today" (Ernst Roehm, *Die Geschichte eines Hochverräters*, 1933, Volksausgabe, p. 284).

[34] SS applicants had to trace their ancestry back to 1750. Applicants for leading positions in the party were asked only three questions: 1. What have you done for the party? 2. Are you absolutely sound, physically, mentally, morally? 3. Is your family tree in order? See *Nazi Primer*.

[35] "One should not overestimate the influence of the press . . . , it decreases in general while the influence of the organization increases" (Hadamovsky, *op. cit.*, p. 64). "The newspapers are helpless when they are supposed to fight against the aggressive force of a living organization" (*ibid.*, p. 65). "Power formations which have their origin in mere propaganda are fluctuating and can disappear quickly unless the violence of an organization supports the propaganda" (*ibid.*, p. 21).

THE TOTALITARIAN MOVEMENT

movement could set itself up as an artificial extension of the mass meeting and rationalize the essentially futile feelings of self-importance and hysterical security that it offered to the isolated individuals of an atomized society.[36]

The same ingenious application of slogans, coined by others and tried out before, was apparent in the Nazis' treatment of other relevant issues. When public attention was equally focused on nationalism on one hand and socialism on the other, when the two were thought to be incompatible and actually constituted the ideological watershed between the Right and the Left, the "National Socialist German Workers' Party" (Nazi) offered a synthesis supposed to lead to national unity, a semantic solution whose double trademark of "German" and "Worker" connected the nationalism of the Right with the internationalism of the Left. The very name of the Nazi movement stole the political contents of all other parties and pretended implicitly to incorporate them all. Combinations of supposedly antagonistic political doctrines (national-socialist, christian-social, etc.) had been tried, and successfully, before; but the Nazis realized their own combination in such a way that the whole struggle in Parliament between the socialists and the nationalists, between those who pretended to be workers first of all and those who were Germans first, appeared as a sham designed to hide ulterior sinister motives—for was not a member of the Nazi movement all these things at once?

It is interesting that even in their beginnings the Nazis were prudent enough never to use slogans which, like democracy, republic, dictatorship, or monarchy, indicated a specific form of government. It is as though, in this one matter, they always intended to be entirely original. Every discussion about the actual form of their future government could be dismissed as empty talk about mere formalities—the state, according to Hitler, being only a "means" for the conservation of the race, as the state, according to Bolshevik propaganda, is only an instrument in the struggle of classes.[37]

In another curious and roundabout way, however, the Nazis gave a propaganda answer to the question of what their future rule would be, and that was in their use of the "Protocols of the Elders of Zion" as a model for the future organization of the German masses for "world empire." The use of the Protocols was not restricted to the Nazis; hundreds of thousands of copies were sold in postwar Germany, and even their open adoption as a

---

[36] "The mass-meeting is the strongest form of propaganda . . . [because] each individual feels more self-confident and more powerful in the unity of a mass" (*ibid.*, p. 47). "The enthusiasm of the moment becomes a principle and a spiritual attitude through organization and systematic training and discipline" (*ibid.*, pp. 21-22).

[37] Hitler repeated many times: "The state is only the means to an end. The end is: Conservation of race" (*Reden*, 1939, p. 125). This, *mutatis mutandis*, is also the core of the complicated double talk which is Stalin's so-called "state theory": "We are in favor of the State dying out, and at the same time we stand for the strengthening of the dictatorship of the proletariat which represents the most powerful and mighty authority of all forms of State which have existed up to the present day. The highest possible development of the power of the State with the object of preparing the conditions for the dying out of the State: that is the Marxist formula" (*op. cit., loc. cit.*).

handbook of politics was not new.[38] Nevertheless, this forgery was mainly used for the purpose of denouncing the Jews and arousing the mob to the dangers of Jewish domination.[39] In terms of mere propaganda, the discovery of the Nazis was that the masses were not so frightened by Jewish world rule as they were interested in how it could be done, that the popularity of the Protocols was based on admiration and eagerness to learn rather than on hatred, and that it would be wise to stay as close as possible to certain of their outstanding formulas, as in the case of the famous slogan: "Right is what is good for the German people," which was copied from the Protocols' "Everything that benefits the Jewish people is morally right and sacred." [40]

The Protocols are a very curious and noteworthy document in many respects. Apart from their cheap Machiavellianism, their essential political characteristic is that in their crackpot manner they touch on every important political issue of the time. They are antinational in principle and picture the nation-state as a colossus with feet of clay. They discard national sovereignty and believe, as Hitler once put it, in a world empire on a national basis.[41] They are not satisfied with revolution in a particular country, but aim at the conquest and rule of the world. They promise the people that, regardless of superiority in numbers, territory, and state power, they will be able to achieve world conquest through organization alone. To be sure, part of their persuasive strength derives from very old elements of superstition. The notion of the uninterrupted existence of an international sect that has

[38] Alexander Stein, *Adolf Hitler, Schüler der "Weisen von Zion,"* Karlsbad, 1936, was the first to analyze by philological comparison the ideological identity of the teachings of the Nazis with that of the "Elders of Zion." See also R. M. Blank, *Adolf Hitler et les "Protocoles des Sages de Sion,"* 1938.

The first to admit indebtedness to the teachings of the Protocols was Theodor Fritsch, the "grand old man" of German postwar antisemitism. He writes in the epilogue to his edition of the *Protocols,* 1924: "Our future statesmen and diplomats will have to learn from the oriental masters of villainy even the ABC of government, and for this purpose, the 'Zionist Protocols' offer an excellent preparatory schooling."

[39] On the history of the Protocols, see John S. Curtiss, *An Appraisal of the Protocols of Zion,* 1942.

The fact that the Protocols were a forgery was irrelevant for propaganda purposes. The Russian publicist S. A. Nilus who published the second Russian edition in 1905 was already well aware of the doubtful character of this "document" and added the obvious: "But if it were possible to show its authenticity by documents or by the testimony of trustworthy witnesses, if it were possible to disclose the persons standing at the head of the world-wide plot . . . then . . . 'the secret iniquity' could be broken. . . ." Translation in Curtiss, *op. cit.*

Hitler did not need Nilus to use the same trick: the best proof of their authenticity is that they have been proved to be a forgery. And he also adds the argument of their "plausibility": "What many Jews may do unconsciously is here consciously made clear. And that is what counts" (*Mein Kampf,* Book I, chapter xi).

[40] Fritsch, *op. cit.,* "[*Der Juden*] oberster Grundsatz lautet: 'Alles, was dem Volke Juda nützt, ist moralisch und ist heilig.'"

[41] "World Empires spring from a national basis, but they expand soon far beyond it" (*Reden*).

pursued the same revolutionary aims since antiquity is very old [42] and has played a role in political backstairs literature ever since the French Revolution, even though it did not occur to anyone writing at the end of the eighteenth century that the "revolutionary sect," this "peculiar nation . . . in the midst of all civilized nations" could be the Jews.[43]

It was the motif of a global conspiracy in the Protocols which appealed most to the masses, for it corresponded so well to the new power situation. (Hitler very early promised that the Nazi movement would "transcend the narrow limits of modern nationalism." [44]) Only world powers seemed still to have a chance of independent survival and only global politics a chance of lasting results. That this situation should frighten the smaller nations who are not world powers is only too understandable. The Protocols seemed to show a way out that did not depend upon objective unalterable conditions, but only on the power of organization.

Nazi propaganda, in other words, discovered in "the supranational because intensely national Jew" [45] the forerunner of the German master of the world and assured the masses that "the nations that have been the first to see through the Jew and have been the first to fight him are going to take his place in the domination of the world." [46] To take away these people's de-

[42] Henri Rollin, *L'Apocalypse de Notre Temps*, Paris, 1939, who considers the popularity of the Protocols to be second only to the Bible (p. 40), shows the similarity between them and the *Monita Secreta*, first published in 1612 and still sold in 1939 on the streets of Paris, which claim to reveal a Jesuit conspiracy "that justifies all villainies and all uses of violence. . . . This is a real campaign against the established order" (p. 32).

[43] This whole literature is well represented by the Chevalier de Malet, *Recherches politiques et historiques qui prouvent l'existence d'une secte révolutionnaire*, 1817, who quotes extensively from earlier authors. The heroes of the French Revolution are to him *"mannequins"* of an *"agence secrète,"* the agents of the Freemasons. But Freemasonry is only the name which his contemporaries have given to a "revolutionary sect" which has existed at all times and whose policy always has been to attack "remaining behind the scenes, manipulating the strings of the marionettes it thought convenient to put on the scene." He starts by saying: "Probably, it will be difficult to believe in a plan which was formed in antiquity and always followed with the same constancy: . . . the authors of the Revolution are no more French than they are German, Italian, English, etc. They constitute a peculiar nation which was born and has grown in darkness, in the midst of all civilized nations, with the aim of subduing them all to its domination."

For an extensive discussion of this literature, see E. Lesueur, *La Franc-Maçonnerie Artésienne au 18e siècle*. Bibliothèque d'Histoire Révolutionnaire, 1914. How persistent these conspiracy legends are in themselves, even under normal circumstances, can be seen by the enormous anti-Freemason crackpot literature in France, which is hardly less extensive than its antisemitic counterpart. A kind of compendium of all theories which saw in the French Revolution the product of secret conspiratory societies can be found in G. Bord, *La Franc-Maçonnerie en France dès Origines à 1815*, 1908.

[44] *Reden*.

[45] *Hitler's Speeches*, ed. Baynes, p. 6.

[46] Goebbels, *op. cit.*, p. 377. This promise, implied in all antisemitic propaganda of the Nazi type, was prepared by Hitler's "The most extreme contrast to the Aryan is the Jew" (*Mein Kampf*, Book I, chapter xi).

lusion that the Jews were masters of the present world would have meant to rob them of the hope of becoming its future rulers. Thus the Protocols presented world conquest as a practical possibility, implied that the whole affair was only a question of inspired or shrewd know-how, and that nobody stood in the way of a German victory over the entire world but a patently small people, the Jews, who ruled it without possessing instruments of violence—an easy opponent, therefore, once their secret was discovered and their method emulated on a larger scale.

Nazi propaganda concentrated all these new and promising vistas in one concept which it labeled *Volksgemeinschaft*. This new community, tentatively realized in the Nazi movement in the pretotalitarian atmosphere, was based on the absolute equality of all Germans, an equality not of rights but of nature, and their absolute difference from all other people.[47] After the Nazis came to power, this concept gradually lost its importance and gave way to a general contempt for the German people (which the Nazis had always harbored but could not very well show publicly before) on one hand,[48] and a great eagerness, on the other, to enlarge their own ranks from "Aryans" of other nations, an idea which had played only a small role in the prepower stage of Nazi propaganda.[49]

To a certain extent, the *Volksgemeinschaft* was the Nazis' attempt to counter the Communist promise of a classless society. The propaganda appeal of the one over the other seems obvious if we disregard all ideological implications. While both promised to level all social and property differences, the classless society had the obvious connotation that everybody would be leveled to the status of a factory worker, while the *Volksgemeinschaft,* with its connotation of conspiracy for world conquest, held out a reasonable hope that every German could eventually become a factory owner. The even greater advantage of the *Volksgemeinschaft,* however, was that its establishment did not have to wait for some future time and did not depend upon objective conditions: it could be realized immediately in the fictitious world of the movement.

✦

[47] Hitler's early promise (*Reden*), "I shall never recognize that other nations have the same right as the German," became official doctrine: "The foundation of the national socialist outlook in life is the perception of the unlikeness of men" (*Nazi Primer*, p. 5).

[48] For instance, Hitler in 1923: "The German people consists for one third of heroes, for another third, of cowards, while the rest are traitors" (*Hitler's Speeches*, ed. Baynes, p. 76).

After the seizure of power this trend became more brutally outspoken. See, for instance, Goebbels in 1934: "Who are the people to criticize? Party members? No. The rest of the German people? They should consider themselves lucky to be still alive. It would be too much of a good thing altogether, if those who live at our mercy should be allowed to criticize." Quoted from Kohn-Bramstedt, *op. cit.*, pp. 178-179.

[49] Himmler in a speech to SS leaders at Kharkov in April, 1943 (*Nazi Conspiracy*, IV, 572 ff.): "I very soon formed a Germanic SS in the various countries. . . ." An early prepower indication of this non-national policy was given by Hitler (*Reden*): "We shall certainly also receive into the new master class representatives of other nations, *i.e.,* those who deserve it because of their participation in our fight."

THE TOTALITARIAN MOVEMENT 351

The true goal of totalitarian propaganda is not persuasion but organization—the "accumulation of power without the possession of the means of violence."⁵⁰ For this purpose, originality in ideological content can only be considered an unnecessary obstacle. It is no accident that the two totalitarian movements of our time, so frightfully "new" in methods of rule and ingenious in forms of organization, have never preached a new doctrine, have never invented an ideology which was not already popular.⁵¹ Not the passing successes of demagogy win the masses, but the visible reality and power of a "living organization."⁵² Hitler's brilliant gifts as a mass orator did not win him his position in the movement but rather misled his opponents into underestimating him as a simple demagogue, and Stalin was able to defeat the greatest orator of the Russian Revolution.⁵³ What distinguishes the totalitarian leaders and dictators is rather the simple-minded, single-minded purposefulness with which they choose those elements from existing ideologies which are best fitted to become the fundaments of another, entirely fictitious world. The fiction of the Protocols was as adequate as the fiction of a Trotskyite conspiracy, for both contained an element of plausibility—the nonpublic influence of the Jews in the past; the struggle for power between Trotsky and Stalin—which not even the fictitious world of totalitarianism can safely do without. Their art consists in using, and at the same time transcending, the elements of reality, of verifiable experiences, in the chosen fiction, and in generalizing them into regions which then are definitely removed from all possible control by individual experience. With such generalizations, totalitarian propaganda establishes a world fit to compete with the real one, whose main handicap is that it is not logical, consistent, and organized. The consistency of the fiction and strictness of the organization make it possible for the generalization eventually to survive the explosion of more specific lies—the power of the Jews after their helpless

⁵⁰ Hadamovsky, *op. cit.*

⁵¹ Heiden, *op. cit.*, p. 139: Propaganda is not "the art of instilling an opinion in the masses. Actually it is the art of receiving an opinion from the masses."

⁵² Hadamovsky, *op. cit.*, *passim*. The term is taken from Hitler, *Mein Kampf* (Book II, chapter xi), where the "living organization" of a movement is contrasted with the "dead mechanism" of a bureaucratic party.

⁵³ It would be a serious error to interpret totalitarian leaders in terms of Max Weber's category of the "charismatic leadership." See Hans Gerth, "The Nazi Party," in *American Journal of Sociology*, 1940, Vol. XLV. (A similar misunderstanding is also the shortcoming of Heiden's biography, *op. cit.*) Gerth describes Hitler as the charismatic leader of a bureaucratic party. This alone, in his opinion, can account for the fact that "however flagrantly actions may have contradicted words, nothing could disrupt the firmly disciplinary organization." (This contradiction, by the way, is much more characteristic of Stalin who "took care always to say the opposite of what he did, and to do the opposite of what he said." Souvarine, *op. cit.*, p. 431.)

For the source of this misunderstanding see the Nazi political theorist Alfred von Martin, "Zur Soziologie der Gegenwart," in *Zeitschrift für Kulturgeschichte*, Band 27, and Arnold Koettgen, "Die Gesetzmässigkeit der Verwaltung im Führerstaat," in *Reichsverwaltungs-Blatt*, 1936, both of whom characterize the Nazi state as a bureaucracy with charismatic leadership.

slaughter, the sinister global conspiracy of Trotskyites after their liquidation in Soviet Russia and the murder of Trotsky.

The stubbornness with which totalitarian dictators have clung to their original lies in the face of absurdity is more than superstitious gratitude to what turned the trick, and, at least in the case of Stalin, cannot be explained by the psychology of the liar whose very success may make him his own last victim. Once these propaganda slogans are integrated into a "living organization," they cannot be safely eliminated without wrecking the whole structure. The assumption of a Jewish world conspiracy was transformed by totalitarian propaganda from an objective, arguable matter into the chief element of the Nazi reality; the point was that the Nazis *acted* as though the world were dominated by the Jews and needed a counterconspiracy to defend itself. Racism for them was no longer a debatable theory of dubious scientific value, but was being realized every day in the functioning hierarchy of a political organization in whose framework it would have been very "unrealistic" to question it. Similarly, Bolshevism no longer needs to win an argument about class struggle, internationalism, and unconditional dependence of the welfare of the proletariat on the welfare of the Soviet Union; the functioning organization of the Comintern is more convincing than any argument or mere ideology could ever be.

The fundamental reason for the superiority of totalitarian propaganda over the propaganda of other parties and movements is that its content, for the members of the movement at any rate, is no longer an objective issue about which people may have opinions, but has become as real and untouchable an element in their lives as the rules of arithmetic. The organization of the entire texture of life according to an ideology can be fully carried out only under a totalitarian regime. In Nazi Germany, questioning the validity of racism and antisemitism when nothing mattered but race origin, when a career depended upon an "Aryan" physiognomy (Himmler used to select the applicants for the SS from photographs) and the amount of food upon the number of one's Jewish grandparents, was like questioning the existence of the world.

The advantages of a propaganda that constantly "adds the power of organization" [54] to the feeble and unreliable voice of argument, and thereby realizes, so to speak, on the spur of the moment, whatever it says, are obvious beyond demonstration. Foolproof against arguments based on a reality which the movements promised to change, against a counterpropaganda disqualified by the mere fact that it belongs to or defends a world which the shiftless masses cannot and will not accept, it can be disproved only by another, a stronger or better, reality.

It is in the moment of defeat that the inherent weakness of totalitarian propaganda becomes visible. Without the force of the movement, its members cease at once to believe in the dogma for which yesterday they still were ready to sacrifice their lives. The moment the movement, that is, the

---

[54] Hadamovsky, *op. cit.*, p. 21.

fictitious world which sheltered them, is destroyed, the masses revert to their old status of isolated individuals who either happily accept a new function in a changed world or sink back into their old desperate superfluousness. The members of totalitarian movements, utterly fanatical as long as the movement exists, will not follow the example of religious fanatics and die the death of martyrs (even though they were only too willing to die the death of robots).[55] Rather they will quietly give up the movement as a bad bet and look around for another promising fiction or wait until the former fiction regains enough strength to establish another mass movement.

The experience of the Allies who vainly tried to locate one self-confessed and convinced Nazi among the German people, 90 per cent of whom probably had been sincere sympathizers at one time or another, is not to be taken simply as a sign of human weakness or gross opportunism. Nazism as an ideology had been so fully "realized" that its content ceased to exist as an independent set of doctrines, lost its intellectual existence, so to speak; destruction of the reality therefore left almost nothing behind, least of all the fanaticism of believers.

II: *Totalitarian Organization*

THE FORMS OF totalitarian organization, as distinguished from their ideological content and propaganda slogans, are completely new.[56] They are designed to translate the propaganda lies of the movement, woven around a central fiction—the conspiracy of the Jews, or the Trotskyites, or 300 families, etc.—into a functioning reality, to build up, even under nontotalitarian circumstances, a society whose members act and react according to the rules of a fictitious world. In this sense, organization and propaganda (rather than terror and propaganda) are two sides of the same coin.[57]

The most strikingly new organizational device of the movements in their prepower stage is the creation of front organizations, the distinction drawn between party members and sympathizers. Compared to this invention, other typically totalitarian features, such as the appointment of functionaries from above and the eventual monopolization of appointments by one man (the so-called "Leader principle") are secondary in importance. These

---

[55] R. Hoehn, one of the outstanding Nazi political theorists, interpreted this lack of a doctrine or even a common set of ideals and beliefs in the movement in his *Reichsgemeinschaft und Volksgemeinschaft,* Hamburg, 1935: "From the point of view of a folk community, every community of values is destructive" (p. 83).

[56] Hitler, discussing the relationship between *Weltanschauung* and organization, admits as a matter of course that the Nazis took over from other groups and parties the "racial idea" (*die völkische Idee*) and acted as though they were its only representatives because they were the first to base a fighting organization on it and to formulate it for practical purposes. *Op. cit.,* Book II, chapter v.

[57] See Hitler, "Propaganda and Organization," in *op. cit.,* Book II, chapter xi.

practices were the result of experience (in the case of Hitler) or of personal shrewdness (in the case of Stalin) rather than of conscious planning.[58]

An anonymity which contributes greatly to the weirdness of the whole phenomenon clouds the beginnings of this new organizational structure. We do not know who first decided to organize fellow-travelers into front organizations, who first saw in vaguely sympathizing masses—upon whom all parties used to count at election day but whom they considered to be too fluctuating for membership—not only a reservoir from which to draw party members, but a decisive force in itself. The early Communist-inspired organizations of sympathizers, such as the Friends of the Soviet Union or the Red Relief associations, developed into front organizations but were originally nothing more or less than what their names indicated: a gathering of sympathizers for financial or other (for instance, legal) help. Hitler was the first to say that each movement should divide the masses which have been won through propaganda into two categories, sympathizers and members. This in itself is interesting enough; even more significant is that he based this division upon a more general philosophy according to which most people are too lazy and cowardly for anything more than mere theoretical insight, and only a minority want to fight for their convictions.[59] Hitler, consequently, was the first to devise a conscious policy of constantly enlarging the ranks of sympathizers while at the same time keeping the number of party members strictly limited.[60] This notion of a minority of party members surrounded by

[58] Heiden, *op. cit.*, p. 292, reports the following difference between the first and the following editions of *Mein Kampf:* The first edition proposes the election of party officials who only after their election are vested with "unlimited power and authority"; all following editions establish appointment of party officials from above by the next higher leader. Naturally, for the stability of totalitarian regimes the appointment from above is a much more important principle than the "unlimited authority" of the appointed official. In practice, the subleaders' authority was decisively limited through the Leader's absolute sovereignty. See below.

Stalin, coming from the conspiratory apparatus of the Bolshevik party, probably never thought this a problem. To him, appointments in the party machine were a question of accumulation of personal power. It must, however, be admitted that he could easily justify these methods by quoting Lenin's theory that "the history of all countries shows that the working class, exclusively by its own effort, is able to develop only trade-union consciousness," and that its leadership therefore necessarily comes from without. (See *What is to be done*, first published in 1902, in *Collected Works*, Vol. IV, Book II.) The point is that Lenin considered the Communist Party as the "most progressive" part of the working class and at the same time "the lever of political organization" which "directs the whole mass of the proletariat," *i.e.*, an organization outside and above the class. (See W. H. Chamberlin, *The Russian Revolution, 1917-1921*, New York, 1935, II, 361.) This theory can easily lead to the introduction of authoritarian principles into the party hierarchy.

[59] Hitler, *op. cit.*, Book II, chapter xi.

[60] *Ibid.* This principle was strictly enforced as soon as the Nazis seized power. Of 7 million members of the Hitler youth only 50,000 were accepted for party membership in 1937. See the preface by H. L. Childs to *The Nazi Primer*.—Compare also Gottfried Neesse, "Die verfassungsrechtliche Gestaltung der Ein-Partei," in *Zeitschrift für die gesamte Staatswissenschaft*, 1938, Band 98, p. 678: "Even the One-Party must never grow to the point where it would embrace the whole population. It is 'total' because of its ideological influence on the nation."

THE TOTALITARIAN MOVEMENT

a majority of sympathizers comes very close to the later reality of front organizations—a term which indeed expresses most aptly their eventual function, and indicates the relationship between members and sympathizers within the movement itself. For the front organizations of sympathizers are no less essential to the functioning of the movement than its actual membership.

The front organizations surround the movements' membership with a protective wall which separates them from the outside, normal world; at the same time, they form a bridge back into normalcy, without which the members in the prepower stage would feel too sharply the differences between their beliefs and those of normal people, between the lying fictitiousness of their own and the reality of the normal world. The ingeniousness of this device during the movements' struggle for power is that the front organizations not only isolate the members but offer them a semblance of outside normalcy which wards off the impact of true reality more effectively than mere indoctrination. It is the difference between his own and the fellow-traveler's attitudes which confirms a Nazi or Bolshevik in his belief in the fictitious explanation of the world, for the fellow-traveler has the same convictions, after all, albeit in a more "normal," *i.e.,* less fanatic, more confused form; so that to the party member it appears that anyone whom the movement has not expressly singled out as an enemy (a Jew, a capitalist, etc.) is on his side, that the world is full of secret allies who merely cannot, as yet, summon up the necessary strength of mind and character to draw the logical conclusions from their own convictions.[61]

The world at large, on the other side, usually gets its first glimpse of a totalitarian movement through its front organizations. The sympathizers, who are to all appearances still innocuous fellow-citizens in a nontotalitarian society, can hardly be called single-minded fanatics; through them, the movements make their fantastic lies more generally acceptable, can spread their propaganda in milder, more respectable forms, until the whole atmosphere is poisoned with totalitarian elements which are hardly recognizable as such but appear to be normal political reactions or opinions. The fellow-traveler organizations surround the totalitarian movements with a mist of normality and respectability that fools the membership about the true character of the outside world as much as it does the outside world about the true character of the movement. The front organization functions both ways: as the façade of the totalitarian movement to the nontotalitarian world, and as the façade of this world to the inner hierarchy of the movement.

Even more striking than this relationship is the fact that it is repeated on different levels within the movement itself. As party members are related to and separated from the fellow-travelers, so are the elite formations of the movement related to and separated from the ordinary members. If the fellow-traveler still appears to be a normal inhabitant of the outside world

---

[61] See Hitler's differentiation between the "radical people" who alone were prepared to become members of the party and hundreds of thousands of sympathizers who were too "cowardly" to make the necessary sacrifice. *Op. cit., loc. cit.*

who has adopted the totalitarian creed as one may adopt the program of an ordinary party, the ordinary member of the Nazi or Bolshevik movement still belongs, in many respects, to the surrounding world: his professional and social relationships are not yet absolutely determined by his party membership, although he may realize—in distinction from the mere sympathizer —that in case of conflict between his party allegiance and his private life, the former is supposed to be decisive. The member of a militant group, on the other hand, is wholly identified with the movement; he has no profession and no private life independent of it. Just as the sympathizers constitute a protective wall around the members of the movement and represent the outside world to them, so the ordinary membership surrounds the militant groups and represents the normal outside world to them.

A definite advantage of this structure is that it blunts the impact of one of the basic totalitarian tenets—that the world is divided into two gigantic hostile camps, one of which is the movement, and that the movement can and must fight the whole world—a claim which prepares the way for the indiscriminate aggressiveness of totalitarian regimes in power. Through a carefully graduated hierarchy of militancy in which each rank is the higher level's image of the nontotalitarian world because it is less militant and its members less totally organized, the shock of the terrifying and monstrous totalitarian dichotomy is vitiated and never fully realized; this type of organization prevents its members' ever being directly confronted with the outside world, whose hostility remains for them a mere ideological assumption. They are so well protected against the reality of the nontotalitarian world that they constantly underestimate the tremendous risks of totalitarian politics.

There is no doubt that the totalitarian movements attack the status quo more radically than did any of the earlier revolutionary parties. They can afford this radicalism, apparently so unsuited to mass organizations, because their organization offers a temporary substitute for ordinary, nonpolitical life, which totalitarianism actually seeks to abolish. The whole world of nonpolitical social relationships, from which the "professional revolutionary" had to cut himself off or had to accept as they were, exists in the form of less militant groups in the movement; within this hierarchically organized world the fighters for world conquest and world revolution are never exposed to the shock inevitably generated by the discrepancy between "revolutionary" beliefs and the "normal" world. The reason why the movements in their prepower, revolutionary stage can attract so many ordinary philistines is that their members live in a fool's paradise of normalcy; the party members are surrounded by the normal world of sympathizers and the elite formations by the normal world of ordinary members.

Another advantage of the totalitarian pattern is that it can be repeated indefinitely and keeps the organization in a state of fluidity which permits it constantly to insert new layers and define new degress of militancy. The whole history of the Nazi party can be told in terms of new formations

THE TOTALITARIAN MOVEMENT

within the Nazi movement.[62] The SA, the stormtroopers (founded in 1922), were the first Nazi formation which was supposed to be more militant than the party itself;[63] in 1926, the SS was founded as the elite formation of the SA; after three years, the SS was separated from the SA and put under Himmler's command; it took Himmler only a few more years to repeat the same game within the SS; one after the other, the Death Head units, the Shock Troops,[64] the Security Service came into being, each more militant than its predecessor, to which the earlier SS-men, now called "General SS," stood in the same relationship as the SA-man to the SS-man, or the party member to the SA-man, or the member of a front organization to a party member.[65]

This fluctuating hierarchy, with its constant addition of new layers and shifts in authority, is well known from secret control bodies, the secret police or espionage services, where new controls are always needed to control the controllers. In the prepower stage of the movements, total espionage is not yet possible; but the fluctuating hierarchy, similar to that of secret services, makes it possible, even without actual power, to degrade any rank or group that wavers or shows signs of decreasing radicalism, by the mere insertion of a new more radical layer, hence driving the older group automatically in the direction of the front organization and away from the center of the movement. Thus, the Nazi elite formations were primarily innerparty organizations: the SA rose to the position of a superparty when the party appeared to lose in radicality and was then in turn and for similar reasons superseded by the SS.

The military value of the totalitarian elite formations, especially of the SA and the SS, are frequently overrated, while their purely inner-party significance has been somewhat neglected.[66] None of the Fascist Shirt-organizations was founded for specific defensive or aggressive purposes, though defense of the leaders or the ordinary party members usually was cited as a pretext.[67] The paramilitary form of Nazi and Fascist elite groups was the

---

[62] Heiden, *op. cit.*, notices this but for the SS only. "The SS was stamped forever by the reason for its founding: Hitler's need to control an undisciplined party by founding a new party" (p. 308).

[63] See Hitler: chapter on the SA in *op. cit.*, Book II, chapter ix, second part.

[64] In translating *Verfügungstruppe*, i.e., the special units of the SS which originally were supposed to be at Hitler's special disposal, as shock troops, I follow O. C. Giles, *The Gestapo*. Oxford Pamphlets on World Affairs, No. 36, 1940.

[65] For the organization and history of the SS see Gunter d'Alquen, *op. cit.*; Giles, *op. cit.*; *Nazi Conspiracy*, II, 173 ff.; Franz Neumann, *Behemoth*, New York, 1942, Appendix.

[66] This, however, was not the fault of Hitler, who always insisted that the very name of the SA (*Sturmabteilung*) indicated that it was only "a section of the movement" just like other party formations such as the propaganda department, the newspaper, the scientific institutes, etc. He also tried to dispel the illusions of the possible military value of a paramilitary formation and wanted training to be carried through according to the needs of the party and not according to the principles of an army. *Op. cit., loc. cit.*

[67] The official reason for the foundation of the SA was protection of Nazi meetings, while the original task of the SS was protection of Nazi leaders.

result of their being founded as "instruments of the ideological fight of the movement" [68] against the widespread pacificism in Europe after the first World War. For totalitarian purposes it was much more important to set up, as "the expression of an aggressive attitude," [69] a fake army which resembled as closely as possible the bogus army of the pacifists (unable to understand the constitutional place of an army within the political body, the pacifists had denounced all military institutions as bands of willful murderers), than to have a troop of well-trained soldiers. The SA and the SS were certainly model organizations for arbitrary violence and murder; they were hardly as well trained as the Black Reichswehr, and they were not equipped for a fight against regular troops. Militaristic propaganda was more popular in postwar Germany than military training, and uniforms did not enhance the military value of paramilitary troops, though they were useful as a clear indication of the abolition of civilian standards and morals; somehow these uniforms eased considerably the consciences of the murderers and also made them even more receptive to unquestioning obedience and unquestioned authority. Despite these militaristic trappings, the inner-party faction of the Nazis, which was primarily nationalistic and militaristc and therefore viewed the paramilitary troops not as mere party formations but as an illegal enlargement of the Reichswehr (which had been limited by the terms of the Versailles Peace Treaty), was the first to be liquidated. Roehm, the leader of the SA stormtroopers, had indeed dreamed of and negotiated for incorporation of his SA into the Reichswehr after the Nazis seized power. He was killed by Hitler because he tried to transform the new Nazi regime into a military dictatorship.[70] Hitler had made it clear several years before that such a development was not desired by the Nazi movement when he dismissed Roehm—a real soldier whose experience in the war and in the organization of the Black Reichswehr would have made him indispensable to a serious military training program—from his position as chief of the SA and chose Himmler, a man without the slightest knowledge of military matters, as reorganizer of the SS.

[68] Hitler, *op. cit., loc. cit.*
[69] Ernst Bayer, *Die SA*, Berlin, 1938. Translation quoted from *Nazi Conspiracy*, IV.
[70] Roehm's autobiography shows clearly how little his political convictions agreed with those of the Nazis. He always desired a *"Soldatenstaat"* and always insisted on the *"Primat des Soldaten vor dem Politiker"* (*op. cit.*, p. 349). Especially telling for his nontotalitarian attitude, or rather for his inability even to understand totalitarianism and its "total" claim, is the following passage: "I don't see why the following three things should not be compatible: my loyalty to the hereditary prince of the house of Wittelsbach and heir to Bavaria's crown; my admiration for the quartermaster-general of the World War [*i.e.*, Ludendorff], who today embodies the conscience of the German people; and my comradeship with the harbinger and bearer of the political struggle, Adolf Hitler" (p. 348).
Within the Nazi party, the possibility of an SA-Reichswehr plot against the rule of the SS and the police apparently never was quite forgotten. Hans Frank, Governor General of Poland, in 1942, eight years after the murder of Roehm and General Schleicher, was suspected of wishing "after the war . . . to inaugurate the greatest fight for justice [against the SS] with the assistance of the Armed Forces and the SA" (*Nazi Conspiracy*, VI, 747).

THE TOTALITARIAN MOVEMENT

Apart from the importance of the elite formations to the organizational structure of the movement, where they comprised the changing nuclei of militancy, their paramilitary character must be understood in connection with other professional party organizations, such as those for teachers, lawyers, physicians, students, university professors, technicians, and workers. All these were primarily duplicates of existing nontotalitarian professional societies, paraprofessional as the stormtroopers were paramilitary. It was characteristic that the more clearly the European Communist parties became branches of a Moscow-directed Bolshevik movement, the more they, too, used their front organizations to compete with existing purely professional groups. The difference between the Nazis and the Bolsheviks in this respect was only that the Nazis had a pronounced tendency to consider these paraprofessional formations as part of the party elite, while the Communists preferred to recruit from them the material for their front organizations. The important factor for the movements is that, even before they seize power, they give the impression that all elements of society are embodied in their ranks. (The ultimate goal of Nazi propaganda was to organize the whole German people as sympathizers.[71]) The Nazis went one step further in this game and set up a series of fake departments which were modeled after the regular state administration, such as their own department of foreign affairs, education, culture, sport, etc. None of these institutions had more professional value than the imitation of the army represented by the stormtroopers, but together they created a perfect world of appearances in which every reality in the nontotalitarian world was slavishly duplicated in the form of humbug.

This technique of duplication, certainly useless for the direct overthrow of government, proved extremely fruitful in the work of undermining actively existing institutions and in the "decomposition of the status quo" [72] which totalitarian organizations invariably prefer to an open show of force. If it is the task of movements "to bore their way like polyps into all positions of power," [73] then they must be ready for any specific social and political position. In accordance with their claim to total domination, every single organized group in the nontotalitarian society is felt to present a specific challenge to the movement to destroy it; every one needs, so to speak, a specific instrument of destruction. The practical value of the fake organizations came to light when the Nazis seized power and were ready at once to destroy the existing teachers' organizations with another teachers' organization, the existing lawyers' clubs with a Nazi-sponsored lawyers' club, etc. They could change overnight the whole structure of German society

---

[71] Hitler, *op. cit.,* Book II, chapter xi, states that propaganda attempts to force a doctrine on the whole people while the organization incorporates only a comparatively small proportion of its more militant members.—Compare also G. Neesse, *op. cit.*

[72] Hitler, *op. cit., loc. cit.*

[73] Hadamovsky, *op. cit.,* p. 28.—Compare also Franz Borkenau, "Die neue Komintern," in *Der Monat,* Berlin, 1949, Heft 4: "If a Communist Party 'dissolves' in a greater unit, this means simply that Communist cells bore their way into a mass organization in order to destroy it from within as a parasite does to his host."

—and not just political life—precisely because they had prepared its exact counterpart within their own ranks. In this respect, the task of the paramilitary formations was finished when the regular military hierarchy could be placed, during the last stages of the war, under the authority of SS generals. The technique of this "co-ordination" was as ingenious and irresistible as the deterioration of professional standards was swift and radical, although these results were more immediately felt in the highly technical and specialized field of warfare than anywhere else.

If the importance of paramilitary formations for totalitarian movements is not to be found in their doubtful military value, neither is it wholly in their fake imitation of the regular army. As elite formations they are more sharply separated from the outside world than any other group. The Nazis realized very early the intimate connection between total militancy and total separation from normality; the stormtroopers were never assigned to duty in their home communities, and the active cadres of the SA in the prepower stage, and of the SS under the Nazi regime, were so mobile and so frequently exchanged that they could not possibly get used to and take root in any other part of the ordinary world.[74] They were organized after the model of criminal gangs and used for organized murder.[75] These murders were publicly paraded and officially admitted by the upper Nazi hierarchy, so that open complicity made it well-nigh impossible for members to quit the movement even under the nontotalitarian government and even if they were not threatened, as they actually were, by their former comrades. In this respect, the function of the elite formations is the very opposite of that of the front organizations: while the latter lend the movement an air of respectability and inspire confidence, the former, by extending complicity, make every party member aware that he has left for good the normal world which outlaws murder and that he will be held accountable for all crimes committed by the elite.[76] This is achieved even in the prepower

---

[74] The Death Head battalions of the SS were placed under the following rules: 1. No brigade is placed in its native district. 2. Every battalion is to change after three weeks' service. 3. Members are never to be sent into the streets alone or ever to display their Death Head insignia in public. See: *Secret Speech by Himmler to the German Army General Staff 1938* (the speech, however, was delivered in 1937, see *Nazi Conspiracy*, IV, 616, where only excerpts are published). Published by the American Committee for Anti-Nazi Literature.

[75] Heinrich Himmler, *Die Schutzstaffel als antibolschewistische Kampforganisation*. Aus dem Schwarzen Korps, No. 3, 1936, said publicly: "I know that there are people in Germany who get sick when they see this black coat. We understand that and don't expect to be loved by too many people."

[76] In his speeches to the SS Himmler always stressed committed crimes, underlining their gravity. About the liquidation of the Jews, for instance, he would say: "I also want to talk to you quite frankly on a very grave matter. Among ourselves it should be mentioned quite frankly, and yet we will never speak of it publicly." On the liquidation of the Polish intelligentsia: ". . . you should hear this but also forget it immediately . . ." (*Nazi Conspiracy*, IV, 558 and 553 respectively).

Goebbels, *op. cit.*, p. 266, notes in a similar vein: "On the Jewish question, especially, we have taken a position from which there is no escape. . . . Experience teaches that a movement and a people who have burned their bridges fight with much greater determination than those who are still able to retreat."

THE TOTALITARIAN MOVEMENT

stage, when the leadership systematically claims responsibility for all crimes and leaves no doubt that they are committed for the ultimate good of the movement.

The artificial creation of civil-war conditions by which the Nazis blackmailed their way into power has more than the obvious advantage of stirring up trouble. For the movement, organized violence is the most efficient of the many protective walls which surround its fictitious world, whose "reality" is proved when a member fears leaving the movement more than he fears the consequences of his complicity in illegal actions, and feels more secure as a member than as an opponent. This feeling of security, resulting from the organized violence with which the elite formations protect the party members from the outside world, is as important to the integrity of the fictitious world of the organization as the fear of its terror.

In the center of the movement, as the motor that swings it into motion, sits the Leader. He is separated from the elite formation by an inner circle of the initiated who spread around him an aura of impenetrable mystery which corresponds to his "intangible preponderance." [77] His position within this intimate circle depends upon his ability to spin intrigues among its members and upon his skill in constantly changing its personnel. He owes his rise to leadership to an extreme ability to handle inner-party struggles for power rather than to demagogic or bureaucratic-organizational qualities. He is distinguished from earlier types of dictators in that he hardly wins through simple violence. Hitler needed neither the SA nor the SS to secure his position as leader of the Nazi movement; on the contrary, Roehm, the chief of the SA and able to count upon its loyalty to his own person, was one of Hitler's inner-party enemies. Stalin won against Trotsky, who not only had a far greater mass appeal but, as chief of the Red Army, held in his hands the greatest power potential in Soviet Russia at the time.[78] Not Stalin, but Trotsky, moreover, was the greatest organizational talent, the ablest bureaucrat of the Russian Revolution.[79] On the other hand, both Hitler and Stalin were masters of detail and devoted themselves in the early stages of their careers almost entirely to questions of personnel, so that after a few years hardly any man of importance remained who did not owe his position to them.

Such personal abilities, however, though an absolute prerequisite for the

---

[77] Souvarine, *op. cit.*, p. 648.—The way the totalitarian movements have kept the private lives of their leaders (Hitler and Stalin) absolutely secret contrasts with the publicity value which all democracies find in parading the private lives of Presidents, Kings, Prime Ministers, etc., in public. Totalitarian methods do not allow for an identification based on the conviction: Even the highest of us is only human.

Souvarine, *op. cit.*, p. xiii, quotes the most frequently used tags to describe Stalin: "Stalin, the mysterious host of the Kremlin"; "Stalin, impenetrable personality"; "Stalin, the Communist Sphinx"; "Stalin, the Enigma," the "insoluble mystery," etc.

[78] "If [Trotsky] had chosen to stage a military *coup d'état* he might perhaps have defeated the triumvirs. But he left office without the slightest attempt at rallying in his defence the army he had created and led for seven years" (Isaac Deutscher, *op. cit.*, p. 297).

[79] The Commissariat for War under Trotsky "was a model institution" and Trotsky was called in in all cases of disorder in other departments. Souvarine, *op. cit.*, p. 288.

first stages of such a career and even later far from insignificant, are no longer decisive when a totalitarian movement has been built up, has established the principle that "the will of the Fuehrer is the Party's law,"[80] and when its whole hierarchy has been efficiently trained for a single purpose—swiftly to communicate the will of the Leader to all ranks. When this has been achieved, the Leader is irreplaceable because the whole complicated structure of the movement would lose its *raison d'être* without his commands. Now, despite eternal cabals in the inner clique and unending shifts of personnel, with their tremendous accumulation of hatred, bitterness, and personal resentment, the Leader's position can remain secure against chaotic palace revolutions not because of his superior gifts, about which the men in his intimate surroundings frequently have no great illusions, but because of these men's sincere and sensible conviction that without him everything would be immediately lost.

The supreme task of the Leader is to impersonate the double function characteristic of each layer of the movement—to act as the magic defense of the movement against the outside world; and at the same time, to be the direct bridge by which the movement is connected with it. The Leader represents the movement in a way totally different from all ordinary party leaders; he claims personal responsibility for every action, deed, or misdeed, committed by any member or functionary in his official capacity. This total responsibility is the most important organizational aspect of the so-called Leader principle, according to which every functionary is not only appointed by the Leader but is his walking embodiment, and every order is supposed to emanate from this one ever-present source. This thorough identification of the Leader with every appointed subleader and this monopoly of responsibility for everything which is being done are also the most conspicuous signs of the decisive difference between a totalitarian leader and an ordinary dictator or despot. A tyrant would never identify himself with his subordinates, let alone with every one of their acts;[81] he might use them as scapegoats and gladly have them criticized in order to save himself from the wrath of the people, but he would always maintain an absolute distance from all his subordinates and all his subjects. The Leader, on the contrary, cannot tolerate criticism of his subordinates, since they act always in his name; if he wants to correct his own errors, he must liquidate those who carried them out; if he wants to blame his mistakes on others, he must kill them.[82]

[80] For a curious legal discussion of this principle, see Neesse, *op. cit.*

[81] Thus Hitler personally cabled his responsibility for the Potempa murder to the SA assassins in 1932. Also interesting in this respect is this formulation from Hitler's speech in 1936 to the SA: "All that you are, you are through me; and all that I am, I am through you alone" (Ernst Bayer, *op. cit.*).

[82] "One of Stalin's distinctive characteristics . . . is systematically to throw his own misdeeds and crimes, as well as his political errors . . . on the shoulders of those whose discredit and ruin he is plotting" (Souvarine, *op. cit.*, p. 655). It is obvious that a totalitarian leader can choose freely whom he wants to impersonate his own errors since all acts committed by subleaders are supposed to be inspired by him, so that anybody can be forced into the role of an impostor.

THE TOTALITARIAN MOVEMENT

For within this organizational framework a mistake can only be a fraud: the impersonation of the Leader by an impostor.

This total responsibility for everything done by the movement and this total identification with every one of its functionaries have the very practical consequence that nobody ever experiences a situation in which he has to be responsible for his own actions or can explain the reasons for them. Since the Leader has monopolized the right and possibility of explanation, he appears to the outside world as the only person who knows what he is doing, *i.e.*, the only representative of the movement with whom one may still talk in nontotalitarian terms and who, if reproached or opposed, cannot say: Don't ask me, ask the Leader. Being in the center of the movement, the Leader can act as though he were above it. It is therefore perfectly understandable (and perfectly futile) for outsiders to set their hopes time and again on a personal talk with the Leader himself when they have to deal with totalitarian movements or governments. The real mystery of the totalitarian Leader resides in an organization which makes it possible for him to assume the total responsibility for all crimes committed by the elite formations of the movement *and* to claim at the same time, the honest, innocent respectability of its most naïve fellow-traveler.[83]

The totalitarian movements have been called "secret societies established in broad daylight." [84] Indeed, little as we know of the sociological structure and the more recent history of secret societies, the structure of the movements, unprecedented if compared with parties and factions, reminds

---

[83] See for instance Admiral Erich Raeder's memo on "My Relationship to Adolf Hitler and to the Party" in *Nazi Conspiracy*, VIII, 707 ff. "When information or rumours arose about radical measures of the Party and the Gestapo, one could come to the conclusion by the conduct of the Fuehrer that such measures were not ordered by the Fuehrer himself. . . . In the course of future years, I gradually came to the conclusion that the Fuehrer himself always leaned toward the more radical solution without letting on outwardly."

In the intraparty struggle which preceded his rise to absolute power, Stalin was careful always to pose as "the man of the golden mean" (see Deutscher, *op. cit.*, pp. 295 ff.); though certainly no "man of compromise," he never abandoned this role altogether. When, for instance, in 1936 a foreign journalist questioned him about the movement's aim of world revolution, he replied: "We have never had such plans and intentions. . . . This is the product of a misunderstanding . . . a comic one, or rather a tragicomic one" (Deutscher, *op. cit.*, p. 422).

[84] See Alexandre Koyré, "The Political Function of the Modern Lie," in *Contemporary Jewish Record*, June, 1945.

Hitler, *op. cit.*, Book II, chapter ix, discusses extensively the pros and cons of secret societies as models for totalitarian movements. His considerations actually led him to Koyré's conclusion, *i.e.*, to adopt the principles of secret societies without their secretiveness and to establish them in "broad daylight." There was, in the prepower stage of the movement, hardly anything which the Nazis consistently kept secret. Later, in the midst of war and surrounded by the whole military hierarchy, the general structure of their organization made it possible for Hitler to act like the secret chief of a band of conspirators. In a lecture delivered by the Chief of the German Staff of the Armed Forces in 1943, this principle was openly stated: "The Fuehrer has ordered that no one may know more or be told more than he needs for his immediate task" (*Nazi Conspiracy*, II, 54).

one of nothing so much as of certain outstanding traits of secret societies.⁸⁵ Secret societies also form hierarchies according to degrees of "initiation," regulate the life of their members according to a secret and fictitious assumption which makes everything look as though it were something else, adopt a strategy of consistent lying to deceive the noninitiated external masses, demand unquestioning obedience from their members who are held together by allegiance to a frequently unknown and always mysterious leader, who himself is surrounded, or supposed to be surrounded, by a small group of initiated who in turn are surrounded by the half-initiated who form a "buffer area" against the hostile profane world.⁸⁶ With secret societies, the totalitarian movements also share the dichotomic division of the world between "sworn blood brothers" and an indistinct inarticulate mass of sworn enemies.⁸⁷ This distinction, based on absolute hostility to the surrounding world, is very different from the ordinary parties' tendency to divide people into those who belong and those who don't. Parties and open societies in general will consider only those who expressly oppose them to be their enemies, while it has always been the principle of secret societies that "whosoever is not expressly included is excluded." ⁸⁸ This esoteric prin-

⁸⁵ The following analysis follows closely Georg Simmel's "Sociology of Secrecy and of Secret Societies," in *The American Journal of Sociology,* Vol. XI, No. 4, January, 1906, which forms chapter v of his *Soziologie,* Leipzig, 1908, selections of which are translated by Kurt H. Wolff under the title *The Sociology of Georg Simmel,* 1950.

⁸⁶ "Precisely because the lower grades of the society constitute a mediating transition to the actual center of the secret, they bring about the gradual compression of the sphere of repulsion around the same, which affords more secure protection than the abruptness of a radical standing wholly without or wholly within could secure" (*ibid.,* p. 489).

⁸⁷ The terms "sworn brothers," "sworn comrades," "sworn community," etc., are repeated *ad nauseam* throughout Nazi literature, partly because of their appeal to juvenile romanticism which was widespread in the German youth movement. It was mainly Himmler who used these terms in a more definite sense, introduced them into the "central watchword," of the SS ("Thus we have fallen in line and march forward to a distant future following the unchangeable laws as a National Socialist order of Nordic men and as a sworn community of their tribes [*Sippen*]" see D'Alquen, *op. cit.*) and gave them their articulate meaning of "absolute hostility" against all others (see Simmel, *op. cit.,* p. 489): "Then when the mass of humanity of 1 to 1½ milliards [*sic!*] lines up against us, the Germanic people, . . ." See Himmler's speech at the meeting of the SS Major Generals at Posen, October 4, 1943, *Nazi Conspiracy,* IV, 558.

⁸⁸ Simmel, *op. cit.,* p. 490.—This, like so many other principles, was adopted by the Nazis after careful reflection on the implications of the "Protocols of the Elders of Zion." Hitler said as early as 1922: "[The gentlemen of the Right] have never yet understood that it is not necessary to be an enemy of the Jew to drag you one day . . . to the scaffold . . . it is quite enough . . . *not to be a Jew:* that will secure the scaffold for you" (*Hitler's Speeches,* p. 12). At that time, nobody could guess that this particular form of propaganda actually meant: One day, it will not be necessary to be an enemy of ours to be dragged to the scaffold; it will be quite enough to be a Jew, or, ultimately, a member of some other people, to be declared "racially unfit" by some Health Commission. Himmler believed and preached that the whole SS was based on the principle that "we must be honest, decent, loyal and comradely to members of our own blood and nobody else" (*op. cit., loc. cit.*).

THE TOTALITARIAN MOVEMENT

ciple seems to be entirely inappropriate for mass organizations; yet the Nazis gave their members at least the psychological equivalent for the initiation ritual of secret societies when, instead of simply excluding Jews from membership, they demanded proof of non-Jewish descent from their members and set up a complicated machine to shed light on the dark ancestry of some 80 million Germans. It was of course a comedy, and even an expensive one, when 80 million Germans set out to look for Jewish grandfathers; yet everybody came out of the examination with the feeling that he belonged to a group of included which stood against an imaginary multitude of ineligibles. The same principle is confirmed in the Bolshevik movement through repeated party purges which inspire in everybody who is not excluded a reaffirmation of his inclusion.

Perhaps the most striking similarity between the secret societies and the totalitarian movements lies in the role of the ritual. The marches around the Red Square in Moscow are in this respect no less characteristic than the pompous formalities of the Nuremberg party days. In the center of the Nazi ritual was the so-called "blood banner," and in the center of the Bolshevik ritual stands the mummified corpse of Lenin, both of which introduce a strong element of idolatry into the ceremony. Such idolatry hardly is proof —as is sometimes asserted—of pseudoreligious or heretical tendencies. The "idols" are mere organizational devices, familiar from the ritual of secret societies, which also used to frighten their members into secretiveness by means of frightful, awe-inspiring symbols. It is obvious that people are more securely held together through the common experience of a secret ritual than by the common sharing of the secret itself. That the secret of totalitarian movements is exposed in broad daylight does not necessarily change the nature of the experience.[89]

These similarities are not, of course, accidental; they cannot simply be explained by the fact that both Hitler and Stalin had been members of modern secret societies before they became totalitarian leaders—Hitler in the secret service of the Reichswehr and Stalin in the conspiratory section of the Bolshevik party. They are to some extent the natural outcome of the conspiracy fiction of totalitarianism whose organizations supposedly have been founded to counteract secret societies—the secret society of the Jews or the conspiratory society of the Trotskyites. What is remarkable in the totalitarian organizations is rather that they could adopt so many organizational devices of secret societies without ever trying to keep their own goal a secret. That the Nazis wanted to conquer the world and establish a world empire, that the Bolsheviks work for the world revolution, was never a secret; these aims, on the contrary, were always part of their propaganda. In other words, the totalitarian movements imitate all the paraphernalia of the secret societies but empty them of the only thing that could excuse, or was supposed to excuse, their methods—the necessity to safeguard a secret.

[89] See Simmel, *op. cit.*, pp. 480-481.

In this, as in so many other respects, Nazism and Bolshevism arrived at the same organizational result from very different historical beginnings. The Nazis started with the fiction of a conspiracy and modeled themselves, more or less consciously, after the example of the secret society of the Elders of Zion, whereas the Bolsheviks came from a revolutionary party, whose aim was one-party dictatorship, passed through a stage in which the party was "entirely apart and above everything" to the moment when the Politburo of the party was "entirely apart from and above everything";[90] finally Stalin imposed upon this party structure the rigid totalitarian rules of its conspiratory sector and only then discovered the need for a central fiction to maintain the iron discipline of a secret society under the conditions of a mass organization. The Nazi development may be more logical, more consistent in itself, but the history of the Bolshevik party offers a better illustration of the essentially fictitious character of totalitarianism, precisely because the fictitious global conspiracies against and according to which the Bolshevik conspiracy is supposedly organized have not been ideologically fixed. They have changed—from the Trotskyites to the 300 families, then to various "imperialisms" and recently to "rootless cosmopolitanism"—and were adjusted to passing needs; yet at no moment and under none of the most various circumstances has it been possible for Bolshevism to do without some such fiction.

The means by which Stalin changed the Russian one-party dictatorship into a totalitarian regime and the revolutionary Communist parties all over the world into totalitarian movements was the liquidation of factions, the abolition of inner-party democracy and the transformation of national Communist parties into Moscow-directed branches of the Comintern. Secret societies in general, and the conspiratory apparatus of revolutionary parties in particular, have always been characterized by absence of factions, suppression of dissident opinions, and absolute centralization of command. All these measures have the obvious utilitarian purpose of protecting the members against persecution and the society against treason; the total obedience asked of each member and the absolute power in the hands of the chief were only inevitable by-products of practical necessities. The trouble, however, is that conspirators have an understandable tendency to think that the most efficient methods in politics in general are those of conspiratory societies and that if one can apply them in broad daylight and support them with a whole nation's instruments of violence, the possibilities for power accumulation become absolutely limitless.[91] The conspiratory sector of a revolutionary party can, as long as the party itself is still intact, be likened to the role of the army within an intact political body: although its own rules of conduct differ radically from those of the civilian body, it serves, remains subject to, and is controlled by it. Just as the danger of a military dictatorship arises when the army no longer serves but wants to dominate the body politic, so

---

[90] Souvarine, *op. cit.*, p. 319, follows a formulation of Bukharin.

[91] Souvarine, *op. cit.*, p. 113, mentions that Stalin "was always impressed by men who brought off 'an affair.' He looked on politics as an 'affair' requiring dexterity."

THE TOTALITARIAN MOVEMENT

the danger of totalitarianism arises when the conspiratory sector of a revolutionary party emancipates itself from the control of the party and aspires to leadership. This is what happened to the Communist parties under the Stalin regime. Stalin's methods were always typical of a man who came from the conspiratory sector of the party: his devotion to detail, his emphasis on the personal side of politics, his ruthlessness in the use and liquidation of comrades and friends. His chief support in the succession struggle after Lenin's death came from the secret police [92] which at that time had already become one of the most important and powerful sections of the party.[93] It was only natural that the Cheka's sympathies should be with the representative of the conspiratory section, with the man who already looked upon it as a kind of secret society and therefore was likely to preserve and to expand its privileges.

The seizure of the Communist parties by their conspiratory sector, however, was only the first step in their transformation into totalitarian movements. It was not enough that the secret police in Russia and its agents in the Communist parties abroad played the same role in the movement as the elite formations which the Nazis had constituted in the form of paramilitary troops. The parties themselves had to be transformed, if the rule of the secret police was to remain stable. Liquidation of factions and inner-party democracy, consequently, was accompanied in Russia by the admission of large, politically uneducated and "neutral" masses to membership, a policy which was quickly followed by the Communist parties abroad after the Popular Front policy had initiated it.

Nazi totalitarianism started with a mass organization which was only gradually dominated by elite formations, while the Bolsheviks started with elite formations and organized the masses accordingly. The result was the same in both cases. The Nazis, moreover, because of their militaristic tradition and prejudices, originally modeled their elite formations after the army, while the Bolsheviks from the beginning endowed the secret police with the exercise of supreme power. Yet after a few years this difference too disappeared: the chief of the SS became the chief of the secret police, and the SS formations were gradually incorporated into and replaced the former personnel of the Gestapo, even though this personnel already consisted of reliable Nazis.[94]

---

[92] In the inner-party struggles during the twenties, "the collaborators of the GPU were almost without exception fanatic adversaries of the Right and adherents of Stalin. The various services of the GPU were at that time the bulwarks of the Stalinist section" (Ciliga, *op. cit.*, p. 48) —Souvarine, *op. cit.*, p. 289, reports that Stalin even before had "continued the police activity he had begun during the Civil War" and been the representative of the Politburo in the GPU.

[93] Immediately after the civil war in Russia, *Pravda* stated "that the formula 'All power to the Soviets' had been replaced by 'All power to the Chekas.' . . . The end of the armed hostilities reduced military control . . . but left a ramified Cheka which perfected itself by simplification of its operation" (Souvarine, *op. cit.*, p. 251).

[94] The Gestapo was set up by Goering in 1933; Himmler was appointed chief of the Gestapo in 1934 and began at once to replace its personnel with his SS-men; at the

It is because of the essential affinity between the functioning of a secret society of conspirators and of the secret police organized to combat it that totalitarian regimes, based on a fiction of global conspiracy and aiming at global rule, eventually concentrate all power in the hands of the police. In the prepower stage, however, the "secret societies in broad daylight" offer other organizational advantages. The obvious contradiction between a mass organization and an exclusive society, which alone can be trusted to keep a secret, is of no importance compared with the fact that the very structure of secret and conspiratory societies could translate the totalitarian ideological dichotomy—the blind hostility of the masses against the existing world regardless of its divergences and differences—into an organizational principle. From the viewpoint of an organization which functions according to the principle that whoever is not included is excluded, whoever is not with me is against me, the world at large loses all the nuances, differentiations, and pluralistic aspects which had in any event become confusing and unbearable to the masses who had lost their place and their orientation in it.[95] What inspired them with the unwavering loyalty of members of secret societies was not so much the secret as the dichotomy between Us and all others. This could be kept intact by imitating the secret societies' organizational structure and emptying it of its rational purpose of safeguarding a secret. Nor did it matter if a conspiracy ideology was the origin of this development, as in the case of the Nazis, or a parasitic growth of the conspiratory sector of a revolutionary party, as in the case of the Bolsheviks. The claim inherent in totalitarian organization is that everything outside the movement is "dying," a claim which is drastically realized under the murderous conditions of totalitarian rule, but which even in the prepower stage appears plausible to the masses who escaped from disintegration and disorientation into the fictitious home of the movement.

Totalitarian movements have proved time and again that they can command the same total loyalty in life and death which had been the prerogative of secret and conspiratory societies.[96] The complete absence of resistance in a thoroughly trained and armed troop like the SA in the face of the murder of a beloved leader (Roehm) and hundreds of close comrades was a curious spectacle. At that moment probably Roehm, and not Hitler, had

---

end of the war, 75 per cent of all Gestapo agents were SS-men. It must also be considered that the SS units were particularly qualified for this job as Himmler had organized them, even in the prepower stage, for espionage duty among party members (Heiden, *op. cit.*, p. 308). For the history of the Gestapo, see Giles, *op. cit.*, and also *Nazi Conspiracy*, Vol. II, chapter xii.

[95] It was probably one of the decisive ideological errors of Rosenberg, who fell from the Fuehrer's favor and lost his influence in the movement to men like Himmler, Bormann, and even Streicher, that his *Myth of the Twentieth Century* admits a racial pluralism from which only the Jews were excluded. He thereby violated the principle that whoever is not included ("the Germanic people") is excluded ("the mass of humanity"). Cf. note 87.

[96] Simmel, *op. cit.*, p. 492, enumerates secret criminal societies in which the members voluntarily set up one commander whom they obey from then on without criticism and without limitation.

THE TOTALITARIAN MOVEMENT

the power of the Reichswehr behind him. But these incidents in the Nazi movement have by now been overshadowed by the ever-repeated spectacle of self-confessed "criminals" in the Bolshevik parties. Trials based on absurd confessions have become part of an internally all-important and externally incomprehensible ritual. But, no matter how the victims are being prepared today, this ritual owes its existence to the probably unfabricated confessions of the old Bolshevik guard in 1936. Long before the time of the Moscow Trials men condemned to death would receive their sentences with great calm, an attitude "particularly prevalent among members of the Cheka." [97] So long as the movement exists, its peculiar form of organization makes sure that at least the elite formations can no longer conceive of a life outside the closely knit band of men who, even if they are condemned, still feel superior to the rest of the uninitiated world. And since this organization's exclusive aim has always been to deceive and fight and ultimately conquer the outside world, its members are satisfied to pay with their lives if only this helps again to fool the world.[98]

The chief value, however, of the secret or conspiratory societies' organizational structure and moral standards for purposes of mass organization does not even lie in the inherent guarantees of unconditional belonging and loyalty, and organizational manifestation of unquestioned hostility to the outside world, but in their unsurpassed capacity to establish and safeguard the fictitious world through consistent lying. The whole hierarchical structure of totalitarian movements, from naïve fellow-travelers to party members, elite formations, the intimate circle around the Leader, and the Leader himself, could be described in terms of a curiously varying mixture of gullibility and cynicism with which each member, depending upon his rank and standing in the movement, is expected to react to the changing lying statements of the leaders and the central unchanging ideological fiction of the movement.

A mixture of gullibility and cynicism had been an outstanding characteristic of mob mentality before it became an everyday phenomenon of masses. In an ever-changing, incomprehensible world the masses had reached the point where they would, at the same time, believe everything and nothing, think that everything was possible and that nothing was true. The mixture in itself was remarkable enough, because it spelled the end of the illusion that gullibility was a weakness of unsuspecting primitive souls and cynicism the vice of superior and refined minds. Mass propaganda discovered that its audience was ready at all times to believe the worst, no matter how ab-

[97] Ciliga, *op. cit.*, pp. 96-97. He also describes how in the twenties even ordinary prisoners in the GPU prison of Leningrad who had been condemned to death allowed themselves to be taken to execution "without a word, without a cry of revolt against the Government that put them to death" (p. 183).

[98] Ciliga reports how the condemned party members "thought that if these executions saved the bureaucratic dictatorship as a whole, if they calmed the rebellious peasantry (or rather if they misled them into error), the sacrifice of their lives would not have been in vain" (*op. cit.*, pp. 96-97).

surd, and did not particularly object to being deceived because it held every statement to be a lie anyhow. The totalitarian mass leaders based their propaganda on the correct psychological assumption that, under such conditions, one could make people believe the most fantastic statements one day, and trust that if the next day they were given irrefutable proof of their falsehood, they would take refuge in cynicism: instead of deserting the leaders who had lied to them, they would protest that they had known all along that the statement was a lie and would admire the leaders for their superior tactical cleverness.

What had been a demonstrable reaction of mass audiences became an important hierarchical principle for mass organizations. A mixture of gullibility and cynicism is prevalent in all ranks of totalitarian movements, and the higher the rank the more cynicism weighs down gullibility. The essential conviction shared by all ranks, from fellow-traveler to leader, is that politics is a game of cheating and that the "first commandment" of the movement: "The Fuehrer is always right," [99] is as necessary for the purposes of world politics, *i.e.,* world-wide cheating, as the rules of military discipline are for the purposes of war.[100]

The machine that generates, organizes, and spreads the monstrous falsehoods of totalitarian movements depends again upon the position of the Leader. To the propaganda assertion that all happenings are scientifically predictable according to the laws of nature or economics, totalitarian organization adds the position of one man who has monopolized this knowledge and whose principal quality is that he "was always right and will always be right." [101] To a member of a totalitarian movement this knowledge has nothing to do with truth and this being right nothing to do with the objective truthfulness of the Leader's statements which cannot be disproved by facts, but only by future success or failure. The Leader is always right in his actions and since these are planned for centuries to come, the ultimate test of what he does has been removed beyond the experience of his contemporaries.[102]

The only group supposed to believe loyally and textually in the Leader's words are the sympathizers whose confidence surrounds the movement with an atmosphere of honesty and simple-mindedness, and helps the Leader to fulfill half his task, that is, to inspire confidence in the movement. The party

---

[99] *Organisationsbuch der NSDAP.*

[100] Goebbels' notion of the role of diplomacy in politics is characteristic: "There is no doubt that one does best if one keeps the diplomats uninformed about the background of politics. . . . Genuineness in playing an appeasement role is sometimes the most convincing argument for their political trustworthiness" (*op. cit.,* p. 87).

[101] Rudolf Hess in a broadcast in 1934. *Nazi Conspiracy,* I, 193.

[102] Werner Best, a Nazi jurist, explained in *Die Deutsche Polizei,* 1940: "Whether the will of the government lays down the 'right' rules . . . is no longer a question of law, but a question of fate. For actual misuses . . . will be punished more surely before history by fate itself with misfortune and overthrow and ruin, because of the violation of the 'laws of life,' than by a State Court of Justice." Translation quoted from *Nazi Conspiracy,* IV, 490.

THE TOTALITARIAN MOVEMENT

members never believe public statements and are not supposed to, but are complimented by totalitarian propaganda on that superior intelligence which supposedly distinguishes them from the nontotalitarian outside world, which, in turn, they know only from the abnormal gullibility of sympathizers. Only Nazi sympathizers believed Hitler when he swore his famous legality oath before the supreme court of the Weimar Republic; members of the movement knew very well that he lied, and trusted him more than ever because he apparently was able to fool public opinion and the authorities. When in later years Hitler repeated the performance for the whole world, when he swore to his good intentions and at the same time most openly prepared his crimes, the admiration of the Nazi membership naturally was boundless. Similarly, only Bolshevik fellow-travelers believed in the dissolution of the Comintern, and only the nonorganized masses of the Russian people and the fellow-travelers abroad were meant to take at face value Stalin's prodemocratic statements during the war. Bolshevik party members were explicitly warned not to be fooled by tactical maneuvers and were asked to admire their Leader's shrewdness in betraying his allies.[103]

Without the organizational division of the movement into elite formations, membership, and sympathizers, the lies of the Leader would not work. The graduation of cynicism expressed in a hierarchy of contempt is at least as necessary in the face of constant refutation as plain gullibility. The point is that the sympathizers in front organizations despise their fellow-citizens' complete lack of initiation, the party members despise the fellow-travelers' gullibility and lack of radicalism, the elite formations despise for similar reasons the party membership, and within the elite formations a similar hierarchy of contempt accompanies every new foundation and development.[104] The result of this system is that the gullibility of sympathizers makes lies credible to the outside world, while at the same time the graduated cynicism of membership and elite formations eliminates the danger that the Leader will ever be forced by the weight of his own propaganda to make good his own statements and feigned respectability. It has been one of the chief handicaps of the outside world in dealing with totalitarian systems that it ignored this system and therefore trusted that, on one hand, the very enormity of totalitarian lies would be their undoing and that, on the other, it would be possible to take the Leader at his word and force him, regardless of his original intentions, to make it good. The totalitarian system, unfortunately, is foolproof against such normal consequences; its ingeniousness rests precisely on the elimination of that reality which either unmasks the liar or forces him to live up to his pretense.

While the membership does not believe statements made for public consumption, it believes all the more fervently the standard clichés of ideological

---

[103] See Kravchenko, *op. cit.*, p. 422. "No properly indoctrinated Communist felt that the Party was 'lying' in professing one set of policies in public and its very opposite in private."

[104] "The National Socialist despises his fellow German, the SA man the other National Socialists, the SS man the SA man" (Heiden, *op. cit.*, p. 308).

explanation, the keys to past and future history which totalitarian movements took from nineteenth-century ideologies, and transformed, through organization, into a working reality. These ideological elements in which the masses had come to believe anyhow, albeit rather vaguely and abstractly, were turned into factual lies of an all-comprehensive nature (the domination of the world by the Jews instead of a general theory about races, the conspiracy of Wall Street instead of a general theory about classes) and integrated into a general scheme of action in which only the "dying"—the dying classes of capitalist countries or the decadent nations—are supposed to stand in the way of the movement. In contrast to the movements' tactical lies which change literally from day to day, these ideological lies are supposed to be believed like sacred untouchable truths. They are surrounded by a carefully elaborated system of "scientific" proofs which do not have to be convincing for the completely "uninitiated," but still appeal to some vulgarized thirst for knowledge by "demonstrating" the inferiority of the Jews or the misery of people living under a capitalist system.

The elite formations are distinguished from the ordinary party membership in that they do not need such demonstrations and are not even supposed to believe in the literal truth of ideological clichés. These are fabricated to answer a quest for truth among the masses which in its insistence on explanation and demonstration still has much in common with the normal world. The elite is not composed of ideologists; its members' whole education is aimed at abolishing their capacity for distinguishing between truth and falsehood, between reality and fiction. Their superiority consists in their ability immediately to dissolve every statement of fact into a declaration of purpose. In distinction to the mass membership which, for instance, needs some demonstration of the inferiority of the Jewish race before it can safely be asked to kill Jews, the elite formations understand that the statement, all Jews are inferior, means, all Jews should be killed; they know that when they are told that only Moscow has a subway, the real meaning of the statement is that all subways should be destroyed, and are not unduly surprised when they discover the subway in Paris. The tremendous shock of disillusion which the Red Army suffered on its conquering trip to Europe could be cured only by concentration camps and forced exile for a large part of the occupation troops; but the police formations which accompanied the Army were prepared for the shock, not by different and more correct information—there is no secret training school in Soviet Russia which gives out authentic facts about life abroad—but simply by a general training in supreme contempt for all facts and all reality.

This mentality of the elite is no mere mass phenomenon, no mere consequence of social rootlessness, economic disaster, and political anarchy; it needs careful preparation and cultivation and forms a more important, though less easily recognizable, part of the curriculum of totalitarian leadership schools, the Nazi *Ordensburgen* for the SS troops, and the Bolshevik training centers for Comintern agents, than race indoctrination or the techniques of civil war. Without the elite and its artificially induced inability to

THE TOTALITARIAN MOVEMENT

understand facts as facts, to distinguish between truth and falsehood, the movement could never move in the direction of realizing its fiction. The outstanding negative quality of the totalitarian elite is that it never stops to think about the world as it really is and never compares the lies with reality. Its most cherished virtue, correspondingly, is loyalty to the Leader, who, like a talisman, assures the ultimate victory of lie and fiction over truth and reality.

The topmost layer in the organization of totalitarian movements is the intimate circle around the Leader, which can be a formal institution, like the Bolshevik Politburo, or a changing clique of men who do not necessarily hold office, like the entourage of Hitler. To them ideological clichés are mere devices to organize the masses, and they feel no compunction about changing them according to the needs of circumstances if only the organizing principle is kept intact. In this connection, the chief merit of Himmler's reorganization of the SS was that he found a very simple method for "solving the problem of blood by action," that is, for selecting the members of the elite according to "good blood" and preparing them to "carry on a racial struggle without mercy" against everyone who could not trace his "Aryan" ancestry back to 1750, or was less than 5 feet 8 inches tall ("I know that people who have reached a certain height must possess the desired blood to some degree") or did not have blue eyes and blond hair.[105] The importance of this racism in action was that the organization became independent of almost all concrete teachings of no matter what racial "science," independent also of antisemitism insofar as it was a specific doctrine concerning the nature and role of the Jews, whose usefulness would have ended with their extermination.[106] Racism was safe and independent of the scientificality of propaganda once an elite had been selected by a "race commission" and placed under the authority of special "marriage laws," while at the opposite end and under the jurisdiction of this "racial elite," concentration camps existed for the sake of "better demonstration of the laws of inheritance and race."[107] On the strength of this "living organization," the Nazis could dis-

---

[105] Himmler originally selected the candidates of the SS from photographs. Later, a Race Commission, before which the applicant had to appear in person, approved or disapproved of his racial appearance. See Himmler on "Organization and Obligation of the SS and the Police," *Nazi Conspiracy*, IV, 616 ff.

[106] Himmler was well aware of the importance of having eliminated mere antisemitism as the basis of a racial organization. As soon as he was appointed chief of the SS in 1929, he introduced the principle of racial selection and marriage laws and added: "The SS knows very well that this order is of great significance. Taunts, sneers or misunderstanding don't touch us; the future is ours." Quoted from d'Alquen, *op. cit.* And again, fourteen years later, in his speech at Kharkov (*Nazi Conspiracy*, IV, 572 ff.), Himmler reminds his SS leaders that "we were the first really to solve the problem of blood by action . . . and by problem of blood, we of course do not mean antisemitism. Antisemitism is exactly the same as delousing. Getting rid of lice is not a question of ideology. It is a matter of cleanliness. . . . But for us the question of blood was a reminder of our own worth, a reminder of what is actually the basis holding this German people together."

[107] Himmler, *op. cit., Nazi Conspiracy*, IV, 616 ff.

pense with dogmatism and offer friendship to Semitic peoples, like the Arabs, or enter into alliances with the very representatives of the Yellow Danger, the Japanese.

The policy-makers of Bolshevism show the same superiority to their own avowed dogmas. They are quite capable of interrupting every existing class struggle with a sudden alliance with capitalism without undermining the reliability of their cadres or committing treason against their belief in class struggle. The dichotomous principle of class struggle having become an organizational device, having, as it were, petrified into uncompromising hostility against the whole world through the secret police cadres in Russia and the Comintern agents abroad, Bolshevik policy has become remarkably free of "prejudices."

It is this freedom from the content of their own ideologies which characterizes the highest rank of the totalitarian hierarchy. These men consider everything and everybody in terms of organization, and this includes the Leader who to them is neither an inspired talisman nor the one who is infallibly right, but the simple consequence of this type of organization; he is needed, not as a person, but as a function, and as such he is indispensable to the movement. In contrast, however, to other despotic forms of government, where frequently a clique rules and the despot plays only the representative role of a puppet ruler, totalitarian leaders are actually free to do whatever they please and can count on the loyalty of their entourage even if they choose to murder them.

The more technical reason for this suicidal loyalty is that succession to the supreme office is not regulated by any inheritance or other laws. A successful palace revolt would have as disastrous results for the movement as a whole as a military defeat. It is in the nature of the movement that once the Leader has assumed his office, the whole organization is so absolutely identified with him that any admission of a mistake or removal from office would break the spell of infallibility which surrounds the office of the Leader and spell doom to all those connected with the movement. It is not the truthfulness of the Leader's words but the infallibility of his actions which is the basis for the structure. Without it and in the heat of a discussion which presumes fallibility, the whole fictitious world of totalitarianism goes to pieces, overwhelmed at once by the factuality of the real world which only the movement steered in an infallibly right direction by the Leader was able to ward off.

However, the loyalty of those who believe neither in ideological clichés nor in the infallibility of the Leader also has deeper, nontechnical reasons. What binds these men together is a firm and sincere belief in human omnipotence. Their moral cynicism, their belief that everything is permitted, rests on the solid conviction that everything is possible. It is true that these men, few in number, are not easily caught in their own specific lies and that they do not necessarily believe in racism or economics, in the conspiracy of the Jews or of Wall Street. Yet they too are deceived, deceived by their impudent conceited idea that everything can be done and their contemptuous convic-

THE TOTALITARIAN MOVEMENT

tion that everything that exists is merely a temporary obstacle that superior organization will certainly destroy. Confident that power of organization can destroy power of substance, as the violence of a well-organized gang might rob a rich man of ill-guarded wealth, they constantly underestimate the substantial power of stable communities and overestimate the driving force of a movement. Since, moreover, they do not actually believe in the factual existence of a world conspiracy against them, but use it only as an organizational device, they fail to understand that their own conspiracy may eventually provoke the whole world into uniting against them.

Yet no matter how the delusion of human omnipotence through organization is ultimately defeated, within the movement its practical consequence is that the entourage of the Leader, in case of disagreement with him, will never be very sure of their own opinions, since they believe sincerely that their disagreements do not really matter, that even the maddest device has a fair chance of success if properly organized. The point of their loyalty is not that they believe the Leader is infallible, but that they are convinced that everybody who commands the instruments of violence with the superior methods of totalitarian organization can become infallible. This delusion is greatly strengthened when totalitarian regimes hold the power to demonstrate the relativity of success and failure, and to show how a loss in substance can become a gain in organization. (The fantastic mismanagement of industrial enterprise in Soviet Russia led to the atomization of the working class, and the terrifying mistreatment of civilian prisoners in Eastern territories under Nazi occupation, though it caused a "deplorable loss of labor," "thinking in terms of generations, [was] not to be regretted." [108]) Moreover, the decision regarding success and failure under totalitarian circumstances is very largely a matter of organized and terrorized public opinion. While it is objectively true that "never in human history has such a tremendous cynical wickedness ended in such a long, almost uninterrupted series of failures," [109] it is also true that, in a totally fictitious world, failures need not be recorded, admitted, and remembered, and that factuality itself depends for its continued existence upon the existence of the nontotalitarian world.

[108] Himmler in his speech at Posen, *Nazi Conspiracy*, IV, 558.
[109] Franz Borkenau, "Die neue Komintern," *op. cit.*

[7]
Leaders and Followers

THE power impulse has two forms: explicit, in leaders; implicit, in their followers. When men willingly follow a leader, they do so with a view to the acquisition of power by the group which he commands, and they feel that his triumphs are theirs. Most men do not feel in themselves the competence required for leading their group to victory, and therefore seek out a captain who appears to possess the courage and sagacity necessary for the achievement of supremacy. Even in religion this impulse appears. Nietzsche accused Christianity of inculcating a slave-morality, but ultimate triumph was always the goal. 'Blessed are the meek, *for they shall inherit the earth.*' Or as a well-known hymn more explicitly states it:

> The Son of God goes forth to war,
>   A kingly crown to gain.
> His blood-red banner streams afar.
>   Who follows in His train?
>
> Who best can drink his cup of woe,
>   Triumphant over pain,
> Who patient bears his cross below,
>   He follows in His train.

If this is a slave-morality, then every soldier of fortune who endures the rigours of a campaign, and every rank-and-file politician who works hard at electioneering, is to be accounted a slave. But in fact, in every genuinely co-operative enterprise, the follower is psychologically no more a slave than the leader.

It is this that makes endurable the inequalities of power which organization makes inevitable, and which tend to increase rather than diminish as society grows more organic.

Inequality in the distribution of power has always existed in human communities, as far back as our knowledge extends. This is due partly to external necessity, partly to causes which are to be found in human nature. Most collective enterprises are only possible if they are directed by some governing body. If a house

LEADERS AND FOLLOWERS 13

is to be built, some one must decide on the plans; if trains are to run on a railway, the time-table cannot be left to the caprices of engine-drivers; if a new road is to be constructed, some one must decide where it is to go. Even a democratically elected government is still a government, and therefore, on grounds that have nothing to do with psychology, there must, if collective enterprises are to succeed, be some men who give orders and others who obey them. But the fact that this is possible, and still more the fact that the actual inequalities of power exceed what is made necessary by technical causes, can only be explained in terms of individual psychology and physiology. Some men's characters lead them always to command, others always to obey; between these extremes lie the mass of average human beings, who like to command in some situations, but in others prefer to be subject to a leader.

Adler, in his book on *Understanding Human Nature*, distinguishes a submissive type and an imperious type. 'The servile individual,' he says, 'lives by the rules and laws of others, and this type seeks out a servile position almost compulsively.' On the other hand, he continues, the imperious type, which asks: 'How can I be superior to everyone?' is found whenever a director is needed, and rises to the top in revolutions. Adler regards both types as undesirable, at any rate in their extreme forms, and he considers both as products of education. 'The greatest disadvantage of an authoritative education,' he says, 'lies in the fact that it gives the child an ideal of power, and shows him the pleasures which are connected with the possession of power.' Authoritative education, we may add, produces the slave type as well as the despotic type, since it leads to the feeling that the only possible relation between two human beings who cooperate is that in which one issues orders and the other obeys them.

Love of power, in various limited forms, is almost universal, but in its absolute form it is rare. A woman who enjoys power in the management of her house is likely to shrink from the sort of political power enjoyed by a Prime Minister; Abraham Lincoln, on the contrary, while not afraid to govern the United States, could not face civil war in the home. Perhaps Napoleon, if the *Bellerophon* had suffered shipwreck, would have tamely obeyed the orders of British officers as to escaping in boats. Men like power so long as they believe in their own competence to handle the business in question, but when they know themselves incompetent they prefer to follow a leader.

14 POWER

The impulse of submission, which is just as real and just as common as the impulse to command, has its roots in fear. The most unruly gang of children ever imagined will become completely amenable to the orders of a competent adult in an alarming situation, such as a fire; when the War came, the Pankhursts made their peace with Lloyd George. Whenever there is acute danger, the impulse of most people is to seek out Authority and submit to it; at such moments, few would dream of revolution. When war breaks out, people have similar feelings towards the Government.

Organizations may or may not be designed for the purpose of meeting dangers. Economic organizations in some cases, such as coal mines, involve dangers, but these are incidental, and if they were eliminated the organizations would flourish all the better. In general, meeting dangers is no part of the essential purpose of economic organizations, or of governmental organizations concerned with internal affairs. But lifeboats and fire-brigades, like armies and navies, are constructed for the purpose of meeting dangers. In a certain less immediate sense, this is also true of religious bodies, which exist in part to allay the metaphysical fears that are buried deep in our nature. If anyone feels inclined to question this, let him think of such hymns as:

> Rock of Ages, cleft for me,
> Let me hide myself in thee;

or

> Jesu, lover of my soul,
> Let me to thy bosom fly,
> While the gathering waters roll,
> While the tempest still is high.

In submission to the Divine Will there is a sense of ultimate safety, which has led to religious abasement in many monarchs who could not submit to any merely earthly being. All submissiveness is rooted in fear, whether the leader to whom we submit be human or divine.

It has become a commonplace that aggressiveness also often has its roots in fear. I am inclined to think that this theory has been pushed too far. It is true of a certain kind of aggressiveness, for instance, that of D. H. Lawrence. But I greatly doubt whether the men who become pirate chiefs are those who are filled with

LEADERS AND FOLLOWERS

retrospective terror of their fathers, or whether Napoleon, at Austerlitz, really felt that he was getting even with Madame Mère. I know nothing of the mother of Attila, but I rather suspect that she spoilt the little darling, who subsequently found the world irritating because it sometimes resisted his whims. The type of aggressiveness that is the outcome of timidity is not, I think, that which inspires great leaders; the great leaders, I should say, have an exceptional self-confidence which is not only on the surface, but penetrates deep into the subconscious.

The self-confidence necessary to a leader may be caused in various ways. Historically, one of the commonest has been a hereditary position of command. Read, for example, the speeches of Queen Elizabeth in moments of crisis: you will see the monarch over-riding the woman, convincing her and through her the nation, that she knows what must be done, as no mere commoner can hope to do. In her case, the interests of the nation and the sovereign were in harmony; that is why she was 'Good Queen Bess'. She could even praise her father without arousing indignation. There is no doubt that the habit of command makes it easier to bear responsibilities and to take quick decisions. A clan which follows its hereditary chief probably does better than if it chose its chief by lot. On the other hand, a body like the mediaeval church, which chose its chief on account of conspicuous merits, and usually after he had had considerable experience of important administrative posts, secured, on the average, considerably better results than were secured, in the same period, in hereditary monarchies.

Some of the ablest leaders known to history have arisen in revolutionary situations. Let us consider, for a moment, the qualities which brought success to Cromwell, Napoleon, and Lenin. All three, in difficult times, dominated their respective countries, and secured the willing service of able men who were not by nature submissive. All three had boundless courage and self-confidence, combined with what their colleagues considered sound judgment at difficult moments. Of the three, however, Cromwell and Lenin belonged to one type, and Napoleon to another. Cromwell and Lenin were men of profound religious faith, believing themselves to be the appointed ministers of a non-human purpose. Their power-impulses thus seemed to themselves indubitably righteous, and they cared little for those rewards of power—such as luxury and ease—which could not be harmonized with their identification with the cosmic purpose.

This is specially true of Lenin, for Cromwell, in his last years, was conscious of falling into sin. Nevertheless, in both cases it was the combination of faith with great ability that gave them courage, and enabled them to inspire their followers with confidence in their leadership.

Napoleon, as opposed to Cromwell and Lenin, is the supreme example of the soldier of fortune. The Revolution suited him, since it made his opportunity, but otherwise he was indifferent to it. Though he gratified French patriotism and depended upon it, France, like the Revolution, was to him merely an opportunity; he had even, in his youth, toyed with the idea of fighting for Corsica against France. His success was due, not so much to any exceptional qualities of character, as to his technical skill in war: when other men would have been defeated, he was victorious. At crucial moments, such as the 18 Brumaire and Marengo, he depended upon others for success; but he had the spectacular gifts that enabled him to annex the achievements of his coadjutors. The French army was full of ambitious young men; it was Napoleon's cleverness, not his psychology, that gave him the power to succeed where the others failed. His belief in his star, which finally led to his downfall, was the effect of his victories, not their cause.

To come to our own day, Hitler must be classed, psychologically, with Cromwell and Lenin, Mussolini with Napoleon.

The soldier of fortune, or pirate chief, is a type of more importance in history than is thought by 'scientific' historians. Sometimes, like Napoleon, he succeeds in making himself the leader of bodies of men who have purposes that are in part impersonal: the French revolutionary armies conceived of themselves as the liberators of Europe, and were so regarded in Italy as well as by many in Western Germany, but Napoleon himself never brought any more liberation than seemed useful for his own career. Very often there is no pretence of impersonal aims. Alexander may have set to work to hellenize the East, but it is doubtful whether his Macedonians were much interested in this aspect of his campaigns. Roman generals, during the last hundred years of the Republic, were mainly out for cash, and secured their soldiers' loyalty by distributions of land and treasure. Cecil Rhodes professed a mystical belief in the British Empire, but the belief yielded good dividends, and the troopers whom he engaged for the conquest of Matabeleland were offered nakedly pecuniary inducements. Organized greed, with little or no disguise, has played a very large part in the world's wars.

The ordinary quiet citizen, we said, is led largely by fear when he submits to a leader. But this can hardly be true of a gang of pirates, unless no more peaceable profession was open to them. When once the leader's authority is established, he may inspire fear in mutinous individuals; but until he is a leader, and is recognized as such by the majority, he is not in a position to inspire fear. To acquire the position of leader, he must excel in the qualities that confer authority: self-confidence, quick decision, and skill in deciding upon the right measures. Leadership is relative: Caesar could make Antony obey him, but no one else could. Most people feel that politics is difficult, and that they had better follow a leader—they feel this instinctively and unconsciously, as dogs do with their masters. If this were not the case, collective political action would scarcely be possible.

Thus love of power, as a motive, is limited by timidity, which also limits the desire for self-direction. Since power enables us to realize more of our desires than would otherwise be possible, and since it secures deference from others, it is natural to desire power except in so far as timidity interferes. This sort of timidity is lessened by the habit of responsibility, and accordingly responsibilities tend to increase the desire for power. Experience of cruelty and unfriendliness may operate in either direction: with those who are easily frightened it produces the wish to escape observation, while bolder spirits are stimulated to seek positions in which they can inflict cruelties rather than suffer them.

After anarchy, the natural first step is despotism, because this is facilitated by the instinctive mechanisms of domination and submission; this has been illustrated in the family, in the State, and in business. Equal co-operation is much more difficult than despotism, and much less in line with instinct. When men attempt equal co-operation, it is natural for each to strive for complete mastery, since the submissive impulses are not brought into play. It is almost necessary that all the parties concerned should acknowledge a common loyalty to something outside all of them. In China, family businesses often succeed because of Confucian loyalty to the family; but impersonal joint-stock companies are apt to prove unworkable, because no one has any compelling motive for honesty towards the other shareholders. Where there is government by deliberation, there must, for success, be a general respect for the law, or for the nation, or for some principle which all parties respect. The Society of Friends,

18   POWER

when any doubtful matter has to be decided, do not take a vote and abide by the majority: they discuss until they arrive at 'the sense of the meeting,' which used to be regarded as prompted by the Holy Spirit. In their case we are concerned with an unusually homogeneous community, but without some degree of homogeneity government by discussion is unworkable.

A sense of solidarity sufficient to make government by discussion possible can be generated without much difficulty in a family, such as the Fuggers or Rothschilds, in a small religious body such as the Quakers, in a barbarous tribe, or in a nation at war or in danger of war. But outside pressure is all but indispensable: the members of a group hang together for fear of hanging separately. A common peril is much the easiest way of producing homogeneity. This, however, affords no solution of the problem of power in the world as a whole. We wish to prevent the perils—e.g. war—which at present cause cohesion, but we do not wish to destroy social co-operation. This problem is difficult psychologically as well as politically, and if we may judge by analogy, it is likely to be solved, if at all, by an initial despotism of some one nation. Free co-operation among nations, accustomed as they are to the *liberum veto*, is as difficult as among the Polish aristocracy before the Partition. Extinction, in this case as in that, is likely to be thought preferable to common sense. Mankind need government, but in regions where anarchy has prevailed they will, at first, submit only to despotism. We must therefore seek first to secure government, even though despotic, and only when government has become habitual can we hope successfully to make it democratic. 'Absolute power is useful in building the organization. More slow, but equally sure, is the development of social pressure demanding that the power shall be used for the benefit of all concerned. This pressure, constant in ecclesiastical and political history, is already making its appearance in the economic field.'[1]

I have spoken hitherto of those who command and those who obey, but there is a third type, namely, those who withdraw. There are men who have the courage to refuse submission without having the imperiousness that causes the wish to command. Such men do not fit readily into the social structure, and in one way or another they seek a refuge where they can enjoy a more or less solitary freedom. At times, men with this tempera-

[1] Berle and Means, *The Modern Corporation and Private Property*, p. 353. They are speaking of industrial corporations.

ment have been of great historical importance; the early Christians and the American pioneers represent two species of the genus. Sometimes the refuge is mental, sometimes physical; sometimes it demands the complete solitude of a hermitage, sometimes the social solitude of a monastery. Among mental refugees are those who belong to obscure sects, those whose interests are absorbed by innocent fads, and those who occupy themselves with recondite and unimportant forms of erudition. Among physical refugees are men who seek the frontier of civilization, and such explorers as Bates, the 'naturalist on the Amazon,' who lived happily for fifteen years without other society than the Indians. Something of the hermit's temper is an essential element in many forms of excellence, since it enables men to resist the lure of popularity, to pursue important work in spite of general indifference or hostility, and to arrive at opinions which are opposed to prevalent errors.

Of those who withdraw, some are not genuinely indifferent to power, but only unable to obtain it by the usual methods. Such men may become saints or heresiarchs, founders of monastic orders or of new schools in art or literature. They attach to themselves as disciples people who combine a love of submission with an impulse to revolt; the latter prevents orthodoxy, while the former leads to uncritical adoption of the new tenets. Tolstoy and his followers illustrate this pattern. The genuine solitary is quite different. A perfect example of his type is the melancholy Jacques, who shares exile with the good Duke because it is exile, and afterwards remains in the forest with the bad Duke rather than return to Court. Many American pioneers, after suffering long hardship and privation, sold their farms and moved further West as soon as civilization caught up with them. For men of this temperament, the world affords fewer and fewer opportunities. Some drift into crime, some into a morose and anti-social philosophy. Too much contact with their fellow-men produces misanthropy, which, when solitude is unattainable, turns naturally towards violence.

Among the timid, organization is promoted, not only by submission to a leader, but by the reassurance which is felt in being one of a crowd who all feel alike. In an enthusiastic public meeting with whose purpose one is in sympathy, there is a sense of exaltation, combined with warmth and safety: the emotion which is shared grows more and more intense until it crowds out all other feelings except an exultant sense of power produced by the multiplication of the *ego*. Collective excitement is a delicious intoxication, in which sanity, humanity, and even self-preservation are easily forgotten, and in which atrocious massacres and heroic martyrdom are equally possible. This kind of intoxication, like others, is hard to resist when its delights have once been experienced, but leads in the end to apathy and weariness, and to the need for a stronger and stronger stimulus if the former fervour is to be reproduced.

Although a leader is not essential to this emotion, which can be produced by music, and by some exciting event which is seen by a crowd, the words of an orator are the easiest and most usual method of inducing it. The pleasure of collective excitement is, therefore, an important element in the power of leaders. The leader need not share in the feelings which he arouses; he may say to himself, like Shakespeare's Antony:

> Now let it work: mischief, thou art afoot,
> Take thou what course thou wilt!

But the leader is hardly likely to be successful unless he enjoys his power over his followers. He will therefore be led to a preference for the kind of situation, and the kind of mob, that makes his success easy. The best situation is one in which there is a danger sufficiently serious to make men feel brave in combating it, but not so terrifying as to make fear predominant—such a situation, for example, as the outbreak of war against an enemy who is thought formidable but not invincible. A skilful orator, when he wishes to stimulate warlike feeling, produces in his audience two layers of belief: a superficial layer, in which the power of the enemy is magnified so as to make great courage seem necessary, and a deeper layer, in which there is a firm conviction of victory. Both are embodied in such a slogan as 'right will prevail over might'.

The kind of mob that the orator will desire is one more given to emotion than to reflection, one filled with fears and consequent hatreds, one impatient of slow and gradual methods, and at once exasperated and hopeful. The orator, if he is not a complete cynic, will acquire a set of beliefs that justify his activities. He will think that feeling is a better guide than reason, that our opinions should be formed with the blood rather than the brain, that the best elements in human life are collective rather than individual. If he controls education, he will make it consist of an alternation of drill and collective intoxication, while knowledge

LEADERS AND FOLLOWERS

and judgment will be left to the cold devotees of inhuman science.

Power-loving individuals, however, are not all of the orator type. There are men of quite a different kind, whose love of power has been fed by control over mechanism. Take, for example, Bruno Mussolini's account of his exploits from the air in the Abyssinian war:

'We had to set fire to the wooded hills, to the fields and little villages. ... It was all most diverting. ... The bombs hardly touched the earth before they burst out into white smoke and an enormous flame and the dry grass began to burn. I thought of the animals: God, how they ran ... After the bomb-racks were emptied I began throwing bombs by hand. ... It was most amusing: a big Zariba surrounded by tall trees was not easy to hit. I had to aim carefully at the straw roof and only succeeded at the third shot. The wretches who were inside, seeing their roof burning, jumped out and ran off like mad.

'Surrounded by a circle of fire about five thousand Abyssinians came to a sticky end. It was like hell.'

While the orator needs much intuitive psychology for his success, the aviator of Bruno Mussolini's type can get his pleasure with no more psychology than is involved in knowing that it is unpleasant to burn to death. The orator is an ancient type; the man whose power is based on mechanism is modern. Not wholly: read, for example, how Carthaginian elephants were used, at the end of the first Punic War, to trample mutinous mercenaries to death, where the psychology, though not the science, is the same as Bruno Mussolini's.[1] But speaking comparatively, mechanical power is more characteristic of our age than of any previous time.

The psychology of the oligarch who depends upon mechanical power is not, as yet, anywhere fully developed. It is, however, an imminent possibility, and quantitatively, though not qualitatively, quite new. It would now be feasible for a technically trained oligarchy, by controlling aeroplanes, navies, power stations, motor transport, and so on, to establish a dictatorship demanding almost no conciliation of subjects. The empire of Laputa was maintained by its power of interposing itself between the sun and a rebellious province; something almost equally drastic would be possible for a union of scientific technologists. They could starve a recalcitrant region, and deprive it of light and heat and electrical power after encouraging dependence on

[1] Diodorus Siculus, Bk. XXV (fragment). See Flaubert's *Salammbo*.

these sources of comfort; they could flood it with poison gas or with bacteria. Resistance would be utterly hopeless. And the men in control, having been trained on mechanism, would view human material as they had learnt to view their own machines, as something unfeeling governed by laws which the manipulator can operate to his advantage. Such a régime would be characterized by a cold inhumanity surpassing anything known in previous tyrannies.

Power over men, not power over matter, is my theme in this book; but it is possible to establish a technicological power over men which is based upon power over matter. Those who have the habit of controlling powerful mechanisms, and through this control have acquired power over human beings, may be expected to have an imaginative outlook towards their subjects which will be completely different from that of men who depend upon persuasion, however dishonest. Most of us have, at some time, wantonly disturbed an ants' nest, and watched with mild amusement the scurrying confusion that resulted. Looking down from the top of a sky-scraper on the traffic of New York, the human beings below cease to seem human, and acquire a faint absurdity. If one were armed, like Jove, with a thunderbolt, there would be a temptation to hurl it into the crowd, from the same motive as in the case of the ants' nest. This was evidently Bruno Mussolini's feeling, as he looked down upon the Abyssinians from his aeroplane. Imagine a scientific government which, from fear of assassination, lives always in aeroplanes, except for occasional descents on to landing stages on the summits of high towers or rafts on the sea. Is it likely that such a government will have any profound concern for the happiness of its subjects? Is it not, on the contrary, practically certain that it will view them, when all goes well, in the impersonal manner in which it views its machines, but that, when anything happens to suggest that after all they are not machines, it will feel the cold rage of men whose axioms are questioned by underlings, and will exterminate resistance in whatever manner involves least trouble?

All this, the reader may think, is mere unnecessary nightmare. I wish I could share this view. Mechanical power, I am convinced, tends to generate a new mentality, which makes it more important than in any former age to find ways of controlling governments. Democracy may have become more difficult owing to technical developments, but it has also become more important. The man who has vast mechanical power at his

LEADERS AND FOLLOWERS 23

command is likely, if uncontrolled, to feel himself a god—not a Christian God of Love, but a pagan Thor or Vulcan.

Leopardi describes what volcanic action has achieved on the slopes of Vesuvius:

> These lands that now are strewn
> With sterilizing cinders, and embossed
> With lava frozen to stone,
> That echoes to the lonely pilgrim's foot;
> Where nestling in the sun the snake lies coiled,
> And where in some cleft
> In cavernous rocks the rabbit hurries home—
> Here once were happy farms,
> And tilth, and yellowing harvests, and the sound
> Of lowing herds; here too
> Gardens and palaces:
> Retreats dear to the leisure
> Of powerful lords; and here were famous towns,
> Which the implacable mountain, thundering forth
> Molten streams from its fiery mouth, destroyed
> With all their habitants. Now all around
> Lies crushed 'neath one vast ruin.[1]

These results can now be achieved by men. They have been achieved at Guernica; perhaps before long they will be achieved where as yet London stands. What good is to be expected of an oligarchy which will have climbed to dominion through such destruction? And if it were Berlin and Rome, not London and Paris, that were destroyed by the thunderbolts of the new gods, could any humanity survive in the destroyers after such a deed?

[1] Questi campi cosparsi
Di ceneri infeconde, e ricoperti
Dall' impietrata lava,
Che sotto i passi al peregrin risona;
Dove s'annida e si contorce al sole
La serpe, e dove al noto
Cavernoso covil torna il coniglio;
Fur liete ville e colti,
E biondeggiàr di spiche, e risonaro
Di muggito d'armenti;
Fur giardini e palagi,
Agli ozi de' potenti
Gradito ospizio, e fur città famose,
Che coi torrenti suoi l' altero monte
Dall' ignea bocca fulminando oppresse
Con gli abitanti insieme. Or tutto intorno
Una ruina involve.

I owe the above translation to the kindness of my friend, Mr R. C. Trevelyan.

24   POWER

Would not those who had human feelings to begin with be driven mad by suppressed pity, and become even worse than those who had no need of suppressing their compassion?

In former days, men sold themselves to the Devil to acquire magical powers. Nowadays they acquire these powers from science, and find themselves compelled to become devils. There is no hope for the world unless power can be tamed, and brought into the service, not of this or that group of fanatical tyrants, but of the whole human race, white and yellow and black, fascist and communist and democrat; for science has made it inevitable that all must live or all must die.

[8]
Panopticism

The following, according to an order published at the end of the seventeenth century, were the measures to be taken when the plague appeared in a town.[1]

First, a strict spatial partitioning: the closing of the town and its outlying districts, a prohibition to leave the town on pain of death, the killing of all stray animals; the division of the town into distinct quarters, each governed by an intendant. Each street is placed under the authority of a syndic, who keeps it under surveillance; if he leaves the street, he will be condemned to death. On the appointed day, everyone is ordered to stay indoors: it is forbidden to leave on pain of death. The syndic himself comes to lock the door of each house from the outside; he takes the key with him and hands it over to the intendant of the quarter; the intendant keeps it until the end of the quarantine. Each family will have made its own provisions; but, for bread and wine, small wooden canals are set up between the street and the interior of the houses, thus allowing each person to receive his ration without communicating with the suppliers and other residents; meat, fish and herbs will be hoisted up into the houses with pulleys and baskets. If it is absolutely necessary to leave the house, it will be done in turn, avoiding any meeting. Only the intendants, syndics and guards will move about the streets and also, between the infected houses, from one corpse to another, the 'crows', who can be left to die: these are 'people of little substance who carry the sick, bury the dead, clean and do many vile and abject offices'. It is a segmented, immobile, frozen space. Each individual is fixed in his place. And, if he moves, he does so at the risk of his life, contagion or punishment.

Inspection functions ceaselessly. The gaze is alert everywhere: 'A considerable body of militia, commanded by good officers and men

Discipline

of substance', guards at the gates, at the town hall and in every quarter to ensure the prompt obedience of the people and the most absolute authority of the magistrates, 'as also to observe all disorder, theft and extortion'. At each of the town gates there will be an observation post; at the end of each street sentinels. Every day, the intendant visits the quarter in his charge, inquires whether the syndics have carried out their tasks, whether the inhabitants have anything to complain of; they 'observe their actions'. Every day, too, the syndic goes into the street for which he is responsible; stops before each house: gets all the inhabitants to appear at the windows (those who live overlooking the courtyard will be allocated a window looking onto the street at which no one but they may show themselves); he calls each of them by name; informs himself as to the state of each and every one of them – 'in which respect the inhabitants will be compelled to speak the truth under pain of death'; if someone does not appear at the window, the syndic must ask why: 'In this way he will find out easily enough whether dead or sick are being concealed.' Everyone locked up in his cage, everyone at his window, answering to his name and showing himself when asked – it is the great review of the living and the dead.

This surveillance is based on a system of permanent registration: reports from the syndics to the intendants, from the intendants to the magistrates or mayor. At the beginning of the 'lock up', the role of each of the inhabitants present in the town is laid down, one by one; this document bears 'the name, age, sex of everyone, notwithstanding his condition': a copy is sent to the intendant of the quarter, another to the office of the town hall, another to enable the syndic to make his daily roll call. Everything that may be observed during the course of the visits – deaths, illnesses, complaints, irregularities – is noted down and transmitted to the intendants and magistrates. The magistrates have complete control over medical treatment; they have appointed a physician in charge; no other practitioner may treat, no apothecary prepare medicine, no confessor visit a sick person without having received from him a written note 'to prevent anyone from concealing and dealing with those sick of the contagion, unknown to the magistrates'. The registration of the pathological must be constantly centralized. The relation of each individual to his

Panopticism

disease and to his death passes through the representatives of power, the registration they make of it, the decisions they take on it.

Five or six days after the beginning of the quarantine, the process of purifying the houses one by one is begun. All the inhabitants are made to leave; in each room 'the furniture and goods' are raised from the ground or suspended from the air; perfume is poured around the room; after carefully sealing the windows, doors and even the keyholes with wax, the perfume is set alight. Finally, the entire house is closed while the perfume is consumed; those who have carried out the work are searched, as they were on entry, 'in the presence of the residents of the house, to see that they did not have something on their persons as they left that they did not have on entering'. Four hours later, the residents are allowed to re-enter their homes.

This enclosed, segmented space, observed at every point, in which the individuals are inserted in a fixed place, in which the slightest movements are supervised, in which all events are recorded, in which an uninterrupted work of writing links the centre and periphery, in which power is exercised without division, according to a continuous hierarchical figure, in which each individual is constantly located, examined and distributed among the living beings, the sick and the dead – all this constitutes a compact model of the disciplinary mechanism. The plague is met by order; its function is to sort out every possible confusion: that of the disease, which is transmitted when bodies are mixed together; that of the evil, which is increased when fear and death overcome prohibitions. It lays down for each individual his place, his body, his disease and his death, his well-being, by means of an omnipresent and omniscient power that subdivides itself in a regular, uninterrupted way even to the ultimate determination of the individual, of what characterizes him, of what belongs to him, of what happens to him. Against the plague, which is a mixture, discipline brings into play its power, which is one of analysis. A whole literary fiction of the festival grew up around the plague: suspended laws, lifted prohibitions, the frenzy of passing time, bodies mingling together without respect, individuals unmasked, abandoning their statutory identity and the figure under which they had been recognized, allowing a quite different truth to appear. But there was also a political dream of the

Discipline

plague, which was exactly its reverse: not the collective festival, but strict divisions; not laws transgressed, but the penetration of regulation into even the smallest details of everyday life through the mediation of the complete hierarchy that assured the capillary functioning of power; not masks that were put on and taken off, but the assignment to each individual of his 'true' name, his 'true' place, his 'true' body, his 'true' disease. The plague as a form, at once real and imaginary, of disorder had as its medical and political correlative discipline. Behind the disciplinary mechanisms can be read the haunting memory of 'contagions', of the plague, of rebellions, crimes, vagabondage, desertions, people who appear and disappear, live and die in disorder.

If it is true that the leper gave rise to rituals of exclusion, which to a certain extent provided the model for and general form of the great Confinement, then the plague gave rise to disciplinary projects. Rather than the massive, binary division between one set of people and another, it called for multiple separations, individualizing distributions, an organization in depth of surveillance and control, an intensification and a ramification of power. The leper was caught up in a practice of rejection, of exile-enclosure; he was left to his doom in a mass among which it was useless to differentiate; those sick of the plague were caught up in a meticulous tactical partitioning in which individual differentiations were the constricting effects of a power that multiplied, articulated and subdivided itself; the great confinement on the one hand; the correct training on the other. The leper and his separation; the plague and its segmentations. The first is marked; the second analysed and distributed. The exile of the leper and the arrest of the plague do not bring with them the same political dream. The first is that of a pure community, the second that of a disciplined society. Two ways of exercising power over men, of controlling their relations, of separating out their dangerous mixtures. The plague-stricken town, traversed throughout with hierarchy, surveillance, observation, writing; the town immobilized by the functioning of an extensive power that bears in a distinct way over all individual bodies – this is the utopia of the perfectly governed city. The plague (envisaged as a possibility at least) is the trial in the course of which one may define ideally the exercise of disciplinary power. In order to make rights and laws function according to pure theory, the jurists place themselves in imagination in the state of nature; in order to see perfect disciplines functioning, rulers dreamt of the state of plague. Underlying disciplinary projects the image of the plague stands for all forms of confusion and disorder; just as the image of the leper, cut off from all human contact, underlies projects of exclusion.

They are different projects, then, but not incompatible ones. We see them coming slowly together, and it is the peculiarity of the nineteenth century that it applied to the space of exclusion of which the leper was the symbolic inhabitant (beggars, vagabonds, madmen and the disorderly formed the real population) the technique of power proper to disciplinary partitioning. Treat 'lepers' as 'plague victims', project the subtle segmentations of discipline onto the confused space of internment, combine it with the methods of analytical distribution proper to power, individualize the excluded, but use procedures of individualization to mark exclusion – this is what was operated regularly by disciplinary power from the beginning of the nineteenth century in the psychiatric asylum, the penitentiary, the reformatory, the approved school and, to some extent, the hospital. Generally speaking, all the authorities exercising individual control function according to a double mode; that of binary division and branding (mad/sane; dangerous/harmless; normal/abnormal); and that of coercive assignment, of differential distribution (who he is; where he must be; how he is to be characterized; how he is to be recognized; how a constant surveillance is to be exercised over him in an individual way, etc.). On the one hand, the lepers are treated as plague victims; the tactics of individualizing disciplines are imposed on the excluded; and, on the other hand, the universality of disciplinary controls makes it possible to brand the 'leper' and to bring into play against him the dualistic mechanisms of exclusion. The constant division between the normal and the abnormal, to which every individual is subjected, brings us back to our own time, by applying the binary branding and exile of the leper to quite different objects; the existence of a whole set of techniques and institutions for measuring, supervising and correcting the abnormal brings into play the disciplinary mechanisms to which the fear of the plague gave rise. All the mechanisms of power which, even today, are disposed around the abnormal individual, to brand him and to alter

Discipline

him, are composed of those two forms from which they distantly derive.

Bentham's *Panopticon* is the architectural figure of this composition. We know the principle on which it was based: at the periphery, an annular building; at the centre, a tower; this tower is pierced with wide windows that open onto the inner side of the ring; the peripheric building is divided into cells, each of which extends the whole width of the building; they have two windows, one on the inside, corresponding to the windows of the tower; the other, on the outside, allows the light to cross the cell from one end to the other. All that is needed, then, is to place a supervisor in a central tower and to shut up in each cell a madman, a patient, a condemned man, a worker or a schoolboy. By the effect of backlighting, one can observe from the tower, standing out precisely against the light, the small captive shadows in the cells of the periphery. They are like so many cages, so many small theatres, in which each actor is alone, perfectly individualized and constantly visible. The panoptic mechanism arranges spatial unities that make it possible to see constantly and to recognize immediately. In short, it reverses the principle of the dungeon; or rather of its three functions – to enclose, to deprive of light and to hide – it preserves only the first and eliminates the other two. Full lighting and the eye of a supervisor capture better than darkness, which ultimately protected. Visibility is a trap.

To begin with, this made it possible – as a negative effect – to avoid those compact, swarming, howling masses that were to be found in places of confinement, those painted by Goya or described by Howard. Each individual, in his place, is securely confined to a cell from which he is seen from the front by the supervisor; but the side walls prevent him from coming into contact with his companions. He is seen, but he does not see; he is the object of information, never a subject in communication. The arrangement of his room, opposite the central tower, imposes on him an axial visibility; but the divisions of the ring, those separated cells, imply a lateral invisibility. And this invisibility is a guarantee of order. If the inmates are convicts, there is no danger of a plot, an attempt at collective escape, the planning of new crimes for the future, bad reciprocal influences; if they are patients, there is no danger of

Panopticism

contagion; if they are madmen there is no risk of their committing violence upon one another; if they are schoolchildren, there is no copying, no noise, no chatter, no waste of time; if they are workers, there are no disorders, no theft, no coalitions, none of those distractions that slow down the rate of work, make it less perfect or cause accidents. The crowd, a compact mass, a locus of multiple exchanges, individualities merging together, a collective effect, is abolished and replaced by a collection of separated individualities. From the point of view of the guardian, it is replaced by a multiplicity that can be numbered and supervised; from the point of view of the inmates, by a sequestered and observed solitude (Bentham, 60–64).

Hence the major effect of the Panopticon: to induce in the inmate a state of conscious and permanent visibility that assures the automatic functioning of power. So to arrange things that the surveillance is permanent in its effects, even if it is discontinuous in its action; that the perfection of power should tend to render its actual exercise unnecessary; that this architectural apparatus should be a machine for creating and sustaining a power relation independent of the person who exercises it; in short, that the inmates should be caught up in a power situation of which they are themselves the bearers. To achieve this, it is at once too much and too little that the prisoner should be constantly observed by an inspector: too little, for what matters is that he knows himself to be observed; too much, because he has no need in fact of being so. In view of this, Bentham laid down the principle that power should be visible and unverifiable. Visible: the inmate will constantly have before his eyes the tall outline of the central tower from which he is spied upon. Unverifiable: the inmate must never know whether he is being looked at at any one moment; but he must be sure that he may always be so. In order to make the presence or absence of the inspector unverifiable, so that the prisoners, in their cells, cannot even see a shadow, Bentham envisaged not only venetian blinds on the windows of the central observation hall, but, on the inside, partitions that intersected the hall at right angles and, in order to pass from one quarter to the other, not doors but zig-zag openings; for the slightest noise, a gleam of light, a brightness in a half-opened door would betray the presence of the guardian.[2] The Panopticon is a machine for dissociating the see/being seen dyad: in the peripheric ring, one is totally seen, without ever seeing; in the central tower, one sees everything without ever being seen.[3]

It is an important mechanism, for it automatizes and disindividualizes power. Power has its principle not so much in a person as in a certain concerted distribution of bodies, surfaces, lights, gazes; in an arrangement whose internal mechanisms produce the relation in which individuals are caught up. The ceremonies, the rituals, the marks by which the sovereign's surplus power was manifested are useless. There is a machinery that assures dissymmetry, disequilibrium, difference. Consequently, it does not matter who exercises power. Any individual, taken almost at random, can operate the machine: in the absence of the director, his family, his friends, his visitors, even his servants (Bentham, 45). Similarly, it does not matter what motive animates him: the curiosity of the indiscreet, the malice of a child, the thirst for knowledge of a philosopher who wishes to visit this museum of human nature, or the perversity of those who take pleasure in spying and punishing. The more numerous those anonymous and temporary observers are, the greater the risk for the inmate of being surprised and the greater his anxious awareness of being observed. The Panopticon is a marvellous machine which, whatever use one may wish to put it to, produces homogeneous effects of power.

A real subjection is born mechanically from a fictitious relation. So it is not necessary to use force to constrain the convict to good behaviour, the madman to calm, the worker to work, the schoolboy to application, the patient to the observation of the regulations. Bentham was surprised that panoptic institutions could be so light: there were no more bars, no more chains, no more heavy locks; all that was needed was that the separations should be clear and the openings well arranged. The heaviness of the old 'houses of security', with their fortress-like architecture, could be replaced by the simple, economic geometry of a 'house of certainty'. The efficiency of power, its constraining force have, in a sense, passed over to the other side – to the side of its surface of application. He who is subjected to a field of visibility, and who knows it, assumes responsibility for the constraints of power; he makes them play spontaneously upon himself; he inscribes in himself the power relation in which he simultaneously plays both roles; he becomes the principle of his own subjection. By this very fact, the external power may throw off its physical weight; it tends to the non-corporal; and, the more it approaches this limit, the more constant, profound and permanent are its effects: it is a perpetual victory that avoids any physical confrontation and which is always decided in advance.

Bentham does not say whether he was inspired, in his project, by Le Vaux's menagerie at Versailles: the first menagerie in which the different elements are not, as they traditionally were, distributed in a park (Loisel, 104–7). At the centre was an octagonal pavilion which, on the first floor, consisted of only a single room, the king's *salon*; on every side large windows looked out onto seven cages (the eighth side was reserved for the entrance), containing different species of animals. By Bentham's time, this menagerie had disappeared. But one finds in the programme of the Panopticon a similar concern with individualizing observation, with characterization and classification, with the analytical arrangement of space. The Panopticon is a royal menagerie; the animal is replaced by man, individual distribution by specific grouping and the king by the machinery of a furtive power. With this exception, the Panopticon also does the work of a naturalist. It makes it possible to draw up differences: among patients, to observe the symptoms of each individual, without the proximity of beds, the circulation of miasmas, the effects of contagion confusing the clinical tables; among schoolchildren, it makes it possible to observe performances (without there being any imitation or copying), to map aptitudes, to assess characters, to draw up rigorous classifications and, in relation to normal development, to distinguish 'laziness and stubbornness' from 'incurable imbecility'; among workers, it makes it possible to note the aptitudes of each worker, compare the time he takes to perform a task, and if they are paid by the day, to calculate their wages (Bentham, 60–64).

So much for the question of observation. But the Panopticon was also a laboratory; it could be used as a machine to carry out experiments, to alter behaviour, to train or correct individuals. To experiment with medicines and monitor their effects. To try out different punishments on prisoners, according to their crimes and character, and to seek the most effective ones. To teach different techniques

Discipline

simultaneously to the workers, to decide which is the best. To try out pedagogical experiments – and in particular to take up once again the well-debated problem of secluded education, by using orphans. One would see what would happen when, in their sixteenth or eighteenth year, they were presented with other boys or girls; one could verify whether, as Helvetius thought, anyone could learn anything; one would follow 'the genealogy of every observable idea'; one could bring up different children according to different systems of thought, making certain children believe that two and two do not make four or that the moon is a cheese, then put them together when they are twenty or twenty-five years old; one would then have discussions that would be worth a great deal more than the sermons or lectures on which so much money is spent; one would have at least an opportunity of making discoveries in the domain of metaphysics. The Panopticon is a privileged place for experiments on men, and for analysing with complete certainty the transformations that may be obtained from them. The Panopticon may even provide an apparatus for supervising its own mechanisms. In this central tower, the director may spy on all the employees that he has under his orders: nurses, doctors, foremen, teachers, warders; he will be able to judge them continuously, alter their behaviour, impose upon them the methods he thinks best; and it will even be possible to observe the director himself. An inspector arriving unexpectedly at the centre of the Panopticon will be able to judge at a glance, without anything being concealed from him, how the entire establishment is functioning. And, in any case, enclosed as he is in the middle of this architectural mechanism, is not the director's own fate entirely bound up with it? The incompetent physician who has allowed contagion to spread, the incompetent prison governor or workshop manager will be the first victims of an epidemic or a revolt. ' "By every tie I could devise", said the master of the Panopticon, "my own fate had been bound up by me with theirs" ' (Bentham, 177). The Panopticon functions as a kind of laboratory of power. Thanks to its mechanisms of observation, it gains in efficiency and in the ability to penetrate into men's behaviour; knowledge follows the advances of power, discovering new objects of knowledge over all the surfaces on which power is exercised.

Panopticism

The plague-stricken town, the panoptic establishment – the differences are important. They mark, at a distance of a century and a half, the transformations of the disciplinary programme. In the first case, there is an exceptional situation: against an extraordinary evil, power is mobilized; it makes itself everywhere present and visible; it invents new mechanisms; it separates, it immobilizes, it partitions; it constructs for a time what is both a counter-city and the perfect society; it imposes an ideal functioning, but one that is reduced, in the final analysis, like the evil that it combats, to a simple dualism of life and death: that which moves brings death, and one kills that which moves. The Panopticon, on the other hand, must be understood as a generalizable model of functioning; a way of defining power relations in terms of the everyday life of men. No doubt Bentham presents it as a particular institution, closed in upon itself. Utopias, perfectly closed in upon themselves, are common enough. As opposed to the ruined prisons, littered with mechanisms of torture, to be seen in Piranese's engravings, the Panopticon presents a cruel, ingenious cage. The fact that it should have given rise, even in our own time, to so many variations, projected or realized, is evidence of the imaginary intensity that it has possessed for almost two hundred years. But the Panopticon must not be understood as a dream building: it is the diagram of a mechanism of power reduced to its ideal form; its functioning, abstracted from any obstacle, resistance or friction, must be represented as a pure architectural and optical system: it is in fact a figure of political technology that may and must be detached from any specific use.

It is polyvalent in its applications; it serves to reform prisoners, but also to treat patients, to instruct schoolchildren, to confine the insane, to supervise workers, to put beggars and idlers to work. It is a type of location of bodies in space, of distribution of individuals in relation to one another, of hierarchical organization, of disposition of centres and channels of power, of definition of the instruments and modes of intervention of power, which can be implemented in hospitals, workshops, schools, prisons. Whenever one is dealing with a multiplicity of individuals on whom a task or a particular form of behaviour must be imposed, the panoptic schema may be used. It is – necessary modifications apart – applicable 'to all establishments whatsoever, in which, within a space not too large

Discipline

to be covered or commanded by buildings, a number of persons are meant to be kept under inspection' (Bentham, 40; although Bentham takes the penitentiary house as his prime example, it is because it has many different functions to fulfil – safe custody, confinement, solitude, forced labour and instruction).

In each of its applications, it makes it possible to perfect the exercise of power. It does this in several ways: because it can reduce the number of those who exercise it, while increasing the number of those on whom it is exercised. Because it is possible to intervene at any moment and because the constant pressure acts even before the offences, mistakes or crimes have been committed. Because, in these conditions, its strength is that it never intervenes, it is exercised spontaneously and without noise, it constitutes a mechanism whose effects follow from one another. Because, without any physical instrument other than architecture and geometry, it acts directly on individuals; it gives 'power of mind over mind'. The panoptic schema makes any apparatus of power more intense: it assures its economy (in material, in personnel, in time); it assures its efficacy by its preventative character, its continuous functioning and its automatic mechanisms. It is a way of obtaining from power 'in hitherto unexampled quantity', 'a great and new instrument of government . . .; its great excellence consists in the great strength it is capable of giving to *any* institution it may be thought proper to apply it to' (Bentham, 66).

It's a case of 'it's easy once you've thought of it' in the political sphere. It can in fact be integrated into any function (education, medical treatment, production, punishment); it can increase the effect of this function, by being linked closely with it; it can constitute a mixed mechanism in which relations of power (and of knowledge) may be precisely adjusted, in the smallest detail, to the processes that are to be supervised; it can establish a direct proportion between 'surplus power' and 'surplus production'. In short, it arranges things in such a way that the exercise of power is not added on from the outside, like a rigid, heavy constraint, to the functions it invests, but is so subtly present in them as to increase their efficiency by itself increasing its own points of contact. The panoptic mechanism is not simply a hinge, a point of exchange between a mechanism of power and a function; it is a way of making

Panopticism

power relations function in a function, and of making a function function through these power relations. Bentham's Preface to *Panopticon* opens with a list of the benefits to be obtained from his 'inspection-house': '*Morals reformed – health preserved – industry invigorated – instruction diffused – public burthens lightened* – Economy seated, as it were, upon a rock – the gordian knot of the Poor-Laws not cut, but untied – all by a simple idea in architecture!' (Bentham, 39).

Furthermore, the arrangement of this machine is such that its enclosed nature does not preclude a permanent presence from the outside: we have seen that anyone may come and exercise in the central tower the functions of surveillance, and that, this being the case, he can gain a clear idea of the way in which the surveillance is practised. In fact, any panoptic institution, even if it is as rigorously closed as a penitentiary, may without difficulty be subjected to such irregular and constant inspections: and not only by the appointed inspectors, but also by the public; any member of society will have the right to come and see with his own eyes how the schools, hospitals, factories, prisons function. There is no risk, therefore, that the increase of power created by the panoptic machine may degenerate into tyranny; the disciplinary mechanism will be democratically controlled, since it will be constantly accessible 'to the great tribunal committee of the world'.[4] This Panopticon, subtly arranged so that an observer may observe, at a glance, so many different individuals, also enables everyone to come and observe any of the observers. The seeing machine was once a sort of dark room into which individuals spied; it has become a transparent building in which the exercise of power may be supervised by society as a whole.

The panoptic schema, without disappearing as such or losing any of its properties, was destined to spread throughout the social body; its vocation was to become a generalized function. The plague-stricken town provided an exceptional disciplinary model: perfect, but absolutely violent; to the disease that brought death, power opposed its perpetual threat of death; life inside it was reduced to its simplest expression; it was, against the power of death, the meticulous exercise of the right of the sword. The Panopticon, on the other hand, has a role of amplification; although it arranges power, although it is intended to make it more economic and more effective,

Discipline

it does so not for power itself, nor for the immediate salvation of a threatened society: its aim is to strengthen the social forces – to increase production, to develop the economy, spread education, raise the level of public morality; to increase and multiply.

How is power to be strengthened in such a way that, far from impeding progress, far from weighing upon it with its rules and regulations, it actually facilitates such progress? What intensificator of power will be able at the same time to be a multiplicator of production? How will power, by increasing its forces, be able to increase those of society instead of confiscating them or impeding them? The Panopticon's solution to this problem is that the productive increase of power can be assured only if, on the one hand, it can be exercised continuously in the very foundations of society, in the subtlest possible way, and if, on the other hand, it functions outside these sudden, violent, discontinuous forms that are bound up with the exercise of sovereignty. The body of the king, with its strange material and physical presence, with the force that he himself deploys or transmits to some few others, is at the opposite extreme of this new physics of power represented by panopticism; the domain of panopticism is, on the contrary, that whole lower region, that region of irregular bodies, with their details, their multiple movements, their heterogeneous forces, their spatial relations; what are required are mechanisms that analyse distributions, gaps, series, combinations, and which use instruments that render visible, record, differentiate and compare: a physics of a relational and multiple power, which has its maximum intensity not in the person of the king, but in the bodies that can be individualized by these relations. At the theoretical level, Bentham defines another way of analysing the social body and the power relations that traverse it; in terms of practice, he defines a procedure of subordination of bodies and forces that must increase the utility of power while practising the economy of the prince. Panopticism is the general principle of a new 'political anatomy' whose object and end are not the relations of sovereignty but the relations of discipline.

The celebrated, transparent, circular cage, with its high tower, powerful and knowing, may have been for Bentham a project of a perfect disciplinary institution; but he also set out to show how one may 'unlock' the disciplines and get them to function in a diffused,

Panopticism

multiple, polyvalent way throughout the whole social body. These disciplines, which the classical age had elaborated in specific, relatively enclosed places – barracks, schools, workshops – and whose total implementation had been imagined only at the limited and temporary scale of a plague-stricken town, Bentham dreamt of transforming into a network of mechanisms that would be everywhere and always alert, running through society without interruption in space or in time. The panoptic arrangement provides the formula for this generalization. It programmes, at the level of an elementary and easily transferable mechanism, the basic functioning of a society penetrated through and through with disciplinary mechanisms.

Notes

3. *Panopticism*

1. Archives militaires de Vincennes, A 1,516 91 sc. Pièce. This regulation is broadly similar to a whole series of others that date from the same period and earlier.
2. In the *Postscript to the Panopticon*, 1791, Bentham adds dark inspection galleries painted in black around the inspector's lodge, each making it possible to observe two storeys of cells.
3. In his first version of the Panopticon, Bentham had also imagined an acoustic surveillance, operated by means of pipes leading from the cells to the central tower. In the *Postscript* he abandoned the idea, perhaps because he could not introduce into it the principle of dis-symmetry and prevent the prisoners from hearing the inspector as well as the inspector hearing them. Julius tried to develop a system of dis-symmetrical listening (Julius, 18).
4. Imagining this continuous flow of visitors entering the central tower by an underground passage and then observing the circular landscape of the Panopticon, was Bentham aware of the Panoramas that Barker was constructing at exactly the same period (the first seems to have dated from 1787) and in which the visitors, occupying the central place, saw unfolding around them a landscape, a city or a battle. The visitors occupied exactly the place of the sovereign gaze.

References

Bentham, J., *Works*, ed. Bowring, IV, 1843.
Julius, N. H., *Leçons sur les prisons*, I, 1831 (Fr. trans).
Loisel, G., *Histoire des ménageries*, II, 1912.
Servan, J., *Le Soldat citoyen*, 1780.

[9]

Using Power/Fighting Power: The Polity

JANE MANSBRIDGE

Coercion and Persuasion

In the last two decades, theorists of deliberative democracy have stressed the democratic potential for reasoned persuasion to the almost complete exclusion of the independently justifiable arguments for power as coercion in democratic life. Yet democracies must have their coercive as well as their deliberative moments.

Against deliberative theorists who associate the coercion in democracy with "violence" and make that coercion at best tangential to the democratic process, this essay argues that coercion must play a large, valuable, and relatively legitimate role in almost any democracy that functions well. But against those who assume the full legitimacy of coercion in conditions of lasting disagreement, this essay argues that any justification for coercion will necessarily be incomplete. In conditions of lasting disagreement there is no unquestionably fair procedure for producing a decision to coerce. Moreover, much coercion in existing democracies will be far from fair, and policies requiring coercion will often have features that are far from just.

Recognizing the need for coercion, and recognizing too that no coercion can be either incontestably fair or predictably just, democracies must find ways of fighting, while they use it, the very coercion that they need.

Democracies usually fight their own coercive power by girding that power about with the institutional safeguards of individual rights, free speech and association, and other features of the "rule of law," sometimes including constitutional requirements that every policy have at least a nominal "public purpose." Along with these safeguards, democracies need political parties, interest groups, and other traditional institutions that can serve as instruments of formal opposition. Less obviously, this essay argues that democracies also

I would like to thank Joshua Cohen and Thomas McCarthy for comments at and after the conference on "Democracy and Difference" at Yale University, and Nancy Fraser, Jürgen Habermas, Bonnie Honig, David Kahane, Cass Sunstein, Iris Young, and participants in a seminar at the London School of Economics for helpful comments and criticisms on an earlier draft of this essay.

need to foster and value informal deliberative enclaves of resistance in which those who lose in each coercive move can rework their ideas and their strategies, gathering their forces and deciding in a more protected space in what way or whether to continue the battle.

Why Democracies Need Coercion

By "power" in this essay I mean coercion. In other contexts I would define power more broadly as "the actual or potential causal relation between the interests of an actor or set of actors and the outcome itself." This broad definition usefully focuses on cause; it is neutral regarding intent; it includes anticipated reactions; and, unlike the narrower meaning of power I will adopt here, it covers what Mary Parker Follett, William Connolly, and many feminists like to call "power to" or "power with" as well as "power over."[1]

In contrast to this broader definition, I will use the word "power" in this essay, interchangeably with "coercion," to mean an actual or potential causal relation between the interests of an actor or set of actors and an outcome, in which cause operates specifically through the use of force or the threat of sanction.[2]

Democracies need coercion primarily to take action without overly privileging the status quo. When individual interests[3] come in what gives every indication of being an irreconcilable conflict, a democratic polity must either reinforce the status quo by taking no action or, by taking action, force or threaten (coerce) some of its citizens into situations or actions not in their interests. Majority rule is one standard mechanism for achieving a relatively fair form of democratic coercion.

Democracies can undoubtedly settle some or many of their conflicts through deliberation. Deliberation can help transform interests and reveal previously unrealized areas of agreement. It can also sharpen participants' understandings of their conflicts. In a good democracy, large or small, the deliberative arena should ideally be equally open to all, and power—in the sense of the threat of sanction or the use of force—should not interfere with the impact of the better argument.

At some point and on some issues, however, deliberation will not lead to agreement. Good deliberation will have opened areas of agreement and will have clarified the remaining areas of conflict. The participants will have come to understand their interests, including their conflicting interests, better than before deliberation. But material interests, and interests in one's deepest values, cannot always be reconciled with the interests, material and ideal, of others. At this point, when conflict remains after good deliberation, a democracy has two choices—to remain at the status quo or to act, by coercing some to go along with others.

When a new highway destroys an old neighborhood or when a government takes a symbolic stand that some citizens find deeply abhorrent, the coercion inherent in democratic decision lets some citizens or their representatives use force or the threat of sanction to cause outcomes that other citizens oppose. Members of the losing group will henceforth, for example, unwillingly live across a noisy highway from their past neighbors or have to dissociate themselves from stands that others attribute to them as members of that polity. In the quintessential example of enforced taxation, a strong welfare state requires coercion to collect taxes from those who are unalterably opposed to extensive social welfare policies, both in principle and as a result of pursuing their own material interests.

Even regulations that succeed primarily because citizens cooperate freely from public-spirited motivation usually need some coercion around the edges to keep the occasional defector from turning the majority of cooperators into suckers.[4] Democracies need to use coercion not only for the reasons of security that Thomas Hobbes recognized and that finally even Robert Nozick, after the most extraordinary twists and turns, recognized as well, but also for the hundreds of thousands of occasions, in a complex, interdependent society, in which collective action requires some degree of coercion to attain even unanimously approved collective ends. And because in a large society with a number of conflicting interests the requirement of unanimity will give almost total power to those who benefit from the status quo, democracies committed to some rough approximation to equal power will require some forms of nonunanimously approved coercion to attain ends that most of their citizens approve.

Coming to Grips with Coercion

Many of the best contemporary political theorists have not faced squarely the role of conflicting interests, and consequently of coercion, in any democratic polity. Thinkers as diverse as Hannah Arendt, Sheldon Wolin, Michael Walzer, and Jürgen Habermas have conceived of democracy in ways that extol the role of democratic deliberation in discovering, creating, and maintaining commonality, while implicitly or explicitly denigrating the role of democratic coercion when interests conflict.

Hannah Arendt is the least subtle and, I believe, the most misguided of these deliberative theorists. Arendt denounced as illegitimate, calling it "violence," the kind of coercion I consider a critical tool of democracy. She contrasted this coercion, or "violence," of which she disapproved, to what she approvingly called "power," defined to mean the power of a united people moving to achieve common ends.[5]

Arendt joined her denunciation of coercion as violence to an insistence that private and material interests should not "invade the public domain."[6] In her view, a voter who uses public coercion (through pressure groups, for example) "out of concern with his private life and well-being" acts as a "blackmailer," not a member of the public (273).

Against Arendt, I contend that concerns with one's private life and well-being, including one's "interest and welfare," are appropriate, important, and valuable material for political deliberation and decision (see n. 36). Such concerns do not constitute the only material for political deliberation and decision. But they have a legitimate place in politics and public life. When such concerns conflict irreconcilably, as when values conflict irreconcilably, and when inaction would unfairly sustain the status quo, democracies need the kind of coercion by which, in Arendt's derogatory phrase, voters "force their representatives to execute their wishes at the expense of other groups of voters" (273). By simply defining any such coercion as violence and ruling it out of the democratic process, Arendt forestalls democratic attempts both to make the coercion as legitimate as possible and, after accepting its necessity, to find ways of containing, restricting and fighting it at the very moment of using it.

The other deliberative theorists to whom I now turn have positions less strong than Arendt's and more subtle. These positions are also sometimes less well worked out, in part because the theorists were not centrally concerned with the problems I address in this essay. With these theorists more than with Arendt I have primarily a disagreement in emphasis.

In *Politics and Vision*, Sheldon Wolin defined the "political" along Arendtian lines as "uniquely concerned with what is 'common' to the whole community."[7] Like Arendt, Wolin also considered material interests "essentially private," "radically individual," and "fundamentally unsharable" (277). But Wolin stopped short of excluding material interests from the public domain. Rather, he objected reasonably to placing these interests "at the center of the political association" (277) and making them "supreme" (280). For Wolin, interests were "*least* capable of representation at the public level" (277, my emphasis), not, as for Arendt, *incapable* of such representation.

Wolin wanted to integrate "politics" (his word for "the struggle for competitive advantage" [42, 10]) with the "political," defined by commonality. His vision of integration takes conflict and antagonism as "the raw material for creating areas of agreement, or, if this fails, to make it possible for competing forces to compromise." It confines "imposition . . . to those situations where no other alternative exists" (43).[8] The rest of the book fleshes out this unexceptionable but relatively empty formulation by never portraying "imposition," or coercion, as a valued component of democracy.

A similar normative abhorrence of coercion informs Wolin's understanding of "compromise," which fails to capture the ways that more and less legitimate uses of coercive power, as well as considerations of principle and the common good, lie behind most viable political compromises. When, say, environmentalists compromise with the proponents of growth on a particular policy, the result derives not only from reasoning together on the merits of their various arguments regarding the common good but also from weighing implicitly or explicitly the number of votes each group can muster in the next election, the relative size of their advertising budgets, the efficiency of their relative political organizations, the harm each can do the other in the media, the alliances each has with other groups, and the degree to which each can appeal to different sectors in the ownership of capital. These considerations are not all illegitimate in a normative understanding of democracy. Some, such as the number of votes each can muster in the next election, have strong claims to democratic legitimacy. By taking an overall stance that refuses normative legitimacy to any of these coercion-related contributions to a compromise, we keep ourselves from asking to what degree each factor could be legitimate, and what criteria for legitimacy we might bring to bear in each case. We also keep ourselves from asking what safeguards we need to institute against the coercion involved in and emanating from such compromises.

Although further removed than Wolin from the Arendtian tradition, Michael Walzer also contends that in democracy, "what counts is argument among the citizens. Democracy puts a premium on speech, persuasion, rhetorical skill. Ideally, the citizen who makes the most persuasive argument— that is the argument that actually persuades the largest number of citizens— gets his way. But he can't use force."[9] Through the deft move of defining "force" as "power used in violation of its social meaning" (282), Walzer simply stipulates its illegitimacy. The reader takes, however, the message that force as coercion—and power as coercion—has no valued role in Walzer's understanding of democracy.

Walzer's emphasis on persuasion leaves him, for example, ill at ease with the vote. He wants to conclude that "power 'belongs to' persuasiveness,"[10] and not to coercive institutions like the vote. Asking rhetorically, "But isn't the vote itself a kind of power?" he hedges: "A kind of power perhaps. . . . But choices . . . still depend not on single votes but on the accumulation of votes—hence on influence, persuasion, pressure, bargaining, organization, and so on" (305–6). Walzer never considers the normative justifications for deciding through the coercive powers of a vote alone when persuasion has been exhausted.

Two decades ago Jürgen Habermas addressed some of these issues in a subtle critique and appreciation of Hannah Arendt.[11] In this essay, Habermas first welcomed Arendt's break with Max Weber and others who defined power only in terms of the "purposefully rational agent, who is exclusively interested in the success of his action" (73), that is, an agent who operates in the spheres of "strategic" rather than "communicative" action. He then criticized Arendt for giving strategic action no role at all in the "realm of the political" (112).[12] Yet within this criticism Habermas still deliberately withheld the word "legitimate" from strategic action, with its concern for acquiring and exercising political power. For Habermas, the only "legitimate power arises among those who form common convictions in communication free from coercion" (183). These "common convictions" (Habermas's reformulation of Arendt's "power") *create* the legitimate power for which strategic actors then *compete*. Competition among strategic actors can be "normalized" (182) and "institutionalized" (183), but it can never become "legitimate power."[13]

One must agree with Habermas that common convictions formed through mutual communication differ dramatically from decisions arrived at through mutual coercion. Even democratic coercion can never be fully legitimate. Only genuine agreement, arrived at in conditions free from coercion, can produce fully legitimate outcomes. I differ with him, however, in one point of emphasis and one of substance. I would emphasize that in the real world—as Foucault reminds us and Habermas grants—there are no conditions free from the threat of sanction or use of force. The ideal of coercion-free deliberation resembles many important and useful democratic ideals in being impossible to achieve fully, although possible to approach. If, as I believe, the structure of language and culture makes it impossible fully to eliminate "illusionary" convictions, produced by the capacity of some to keep others from perceiving their interests (186, 183),[14] then in Habermas's own terms *fully* legitimate power, arrived at through deliberation, is a practical impossibility. Polities can and do differ in the degree to which they approach that ideal. My substantive disagreement comes in the next section, where I argue that, much like deliberative agreement, coercion and competition among strategic actors can also be more or less legitimate.

How the Coercion that Democracies Need Can Be Made Relatively Legitimate

Democratic theorists have tried to legitimate coercion through one or more of the following lines of thought.

First, we have tried to legitimate coercion explicitly or implicitly through direct or indirect hypothetical consent. For a few coordination problems, such as devising rules of the road, or even collective action problems, such as ensuring clean air, we could imagine that every sane citizen would agree directly to be coerced into doing his or her part in these matters so long as every other citizen were subjected to a similar coercion. We could even hypothesize that every sane citizen would agree to some decision-rule, such as majority rule within appropriate limiting conditions, to settle most other disagreements, especially if the hypothesized alternative were a war of all against all. This "indirect" consent would legitimate all forms of coercion emanating from the agreed-on rule. The logic of consent, however, produces a dubious and indeterminate legitimacy, because no citizen ever gives actual consent to every decision, and hypothetical consent is, at the least, always open to contest.

In a more subtle version of this argument, coercion might be legitimated to the degree that it derived from procedures to which all affected would agree in conditions of free, equal, and unconstrained deliberation. This criterion for legitimation from hypothetical deliberation is subject to some of the same problems as the other, however, for citizens are likely to disagree strongly, on the basis of irreconcilably opposed value commitments, about the procedures to which they would agree in such conditions.[15]

Second, we might legitimate coercion primarily or only through an appeal to substantive justice. To argue for the legitimacy of the coercion necessary to establish private property rights, for example, one would first judge the justice of the desired end by some substantive standard (i.e., one would argue that the institution of private property rights benefits the greatest number, deviates from equality only in benefiting the least advantaged, or even conforms to the criteria for justice embedded in a local situation or community). One would then judge how necessary coercion was as a means to accomplishing that just end. In this approach, anyone seeking to use coercion would have to identify some plausible conception of the right or the good by which to defend what they propose. In this approach only substantively just outcomes, including those that derive from particular stands on the good and the right (e.g., antidiscrimination laws, endangered species acts, and antismoking requirements), would legitimate the coercion required to achieve them.[16] Serious disagreements over what is substantively just make this criterion for legitimating coercion also, at the least, always open to contest.

Finally, theorists in what I have called the "adversary" tradition have taken an independent tack, approaching democracy as if coercion were legitimated only, or primarily, through fair aggregative, rather than deliberative, procedures.[17] Fair aggregation in this tradition requires some version of one person/one vote, or in more radical formulations the equal power of each individual in the decision. In this tradition some theorists have even defined democracy as "equal power,"[18] or more cautiously, "the equal opportunity to exercise power."[19] Theorists as different as Carole Pateman and Robert Dahl have made equal power in decisions a central ingredient of the ideal of democracy.[20]

Even in the adversary tradition most theorists consider coercion legitimate only if it is exercised in the context of certain limiting conditions, such as the protection of individual rights, the "rule of law," and perhaps the constitutional requirement of some formal "public purpose" for the decision.[21] Although these limiting conditions figure prominently in the ways democracies must fight the very coercion that they use, they only mitigate, rather than eradicate, the necessary and valuable imposition of democratic coercion.

The legitimacy of one person/one vote, or more radically equal power, in the adversary tradition does not derive from the medieval conclusion that a majority is, all things equal, more likely to be substantively right than a minority.[22] Rather, in a rationale that has developed slowly since the seventeenth century, the legitimacy of majority rule (and of equal power in decisions more generally) derives, independently of any postulated outcome of uncoerced communication, from two sources.

First, when conflicting interests erode the bases for any standard other than equality, equality becomes the only mutually acceptable default position. This essentially negative argument, which Isaiah Berlin makes in general terms, is particularly applicable to majority rule. Berlin points out that all norms or rules (without which there can be no society) have a structure such that within the categories created by the rule all individuals are treated equally. This is the meaning of a rule. Members of any society, asked to justify a rule, give reasons for including or excluding individuals from the relevant categories. When no good reason for a distinction can be given, the default presumption is that individuals will be treated equally. Following this logic, struggles over the franchise have taken the form of struggles over reasons for exclusion. Whenever the underlying rationale for traditional exclusions erodes, more previously excluded individuals gain the vote.[23]

Second, when a political culture includes a value of respect for the equal moral worth of each individual, that respect provides a positive standard to legitimate the equal vote. Features of the Judeo-Christian tradition, as well as features of the cultures of other societies, help to make the equal vote—or, more radically, equal power—a public mark of equal worth.

These two reasons underlie the decision of democratic theorists in the adversary tradition to legitimate coercion by, within limiting conditions, giving participants equal power in the decision to coerce whenever fundamental conflicts of material interests or values prevent agreement.[24]

The problem with this criterion is that even if equal power were fully to legitimate the coercion democracies must use, no democratic decision-rule could guarantee that equal power. No formula—majority rule or any other—can produce a system in which, even in theory, each can equally coerce and be coerced in turn.

The ideal is theoretically unreachable because we hold at least three opposed, but equally valid, conceptions of what it means to have equal power. One definition is that one's resources for coercion—one's weapons—be equal to those of any other individual (as in the example of one person/one vote). Another is that, as a member of a group, one succeed in getting the outcome one prefers in proportion to the number of allies one has on the issue (proportional outcomes). A third is that one succeed in getting the outcome one prefers as often as any other individual (equal satisfaction). Absent perfectly equal cross-cutting cleavages, these goals are not compatible. When issues do not arise such that each individual wins exactly as often as every other, equally weighted votes will lead to those with more allies coercing others more often than those with fewer allies.[25]

In addition, scholars since the late eighteenth century have demonstrated that when preferences are not single-peaked, majority rule can produce several equally legitimate but competing outcomes.[26]

For these reasons among others, democratic theorists who have studied the issue in some depth have concluded that democratic coercion can be legitimated only by what Charles Beitz calls "complex proceduralism," deriving from "the irreducible plurality of substantive interests associated with the idea of political fairness."[27] Although equal resources with majority rule often produces the best contender for a procedurally fair decision rule, "theoretical reasoning evidently cannot be made to yield a firm conclusion that majority rule is necessarily superior or inferior to some alternatives to it."[28] The same is true for any other attempt to count individuals equally in a decision.

More important than these theoretical considerations is the raw fact that no large democracy has ever produced a political system in which every member had anything even approximating equal coercive resources, the equal opportunity to exercise coercion, or the experience of exercising coercion equally with all other members of the polity. All existing nation-states are so far from actual political equality as to dwarf the technical problems of capturing in any decision-rule the conflicting implicit mandates of democratic theory.

Even the most internally democratic small collectives cannot in fact achieve equality of power in their decisions.[29] If coercion is legitimated only by equal power in the decision to coerce, and if no real democracy can achieve equal power, then no real democracy—especially no real large-scale democracy—can ever fully justify the coercion it exercises.

In short, none of the criteria for legitimating coercion—whether based on assessments of hypothetical consent, the substantive justice of outcomes, the freedom from coercion or closeness to agreement of the deliberative process that resulted in a decision to coerce, or the equal power that participants exercise in the decision process—can produce in cases of ongoing disagreement an incontestably legitimate result. Nor has any contemporary standard for determining the substantive justice of an outcome been able to prevail by appealing to the pure truth of its premises or the logic of its derivation. Whatever policy an actual democracy adopts on any contested subject, some citizens can reasonably believe that by their standards the procedures that produced the outcome were unfair, and that by their standards the outcomes themselves—or aspects of those outcomes—were unjust.

In practice, actual democracies can produce at best a "rough" or "good enough" legitimacy, based on citizens' generalizable interests in creating conditions of relatively willing cooperation. They will always create only institutions "that are reasonably just in view of the circumstances" or that do not "exceed the limits of tolerable injustice,"[30] determinations that will always depend in part on relatively local judgments about the mitigating character of different circumstances and the limits of the tolerable. People's willingness to accept some coercion as "legitimate enough" or "reasonably just under the circumstances" in turn seldom derives from an explicit or reflectively achieved consensus formed by unconstrained discussion. That willingness derives largely from a conventional and unreflective consensus rooted in the internalization of social and cultural traditions.[31] The discursive base from which people make their decisions on the reasonableness of deviations from justice is permeated with power. Accordingly, even these ad hoc rough decisions on what is "good enough" must be suspect.

I do not want to suggest, however, that the inevitability of contest over standards means giving up on at least provisional determinations of what is procedurally fair and substantively just. Indeed, my own relative certainty that many policy decisions in today's democracies are neither procedurally fair nor substantively just rests on strongly held, although admittedly provisional, convictions. Although the best we may hope for is an "if . . . then" formulation,[32] that formulation must suffice for the present, to be possibly corrected through further deliberation. For example, if we conclude now that a rough approximation to political equality is one ingredient in democratic fairness, then most policy outcomes in today's democracies do not derive from procedures that even approach that standard of fairness. If we conclude now that one or more of the egalitarian features of competing contemporary standards of justice (the greatest good for the greatest number, say, or the difference principle in justice as fairness) captures an important aspect of substantive justice, then most policy outcomes in today's democracies do not approach those standards.

I also do not want to suggest that the contestability of standards, the inevitable failure of any actual society to live up to its ideals, or even the great failure of existing democracies to live up to their ideals justifies, in most cases, civil disobedience. To the contrary, I will assume here that most acts of democratic coercion in modern Western democracies are sufficiently procedurally fair and their outcomes sufficiently just "under the circumstances" to disallow, in most cases, large-scale civil disobedience, individual major acts of civil disobedience, and even minor individual breaches of either the law or public spirit, such as small-scale cheating on the income tax. This is not the place for a full-scale discussion of political obligation, which I see as deriving from several different sources. In this essay I want to direct attention away from the traditional focus in political theory on political obligation and civil disobedience, toward a recognition of the ongoing imperfection of democratic decision. Democracies need ways short of civil disobedience and the breakdown of normatively based mutual cooperation to recognize and fight the ongoing injustice of their procedures and their outcomes.

How Citizens Must Fight the Very Coercion that They Need

When delegitimation walks hand in hand with legitimation, sufficient legitimation must remain to let reasonably just coercion do its good work of helping organize social arrangements and redressing the greater injustices that would emerge without it. Each individual in each society must feel out this delicate balance for herself. The trick is to recognize the importance, particularly to the most disadvantaged, of having a large number of relatively democratic and relatively unchallenged decisions made (and democratic coercion imposed) on a daily, monthly, and yearly basis as a matter of routine, and at the same time to recognize the importance, particularly to the most disadvantaged, of maintaining, in the institutions and culture of the society and in the minds of its citizens, some ongoing recognition and critique of the ways in which those decisions (and that coercion) are unfair and unjust.

Most democracies are capitalist as a rule, and capitalism (like many other economic systems) creates the very inequalities that make decisions in those democracies far from procedurally fair. All democracies except small voluntary women's communities are patriarchal, and patriarchy also creates inequalities that make decisions in those democracies far from procedurally fair. Most democracies are also racist, and classist even without reference to capitalism, with similar results. All real democracies, including the most utopian intentional communities, incorporate inequalities that produce coercive decisions that are procedurally unequal. All real democracies, including the most utopian, produce outcomes with aspects that are substantively unjust.[33] But workers, women, subordinated races, lower classes, and other disadvantaged groups fare far better in those democracies than they would in most cases if the democracies began to fall apart. Raw power, unmitigated by democratic values, usually hurts the disadvantaged far more than does democratic power. The disadvantaged need the relatively just coercion that democracies produce.

To fight that coercion at the same time as using it, democracies can multiply the available deliberative arenas to vary the kinds of power that permeate each one. Different arenas facilitate critiques of power from different directions. C. B. Macpherson and other theorists who excoriate political parties fail to recognize that parties and organized oppositions provide critical arenas for the losers in any given political interaction to rework their understandings of the situation and later return to the fray. Jürgen Habermas and other theorists who deprecate interest groups do not value the deliberative functions these groups can perform.[34]

Expanding opportunities for democratic participation, both by traditional efforts like voter registration and by developing new forms in the untraditional venues of workplaces, neighborhood town meetings, and deliberative referenda,[35] helps citizens fight coercion only when that participation itself does not cloud their understanding. For participation to help people understand their interests better, participants often need issues on which they have direct experience. They also often need a variety of different arenas for deliberation. They may need, for example, to oscillate between protected enclaves, in which they can explore their ideas in an environment of mutual encouragement, and more hostile but also broader surroundings in which they can test those ideas against the reigning reality.

Interest groups, political parties, and social movements, as well as churches, workplaces, ad hoc political collectives, and consciousness-raising groups, provide different forms of protected enclaves, in which members legitimately consider in their deliberations not only what is good for the whole polity but also what is good for themselves individually (their private lives and well-being, in Arendt's words) and for their group. Members of these groups may legitimately take particularist as well as universalist stands, as they may legitimately challenge the underlying assumptions of the forms of universalism they see around them. Only by making material interest and self-interest legitimate in these and other deliberations can the democracy succeed in encouraging a thorough "probing of volitions," which subjects "every pressing issue to continuous examination and possible reformulation."[36]

The present reigning hostility to "identity politics" does not recognize the value to democracy of deliberative enclaves in which the relatively like-minded can consult easily with one another. Karl Marx saw that capitalist factories, which had the unexpected attribute of bringing workers together in close quarters to share their experiences, helped transform the workers into the "gravediggers" of capitalism.[37] The black colleges that began the sit-ins of the southern civil rights movement in the United States, the early women's consciousness-raising groups and women's centers, and the bookstores and cafés that now support enclaves of identity politics all harbored and still harbor relatively safe spaces in which the like-minded can make their own sense of what they see.[38] In a more ephemeral example, some working-class citizens in a small town I studied felt the need to meet one night before the town meeting for a session that was one part strategy, including parsing out the dimensions of the problem, and five parts mutual support.[39]

Much contemporary work on civil society recognizes how partial, conflicting deliberative spaces, which yield partial and conflicting accounts of self-interest as well as conflicting accounts of the common good, must supplement both mainstream discourse about the common good and the formal deliberations that take place in local and national governments. What Nancy Fraser aptly terms "subaltern counterpublics" allow subordinated social groups to "invent and circulate counterdiscourses, which in turn permit them to formulate oppositional interpretations of their identities, interests and needs."[40]

James Scott writes of the importance for subordinated groups of "sequestered settings where, in principle, a shared critique of domination may develop."[41]

The goals of these counterpublics include understanding themselves better, forging bonds of solidarity, preserving the memories of past injustices, interpreting and reinterpreting the meanings of those injustices, working out alternative conceptions of self, of community, of justice, and of universality, trying to make sense of both the privileges they wield and the oppressions they face, understanding the strategic configurations for and against their desired ends, deciding what alliances to make both emotionally and strategically, deliberating on ends and means, and deciding how to act, individually and collectively.

Even the most just societies need these enclaves of protected discourse and action, because each institution of new forms of power and participation unsettles past patterns of power in ways that are not simply just. Each balance of power creates a new underdog, each settlement a new group who would benefit from unsettling. Each settlement accordingly creates not only the necessary capacity for action but also the need to protect and facilitate in some way those who have lost.[42] Because no democracy ever reaches the point at which justice is simply done, democracies need to recognize and foster enclaves of resistance. Suggestions to improve democracy, such as democratic neocorporatism,[43] therefore need to show not only how well they foster deliberation in general but also how they facilitate or impede enclaves of oppositional discourse.

This "enclave" model of democratic deliberation and action generates at least two problems. First come the dangers that arise when members of any group speak only to one another. When white supremacists speak mostly to white supremacists, Serbs to Serbs, feminists to feminists, and political philosophers to political philosophers, they encourage one another not to hear anyone else. They do not learn how to put what they want to say in words that others can hear and understand. The enclaves, which produce insights that less protected spaces would have prevented, also protect those insights from reasonable criticism. Yet most people, and particularly those disadvantaged in the larger society, need some such protection in order to think more critically and carefully. We also need this protection to help us develop confidence in our ideas, marshal our forces, and feel supported by others.[44]

For most people, spending time both in an oppositional enclave and outside it promotes weighing the lessons of each venue against the other. It allows the straddling individual to gain the confidence of others' support but temper that support against the light and heat of outside opposition. A division of labor also helps, in which some individuals immerse themselves in enclave life and thought while others span the spectrum between the enclave and the outside world. The danger comes when large numbers live only in their conceptual enclaves, reinforcing one another in their mutual *folie*. Then the translators need to work with a vengeance.

The second, and equally important, problem is that facilitating enclaves can contravene other values, such as the triumph of the right and the good. When the Ku Klux Klan loses influence in the deliberative arena and is outvoted in the coercive one, the racism it espouses ought normatively eventually to disappear entirely from the array of conceptual possibilities to which citizens have access. The case for enclaves must be much like that for free speech, which also must be balanced against other rights and goods. Just as a democracy should affirmatively promote enclaves of speech by postal subsidies for magazines and newspapers regardless of their content, along with subsidies of Internet communication, so too, all other things equal, the public culture of democracy should recognize the value of organizational and deliberative enclaves where oppositional thought can grow.

Facilitating opposition in general may be a luxury open only to relatively settled democracies whose populations find most decisions sufficiently just to let the necessary degree of democratic coercion do its work. Each society must work out the relative values of using and fighting power through constant balancing and testing, sacrificing neither. Normative political thought can help by recognizing as democratic values both reasonably just coercion and opposition to the injustice within that coercion.

Living with the Tension

The tensions we should keep alive in democratic practice resemble the tensions we should keep alive within ourselves when we try to use the power that has made us who we are and yet fight that power at the same time.[45] We need worry far less about the compromises we make between the good and the best, or between the bad-but-livable and the better, when those compromises are, roughly speaking, utility-driven—when we are only giving up one good to get another. But when we compromise with justice, we must design our lives and our institutions so that the justice that is compromised remains nagging, in the margin somewhere, in a bracket that does not go away, to pique our souls and goad us into future action.

In the polity we can best preserve these irritants by encouraging "affirmative pluralism" in democratic talk. In our democracies, we need to find ways of removing coercion as much as possible from the arenas in which we struggle to understand what is just and unjust. This means a public discourse not completely overwhelmed with the massive resources of existing forms of domination.

But we must remember that in their decision-making functions democracies need coercion, that the coercion needed is usually far from fully legitimate, and that in using power, we must also fight it at the same time. To fight power means affirmatively encouraging oppositional discourses and oppositional cultures. Those discourses and cultures have evolved in part for the purpose of reminding their participants and, through them, the other members of the society, of the illegitimate coercion and substantive injustice that pervades any existing democracy. These discourses and cultures make it easier to investigate different ends from those the larger polity is pursuing, and different means to similar ends. The different ways the cultures work and the different avenues they explore may later replace or supplement the ways that reign at present.

The injustices we commit as we act collectively—for not to act coercively would in many cases create a greater injustice than to act and coerce some unfairly—should not be forgotten and put behind us. Our collective deliberations should find ways to recognize, store, and rethink our understandings of these actions, so that we do not foreclose the opportunity of making reparation, or of someday understanding how to make the coercion we must use more procedurally fair and its outcomes more substantively just.

Notes

1. I have adapted to systemic power the definition devised by Jack H. Nagel, *The Descriptive Analysis of Power* (New Haven: Yale University Press, 1975), 29, by substituting "interests" for his "preferences" and adding "a set of actors." By focusing on cause, Nagel's definition avoids imputations of intent and allows anticipations of future events (e.g., the next election) to cause present behavior.

For an emphasis on the relatively benign "power to," "power with," "power as energy," and "power-from-within," in contrast to the "power over" that I emphasize in this essay, see Mary Parker Follett, "Power" (1975), in *Dynamic Administration: The Collected Papers of Mary Parker Follett*, ed. Henry C. Metcalf (New York: Harper, 1942); William E. Connolly, "Power and Responsibility," in *The Terms of Political Discourse* (Lexington: D. C. Heath, 1974); Nancy Hartsock, "Political Change: Two Perspectives on Power," *Quest* 1 (1974): 10–25, reprinted in Charlotte Bunch, ed., *Building Feminist Theory: Essays from Quest* (New York: Longman, 1981); and, among more recent feminist theorists, Starhawk, *Truth or Dare* (1987) (New York: HarperCollins, 1990), 8–19.

2. Power therefore means here "power over" other human beings. In this definition I draw not only on Nagel, *Descriptive Analysis*, but also on distinctions in Peter Bachrach and Morton Baratz, "Decisions and Non-Decisions: An Analytic Framework," *American Political Science Review* 57 (1963): 632–44; and Steven Lukes, *Power: A Radical View* (London: Macmillan, 1974). Unlike the threat of sanction, "force" as I use it here involves no element of the will of the other. If I carry you out of the room and your will is irrelevant, my action involves force; if I tell you I will shoot you unless you leave, my getting what I desire (your leaving) involves, to a small degree, your will. (You can always refuse to leave, and although I shoot you, I will not have gained your leaving.) Force, which does not involve will, is implicated in many systemic attributes such as language. Accordingly, although power as the threat of sanction always involves resistance or the possibility of resistance, power as force is sometimes impossible to resist.

(Michel Foucault may not have recognized this distinction.) To keep the argument relatively simple, the definition of coercion in this essay does not encompass positive inducement, although if asymmetries are great enough, positive inducements may count as forms of coercion. See Brian Barry, "Power: An Economic Analysis" (1975), in *Democracy and Power*, vol. 1 of *Essays in Political Theory* (Oxford: Oxford University Press, 1991).

3. I use the word "interest" here to mean a deliberatively considered conclusion on a policy preference. That conclusion may be self-interested or public-spirited. The conclusion is also always open to contest and to the possibility of reaching different conclusions after further thought, action, and political struggle. The word "interest" often connotes both self-interest and objective, static, or eternal states, discoverable through revolutionary action or through reason and revealed by removing the sources of oppression or repression. I want to discard these connotations, while retaining some distinction between surface preferences (or prereflective understandings) and understandings that are more considered, emotionally and rationally, and more thoroughly tested in action. One test of a considered understanding in this sense might be its formation in as close an approximation as possible to free, equal and unconstrained communication. Another test, which I suggest throughout, might be the vitality of the contest for adopting alternatives within which a given understanding developed, including the divergence of opposing ideas in that contest and the degree of life subsequently preserved in the excluded alternatives. European readers uncomfortable with the frequent American usage of incorporating value orientations into the conception of interests are requested mentally to substitute the phrase "interests and value orientations" whenever the word "interests" appears in this text.

4. Jane Mansbridge, "Public Spirit in Political Systems," in Henry J. Aaron, Thomas E. Mann, and Timothy Taylor, eds., *Values and Public Policy* (Washington: Brookings, 1994); Ian Ayers and John Braithwaite, *Responsive Regulation: Transcending the Deregulation Debate* (New York: Oxford University Press, 1992).

5. This opposition of coercion to "power" permeates Arendt's writing. In *On Revolution* (1963; reprint, New York: Viking, 1965), Arendt defined power, in contradistinction to "pre-political natural violence" (181), as follows: "Power comes into being only if and when men join themselves together for the purpose of action, and it will disappear when, for whatever reason, they disperse and desert one another" (174; see also 145, 148–49, 150–52, 155, 162, 163–67, 170, 175, 179, 181–82).

In her later *On Violence* (New York: Harvest/HBJ, 1970), Arendt consistently elided violence and coercion, attributing to all forms of instrumental coercion the psychology and substantive outcomes of physical violence. Her elision of the two in English reflected the double meaning of violence and coercive power inherent in the German *Gewalt*, which Max Weber and others had used to express the power of the state. The book's earliest section sets the pattern by first making violence quintessentially instrumental, "ruled by the means-end category" (4; also 46, 51, 79), then situating it immediately in the context of the battlefield, the sword, war, guns, shooting, extermination camps, genocide, torture, and nuclear doomsday (4, 5, 6, 11, 13, 14, 17). The second section, introducing "the question of violence in the political realm" (35), first identifies violence with coercion in general (36), then associates violence, rule, and command with the specific psychological feelings that come from imposing oneself on others, making others the instruments of one's will, asserting one's own will against the resistance of others, and desiring to exercise power over others. The third, last section links violence again with the imagery of aggressiveness, rage, and the battlefield (59–61, 63, 67). Arendt never explores the everyday nonviolent forms of coercion that I argue make complex and relatively just interdependence possible. (In *On Violence* Arendt's "power" remains the "living power of the people" acting "in concert" [40–41, 44].)

6. Arendt, *On Revolution*, 255. Arendt distinguished sharply between the "political" realm of "opinions," to which public "power" in her definition applied, and the "social and economic" realms of mere material interest (278). In *Contradictions of the Welfare State* (Cambridge, Mass.: MIT Press, 1984) Claus Offe similarly defines politics as having to do *not* with negotiations among interests but rather with "the working out of visions about the just order of social life, and the conflict among visions of that order" (173). See also Iris Marion Young, *Justice and the Politics of Difference* (Princeton: Princeton University Press, 1990), 72–74.

7. *Politics and Vision* (Boston: Little, Brown, 1960), 277, 2; also 3, 9–10, 60–66, 191, 429–34 on the political as "general and integrative." See also Wolin's "Fugitive Democracy," this volume, 31.

8. On politics, interests, and "the primordial fact that the hard core of power is violence" (220), see also *Politics and Vision*, 42, 86–92, 115–18, 201, 214–23, 232–36, 241, 272–85, 338–42.

9. *Spheres of Justice* (New York: Basic Books, 1983), 304.

10. Ibid., 306. Because he wants to make "power" belong only to persuasiveness, Walzer refuses to call television referenda an "exercise of power." He is "inclined to say, instead, that it is only another example of the erosion of value" (307). Similarly, he writes that "democracy requires equal rights, not equal power" (309). Although in one passage he agrees that a citizen can legitimately aim "to win—that is, to exercise *unequaled* power" (309), he does not explore the implications of this thought for a politics of relatively legitimate coercion.

11. Jürgen Habermas, "Hannah Arendt's Communications Concept of Power" (1976), in Jürgen Habermas, *Philosophical-Political Profiles*, trans. Frederick G. Lawrence (Cambridge, Mass.: MIT Press, 1985).

12. As Habermas carefully enunciated his position, strategic action "has taken place also within the city walls" (182). In another careful formulation, "We cannot exclude the element of strategic action from the concept of the political" (183).

13. For Habermas's evolving thought on this issue, see "Further Reflections on the Public Sphere," in Craig Calhoun, ed., *Habermas and the Public Sphere* (Cambridge, Mass.: MIT Press, 1992), 421–61, esp. 446–50, and "Three Normative Models of Democracy" in this volume, 21–30. For a critique, see my "Ugliness in Democratic Life," forthcoming in *Constellations*.

14. Habermas calls the capacity to keep other individuals or groups from perceiving their interests "violence" (183). He calls "structural violence" the capacity to keep others from perceiving their interests that is built into social and political institutions and "blocks in an unnoticed fashion those communications in which are shaped and propagated the convictions effective for legitimation" (186). This is in my terminology a form of "force" (see n. 2).

15. For example, decisions on majority rule vs. unanimity as a decision rule depend in part on commitments to equality as opposed to a conception of liberty that naturalizes the status quo. Seyla Benhabib, in "Toward a Deliberative Model of Democratic

Legitimacy" (this volume), applies this kind of legitimating criterion of hypothetical deliberation not to coercion per se but to "methods for articulating, sifting through, weighing conflicting interests" (73). In context, her "weighing" involves weighing the merits of arguments for different interests, not the numbers of interest-bearers. The criterion of hypothetical deliberation differs from the criterion of hypothetical consent by making the act of agreement collective, mutual, considered, and subject to the strong constraints of the deliberative ideal (see p. 70 in this volume for features of that ideal).

16. I am indebted to Cass Sunstein for these examples and helpful clarifications. Using this criterion for legitimation, one could also define as just whatever outcome a group of affected individuals would agree (or hypothetically agree) was just after uncoerced deliberation in which only the merit of the better argument prevailed; coercion would be more or less legitimate as the outcome was more or less just. Brian Barry, in "Is Democracy Special?" (1979; in *Democracy and Power*), points out that legitimation from substantive outcomes is insufficient for democratic theory, giving several reasons why "a law's having been enacted (or not repealed) by a democratic procedure adds a reason for obeying it to whatever reasons exist independently of that" (25).

17. Jane Mansbridge, *Beyond Adversary Democracy* (1980; reprint, Chicago: University of Chicago Press, 1983). Readers of that book will recognize in this essay a defense of the (partial) legitimacy of adversary democracy.

18. E.g., Jack Lively, *Democracy* (1975; reprint, New York: Putnam, 1977), 8.

19. Robert Dahl, "The Analysis of Influence in Local Communities" (1960), in Bernard J. Frieden and Robert Morris, ed., *Urban Planning and Social Policy* (New York: Basic Books, 1968), 225, 227. In his more recent work, *Democracy and Its Critics* (New Haven: Yale University Press, 1989), Dahl prefers the formulation, "At the decisive stage of collective decisions, each citizen must be ensured an equal opportunity to express a choice that will be counted as equal in weight to the choice expressed by other citizens" (109).

20. For the many theorists who make some version of equal power or the equal opportunity to exercise power a central element in democracy or, more broadly, in political fairness, see my "Using Power/Fighting Power," *Constellations* 1 (1994): 53–73, n. 19.

21. The exact content of these limiting conditions will always be a matter of contention. For English understandings of the rule of law, see A. V. Dicey, *Introduction to the Study of the Law of the Constitution*, ed. E.C.S. Wade (1885; reprint, London: Macmillan, 1939); Geoffrey Marshall, "Rule of law," in David Miller, ed., *The Blackwell Encyclopedia of Political Thought* (Oxford: Blackwell, 1987); and Don Herzog, *Happy Slaves* (Chicago: University of Chicago Press, 1989), chap. 4. For the ways the constitution of the United States prohibits the majoritarian imposition of the "naked preferences" of one group on another without at least nominal deference to a public purpose, see Cass R. Sunstein, "Naked Preferences and the Constitution," *Columbia Law Review* 84 (1984): 1689–1732.

22. For the argument in canon law, see Gierke, "Über die Geschichte des Majoritätsprinzips" (1913), cited in John Gilbert Heinberg, "History of the Majority Principle," *American Political Science Review* 20 (1926): 52–68, 59. The ancient Greeks may also have had a rationale for majority rule as a curtailed form of deliberation. Willmoore Kendall considers this claim implicit in John Locke's argument for majority rule: *John Locke and the Doctrine of Majority Rule* (Urbana: University of Illinois Press, 1941); and

Elaine Spitz (*Majority Rule* [Chatham, N.J.: Chatham House Publishers, 1984]) also upholds a relatively deliberative justification for majority rule, describing it as a complex social practice in which, at least in the early stages, "discussion, not voting, lies at the heart of the procedures" (xiii). For more recent conceptualizations of majority rule as "discursive as circumstances permit [subject to] temporal constraints," see Habermas, "Further Reflections," 449–50, and Benhabib, "Deliberative Rationality,".72.

23. For the general argument, see Isaiah Berlin, "Equality," *Proceedings of the Aristotelian Society* 56 (1955–56). A version of utilitarianism also provides a numerical argument for majority rule, as when even Willmoore Kendall in his later work justified majority rule as simply a lesser evil (producing fewer coerced individuals) than minority rule: Austin Ranney and Willmoore Kendall, *Democracy and the American Party System* (New York: Harcourt, Brace, 1956), 32.

24. This criterion of legitimation is conceptually independent from the discursive criterion, although if equality is the default position inherent in the concept of a rule, one would expect individuals in conditions of free and equal deliberation to agree on this position in the absence of good reasons for exclusion. The point is that discursive agreement would follow from reasons independent of the discursive agreement itself. These reasons are analytically independent of the discursive agreement even though in order to be persuaded that the criterion of equal power has its own internally compelling rationale, we have to point to the results of actual discursive processes, judged according to the criteria for ideal deliberation. By analogy, when we ask why we should believe a given result in the work of the physical sciences we point to social processes whose degree of closeness to a discursive ideal leads us to have more or less confidence in their conclusions. But those social conclusions in turn are based on criteria that are to some degree independent of the discursive process. In the legitimating loop, the deliberative process and the other criteria have independent but reinforcing status.

25. See Mansbridge, *Beyond Adversary Democracy*, 266–68 and accompanying notes, and Charles R. Beitz, *Political Equality* (Princeton: Princeton University Press, 1989), 8–11 and notes. This problem is particularly severe when segmented rather than cross-cutting cleavages produce permanent minorities. See, e.g., John C. Calhoun, *A Disquisition on Government* (1853) (New York: Bobbs-Merrill, 1953); Arend Lijphart, *The Politics of Accommodation* (Berkeley and Los Angeles: University of California Press, 1968); Lani Guinier, *The Tyranny of the Majority* (New York: Free Press, 1994); and commentaries such as Ian Shapiro's "Democratic Innovation," *World Politics* 46 (1993): 121–50.

26. See, e.g., Duncan Black, *The Theory of Committees and Elections* (1958; reprint, Cambridge: Cambridge University Press, 1963), expanding on the work of Condorcet and C. L. Dodgson; Kenneth J. Arrow, *Social Choice and Individual Values* (New York: John Wiley, 1963); William H. Riker, *Liberalism against Populism* (Prospect Heights, Ill.: Waveland Press, 1982).

27. Beitz, *Political Equality*, xiii.

28. Dahl, *Democracy and Its Critics*, 156. Dahl himself generates five criteria for "political equality" or, more generally, for "a democratic process." In "Is Democracy Special?" Brian Barry gives an excellent account of these problems.

29. See Mansbridge, *Beyond Adversary Democracy*, for evidence of systematic unequal power even in a highly egalitarian, highly democratic, and ideologically committed forty-one-person collective.

30. John Rawls, *A Theory of Justice* (Cambridge, Mass.: Harvard University Press, 1971), 112, regarding obligations to do one's part to maintain just cooperative arrangements in which others are cooperating and from which one benefits. See also "as just as it is reasonable to expect in the circumstances" (115), regarding the natural duty to support and comply with just institutions.

31. I take this formulation from Nancy Fraser, "What's Critical about Critical Theory?" chap. 6 of her *Unruly Practices* (Minneapolis: University of Minnesota Press, 1989), 120.

32. Compare the celebrated first sentence of H.L.A. Hart's "Are There Any Natural Rights?" *Philosophical Review* 64 (1958): 175–19.

33. In regard to justice, Iris Young has suggested the example of a universal health care bill that omitted coverage for victims of AIDS. In a country previously without universal coverage, the overall thrust of the policy would be in the direction of social justice, while parts of its operation would be, by most standards, unjust.

34. For a defense of the potential deliberative capacities of interest groups, see Mansbridge, "A Deliberative Theory of Interest Representation."

35. See the suggestions for participatory innovation in Benjamin Barber, *Strong Democracy* (Berkeley and Los Angeles: University of California Press, 1984).

36. The phrase "probing of volitions" comes from Charles E. Lindblom, *Inquiry and Change* (New Haven: Yale University Press, 1990); and the mandate to subject every issue to continuous reexamination is from Barber, *Strong Democracy*, 182. This is not the place for a full defense of my claim that narrow, material self-interest ought to play a role, in some cases an important role, in democratic deliberation (see my "Feminism and Democracy," "A Deliberative Theory of Interest Representation," and "On the Relation of Altruism and Self-Interest," in Mansbridge, ed., *Beyond Self-Interest* [Chicago: University of Chicago Press, 1990]). My claim derives from two kinds of experience. The first is the experience of "consciousness-raising," which Pamela Allen described as follows: "Although we are not sure that full autonomy is a possible goal, we believe that our hope lies in developing as individuals who understand themselves, their own needs, the workings of our society, and the needs of others" (Pamela Allen, "Free Space" [1970], in Anne Koedt et al., eds., *Radical Feminism* [New York: Quadrangle Press, 1973], 271–72). We cannot understand our "own needs" better without also understanding better our narrow material self-interested needs as well as other kinds of needs. The second is the experience of collective decision-making, from which I conclude that deliberations that force participants into describing their needs and desires only in terms of the collective "we" gravely distort the process of communication and keep participants from seeing as accurately as possible when they ought to strive for consensus on the basis of discovering or creating common interests and when they ought to deal with the issues by recognizing underlying conflicts and settling those conflicts provisionally through the fairest available "adversary" democratic procedures. See also Laura Stoker, "Interests and Ethics in Politics," *American Political Science Review* 86 (1992): 369–80.

37. *Capital* (1867) (New York: International Publishers, 1967), vol. 1, 763; Karl Marx and Friedrich Engels, *The Communist Manifesto* (1848) (Chicago: Henry Regnery, 1954), 32. Jon Elster, *Making Sense of Marx* (Cambridge: Cambridge University Press, 1985), 355, points out that Marx did not say explicitly that concentration in the factory rather than in housing and residence was the decisive factor in producing worker soli-

darity, "but from what he says elsewhere about the importance of trade unions this can reasonably be inferred."

38. For examples of such enclaves, see Verta Taylor, "Social Movement Continuity: The Women's Movement In Abeyance," *American Sociological Review* 54 (1989): 761–75, and Verta Taylor and Nancy Whittier, "Collective Identity in Social Movement Communities," in Aldon D. Morris and Carol McClurg Mueller, eds., *Frontiers in Social Movement Theory* (New Haven: Yale University Press, 1992). For an early description of the importance of "a place in which to think," see Pamela Allen, "Free Space," 271–79. On social movements politicizing culture, see Iris Marion Young, *Justice and the Politics of Difference*, 86–88.

39. Mansbridge, *Beyond Adversary Democracy*, 62–63.

40. "Rethinking the Public Sphere: A Contribution to the Critique of Actually Existing Democracy," in Craig Calhoun, ed., *Habermas and the Public Sphere*, 123.

41. James C. Scott, *Domination and the Arts of Resistance: Hidden Transcripts* (New Haven: Yale University Press, 1990).

42. See Bonnie Honig, *Political Theory and the Displacement of Politics* (Ithaca: Cornell University Press, 1993), esp. chap. 1, on both the reality and the affirmative dimensions of "perpetual contest." Honig argues that "every politics has its remainders," or competing possibilities that are "produced by the process of division itself" but are often successfully suppressed by that process (3, 15, and 213, n. 1). Honig's argument has influenced both my own insistence on the need to keep contest alive and my stress, contrary to her overall thrust, on the importance, particularly for the disadvantaged, of ongoing stable coercion.

43. Joshua Cohen and Joel Rogers, "Secondary Associations and Democratic Governance," *Politics and Society* 20 (1992): 393–472; Philippe Schmitter, "The Irony of Modern Democracy and Efforts to Improve Its Practice," *Politics and Society* 20 (1992): 507–12. On group representation see also Young, *Justice and the Politics of Difference*.

44. Scott, *Domination and the Arts of Resistance*.

45. Mansbridge, "Using Power, Fighting Power," 54–55, 65–67.

Part III
Ethics, Values and Leadership

[10]
THE PURSUIT OF THE IDEAL

I

THERE ARE, in my view, two factors that, above all others, have shaped human history in this century. One is the development of the natural sciences and technology, certainly the greatest success story of our time – to this, great and mounting attention has been paid from all quarters. The other, without doubt, consists in the great ideological storms that have altered the lives of virtually all mankind: the Russian Revolution and its aftermath – totalitarian tyrannies of both right and left and the explosions of nationalism, racism, and, in places, of religious bigotry, which, interestingly enough, not one among the most perceptive social thinkers of the nineteenth century had ever predicted.

When our descendants, in two or three centuries' time (if mankind survives until then), come to look at our age, it is these two phenomena that will, I think, be held to be the outstanding characteristics of our century, the most demanding of explanation and analysis. But it is as well to realise that these great movements began with ideas in people's heads: ideas about what relations between men have been, are, might be, and should be; and to realise how they came to be transformed in the name of a vision of some supreme goal in the minds of the leaders, above all of the prophets with armies at their backs. Such ideas are the substance of ethics. Ethical thought consists of the systematic examination of the relations of human beings to each other, the conceptions, interests and ideals from which human ways of treating one another spring, and the systems of value on which

The Pursuit of the Ideal

such ends of life are based. These beliefs about how life should be lived, what men and women should be and do, are objects of moral inquiry; and when applied to groups and nations, and, indeed, mankind as a whole, are called political philosophy, which is but ethics applied to society.

If we are to hope to understand the often violent world in which we live (and unless we try to understand it, we cannot expect to be able to act rationally in it and on it), we cannot confine our attention to the great impersonal forces, natural and man-made, which act upon us. The goals and motives that guide human action must be looked at in the light of all that we know and understand; their roots and growth, their essence, and above all their validity, must be critically examined with every intellectual resource that we have. This urgent need, apart from the intrinsic value of the discovery of truth about human relationships, makes ethics a field of primary importance. Only barbarians are not curious about where they come from, how they came to be where they are, where they appear to be going, whether they wish to go there, and if so, why, and if not, why not.

The study of the variety of ideas about the views of life that embody such values and such ends is something that I have spent forty years of my long life in trying to make clear to myself. I should like to say something about how I came to become absorbed by this topic, and particularly about a turning-point which altered my thoughts about the heart of it. This will, to some degree, inevitably turn out to be somewhat autobiographical – for this I offer my apologies, but I do not know how else to give an account of it.

II

When I was young I read *War and Peace* by Tolstoy, much too early. The real impact on me of this great novel came only later, together with that of other Russian writers, both novelists and

The Pursuit of the Ideal

social thinkers, of the mid-nineteenth century. These writers did much to shape my outlook. It seemed to me, and still does, that the purpose of these writers was not principally to give realistic accounts of the lives and relationships to one another of individuals or social groups or classes, not psychological or social analysis for its own sake – although, of course, the best of them achieved precisely this, incomparably. Their approach seemed to me essentially moral: they were concerned most deeply with what was responsible for injustice, oppression, falsity in human relations, imprisonment whether by stone walls or conformism – unprotesting submission to man-made yokes – moral blindness, egoism, cruelty, humiliation, servility, poverty, helplessness, bitter indignation, despair, on the part of so many. In short, they were concerned with the nature of these experiences and their roots in the human condition; the condition of Russia in the first place, but, by implication, of all mankind. And conversely they wished to know what would bring about the opposite of this, a reign of truth, love, honesty, justice, security, personal relations based on the possibility of human dignity, decency, independence, freedom, spiritual fulfilment.

Some, like Tolstoy, found this in the outlook of simple people, unspoiled by civilisation; like Rousseau, he wished to believe that the moral universe of peasants was not unlike that of children, not distorted by the conventions and institutions of civilisation, which sprang from human vices – greed, egoism, spiritual blindness; that the world could be saved if only men saw the truth that lay at their feet; if they but looked, it was to be found in the Christian gospels, the Sermon on the Mount. Others among these Russians put their faith in scientific rationalism, or in social and political revolution founded on a true theory of historical change. Others again looked for answers in the teachings of the Orthodox theology, or in liberal western democracy, or in a return to ancient Slav values, obscured by the reforms of Peter the Great and his successors.

What was common to all these outlooks was the belief that

The Pursuit of the Ideal

solutions to the central problems existed, that one could discover them, and, with sufficient selfless effort, realise them on earth. They all believed that the essence of human beings was to be able to choose how to live: societies could be transformed in the light of true ideals believed in with enough fervour and dedication. If, like Tolstoy, they sometimes thought that man was not truly free but determined by factors outside his control, they knew well enough, as he did, that if freedom was an illusion it was one without which one could not live or think. None of this was part of my school curriculum, which consisted of Greek and Latin authors, but it remained with me.

When I became a student at the University of Oxford, I began to read the works of the great philosophers, and found that the major figures, especially in the field of ethical and political thought, believed this too. Socrates thought that if certainty could be established in our knowledge of the external world by rational methods (had not Anaxagoras arrived at the truth that the moon was many times larger than the Peloponnese, however small it looked in the sky?) the same methods would surely yield equal certainty in the field of human behaviour – how to live, what to be. This could be achieved by rational argument. Plato thought that an élite of sages who arrived at such certainty should be given the power of governing others intellectually less well endowed, in obedience to patterns dictated by the correct solutions to personal and social problems. The Stoics thought that the attainment of these solutions was in the power of any man who set himself to live according to reason. Jews, Christians, Muslims (I knew too little about Buddhism) believed that the true answers had been revealed by God to his chosen prophets and saints, and accepted the interpretation of these revealed truths by qualified teachers and the traditions to which they belonged.

The rationalists of the seventeenth century thought that the answers could be found by a species of metaphysical insight, a special application of the light of reason with which all men were endowed. The empiricists of the eighteenth century,

The Pursuit of the Ideal

impressed by the vast new realms of knowledge opened by the natural sciences based on mathematical techniques, which had driven out so much error, superstition, dogmatic nonsense, asked themselves, like Socrates, why the same methods should not succeed in establishing similar irrefutable laws in the realm of human affairs. With the new methods discovered by natural science, order could be introduced into the social sphere as well – uniformities could be observed, hypotheses formulated and tested by experiment; laws could be based on them, and then laws in specific regions of experience could be seen to be entailed by wider laws; and these in turn to be entailed by still wider laws, and so on upwards, until a great harmonious system, connected by unbreakable logical links and capable of being formulated in precise – that is, mathematical – terms, could be established.

The rational reorganisation of society would put an end to spiritual and intellectual confusion, the reign of prejudice and superstition, blind obedience to unexamined dogmas, and the stupidities and cruelties of the oppressive regimes which such intellectual darkness bred and promoted. All that was wanted was the identification of the principal human needs and discovery of the means of satisfying them. This would create the happy, free, just, virtuous, harmonious world which Condorcet so movingly predicted in his prison cell in 1794. This view lay at the basis of all progressive thought in the nineteenth century, and was at the heart of much of the critical empiricism which I imbibed in Oxford as a student.

III

At some point I realised that what all these views had in common was a Platonic ideal: in the first place that, as in the sciences, all genuine questions must have one true answer and one only, all the rest being necessarily errors; in the second place, that there must be a dependable path towards the

The Pursuit of the Ideal

discovery of these truths; in the third place, that the true answers, when found, must necessarily be compatible with one another and form a single whole, for one truth cannot be incompatible with another – that we knew *a priori*. This kind of omniscience was the solution of the cosmic jigsaw puzzle. In the case of morals, we could then conceive what the perfect life must be, founded as it would be on a correct understanding of the rules that governed the universe.

True, we might never get to this condition of perfect knowledge – we may be too feeble-witted, or too weak or corrupt or sinful, to achieve this. The obstacles, both intellectual and those of external nature, may be too many. Moreover, opinions, as I said, had widely differed about the right path to pursue – some found it in churches, some in laboratories; some believed in intuition, others in experiment, or in mystical visions, or in mathematical calculation. But even if we could not ourselves reach these true answers, or indeed, the final system that interweaves them all, the answers must exist – else the questions were not real. The answers must be known to someone: perhaps Adam in Paradise knew; perhaps we shall only reach them at the end of days; if men cannot know them, perhaps the angels know; and if not the angels, then God knows. These timeless truths must in principle be knowable.

Some nineteenth-century thinkers – Hegel, Marx – thought it was not quite so simple. There were no timeless truths. There was historical development, continuous change; human horizons altered with each new step in the evolutionary ladder; history was a drama with many acts; it was moved by conflicts of forces in the realms of both ideas and reality, sometimes called dialectical, which took the form of wars, revolutions, violent upheavals of nations, classes, cultures, movements. Yet after inevitable setbacks, failures, relapses, returns to barbarism, Condorcet's dream would come true. The drama would have a happy ending – man's reason had achieved triumphs in the past, it could not be held back for ever. Men would no longer be victims of nature or of their own largely irrational societies:

The Pursuit of the Ideal

reason would triumph; universal harmonious cooperation, true history, would at last begin.

For if this was not so, do the ideas of progress, of history, have any meaning? Is there not a movement, however tortuous, from ignorance to knowledge, from mythical thought and childish fantasies to perception of reality face to face, to knowledge of true goals, true values as well as truths of fact? Can history be a mere purposeless succession of events, caused by a mixture of material factors and the play of random selection, a tale full of sound and fury signifying nothing? This was unthinkable. The day would dawn when men and women would take their lives in their own hands and not be self-seeking beings or the playthings of blind forces that they did not understand. It was, at the very least, not impossible to conceive what such an earthly paradise could be; and if conceivable we could, at any rate, try to march towards it. That has been at the centre of ethical thought from the Greeks to the Christian visionaries of the Middle Ages, from the Renaissance to progressive thought in the last century; and indeed, is believed by many to this day.

IV

At a certain stage in my reading, I naturally met with the principal works of Machiavelli. They made a deep and lasting impression upon me, and shook my earlier faith. I derived from them not the most obvious teachings – on how to acquire and retain political power, or by what force or guile rulers must act if they are to regenerate their societies, or protect themselves and their states from enemies within or without, or what the principal qualities of rulers on the one hand, and of citizens on the other, must be, if their states are to flourish – but something else. Machiavelli was not a historicist: he thought it possible to restore something like the Roman Republic or Rome of the early Principate. He believed that to do this one needed a ruling class of brave, resourceful, intelligent, gifted men who knew

The Pursuit of the Ideal

how to seize opportunities and use them, and citizens who were adequately protected, patriotic, proud of their state, epitomes of manly, pagan virtues. That is how Rome rose to power and conquered the world, and it is the absence of this kind of wisdom and vitality and courage in adversity, of the qualities of both lions and foxes, that in the end brought it down. Decadent states were conquered by vigorous invaders who retained these virtues.

But Machiavelli also sets, side by side with this, the notion of Christian virtues – humility, acceptance of suffering, unworldliness, the hope of salvation in an afterlife – and he remarks that if, as he plainly himself favours, a state of a Roman type is to be established, these qualities will not promote it: those who live by the precepts of Christian morality are bound to be trampled on by the ruthless pursuit of power by men who alone can re-create and dominate the republic which he wants to see. He does not condemn Christian virtues. He merely points out that the two moralities are incompatible, and he does not recognise any overarching criterion whereby we are enabled to decide the right life for men. The combination of *virtù* and Christian values is for him an impossibility. He simply leaves you to choose – he knows which he himself prefers.

The idea that this planted in my mind was the realisation, which came as something of a shock, that not all the supreme values pursued by mankind now and in the past were necessarily compatible with one another. It undermined my earlier assumption, based on the *philosophia perennis*, that there could be no conflict between true ends, true answers to the central problems of life.

Then I came across Giambattista Vico's *Scienza nuova*. Scarcely anyone in Oxford had then heard of Vico, but there was one philosopher, Robin Collingwood, who had translated Croce's book on Vico, and he urged me to read it. This opened my eyes to something new. Vico seemed to be concerned with the succession of human cultures – every society had, for him, its own vision of reality, of the world in which it lived, and of

The Pursuit of the Ideal

itself and of its relations to its own past, to nature, to what it strove for. This vision of a society is conveyed by everything that its members do and think and feel — expressed and embodied in the kinds of words, the forms of language that they use, the images, the metaphors, the forms of worship, the institutions that they generate, which embody and convey their image of reality and of their place in it; by which they live. These visions differ with each successive social whole — each has its own gifts, values, modes of creation, incommensurable with one another: each must be understood in its own terms — understood, not necessarily evaluated.

The Homeric Greeks, the master class, Vico tells us, were cruel, barbarous, mean, oppressive to the weak; but they created the *Iliad* and the *Odyssey*, something we cannot do in our more enlightened day. Their great creative masterpieces belong to them, and once the vision of the world changes, the possibility of that type of creation disappears also. We, for our part, have our sciences, our thinkers, our poets, but there is no ladder of ascent from the ancients to the moderns. If this is so, it must be absurd to say that Racine is a better poet than Sophocles, that Bach is a rudimentary Beethoven, that, let us say, the Impressionist painters are the peak to which the painters of Florence aspired but did not reach. The values of these cultures are different, and they are not necessarily compatible with one another. Voltaire, who thought that the values and ideals of the enlightened exceptions in a sea of darkness — of classical Athens, of Florence of the Renaissance, of France in the *grand siècle* and of his own time — were almost identical, was mistaken.[1] Machiavelli's Rome did not, in fact, exist. For Vico there is a plurality of civilisations (repetitive cycles of them, but that is unimportant), each with its own unique pattern.

---

[1] Voltaire's conception of enlightenment as being identical in essentials wherever it is attained seems to lead to the inescapable conclusion that, in his view, Byron would have been happy at table with Confucius, and Sophocles would have felt completely at ease in quattrocento Florence, and Seneca in the *salon* of Madame du Deffand or at the court of Frederick the Great.

The Pursuit of the Ideal

Machiavelli conveyed the idea of two incompatible outlooks; and here were societies the cultures of which were shaped by values, not means to ends but ultimate ends, ends in themselves, which differed, not in all respects – for they were all human – but in some profound, irreconcilable ways, not combinable in any final synthesis.

After this I naturally turned to the German eighteenth-century thinker Johann Gottfried Herder. Vico thought of a succession of civilisations, Herder went further and compared national cultures in many lands and periods, and held that every society had what he called its own centre of gravity, which differed from that of others. If, as he wished, we are to understand Scandinavian sagas or the poetry of the Bible, we must not apply to them the aesthetic criteria of the critics of eighteenth-century Paris. The ways in which men live, think, feel, speak to one another, the clothes they wear, the songs they sing, the gods they worship, the food they eat, the assumptions, customs, habits which are intrinsic to them – it is this that creates communities, each of which has its own 'life-style'. Communities may resemble each other in many respects, but the Greeks differ from Lutheran Germans, the Chinese differ from both; what they strive after and what they fear or worship are scarcely ever similar.

This view has been called cultural or moral relativism – this is what that great scholar, my friend Arnaldo Momigliano, whom I greatly admired, supposed both about Vico and about Herder. He was mistaken. It is not relativism. Members of one culture can, by the force of imaginative insight, understand (what Vico called *entrare*) the values, the ideals, the forms of life of another culture or society, even those remote in time or space. They may find these values unacceptable, but if they open their minds sufficiently they can grasp how one might be a full human being, with whom one could communicate, and at the same time live in the light of values widely different from one's own, but which nevertheless one can see to be values, ends of life, by the realisation of which men could be fulfilled.

The Pursuit of the Ideal

'I prefer coffee, you prefer champagne. We have different tastes. There is no more to be said.' That is relativism. But Herder's view, and Vico's, is not that: it is what I should describe as pluralism – that is, the conception that there are many different ends that men may seek and still be fully rational, fully men, capable of understanding each other and sympathising and deriving light from each other, as we derive it from reading Plato or the novels of medieval Japan – worlds, outlooks, very remote from our own. Of course, if we did not have any values in common with these distant figures, each civilisation would be enclosed in its own impenetrable bubble, and we could not understand them at all; this is what Spengler's typology amounts to. Intercommunication between cultures in time and space is only possible because what makes men human is common to them, and acts as a bridge between them. But our values are ours, and theirs are theirs. We are free to criticise the values of other cultures, to condemn them, but we cannot pretend not to understand them at all, or to regard them simply as subjective, the products of creatures in different circumstances with different tastes from our own, which do not speak to us at all.

There is a world of objective values. By this I mean those ends that men pursue for their own sakes, to which other things are means. I am not blind to what the Greeks valued – their values may not be mine, but I can grasp what it would be like to live by their light, I can admire and respect them, and even imagine myself as pursuing them, although I do not – and do not wish to, and perhaps could not if I wished. Forms of life differ. Ends, moral principles, are many. But not infinitely many: they must be within the human horizon. If they are not, then they are outside the human sphere. If I find men who worship trees, not because they are symbols of fertility or because they are divine, with a mysterious life and powers of their own, or because this grove is sacred to Athena – but only because they are made of wood; and if when I ask them why they worship wood they say 'Because it is wood' and give no other answer; then I do not

The Pursuit of the Ideal

know what they mean. If they are human, they are not beings with whom I can communicate – there is a real barrier. They are not human for me. I cannot even call their values subjective if I cannot conceive what it would be like to pursue such a life.

What is clear is that values can clash – that is why civilisations are incompatible. They can be incompatible between cultures, or groups in the same culture, or between you and me. You believe in always telling the truth, no matter what; I do not, because I believe that it can sometimes be too painful and too destructive. We can discuss each other's point of view, we can try to reach common ground, but in the end what you pursue may not be reconcilable with the ends to which I find that I have dedicated my life. Values may easily clash within the breast of a single individual; and it does not follow that, if they do, some must be true and others false. Justice, rigorous justice, is for some people an absolute value, but it is not compatible with what may be no less ultimate values for them – mercy, compassion – as arises in concrete cases.

Both liberty and equality are among the primary goals pursued by human beings through many centuries; but total liberty for wolves is death to the lambs, total liberty of the powerful, the gifted, is not compatible with the rights to a decent existence of the weak and the less gifted. An artist, in order to create a masterpiece, may lead a life which plunges his family into misery and squalor to which he is indifferent. We may condemn him and declare that the masterpiece should be sacrificed to human needs, or we may take his side – but both attitudes embody values which for some men or women are ultimate, and which are intelligible to us all if we have any sympathy or imagination or understanding of human beings. Equality may demand the restraint of the liberty of those who wish to dominate; liberty – without some modicum of which there is no choice and therefore no possibility of remaining human as we understand the word – may have to be curtailed in order to make room for social welfare, to feed the hungry, to clothe the naked, to shelter the homeless, to leave room

The Pursuit of the Ideal

for the liberty of others, to allow justice or fairness to be exercised.

Antigone is faced with a dilemma to which Sophocles implies one solution, Sartre offers the opposite, while Hegel proposes 'sublimation' on to some higher level – poor comfort to those who are agonised by dilemmas of this kind. Spontaneity, a marvellous human quality, is not compatible with capacity for organised planning, for the nice calculation of what and how much and where – on which the welfare of society may largely depend. We are all aware of the agonising alternatives in the recent past. Should a man resist a monstrous tyranny at all costs, at the expense of the lives of his parents or his children? Should children be tortured to extract information about dangerous traitors or criminals?

These collisions of values are of the essence of what they are and what we are. If we are told that these contradictions will be solved in some perfect world in which all good things can be harmonised in principle, then we must answer, to those who say this, that the meanings they attach to the names which for us denote the conflicting values are not ours. We must say that the world in which what we see as incompatible values are not in conflict is a world altogether beyond our ken; that principles which are harmonised in this other world are not the principles with which, in our daily lives, we are acquainted; if they are transformed, it is into conceptions not known to us on earth. But it is on earth that we live, and it is here that we must believe and act.

The notion of the perfect whole, the ultimate solution, in which all good things coexist, seems to me to be not merely unattainable – that is a truism – but conceptually incoherent; I do not know what is meant by a harmony of this kind. Some among the Great Goods cannot live together. That is a conceptual truth. We are doomed to choose, and every choice may entail an irreparable loss. Happy are those who live under a discipline which they accept without question, who freely obey the orders of leaders, spiritual or temporal, whose word is fully

The Pursuit of the Ideal

accepted as unbreakable law; or those who have, by their own methods, arrived at clear and unshakeable convictions about what to do and what to be that brook no possible doubt. I can only say that those who rest on such comfortable beds of dogma are victims of forms of self-induced myopia, blinkers that may make for contentment, but not for understanding of what it is to be human.

V

So much for the theoretical objection, a fatal one, it seems to me, to the notion of the perfect state as the proper goal of our endeavours. But there is in addition a more practical socio-psychological obstacle to this, an obstacle that may be put to those whose simple faith, by which humanity has been nourished for so long, is resistant to philosophical arguments of any kind. It is true that some problems can be solved, some ills cured, in both the individual and social life. We can save men from hunger or misery or injustice, we can rescue men from slavery or imprisonment, and do good – all men have a basic sense of good and evil, no matter what cultures they belong to; but any study of society shows that every solution creates a new situation which breeds its own new needs and problems, new demands. The children have obtained what their parents and grandparents longed for – greater freedom, greater material welfare, a juster society; but the old ills are forgotten, and the children face new problems, brought about by the very solutions of the old ones, and these, even if they can in turn be solved, generate new situations, and with them new requirements – and so on, for ever – and unpredictably.

We cannot legislate for the unknown consequences of consequences of consequences. Marxists tell us that once the fight is won and true history has begun, the new problems that may arise will generate their own solutions, which can be peacefully realised by the united powers of harmonious, classless society.

The Pursuit of the Ideal

This seems to me a piece of metaphysical optimism for which there is no evidence in historical experience. In a society in which the same goals are universally accepted, problems can be only of means, all soluble by technological methods. That is a society in which the inner life of man, the moral and spiritual and aesthetic imagination, no longer speaks at all. Is it for this that men and women should be destroyed or societies enslaved? Utopias have their value – nothing so wonderfully expands the imaginative horizons of human potentialities – but as guides to conduct they can prove literally fatal. Heraclitus was right, things cannot stand still.

So I conclude that the very notion of a final solution is not only impracticable but, if I am right, and some values cannot but clash, incoherent also. The possibility of a final solution – even if we forget the terrible sense that these words acquired in Hitler's day – turns out to be an illusion; and a very dangerous one. For if one really believes that such a solution is possible, then surely no cost would be too high to obtain it: to make mankind just and happy and creative and harmonious for ever – what could be too high a price to pay for that? To make such an omelette, there is surely no limit to the number of eggs that should be broken – that was the faith of Lenin, of Trotsky, of Mao, for all I know of Pol Pot. Since I know the only true path to the ultimate solution of the problems of society, I know which way to drive the human caravan; and since you are ignorant of what I know, you cannot be allowed to have liberty of choice even within the narrowest limits, if the goal is to be reached. You declare that a given policy will make you happier, or freer, or give you room to breathe; but I know that you are mistaken, I know what you need, what all men need; and if there is resistance based on ignorance or malevolence, then it must be broken and hundreds of thousands may have to perish to make millions happy for all time. What choice have we, who have the knowledge, but to be willing to sacrifice them all?

Some armed prophets seek to save mankind, and some only their own race because of its superior attributes, but whichever

The Pursuit of the Ideal

the motive, the millions slaughtered in wars or revolutions – gas chambers, gulag, genocide, all the monstrosities for which our century will be remembered – are the price men must pay for the felicity of future generations. If your desire to save mankind is serious, you must harden your heart, and not reckon the cost.

The answer to this was given more than a century ago by the Russian radical Alexander Herzen. In his essay *From the Other Shore*, which is in effect an obituary notice of the revolutions of 1848, he said that a new form of human sacrifice had arisen in his time – of living human beings on the altars of abstractions – nation, church, party, class, progress, the forces of history – these have all been invoked in his day and in ours: if these demand the slaughter of living human beings, they must be satisfied. These are his words:

> If progress is the goal, for whom are we working? Who is this Moloch who, as the toilers approach him, instead of rewarding them, draws back; and as a consolation to the exhausted and doomed multitudes, shouting 'morituri te salutant', can only give the . . . mocking answer that after their death all will be beautiful on earth. Do you truly wish to condemn the human beings alive today to the sad role . . . of wretched galley slaves who, up to their knees in mud, drag a barge . . . with . . . 'progress in the future' upon its flag? . . . a goal which is infinitely remote is no goal, only . . . a deception; a goal must be closer – at the very least the labourer's wage, or pleasure in work performed.

The one thing that we may be sure of is the reality of the sacrifice, the dying and the dead. But the ideal for the sake of which they die remains unrealised. The eggs are broken, and the habit of breaking them grows, but the omelette remains invisible. Sacrifices for short-term goals, coercion, if men's plight is desperate enough and truly requires such measures, may be justified. But holocausts for the sake of distant goals, that is a cruel mockery of all that men hold dear, now and at all times.

The Pursuit of the Ideal

VI

If the old perennial belief in the possibility of realising ultimate harmony is a fallacy, and the positions of the thinkers I have appealed to – Machiavelli, Vico, Herder, Herzen – are valid, then, if we allow that Great Goods can collide, that some of them cannot live together, even though others can – in short, that one cannot have everything, in principle as well as in practice – and if human creativity may depend upon a variety of mutually exclusive choices: then, as Chernyshevsky and Lenin once asked, 'What is to be done?' How do we choose between possibilities? What and how much must we sacrifice to what? There is, it seems to me, no clear reply. But the collisions, even if they cannot be avoided, can be softened. Claims can be balanced, compromises can be reached: in concrete situations not every claim is of equal force – so much liberty and so much equality; so much for sharp moral condemnation, and so much for understanding a given human situation; so much for the full force of the law, and so much for the prerogative of mercy; for feeding the hungry, clothing the naked, healing the sick, sheltering the homeless. Priorities, never final and absolute, must be established.

The first public obligation is to avoid extremes of suffering. Revolutions, wars, assassinations, extreme measures may in desperate situations be required. But history teaches us that their consequences are seldom what is anticipated; there is no guarantee, not even, at times, a high enough probability, that such acts will lead to improvement. We may take the risk of drastic action, in personal life or in public policy, but we must always be aware, never forget, that we may be mistaken, that certainty about the effect of such measures invariably leads to avoidable suffering of the innocent. So we must engage in what are called trade-offs – rules, values, principles must yield to each other in varying degrees in specific situations. Utilitarian solutions are sometimes wrong, but, I suspect, more often beneficent. The best that can be done, as a general rule, is to

The Pursuit of the Ideal

maintain a precarious equilibrium that will prevent the occurrence of desperate situations, of intolerable choices – that is the first requirement for a decent society; one that we can always strive for, in the light of the limited range of our knowledge, and even of our imperfect understanding of individuals and societies. A certain humility in these matters is very necessary.

This may seem a very flat answer, not the kind of thing that the idealistic young would wish, if need be, to fight and suffer for, in the cause of a new and nobler society. And, of course, we must not dramatise the incompatibility of values – there is a great deal of broad agreement among people in different societies over long stretches of time about what is right and wrong, good and evil. Of course traditions, outlooks, attitudes may legitimately differ; general principles may cut across too much human need. The concrete situation is almost everything. There is no escape: we must decide as we decide; moral risk cannot, at times, be avoided. All we can ask for is that none of the relevant factors be ignored, that the purposes we seek to realise should be seen as elements in a total form of life, which can be enhanced or damaged by decisions.

But, in the end, it is not a matter of purely subjective judgement: it is dictated by the forms of life of the society to which one belongs, a society among other societies, with values held in common, whether or not they are in conflict, by the majority of mankind throughout recorded history. There are, if not universal values, at any rate a minimum without which societies could scarcely survive. Few today would wish to defend slavery or ritual murder or Nazi gas chambers or the torture of human beings for the sake of pleasure or profit or even political good – or the duty of children to denounce their parents, which the French and Russian revolutions demanded, or mindless killing. There is no justification for compromise on this. But on the other hand, the search for perfection does seem to me a recipe for bloodshed, no better even if it is demanded by the sincerest of idealists, the purest of heart. No more rigorous moralist than Immanuel Kant has ever lived, but even he said,

The Pursuit of the Ideal

in a moment of illumination, 'Out of the crooked timber of humanity no straight thing was ever made.' To force people into the neat uniforms demanded by dogmatically believed-in schemes is almost always the road to inhumanity. We can only do what we can: but that we must do, against difficulties.

Of course social or political collisions will take place; the mere conflict of positive values alone makes this unavoidable. Yet they can, I believe, be minimised by promoting and preserving an uneasy equilibrium, which is constantly threatened and in constant need of repair – that alone, I repeat, is the precondition for decent societies and morally acceptable behaviour, otherwise we are bound to lose our way. A little dull as a solution, you will say? Not the stuff of which calls to heroic action by inspired leaders are made? Yet if there is some truth in this view, perhaps that is sufficient. An eminent American philosopher of our day once said, 'There is no *a priori* reason for supposing that the truth, when it is discovered, will necessarily prove interesting.' It may be enough if it is truth, or even an approximation to it; consequently I do not feel apologetic for advancing this. Truth, said Tolstoy, 'has been, is and will be beautiful'. I do not know if this is so in the realm of ethics, but it seems to me near enough to what most of us wish to believe not to be too lightly set aside.

[11]
THE STRUCTURE OF MORAL LEADERSHIP

"We have many wants," Plato said, and society and government arose out of these needs as people began to exchange things that they made. Necessity is the mother of invention, Plato went on. "Now the first and greatest necessity is food, which is the condition of life and existence. . . . The second is a dwelling, and the third clothing and the like. . . ." Once a family had these things, then "noble cakes and loaves" would be served up on a mat of reeds or clean leaves, the parents "reclining the while upon beds strewn with yew or myrtle. And they and their children will feast, drinking of the wine which they have made, wearing garlands on their heads, and hymning the praises of the gods, in happy converse with one another. . . ."

With these words Plato posed a question that has challenged philosophers and scientists to this day: whether people the world over share common wants and needs. As some wants are satisfied are other—"higher"—wants created? Are wants and needs arranged in roughly the same hierarchies in most or all cultures? Common sense tells us that any person, whether Eskimo or Hottentot, Zuni or Kpelle, Brooklynite or East End Londoner, puts first things first—breathing before eating, human life above property, basic nourishment before the "sauces and sweets" that Plato proposed as the climax of the meal. The same would seem to be true of "higher needs"—for survival needs before social acceptance, and social needs—love and esteem—before aesthetic. Yet anthropologists have identified countless cultures with the most remarkable varieties of wants and needs. Consider the assumed top priority of sheer survival. Some societies kill their infants to protect their food reserves. In others, men kill themselves (Wall Street, 1929) when they lose their property. In India women burned themselves on funeral pyres when they lost their husbands.

For students of leadership an even more urgent question arises. Supposing we could find species-wide commonalities among hierarchies of wants and needs, could we also find common stages and levels of moral development and reasoning emerging out of those wants and needs? If so, we could assume common foundations for leadership. If we define leadership as not merely a property or activity of leaders but as *relationship* between leaders and a multitude of followers of many types, if we see leaders as interacting with followers in a great merging of motivations and purposes of both, and if in turn we find that many of those motivations and purposes are common to vast numbers of humankind in many cultures, then could we expect to identify patterns of leadership behavior permitting plausible generalizations about the ways in which leaders generally behave?

During the last decade or so, researches in the field of moral development have uncovered remarkable uniformities in hierarchies of moral reasoning across a number of cultures. The research is far from complete; certain cultural relativists hold that the findings and implications are overgeneralized; and it is alleged that the values considered to be universal have in fact a Western bias. But, as Harry Girvetz has said: "In rejecting moral dogmatism are we to be driven to moral skepticism?" Identification of leadership patterns does not depend on finding absolutely universal motives and values. Universal patterns simply assume strong probabilities that most leaders in interacting with followers will behave in similar ways most of the time. In dealing with the structure of moral leadership in this chapter, we will be summarizing more extensive findings to be presented more fully in the next chapter. Here we must note how levels of wants and needs and other motivations, combined with hierarchies of values, and sharpened by conflict, undergird the dynamics of leadership.

> *Erst kommt das Fressen, dann Kommt die Moral.*
> First comes the belly, then morality.
> Bertolt Brecht, *Three-Penny Opera*

The Power and Sources of Values

Like Plato, we can see the role of power and values in every-day life.

A thousand years ago, according to Soviet Armenian legend, Moslem invaders tried to find a way to lower the water level of Lake Sevan. Their aim was to make a land attack on an island fortress and monastery in the lake, located halfway between the Black Sea and the lower Caspian. In the 1930s Soviet engineers accomplished this feat not for military but for economic purposes; by tapping the lake's waters they were able to create new farmland and to generate electric power for local industrial development. They succeeded, but the lowered water level caused extensive ecological and aesthetic damage. Forty years later Soviet construction crews were digging a huge, thirty-mile tunnel from a nearby river to replenish the lake.

"When we were poor," a local water power official observed, "Lake Sevan helped us to stand on our feet. But when we became richer, we began to think how we had to help Sevan, this beauty of nature."

In New York City not long ago a construction crew, chain saws in hand, suddenly appeared on East 63rd Street and fell upon a dozen or so spreading sycamores. The tearing, growling noise of the saws brought residents to their windows. One woman hurled a plastic bag filled with water at a foreman; another woman burst into tears as she watched. She was not propitiated by the setting up of some potted trees where the sycamores had stood.

"They were beautiful old trees, so old, so fresh," she said later, "you looked up at them and regardless of your depression, you simply thought, oh isn't that lovely."

"I'll tell you, to be very honest, I was mad," the foreman said. "We're poor people, but we're human beings." Pointing to the replacement trees, he added: "You see what the poor people do for the rich people."

"I must study politics and war, that my sons may have liberty to study mathematics and philosophy," John Adams said. "My sons ought to study mathematics and philosophy, geography, natural history and naval architecture, in order to give their children a right to study painting, poetry, music, architecture, statuary, tapestry and porcelain." A Thai boy scout, recruited to combat "communism," bespoke the value he was scheduled to embrace. "Once we get trained, we are united. So it is very difficult for other types of ideas to come in. We stress love of our king, of our country, of religion." Oh, there was no ideology, he added; they did not mention Communism, "but it works automatically."

We must not put groups or societies into conceptual straitjackets. Sometimes the people seem to "skip" a level and advance to a higher one apparently inappropriate to present need. In the 1976 electoral revolt against Indira Gandhi and the Congress party, India voted against suppressors of liberty despite the emphasis of the Congress party on basic needs for food, shelter, and land. Ordinarily, however, economic want and social disarray are stultifying, causing people's aspirations to turn downward and inward; only after physical survival and economic security are assured do people turn to higher needs and hopes.

The long relationship between Franklin D. Roosevelt and Joseph P. Kennedy illustrates the complex interplay of power and values, and suggests that ultimately the role of values may be crucial, even in the "practical" relationships of leaders. Both were Harvard men, but otherwise their backgrounds contrasted sharply: Roosevelt the product of a benign, secure and small patrician world on the banks of the Hudson, Kennedy of the striving, competitive, vulnerable world of the Irish immigrant on the urban East Coast. The two men were thrown into a personal confrontation in World War I when Roosevelt, the assistant secretary of the navy, asked Kennedy, assistant manager of the Fore River shipyard in Massachusetts, to deliver several battleships Fore River had built for the Argentine government. Kennedy refused to release the ships because the Argentinians had not yet paid the bill. After appealing in vain to Kennedy's sense of patriotism in wartime, Roosevelt threatened to have the navy tow the ships away. Kennedy left fuming and defeated; he was so upset on leaving Roosevelt's office, he admitted later, that "I broke down and cried."

More than two decades later, during another great European war, Kennedy and Roosevelt confronted each other once again, under a very different set of circumstances. Having joined the Roosevelt bandwagon well before the Chicago convention of 1932, Kennedy had headed the Securities and Exchange Commission and the Maritime Commission and then eagerly accepted an appointment by Roosevelt as ambassador to Britain. But as Europe plunged into war, disquieting reports trickled into Washington about the ambassador's "defeatist" view of Britain's ability to withstand Nazi attack and about his veiled but pungent criticism of Roosevelt and his administration. As the 1940 presidential campaign got under way, Kennedy seemed to hold a pivotal political position. To fight off a hard drive by Wendell Willkie, Roosevelt was picking out a tortuous path between the interventionists and the America Firsters. A resignation by such a prominent Roosevelt ambassador as Kennedy and a return home to join Willkie's "crusade"—or even a Kennedy warning against the administration's "interventionism"—might have tipped the scales in favor of the Republicans. Kennedy's conspicuous Catholicism gave him considerable leverage with the Irish and other ethnic voters who might be pivotal in some of the Northeastern states. He could help the President a lot—or hurt him a lot.

The problem for the President was to persuade Kennedy either to remain in London or to declare for Roosevelt with the right kind of endorsement. First Roosevelt directed that Kennedy be ordered to remain at his post, but when Kennedy threatened to release a statement critical of the administration if not allowed home, the President granted his envoy home leave, with repeated instructions not to say a word about politics or diplomacy on the way back to America. Presidential agents intercepted Kennedy at LaGuardia Field and in effect cordoned him off from Willkie emissaries who had hoped to bring the ambassador into the Republican campaign. A red carpet awaited Kennedy at the

White House, where Roosevelt greeted him effusively and invited him to talk. The ambassador proceeded to pour out his grievances against the State Department and against the White House for asking him to perform favors and then not reciprocating. Roosevelt made no defense of his subordinates or of himself. On the contrary, he nodded understandingly, adding that he knew exactly how Kennedy felt and promising that State Department bureaucrats would not be permitted to treat old and valued envoys so outrageously in the future. The President even—or so the ambassador was led to believe—made some "offer" to Kennedy of the Democratic party nomination in 1944. The carrot was dangled, but so perhaps was the stick—according to a British secret service agent, Roosevelt brought out transcripts of Kennedy's London denunciations of the President. Now his chief asked him to support him publicly for re-election, and Kennedy gave in. A few nights later Kennedy endorsed Roosevelt in a nationwide radio address. The President defeated Willkie, and after the election, Kennedy resigned in expectation of another presidential appointment. No word came from the White House. A year later, after Pearl Harbor, Kennedy volunteered his services for an important war job, but he never received one. Roosevelt exerted the power of *inaction*.

Leadership in the shaping of private and public opinion, leadership of reform and revolutionary movements—that is, transformational leadership—seems to take on significant and collective proportions historically, but at the time and point of action leadership is intensely individual and personal. Leadership becomes a matter of all-too-human motivation and goals, of conflict and competition that seem to be dominated by the petty quest for esteem and prestige. In the battle of the battleships Kennedy and Roosevelt seemed to be engaged in a naked power fight, and the bigger battalions—in this case, battleships—won. Roosevelt finally got his way not by appealing to Kennedy's motives of patriotism or personal advancement; he got it through direct exercise of power. In the crux Kennedy had no recourse. Conceivably he might have appealed to the head of Bethlehem Steel, who owned the Fore River yard, but Bethlehem would hardly have challenged the administration in time of war. Or he might have appealed to shipyard workers to cordon off the battleships against the navy, but the workers hardly shared Kennedy's obsession with cash on the barrelhead. Kennedy built warships but Roosevelt disposed of them. No wonder Kennedy cried.

Roosevelt's bringing Kennedy back into camp in 1940 is a contrasting kind of power-wielding. Once again Roosevelt seemed to exert his will, but this time Kennedy had considerable freedom of choice. The President could try to exploit the ambassador's motives of self-esteem and patriotism, but Kennedy could achieve self-esteem through the esteem of others beside Roosevelt—of the Willkieites, for example—and he had his own notion of patriotism. If Roosevelt blocked his hopes of becoming a wartime czar, Kennedy had other means of achieving recognition.

What ultimately dominated World War II politics and strategy, however, was the moral issue of aid to the allies who were fighting Nazism. It was because Roosevelt's fundamental values were deeply humane and democratic that he was able, despite his earlier compromises and evasions, to act when action was imperative. Within a few weeks of his re-election in 1940 he was hard at work on a program—Lend Lease—that was to have an extraordinary impact on war and post-war outcomes. Testifying on the Lend Lease bill before the House Foreign Affairs committee, Kennedy was so inconclusive and self-contradictory that he gave no clear lead to friend or foe. Kennedy never seemed to see a transcending moral issue in the war. Because Roosevelt did, he was able to act with moral impact—to act with power.

Clearly the leader who commands compelling causes has an extraordinary potential influence over followers. Followers armed by moral inspiration, mobilized and purposeful, become zealots and leaders in their own right. How do values come to hold such power over certain leaders? What theories of human development cast light on the sources of such values in both leaders and followers? Do some leaders respond to followers' values without sharing them?

The need for social esteem, we have noted, is a powerful one. Mature leaders may have such a voracious need for affection that they seek it and accept it from every source, without discrimination; Lyndon B. Johnson seemed to want every member of the Senate to love him when he was majority leader and every American to love him when he was President. No matter how strong this longing for unanimity, however, almost all leaders, at least at the national level, must settle for far less than universal affection. They must be willing *to make enemies*—to deny themselves the affection of their adversaries. They must accept conflict. They must be willing and able to be unloved. It is hard to pick one's friends, harder to pick one's enemies.

On what basis is the decision *not* to win friends made? The calculus may seem purely pragmatic; leaders may need to win only enough support to gain a party nomination, build an electoral majority, put a bill through the legislature, bring off a revolution. But even in the most practical terms leaders must decide what side they will take, which group they will lead, what party they will utilize, what kind of revolution they will command. They will, in short, be influenced by considerations of *purpose* or *value* that may lie beyond calculations of personal advancement. Can we trace the origins of the shaping and sharing of values back to various needs of childhood, or is purpose and influence built into the potential leader by social and political processes only during later years? Is it in some measure independent of psychological need and environmental cause—objectively based in process of mind? How deep are the roots of values held strongly by leaders and the led?

The roots lie very deep, entwined with guilt feelings that arise out of the child's early confrontation with parental authority, too deep to disentangle them completely. In Freudian theory the superego develops as part of the resolution of Oedipal conflicts, as the child internalizes prohibitions expressed in the form of parental chidings and warnings. In need of urgent instant gratification, anxious also to identify with the parents and gain their affection, the child learns to evade parental displeasure and punishment by repressing the behavior that would invoke these penalties. Typically the superego manifested itself in feelings of conscience early in childhood. Jean Piaget noted that children internalized rules and standards so automatically that they grew literal and absolutist about them; rules they saw as ends—almost as objects—in themselves, to be responded to indiscriminately. In some persons these moralistic rigidities carried on into later years without adequate transformation of rule into values. In most cases they were altered by socializing forces.

Out of these elemental but powerful influences of the superego values emerge. The question is how the child makes the transition from rules dictated by Oedipal and other conflict, articulated and enforced by parents, and internalized by the child to the shaping of values. This question has divided the analysts. Freud doubted that the early configurations of conscience and standards could be substantially changed in adult life, except perhaps through psychoanalysis, for they were determined by an iron law of biological and child-parent relations. Carl Jung criticized the "Viennese idea of sexuality with all its vague omnipotence," the notion that the brain was merely an appendage of the genital glands, and the entire mechanistic approach to causation. Persons, Jung insisted, acted not only in response to causal (i.e., mechanistic) forces but to ends or aims (*fines*) as well. Julian Huxley wrote that the evolution of "the primitive super-ego" into a "more rational and less cruel mechanism" is "the central ethical problem confronting every human individual." Erik Erikson said: "The great governor of initiative is conscience. . . . But . . . the conscience of the child can be primitive, cruel, and uncompromising. . . ." Talcott Parsons contended that Freud's view while correct was too narrow, that not only moral standards but all the components of the common culture become rooted in personality structure.

Of these views on the origins of values, Freud's theory of Oedipal conflict, as applied to broader social processes, and Jung's concern with ends, or purposes, are together most useful to students of leadership, for they make possible a concept of values forged and hardened by *conflict*.

Conflict and Consciousness

Leadership is a process of morality to the degree that leaders engage with followers on the basis of shared motives and values and goals—on the basis, that is, of the followers' "true" needs as well as those of leaders: psychological, economic, safety, spiritual, sexual, aesthetic, or physical. Friends, relatives, teachers, officials, politicians, ministers, and others will supply a variety of initiatives, but only the followers themselves can ultimately define their own true needs. And they can do so only when they have been exposed to the competing diagnoses, claims, and values of would-be leaders, only when the followers can make an informed choice among competing "prescriptions," only when—in the political arena at least—followers have had full opportunity to perceive, comprehend, evaluate, and finally experience alternatives offered by those professing to be their "true" representatives. Ultimately the moral legitimacy of transformational leadership, and to a lesser degree transactional leadership, is grounded in *conscious choice among real alternatives*. Hence leadership assumes competition and conflict, and brute power denies it.

Conflict has become the stepchild of political thought. Philosophical concern with conflict reaches back to Hobbes and even Heraclitus, and men who spurred revolutions in Western thought—Machiavelli and Hegel, Marx and Freud—recognized the vital role of conflict in the relations among persons or in the ambivalences within them. The seventeenth-century foes of absolute monarchy, the eighteenth-century Scottish moralists, the nineteenth-century Social Darwinists—these and other schools of thought dealt directly with questions of power and conflict, and indirectly at least with the nature of leadership. The theories of Pareto, Durkheim, Weber, and others, while not centrally concerned with problems of social conflict, "contain many concepts, assumptions, and hypotheses which greatly influenced later writers who did attempt to deal with conflict in general." Georg Simmel and others carried theories of conflict into the twentieth century.

It was, curiously, in this same century—an epoch of the bloodiest world wars, mightiest revolutions, and most savage civil wars—that social science, at least in the West, became most entranced with doctrines of harmony, adjustment, and stability. Perhaps this was the result of relative affluence, or of the need to unify people to conduct total war or consolidate revolutions, or of the co-option of scholars to advise on mitigating hostility among interest groups such as labor and management or racial groups such as blacks and whites. Whatever the cause, the "static bias" afflicted scholarly research with a tendency to look on conflict as an aberration, if not a perversion, of the agreeable and harmonious interactions that were seen as actually making up organized society. More recently Western scholarship has shown a quickened interest in the role of conflict in establishing boundaries, channeling hostility, counteracting social ossification, invigorating class and group interests, encouraging innovation, and defining and empowering leadership.

The static bias among scholars doubtless encouraged and reflected the pronouncements of political authority. Communist leaders apotheosized conflict as the engine of the process of overthrowing bourgeois regimes and then banned both the profession and the utilization of conflict in the new "classless" societies. Western leaders, especially in the United States, make a virtual fetish of "national unity," "party harmony," and foreign policy bipartisanship even while they indulge in—and virtually live off—contested elections and divisive policy issues. Jefferson proclaimed at his first Inaugural, "We are all Federalists, we are all Republicans." Few American presidents have aroused and inflamed popular attitudes as divisively as Franklin D. Roosevelt with his assaults on conservatives in both parties, his New Deal innovations, and his efforts to pack the Supreme Court and purge the Democratic party, yet few American presidents have devoted so many addresses to sermonlike calls for transcending differences and behaving as one nation and one people.

The potential for conflict permeates the relations of humankind, and that potential is a force for health and growth as well as for destruction and barbarism. No group can be wholly harmonious, as Simmel said, for such a group would be empty of process and structure. The smooth interaction of people is continually threatened by disparate rates of change, technological innovation, mass deprivation, competition for scarce resources, and other ineluctable social forces and by ambivalences, tensions, and conflicts within individuals' personalities. One can imagine a society—in ancient Egypt, perhaps, or in an isolated rural area today—in which the division of labor, the barriers against external influence, the structure of the family, the organization of the value system, the acceptance of authority, and the decision-making by leaders all interact smoothly and amiably with one another. But the vision of such a society would be useful only as an imaginary construct at one end of a continuum from cohesion to conflict. Indeed, the closer, the more intimate the relations within a group, the more hostility as well as harmony may be generated. The smaller the cooperative group—even if united by language and thrown closely together by living arrangements—"the easier it is for them to be mutually irritated and to flare up in anger," Bronislaw Malinowski said. Some conflict over valued goals and objects is almost inevitable. Even small, isolated societies cannot indefinitely dike off the impact of internal changes such as alteration of the birth rate or the disruption caused by various forms of innovation.

The question, then, is not the inevitability of conflict but the function of leadership in expressing, shaping, and curbing it. Leadership as conceptualized here is grounded in the seedbed of conflict. Conflict is intrinsically compelling; it galvanizes, prods, motivates people. Every person, group, and society has latent tension and hostility, forming a variety of psychological and political patterns across social situations. Leadership acts as an inciting and triggering force in the conversion of conflicting demands, values, and goals into significant behavior. Since leaders have an interest of their own, whether opportunistic or ideological or both, in expressing and exploiting followers' wants, needs, and aspirations, they act as catalytic agents in arousing followers' consciousness. They discern signs of dissatisfaction, deprivation, and strain; they take the initiative in making connections with their followers; they plumb the character and intensity of their potential for mobilization; they articulate grievances and wants; and they act for followers in their dealings with other clusters of followers.

Conflicts vary in origin—in and between nations, races, regions, religions, economic enterprises, labor unions, communities, kinship groups, families, and individuals themselves. Conflicts show various degrees and qualities of persistence, direction, intensity, volatility, latency, scope. The last alone may be pivotal; the outcome of every conflict, E. E. Schattschneider wrote, "is determined by the *scope* of its contagion. The number of people involved in any conflict determines what happens; every change in the number of participants . . . affects the results . . . . The moral of this is: If a fight starts, watch the crowd, because the crowd plays the decisive role." But it is leadership that draws the crowd into the incident, that changes the number of participants, that closely affects the manner of the spread of the conflict, that constitutes the main "processes" of relating the wider public to the conflict.

The root causes of conflict are as varied as their origins. No one has described these causes as cogently as James Madison.

> The latent causes of faction are thus sown in the nature of man; and we see them every where brought into different degrees of activity, according to the different circumstances of civil society. A zeal for different opinions concerning religion, concerning government and many other points, as well of speculation as of practice, an attachment to different leaders ambitiously contending for preeminence and power; or to persons of other descriptions whose fortunes have been interesting to the human passions, have in turn divided mankind into parties, inflamed them with mutual animosity, and rendered them much more disposed to vex and oppress each other, than to co-operate for their common good. So strong is this propensity of mankind to fall into mutual animosities, that where no substantial occasion presents itself, the most frivolous and fanciful distinctions have

been sufficient to kindle their unfriendly passions, and excite their most violent conflicts. But the most common and durable source of factions, has been the various and unequal distribution of property.

Not only "attachment to different leaders" but all these forces for conflict are expressed and channeled through many different types of leaders "ambitiously contending for pre-eminence and power."

Leaders, whatever their professions of harmony, do not shun conflict; they confront it, exploit it, ultimately embody it. Standing at the points of contact among latent conflict groups, they can take various roles, sometimes acting directly for their followers, sometimes bargaining with others, sometimes overriding certain motives of followers and summoning others into play. The smaller and more homogeneous the group for which they act, the more probable that they will have to deal with the leaders of other groups with opposing needs and values. The larger, more heterogeneous their collection of followers, the more probable that they will have to embrace competing interests and goals within their constituency. At the same time, their marginality supplies them with a double leverage, since in their status as leaders they are expected by their followers and by other leaders to deviate, to innovate, and to mediate between the claims of their groups and those of others.

But leaders shape as well as express and mediate conflict. They do this largely by influencing the intensity and scope of conflict. Within limits they can soften or sharpen the claims and demands of their followers, as they calculate their own political resources in dealing with competing leaders within their own constituencies and outside. They can amplify the voice and pressure of their followers, to the benefit of their bargaining power perhaps, but at the possible price of freedom to maneuver—less freedom to protect themselves against their followers—as they play in games of broader stakes. Similarly, they can narrow or broaden the scope of conflict as they seek to limit or multiply the number of entrants into a specific political arena.

Franklin Roosevelt demonstrated the fine art of controlling entry in the presidential nomination race in 1940. There was widespread uncertainty as to whether he would run for a third term. He himself was following the development of public opinion at the same time that he was influencing it. Leaders in his own party were divided; onetime stalwarts like James A. Farley and Cordell Hull opposed a third term. It was supposed that FDR would discourage Democrats from entering the nomination race. On the contrary, he welcomed them. Secondary figures like Joseph Kennedy, coming to the Oval Office to sound out Roosevelt on his intentions and on their own chances, found themselves flattered and rated as serious and deserving possibilities. The effect was to broaden the field of possible adversaries and hence divide and weaken the opposition. FDR had little trouble winning the nomination.

The essential strategy of leadership in mobilizing power is to recognize the arrays of motives and goals in potential followers, to appeal to those motives by words and action, and to strengthen those motives and goals in order to increase the power of leadership, thereby changing the environment within which both followers and leaders act. Conflict—disagreement over goals within an array of followers, fear of outsiders, competition for scarce resources—immensely invigorates the mobilization of consensus and dissensus. But the fundamental process is a more elusive one; it is, in large part, *to make conscious what lies unconscious among followers.*

The purposeful awakening of persons into a state of political consciousness is a familiar problem for philosophers and psychologists and one that has stimulated thought in other disciplines. For the student of leadership the concept of political consciousness is as primitive as it is fertile. That "conflict produces consciousness" was fundamental in the doctrine of Hegel, Marx, and other nineteenth-century theorists, but they differed over the cardinal question: consciousness of *what?* They recognized the essential human needs but differed as to the nature of those needs. Feuerbach, an intellectual leader of the young Marx, conceived humanity as imbued with real, tangible, solid needs arising from Nature. Marx compared human consciousness with that of animals, which had no consciousness of the world as something objective and real apart from the animal's own existence and needs. But *human* labor, rather than leading to direct satisfaction of need, generates human consciousness and self-consciousness. Thus the early Marx had some understanding of the variety and inexhaustibility of human needs.

It was a marvelous insight, but Marx came to be identified with the doctrine that *true* consciousness, to be achieved through unremitting conflict, was always of *class.* Felt, palpable human needs, however, did not seem to be translated into a rising class consciousness in the capitalist environment of the mid-nineteenth century. Marx and Engels railed at the "false consciousness" of religion and nationalism and the other diversions and superficialities that seemed to engage men who were caught in the iron grip of material deprivation. The progress toward class consciousness was slow, irregular, uneven. The almost automatic movement toward revolution, emerging out of the "spontaneous class-organization of the proletariat," simply did not come about in the great bourgeois societies; ultimately revolution would need to be spurred by militant leadership and iron party discipline.

In the fiery intellectual and political conflict of the nineteenth century both Marxists and their adversaries assumed too much about the central springs of human behavior without knowing enough about motivation or the complex relations between motives and behavior. Few perceived that if people did not behave the way they were supposed to, the fault might lie in the suppositions rather than in the people. One of the suppositions was that ultimately humans would respond rationally and "realistically" to "objective" social conditions. But what was real and rational? If Marx had turned Hegel's dialectic of ideas on its head, Freud turned Marx's Consciousness upside down. Freud was drawn to the function of the unconscious rather than the conscious or the preconscious; for him the unconscious was the "true psychic reality," betrayed by dreams, fantasies, accidents, and curious slips of the tongue. Consciousness and related concepts of alienation and identity have continued to be variously defined and heatedly debated. During the ferment of the 1960s that reached across the Western world, young people were urged to "expand consciousness" and "consciousness-raising" became something of a fad and a profession.

If the first task of leadership is to bring to consciousness the followers' sense of their own needs, values, and purposes, the question remains: consciousness of what? Which of these motives and goals are to be tapped? Leaders, for example, can make followers more conscious of aspects of their *identity* (sexual, communal, ethnic, class, national, ideological). Georges Sorel argued that only through leadership and conflict, including "terrifying violence," could the working class become conscious of its true identity—and hence of its power. But to what extent was Sorel imposing his own values and goals on workers who might have very different, even idiosyncratic, ones? We return to the dilemma: to what degree do leaders, through their command of personal influence, substitute their own motives and goals for those of the followers? Should they whip up chauvinism, feelings of ethnic superiority, regional prejudice, economic rivalry? What must they accept among followers as being durable and valid rather than false and transient? And we return to the surmise here: leaders with relevant motives and goals of their own respond to followers' needs and wants and goals in such a way as to meet those motivations and to bring changes consonant with those of both leaders and followers, and with the values of both.

The Elevating Power of Leadership

Mobilized and shaped by gifted leadership, sharpened and strengthened by conflict, values can be the source of vital change. The question is: at what level of need or stage of morality do leaders operate to elevate their followers? At levels of safety and security, followers tend to conform to group expectations and to support and justify the social order. At a certain stage Kohlberg finds a "law and order" orientation toward authority, fixed rules, and maintenance of the social order for its own sake. At a higher stage Simpson found a significant relation between tendencies toward self-esteem and positive law values (belief that the authority for judgments rests in the laws and norms humans have developed collectively). This is the level of "social contract morality."

At the highest stage of moral development persons are guided by near-universal ethical principles of justice such as equality of human rights and respect for individual dignity. This stage sets the opportunity for rare and creative leadership. Politicians who operate at the lower and middle levels of need and moral development are easily understood, but what kind of leadership reaches into the need and value structures, mobilizing and directing support for such values as justice and empathy?

First, it is the kind of leadership that *operates at need and value levels higher than those of the potential follower* (but not so much higher as to lose contact). This kind of leadership need be neither doctrinaire nor indoctrinative (in the ordinary sense of preaching). In its most effective form it appeals to the higher, more general and comprehensive values that express followers' more fundamental and enduring needs. The appeal may be more potent when a polity faces danger from outside, as from an invasion, or from inside, as in social breakdown, civil war, or natural catastrophe. "If inefficiencies and corruption of governmental and social leadership go beyond 'normal,' if demands are constantly frustrated by incapacities, which can be readily laid at some human door, if all of this is compounded by a rising consciousness of discrimination and sense of justice," according to a four-nation study, "then people can experience great and often very sudden transformation of values, or those values that were subdued can become the basis for vigorous action." No single force, such as economic conditions, predetermines change, this study concluded; other factors—notably the quality of leadership—intervene, so the role of values in social change varies from culture to culture. Among the nations studied (India, Poland, the United States, Yugoslavia) similarities were found in leaders' espousal of innovative change, economic development, and the norms of selflessness (commitment to the general welfare) and honesty.

Second, it is the kind of leadership that *can exploit conflict and tension within persons' value structures*. Contradictions can be expected among competing substantive values, such as liberty and equality, or between those values and moral values like honesty, or between terminal values and instrumental values. "All contemporary theories in social psychology would probably agree that a necessary prerequisite to cognitive change is the presence of some state of imbalance within the system,'' Rokeach says.

Leaders may simply help a follower see these types of contradictions, or they might actively arouse a sense of dissatisfaction by making the followers aware of contradictions in or inconsistencies between values and behavior. The more contradictions challenge self-conceptions, according to Rokeach, the more dissatisfaction will be aroused. And such dissatisfactions are the source of changes that the leader can influence. There is an implication in Rokeach that the contradictions in themselves cause change, simply on the basis of self-cognition. Typically, however, an outside influence is required in the form of a leader, preferably "one step above." Rokeach bases much of his analysis on experimental situations in which the subjects are exposed to close direction and restraint—certainly a context of manipulation if not of leadership. Autonomous cognition usually is not enough to enable persons to break out of their imprisoning value structures. Experimenters may assume a leadership role.

Given the right conditions of value conflict, leaders hold enhanced influence at the higher levels of the need and value hierarchies. They can appeal to the more widely and deeply held values, such as justice, liberty, and brotherhood. They can expose followers to the broader values that contradict narrower ones or inconsistent behavior. They can redefine aspirations and gratifications to help followers see their stake in new, program-oriented social movements. Most important, they can gratify lower needs so that higher motivations will arise to elevate the conscience of men and women. To be sure, leadership may be frustrated and weakened at the higher levels as well as the lower. Potential support may thin out when immediate parochial needs and values threaten to weaken higher, more general ones. Substantive values, such as liberty or equality, may compete with one another, and, however logically compelling the leader's value priorities may look, they may not co-exist so harmoniously in the political arena. Perhaps the most disruptive force in competitive politics is conflict between *modal values* such as fair play and due process and *end-values* such as equality. Roosevelt's court-packing plan, with its use of dubious means to attain high ends, is a case in point. Some of those believing in equal opportunity today may also believe in certain modes of conduct—endless debate, for example, or elaborate procedures for judicial review—that make the attainment of equal opportunity far less certain.

The potential for influence through leadership is usually immense. The essence of leadership in any polity is the recognition of real need, the uncovering and exploiting of contradictions among values and between values and practice, the realigning of values, the reorganization of institutions where necessary, and the governance of change. Essentially the leader's task is consciousness-raising on a wide plane. "Values exist only when there is consciousness," Susanne Langer has said. "Where nothing is felt, nothing matters." The leader's fundamental act is to induce people to be aware or conscious of what they feel—to feel their true needs so strongly, to define their values so meaningfully, that they can be moved to purposeful action.

A congruence between the need and value hierarchies would produce a powerful potential for the exercise of purposeful leadership. When these hierarchies are combined with stage theories—for example, Erikson's eight psychosocial stages of man, with its emphasis on trust versus mistrust, autonomy versus shame, role experimentation versus negative identity—leadership, with its capacity to exploit tension and conflict, finds an even more durable foundation. While both Maslow's and Kohlberg's hierarchies imply *uni-directionality* and *irreversibility*—persons move through the levels at varying rates of speed but in only one direction—we know that people can and do regress. Still, for four values in particular—the end-values of equality, freedom, and a world of beauty (Rokeach's "terminal" values) and the instrumental value of self-control—the long-term changes have been documented in several studies as leading toward heavier impact of values. These findings suggest one of the most vital aspects of leadership: it cannot influence people "downward" on the need or value hierarchy without a reinforcing environment. The functioning of some persons at the levels of principle or self-actualization would not easily regress to the conventional level (e.g., need for social esteem). *Stasis* operates to prevent slippage to an earlier stage. If leaders reflecting more widely and deeply held values compete for support among followers who are moving toward more socially responsible levels in the hierarchies, leadership itself tends to move on to still broader and "higher" values.

This phenomenon provides the theoretical foundation for Gunnar Myrdal's brilliant analysis of the likely course of the conflict between egalitarian values and practice in the United States. Just as most persons strive for some coherence and consistency within their value hierarchies, so value systems in whole societies, reflecting the cognitive-affective-behavioral factors described above, tend toward some structuring. As societies, like persons, confront challenges, crises, and conflict, there is a tendency toward consistency. A rough hierarchy of values develops as lower and higher priorities develop (or are assigned) in circumstances where people cannot equally embrace all the end-values and modal values that they might wish. In the process of the moral criticism that men make upon each other, Myrdal notes, "the valuations of the higher and more general planes—referring to *all* human beings and *not* to specific small groups—are regularly invoked by one party or the other, simply because they are held in common among all groups in society, and also because of the supreme prestige they are traditionally awarded. . . . Specific attitudes and forms of behavior are then reconciled to the more general moral principles. . . ." There are, of course, limits to the tendency toward congruency in societies—and probably in persons as well. The four-nation study found an unexpectedly high degree of conflict *within* the countries studied, not merely conflict among the countries. At societal levels, however, such conflict is not random but assumes some kind of form and persistence. And conflict, as we understand it here, is necessary for leadership and, indeed, for higher levels of coherence, in a kind of dialectical and synthesis response.

In a famous distinction Max Weber contrasted the "ethic of responsibility" with the "ethic of ultimate ends." The latter measured persons' behavior by the extent of their adherence to good ends or high purposes; the former measured action by persons' capacity to take a calculating, prudential, rationalistic approach, making choices in terms of not one supreme value or value hierarchy alone but many values, attitudes, and interests, seeing the implication of choice for the means of attaining it—the price paid to achieve it, the relation of one goal to another, the direct and indirect effects of different goals for different persons and interests, all in a context of specificity and immediacy, and with an eye to actual *consequences* rather than lofty intent.

This dualism is of course oversimplified; most leaders and followers shift back and forth from specific, self-involved values to broader, public-involved ones. But the perception of dualism poses sharply the dilemmas facing leaders who embrace and respond to popular needs and values. The ethic of responsibility, whatever its appeal to moral rationalists like Weber, opened the floodgates to such a variety of discrete, multiple, relativistic, individualistic values as to allow a person observing this ethic to legitimate an enormous variety of actions. This ethic, by extension, permitted expedient, opportunistic, and highly self-serving action because the concept of responsibility could easily be stretched to authorize the kind of opportunism that we associate, for example, with nineteenth-century "rugged individualism." If leaders are encouraged to follow immediate, specific, calculable interests, they can end up serving their narrow, short-run interests alone, rationalizing the consequences in terms of responsibility to themselves, to their families, or to a relatively narrow group. Leaders holding this ethic, or representing persons holding this ethic, would act amid such a plethora of responsibilities as to legitimate both high-minded and self-serving behavior, action both for broad, general interests and for parochial ones, action that might be self-limiting contrasted with action that in the long run might be self-fulfilling (by the standards of the highest level of moral development). Worse, leaders might lack useful standards for distinguishing between the two sets of alternatives.

By the same token, Weber's ethic of ultimate ends emphasizes the demands of an overriding, millenarian kind of value system at the expense of the far more typical situation (at least in pluralistic societies) in which choices must be made among a number of compelling end-values, modal values, and instrumental values. And the ethic of responsibility could rather be seen as the day-to-day measured application of the "ethic of ultimate ends" to complex circumstance.

For the study of leadership, the dichotomy is not between Weber's two ethics but between the leader's commitment to a number of overriding, general welfare-oriented values on the one hand and his encouragement of, and entanglement in, a host of lesser values and "responsibilities" on the other. The four-nation study notes the "most important motivational distinction among leaders desiring change—the distinction between those who see progress primarily in terms of political opportunity and those who nurse a feeling of social injustice arising out of the gap between the economically deprived and the privileged," even though no consistent relationship seemed to explain it. The great bulk of leadership activity consists of the day-to-day interaction of leaders and followers characterized by the processes described above. But the ultimate test of moral leadership is its capacity to transcend the claims of the multiplicity of everyday wants and needs and expectations, to respond to the higher levels of moral development, and to relate leadership behavior—its roles, choices, style, commitments—to a set of reasoned, relatively explicit, conscious values.

SOURCES: *Pages 25–35*   469

2. THE STRUCTURE OF MORAL LEADERSHIP

Plato on needs and wants: *The Republic of Plato*, B. Jowett, trans. (Oxford: Clarendon Press, 1888), Book II, pp. 49–53.

Critical analysis of moral development theory: Elizabeth Léonie Simpson, "Moral Development Research: A Case Study of Scientific Cultural Bias," *Human Development*, Vol. 17 (1974), 81–106; Jane Loevinger, *Ego Development* (San Francisco: Jossey-Bass, 1976), esp. chs. 9, 10.

Girvetz on moral dogmatism: Harry K. Girvetz, *Beyond Right and Wrong* (New York: Free Press, 1973), p. 3.

Bertolt Brecht, "Die Dreigroschenoper" in *Stücke für das Theater am Schiffbauer damm* (Berlin: Suhrkamp Verlag, 1962).

The Power and Sources of Values

Tapping Lake Sevan: *New York Times*, May 29, 1977, p. 9.

Sycamore tree incident: *New York Times*, May 25, 1976, p. 33.

John Adams on studying politics and war: James Truslow Adams, *The Adams Family* (Boston: Little, Brown, 1930), p. 67.

Thai boy scout and his ideology: *New York Times*, November 29, 1976, p. 8.

The relationship of Franklin D. Roosevelt and Joseph P. Kennedy: Michael R. Beschloss, "Joseph Kennedy and Franklin Roosevelt: A Study in Power and Leadership," Williams College, 1977. Joseph Kennedy's Lend Lease testimony: Richard J. Whalen, *The Founding Father* (New York: New American Library, 1964), pp. 352–355.

Piaget on children's internalization of values: Jean Piaget, *The Moral Judgment of the Child* (New York: Harcourt, Brace, 1932).

Jung on ends: C. C. Jung, *Collected Papers on Analytical Psychology* (London: Baillière, Tindall and Cox, 1922), pp. x, xiv.

Huxley on the superego: T. H. Huxley and J. S. Huxley, *Touchstone for Ethics* (New York: Harper & Brothers, 1947), p. 256.

Erikson on conscience: Erik H. Erikson, *Identity: Youth and Crisis* (New York: Norton, 1968), p. 119.

Parsons on Freud's view: Talcott Parsons, *Social Structure and Personality* (New York: Free Press, 1964), passim.

470   SOURCES: *Pages 36–42*

Conflict and Consciousness

Influence of Pareto, Durkheim, Weber, etc.: Clinton F. Fink, "Some Conceptual Difficulties in the Theory of Social Conflict," *Journal of Conflict Resolution,* Vol. 12, No. 4 (December 1968), 425; see also Anthony Oberschall, *Social Conflict and Social Movements* (Englewood Cliffs, N.J.: Prentice-Hall, 1973), esp. pp. 1–8.

Simmel: Georg Simmel, "The Sociology of Conflict," *American Journal of Sociology,* Vol. 9, No. 4 (1903–04), 490–525; Simmel, *Conflict and the Web of Group Affiliations,* Kurt H. Wolff and Reinhard Bendix, trs. (Glencoe, Ill.: Free Press, 1955.)

Recent scholarly interest in conflict: Lewis A. Coser, *The Functions of Social Conflict* (Glencoe, Ill.: Free Press, 1956); Ralf Dahrendorf, *Class and Class Conflict in Industrial Society* (Stanford: Stanford University Press, 1959); Louis Kriesberg, *The Sociology of Social Conflicts* (Englewood Cliffs, N.J.: Prentice-Hall, 1973).

Simmel on group harmony: Paraphrased by Coser, p. 31, from opening pages of Simmel, *Conflict.*

Conflict within individuals: see, for example, Muzafer Sherif, *An Outline of Social Psychology* (New York: Harper & Brothers, 1948), esp. chs. 10, 15–17.

Malinowski on conflict in small groups: Bronislaw Malinowski, "An Anthropological Analysis of War," *Magic, Science and Religion* (Glencoe, Ill.: Free Press, 1948), p. 285, quoted by Coser, p. 63. See also Fink, pp. 445–456.

Schattschneider on scope of conflict: E. E. Schattschneider, *The Semi-Sovereign People* (New York: Holt, Rinehart and Winston, 1960), pp. 2–3.

Madison on conflict: *The Federalist,* Jacob E. Cooke, ed. (Middletown, Conn.: Wesleyan University Press, 1961), No. 10, pp. 58–59.

Leaders and their followings: cf. Andrew McFarland, *Power and Leadership in Pluralist Systems* (Stanford: Stanford University Press, 1969), pp. 189–191.

For other sources on conflict see Peter W. Sperlich, *Conflict and Harmony in Human Affairs* (Chicago: Rand McNally, 1971); Anthony de Reuck and Julie Knight, eds., *Conflict in Society* (Boston: Little, Brown, 1966); *Journal of Conflict Resolution,* Vol. 12 (1968), passim; Walter Korpi, "Conflict, Power and Relative Deprivation," *American Political Science Review,* Vol. 68, No. 4 (December 1974), 1569–1578.

Hegel, Feuerbach, and Marx on consciousness and on needs: Gyorgy Márkus, *The Marxian Concept of Consciousness, Political Science Syllabus;* Henri Lefebvre, *Dialectical Materialism* (London: Jonathan Cape, 1968); A. James Gregor, *A Survey of Marxism* (New York: Random House, 1965). Marx on "fresh needs": from Karl Marx and Friedrich Engels, *The German Ideology* (New York: International Publishers, 1947), as summarized in Lefebvre, p. 70.

On consciousness see also Pratima Bowes, *Consciousness and Freedom* (London: Methuen 1971).

Sorel on violence and class identity: Georges Sorel, *Reflections on Violence,* T. E. Hulme, tr. (New York: B. W. Huebsch, 1914).

The Elevating Power of Leadership

Need of safety and security as counterparts of conforming to and maintaining the social order: Lawrence Kohlberg "The Cognitive-Developmental Approach to Moral Education," *Phi Delta Kappan* (June 1975), 671; cf. Elizabeth Simpson, "A Holistic Approach to Moral Development and Behavior," in T. Lickona, ed. *Moral Development and Behavior* (New York: Holt, Rinehart and Winston, 1976), passim.

Simpson on relation of esteem needs and natural-law values: Elizabeth Léonie Simpson, *Democracy's Stepchildren* (San Francisco: Jossey-Bass, 1971), p. 126.

Four-nation study on transformations of values: *Values and the Active Community* (New

York: Free Press, 1971), pp. 13, 72–79. The four nations studied are India, Poland, the United States, and Yugoslavia.

Rokeach on imbalance within value systems: Milton Rokeach, *The Nature of Human Values* (New York: Free Press, 1973), p. 217.

Rokeach on contradictions and self-conception: Rokeach, pp. 226, 229–233.

Experimenters as leaders: Bernard M. Bass, *Leadership, Psychology and Organizational Behavior* (New York: Harper & Brothers, 1960), p. 97.

Susanne Langer on consciousness: quoted in Simpson, *Democracy's Stepchildren*, p. 73.

Erikson's eight stages of man: Erik H. Erikson, "The Problem of Ego Identity," *Journal of the American Psychoanalytic Association*, Vol. 4 (1956), 56–121.

Studies on irreversibility of movement toward four general values: cited in Rokeach, p. 328.

Myrdal on higher valuations: Gunnar Myrdal, *An American Dilemma* (New York: Harper & Brothers, 1944), p. 1029.

Max Weber's two ethics: Max Weber, "Politics as a Vocation," reprinted in H. H. Gerth and C. Wright Mills, *From Max Weber: Essays in Sociology* (New York: Oxford University Press, 1953), pp. 77–128.

MICHAEL WALZER

[12]

Political Action:
The Problem of Dirty Hands[1]

In an earlier issue of *Philosophy & Public Affairs* there appeared a symposium on the rules of war which was actually (or at least more importantly) a symposium on another topic.[2] The actual topic was whether or not a man can ever face, or ever has to face, a moral dilemma, a situation where he must choose between two courses of action both of which it would be wrong for him to undertake. Thomas Nagel worriedly suggested that this could happen and that it did happen whenever someone was forced to choose between upholding an important moral principle and avoiding some looming disaster.[3] R. B. Brandt argued that it could not possibly happen, for there were guidelines we might follow and calculations we might go through which would necessarily yield the conclusion that one or the other course of action was the right one to undertake in the circumstances (or that it did not matter which we undertook). R. M. Hare explained how it was

1. An earlier version of this paper was read at the annual meeting of the Conference for the Study of Political Thought in New York, April 1971. I am indebted to Charles Taylor, who served as commentator at that time and encouraged me to think that its arguments might be right.

2. *Philosophy & Public Affairs* 1, no. 2 (Winter 1971/72): Thomas Nagel, "War and Massacre," pp. 123-144; R. B. Brandt, "Utilitarianism and the Rules of War," pp. 145-165; and R. M. Hare, "Rules of War and Moral Reasoning," pp. 166-181.

3. For Nagel's description of a possible "moral blind alley," see "War and Massacre," pp. 142-144. Bernard Williams has made a similar suggestion, though without quite acknowledging it as his own: "many people can recognize the thought that a certain course of action is, indeed, the best thing to do on the whole in the circumstances, but that doing it involves doing something wrong" (*Morality: An Introduction to Ethics* [New York, 1972], p. 93).

161   *Political Action:*
                             The Problem of Dirty Hands

that someone might wrongly suppose that he was faced with a moral dilemma: sometimes, he suggested, the precepts and principles of an ordinary man, the products of his moral education, come into conflict with injunctions developed at a higher level of moral discourse. But this conflict is, or ought to be, resolved at the higher level; there is no real dilemma.

I am not sure that Hare's explanation is at all comforting, but the question is important even if no such explanation is possible, perhaps especially so if this is the case. The argument relates not only to the coherence and harmony of the moral universe, but also to the relative ease or difficulty—or impossibility—of living a moral life. It is not, therefore, merely a philosopher's question. If such a dilemma can arise, whether frequently or very rarely, any of us might one day face it. Indeed, many men have faced it, or think they have, especially men involved in political activity or war. The dilemma, exactly as Nagel describes it, is frequently discussed in the literature of political action—in novels and plays dealing with politics and in the work of theorists too.

In modern times the dilemma appears most often as the problem of "dirty hands," and it is typically stated by the Communist leader Hoerderer in Sartre's play of that name: "I have dirty hands right up to the elbows. I've plunged them in filth and blood. Do you think you can govern innocently?"[4] My own answer is no, I don't think I could govern innocently; nor do most of us believe that those who govern us are innocent—as I shall argue below—even the best of them. But this does not mean that it isn't possible to do the right thing while governing. It means that a particular act of government (in a political party or in the state) may be exactly the right thing to do in utilitarian terms and yet leave the man who does it guilty of a moral wrong. The innocent man, afterwards, is no longer innocent. If on the other hand he remains innocent, chooses, that is, the "absolutist" side of Nagel's dilemma, he not only fails to do the right thing (in utilitarian terms), he may also fail to measure up to the duties of his office (which imposes on him a considerable responsibility for consequences and outcomes). Most often, of course, political leaders accept the utilitarian

    4. Jean-Paul Sartre, *Dirty Hands*, in *No Exit and Three Other Plays*, trans. Lionel Abel (New York, n.d.), p. 224.

calculation; they try to measure up. One might offer a number of sardonic comments on this fact, the most obvious being that by the calculations they usually make they demonstrate the great virtues of the "absolutist" position. Nevertheless, we would not want to be governed by men who consistently adopted that position.

The notion of dirty hands derives from an effort to refuse "absolutism" without denying the reality of the moral dilemma. Though this may appear to utilitarian philosophers to pile confusion upon confusion, I propose to take it very seriously. For the literature I shall examine is the work of serious and often wise men, and it reflects, though it may also have helped to shape, popular thinking about politics. It is important to pay attention to that too. I shall do so without assuming, as Hare suggests one might, that everyday moral and political discourse constitutes a distinct level of argument, where content is largely a matter of pedagogic expediency.[5] If popular views are resistant (as they are) to utilitarianism, there may be something to learn from that and not merely something to explain about it.

I

Let me begin, then, with a piece of conventional wisdom to the effect that politicians are a good deal worse, morally worse, than the rest of us (it is the wisdom of the rest of us). Without either endorsing it or pretending to disbelieve it, I am going to expound this convention. For it suggests that the dilemma of dirty hands is a central feature of political life, that it arises not merely as an occasional crisis in the career of this or that unlucky politician but systematically and frequently.

Why is the politician singled out? Isn't he like the other entrepreneurs in an open society, who hustle, lie, intrigue, wear masks, smile and are villains? He is not, no doubt for many reasons, three of which I need to consider. First of all, the politician claims to play a different part than other entrepreneurs. He doesn't merely cater to our interests; he acts on our behalf, even in our name. He has purposes in mind, causes and projects that require the support and redound to the bene-

5. Hare, "Rules of War and Moral Reasoning," pp. 173-178, esp. p. 174: "the simple principles of the deontologist . . . have their place at the level of character-formation (moral education and self-education)."

163   *Political Action:*
The Problem of Dirty Hands

fit, not of each of us individually, but of all of us together. He hustles, lies, and intrigues *for us*—or so he claims. Perhaps he is right, or at least sincere, but we suspect that he acts for himself also. Indeed, he cannot serve us without serving himself, for success brings him power and glory, the greatest rewards that men can win from their fellows. The competition for these two is fierce; the risks are often great, but the temptations are greater. We imagine ourselves succumbing. Why should our representatives act differently? Even if they would like to act differently, they probably can not: for other men are all too ready to hustle and lie for power and glory, and it is the others who set the terms of the competition. Hustling and lying are necessary because power and glory are so desirable—that is, so widely desired. And so the men who act for us and in our name are necessarily hustlers and liars.

Politicians are also thought to be worse than the rest of us because they rule over us, and the pleasures of ruling are much greater than the pleasures of being ruled. The successful politician becomes the visible architect of our restraint. He taxes us, licenses us, forbids and permits us, directs us to this or that distant goal—all for our greater good. Moreover, he takes chances for our greater good that put us, or some of us, in danger. Sometimes he puts himself in danger too, but politics, after all, is his adventure. It is not always ours. There are undoubtedly times when it is good or necessary to direct the affairs of other people and to put them in danger. But we are a little frightened of the man who seeks, ordinarily and every day, the power to do so. And the fear is reasonable enough. The politician has, or pretends to have, a kind of confidence in his own judgment that the rest of us know to be presumptuous in any man.

The presumption is especially great because the victorious politician uses violence and the threat of violence—not only against foreign nations in our defense but also against us, and again ostensibly for our greater good. This is a point emphasized and perhaps overemphasized by Max Weber in his essay "Politics as a Vocation."[6] It has not, so far as I can tell, played an overt or obvious part in the development of the convention I am examining. The stock figure is the lying, not the murderous, politician—though the murderer lurks in the background,

---

6. In *From Max Weber: Essays in Sociology*, trans. and ed. Hans H. Gerth and C. Wright Mills (New York, 1946), pp. 77-128.

appearing most often in the form of the revolutionary or terrorist, very rarely as an ordinary magistrate or official. Nevertheless, the sheer weight of official violence in human history does suggest the kind of power to which politicians aspire, the kind of power they want to wield, and it may point to the roots of our half-conscious dislike and unease. The men who act for us and in our name are often killers, or seem to become killers too quickly and too easily.

Knowing all this or most of it, good and decent people still enter political life, aiming at some specific reform or seeking a general reformation. They are then required to learn the lesson Machiavelli first set out to teach: "how not to be good."[7] Some of them are incapable of learning; many more profess to be incapable. But they will not succeed unless they learn, for they have joined the terrible competition for power and glory; they have chosen to work and struggle as Machiavelli says, among "so many who are not good." They can do no good themselves unless they win the struggle, which they are unlikely to do unless they are willing and able to use the necessary means. So we are suspicious even of the best of winners. It is not a sign of our perversity if we think them only more clever than the rest. They have not won, after all, because they were good, or not only because of that, but also because they were not good. No one succeeds in politics without getting his hands dirty. This is conventional wisdom again, and again I don't mean to insist that it is true without qualification. I repeat it only to disclose the moral dilemma inherent in the convention. For sometimes it is right to try to succeed, and then it must also be right to get one's hands dirty. But one's hands get dirty from doing what it is wrong to do. And how can it be wrong to do what is right? Or, how can we get our hands dirty by doing what we ought to do?

II

It will be best to turn quickly to some examples. I have chosen two, one relating to the struggle for power and one to its exercise. I should stress that in both these cases the men who face the dilemma of dirty hands have in an important sense chosen to do so; the cases tell us

---

7. See *The Prince*, chap. XV; cf. *The Discourses*, bk. I, chaps. IX and XVIII. I quote from the Modern Library edition of the two works (New York, 1950), p. 57.

165   *Political Action:*
                           The Problem of Dirty Hands

nothing about what it would be like, so to speak, to fall into the dilemma; nor shall I say anything about that here. Politicians often argue that they have no right to keep their hands clean, and that may well be true of them, but it is not so clearly true of the rest of us. Probably we do have a right to avoid, if we possibly can, those positions in which we might be forced to do terrible things. This might be regarded as the moral equivalent of our legal right not to incriminate ourselves. Good men will be in no hurry to surrender it, though there are reasons for doing so sometimes, and among these are or might be the reasons good men have for entering politics. But let us imagine a politician who does not agree to that: he wants to do good only by doing good, or at least he is certain that he can stop short of the most corrupting and brutal uses of political power. Very quickly that certainty is tested. What do we think of him then?

He wants to win the election, someone says, but he doesn't want to get his hands dirty. This is meant as a disparagement, even though it also means that the man being criticized is the sort of man who will not lie, cheat, bargain behind the backs of his supporters, shout absurdities at public meetings, or manipulate other men and women. Assuming that this particular election ought to be won, it is clear, I think, that the disparagement is justified. If the candidate didn't want to get his hands dirty, he should have stayed at home; if he can't stand the heat, he should get out of the kitchen, and so on. His decision to run was a commitment (to all of us who think the election important) to try to win, that is, to do within rational limits whatever is necessary to win. But the candidate is a moral man. He has principles and a history of adherence to those principles. That is why we are supporting him. Perhaps when he refuses to dirty his hands, he is simply insisting on being the sort of man he is. And isn't that the sort of man we want?

Let us look more closely at this case. In order to win the election the candidate must make a deal with a dishonest ward boss, involving the granting of contracts for school construction over the next four years. Should he make the deal? Well, at least he shouldn't be surprised by the offer, most of us would probably say (a conventional piece of sarcasm). And he should accept it or not, depending on exactly what is at stake in the election. But that is not the candidate's view. He is extremely reluctant even to consider the deal, puts off his aides when they remind him of it, refuses to calculate its possible effects upon the campaign. Now, if he is acting this way because the very thought of bargaining with that particular ward boss makes him feel unclean, his reluctance isn't very interesting. His feelings by themselves are not important. But he may also have reasons for his reluctance. He may know, for example, that some of his supporters support him precisely because they believe he is a good man, and this means to them a man who won't make such deals. Or he may doubt his own motives for considering the deal, wondering whether it is the political campaign or his own candidacy that makes the bargain at all tempting. Or he may believe that if he makes deals of this sort now he may not be able later on to achieve those ends that make the campaign worthwhile, and he may not feel entitled to take such risks with a future that is not only his own future. Or he may simply think that the deal is dishonest and therefore wrong, corrupting not only himself but all those human relations in which he is involved.

Because he has scruples of this sort, we know him to be a good man. But we view the campaign in a certain light, estimate its importance in a certain way, and hope that he will overcome his scruples and make the deal. It is important to stress that we don't want just *anyone* to make the deal; we want *him* to make it, precisely because he has scruples about it. We know he is doing right when he makes the deal because he knows he is doing wrong. I don't mean merely that he will feel badly or even very badly after he makes the deal. If he is the good man I am imagining him to be, he will feel guilty, that is, he will believe himself to be guilty. That is what it means to have dirty hands.

All this may become clearer if we look at a more dramatic example, for we are, perhaps, a little blasé about political deals and disinclined to worry much about the man who makes one. So consider a politician who has seized upon a national crisis—a prolonged colonial war—to reach for power. He and his friends win office pledged to decolonization and peace; they are honestly committed to both, though not without some sense of the advantages of the commitment. In any case, they have no responsibility for the war; they have steadfastly opposed it. Immediately, the politician goes off to the colonial capital to open negotiations with the rebels. But the capital is in the grip of a terrorist

167   *Political Action:*
                          The Problem of Dirty Hands

campaign, and the first decision the new leader faces is this: he is asked to authorize the torture of a captured rebel leader who knows or probably knows the location of a number of bombs hidden in apartment buildings around the city, set to go off within the next twenty-four hours. He orders the man tortured, convinced that he must do so for the sake of the people who might otherwise die in the explosions—even though he believes that torture is wrong, indeed abominable, not just sometimes, but always.[8] He had expressed this belief often and angrily during his own campaign; the rest of us took it as a sign of his goodness. How should we regard him now? (How should he regard himself?)

Once again, it does not seem enough to say that he should feel very badly. But why not? Why shouldn't he have feelings like those of St. Augustine's melancholy soldier, who understood both that his war was just and that killing, even in a just war, is a terrible thing to do?[9] The difference is that Augustine did not believe that it was wrong to kill in a just war; it was just sad, or the sort of thing a good man would be saddened by. But he might have thought it wrong to torture in a just war, and later Catholic theorists have certainly thought it wrong. Moreover, the politician I am imagining thinks it wrong, as do many of us who supported him. Surely we have a right to expect more than melancholy from him now. When he ordered the prisoner tortured, he committed a moral crime and he accepted a moral burden. Now he is a guilty man. His willingness to acknowledge and bear (and perhaps to repent and do penance for) his guilt is evidence, and it is the only evidence he can offer us, both that he

     8. I leave aside the question of whether the prisoner is himself responsible for the terrorist campaign. Perhaps he opposed it in meetings of the rebel organization. In any case, whether he deserves to be punished or not, he does not deserve to be tortured.

     9. Other writers argued that Christians must never kill, even in a just war; and there was also an intermediate position which suggests the origins of the idea of dirty hands. Thus Basil The Great (Bishop of Caesarea in the fourth century A.D.): "Killing in war was differentiated by our fathers from murder . . . nevertheless, perhaps it would be well that those whose hands are unclean abstain from communion for three years." Here dirty hands are a kind of impurity or unworthiness, which is not the same as guilt, though closely related to it. For a general survey of these and other Christian views, see Roland H. Bainton, *Christian Attitudes Toward War and Peace* (New York, 1960), esp. chaps. 5-7.

is not too good for politics and that he is good enough. Here is the moral politician: it is by his dirty hands that we know him. If he were a moral man and nothing else, his hands would not be dirty; if he were a politician and nothing else, he would pretend that they were clean.

III

Machiavelli's argument about the need to learn how not to be good clearly implies that there are acts known to be bad quite apart from the immediate circumstances in which they are performed or not performed. He points to a distinct set of political methods and stratagems which good men must study (by reading his books), not only because their use does not come naturally, but also because they are explicitly condemned by the moral teachings good men accept—and whose acceptance serves in turn to mark men as good. These methods may be condemned because they are thought contrary to divine law or to the order of nature or to our moral sense, or because in prescribing the law to ourselves we have individually or collectively prohibited them. Machiavelli does not commit himself on such issues, and I shall not do so either if I can avoid it. The effects of these different views are, at least in one crucial sense, the same. They take out of our hands the constant business of attaching moral labels to such Machiavellian methods as deceit and betrayal. Such methods are simply bad. They are the sort of thing that good men avoid, at least until they have learned how not to be good.

Now, if there is no such class of actions, there is no dilemma of dirty hands, and the Machiavellian teaching loses what Machiavelli surely intended it to have, its disturbing and paradoxical character. He can then be understood to be saying that political actors must sometimes overcome their moral inhibitions, but not that they must sometimes commit crimes. I take it that utilitarian philosophers also want to make the first of these statements and to deny the second. From their point of view, the candidate who makes a corrupt deal and the official who authorizes the torture of a prisoner must be described as good men (given the cases as I have specified them), who ought, perhaps, to be honored for making the right decision when it was a hard decision to make. There are three ways of developing this argument.

169   *Political Action:*
                              The Problem of Dirty Hands

First, it might be said that every political choice ought to be made solely in terms of its particular and immediate circumstances—in terms, that is, of the reasonable alternatives, available knowledge, likely consequences, and so on. Then the good man will face difficult choices (when his knowledge of options and outcomes is radically uncertain), but it cannot happen that he will face a moral dilemma. Indeed, if he always makes decisions in this way, and has been taught from childhood to do so, he will never have to overcome his inhibitions, whatever he does, for how could he have acquired inhibitions? Assuming further that he weighs the alternatives and calculates the consequences seriously and in good faith, he cannot commit a crime, though he can certainly make a mistake, even a very serious mistake. Even when he lies and tortures, his hands will be clean, for he has done what he should do as best he can, standing alone in a moment of time, forced to choose.

This is in some ways an attractive description of moral decision-making, but it is also a very improbable one. For while any one of us may stand alone, and so on, when we make this or that decision, we are not isolated or solitary in our moral lives. Moral life is a social phenomenon, and it is constituted at least in part by rules, the knowing of which (and perhaps the making of which) we share with our fellows. The experience of coming up against these rules, challenging their prohibitions, and explaining ourselves to other men and women is so common and so obviously important that no account of moral decision-making can possibly fail to come to grips with it. Hence the second utilitarian argument: such rules do indeed exist, but they are not really prohibitions of wrongful actions (though they do, perhaps for pedagogic reasons, have that form). They are moral guidelines, summaries of previous calculations. They ease our choices in ordinary cases, for we can simply follow their injunctions and do what has been found useful in the past; in exceptional cases they serve as signals warning us against doing too quickly or without the most careful calculations what has not been found useful in the past. But they do no more than that; they have no other purpose, and so it cannot be the case that it is or even might be a crime to override them.[10] Nor is it

---

10. Brandt's rules do not appear to be of the sort that can be overridden—except perhaps by a soldier who decides that he just *won't* kill any more civil-

necessary to feel guilty when one does so. Once again, if it is right to break the rule in some hard case, after conscientiously worrying about it, the man who acts (especially if he knows that many of his fellows would simply worry rather than act) may properly feel pride in his achievement.

But this view, it seems to me, captures the reality of our moral life no better than the last. It may well be right to say that moral rules ought to have the character of guidelines, but it seems that in fact they do not. Or at least, we defend ourselves when we break the rules as if they had some status entirely independent of their previous utility (and we rarely feel proud of ourselves). The defenses we normally offer are not simply justifications; they are also excuses. Now, as Austin says, these two can *seem* to come very close together—indeed, I shall suggest that they can appear side by side in the same sentence—but they are conceptually distinct, differentiated in this crucial respect: an excuse is typically an admission of fault; a justification is typically a denial of fault and an assertion of innocence.[11] Consider a well-known defense from Shakespeare's *Hamlet* that has often reappeared in political literature: "I must be cruel only to be kind."[12] The words are spoken on an occasion when Hamlet is actually being cruel to his mother. I will leave aside the possibility that she deserves to hear (to be forced to listen to) every harsh word he utters, for Hamlet himself makes no such claim—and if she did indeed deserve that, his words might not be cruel or he might not be cruel for speaking them. "I must be cruel" contains the excuse, since it both admits a fault and suggests that Hamlet has no choice but to commit it. He is doing what he has to do; he can't help himself (given the ghost's command, the rotten state of Denmark, and so on). The rest of the sentence is a justification, for it suggests that Hamlet intends and expects kindness to be the outcome of his actions—we must assume that

---

ians, no matter what cause is served—since all they require is careful calculation. But I take it that rules of a different sort, which have the form of ordinary injunctions and prohibitions, can and often do figure in what is called "rule-utilitarianism."

11. J. L. Austin, "A Plea for Excuses," in *Philosophical Papers*, ed. J. O. Urmson and G. J. Warnock (Oxford, 1961), pp. 123-152.

12. *Hamlet* 3.4.178.

171   *Political Action:*
                              The Problem of Dirty Hands

he means greater kindness, kindness to the right persons, or some such. It is not, however, so complete a justification that Hamlet is able to say that he is not *really* being cruel. "Cruel" and "kind" have exactly the same status; they both follow the verb "to be," and so they perfectly reveal the moral dilemma.[13]

When rules are overridden, we do not talk or act as if they had been set aside, canceled, or annulled. They still stand and have this much effect at least: that we know we have done something wrong even if what we have done was also the best thing to do on the whole in the circumstances.[14] Or at least we feel that way, and this feeling is itself a crucial feature of our moral life. Hence the third utilitarian argument, which recognizes the usefulness of guilt and seeks to explain it. There are, it appears, good reasons for "overvaluing" as well as for overriding the rules. For the consequences might be very bad indeed if the rules were overridden every time the moral calculation seemed to go against them. It is probably best if most men do not calculate too nicely, but simply follow the rules; they are less likely to make mistakes that way, all in all. And so a good man (or at least an ordinary good man) will respect the rules rather more than he would if he thought them merely guidelines, and he will feel guilty when he overrides them. Indeed, if he did not feel guilty, "he would not be such a good man."[15] It is by his feelings that we know him. Because of those feelings he will never be in a hurry to override the rules, but will wait until there is no choice, acting only to avoid consequences that are both imminent and almost certainly disastrous.

The obvious difficulty with this argument is that the feeling whose usefulness is being explained is most unlikely to be felt by someone who is convinced only of its usefulness. He breaks a utilitarian rule (guideline), let us say, for good utilitarian reasons: but can he then

---

13. Compare the following lines from Bertold Brecht's poem "To Posterity": "Alas, we/ Who wished to lay the foundations of kindness/ Could not ourselves be kind ..." (*Selected Poems*, trans. H. R. Hays [New York, 1969], p. 177). This is more of an excuse, less of a justification (the poem is an *apologia*).

14. Robert Nozick discusses some of the possible effects of overriding a rule in his "Moral Complications and Moral Structures," *Natural Law Forum* 13 (1968): 34-35 and notes. Nozick suggests that what may remain after one has broken a rule (for good reasons) is a "duty to make reparations." He does not call this "guilt," though the two notions are closely connected.

15. Hare, "Rules of War and Moral Reasoning," p. 179.

feel guilty, also for good utilitarian reasons, when he has no reason for believing that he *is* guilty? Imagine a moral philosopher expounding the third argument to a man who actually does feel guilty or to the sort of man who is likely to feel guilty. Either the man won't accept the utilitarian explanation as an account of his feeling about the rules (probably the best outcome from a utilitarian point of view) or he will accept it and then cease to feel that (useful) feeling. But I do not want to exclude the possibility of a kind of superstitious anxiety, the possibility, that is, that some men will continue to feel guilty even after they have been taught, and have agreed, that they cannot possibly *be* guilty. It is best to say only that the more fully they accept the utilitarian account, the less likely they are to feel that (useful) feeling. The utilitarian account is not at all useful, then, if political actors accept it, and that may help us to understand why it plays, as Hare has pointed out, so small a part in our moral education.[16]

16. There is another possible utilitarian position, suggested in Maurice Merleau-Ponty's *Humanism and Terror*, trans. John O'Neill (Boston, 1970). According to this view, the agony and the guilt feelings experienced by the man who makes a "dirty hands" decision derive from his radical uncertainty about the actual outcome. Perhaps the awful thing he is doing will be done in vain; the results he hopes for won't occur; the only outcome will be the pain he has caused or the deceit he has fostered. Then (and only then) he will indeed have committed a crime. On the other hand, if the expected good does come, then (and only then) he can abandon his guilt feelings; he can say, and the rest of us must agree, that he is justified. This is a kind of delayed utilitarianism, where justification is a matter of actual and not at all of predicted outcomes. It is not implausible to imagine a political actor anxiously awaiting the "verdict of history." But suppose the verdict is in his favor (assuming that there is a *final* verdict or a statute of limitations on possible verdicts): he will surely feel relieved—more so, no doubt, than the rest of us. I can see no reason, however, why he should think himself justified, if he is a good man and knows that what he did was wrong. Perhaps the victims of his crime, seeing the happy result, will absolve him, but history has no powers of absolution. Indeed, history is more likely to play tricks on our moral judgment. Predicted outcomes are at least thought to follow from our own acts (this is the prediction), but actual outcomes almost certainly have a multitude of causes, the combination of which may well be fortuitous. Merleau-Ponty stresses the risks of political decision-making so heavily that he turns politics into a gamble with time and circumstance. But the anxiety of the gambler is of no great moral interest. Nor is it much of a barrier, as Merleau-Ponty's book makes all too clear, to the commission of the most terrible crimes.

Political Action:
The Problem of Dirty Hands

IV

One further comment on the third argument: it is worth stressing that to feel guilty is to suffer, and that the men whose guilt feelings are here called useful are themselves innocent according to the utilitarian account. So we seem to have come upon another case where the suffering of the innocent is permitted and even encouraged by utilitarian calculation.[17] But surely an innocent man who has done something painful or hard (but justified) should be helped to avoid or escape the sense of guilt; he might reasonably expect the assistance of his fellow men, even of moral philosophers, at such a time. On the other hand, if we intuitively think it true of some other man that he *should* feel guilty, then we ought to be able to specify the nature of his guilt (and if he is a good man, win his agreement). I think I can construct a case which, with only small variation, highlights what is different in these two situations.

Consider the common practice of distributing rifles loaded with blanks to some of the members of a firing squad. The individual men are not told whether their own weapons are lethal, and so though all of them look like executioners to the victim in front of them, none of them know whether they are really executioners or not. The purpose of this stratagem is to relieve each man of the sense that he is a killer. It can hardly relieve him of whatever moral responsibility he incurs by serving on a firing squad, and that is not its purpose, for the execution is not thought to be (and let us grant this to be the case) an immoral or wrongful act. But the inhibition against killing another human being is so strong that even if the men believe that what they are doing is right, they will still feel guilty. Uncertainty as to their actual role apparently reduces the intensity of these feelings. If this is so, the stratagem is perfectly justifiable, and one can only rejoice in every case where it succeeds—for every success subtracts one from the number of innocent men who suffer.

But we would feel differently, I think, if we imagine a man who believes (and let us assume here that we believe also) either that capital

17. Cf. the cases suggested by David Ross, *The Right and the Good* (Oxford, 1930), pp. 56-57, and E. F. Carritt, *Ethical and Political Thinking* (Oxford, 1947), p. 65.

punishment is wrong or that this particular victim is innocent, but who nevertheless agrees to participate in the firing squad for some overriding political or moral reason—I won't try to suggest what that reason might be. If he is comforted by the trick with the rifles, then we can be reasonably certain that his opposition to capital punishment or his belief in the victim's innocence is not morally serious. And if it is serious, he will not merely feel guilty, he will know that he is guilty (and we will know it too), though he may also believe (and we may agree) that he has good reasons for incurring the guilt. Our guilt feelings can be tricked away when they are isolated from our moral beliefs, as in the first case, but not when they are allied with them, as in the second. The beliefs themselves and the rules which are believed in can only be *overridden*, a painful process which forces a man to weigh the wrong he is willing to do in order to do right, and which leaves pain behind, and should do so, even after the decision has been made.

V

That is the dilemma of dirty hands as it has been experienced by political actors and written about in the literature of political action. I don't want to argue that it is only a political dilemma. No doubt we can get our hands dirty in private life also, and sometimes, no doubt, we should. But the issue is posed most dramatically in politics for the three reasons that make political life the kind of life it is, because we claim to act for others but also serve ourselves, rule over others, and use violence against them. It is easy to get one's hands dirty in politics and it is often right to do so. But it is not easy to teach a good man how not to be good, nor is it easy to explain such a man to himself once he has committed whatever crimes are required of him. At least, it is not easy once we have agreed to use the word "crimes" and to live with (because we have no choice) the dilemma of dirty hands. Still, the agreement is common enough, and on its basis there have developed three broad traditions of explanation, three ways of thinking about dirty hands, which derive in some very general fashion from neoclassical, Protestant, and Catholic perspectives on politics and morality. I want to try to say something very briefly about each of them, or rather about a representative example of each of

175 *Political Action:
The Problem of Dirty Hands*

them, for each seems to me partly right. But I don't think I can put together the compound view that might be wholly right.

The first tradition is best represented by Machiavelli, the first man, so far as I know, to state the paradox that I am examining. The good man who aims to found or reform a republic must, Machiavelli tells us, do terrible things to reach his goal. Like Romulus, he must murder his brother; like Numa, he must lie to the people. Sometimes, however, "when the act accuses, the result excuses."[18] This sentence from *The Discourses* is often taken to mean that the politician's deceit and cruelty are justified by the good results he brings about. But if they were justified, it wouldn't be necessary to learn what Machiavelli claims to teach: how not to be good. It would only be necessary to learn how to be good in a new, more difficult, perhaps roundabout way. That is not Machiavelli's argument. His political judgments are indeed consequentialist in character, but not his moral judgments. We know whether cruelty is used well or badly by its effects over time. But that it is bad to use cruelty we know in some other way. The deceitful and cruel politician is excused (if he succeeds) only in the sense that the rest of us come to agree that the results were "worth it" or, more likely, that we simply forget his crimes when we praise his success.

It is important to stress Machiavelli's own commitment to the existence of moral standards. His paradox depends upon that commitment as it depends upon the general stability of the standards—which he upholds in his consistent use of words like good and bad.[19] If he wants the standards to be disregarded by good men more often than they are, he has nothing with which to replace them and no other way of recognizing the good men except by their allegiance to those same standards. It is exceedingly rare, he writes, that a good man is willing to employ bad means to become prince.[20] Machiavelli's purpose is to persuade such a person to make the attempt, and he holds out the supreme political rewards, power and glory, to the man who does so and succeeds. The good man is not rewarded (or excused), how-

---

18. *The Discourses*, bk. I, chap. IX (p. 139).
19. For a very different view of Machiavelli, see Isaiah Berlin, "The Question of Machiavelli," *The New York Review of Books*, 4 November 1971.
20. *The Discourses*, bk. I, chap. XVIII (p. 171).

ever, merely for his willingness to get his hands dirty. He must do bad things well. There is no reward for doing bad things badly, though they are done with the best of intentions. And so political action necessarily involves taking a risk. But it should be clear that what is risked is not personal goodness—*that is thrown away*—but power and glory. If the politician succeeds, he is a hero; eternal praise is the supreme reward for not being good.

What the penalties are for not being good, Machiavelli doesn't say, and it is probably for this reason above all that his moral sensitivity has so often been questioned. He is suspect not because he tells political actors they must get their hands dirty, but because he does not specify the state of mind appropriate to a man with dirty hands. A Machiavellian hero has no inwardness. What he thinks of himself we don't know. I would guess, along with most other readers of Machiavelli, that he basks in his glory. But then it is difficult to account for the strength of his original reluctance to learn how not to be good. In any case, he is the sort of man who is unlikely to keep a diary and so we cannot find out what he thinks. Yet we do want to know; above all, we want a record of his anguish. That is a sign of our own conscientiousness and of the impact on us of the second tradition of thought that I want to examine, in which personal anguish sometimes seems the only acceptable excuse for political crimes.

The second tradition is best represented, I think, by Max Weber, who outlines its essential features with great power at the very end of his essay "Politics as a Vocation." For Weber, the good man with dirty hands is a hero still, but he is a tragic hero. In part, his tragedy is that though politics is his vocation, he has not been called by God and so cannot be justified by Him. Weber's hero is alone in a world that seems to belong to Satan, and his vocation is entirely his own choice. He still wants what Christian magistrates have always wanted, both to do good in the world and to save his soul, but now these two ends have come into sharp contradiction. They are contradictory because of the necessity for violence in a world where God has not instituted the sword. The politician takes the sword himself, and only by doing so does he measure up to his vocation. With full consciousness of what he is doing, he does bad in order to do good, and surrenders his soul. He "lets himself in," Weber says, "for the diabolic forces lurking in all violence." Perhaps Machiavelli also meant to suggest that his hero surrenders salvation in exchange for glory, but he does not explicitly say so. Weber is absolutely clear: "the genius or demon of politics lives in an inner tension with the god of love . . . [which] can at any time lead to an irreconcilable conflict."[21] His politician views this conflict when it comes with a tough realism, never pretends that it might be solved by compromise, chooses politics once again, and turns decisively away from love. Weber writes about this choice with a passionate high-mindedness that makes a concern for one's soul seem no more elevated than a concern for one's flesh. Yet the reader never doubts that his mature, superbly trained, relentless, objective, responsible, and disciplined political leader is also a suffering servant. His choices are hard and painful, and he pays the price not only while making them but forever after. A man doesn't lose his soul one day and find it the next.

The difficulties with this view will be clear to anyone who has ever met a suffering servant. Here is a man who lies, intrigues, sends other men to their death—and suffers. He does what he must do with a heavy heart. None of us can know, he tells us, how much it costs him to do his duty. Indeed, we cannot, for he himself fixes the price he pays. And that is the trouble with this view of political crime. We suspect the suffering servant of either masochism or hypocrisy or both, and while we are often wrong, we are not always wrong. Weber attempts to resolve the problem of dirty hands entirely within the confines of the individual conscience, but I am inclined to think that this is neither possible nor desirable. The self-awareness of the tragic hero is obviously of great value. We want the politician to have an inner life at least something like that which Weber describes. But sometimes the hero's suffering needs to be socially expressed (for like punishment, it confirms and reinforces our sense that certain acts are wrong). And equally important, it sometimes needs to be socially limited. We don't want to be ruled by men who have lost their souls.

21. "Politics as a Vocation," pp. 125-126. But sometimes a political leader does choose the "absolutist" side of the conflict, and Weber writes (p. 127) that it is "immensely moving when a *mature* man . . . aware of a responsibility for the consequences of his conduct . . . reaches a point where he says: 'Here I stand; I can do no other.' " Unfortunately, he does not suggest just where that point is or even where it might be.

A politician with dirty hands needs a soul, and it is best for us all if he has some hope of personal salvation, however that is conceived. It is not the case that when he does bad in order to do good he surrenders himself forever to the demon of politics. He commits a determinate crime, and he must pay a determinate penalty. When he has done so, his hands will be clean again, or as clean as human hands can ever be. So the Catholic Church has always taught, and this teaching is central to the third tradition that I want to examine.

Once again I will take a latter-day and a lapsed representative of the tradition and consider Albert Camus' *The Just Assassins*. The heroes of this play are terrorists at work in nineteenth-century Russia. The dirt on their hands is human blood. And yet Camus' admiration for them, he tells us, is complete. We consent to being criminals, one of them says, but there is nothing with which anyone can reproach us. Here is the dilemma of dirty hands in a new form. The heroes are innocent criminals, just assassins, because, having killed, they are prepared to die—*and will die*. Only their execution, by the same despotic authorities they are attacking, will complete the action in which they are engaged: dying, they need make no excuses. That is the end of their guilt and pain. The execution is not so much punishment as self-punishment and expiation. On the scaffold they wash their hands clean and, unlike the suffering servant, they die happy.

Now the argument of the play when presented in so radically simplified a form may seem a little bizarre, and perhaps it is marred by the moral extremism of Camus' politics. "Political action has limits," he says in a preface to the volume containing *The Just Assassins*, "and there is no good and just action but what recognizes those limits and if it must go beyond them, at least accepts death."[22] I am less interested here in the violence of that "at least"—what else does he have in mind?—than in the sensible doctrine that it exaggerates. That doctrine might best be described by an analogy: just assassination, I want to suggest, is like civil disobedience. In both men violate a set of rules, go beyond a moral or legal limit, in order to do what they believe they should do. At the same time, they acknowledge their responsibility for the violation by accepting punishment or doing penance. But

---

22. *Caligula and Three Other Plays* (New York, 1958), p. x. (The preface is translated by Justin O'Brian, the plays by Stuart Gilbert.)

Political Action: The Problem of Dirty Hands

there is also a difference between the two, which has to do with the difference between law and morality. In most cases of civil disobedience the laws of the state are broken for moral reasons, and the state provides the punishment. In most cases of dirty hands moral rules are broken for reasons of state, and no one provides the punishment. There is rarely a Czarist executioner waiting in the wings for politicians with dirty hands, even the most deserving among them. Moral rules are not usually enforced against the sort of actor I am considering, largely because he acts in an official capacity. If they were enforced, dirty hands would be no problem. We would simply honor the man who did bad in order to do good, and at the same time we would punish him. We would honor him for the good he has done, and we would punish him for the bad he has done. We would punish him, that is, for the same reasons we punish anyone else; it is not my purpose here to defend any particular view of punishment. In any case, there seems no way to establish or enforce the punishment. Short of the priest and the confessional, there are no authorities to whom we might entrust the task.

I am nevertheless inclined to think Camus' view the most attractive of the three, if only because it requires us at least to imagine a punishment or a penance that fits the crime and so to examine closely the nature of the crime. The others do not require that. Once he has launched his career, the crimes of Machiavelli's prince seem subject only to prudential control. And the crimes of Weber's tragic hero are limited only by *his* capacity for suffering and not, as they should be, by *our* capacity for suffering. In neither case is there any explicit reference back to the moral code, once it has, at great personal cost to be sure, been set aside. The question posed by Sartre's Hoerderer (whom I suspect of being a suffering servant) is rhetorical, and the answer is obvious (I have already given it), but the characteristic sweep of both is disturbing. Since it is concerned only with those crimes that ought to be committed, the dilemma of dirty hands seems to exclude questions of degree. Wanton or excessive cruelty is not at issue, any more than is cruelty directed at bad ends. But political action is so uncertain that politicians necessarily take moral as well as political risks, committing crimes that they only think ought to be committed. They override the rules without ever being certain that they have found the best way to the results they hope to achieve, and we don't want them to do that too quickly or too often. So it is important that the moral stakes be very high—which is to say, that the rules be rightly valued. That, I suppose, is the reason for Camus' extremism. Without the executioner, however, there is no one to set the stakes or maintain the values except ourselves, and probably no way to do either except through philosophic reiteration and political activity.

"We shall not abolish lying by refusing to tell lies," says Hoerderer, "but by using every means at hand to abolish social classes."[23] I suspect we shall not abolish lying at all, but we might see to it that fewer lies were told if we contrived to deny power and glory to the greatest liars—except, of course, in the case of those lucky few whose extraordinary achievements make us forget the lies they told. If Hoerderer succeeds in abolishing social classes, perhaps he will join the lucky few. Meanwhile, he lies, manipulates, and kills, and we must make sure he pays the price. We won't be able to do that, however, without getting our own hands dirty, and then we must find some way of paying the price ourselves.

23. *Dirty Hands*, p. 223.

[13]
Servility and self-respect

Several motives underlie this paper.[1] In the first place, I am curious to see if there is a legitimate source for the increasingly common feeling that servility can be as much a vice as arrogance. There seems to be something morally defective about the Uncle Tom and the submissive housewife; and yet, on the other hand, if the only interests they sacrifice are their own, it seems that we should have no right to complain. Secondly, I have some sympathy for the now unfashionable view that each person has duties to himself as well as to others. It does seem absurd to say that a person could literally violate his own rights or owe himself a debt of gratitude, but I suspect that the classic defenders of duties to oneself had something different in mind. If there are duties to oneself, it is natural to expect that a duty to avoid being servile would have a prominent place among them. Thirdly, I am interested in making sense of Kant's puzzling, but suggestive, remarks about respect for persons and respect for the moral law. On the usual reading, these remarks seem unduly moralistic; but, viewed in another way, they suggest an argument for a kind of self-respect which is incompatible with a servile attitude.

My procedure will not be to explicate Kant directly. Instead I shall try to isolate the defect of servility and sketch an argument to show why it is objectionable, noting only in passing how this relates to Kant and the controversy about duties to oneself. What I say about self-respect is far from the whole story. In particular, it is not concerned with esteem for one's special abilities and achievements or with the self-confidence which characterizes the especially autonomous person. Nor is my concern with the psychological antecedents and effects of self-respect. Nevertheless, my conclusions, if correct, should be of interest; for they imply that, given a common view of morality, there are nonutilitarian moral reasons for each person, regardless of his merits, to respect himself. To avoid servility to the extent that one can is not simply a right but a duty, not simply a duty to others but a duty to oneself.

---

1 An earlier version of this paper was presented at the meetings of the American Philosophical Association, Pacific Division. A number of revisions have been made as a result of the helpful comments of others, especially Norman Dahl, Sharon Hill, Herbert Morris, and Mary Mothersill.

SERVILITY AND SELF-RESPECT

I

Three examples may give a preliminary idea of what I mean by *servility*. Consider, first, an extremely deferential black, whom I shall call the *Uncle Tom*. He always steps aside for white men; he does not complain when less qualified whites take over his job; he gratefully accepts whatever benefits his all-white government and employers allot him, and he would not think of protesting its insufficiency. He displays the symbols of deference to whites, and of contempt towards blacks: he faces the former with bowed stance and a ready "sir" and "Ma'am"; he reserves his strongest obscenities for the latter. Imagine, too, that he is not playing a game. He is not the shrewdly prudent calculator, who knows how to make the best of a bad lot and mocks his masters behind their backs. He accepts without question the idea that, as a black, he is owed less than whites. He may believe that blacks are mentally inferior and of less social utility, but that is not the crucial point. The attitude which he displays is that what he values, aspires for, and can demand is of less importance than what whites value, aspire for, and can demand. He is far from the picture book's carefree, happy servant, but he does not feel that he has a right to expect anything better.

Another pattern of servility is illustrated by a person I shall call the *Self-Deprecator*. Like the Uncle Tom, he is reluctant to make demands. He says nothing when others take unfair advantage of him. When asked for his preferences or opinions, he tends to shrink away as if what he said should make no difference. His problem, however, is not a sense of racial inferiority but rather an acute awareness of his own inadequacies and failures as an individual. These defects are not imaginary: he has in fact done poorly by his own standards and others'. But, unlike many of us in the same situation, he acts as if his failings warrant quite unrelated maltreatment even by strangers. His sense of shame and self-contempt make him content to be the instrument of others. He feels that nothing is owed him until he has earned it and that he has earned very little. He is not simply playing a masochist's game of winning sympathy by disparaging himself. On the contrary, he assesses his individual merits with painful accuracy.

A rather different case is that of the *Deferential Wife*. This is a woman who is utterly devoted to serving her husband. She buys the clothes *he* prefers, invites the guests *he* wants to entertain, and makes love whenever *he* is in the mood. She willingly moves to a new city in order for him to have a more attractive job, counting her own friendships and geographical preferences insignificant by comparison. She loves her husband, but her conduct is not simply an expression of love. She is happy, but she does not subordinate herself as a means to happiness. She does not simply defer to her husband in certain spheres as a trade-off for his deference in other spheres. On the contrary, she tends not to form her own interests, values, and ideals; and, when she does, she counts them as less important than her husband's. She readily responds to appeals from Women's Liberation

AUTONOMY AND SELF-RESPECT

that she agrees that women are mentally and physically equal, if not superior, to men. She just believes that the proper role for a woman is to serve her family. As a matter of fact, much of her happiness derives from her belief that she fulfills this role very well. No one is trampling on her rights, she says; for she is quite glad, and proud, to serve her husband as she does.

Each one of these cases reflects the attitude which I call servility.[2] It betrays the absence of a certain kind of self-respect. What I take this attitude to be, more specifically, will become clearer later on. It is important at the outset, however, not to confuse the three cases sketched above with other, superficially similar cases. In particular, the cases I have sketched are not simply cases in which someone refuses to press his rights, speaks disparagingly of himself, or devotes himself to another. A black, for example, is not necessarily servile because he does not demand a just wage; for, seeing that such a demand would result in his being fired, he might forbear for the sake of his children. A self-critical person is not necessarily servile by virtue of bemoaning his faults in public; for his behavior may be merely a complex way of satisfying his own inner needs quite independent of a willingness to accept abuse from others. A woman need not be servile whenever she works to make her husband happy and prosperous; for she might freely and knowingly choose to do so from love or from a desire to share the rewards of his success. If the effort did not require her to submit to humiliation or maltreatment, her choice would not mark her as servile. There may, of course, be grounds for objecting to the attitudes in these cases, but the defect is not servility of the sort I want to consider. It should also be noted that my cases of servility are not simply instances of deference to superior knowledge or judgment. To defer to an expert's judgment on matters of fact is not to be servile; to defer to his every wish and whim is. Similarly, the belief that one's talents and achievements are comparatively low does not, by itself, make one servile. It is no vice to acknowledge the truth, and one may in fact have achieved less, and have less ability, than others. To be servile is not simply to hold certain empirical beliefs but to have a certain attitude concerning one's rightful place in a moral community.

II

Are there grounds for regarding the attitudes of the Uncle Tom, the Self-Deprecator, and the Deferential Wife as morally objectionable? Are there moral

---

2 Each of the cases is intended to represent only one possible pattern of servility. I make no claims about how often these patterns are exemplified, nor do I mean to imply that only these patterns could warrant the labels "Deferential Wife," "Uncle Tom," etc. All the more, I do not mean to imply any comparative judgments about the causes or relative magnitude of the problems of racial and sexual discrimination. One person, e.g., a self-contemptuous woman with a sense of racial inferiority, might exemplify features of several patterns at once; and, of course, a person might view her being a woman the way an Uncle Tom views his being black, etc.

SERVILITY AND SELF-RESPECT

arguments we could give them to show that they ought to have more self-respect? None of the more obvious replies is entirely satisfactory.

One might, in the first place, adduce utilitarian considerations. Typically the servile person will be less happy than he might be. Moreover, he may be less prone to make the best of his own socially useful abilities. He may become a nuisance to others by being overly dependent. He will, in any case, lose the special contentment that comes from standing up for one's rights. A submissive attitude encourages exploitation, and exploitation spreads misery in a variety of ways. These considerations provide a prima facie case against the attitudes of the Uncle Tom, the Deferential Wife, and the Self-Deprecator, but they are hardly conclusive. Other utilities tend to counterbalance the ones just mentioned. When people refuse to press their rights, there are usually others who profit. There are undeniable pleasures in associating with those who are devoted, understanding, and grateful for whatever we see fit to give them — as our fondness for dogs attests. Even the servile person may find his attitude a source of happiness, as the case of the Deferential Wife illustrates. There may be comfort and security in thinking that the hard choices must be made by others, that what I would say has little to do with what ought to be done. Self-condemnation may bring relief from the pangs of guilt even if it is not deliberately used for that purpose. On balance, then, utilitarian considerations may turn out to favor servility as much as they oppose it.

For those who share my moral intuitions, there is another sort of reason for not trying to rest a case against servility on utilitarian considerations. Certain utilities seem irrelevant to the issue. The utilitarian must weigh them along with others, but to do so seems morally inappropriate. Suppose, for example, that the submissive attitudes of the Uncle Tom and the Deferential Wife result in positive utilities for those who dominate and exploit them. Do we need to tabulate *these* utilities before conceding that servility is objectionable? The Uncle Tom, it seems, is making an error, a moral error, quite apart from consideration of how much others in fact profit from his attitude. The Deferential Wife may be quite happy; but if her happiness turns out to be contingent on her distorted view of her own rights and worth as a person, then it carries little moral weight against the contention that she ought to change that view. Suppose I could cause a woman to find her happiness in denying all her rights and serving my every wish. No doubt I could do so only by nonrational manipulative techniques, which I ought not to use. But is this the only objection? My efforts would be wrong, it seems, not only because of the techniques they require but also because the resultant attitude is itself objectionable. When a person's happiness stems from a morally objectionable attitude, it ought to be discounted. That a sadist gets pleasure from seeing others suffer should not count even as a partial justification for his attitude. That a servile person derives pleasure from denying her moral status, for similar reasons, cannot make her attitude acceptable. These

AUTONOMY AND SELF-RESPECT

brief intuitive remarks are not intended as a refutation of utilitarianism, with all its many varieties, but they do suggest that it is well to look elsewhere for adequate grounds for rejecting the attitudes of the Uncle Tom, the Self-Deprecator, and the Deferential Wife.

One might try to appeal to meritarian considerations. That is, one might argue that the servile person *deserves* more than he allows himself. This line of argument, however, is no more adequate than the utilitarian one. It may be wrong to deny others what they deserve, but it is not so obviously wrong to demand less for oneself than one deserves. In any case, the Self-Deprecator's problem is not that he underestimates his merits. By hypothesis, he assesses his merits quite accurately. We cannot reasonably tell him to have more respect for himself because he *deserves* more respect; he knows that he has not *earned* better treatment. His problem, in fact, is that he thinks of his moral status with regard to others as entirely dependent upon his merits. His interests and choices are important, he feels, only if he has earned the right to make demands; or if he had rights by birth, they were forfeited by his subsequent failures and misdeeds. My Self-Deprecator is no doubt an atypical person, but nevertheless he illustrates an important point. Normally when we find a self-contemptuous person, we can plausibly argue that he is not so bad as he thinks, that his self-contempt is an overreaction prompted more by inner needs than by objective assessment of his merits. Because this argument cannot work with the Self-Deprecator, his case draws attention to a distinction, applicable in other cases as well, between saying that someone deserves respect for his merits and saying that he is owed respect as a person. On meritarian grounds we can only say "You deserve better than this," but the defect of the servile person is not merely failure to recognize his merits.

Other common arguments against the Uncle Tom, et al., may have some force but seem not to strike to the heart of the problem. For example, philosophers sometimes appeal to the value of human potentialities. As a human being, it is said, one at least has a capacity for rationality, morality, excellence, or autonomy, and this capacity is worthy of respect. Although such arguments have the merit of making respect independent of a person's actual deserts, they seem quite misplaced in some cases. There comes a time when we have sufficient evidence that a person is not ever going to *be* rational, moral, excellent, or autonomous even if he still has a capacity, in some sense, for being so. As a person approaches death with an atrocious record so far, the chances of his realizing his diminishing capacities become increasingly slim. To make these capacities the basis of his self-respect is to rest it on a shifting and unstable ground. We do, of course, respect persons for capacities which they are not exercising at the moment; for example, I might respect a person as a good philosopher even though he is just now blundering into gross confusion. In these cases, however, we respect the person for an active capacity, a ready disposition, which he had displayed on

SERVILITY AND SELF-RESPECT

many occasions. On this analogy, a person should have respect for himself only when his capacities are developed and ready, needing only to be triggered by an appropriate occasion or the removal of some temporary obstacle. The Uncle Tom and the Deferential Wife, however, may in fact have quite limited capacities of this sort, and, since the Self-Deprecator is already overly concerned with his own inadequacies, drawing attention to his capacities seems a poor way to increase his self-respect. In any case, setting aside the Kantian nonempirical capacity for autonomy, the capacities of different persons vary widely; but what the servile person seems to overlook is something by virtue of which he is equal with every other person.

III

Why, then, is servility a moral defect? There is, I think, another sort of answer which is worth exploring. The first part of this answer must be an attempt to isolate the objectionable features of the servile person; later we can ask why these features are objectionable. As a step in this direction, let us examine again our three paradigm cases. The moral defect in each case, I suggest, is a failure to understand and acknowledge one's own moral rights. I assume, without argument here, that each person has moral rights.[3] Some of these rights may be basic human rights; that is, rights for which a person needs only to be human to qualify. Other rights will be derivative and contingent upon his special commitments, institutional affiliations, etc. Most rights will be prima facie ones; some may be absolute. Most can be waived under appropriate conditions; perhaps some cannot. Many rights can be forfeited; but some, presumably, cannot. The servile person does not, strictly speaking, violate his own rights. At least in our paradigm cases he fails to acknowledge fully his own moral status because he does not fully understand what his rights are, how they can be waived, and when they can be forfeited.

The defect of the Uncle Tom, for example, is that he displays an attitude that denies his moral equality with whites. He does not realize, or apprehend in an effective way, that he has as much right to a decent wage and a share of political power as any comparable white. His gratitude is misplaced; he accepts benefits which are his by right as if they were gifts. The Self-Deprecator is servile in a more complex way. He acts as if he has forfeited many important rights which in fact he has not. He does not understand, or fully realize in his own case, that certain rights to fair and decent treatment do not have to be earned. He sees his

---

3 As will become evident, I am also presupposing some form of cognitive or "naturalistic" interpretation of rights. If, to accommodate an emotivist or prescriptivist, we set aside talk of moral knowledge and ignorance, we might construct a somewhat analogous case against servility from the point of view of those who adopt principles ascribing rights to all; but the argument, I suspect, would be more complex and less persuasive.

AUTONOMY AND SELF-RESPECT

merits clearly enough, but he fails to see that what he can expect from others is not merely a function of his merits. The Deferential Wife *says* that she understands her rights vis-à-vis her husband, but what she fails to appreciate is that her consent to serve him is a valid waiver of her rights only under certain conditions. If her consent is coerced, say, by the lack of viable options for women in her society, then her consent is worth little. If socially fostered ignorance of her own talents and alternatives is responsible for her consent, then her consent should not count as a fully legitimate waiver of her right to equal consideration within the marriage. All the more, her consent to defer constantly to her husband is not a legitimate setting aside of her rights if it results from her mistaken belief that she has a moral duty to do so. (Recall: "The *proper* role for a woman is to serve her family.") If she believes that she has a *duty* to defer to her husband, then, whatever she may say, she cannot fully understand that she has a *right* not to defer to him. When she says that she freely gives up such a right, she is confused. Her confusion is rather like that of a person who has been persuaded by an unscrupulous lawyer that it is legally incumbent on him to refuse a jury trial but who nevertheless tells the judge that he understands that he has a right to a jury trial and freely waives it. He does not really understand what it is to have and freely give up the right if he thinks that it would be an offense for him to exercise it.

Insofar as servility results from moral ignorance or confusion, it need not be something for which a person is to blame. Even self-reproach may be inappropriate; for at the time a person is in ignorance he cannot feel guilty about his servility, and later he may conclude that his ignorance was unavoidable. In some cases, however, a person might reasonably believe that he should have known better. If, for example, the Deferential Wife's confusion about her rights resulted from a motivated resistance to drawing the implications of her own basic moral principles, then later she might find some ground for self-reproach. Whether blameworthy or not, servility could still be morally objectionable at least in the sense that it ought to be discouraged, that social conditions which nourish it should be reformed, and the like. Not all morally undesirable features of a person are ones for which he is responsible, but that does not mean that they are defects merely from an aesthetic or prudential point of view.

In our paradigm cases, I have suggested, servility is a kind of deferential attitude towards others resulting from ignorance or misunderstanding of one's moral rights. A sufficient remedy, one might think, would be moral enlightenment. Suppose, however, that our servile persons come to know their rights but do not substantially alter their behavior. Are they not still servile in an objectionable way? One might even think that reproach is more appropriate now because they know what they are doing.

The problem, unfortunately, is not as simple as it may appear. Much depends on what they tolerate and why. Let us set aside cases in which a person merely

SERVILITY AND SELF-RESPECT

refuses to *fight* for his rights, chooses not to exercise certain rights, or freely waives many rights which he might have insisted upon. Our problem concerns the previously servile person who continues to display the same marks of deference even after he fully knows his rights. Imagine, for example, that even after enlightenment our Uncle Tom persists in his old pattern of behavior, giving all the typical signs of believing that the injustices done to him are not really wrong. Suppose, too, that the newly enlightened Deferential Wife continues to defer to her husband, refusing to disturb the old way of life by introducing her new ideas. She acts as if she accepts the idea that she is merely doing her duty though actually she no longer believes it. Let us suppose, further, that the Uncle Tom and the Deferential Wife are not merely generous with their time and property; they also accept without protest, and even appear to sanction, treatment which is humiliating and degrading. That is, they do not simply consent to waive mutually acknowledged rights; they tolerate violations of their rights with apparent approval. They pretend to give their permission for subtle humiliations which they really believe no permission can make legitimate. Are such persons still servile despite their moral knowledge?

The answer, I think, should depend upon why the deferential role is played. If the motive is a morally commendable one, or a desire to avert dire consequences to oneself, or even an ambition to set an oppressor up for a later fall, then I would not count the role player as servile. The Uncle Tom, for instance, is not servile in my sense if he shuffles and bows to keep the Klan from killing his children, to save his own skin, or even to buy time while he plans the revolution. Similarly, the Deferential Wife is not servile if she tolerates an abusive husband because he is so ill that further strain would kill him, because protesting would deprive her of her only means of survival, or because she is collecting atrocity stories for her book against marriage. If there is fault in these situations, it seems inappropriate to call it *servility*. The story is quite different, however, if a person continues in his deferential role just from laziness, timidity, or a desire for some minor advantage. He shows too little concern for his moral status as a person, one is tempted to say, if he is willing to deny it for a small profit or simply because it requires some effort and courage to affirm it openly. A black who plays the Uncle Tom merely to gain an advantage over other blacks is harming them, of course; but he is also displaying disregard for his own moral position as an equal among human beings. Similarly, a woman throws away her rights too lightly if she continues to play the subservient role because she is used to it or is too timid to risk a change. A Self-Deprecator who readily accepts what he knows are violations of his rights may be indulging his peculiar need for punishment at the expense of denying something more valuable. In these cases, I suggest, we have a kind of servility independent of any ignorance or confusion about one's rights. The person who has it may or may not be blameworthy, depending on many factors; and the line between servile and nonservile role

AUTONOMY AND SELF-RESPECT

playing will often be hard to draw. Nevertheless, the objectionable feature is perhaps clear enough for present purposes: it is a willingness to disavow one's moral status, publicly and systematically, in the absence of any strong reason to do so.

My proposal, then, is that there are at least two types of servility: one resulting from misunderstanding of one's rights and the other from placing a comparatively low value on them. In either case, servility manifests the absence of a certain kind of self-respect. The respect which is missing is not respect for one's merits but respect for one's rights. The servile person displays this absence of respect not directly by acting contrary to his own rights but indirectly by acting as if his rights were nonexistent or insignificant. An arrogant person ignores the rights of others, thereby arrogating for himself a higher status than he is entitled to; a servile person denies his own rights, thereby assuming a lower position than he is entitled to. Whether rooted in ignorance or simply lack of concern for moral rights, the attitudes in both cases may be incompatible with a proper regard for morality. That this is so is obvious in the case of arrogance, but to see it in the case of servility requires some further argument.

IV

The objectionable feature of the servile person, as I have described him, is his tendency to disavow his own moral rights either because he misunderstands them or because he cares little for them. The question remains: why should anyone regard this as a moral defect? After all, the rights which he denies are his own. He may be unfortunate, foolish, or even distasteful; but why *morally* deficient? One sort of answer, quite different from those reviewed earlier, is suggested by some of Kant's remarks. Kant held that servility is contrary to a perfect non-juridical duty to oneself.[4] To say that the duty is perfect is roughly to say that it is stringent, never overridden by other considerations (e.g., beneficence). To say that the duty is nonjuridical is to say that a person cannot legitimately be coerced to comply. Although Kant did not develop an explicit argument for this view, an argument can easily be constructed from materials which reflect the spirit, if not the letter, of his moral theory. The argument which I have in mind is prompted by Kant's contention that respect for persons, strictly speaking, is respect for the moral law.[5] If taken as a claim about all sorts of respect, this

---

[4] See Immanuel Kant, *The Doctrine of Virtue*, Part II of *The Metaphysics of Morals*, ed. by Mary J. Gregor (New York: Harper & Row, 1964), pp. 99–103; Prussian Academy edition, Vol. VI, pp. 434–7.

[5] Immanuel Kant, *Groundwork of the Metaphysic of Morals*, ed. by H. J. Paton (New York: Harper & Row, 1964), p. 69; Prussian Academy edition, Vol. IV, p. 401; *The Critique of Practical Reason*, ed. by Lewis W. Beck (New York: Bobbs-Merrill, 1956), pp. 81, 84; Prussian Academy edition, Vol. V, pp. 78, 81. My purpose here is not to interpret what Kant meant but to give a sense to his remark.

SERVILITY AND SELF-RESPECT

seems quite implausible. If it means that we respect persons only for their moral character, their capacity for moral conduct, or their status as "authors" of the moral law, then it seems unduly moralistic. My strategy is to construe the remark as saying that at least one sort of respect for persons is respect for the rights which the moral law accords them. If one respects the moral law, then one must respect one's own moral rights; and this amounts to having a kind of self-respect incompatible with servility.

The premises for the Kantian argument, which are all admittedly vague, can be sketched as follows:

First, let us assume, as Kant did, that all human beings have equal basic human rights. Specific rights vary with different conditions, but all must be justified from a point of view under which all are equal. Not all rights need to be earned, and some cannot be forfeited. Many rights can be waived but only under certain conditions of knowledge and freedom. These conditions are complex and difficult to state; but they include something like the condition that a person's consent releases others from obligation only if it is autonomously given, and consent resulting from underestimation of one's moral status is not autonomously given. Rights can be objects of knowledge, but also of ignorance, misunderstanding, deception, and the like.

Second, let us assume that my account of servility is correct; or, if one prefers, we can take it as a definition. That is, in brief, a servile person is one who tends to deny or disavow his own moral rights because he does not understand them or has little concern for the status they give him.

Third, we need one formal premise concerning moral duty, namely, that each person ought, as far as possible, to respect the moral law. In less Kantian language, the point is that everyone should approximate, to the extent that he can, the ideal of a person who fully adopts the moral point of view. Roughly, this means not only that each person ought to do what is morally required and refrain from what is morally wrong but also that each person should treat all the provisions of morality as valuable – worth preserving and prizing as well as obeying. One must, so to speak, take up the spirit of morality as well as meet the letter of its requirements. To keep one's promises, avoid hurting others, and the like, is not sufficient; one should also take an attitude of respect towards the principles, ideals, and goals of morality. A respectful attitude towards a system of rights and duties consists of more than a disposition to conform to its definite rules of behavior; it also involves holding the system in esteem, being unwilling to ridicule it, and being reluctant to give up one's place in it. The essentially Kantian idea here is that morality, as a system of equal fundamental rights and duties, is worthy of respect, and hence a completely moral person would respect it in word and manner as well as in deed. And what a completely moral person would do, in Kant's view, is our duty to do so far as we can.

AUTONOMY AND SELF-RESPECT

The assumptions here are, of course, strong ones, and I make no attempt to justify them. They are, I suspect, widely held though rarely articulated. In any case, my present purpose is not to evaluate them but to see how, if granted, they constitute a case against servility. The objection to the servile person, given our premises, is that he does not satisfy the basic requirement to respect morality. A person who fully respected a system of moral rights would be disposed to learn his proper place in it, to affirm it proudly, and not to tolerate abuses of it lightly. This is just the sort of disposition that the servile person lacks. If he does not understand the system, he is in no position to respect it adequately. This lack of respect may be no fault of his own, but it is still a way in which he falls short of a moral ideal. If, on the other hand, the servile person knowingly disavows his moral rights by pretending to approve of violations of them, then, barring special explanations, he shows an indifference to whether the provisions of morality are honored and publicly acknowledged. This avoidable display of indifference, by our Kantian premises, is contrary to the duty to respect morality. The disrespect in this second case is somewhat like the disrespect a religious believer might show towards his religion if, to avoid embarrassment, he laughed congenially while nonbelievers were mocking the beliefs which he secretly held. In any case, the servile person, as such, does not express disrespect for the system of moral rights in the obvious way by violating the rights of others. His lack of respect is more subtly manifested by his acting before others as if he did not know or care about his position of equality under that system.

The central idea here may be illustrated by an analogy. Imagine a club, say, an old German dueling fraternity. By the rules of the club, each member has certain rights and responsibilities. These are the same for each member regardless of what titles he may hold outside the club. Each has, for example, a right to be heard at meetings, a right not to be shouted down by the others. Some rights cannot be forfeited: for example, each may vote regardless of whether he has paid his dues and satisfied other rules. Some rights cannot be waived: for example, the right to be defended when attacked by several members of the rival fraternity. The members show respect for each other by respecting the status which the rules confer on each member. Now one new member is careful always to allow the others to speak at meetings; but when they shout him down, he does nothing. He just shrugs as if to say, 'Who am I to complain?' When he fails to stand up in defense of a fellow member, he feels ashamed and refuses to vote. He does not deserve to vote, he says. As the only commoner among illustrious barons, he feels that it is his place to serve them and defer to their decisions. When attackers from the rival fraternity come at him with swords drawn, he tells his companions to run and save themselves. When they defend him, he expresses immense gratitude – as if they had done him a gratuitous favor. Now one might argue that our new member fails to show respect for the fraternity and its rules. He does not actually violate any of the rules by refusing to vote, asking others

SERVILITY AND SELF-RESPECT

not to defend him, and deferring to the barons, but he symbolically disavows the equal status which the rules confer on him. If he ought to have respect for the fraternity, he ought to change his attitude. Our servile person, then, is like the new member of the dueling fraternity in having insufficient respect for a system of rules and ideals. The difference is that everyone ought to respect morality whereas there is no comparable moral requirement to respect the fraternity.

The conclusion here is, of course, a limited one. Self-sacrifice is not always a sign of servility. It is not a duty always to press one's rights. Whether a given act is evidence of servility will depend not only on the attitude of the agent but also on the specific nature of his moral rights, a matter not considered here. Moreover, the extent to which a person is responsible, or blameworthy, for his defect remains an open question. Nevertheless, the conclusion should not be minimized. In order to avoid servility, a person who gives up his rights must do so with a full appreciation for what they are. A woman, for example, may devote herself to her husband if she is uncoerced, knows what she is doing, and does not pretend that she has no decent alternative. A self-contemptuous person may decide not to press various unforfeited rights but only if he does not take the attitude that he is too rotten to deserve them. A black may demand less than is due to him provided he is prepared to acknowledge that no one has a right to expect this of him. Sacrifices of this sort, I suspect, are extremely rare. Most people, if they fully acknowledged their rights, would not autonomously refuse to press them.

An even stronger conclusion would emerge if we could assume that some basic rights cannot be waived. That is, if there are some rights that others are bound to respect regardless of what we say, then, barring special explanation, we would be obliged not only to acknowledge these rights but also to avoid any appearance of consenting to give them up. To act as if we could release others from their obligation to grant these rights, apart from special circumstances, would be to fail to respect morality. Rousseau held, for example, that at least a minimal right to liberty cannot be waived. A man who consents to be enslaved, giving up liberty without *quid pro quo*, thereby displays a conditioned slavish mentality that renders his consent worthless. Similarly, a Kantian might argue that a person cannot release others from the obligation to refrain from killing him: consent is no defense against the charge of murder. To accept principles of this sort is to hold that rights to life and liberty are, as Kant believed, rather like a trustee's rights to preserve something valuable entrusted to him: he has not only a right but a duty to preserve it.

Even if there are no specific rights which cannot be waived, there might be at least one formal right of this sort. This is the right to some minimum degree of respect from others. No matter how willing a person is to submit to humiliation by others, they ought to show him some respect as a person. By analogy with self-respect, as presented here, this respect owed by others would consist of a

AUTONOMY AND SELF-RESPECT

willingness to acknowledge fully, in word as well as action, the person's basically equal moral status as defined by his other rights. To the extent that a person gives even tacit consent to humiliations incompatible with this respect, he will be acting as if he waives a right which he cannot in fact give up. To do this, barring special explanations, would mark one as servile.

V

Kant held that the avoidance of servility is a duty to oneself rather than a duty to others. Recent philosophers, however, tend to discard the idea of a duty to oneself as a conceptual confusion. Although admittedly the analogy between a duty to oneself and a duty to others is not perfect, I suggest that something important is reflected in Kant's contention.

Let us consider briefly the function of saying that a duty is *to* someone. *First*, to say that a duty is *to* a given person sometimes merely indicates who is the object of that duty. That is, it tells us that the duty is concerned with how that person is to be treated, how his interests and wishes are to be taken into account, and the like. Here we might as well say that we have a duty *towards*, or *regarding* that person. Typically the person in question is the beneficiary of the fulfillment of the duty. For example, in this sense I have a duty to my children and even a duty to a distant stranger if I promised a third party that I would help that stranger. Clearly a duty to avoid servility would be a duty to oneself at least in this minimal sense, for it is a duty to avoid, so far as possible, the denial of one's own moral status. The duty is concerned with understanding and affirming one's rights, which are, at least as a rule, for one's own benefit.

Second, when we say that a duty is *to* a certain person, we often indicate thereby the person especially entitled to complain in case the duty is not fulfilled. For example, if I fail in my duty to my colleagues, then it is they who can most appropriately reproach me. Others may sometimes speak up on their behalf, but, for the most part, it is not the business of strangers to set me straight. Analogously, to say that the duty to avoid servility is a duty to oneself would indicate that, though sometimes a person may justifiably reproach himself for being servile, others are not generally in the appropriate position to complain. Outside encouragement is sometimes necessary, but, if any blame is called for, it is primarily self-recrimination and not the censure of others.

Third, mention of the person to whom a duty is owed often tells us something about the source of that duty. For example, to say that I have a duty to another person may indicate that the argument to show that I have such a duty turns upon a promise to that person, his authority over me, my having accepted special benefits from him, or, more generally, his rights. Accordingly, to say that the duty to avoid servility is a duty to oneself would at least imply that it is not entirely based upon promises to others, their authority, their beneficence, or an

SERVILITY AND SELF-RESPECT

obligation to respect their rights. More positively, the assertion might serve to indicate that the source of the duty is one's own rights rather than the rights of others, etc. That is, one ought not to be servile because, in some broad sense, one ought to respect one's own rights as a person. There is, to be sure, an asymmetry: one has certain duties to others because one ought not to violate their rights, and one has a duty to oneself because one ought to affirm one's own rights. Nevertheless, to dismiss duties to oneself out of hand is to overlook significant similarities.

Some familiar objections to duties to oneself, moreover, seem irrelevant in the case of servility. For example, some place much stock in the idea that a person would have no duties if alone on a desert island. This can be doubted, but in any case is irrelevant here. The duty to avoid servility is a duty to take a certain stance towards others and hence would be inapplicable if one were isolated on a desert island. Again, some suggest that if there were duties to oneself then one could make promises to oneself or owe oneself a debt of gratitude. Their paradigms are familiar ones. Someone remarks, "I promised myself a vacation this year" or "I have been such a good boy I owe myself a treat." Concentration on these facetious cases tends to confuse the issue. In any case the duty to avoid servility, as presented here, does not presuppose promises to oneself or debts of gratitude to oneself. Other objections stem from the intuition that a person has no duty to promote his own happiness. A duty to oneself, it is sometimes assumed, must be a duty to promote one's own happiness. From a utilitarian point of view, in fact, this is what a duty to oneself would most likely be. The problems with such alleged duties, however, are irrelevant to the duty to avoid servility. This is a duty to understand and affirm one's rights, not to promote one's own welfare. While it is usually in the interest of a person to affirm his rights, our Kantian argument against servility was not based upon this premise. Finally, a more subtle line of objection turns on the idea that, given that rights and duties are correlative, a person who acted contrary to a duty to oneself would have to be violating his own rights, which seems absurd.[6] This objection raises issues too complex to examine here. One should note, however, that I have tried to give a sense to saying that servility is contrary to a duty to oneself without presupposing that the servile person violates his own rights. If acts contrary to duties to others are always violations of their rights, then duties to oneself are not parallel with duties to others to that extent. But this does not mean that it is empty or pointless to say that a duty is to oneself.

My argument against servility may prompt some to say that the duty is "to morality" rather than "to oneself." All this means, however, is that the duty is derived from a basic requirement to respect the provisions of morality; and in

---

[6] This, I take it, is part of M. G. Singer's objection to duties to oneself in *Generalization in Ethics* (New York: Alfred A. Knopf, 1961), pp. 311–18. Singer's objections are discussed in the essay "Promises to Oneself," in this volume.

AUTONOMY AND SELF-RESPECT

this sense every duty is a duty "to morality." My duties to my children are also derivative from a general requirement to respect moral principles, but they are still duties *to* them.

Kant suggests that duties to oneself are a precondition of duties to others. On our account of servility, there is at least one sense in which this is so. Insofar as the servile person is ignorant of his own rights, he is not in an adequate position to appreciate the rights of others. Misunderstanding the moral basis for his equal status with others, he is necessarily liable to underestimate the rights of those with whom he classifies himself. On the other hand, if he plays the servile role knowingly, then, barring special explanation, he displays a lack of concern to see the principles of morality acknowledged and respected and thus the absence of one motive which can move a moral person to respect the rights of others. In either case, the servile person's lack of self-respect necessarily puts him in a less than ideal position to respect others. Failure to fulfill one's duty to oneself, then, renders a person liable to violate duties to others. This, however, is a consequence of our argument against servility, not a presupposition of it.

A Kantian theory of leadership

Norman Bowie
Elmer L. Andersen Chair of Corporate Responsibility, University of Minnesota, USA, and Dixons Professor of Business Ethics and Social Responsibility, London Business School, UK

Keywords
Leadership, Ethics, Autonomy

Abstract
Uses Kant's moral philosophy to provide a normative theory of leadership. First shows how Kant's philosophy would reject instrumental theories of leadership and most charismatic theories of leadership. Perhaps somewhat more surprisingly, it questions some of the assumptions of servant leadership and puts constraints on transformational leadership and the leader as educator. The central concept of Kant's moral philosophy is the dignity given to autonomy. Thus a good leader ought to respect and enrich the autonomy of followers. The Kantian leader turns followers into leaders.

One might think that a Kantian theory of leadership is as much an oxymoron as business ethics itself. After all, it is a conceptual truth that a leader must have followers. Moreover, people tend to think that a follower is of lesser rank than a leader. For many the term "leader" has hierarchical and even élitist connotations. Kant's moral philosophy, on the other hand, is basically egalitarian. It is Kant who provides the intellectual justification for the respect for persons principle. Kant points out that each person thinks of himself or herself as a rational creature who is entitled to dignity and respect. Consistency then requires that each person recognize the rational nature of other persons and thus recognize that other persons are also entitled to be treated with dignity and respect. This is why Kant argues that one cannot use another as a means merely. In yet another formulation of the categorical imperative Kant argues that in a community or organization we are bound by rules but by rules that we ourselves would accept as rational legislators. Thus in such communities, which Kant calls kingdoms of ends, the members are all equally subject and sovereign. Given these egalitarian commitments, how can Kant provide a theory of leadership when "leadership" has connotations of élitism and hierarchy? Suggesting a way out of this dilemma is the subject of this paper.

Section I. What leadership is not

First, it should be pointed out that leaders need not violate the respect for persons formulation of the categorical imperative. Leaders need not use followers as means to their own ends. The fact that many leaders do behave in that way cannot count against the normative claim that they ought not to behave in that way. As a matter of logic this point is certainly correct. However, I must admit that there are many temptations in business life to use followers as means. In finance capitalism and under the influence of Wall Street, the leaders of publicly held firms are under great pressure to increase the "value" of the firm, i.e. to increase the stock price and hence shareholder wealth. With such pressure on contemporary managers it is hard to avoid using the other corporate stakeholders as a mere means for the ends of the stockholders.

Despite the temptation, competitive pressures may not provide even a prudent basis for using stakeholders as a means to stockholder profits and unsophisticated versions of finance capitalism that argue the contrary have not gone unchallenged on this point. Aggressive attempts to subordinate the interests of employees, customers, and suppliers to achieve greater financial returns can be self-defeating. As critics of Al Dunlop's management philosophy point out, there is considerable empirical evidence that companies that also address the interests of employees, customers, suppliers, and the local communities in which they do business have better financial returns than those that do not. This thesis is articulated in books such as *Built to Last*, (Collins and Porras, 1994); *The Loyalty Effect* (Reichheld, 1996), and *The Human Equation* (Pfeffer, 1998). Defenders of this thesis endorse a number of enlightened management practices such as quality circles, teamwork, participative management, and empowerment. However, the adoption of such enlightened management practices does not resolve the issue for the Kantian. If the motivation for adopting such techniques were simply to increase shareholder wealth, then the adoption of such practices would not be genuinely moral acts. Such actions would not result from a good will. They would not be done out of duty but rather would be done out of prudence. They have no more moral value

Norman Bowie
A Kantian theory of leadership
The Leadership & Organization Development Journal
21/4 [2000] 185–193

than the act of truth telling on the part of the shopkeeper, in the *Foundations of the Metaphysics of Morals* (Kant, 1963), who is honest in order to maintain his reputation[1]. Thus a Kantian can agree with Joanne Ciulla when she refers to such enlightened management techniques as "bogus empowerment" (Ciulla, 1998). If leadership involves the adoption of such enlightened management practices, and I will argue that it does, then such practices must not be implemented simply to raise profits for stockholders. Otherwise they use people as means and are, from the moral point of view, merely bogus.

The fact that a Kantian leader must act from a moral motive means that he or she cannot adopt a purely instrumental philosophy? A Kantian cannot take advice on how to be a good leader from Machiavelli. For Machiavelli the sole purpose of leadership is power. The leader seeks to maintain his power and *The Prince* can be considered a handbook for staying in power. Should a leader be kind or cruel? The only way to answer that question from Machiavelli's perspective is to ask whether cruelty or kindness will enable the leader to maintain power. As one might expect the answer will vary according to the situation.

It seems obvious that a Kantian cannot take an instrumental view of leadership. The reason for that is because an instrumental view requires that we use the most efficient means necessary to achieve the end. Now an instrumental view would require us to use people merely as a means if the end required it. But that is not permitted on Kantian moral theory and for Kant the moral point of view trumps all other points of view. We are not permitted to use immoral means to achieve our ends.

This conclusion has interesting results. If leadership theorists were asked to identify persons who were called leaders who subscribed to an instrumental view, two names would be prominent. Henry Kissinger would be the chief example from the world of politics and Jack Welch the CEO of General Electric might well be the chief example from the world of business. Kissinger has been prominently identified as a realist in political affairs so I think the attribution to Kissinger is indeed fair. The attribution to Welch may require a bit of explanation. In his early days at General Electric Welch's aim was to increase shareholder value. To do that he believed that each division at General Electric had to be first or second in its class. Otherwise it should be shut down. Welch also established strict financial goals for his managers and he expected managers to meet those goals or forfeit their positions. Welch was considered a demanding boss and was prominently listed on Fortune's list of the most difficult bosses to work for. He certainly appeared to use subordinates, if not solely as a means for his own end, then solely as a means to increase the wealth of GE shareholders (and at that Welch has certainly been successful). However, Welch would be disqualified as a leader in Kant's sense on those grounds alone. However in the mid-1990s, Welch discovered the human relations function and enlightened management techniques. He no longer believed that being characterized as one of the most difficult bosses to work for was the best way to contribute to the bottom line. Did Jack Welch become a Kantian leader in the 1990s? I think a Kantian would have to say he did not. It is reported that Welch was asked if he would give up his enlightened management techniques if he thought that they were no longer the most efficient way to contribute to the bottom line. He said he would. Welch's management techniques were purely instrumental. If using enlightened human resource techniques contributed to the bottom line, he would use them. If they did not, he would not. But in either case it seems fair to say that subordinates were used solely as a means to contribute to the bottom line. Welch used people as a means whether he was one of the most difficult bosses or not. For that reason a Kantian could not consider Welch a true leader despite the fact that almost everyone in the management field does. A Kantian theory of leadership is not without bite.

A characteristic frequently associated with leadership is charisma[2]. Charisma is defined as "a rare personal quality of leaders who arouse fervent popular devotion and enthusiasm". It is also defined as "personal magnetism or charm". As one can see from the definition, charisma is a quality that elicits powerful emotional responses in followers. A Kantian should be especially nervous about charisma. First, a Kantian requires moral actions to be the result of autonomous choices and an action cannot be an autonomous choice if it is merely an emotional response and nothing more. Such an action would be heteronomous rather than autonomous. Second, a necessary condition for a moral action according to Kant is that it be consistent with reason. By that I mean that the action must be based on a maxim that can be universally endorsed and followed. Otherwise the action is in violation of the first formulation of the categorical imperative. When a leader uses charisma to get his or her followers to act, it

Norman Bowie
A Kantian theory of leadership
The Leadership & Organization Development Journal
21/4 [2000] 185–193

seems as if the response of the followers is merely emotional. Their action might be consistent with principles that could be rationally adopted universally, but their rationality would be purely accidental. Thus even when the charismatic leader whips up his or her followers in a frenzy for an acknowledged good action, neither the followers nor the leader are behaving morally in a Kantian sense. It must also be pointed out that the charismatic leader may not use his or her charismatic quality for good ends. Followers respond to charismatic leaders who endorse the most vicious and immoral actions. This is the so-called Hitler problem (see Ciulla, 1998). For Kant, charisma is neither a necessary or sufficient condition for leadership. Moreover, on balance charisma is dangerous because it motivates followers to act on non-rational grounds rather than rational ones. Do not look for charisma in a Kantian theory of leadership.

In passing it should be noted that even some of those who allow emotion into ethical judgment share the concerns of Kantians with charismatic leadership. For example, Robert Solomon, who defines leadership as "an emotional relationship of trust", is critical of charismatic leadership (Solomon, 1998).

Perhaps a Kantian would endorse a theory of leadership that specifically eschews the notion that the leader is somehow superior to his or her followers. Servant leadership is one such theory. The chief intellectual spokesperson for servant leadership is Greenleaf (1977). Greenleaf begins his classic text by indicating that the idea for servant leadership came from reading Herman Hesse's *Journey to the East*. In that book, the central figure Leo turns out to be a leader, because, although he does menial chores, only Leo can make it possible for the group to conclude its journey. Greenleaf then goes on to say:

> But to me, this story clearly says that the great leader is seen as a servant first, and that simple fact is the key to his greatness. Leo was actually the leader all of the time, but he was servant first because that was what he was, deep down inside. Leadership was bestowed upon a man who was by nature a servant. It was something given or assumed that could be taken away. His servant nature was the real man, not bestowed, not assumed, that could be taken away. He was servant first.

The notion of servant leadership has become a classic in leadership literature. Greenleaf went on to establish a center, the Greenleaf Servant Leadership Center, and in 1998 he published a follow-up book entitled *The Power of Servant Leadership*. That book won endorsement from many of the great names in leadership including Max DePree, Peter Senge, Margaret J. Wheatley, Warren Bennis, and Frances Hesselbein.

What would Kant's position be on servant leadership? Certainly, the servant leader would not merely use followers to achieve his or her own ends. That, in this form of leadership at least, is a conceptual truth. But, despite this, I do not think that Kant would be on the list of endorsees. Given the emphasis on autonomy in Kant's philosophy and given the connotations of the word "servant", I think we must make sure that the servant leader is not allowing himself or herself to be used as merely a means to the goals of those he or she serves. Kant would no more permit an agent to use himself or herself as a means merely than he would allow one to merely use another. That an agent cannot use himself or herself as a means is part of the point of at least two of the four examples in the *Foundations of the Metaphysics of Morals* (Kant, 1990). Kant argues that it is immoral for a person to commit suicide or to fail to develop his or her talents. With respect to suicide Kant says, "man, however, is not a thing, and thus not something to be used merely as a means; he must always be regarded in all his actions as an end in himself. Therefore I cannot dispose of man in my own person so as to mutilate, corrupt or kill him". His comments about the obligation not to waste one's talents are more indirect with respect to not using oneself as a means. He points out in his discussion that it is not enough that our actions not conflict with persons as rational agents; our actions must also harmonize with persons as ends as well. And failure to develop one's talents will not harmonize with one's nature as a rational end. Finally, Kant specifically rejects the notion of servility as an acceptable stance for any person-leader or otherwise.

> A low opinion of oneself in relation to others is no humility; it is a sign of a little spirit and of a servile character. To flatter oneself that this is a virtue is to mistake an imitation for the genuine article; it is a monk's virtue and not at all natural; this form of humility is in fact a form of pride. There is nothing unjust or unreasonable in self-esteem (Kant, 1963).

Now it can be plausibly argued Greenleaf's account of servant leadership is not servile in Kant's sense. As we shall see there are many passages in Greenleaf that would fit with a Kantian theory of leadership. Moreover, even if the classical formulations were servile in tone, a theory of servant leadership can be developed that is not servile. However, a review of the Greenleaf quotation above

Norman Bowie
A Kantian theory of leadership
The Leadership & Organization Development Journal
21/4 [2000] 185–193

certainly seems to endorse the servility as a virtue. That aspect of Greenleaf's view of servant leadership would not be acceptable to Kant.

One of the best known theories of leadership is that leaders are transformational. Its leading exponent is James MacGregor Burns. Burns begins by distinguishing transformational leadership from the more typically practiced transactional leadership. Transactional leadership occurs when one person (the leader) sees possibilities for exchange. Thus the "transactional leader approaches followers with an eye to exchanging one thing for another: jobs for votes or subsidies for campaign contributions". Burns notes that the exchanges under transactional leadership can be economic, political or psychological in nature (Burns, 1978). Now the mere fact that a relationship is one of mutual exchange initiated by the transactional leader does not mean that the transactional leader uses the other person or persons in the exchange is a means merely. He or she may but need not. However, the Kantian would be in agreement with Burns who finds transactional leadership anemic. Transactional leadership may not use a person as a means but it does not respect a person either. There is no concern with the development of the follower as an autonomous, rational, responsible person.

Transformational leadership which Burns defines in one place as a "relationship of mutual stimulation and elevation that converts followers into leaders and may convert leaders into moral agents" (1978, p. 5) is very different. Under transformational leadership the follower (and the leader) are changed for the better. Burns argues that transformational leadership is not based simply on power or authority (although Burns clearly recognizes that conflict and power have a role to play in the dynamics of leadership). Leaders do induce followers to act for certain goals, but these goals "... represent the values and the motivations – the wants and needs, the aspirations and expectations – *of both the leaders and followers*" (p. 19). Leadership seeks to elevate the consciousness of followers. It does this by operating at need and value levels higher than those of the followers and by exploiting conflict and tensions within followers' value structures (p. 42). Burns had been strongly influenced by Lawrence Kohlberg and the moral development school (pp. 42, 46). Thus another way to characterize transformational leadership is to say that it raises the moral development of followers to a higher level on Kohlberg's scale. How is this achieved? Burns clearly rejects indoctrination. It succeeds by appealing to higher values. Followers realize they can become better than they are. For example in cases where values conflict, one of the tasks of the leader is to mediate that value conflict. To do that the leader appeals to "more widely and deeply held values, such as justice, liberty, and brotherhood" (p. 43).

To what extent would Kant endorse transformational leadership? There are many aspects of transformational leadership that would appeal to a Kantian. A Kantian would endorse the respect that is given to the needs and values of followers and as we shall see a Kantian would find the notion that leaders turn followers into leaders an especially desirable feature of leadership. The concerns would focus on how the transformation to higher values takes place. Burns' rejection of indoctrination would earn high marks. However, some commentators remain concerned about whether transformational leadership is sufficiently respectful of the autonomy of the followers. So much depends on how the transformation takes place.

Michael Keeley has expressed an important concern regarding transformational leadership (Keeley, 1995). There is a danger that the unity of purpose will be achieved by silencing the voices of a minority. Drawing on the political philosophy of James Madison, Keeley argues that transformational leadership can in effect turn into the tyranny of the majority. Keeley says:

> The conclusion drawn by Madison is a flat-out repudiation of transformational leadership ... unless leaders are able to transform everyone and create absolute unanimity of interests (a very special case), transformational leadership produces simply a majority will that represents the interests of the strongest faction. Sometimes that will is on the side of the good – as in Ghandi's case. Sometimes it is on the side of evil – as in Hitler's case. In any case, might is an arbitrary guide to right, as Madison clearly understood (1995, p. 77).

A Kantian theory of leadership will insist on more participation on the part of the followers and will be more protective of the interests of dissenting voices. The Kantian leader is not so naïve as to believe that there can be unanimity regarding all the decisions that an organization makes, but the rules that govern decision-making should be rules that everyone living under them has had a hand in making and can endorse. As Kant says one ought to act as if one were a member of a kingdom of ends in which one were both subject and sovereign at the same time. If there is a common purpose, it must be arrived at by rules or principles which are both rational and which have the support of those who must live under them. Transformational leadership must be constrained in that way if it is to be endorsed by the Kantian leader.

Finally some have argued that the leader is primarily an educator. How would Kant respond to that? As Newton points out, education can take place in two ways: some educators try to impose the correct beliefs and values in students. Others think education involves getting students to think for themselves (Newton, 1985). In this vein Newton is following Burns who points out that students should not be used instrumentally nor coerced, but should be treated as joint seekers after truth (Burns, 1978). But what is so valuable about thinking for oneself? I think the answer to that is that learning to think for oneself is one of the fundamental ways of exercising one's autonomy. Thinking for oneself is important because autonomy is important. Education contributes to the development of autonomy. But it also should contribute to the development of personal responsibility. That personal responsibility is played out in one's community. In fact many have argued that the liberal arts education is designed to prepare one for leadership. So education prepares one for leadership and the leader, on this view, is an educator. Again a Kantian would find much to accept from those who argue that a leader is an educator so long as the guiding philosophy of education was the support and development of individual autonomy. After all it is autonomy that gives persons a dignity that is without price. Indeed respect for the autonomy of persons is, I shall argue, the chief building block for a positive theory of leadership. But what of content? What is it that the educator leader teaches? I shall argue in the next section that the educator leader teaches followers to be leaders. Thus I shall argue that a Kantian leader is a teacher who enhances the autonomy of followers by teaching them to be leaders.

Section II. what leadership is: a Kantian theory

In this section I defend the claim that Kantian leadership supports the development of autonomy both in his or her followers as well as in himself or herself. The implementation of such a view requires that the leader turn followers into leaders. In other words the leader transforms the relationships in an organization so that those who had been followers could now be considered leaders.

Thus far the Kantian theory of leadership I have presented has been negative. I have shown that certain well-received views of leadership are not acceptable on Kantian grounds. Prominent among these failed views are charismatic leadership, servant leadership, and instrumental leadership. Theories of transformational leadership and the leader as teacher have proved more promising, but only if constrained by certain features of Kant's moral philosophy. However, I think a Kantian theory of leadership is more robust than standard transformational or leader as teacher theories. I believe that Kantian moral theory provides the tools to construct a positive theory of leadership that shares many features with transformational leadership and with the model of the leader as a teacher but that is unique in its own right.

I propose that the kingdom of ends formulation of the categorical imperative is the key to a positive theory of leadership just as the second formulation was the key for a negative theory (a theory of telling us what leadership is not). The kingdom of ends formulation asserts that "One should act as if one were a member of an ideal kingdom of ends in which one was subject and sovereign at the same time". Kant recognized that human beings interacted with other human beings (ends). Thus the arena of interaction was called a "kingdom of ends". A business organization, like any other organization, is composed of individual persons and since persons are moral creatures, the interactions of persons in an organization are moral interactions and thus are subject to moral law. On Kant's view a business relationship cannot be simply economic; business interactions are interactions among persons and thus they are always subject to morality as well. And as we have seen the relation between leaders and followers cannot simply be transactional.

What are the laws, which govern those interactions? Kant maintained that since those interactions were the interactions of human beings and not billiard balls, laws made by human beings themselves should govern them. Thus the laws should reflect the fact that the members of the organization are autonomous and rational in the practical sense. The laws that govern the interactions of persons should be self-legislated. Of course those laws ought to be consistent with the requirements of morality as spelled out in the first two formulations of the categorical imperative. Thus the laws must be capable of

Norman Bowie
A Kantian theory of leadership
The Leadership & Organization Development Journal
21/4 [2000] 185-193

being universally applied and respect the humanity in a person as an end rather than as a means merely.

Subjection to moral law equally applies when the interaction is within an organization including business organizations. Leaders interact with followers and thus these interactions are subject to moral rules. From the negative point of view or in the sense of things forbidden, leadership interactions cannot violate the categorical imperative. But interactions between leaders and followers need more guiding norms than that. The third formulation of the categorical imperative provides the moral requirement for adopting these other norms. It provides a positive view of what the norms governing a kingdom of ends should be. Basically it says these norms cannot be simply imposed on the basis of power or superiority of position. The norm must be the kind of norm that could in principle receive the assent of all rational moral beings. Thus there is a sense in which the norms that govern an organization must be acceptable to all. That is what it means to say that all individuals including leaders and followers are both subject and sovereign with respect to the norms that govern them.

The third formulation acts as a significant restraint on leadership as it is traditionally understood. Many think of the leader as the boss – as the person who makes the decisions. A Kantian does not accept that view. To be consistent with the kingdom of ends formulation of the categorical imperative, the leader is a decision proposer rather than a decision imposer. The leader in an organization can propose ends as well as means for reaching those ends. He or she can propose decision-making rules as well. But the leader should not order these things or impose them on the basis of his or her power. In management terms the leader creates the conditions for participative management. In less scholarly terminology, the Kantian leader gets buy-in. But the buy-in is not based on charisma. Neither is it based on power or position. Rather it is based on the merits of the proposal. The rules that govern human interactions should be rules that are acceptable to all.

But isn't participative management the abandonment of leadership? And even if it weren't, wouldn't such leadership lead to chaos. If you need universal buy-in for every decision that is made in an organization, you have anarchy and the organization will surely fail. That is certainly true, but universal buy-in is not required for every decision under a Kantian theory of leadership. We need to distinguish among the following:
1 the individual decision, e.g. how many motors should we order,
2 the norm for making a decision, e.g. should that decision be left to the purchasing department; and
3 how should we decide how the norms in (2) should be made.

At a minimum I think a Kantian theory of leadership requires that the norms in (3) meet the conditions of the third formulation of the categorical imperative. Respecting a legislator in the kingdom of ends requires at least that much. Moreover, I think that as an ideal the Kantian leader should get assent for norms and decisions as often as possible and as far down into the organization as possible. The following principles may guide a leader as he or she attempts to transform an organization into a kingdom of ends:
1 The leader should consider the interests of all the affected stakeholders in any decision it makes.
2 The leader should have those affected by the firm's rules and policies participate in the determination of those rules and policies before they are implemented.
3 It should not be the case that the leader always gives the interests of one stakeholder group priority.
4 When a situation arises where it appears that the humanity of one set of stakeholders must be sacrificed for the humanity of another set of stakeholders, the leader cannot make the decision on the grounds that there is a greater number of people in one stakeholder group than in another.
5 Every leader must in cooperation with others in the organization establish procedures to ensure that relations among stakeholders are governed by rules of justice.

The first principle is a straightforward requirement that leaders take respect for persons seriously. The criterion says that leaders should take the moral point of view. Most philosophers agree that the moral point of view involves at least the commitment to take into account the interests of those affected by our actions. It seems to me that it is a principle that all rational persons would adopt.

The second principle provides a practical way for the leader to respect the autonomy of followers. Rather than simply give orders, the leader encourages followers to participate and thus the leader begins the transformation from mere followers, that is from followers who follow blindly, to persons

Norman Bowie
A Kantian theory of leadership
The Leadership & Organization Development Journal
21/4 [2000] 185-193

who can coordinate their goals and interests with others so that the objectives of the organization are obtained.

The third principle functions as a principle of legitimacy. It insures that all those involved in the firm receive some minimum benefit from being part of the organization. The principle reminds us that the task of the leader is not to use participants to achieve the greater good when those participants receive no benefit from the public good.

The fourth principle is an anti-utilitarian criterion and principle 5 ensures that where there is disagreement about the laws or norms that should govern an organization, the disagreement should be settled on grounds of justice. Principle 5 is a further check on authoritarian tendencies in leaders. Some believe that it is the task of the leader to resolve such disagreements. But not a Kantian. The Kantian leader assists in the resolution of disagreement, but he or she does not make the decision herself. To do so would violate the autonomy of the other members of the organization. It seems to me that these criteria for leadership could win universal assent and would meet Kant's requirement that they be norms to which all members of the community may be both subject and sovereign.

What I am really arguing is that the basis of a Kantian theory of leadership is autonomy. What should the relation of a Kantian leader to his or her followers be? The leader should enhance the autonomy of his or her followers. At the extreme the leader transforms followers into leaders. The leader drives leadership down through the organization by making people at lower levels in the hierarchy decision-maker leaders themselves rather than mere followers.

The Harvard Business School case, ABB's Relays Business, is often used as a case study for the development of the matrix organization but it can also be used as a case study for a Kantian theory of leadership. Here is how the case unfolds: the CEO of Asea Brown Boveri (ABB) is Percy Barnevik, the most cited non-American international business leader in American leadership literature. In this case, Barnevik is the person who exemplifies leadership. Yet after page two, Barnevik disappears and is never heard from again. However this HBR case is 12 pages long excluding appendices. If this case is about Barnevik's leadership, where is he? By page two, the actor on center stage is Goran Lindahl, Asea's executive vice-president. As the case unfolds, it is clear Barnevik has made Lindahl a leader. For example Lindahl is responsible for communicating the new philosophy and principles including the guiding principle of decentralization. He also wanted to emphasize the importance of individual accountability. He delegated a series of tasks to managers at lower levels. By page six Lindahl disappears and Ulf Gundemark who becomes ABB's business head for the worldwide relay business is at the center of action. Leadership is being pushed down the organizational chart. A focal point event in the case centers on the allocation of export markets. The Swiss company had been given responsibility for coordinating sales into Mexico but a dispute arose concerning shortening the company's lines to its customers and minimizing the non-value added work in the system. Gundemark delegated this to a team of four marketing managers. After much negotiation they reported back to Gundemark that they could not reach a decision. Rather than make the decision himself, Gundemark sent them back for further discussion. Several days later after exhausting negotiations, they reported they had reached a majority decision of three to one. Gundemark wanted a unanimous decision and sent them back yet again. Finally after three more days of intense negotiation, the marketing team comes back with a unanimous recommendation. Talk about a decision where you are subject and sovereign at the same time. A Kantian leader, contrary to a popular stereotype, is not one to whom you look for a decision. The Kantian leader empowers others in the organization to take responsibility for making a decision. In so doing Barnevik, at least in part, exemplifies what it means to be a Kantian leader.

Yet another Kantian leader is Jan Carlzon former head of SAS airlines. When Carlzon took over as CEO of SAS, the company had lost its way and was floundering. He undertook a number of steps that brought popularity and thus profitability to the airline. A characteristic of his leadership style was to empower others in the organization to make decisions. One story in particular reflects Carlzon's leadership style. Carlzon realized he had not succeeded in providing adequate leadership for the company when he finally went on vacation. Throughout his vacation there were constant phone calls asking him to make a decision. Carlzon realized that he would only succeed when he went on vacation and no one called to seek his advice. His job as a leader was to encourage subordinates to make decisions on their own. In that way they increased their autonomy on the job. Eventually he went on vacation and no one called. Carlzon begins

Norman Bowie
A Kantian theory of leadership

The Leadership & Organization Development Journal
21/4 [2000] 185-193

his book *Moments of Truth* with the following quotations:

> Everyone needs to know and feel that he is needed. Everyone wants to be treated as an individual. Giving someone the freedom to take responsibility releases resources that would otherwise remain concealed. An individual without information cannot take responsibility; an individual who is given information cannot help but take responsibility (Carlzon, 1987).

These two cases illustrate the central thesis of a Kantian theory of leadership. A central task of the leader is to respect and enhance the autonomy of followers. In many organizational contexts, especially in business, having the followers become leaders themselves enhances autonomy. The Kantian leader teaches followers to become leaders.

Does this type of leadership, which I identify as Kantian, have contemporary supporters in addition to Barnevik and Carlzon? Quite candidly my own research as well as my personal experience indicates that the number of enlightened leaders are few in number and that the number of genuine Kantian leaders are yet a rarer breed. Although many putative leaders and even leadership organizations that claim to teach leadership are hierarchical and authoritarian, there are some additional executives who speak like Kantian leaders. However, I acknowledge that some of those I quote are not Kantian leaders in the full sense. I should like to close this essay with some quotations from contemporary leadership authorities that sound like Kantians – at least some of the time!

> The signs of outstanding leadership appear primarily among the followers. Are the followers reaching their potential? Are they learning? Serving? Do they achieve the required results? Do they change with grace? Manage conflict? (DePree, 1989, p. 12).

> Two general themes ran through all our education and communication programmes when we set them up. The first was that information was power. Staff were constantly invited to challenge the rules, to question the status quo and things we took for granted, and never to accept that a manager, simply because he or she was a manager, necessarily knew better. We stressed the importance of the individual and the fact that we wanted to hear from everyone, no matter what their position in the organization. .We were always saying to them: "tell us how we can make things better, how we can ennoble your lives, how we can make your spirits sing" (Roddick, 1991, p. 148).

> First of all we are a democratic organization ... we are not authoritarian, autocratic or paternalistic ... here has to be delegation of authority down the line... We endeavor to create an environment in which responsibility can be exercised effectively at all levels (Pillay, in Stewart, 1988).

> A leadership that is concentrated on the ideas of one person is very limited. Genuine leadership involves getting all the wisdom that is available in a group come to a better decision than any one of its members would have been able to achieve himself (Miller, in Bollier, 1996, p. 302).

> The "how to be" leader knows that people are the organization's greatest asset and in a word, behavior, and relationships she or he demonstrates this powerful philosophy. The leader long ago banned the hierarchy and, involving many heads and hands, built a new kind of structure. The new design took people out of the boxes of the old hierarchy and moved them into a more circular, flexible, and fluid management system that spelled liberation of the human spirit and endeavor (Frances Hesselbein in Hesselbein *et. al.*, 1996, p. 122).

> The leader of the future... will learn to care little about defending the traditional hierarchy. As a result, she or he will be willing to turn the pyramid upside down to implement a vision... Although it seems minor, this one change makes a major difference. The difference is between who is responsible and who is responsive. In the traditional pyramid, the boss is always responsible, and the subordinates are supposed to be responsive to the boss. When you turn the pyramid upside down the roles are reversed. The people become responsible and the job of management is to be responsive to them (Blanchard in Hesselbein *et al.*, 1996).

> Co-leadership is not a fuzzy-minded buzzword... rather it is a tough minded strategy that will unleash the hidden talent in any enterprise. Above all co-leadership is inclusive, not exclusive... co-leadership should permeate every organization at every level... in this new organizational galaxy, power doesn't reside in a single person or corner office. Rather power and responsibility are dispersed, giving the organization a whole constellation of costars (Heenan and Bennis, 1999, p. 5).

A common theme in all these quotations is the belief that leaders ought to contribute to the autonomy of the followers. A Kantian leader does not look for those who will simply follow orders to achieve a purpose laid down by the leader. Rather, the Kantian leader seeks to increase the autonomy and responsibility of followers so that they in turn become leaders in their own right.

Notes

1 I leave open the question as to whether the adoption of enlightened management practices both out of duty and because such

practices increase profits would be genuine moral actions for Kant.

2 The scholar who has contributed the most to our understanding of leadership is Jay Conger. See *The Charasmatic Leader: Beyond the Myth of Exceptional Leadership* (1989), Jossey-Bass Publishers, San Francisco, CA.

References

Bollier, D. (1996), *Aiming Higher*, AMACOM, New York, NY.

Burns, J.M. (1978), *Leadership*, Harper & Row, New York, NY.

Carlzon, J. (1987), *Moments of Truth*, Ballinger, Cambridge, MA.

Ciulla, J. (1998), *Ethics: The Heart of Leadership*, Praeger, Westport, CT.

Collins, J. and Porras, J. (1994), *Built to Last*, Harper Business, New York, NY.

DePree, M. (1989), *Leadership as an Art*, Dell Publishing, New York, NY.

Greenleaf, R., (1977), *Servant Leadership*, Paulist Press, New York, NY.

Heenan, D. and Bennis, W. (1999), *Co-Leaders*, John Wiley & Sons, New York, NY.

Hesselbein, F., Goldsmith, M. and Beckhard, R. (Eds) (1996), *The Leader of the Future*, Jossey-Bass, San Francisco, CA.

Kant, I. (1963), *Lectures on Ethics*, Louis Infield Trans., Harper & Row, New York, NY.

Kant, I. (1785, 1990), *Foundations of the Metaphysics of Morals*, Macmillan, New York, NY.

Keeley, M. (1995), "The trouble with transformational leadership", *Business Ethics Quarterly*, Vol. 5 No. 1, pp. 67-96.

Newton, L. (1985), "Moral leadership in business: the role of structure", *Business and Professional Ethics Journal*, Vol. 5 Nos 3 and 4, pp. 74-90.

Pfeffer, J. (1998), *The Human Equation*, Harvard Business School Press, Boston, MA.

Reichheld, F. (1996), *The Loyalty Effect*, Bain and Company, Boston, MA.

Roddick, A. (1991), *Body and Soul*, Ebony Press, Crown Publications, London.

Solomon, R. (1998), "Ethical leadership, emotions and trust: beyond charisma", in Ciulla, J., *Ethics the Heart of Leadership* (1998), Praeger, Westport, CT.

Stewart, T.A. (1998), "Why leadership matters", *Fortune*, 2 March, p. 112.

[15]
Leadership Ethics: Mapping the Territory

Joanne B. Ciulla

We live in a world where leaders are often morally disappointing. Even the greats of the past, such as Martin Luther King, Jr., and George Washington, are diminished by probing biographers who document their ethical shortcomings. It's hard to have heroes in a world where every wart and wrinkle of a person's life is public. Ironically, the increase in information that we have about leaders has increased the confusion over the ethics of leadership. The more defective our leaders are, the greater our longing to have highly ethical leaders. The ethical issues of leadership are found not only in public debates, they also lie embedded below the surface of the existing leadership literature.

Most scholars and practitioners who write about leadership genuflect at the altar of ethics and speak with hushed reverence about its importance to leadership. Somewhere in almost any book devoted to the subject, there are either a few sentences, paragraphs, pages, or even a chapter on how integrity and strong ethical values are crucial to leadership. Yet, given the central role of ethics in the practice of leadership, it's remarkable that there has been little in the way of sustained and systematic treatment of the subject by scholars. A literature search of 1,800 article abstracts from psychology, business, religion, philosophy, anthropology, sociology, and political science yielded only a handful of articles that offered any in-depth discussion of ethics and leadership.[1] Articles on ethics and leadership are either about a particular kind of leadership (for example, business leadership or political leadership), or a particular problem or aspect of leadership, or they are laudatory articles about the importance of honesty and integrity in leadership. There are also a number of studies that measure the moral development of managers.[2] The state of research on leadership ethics is similar to the state of business ethics twenty years ago. For the most part, the discussion of ethics in the leadership literature is fragmented, there is little reference to other works on the subject, and one gets the sense that most authors write as if they were starting from scratch.

In this chapter I map the place of ethics in the study of leadership. I argue that ethics is located in the heart of leadership studies and not in an appendage. This chapter consists of three parts. In the first part, I discuss the treatment of ethics within existing research in leadership studies. In the second part I look at some discussions concerning the definition of leadership and locate the place of ethics in those discussions. In the third part I examine two normative leadership theories and use them to illustrate how more rigorous work in the area of leadership ethics will give us a more complete understanding of leadership itself.

Throughout the chapter I use the term *leadership ethics* to refer to the study of the ethical issues related to leadership and the ethics of leadership. The study of ethics generally consists of the examination of right, wrong, good, evil, virtue, duty, obligation, rights, justice, fairness, and so on, in human relationships with each other and other living things. Leadership studies, either directly or indirectly, tries to understand what leadership is and how and why the leader-follower relationship works (What is a leader and what does it mean to exercise leadership? How do leaders lead? What do leaders do? and Why do people follow?).[3] Because leadership entails very distinctive kinds of human relationships with distinctive sets of moral problems, I thought it appropriate to refer to the subject as *leadership ethics*; however, my main reason for using the term is that it is less awkward than using expressions like *leadership and ethics*.

PART I: TREATMENT OF ETHICS IN LEADERSHIP STUDIES

Ethics without Effort

Ethics is one of those subjects that people rightfully feel they know about from experience. Most people think of ethics as practical knowledge, not theoretical knowledge. One problem that exists in applied ethics is that scholars sometimes feel that their practical knowledge and common sense (and exemplary moral character) are adequate for discussion of ethics in their particular field. The results of research that uses this approach are sometimes good, sometimes awful, but most of the time just not very informative. Philosophic writings on ethics are frequently (and understandably) ignored or rejected because they appear obtuse and irrelevant to people writing about ethics in their own area of research or practice.[4]

What is striking about leadership studies is not the absence of philosophic writings on ethics, but the fact that authors expend so little energy on researching ethics from any discipline. To some extent this is even true of Joseph Rost's book, *Leadership for the Twenty-First Century*, which contains one of the best critiques of the field of leadership studies. I frequently comment on Rost's book in this chapter because it is an important new contribution to the field. It is extensively researched and contains a terrific twenty-four-page bibliography. However, the chapter on ethics stands out because of its paucity of references. After a very quick run through utilitarian, deontic, relativistic, and contractarian ethics, Rost concludes that "none of the ethical systems is particularly valuable in helping leaders and followers make decisions about the ethics of the changes they intend for an organization or society."[5] He condemns all ethical theories as useless, using only two books, James Rachels's *The Elements of Moral Philosophy* and Mark Pastin's *The Hard Problems of Management*.[6,7]

Scholars who either reject or ignore writings on ethics usually end up either reinventing fairly standard philosophic distinctions and ethical theories or doing without them and proceeding higgledy-piggledy with their discussion. Rost concludes his chapter on ethics by saying, "Clearly, the systems of ethical thought people have used in the past and that are still in use are inadequate to the task of making moral judgments about the content of leadership."[8] Citing the work of Robert Bellah et. al., William Sullivan, and Alasdair MacIntyre, Rost proposes "a new language of civic virtue to discuss and make moral evaluations of the changes they [leaders] intend."[9] After dismissing ethical theory, he goes on to say that out of this new language there will "evolve a new ethical framework of leadership content, a system of ethical thought applied to the content of leadership, that actually works."[10] Rost does not really tell us what will take the place of all the theories that he has dismissed, but rather he assures us that a new system of ethics will emerge. At least Rost pays some attention to the literature in ethics; however, he spends most of his time throwing it out and then runs out of steam when it comes

6   Ethics, the Heart of Leadership

to offering anything concrete in regard to leadership, except for some form of communitarianism.

Another more significant example of the paucity of research energy expended on ethics is *Bass & Stogdill's Handbook of Leadership*, hailed by reviewers as "the most complete work on leadership" and "encyclopedic."[11] This is considered the source book on the study of leadership. The text is 914 pages long and contains a 162-page bibliography. There are 37 chapters in this book, none of which treats the question of ethics in leadership. If you look up ethics in the index, 5 pages are listed. Page 569 contains a brief discussion of different work ethics, page 723 is a reference to the gender differences in values, and page 831 refers to a question raised about whether sensitivity training is unethical. The reader has to go to the last chapter of the book, called "Leadership in the Twenty-First Century," to get to the 2-page exposition on ethics. What we are treated to on the first page of the handbook is a meager grabbag of empirical studies and one fleeting reference to the argument of James MacGregor Burns that transformational leaders foster moral virtue.[12]

The empirical studies include a 1988 Harris poll of 1,031 office workers that revealed that 89 percent of employees thought it was important for managers to be, for example, honest and upright; J. Weber's study of 37 managers, which led to the conclusion that managers reasoned to conform to majority opinion rather than universal rules;[13] and Kuhnert and Lewis's discussion of how transformational leaders develop and move up Kohlberg's scale from concern for personal goals to higher levels of values and obligations.[14] Final references are to a study of seven mainland Chinese factories, hospitals, and agencies, which included, among many other questions, survey questions on the character function of leadership and moral character.[15] The last part of this subsection on ethics contains a paragraph on how professional associations such as the American Psychological Association set standards of ethical behavior.

The second section on ethics, "A Model for Ethical Analysis," sounds more promising. Bass, the author, defines ethics as a "creative searching for human fulfillment and choosing it as good and beautiful." He goes on to argue that professional ethics focuses too much on negative vices and not on the good things. Bass's definition of ethics and sole reference on ethics in this section is taken from *The Paradox of Poverty: A Reprisal of Economic Development Policy* by P. Steidlmeier.[16] The model for ethical analysis that it suggests is one that "determines the connection between moral reasoning and moral behavior and how each depends on the issue involved."[17] After reading these two pages, one gets little information about the area of ethics and leadership.[18] What is most remarkable about this section of the book is that it offers little insight into what the questions are in this area. It is not surprising that the standard reference work on leadership does not carry much information on ethics, in part because there isn't much research on it.[19] Nonetheless, for all the research that went into his book, Bass seems to wing it when it comes to talking about ethics.

Leadership and the Rosetta Stone

As Rost points out in his book, one of the problems with leadership studies is that most of the work has been done from one discipline and a large part of the research rests on what he calls the industrial paradigm, which views leadership as good management.[20] (Bass and Stogdill are both management scholars.) Rost also criticizes the field for overemphasis on things that are peripheral to leadership such as traits, group facilitation, effectiveness, or the content of leadership, which includes the things that leaders must know in order to be effective.[21] This is clearly the case if you look at the contents of Bass and Stogdill. The largest section in the book is on the personal attributes of leaders.

Marta Calas and Linda Smircich also offer a provocative critique of the field that indirectly helps to explain why there has been little work on ethics in leadership studies. Along with Rost, they point out the positivist slant in much of the leadership research (particularly research on leadership in psychology and business). According to Calas and Smircich, the "saga" of leadership researchers is to find the Rosetta stone of leadership and break its codes. They argue that because the research community believes that society puts a premium on science, researchers' attempts to break the Rosetta stone have to be "scientific." Hence the "scientists" keep breaking leadership into smaller and smaller pieces until the main code has been lost and can't be put back together.[22] This fragmentation accounts for one of the reasons why Rost urges us to focus on the essence of leadership, and it also explains why there is so little work on ethics and leadership. Ethical analysis generally requires a broad perspective on a practice. For example, in business, ethical considerations of a problem often go hand in hand with taking a long-term view of a problem and the long-term interests of an organization.

Calas and Smircich also observe that the leadership literature seems irrelevant to practitioners, whereas researchers don't feel like they are getting anywhere—nobody seems happy. They believe that leadership researchers are frustrated because they are trying to do science but they know that they aren't doing good science. The researchers are also trying to do narrative, but the narrative is more concerned

8   Ethics, the Heart of Leadership

with sustaining the community of researchers instead of helping explicate leadership. Calas and Smircich, like Rost, point to the necessity of a multidisciplinary approach to leadership. All three scholars emphasize the importance of narratives, such as case studies, mythology, and biography, in understanding leadership.

It is interesting to note that the two most respected and quoted figures in leadership studies, John W. Gardner and James MacGregor Burns, both do take a somewhat multidisciplinary approach to the subject. John W. Gardner's book, *On Leadership,* is a simple and readable outline of the basic issues in leadership studies. Gardner writes as a practitioner. He has held many distinguished posts in the government and in business and currently teaches at Stanford University. He offers a good, common-sense discussion of ethics and leadership in his chapter "The Moral Dimension." It is interesting to note that the phrase, "the moral dimension of leadership," is now frequently used in the leadership literature; a recent conference on ethics and leadership used this phrase as its title. The conceptualization of morality as a dimension of leadership rather than a part or element is significant in that it implies that it is another way of seeing the whole of leadership rather than simply investigating a part of it.[23]

Gardner's chapter on ethics is a thoughtful piece that uses examples from several disciplines. One reason why it is often quoted is because he is a talented wordsmith, he uses engaging examples, and he offers wisdom that comes from experience. Gardner lines up the usual suspects of evil leadership, such as Hitler and the Ku Klux Klan, and peppers his discussion with a diverse set of examples from history and politics. For the most part, his discussion of ethics is hortatory. He says that we should hope that "our leaders will keep alive values that are not so easy to embed in laws—our feeling about individual moral responsibility, about caring for others, about honor and integrity, about tolerance and mutual respect, and about human fulfillment within a framework of values."[24] Gardner offers some good advice on ethics, but that's about all.

James MacGregor Burns's book *Leadership* is considered by many to be the best book to date on leadership. Burns, a political scientist, historian, and biographer, is probably the most referenced author in leadership studies. Burns's theory of transforming leadership is one that is built around a set of moral commitments. I discuss Burns's work later in this chapter because his work is central to my contention that ethics is at the heart of leadership.

In this section, I have discussed some representative examples of the ways in which ethics has been treated in the leadership literature. Most of what is considered leadership literature comes from the social sciences of psychology, business, and political science. The scarcity of work done on leadership in the humanities is another reason why there is little done on ethics. Burns, the most quoted scholar in the field, takes a multidisciplinary approach to leadership. However, it is not the number of disciplines that makes Burns's work compelling—it is the fact that he tries to understand leadership as a whole and not as a combination of small fragments.

Paradigm, Shifting Paradigm, or Shifty Paradigm?

For an investigation into leadership ethics to be meaningful and useful, it has to be embedded in the study of leadership. Again, it is worthwhile to make an analogy to business ethics. If courses and research on business ethics ignored existing business research and practice, then the subject of ethics would become a mere appendage, a nice but not a crucial addition to our knowledge about business and a business school curriculum. Research and teaching in areas like business ethics and leadership ethics should aim not only at making businesspeople and leaders more ethical but also at reconceptualizing the way that we think about the theory and practice of business and leadership. This is why both areas of applied ethics have to embed themselves into their respective fields.[25]

Using Thomas Kuhn's analysis in *The Structure of Scientific Revolutions*, one might argue that there exists a paradigm of leadership studies, based primarily on the work done in business and psychology.[26] Kuhn says that one way you can tell if a paradigm has been established is if scientists enhance their reputations by writing journal articles that are "addressed only to professional colleagues, the men whose knowledge of a shared paradigm can be assumed." Prior to the establishment of a paradigm, writing a textbook would be prestigious, because you would be making a new contribution to the field.[27,28] Using Kuhn's criteria, there is evidence for the existence of a paradigm of leadership studies: Bass and Stogdill's handbook (now in its third edition), various symposia on leadership,[29] the kinds of leadership articles that are accepted to journals, and the literature that is cross-referenced in these journals.

According to Kuhn, when a paradigm is established and researchers engage in "normal science," there is little discussion of rules or definitions because they become internalized by researchers working in that paradigm. Kuhn says, "lack of a standard interpretation or of an agreed reduction to rules will not prevent a paradigm from guiding research."[30] He points out that over time the meaning of important terms can shift along with theories, which seems to be what has happened in leadership studies. Kuhn believes that scientific progress would be impeded if the meanings of terms were overly rigid.

Rost criticizes some research in leadership studies because researchers don't define leadership. But as Kuhn points out, this sort of definition is not really necessary if researchers are working in a paradigm, because definitions are internalized and unarticulated. Rost's second charge is that researchers all have different definitions of leadership and that the field cannot progress unless there is a shared definition of leadership.[31] If Rost is correct and researchers have radically different definitions of leadership (meaning that leadership denotes radically different things), then either there never was a well-formed paradigm (so leadership studies is in a pre-paradigm phase), or there exists a paradigm, and that paradigm is shifting. In both cases, there would be considerable debate over definitions. However, if there is a paradigm of sorts and researchers are still arguing over definitions, then there is a paradigm of leadership studies but it is a shifty one. By this I mean that scholars don't really trust this paradigm, but they nonetheless stick to it and keep doing research in the same old way.[32]

PART II: LOCATING ETHICS

What Do the Definitions Really Tell Us?

Leadership scholars have spent a large amount of time and trouble worrying about the definition of leadership. Rost analyzes 221 definitions to make his point that there is not a common definition of leadership. What Rost does not make clear is what he means by a definition. Sometimes he sounds as if a definition supplies necessary and sufficient conditions for identifying leadership. He says, "neither scholars nor the practitioners have been able to define leadership with precision, accuracy, and conciseness so that people are able to label it correctly when they see it happening or when they engage in it."[33] He goes on to say that the various publications and the media all use leadership to mean different things that have little to do with what leadership really is.[34] In places Rost uses the word *definition* as if it were a theory or perhaps a paradigm. He says that a shared definition implies that there is a "school" of leadership. When the definition changes, there is a "paradigm shift."[35]

Rost's claim that what leadership studies needs is a common definition of leadership is off the mark for two reasons. One would be hard-pressed to find a group of sociologists or historians who shared the exact same definition of sociology or history. It is also not clear that the various definitions that Rost examines are that different in terms of what they denote. I selected the following definitions from Rost's book on the basis of what Rost says are definitions most representative of each particular era. We need to look at these definitions and ask, Are these definitions so different that there is no family resemblance between them, that is, would researchers be talking about different things?[36] Lastly I look at what these definitions tell us about the place of ethics in leadership studies.

1920s [Leadership is] the ability to impress the will of the leader on those led and induce obedience, respect, loyalty, and cooperation.[37]

1930s Leadership is a process in which the activities of many are organized to move in a specific direction by one.[38]

1940s Leadership is the result of an ability to persuade or direct men, apart from the prestige or power that comes from office or external circumstance.[39]

1950s [Leadership is what leaders do in groups.] The leader's authority is spontaneously accorded him by his fellow group members.[40]

1960s [Leadership is] acts by a person that influence other persons in a shared direction.[41]

1970s Leadership is defined in terms of discretionary influence. Discretionary influence refers to those leader behaviors under control of the leader which he may vary from individual to individual.[42]

1980s Regardless of the complexities involved in the study of leadership, its meaning is relatively simple. Leadership means to inspire others to undertake some form of purposeful action as determined by the leader.[43]

1990s Leadership is an influence relationship between leaders and followers who intend real changes that reflect their mutual purposes.[44]

If we look at the sample of definitions from different periods, we see that the problem of definition is not that scholars have radically different meanings of leadership. Leadership does not denote radically different things for different scholars. One can detect a family resemblance between the different definitions. All of them talk about leadership as some kind of process, act, or influence that in some way gets people to do something. A roomful of people, each holding one of these definitions, would understand each other.

Where the definitions differ is in their connotation, particularly in terms of their implications for the leader-follower relationship. In other words, how leaders get people to do things (impress, organize, persuade, influence, and inspire) and how what is to be done is decided (obedience, voluntary consent, determined by the leader, and reflection of mutual purposes) have normative implications. So perhaps what Rost is really talking about is not definitions, but theories about how people lead (or how people should lead) and the relationship of leaders and those who are led. His critique of particular definitions is really a

12 Ethics, the Heart of Leadership

critique of the way they do or don't describe the underlying moral commitments of the leader-follower relationship.[45]

If the above definitions imply that leadership is some sort of relationship between leaders and followers in which something happens or gets done, then the next question is How do we describe this relationship? For people who believe in the values of a democratic society such as freedom and equality, the most morally unattractive definitions are those that appear to be coercive and manipulative and disregard the input of followers. Rost clearly dislikes the theories from the 1920s, 1970s, and 1980s, not because they are inaccurate, but because he rejects the authoritarian values inherent in them.[46] Nonetheless, theories such as the ones from the 1920s, 1970s, and 1980s may be quite accurate if we were observe the way some corporate and world leaders behave.

The most morally attractive definitions hail from the 1940s, 1950s, 1960s, and Rost's own definition from the 1990s. They imply a noncoercive, participatory, and democratic relationship between leaders and followers. There are two morally attractive elements of these theories. First, rather than induce, these leaders influence, which implies that leaders recognize the autonomy of followers. Rost's definition uses the word *influence,* which carries an implication that there is some degree of voluntary compliance on the part of followers. In Rost's chapter on ethics he says, "The leadership process is ethical if the people in the relationship (the leaders and followers) *freely* agree that the intended changes fairly reflect their mutual purposes."[47] For Rost consensus is an important part of what makes leadership leadership, and it does so because free choice is morally pleasing. The second morally attractive part of these definitions is that they imply recognition of the beliefs, values, and needs of the followers. Followers are the leader's partner in shaping the goals and purposes of a group or organization.

The morally attractive definitions also speak to a distinction frequently made between leadership and headship (or positional leadership). Holding a formal leadership position or position of power does not necessarily mean that a person exercises leadership. Furthermore, you do not have to hold a formal position in order to exercise leadership. Leaders can wield force or authority using only their position and the resources and power that come with it.[48] This is an important distinction, but it does not get us out of "the Hitler problem." The Hitler problem is answering the question, "Is Hitler a leader?" Under the morally unattractive definitions he is a leader, perhaps even a great leader, albeit an immoral one. Ron Heifetz argues that under the great man and trait theories of leadership you can put Hitler, Lincoln, and

Gandhi in the same category because the underlying value of the theory is that leadership is influence over history.[49] However, under the morally attractive theories, Hitler is not a leader at all. He's a bully or tyrant or simply the head of Germany.

To muddy the waters even further, according to one of Warren Bennis's and Burt Nanus's characterizations of leadership, "The manager does things right and the leader does the right thing," one could argue that Hitler is neither unethical nor a leader, he is a manager.[50] Bennis and Nanus are among those management writers who talk as if all leaders are wonderful and all managers morally flabby drones. However, what appears to be behind this in Bennis and Nanus's work is the idea that leaders are morally a head above everyone else.[51]

So what does this all mean? It looks like we are back to the problem of definition again. The first and obvious meaning is that definitions of leadership have normative implications (the old "there is no such thing as a value-free social science"). Leadership scholars such as Bennis and Nanus are sloppy about the language they use to describe and prescribe. Though it is true that researchers have to be clear about when they are describing and when they are prescribing, the crisp fact/value distinction will not in itself improve our understanding of leadership.

Leadership scholars who worry about constructing the ultimate definition of leadership are asking the wrong question but inadvertently trying to answer the right question. As we have seen from the examination of definitions, the ultimate question in leadership studies is not "What is the definition of leadership?" The ultimate point of studying leadership is What is good leadership?" The use of the word *good* here has two senses, morally good and technically good or effective. These two senses form a logical conjunction. In other words, in order for the statement "She is a good leader" to be true, it must be true that she is effective and that she is ethical.[52] The question of what constitutes a good leader lies at the heart of the public debate on leadership. We want our leaders to be good in both ways. It's easy to judge if they are effective, but more difficult to judge if they are ethical, because there is some confusion over what factors are relevant to making this kind of assessment.

Ethics and Effectiveness

The problem with the existing leadership research is that few studies investigate both senses of good, and when they do, they usually do not fully explore the moral implications of their research questions or their

14 Ethics, the Heart of Leadership

results. The research on leadership effectiveness touches indirectly on the problem of explicitly articulating the normative implications of descriptive research. The Ohio Studies and the Michigan Studies both measured leadership effectiveness in terms of how leaders treated subordinates and how they got the job done. The Ohio Studies measured leadership effectiveness in terms of consideration, the degree to which leaders act in a friendly and supportive manner, and initiating structure, or the way that leaders structure their own role and the role of subordinates in order to obtain group goals.[53] The Michigan Studies measured leaders on the basis of task orientation and relationship orientation.[54] These two studies spawned a number of other research programs and theories, including the situational leadership theory of Hersey and Blanchard, which looks at effectiveness in terms of how leaders adapt their leadership style to the requirements of a situation. Some situations require a task orientation, others a relationship orientation.[55]

Implicit in all these theories and research programs is an ethical question. Are leaders more effective when they are nice to people, or are leaders more effective when they use certain techniques for structuring and ordering tasks?[56] One would hope that the answer is both, but that answer is not conclusive in the studies that have taken place over the last three decades.[57] The interesting question is What if this sort of research shows that you don't have to be kind and considerate of other people to run a country or a profitable organization? Would scholars and practitioners draw an *ought* from the *is* of this research?[58] It's hard to tell, when researchers are not explicit about their ethical commitments. The point is that no matter how much empirical information we get from the "scientific" study of leadership, it will always be inadequate if we neglect the moral implications. The reason why leadership scholarship has not progressed very far is that most of the research focuses on explaining leadership, not on understanding it.[59]

The discussion of definition is intended to locate where some of the ethical problems are in leadership studies. As we have seen, ethical commitments are central to how scholars define leadership and shape their research. Leadership scholars do not need to have one definition of leadership in order to understand each other, they just need to be clear about the values and normative assumptions that lie behind the way that they go about researching leadership.[60] By doing so, we have a better chance of understanding the relationship between what leadership is and what we think leadership ought to be.[61] This state of affairs would represent a marked shift in the existing Bass/Stogdill-type paradigm (and maybe finally put to rest the pretensions of value-free social science).

PART III: THE NORMATIVE THEORIES

Transforming Leadership

So far we have located the place of leadership ethics in definitions and in some of the empirical research on leadership. Now we look at two normative leadership theories.

James MacGregor Burns's theory of transforming leadership is compelling because it rests on a set of moral assumptions about the relationship between leaders and followers.[62] Burns's theory is clearly a prescriptive one about the nature of morally good leadership. Drawing from Abraham Maslow's work on needs, Milton Rokeach's research on values development, and research on moral development from Lawrence Kohlberg, Jean Piaget, Erik Erickson, and Alfred Adler, Burns argues that leaders have to operate at higher need and value levels than those of followers.[63] A leader's role is to exploit tension and conflict within people's value systems and play the role of raising people's consciousness.[64]

On Burns's account, transforming leaders have very strong values. They do not water down their values and moral ideals by consensus, but rather they elevate people by using conflict to engage followers and help them reassess their own values and needs. This is an area where Burns is very different from Rost. Burns writes that "despite his [Rost's] intense and impressive concern about the role of values, ethics and morality in transforming leadership, he underestimates the crucial importance of these variables." Burns goes on to say, "Rost leans towards, or at least is tempted by, consensus procedures and goals that I believe erode such leadership."[65]

The moral questions that drive Burns's theory of transforming leadership come from his work as a biographer and a historian.[66] When biographers or historians study a leader, they struggle with the question of how to judge or keep from judging their subject. Throughout his book, Burns uses examples of a number of incidents where questionable means, such as lying and deception, are used to achieve honorable ends or where the private life of a politician is morally questionable.[67] If you analyze the numerous historical examples in Burns's book, you find that two pressing moral questions shape his leadership theory. The first is the morality of means and ends (and this also includes the moral use of power), and the second is the tension between the public and private morality of a leader. His theory of transforming leadership is an attempt to characterize good leadership by accounting for both of these questions.

Burns's distinction between transforming and transactional leadership and modal and end values offers a way to think about the question

16   Ethics, the Heart of Leadership

"What is a good leader?" in terms of the relationship to followers and the means and ends of actions. Transactional leadership rests on the values found in the means of an act. These are called modal values, which are things like responsibility, fairness, honesty, and promise keeping. Transactional leadership helps leaders and followers reach their own goals by supplying lower-level wants and needs so that they can move up to higher needs. Transforming leadership is concerned with end values, such as liberty, justice, and equality. Transforming leaders raise their followers up through various stages of morality and need.[68] They turn their followers into leaders, and the leader becomes a moral agent.

As a historian, Burns is very concerned with the ends of actions and the change that they initiate. In terms of his ethical theory, at times he appears to be a consequentialist, despite his acknowledgment that "insufficient attention to means can corrupt the ends."[69] However, because Burns does not really offer a systematic theory of ethics in the way that a philosopher might, he is difficult to categorize. Consider for example, Burns's two answers to the Hitler question. In the first part of the book, he says quite simply that after Hitler gained power and crushed all opposition, he was no longer a leader. He was a tyrant.[70] Later in the book, he offers three criteria for judging how Hitler would fare before "the bar of history." Burns says that Hitler would probably argue that he was a transforming leader who spoke for the true values of the German people and elevated them to a higher destiny. First, he would be tested by modal values of honor and integrity or the extent to which he advanced or thwarted the standards of good conduct in humanity. Second, he would be judged by the end values of equality and justice. Lastly, he would be judged on the impact that he had on the well-being of the people whom he touched.[71] According to Burns, Hitler would fail all three tests. Burns doesn't consider Hitler a leader or a transforming leader, because of the means that he used, the ends that he achieved, and the impact of Hitler as a moral agent on his followers during the process of his leadership.[72]

By looking at leadership as a process and not a set of individual acts, Burns's theory of good leadership is difficult to pigeonhole into one ethical theory and warrants closer analysis. The most attractive part of Burns's theory is the idea that a leader elevates his or her followers and makes them leaders. Near the end of his book, he reintroduces this idea with an anecdote about why President Johnson did not run for re-election in 1968. Burns tells us, "Perhaps he did not comprehend that the people he had led—as a part of the impact of his leadership—have created their own fresh leadership, which was now outrunning his." All the people that Johnson helped—the sick, the blacks, and the poor—now had their own leadership. Burns says, "Leadership begat leadership and hardly recognized its offspring." "Followers had become leaders."[73]

Burns's theory has spawned a number of descriptive studies on transformational leadership. For example, Bernard Bass studies transformational leadership in terms of the impact of leaders on their followers. In sharp contrast to Burns, Bass removes Burns's condition that leaders have to appeal to higher-order needs and values. So, Bass is willing to call Hitler a transformational leader.[74] There are a number of other researchers writing about transformational leadership, including Judith Rosner, who uses transformational leadership as a means for understanding how women lead.[75]

The other area of research related to transformational leadership is charismatic leadership. Charismatic leaders, according to Jay Conger, "hold certain keys to transformational processes within organizations."[76] Bass believes that charismatic leadership is a necessary ingredient of transformational leadership.[77] The research on charismatic leadership opens up a wide range of ethical questions because of the powerful emotional and moral impact that charismatic leaders have on followers.[78] Charismatic leadership can be the best and the worst kind of leadership depending on whether you are looking at a Gandhi or a Charles Manson.[79] Leadership ethics clearly finds a place in this literature where the moral problems are near the surface, but not explicitly explored.

Servant Leadership

The second example of a normative theory of leadership is servant leadership. Robert K. Greenleaf's book, *Servant Leadership: A Journey into the Nature of Legitimate Power and Greatness*, presents a view of how leaders ought to be. However, the best way to understand servant leadership is to read *Journey to the East*, by Hermann Hesse.[80] Hesse's story is about a spiritual journey to the East. On the journey a servant named Leo carries the bags and does the travelers' chores. There is something special about Leo. He keeps the group together with his presence and songs. When Leo mysteriously disappears, the group loses its way. Later in the book the main character, HH, discovers that the servant, Leo, was actually the leader. The simple but radical shift in emphasis is from followers serving leaders to leaders serving followers.

Servant leadership has not gotten as much attention as transformational leadership in the literature, but students and businesspeople often find this a compelling characterization of leadership. According to Greenleaf, the servant leader leads because he or she wants to serve others.[81] People follow servant leaders freely because they trust them.

Like the transforming leader, the servant leader elevates people. Greenleaf says a servant leader must pass this test: "Do those served grow as persons? Do they, *while being served*, become healthier, wiser, freer, more autonomous, more likely themselves to become servants?" He goes on and adds a Rawlsian proviso, "*And*, what is the effect on the least privileged in society?"[82] As normative theories of leadership, both servant leadership and transforming leadership are areas of leadership ethics that are open to ethical analysis and provide a rich foundation of ideas for developing future normative theories of leadership.

CONCLUSION: ETHICS AT THE HEART OF LEADERSHIP

In this chapter I have mapped the territory of ethics in leadership studies. I argued that the definition question in leadership studies is not really about the question "What is leadership?" but about the question "What is good leadership?" By *good*, I mean morally good and effective. This is why I think it's fair to say that ethics lies at the heart of leadership studies. Researchers in the field need to get clear on the ethical elements of leadership in order to be clear on what the term *leadership* connotes.

Existing theories and empirical literature have strong normative implications that have not been fully developed by their authors. A second place for ethics in leadership studies is expanding the ethical implications of these theories and research findings. Normative theories of leadership, such as transforming leadership and servant leadership, are not well-developed in terms of their philosophic implications. They need more analysis as ethical theories and more empirical testing. One reason why the body of research on transformational leadership looks promising is because it contains empirical research on a theory that was constructed to address some of the basic moral problems of leadership. It offers a richer understanding of leadership than theories that are just about ethics or just about leader behavior.

Leadership ethics can also serve as a critical theory that opens up new kinds of dialogues among researchers and practitioners. Business ethics has certainly played this role in business studies and practice. Lastly, work in leadership ethics should generate different ways of conceptualizing leadership and new ways of asking research questions. To some extent, the ideas of servant leadership and transforming leadership have done this.

In conclusion, the territory of ethics lies at the heart of leadership studies and has veins in leadership research. Ethics also extends to territories waiting to be explored. As an area of applied ethics, leadership ethics needs to take into account research on leadership, and it should be responsive to the pressing ethical concerns of society. Today the most important and most confusing public debate is over what ethical issues are relevant in judging whether a person should lead and whether a person is capable of leadership. Research into leadership ethics should not only help us with questions like "What sort of person should lead?" and "What are the moral responsibilities of leadership?" It should also give us a better understanding of the nature of leadership.

NOTES

This chapter was originally published by *Business Ethics Quarterly* (Vol. 5, No. 1).

1. The best of these articles will be discussed in a separate annotated bibliography. I owe a debt of gratitude to Litt Maxwell, a University of Richmond librarian, for helping to execute this literature search.

2. These Kohlberg-type studies can be interesting for leadership ethics if you put all these studies together. However, taken one by one, they give a very small snapshot of a group. Kohlberg's work on moral development also has the problems that Carol Gilligan has articulated. A number of philosophers also have problems with Kohlberg's description of the highest stage of development. Nonetheless, some of the most fascinating research that uses this approach is cross-cultural. For example, see Sara Harkness, Carolyn Pope Edwards, and Charles M. Super, "Social Roles and Moral Reasoning, A Case Study in a Rural African Community," in *Developmental Psychology* 17, no. 5 (1981): 595–603. Also see Anne Marie Tietjen and Lawrence J. Walker, "Moral Reasoning and Leadership among Men in a Papua New Guinea Society," *Developmental Psychology* 21, no. 6 (1985): 982–92.

3. Many areas of leadership literature from psychology focus on different types of relationships. For example contingency theories focus on the relationship of the leader and the group in a given situation. See Fred Feidler, *A Theory of Leadership Effectiveness* (New York: McGraw-Hill, 1967) and Victor H. Vroom and Paul W. Yetton, *Leadership and Decision-Making* (Pittsburgh: University of Pittsburgh Press, 1973). The vertical dyad linkage model focuses on dyads such as the relationship between leaders and managers. See Fred Dansereau, Jr., George Graen, and William J. Haga, "Vertical Dyad Linkage Approach to Leadership within Formal Organizations: A Longitudinal Investigation of the Role Making Process," *Organizational Behavior and Human Performance* 13 (1975): 46–78.

4. Some of the most frequently cited ethics texts in leadership articles and books are from business ethics. The reasons for this might be that researchers are often in business schools, business ethics texts are written for a broad audience, and the content of business ethics research into managerial ethics and organizational ethics is relevant to leadership.

5. Joseph Rost, *Leadership for the Twenty-First Century* (New York: Praeger, 1991), 172.

6. James Rachels, *The Elements of Moral Philosophy* (New York: Random House, 1986). Mark Pastin, *The Hard Problems of Management: Gaining the Ethics Edge* (San Francisco: Jossey-Bass, 1986). I am not arguing about the quality of these books but rather the quantity of research done by Rost.

20   Ethics, the Heart of Leadership

   7. The chapter also contains pronouncements and generalizations that are not well supported. For example, he says, "The first thing that I want to emphasize is that the ethics of what is intended by leaders and followers in proposing changes may not be the same as the ethics of those changes once they have been implemented. This troubling distinction is not often developed in books on professional ethics, but it does turn up time and time again in real life" (Rost, 168). A number of Kantians who write about professional ethics would take issue with this claim.
   8. Rost, 177.
   9. Ibid., 77. The works cited in his argument are Robert Bellah et al., *Habits of the Heart* (New York: Harper and Row, 1985); William M. Sullivan, *Reconstructing Public Philosophy* (Berkeley: University of California Press, 1986); and Alasdair MacIntyre, *After Virtue* (Notre Dame, Ind.: University of Notre Dame Press, 1984). Rost seems to miss the point that all three of these books are reapplications of older traditions of ethics. Bellah et al. and Sullivan make this point clear in their books. Rost does not discuss virtue ethics in this chapter, so it is not clear whether he means to discard this too when he rejects "ethical theory."
   10. Ibid., 177.
   11. Bernard M. Bass, *Bass & Stogdill's Handbook of Leadership*, 3rd edition (New York: The Free Press, 1990). The quotes are taken from the back jacket of the book.
   12. From James MacGregor Burns's book, *Leadership* (New York: Harper, 1978).
   13. J. Weber, "Managers and Moral Meaning: An Exploratory Look at Managers' Responses to Moral Dilemmas," *Proceedings of the Academy of Management* (Washington, D.C.: Academy of Management, 1989), 333–37.
   14. K. W. Kuhnert and C. J. Lewis, "Transactional and Transformational Leadership: A Constructive/Developmental Analysis," *Academy of Management Review* 12 (1987): 648-57.
   15. M. F. Peterson, R. L. Phillips, and C. A. Duran, "A Comparison of Chinese Performance Maintenance Measures with U.S. Leadership Scales," *Psychologia—An International Journal of Psychology in the Orient* 32 (1989): 58–70.
   16. P. Steidlmeier, *The Paradox of Poverty: A Reprisal of Economic Development Policy* (Cambridge, Mass.: Ballinger, 1987).
   17. Bass, 906.
   18. This is not to say that the articles cited in Bass and Stogdill are not good, but rather that they are focused studies that taken together would not give the reader much of a perspective on ethics as it pertains to leadership.
   19. For example, John Gardner is well known in the leadership area. His leadership paper, "The Moral Aspect of Leadership," was published in 1987. Burns's book was published in 1978 and contained a wealth of references that might have been useful.
   20. Rost, 27.
   21. Ibid., 3.
   22. Marta Calas and Linda Smircich, "Reading Leadership as a Form of Cultural Analysis," in James G. Hunt, B. Rajaram Baliga, H. Peter Dachler, and Chester A. Schrieshcim, eds., *Emerging Leadership Vistas* (Lexington, Mass.: Lexington Books, 1988), 222–26.
   23. For example, see Thomas Sergiovanni, *Moral Leadership* (San Francisco: Jossey-Bass, 1992), xiii. Sergiovanni argues that "rich leadership practice cannot be developed if one set of values or one basis of authority is simply substituted for

another. What we need is an expanded theoretical and operational foundation for leadership practice that will give balance to a full range of values and bases of authority." He refers to this expanded foundation as the moral dimension in leadership.

24. John Gardner, *On Leadership* (New York: Free Press, 1990), 77.

25. Because most of my work has been in business ethics, I use that field as an example. Few philosophers would attempt to write about a topic in business ethics without doing research into that area of business, yet a number of business scholars over the years have felt no discomfort over writing about business ethics without doing research into ethics. If you look at what is considered the best work in business ethics, you do not find research that is only business or only philosophic ethics. A good example of the ideal mix is Ed Freeman's and Dan Gilbert's *Ethics and Strategy* (Englewood Cliffs, N.J.: Prentice Hall, 1988).

26. Extensive work has been done on leadership in political science, but this research is not well integrated into the business/psychology literature. One might argue that because the discussion of leadership is so much a part of political science, it is not noticeable as a separate field, except perhaps for Presidential Studies. It is, however, interesting to note that Barbara Kellerman's anthology on political leadership is interdisciplinary. See Barbara Kellerman, ed., *Political Leadership: A Source Book* (Pittsburgh: University of Pittsburgh Press, 1986). It draws from political science, philosophy, economics, history, sociology. Yet if one looks at the references in Bass and Stogdill, the lion's share of them are from management and psychology and very few from political science or other fields. Extensive work has also been done on leadership in military academies. For example, see Howard Prince and Associates, eds., *Leadership in Organizations*, 3rd edition (West Point, N.Y.: United States Military Academy, 1985).

27. Thomas Kuhn, *The Structure of Scientific Revolutions* (Chicago: University of Chicago Press, 1970), 20.

28. A recent example of a leadership textbook is Richard Hughes, Robert Ginnett, and Gordon J. Curphy, *Leadership: Enhancing the Lessons of Experience* (New York: Irwin, 1993).

29. James G. Hunt has published eight collections of symposia papers on leadership. Note the language in the titles of these books, "Current Developments," "Leadership Frontiers," "The Cutting Edge," "Beyond Establishment Views," and "Emerging Vistas." One senses that Hunt is trying to capture something that keeps falling through scholars' fingers like sand.

E. A. Fleishman and J. G. Hunt, eds., *Current Developments in the Study of Leadership* (Lexington, Mass.: Lexington Books, 1973).

J. G. Hunt and L. L. Larson, eds., *Contingency Approaches to Leadership* (Lexington, Mass.: Lexington Books, 1974).

J. G. Hunt and L. L. Larson, eds., *Leadership Frontiers* (Kent, Ohio: Kent State University Press, 1975).

J. G. Hunt and L. L. Larson, eds., *Leadership: The Cutting Edge* (Lexington, Mass.: Lexington Books, 1977).

J. G. Hunt and L. L. Larson, eds., *Crosscurrents in Leadership* (Lexington, Mass.: Lexington Books, 1979).

J. G. Hunt, U. Sekaran, and C. A. Schriesheim, eds., *Leadership: Beyond Establishment Views* (Lexington, Mass.: Lexington Books, 1982).

J. G. Hunt, D. M. Hosking, C. A. Schriesheim, and R. Stewart, eds., *Leaders and Managers: International Perspectives on Managerial Behavior and Leadership* (Lexington, Mass.: Lexington Books, 1984).

James G. Hunt, B. Rajaram Baliga, H. Peter Dachler, and Chester A. Schriesheim, eds., *Emerging Leadership Vistas* (Lexington, Mass.: Lexington Books, 1988).

30. Kuhn, 20.
31. Rost, 6–7.
32. In J. G. Hunt's symposia (see note 29) and in other articles on leadership, scholars constantly lament that they have done so much studying and know so little about leadership. Yet these same scholars who lament this fact do little to change the way that they do research.
33. Rost, 6.
34. Ibid.
35. Ibid., 99.
36. The theory of meaning that I have in mind is from Ludwig Wittgenstein, *Philosophical Investigations*, translated by G. E. M. Anscomb, 3rd edition (New York: Macmillan, 1968), 18–20, 241.
37. Rost, 47, from B. V. Moore, "The May Conference on Leadership," *Personnel Journal* 6 (1927): 124.
38. Rost, 47, from E. S. Bogardus, *Leaders and Leadership* (New York: Appleton-Century, 1934), 5.
39. Rost, 48, from Reuter (1941), 133.
40. Rost, 50. The bracket part is Rost's summary of the definition from C. A. Gibb, "Leadership," in G. Lindzey, ed., *Handbook of Social Psychology* 2 (1954): 877–920.
41. Rost, 53, from M. Seeman, *Social Status and Leadership* (Columbus: Ohio State University Bureau of Educational Research, 1960), 127.
42. Rost, 59, from R. N. Osborn and J. G. Hunt, "An Adaptive Reactive Theory of Leadership," in J. G. Hunt and L. L. Larson, eds., *Leadership Frontiers* (Kent, Ohio: Kent State University Press, 1975), 28.
43. Rost, 72. From S. C. Sarkesian, "A Personal Perspective," in R. S. Ruch and L. J. Korb, eds., *Military Leadership* (Beverly Hills, Calif.: Sage, 1979), 243.
44. Rost, 102.
45. Burns criticizes leadership studies for bifurcating literature on leadership and followership. He says that the leadership literature is elitist, projecting heroic leaders against the drab mass of powerless followers. The followership literature, according to Burns, tends to be populist in its approach, linking the masses with small overlapping circles of politicians, military officers, and businesspeople. See Burns, 3.
46. One's choice of a definition can be aesthetic and/or moral and/or political (if you control the definitions, you control the research agenda).
47. Rost, 161.
48. Leaders carry their own normative baggage in their definitions. For example:

- "A leader is a man who has the ability to get other people to do what they don't want to do, and like it." (Harry Truman)
- "Clean examples have a curious method of multiplying themselves." (Gandhi)

- "Whatever goal man has reached is due to his originality plus his brutality." (Adolf Hitler)

- "If we do not win, we will blame neither heaven nor earth, only ourselves." (Mao)

These examples are from G. D. Paige's book, *The Scientific Study of Political Leadership*, 66. They are taken from Barbara Kellerman, *Leadership: Multidisciplinary Perspectives* (Pittsburgh: University of Pittsburgh Press, 1986), 71–72.

49. This is from Ron Heifetz's book manuscript *Leadership without Easy Answers* (Cambridge, Mass.: Belknap/Harvard University Press, 1994), 17–18.

50. See Warren Bennis and Burt Nanus, *Leaders: Strategies for Taking Charge* (New York: Harper Collins, 1985), 45.

51. The leader/manager distinction is a troublesome one in the leadership literature. One problem is that *leadership* is a hot word these days and the current trend is to put leadership in the title of books on traditional management subjects. If we look at the formal positions of leaders and managers in organizations, the leader's job requires a broader perspective on the operation and on the moral significance of policies and actions of the organization (this is part of the "vision thing"). The manager's domain of perspective is usually more narrowly defined as people whose job is to ensure that a set of tasks is completed. In ethical terms this element of leadership boils down to thinking about actions in terms of how they impact on the organization as a whole and in the long run. In the ethics seminars that I have run for corporate managers, I have noticed that the managers who tend to take a big picture view of particular ethical problems are most often the ones who have been identified as having the greatest leadership potential. So Bennis and Nanus do seem to be right. However, it is not that managers are unethical, but rather that they have a narrower moral perspective that is in part dictated by the way in which they respond to the constraints and pressures of their position. Managers are also subject to Kant's old adage that "ought implies can."

52. Here Aristotle's discussion of excellence (areté) would be useful. Aristotle says that excellent actions must be good in themselves and good and noble. See the argument in Aristotle, *Nichomachean Ethics*, Book I, sections 6–8 (1096a12–1098b8). Later in Book II, sections 13–16 (31104b), Aristotle argues that a virtuous person has appropriate emotions along with dispositions to act the right way. Virtue then is being made happy by the right sort of thing.

53. See E. A. Fleishman, "The Description of Supervisory Behavior," *Personnel Psychology* 37: 1–6.

54. Results from the earlier and later Michigan Studies are discussed in R. Leikert, *New Patterns of Management* (New York: McGraw-Hill, 1961) and *The Human Organization: Its Management and Value* (New York: McGraw-Hill, 1967).

55. See P. Hersey and K. H. Blanchard, *The Management of Organizational Behavior*, 5th edition (Englewood Cliffs, N.J.: Prentice Hall, 1993).

56. It would be worthwhile to look at some of the studies and ask how the subjects with high/high orientations solve ethical problems. Do they tend to find themselves trapped in between deontic and consequentialist approaches to the problem? Are people who score high on the task scale consequentialists when it comes to approaching ethical problems? and so on.

57. According to Gary Yukl, the only consistent findings that have come from this research is that considerate leaders usually have more satisfied followers. See

24   Ethics, the Heart of Leadership

Gary Yukl, *Leadership in Organizations,* 2nd edition (Englewood Cliffs, N.J.: Prentice Hall, 1989), 96.

58. Old metaethical problems, such as David Hume's problem of drawing an *ought* from G. E. Moore's naturalistic fallacy, and more recent discussions of ethical realism take on a certain urgency in applied ethics. I find that the more work that I do in applied ethics, the more I lean towards the position that moral discourse is cognitive in that it expresses propositions that have truth value. However, I am still uncomfortable with drawing moral prescriptions from "scientific" studies of leadership. I have not really worked out a coherent position on these points of moral epistemology. For a good discussion of these issues see Geoffrey Sayre-McCord, ed., *Essays on Moral Realism* (Ithaca, N.Y.: Cornell University Press, 1988). I find David Wiggins's and Geoffrey Sayre-McCord's articles on ethical realism to be particularly compelling.

59. This is the argument that the sciences provide explanation and the humanities understanding. See Chapter 1 of G. H. von Wright, *Explanation and Understanding* (Ithaca: Cornell University Press, 1971).

60. In most journal articles, authors, including this one, offer stipulative definitions. These definitions make clear how concepts are being used in the paper. They are not meant to be universal definitions.

61. We need a better picture of what a leader ought to be in order to educate and develop leaders in schools and organizations.

62. Burns uses the terms *transforming* and *transformational* in his book. However, he prefers to refer to his theory as *transforming* leadership.

63. I think that Burns is sometimes overly sanguine about the universal truth of these theories of human development.

64. Burns, 42–43.

65. Rost, xii.

66. I am very grateful to Professor Burns for the discussions that we have had on the ethics of leadership. Burns's reflections on his work as a biographer have lead me to this conclusion.

67. For example, see Burns's discussion of Franklin D. Roosevelt's treatment of Joseph Kennedy, 32–33.

68. One of the problems with using the values approach to ethics is that it requires a very complicated taxonomy of values. The word *value* is also problematic because it encompasses so many different kinds of things. The values approach requires arguments for some sort of hierarchy of values that would serve to resolve conflicts of values. In order to make values something that people do rather than just have, Milton Rokeach offers a very awkward discussion of the ought character of values. "A person phenomenologically experiences 'oughtness' to be objectively required by society in somewhat the same way that he perceives an incomplete circle as objectively requiring closure." See Milton Rokeach, *The Nature of Human Values* (New York: The Free Press, 1973), 9.

69. Burns, 426.

70. Ibid., 3.

71. Ibid., 426.

72. The third test has an Aristotelian twist to it. The relationship of leaders and followers and the ends of that relationship must rest on *eudaimonia* or happiness,

which is understood as human flourishing or, as Aristotle says, "living well and faring well with being happy." Aristotle, *Nicomachean Ethics*, Book I (1095a19), from Jonathan Barnes, ed., *The Complete Works of Aristotle*, vol. II (Princeton: Princeton University Press, 1984), 1730.

73. Burns, 424.

74. Bernard Bass, *Leadership and Performance Beyond Expectations* (New York: Free Press, 1985).

75. Judith Rosner, "Ways Women Lead," in *Harvard Business Review* (November-December 1990), 99–125.

76. Jay Conger, *The Charismatic Leader: Behind the Mystique of the Exceptional Leader* (San Francisco: Jossey-Bass, 1989), xiv.

77. Bass, *Leadership and Performance*, 31.

78. For example, see Robert J. House, William D. Spangler, and James Woycke's "Personality and Charisma in the U.S. Presidency," *Administrative Science Quarterly* 36, no. 3 (September 1991), 334–96. Their study looks at charisma in terms of the bond between leaders and followers and in terms of actual behavior of the presidents (366). The questions that lurk in the background are Is this relationship, in Burns's terms, morally uplifting? Is the behavior ethical? and Does the process that takes place in the relationship between these charismatic presidents and their followers humanly enriching?

79. For a very provocative account of charismatic leadership from an anthropological point of view see Charles Lindholm, *Charisma* (Cambridge, Mass.: Basil Blackwell, 1990). Lindholm includes several case studies, including ones on Charles Manson and Jim Jones.

80. Greenleaf takes his theory from Hesse. See Robert K. Greenleaf, *Servant Leadership: A Journey into the Nature of Legitimate Power and Greatness* (New York: Paulist Press, 1977); and Hermann Hesse, *The Journey to the East* (New York: Farrar, Straus and Giroux, 1991).

81. The Robert K. Greenleaf Center in Indianapolis works with companies to implement this idea of leadership in organizations. The Robert K. Greenleaf Center, 1100 W. 42nd St., Suite 321, Indianapolis, IN 46208.

82. Greenleaf, 13–14.

Part IV
Leadership and Social Change

[16]

Letter from Birmingham City Jail

Dr. King wrote this famous essay (written in the form of an open letter) on 16 April 1963 while in jail. He was serving a sentence for participating in civil rights demonstrations in Birmingham, Alabama. He rarely took time to defend himself against his opponents. But eight prominent "liberal" Alabama clergymen, all white, published an open letter earlier in January that called on King to allow the battle for integration to continue in the local and federal courts, and warned that King's nonviolent resistance would have the effect of inciting civil disturbances. Dr. King wanted Christian ministers to see that the meaning of Christian discipleship was at the heart of the African American struggle for freedom, justice, and equality.

My dear Fellow Clergymen,

While confined here in the Birmingham city jail, I came across your recent statement calling our present activities "unwise and untimely." Seldom, if ever, do I pause to answer criticism of my work and ideas. If I sought to answer all of the criticisms that cross my desk, my secretaries would be engaged in little else in the course of the day, and I would have no time for constructive work. But since I feel that you are men of genuine good will and your criticisms are sincerely set forth, I would like to answer your statement in what I hope will be patient and reasonable terms.

I think I should give the reason for my being in Birmingham, since you have been influenced by the argument of "outsiders coming in." I have the honor of serving as president of the Southern Christian Leadership Conference, an organization operating in every southern state, with headquarters in Atlanta, Georgia. We have some eighty-five affiliate organizations all across the South—one being the Alabama Christian Movement for Human Rights. Whenever necessary and possible we share staff, educational and financial resources with our affiliates. Several months ago our local affiliate here in Birmingham invited us to be on call to engage in a nonviolent direct-action program if such were deemed necessary. We readily consented and when the hour came we lived up to our promises. So I am here, along with several members of

290 / HISTORIC ESSAYS

my staff, because we were invited here. I am here because I have basic organizational ties here.

Beyond this, I am in Birmingham because injustice is here. Just as the eighth century prophets left their little villages and carried their "thus saith the Lord" far beyond the boundaries of their hometowns; and just as the Apostle Paul left his little village of Tarsus and carried the gospel of Jesus Christ to practically every hamlet and city of the Graeco-Roman world, I too am compelled to carry the gospel of freedom beyond my particular hometown. Like Paul, I must constantly respond to the Macedonian call for aid.

Moreover, I am cognizant of the interrelatedness of all communities and states. I cannot sit idly by in Atlanta and not be concerned about what happens in Birmingham. Injustice anywhere is a threat to justice everywhere. We are caught in an inescapable network of mutuality, tied in a single garment of destiny. Whatever affects one directly affects all indirectly. Never again can we afford to live with the narrow, provincial "outside agitator" idea. Anyone who lives in the United States can never be considered an outsider anywhere in this country.

You deplore the demonstrations that are presently taking place in Birmingham. But I am sorry that your statement did not express a similar concern for the conditions that brought the demonstrations into being. I am sure that each of you would want to go beyond the superficial social analyst who looks merely at effects, and does not grapple with underlying causes. I would not hesitate to say that it is unfortunate that so-called demonstrations are taking place in Birmingham at this time, but I would say in more emphatic terms that it is even more unfortunate that the white power structure of this city left the Negro community with no other alternative.

In any nonviolent campaign there are four basic steps: (1) collection of the facts to determine whether injustices are alive, (2) negotiation, (3) self-purification, and (4) direct action. We have gone through all of these steps in Birmingham. There can be no gainsaying of the fact that racial injustice engulfs this community.

Birmingham is probably the most thoroughly segregated city in the United States. Its ugly record of police brutality is known in every section of this country. Its injust treatment of Negroes in the courts is a notorious reality. There have been more unsolved bombings of Negro homes and churches in Birmingham than any city in this nation. These are the hard, brutal and unbelievable facts. On the basis of these conditions Negro leaders sought to negotiate with the city fathers. But the political leaders consistently refused to engage in good faith negotiation.

Then came the opportunity last September to talk with some of the leaders of the economic community. In these negotiating sessions certain promises were made by the merchants—such as the promise to remove the humiliating racial signs from the stores. On the basis of these

LETTER FROM BIRMINGHAM CITY JAIL / 291

promises Rev. Shuttlesworth and the leaders of the Alabama Christian Movement for Human Rights agreed to call a moratorium on any type of demonstrations. As the weeks and months unfolded we realized that we were the victims of a broken promise. The signs remained. Like so many experiences of the past we were confronted with blasted hopes, and the dark shadow of a deep disappointment settled upon us. So we had no alternative except that of preparing for direct action, whereby we would present our very bodies as a means of laying our case before the conscience of the local and national community. We were not unmindful of the difficulties involved. So we decided to go through a process of self-purification. We started having workshops on nonviolence and repeatedly asked ourselves the questions, "Are you able to accept blows without retaliating?" "Are you able to endure the ordeals of jail?" We decided to set our direct-action program around the Easter season, realizing that with the exception of Christmas, this was the largest shopping period of the year. Knowing that a strong economic withdrawal program would be the by-product of direct action, we felt that this was the best time to bring pressure on the merchants for the needed changes. Then it occurred to us that the March election was ahead and so we speedily decided to postpone action until after election day. When we discovered that Mr. Connor was in the run-off, we decided again to postpone action so that the demonstrations could not be used to cloud the issues. At this time we agreed to begin our nonviolent witness the day after the run-off.

This reveals that we did not move irresponsibly into direct action. We too wanted to see Mr. Connor defeated; so we went through postponement after postponement to aid in this community need. After this we felt that direct action could be delayed no longer.

You may well ask, "Why direct action? Why sit-ins, marches, etc.? Isn't negotiation a better path?" You are exactly right in your call for negotiation. Indeed, this is the purpose of direct action. Nonviolent direct action seeks to create such a crisis and establish such creative tension that a community that has constantly refused to negotiate is forced to confront the issue. It seeks so to dramatize the issue that it can no longer be ignored. I just referred to the creation of tension as a part of the work of the nonviolent resister. This may sound rather shocking. But I must confess that I am not afraid of the word tension. I have earnestly worked and preached against violent tension, but there is a type of constructive nonviolent tension that is necessary for growth. Just as Socrates felt that it was necessary to create a tension in the mind so that individuals could rise from the bondage of myths and half-truths to the unfettered realm of creative analysis and objective appraisal, we must see the need of having nonviolent gadflies to create the kind of tension in society that will help men to rise from the dark depths of prejudice and racism to the majestic heights of understanding and brotherhood.

So the purpose of the direct action is to create a situation so crisis-packed that it will inevitably open the door to negotiation. We, therefore, concur with you in your call for negotiation. Too long has our beloved Southland been bogged down in the tragic attempt to live in monologue rather than dialogue.

One of the basic points in your statement is that our acts are untimely. Some have asked, "Why didn't you give the new administration time to act?" The only answer that I can give to this inquiry is that the new administration must be prodded about as much as the outgoing one before it acts. We will be sadly mistaken if we feel that the election of Mr. Boutwell will bring the millennium to Birmingham. While Mr. Boutwell is much more articulate and gentle than Mr. Connor, they are both segregationists, dedicated to the task of maintaining the status quo. The hope I see in Mr. Boutwell is that he will be reasonable enough to see the futility of massive resistance to desegregation. But he will not see this without pressure from the devotees of civil rights. My friends, I must say to you that we have not made a single gain in civil rights without determined legal and nonviolent pressure. History is the long and tragic story of the fact that privileged groups seldom give up their privileges voluntarily. Individuals may see the moral light and voluntarily give up their unjust posture; but as Reinhold Niebuhr has reminded us, groups are more immoral than individuals.

We know through painful experience that freedom is never voluntarily given by the oppressor; it must be demanded by the oppressed. Frankly, I have never yet engaged in a direct action movement that was "well-timed," according to the timetable of those who have not suffered unduly from the disease of segregation. For years now I have heard the words "Wait!" It rings in the ear of every Negro with a piercing familiarity. This "Wait" has almost always meant "Never." It has been a tranquilizing thalidomide, relieving the emotional stress for a moment, only to give birth to an ill-formed infant of frustration. We must come to see with the distinguished jurist of yesterday that "justice too long delayed is justice denied." We have waited for more than 340 years for our constitutional and God-given rights. The nations of Asia and Africa are moving with jetlike speed toward the goal of political independence, and we still creep at horse and buggy pace toward the gaining of a cup of coffee at a lunch counter. I guess it is easy for those who have never felt the stinging darts of segregation to say, "Wait." But when you have seen vicious mobs lynch your mothers and fathers at will and drown your sisters and brothers at whim; when you have seen hate-filled policemen curse, kick, brutalize and even kill your black brothers and sisters with impunity; when you see the vast majority of your twenty million Negro brothers smothering in an airtight cage of poverty in the midst of an affluent society; when you suddenly find your tongue twisted and your speech stammering as you seek to explain to your six-year-old daughter why she can't go to the public amusement park that has just been advertised on television, and see tears welling up in her little eyes when she is told that Funtown is closed to colored children, and see the depressing clouds of inferiority begin to form in her little mental sky, and see her begin to distort her little personality by unconsciously developing a bitterness toward white people; when you have to concoct an answer for a five-year-old son asking in agonizing pathos: "Daddy, why do white people treat colored people so mean?"; when you take a cross-country drive and find it necessary to sleep night after night in the uncomfortable corners of your automobile because no motel will accept you; when you are humiliated day in and day out by nagging signs reading "white" and "colored"; when your first name becomes "nigger" and your middle name becomes "boy" (however old you are) and your last name becomes "John," and when your wife and mother are never given the respected title "Mrs."; when you are harried by day and haunted by night by the fact that you are a Negro, living constantly at tiptoe stance never quite knowing what to expect next, and plagued with inner fears and outer resentments; when you are forever fighting a degenerating sense of "nobodiness"; then you will understand why we find it difficult to wait. There comes a time when the cup of endurance runs over, and men are no longer willing to be plunged into an abyss of injustice where they experience the blackness of corroding despair. I hope, sirs, you can understand our legitimate and unavoidable impatience.

You express a great deal of anxiety over our willingness to break laws. This is certainly a legitimate concern. Since we so diligently urge people to obey the Supreme Court's decision of 1954 outlawing segregation in the public schools, it is rather strange and paradoxical to find us consciously breaking laws. One may well ask, "How can you advocate breaking some laws and obeying others?" The answer is found in the fact that there are two types of laws: there are *just* and there are *unjust* laws. I would agree with Saint Augustine that "An unjust law is no law at all."

Now what is the difference between the two? How does one determine when a law is just or unjust? A just law is a man-made code that squares with the moral law or the law of God. An unjust law is a code that is out of harmony with the moral law. To put it in the terms of Saint Thomas Aquinas, an unjust law is a human law that is not rooted in eternal and natural law. Any law that uplifts human personality is just. Any law that degrades human personality is unjust. All segregation statutes are unjust because segregation distorts the soul and damages the personality. It gives the segregator a false sense of superiority, and the segregated a false sense of inferiority. To use the words of Martin Buber, the great Jewish philosopher, segregation substitutes an "I-it" relationship for the "I-thou" relationship, and ends up relegating persons to the status of things. So segregation is not only politically, economically and sociologically unsound, but it is morally wrong and sinful. Paul Tillich has said that sin is separation. Isn't segregation an existential expression of man's tragic separation, an expression of his awful estrangement, his terrible sinfulness? So I can urge men to disobey segregation ordinances becuase they are morally wrong.

Let us turn to a more concrete example of just and unjust laws. An unjust law is a code that a majority inflicts on a minority that is not binding on itself. This is difference made legal. On the other hand a just law is a code that a majority compels a minority to follow that it is willing to follow itself. This is sameness made legal.

Let me give another explanation. An unjust law is a code inflicted upon a minority which that minority had no part in enacting or creating because they did not have the unhampered right to vote. Who can say that the legislature of Alabama which set up the segregation laws was democratically elected? Throughout the state of Alabama all types of conniving methods are used to prevent Negroes from becoming registered voters and there are some counties without a single Negro registered to vote despite the fact that the Negro constitutes a majority of the population. Can any law set up in such a state be considered democratically structured?

These are just a few examples of unjust and just laws. There are some instances when a law is just on its face and unjust in its application. For instance, I was arrested Friday on a change of parading without a permit. Now there is nothing wrong with an ordinance which requires a permit for a parade, but when the ordinance is used to preserve segregation and to deny citizens the First Amendment privilege of peaceful assembly and peaceful protest, then it becomes unjust.

I hope you can see the distinction I am trying to point out. In no sense do I advocate evading or defying the law as the rabid segregationist would do. This would lead to anarchy. One who breaks an unjust law must do it *openly, lovingly* (not hatefully as the white mothers did in New Orleans when they were seen on television screaming, "nigger, nigger, nigger"), and with a willingness to accept the penalty. I submit that an individual who breaks a law that conscience tells him is unjust, and willingly accepts the penalty by staying in jail to arouse the conscience of the community over its injustice, is in reality expressing the very highest respect for law.

Of course, there is nothing new about this kind of civil disobedience. It was seen sublimely in the refusal of Shadrach, Meshach and Abednego to obey the laws of Nebuchadnezzar because a higher moral law was involved. It was practiced superbly by the early Christians who were willing to face hungry lions and the excruciating pain of chopping blocks, before submitting to certain unjust laws of the Roman Empire. To a degree academic freedom is a reality today because Socrates practiced civil disobedience.

We can never forget that everything Hitler did in Germany was "legal" and everything the Hungarian freedom fighters did in Hungary was "illegal." It was "illegal" to aid and comfort a Jew in Hitler's Germany. But I am sure that if I had lived in Germany during that time I would have aided and comforted my Jewish brothers even though it was illegal. If I lived in a Communist country today where certain principles dear to the Christian faith are suppressed, I believe I would openly advocate disobeying these anti-religious laws. I must make two honest confessions to you, my Christian and Jewish brothers. First, I must confess that over the last few years I have been gravely disappointed with the white moderate. I have almost reached the regrettable conclusion that the Negro's great stumbling block in the stride toward freedom is not the White Citizen's Counciler or the Ku Klux Klanner, but the white moderate who is more devoted to "order" than to justice; who prefers a negative peace which is the absence of tension to a positive peace which is the presence of justice; who constantly says, "I agree with you in the goal you seek, but I can't agree with your methods of direct action"; who paternalistically feels that he can set the timetable for another man's freedom; who lives by the myth of time and who constantly advised the Negro to wait until a "more convenient season." Shallow understanding from people of good will is more frustrating than absolute misunderstanding from people of ill will. Lukewarm acceptance is much more bewildering than outright rejection.

I had hoped that the white moderate would understand that law and order exist for the purpose of establishing justice, and that when they fail to do this they become dangerously structured dams that block the flow of social progress. I had hoped that the white moderate would understand that the present tension of the South is merely a necessary phase of the transition from an obnoxious negative peace, where the Negro passively accepted his unjust plight, to a substance-filled positive peace, where all men will respect the dignity and worth of human personality. Actually, we who engage in nonviolent direct action are not the creators of tension. We merely bring to the surface the hidden tension that is already alive. We bring it out in the open where it can be seen and dealt with. Like a boil that can never be cured as long as it is covered up but must be opened with all its pus-flowing ugliness to the natural medicines of air and light, injustice must likewise be exposed, with all of the tension its exposing creates, to the light of human conscience and the air of national opinion before it can be cured.

In your statement you asserted that our actions, even though peaceful, must be condemned because they precipitate violence. But can this assertion be logically made? Isn't this like condemning the robbed man because his possession of money precipitated the evil act of robbery? Isn't this like condemning Socrates because his unswerving commitment to truth and his philosophical delvings precipitated the misguided popular mind to make him drink the hemlock? Isn't this like condemning Jesus because His unique God-consciousness and never-ceasing devotion to his will precipitated the evil act of crucifixion? We must come to see, as federal courts have consistently affirmed, that it is immoral to urge an individual to withdraw his efforts to gain his basic constitutional rights because the quest precipitates violence. Society must protect the robbed and punish the robber.

I had also hoped that the white moderate would reject the myth of time. I received a letter this morning from a white brother in Texas which said: "All Christians know that the colored people will receive equal rights eventually, but it is possible that you are in too great of a religious hurry. It has taken Christianity almost two thousand years to accomplish what it has. The teachings of Christ take time to come to earth." All that is said here grows out of a tragic misconception of time. It is the strangely irrational notion that there is something in the very flow of time that will inevitably cure all ills. Actually time is neutral. It can be used either destructively or constructively. I am coming to feel that the people of ill will have used time much more effectively than the people of good will. We will have to repent in this generation not merely for the vitriolic words and actions of the bad people, but for the appalling silence of the good people. We must come to see that human progress never rolls in on wheels of inevitability. It comes through the tireless efforts and persistent work of men willing to be co-workers with God, and without this hard word time itself becomes an ally of the forces of social stagnation. We must use time creatively, and forever realize that the time is always ripe to do right. Now is the time to make real the promise of democracy, and transform our pending national elegy into a creative psalm of brotherhood. Now is the time to lift our national policy from the quicksand of racial injustice to the solid rock of human dignity.

You spoke of our activity in Birmingham as extreme. At first I was rather disappointed that fellow clergymen would see my nonviolent efforts as those of the extremist. I started thinking about the fact that I stand in the middle of two opposing forces in the Negro community. One is a force of complacency made up of Negroes who, as a result of long years of oppression, have been so completely drained of self-respect and a sense of "somebodiness" that they have adjusted to segregation, and, of a few Negroes in the middle class who, because of a degree of academic and economic security, and because at points they profit by segregation, have unconsciously become insensitive to the problems of the masses. The other force is one of bitterness and hatred, and comes perilously close to advocating violence. It is expressed in the various black nationalist groups that are springing up over the nation, the largest and best known being Elijah Muhammad's Muslim movement. This movement is nourished by the contemporary frustration over the continued existence of racial discrimination. It is made up of people who have lost faith in America, who have absolutely repudiated Christianity,

LETTER FROM BIRMINGHAM CITY JAIL / 297

and who have concluded that the white man is an incurable "devil." I have tried to stand between these two forces, saying that we need not follow the "do-nothingism" of the complacent or the hatred and despair of the black nationalist. There is the more excellent way of love and nonviolent protest. I'm grateful to God that, through the Negro church, the dimension of nonviolence entered our struggle. If this philosophy had not emerged, I am convinced that by now many streets of the South would be flowing with floods of blood. And I am further convinced that if our white brothers dismiss us as "rabble-rousers" and "outside agitators" those of us who are working through the channels of nonviolent direct action and refuse to support our nonviolent efforts, millions of Negroes, out of frustration and despair, will seek solace and security in black nationalist ideologies, a development that will lead inevitably to a frightening racial nightmare.

Oppressed people cannot remain oppressed forever. The urge for freedom will eventually come. This is what happened to the American Negro. Something within has reminded him of his birthright of freedom; something without has reminded him that he can gain it. Consciously and unconsciously, he has been swept in by what the Germans call the *Zeitgeist*, and with his black brothers of Africa, and his brown and yellow brothers of Asia, South America and the Caribbean, he is moving with a sense of cosmic urgency toward the promised land of racial justice. Recognizing this vital urge that has engulfed the Negro community, one should readily understand public demonstrations. The Negro has many pent-up resentments and latent frustrations. He has to get them out. So let him march sometime; let him have his prayer pilgrimages to the city hall; understand why he must have sit-ins and freedom rides. If his repressed emotions do not come out in these nonviolent ways, they will come out in ominous expressions of violence. This is not a threat; it is a fact of history. So I have not said to my people "get rid of your discontent." But I have tried to say that this normal and healthy discontent can be channelized through the creative outlet of nonviolent direct action. Now this approach is being dismissed as extremist. I must admit that I was initially disappointed in being so categorized.

But as I continued to think about the matter I gradually gained a bit of satisfaction from being considered an extremist. Was not Jesus an extremist in love—"Love your enemies, bless them that curse you, pray for them that despitefully use you." Was not Amos an extremist for justice—"Let justice roll down like waters and righteousness like a mighty stream." Was not Paul an extremist for the gospel of Jesus Christ—"I bear in my body the marks of the Lord Jesus." Was not Martin Luther an extremist—"Here I stand; I can do none other so help me God." Was not John Bunyan an extremist—"I will stay in jail to the end of my days before I make a butchery of my conscience." Was not Abraham Lincoln an extremist—"This nation cannot survive half slave and half

298 / HISTORIC ESSAYS

free." Was not Thomas Jefferson an extremist—"We hold these truths to be self-evident, that all men are created equal." So the question is not whether we will be extremist but what kind of extremist will we be. Will we be extremists for hate or will we be extremists for love? Will we be extremists for the preservation of injustice—or will we be extremists for the cause of justice? In that dramatic scene on Calvary's hill, three men were crucified. We must not forget that all three were crucified for the same crime—the crime of extremism. Two were extremists for immorality, and thusly fell below their environment. The other, Jesus Christ, was an extremist for love, truth and goodness, and thereby rose above his environment. So, after all, maybe the South, the nation and the world are in dire need of creative extremists.

I had hoped that the white moderate would see this. Maybe I was too optimistic. Maybe I expected too much. I guess I should have realized that few members of a race that has oppressed another race can understand or appreciate the deep groans and passionate yearnings of those that have been oppressed and still fewer have the vision to see that injustice must be rooted out by strong, persistent and determined action. I am thankful, however, that some of our white brothers have grasped the meaning of this social revolution and committed themselves to it. They are still all too small in quantity, but they are big in quality. Some like Ralph McGill, Lillian Smith, Harry Golden and James Dabbs have written about our struggle in eloquent, prophetic and understanding terms. Others have marched with us down nameless streets of the South. They have languished in filthy roach-infested jails, suffering the abuse and brutality of angry policemen who see them as "dirty nigger-lovers." They, unlike so many of their moderate brothers and sisters, have recognized the urgency of the moment and sensed the need for powerful "action" antidotes to combat the disease of segregation.

Let me rush on to mention my other disappointment. I have been so greatly disappointed with the white church and its leadership. Of course, there are some notable exceptions. I am not unmindful of the fact that each of you has taken some significant stands on this issue. I commend you, Rev. Stallings, for your Christian stance on this past Sunday, in welcoming Negroes to your worship service on a non-segregated basis. I commend the Catholic leaders of this state for integrating Springhill College several years ago.

But despite these notable exceptions I must honestly reiterate that I have been disappointed with the church. I do not say that as one of the negative critics who can always find something wrong with the church. I say it as a minister of the gospel, who loves the church; who was nurtured in its bosom; who has been sustained by its spiritual blessings and who will remain true to it as long as the cord of life shall lengthen.

I had the strange feeling when I was suddenly catapulted into the leadership of the bus protest in Montgomery several years ago that we would have the support of the white church. I felt that the white ministers, priests and rabbis of the South would be some of our strongest allies. Instead, some have been outright opponents, refusing to understand the freedom movement and misrepresenting its leaders; all too many others have been more cautious than courageous and have remained silent behind the anesthetizing security of the stained-glass windows.

In spite of my shattered dreams of the past, I came to Birmingham with the hope that the white religious leadership of this community would see the justice of our cause, and with deep moral concern, serve as the channel through which our just grievances would get to the power structure. I had hoped that each of you would understand. But again I have been disappointed. I have heard numerous religious leaders of the South call upon their worshippers to comply with a desegregation decision because it is the *law*, but I have longed to hear white ministers say, "Follow this decree because integration is morally *right* and the Negro is your brother." In the midst of blatant injustices inflicted upon the Negro, I have watched white churches stand on the sideline and merely mouth pious irrelevancies and sanctimonious trivialities. In the midst of a mighty struggle to rid our nation of racial and economic injustice, I have heard so many ministers say, "Those are social issues with which the gospel has no real concern," and I have watched so many churches commit themselves to a completely otherworldly religion which made a strange distinction between body and soul, the sacred and the secular.

So here we are moving toward the exit of the twentieth century with a religious community largely adjusted to the status quo, standing as a taillight behind other community agencies rather than a headlight leading men to higher levels of justice.

I have traveled the length and breadth of Alabama, Mississippi and all the other southern states. On sweltering summer days and crisp autumn mornings I have looked at her beautiful churches with their lofty spires pointing heavenward. I have beheld the impressive outlay of her massive religious education buildings. Over and over again I have found myself asking: "What kind of people worship here? Who is their God? Where were their voices when the lips of Governor Barnett dripped with words of interposition and nullification? Where were they when Governor Wallace gave the clarion call for defiance and hatred? Where were their voices of support when tired, bruised and weary Negro men and women decided to rise from the dark dungeons of complacency to the bright hills of creative protest?"

Yes, these questions are still in my mind. In deep disappointment, I have wept over the laxity of the church. But be assured that my tears have been tears of love. There can be no deep disappointment where there is not deep love. Yes, I love the church; I love her sacred walls. How could I do otherwise? I am in the rather unique position of being the son, the grandson and the great-grandson of preachers. Yes, I see the church as the body of Christ. But, oh! How we have blemished and scarred that body through social neglect and fear of being nonconformists.

There was a time when the church was very powerful. It was during that period when the early Christians rejoiced when they were deemed worthy to suffer for what they believed. In those days the church was not merely a thermometer that recorded the ideas and principles of popular opinion; it was a thermostat that transformed the mores of society. Wherever the early Christians entered a town the power structure got disturbed and immediately sought to convict them for being "disturbers of the peace" and "outside agitators." But they went on with the conviction that they were "a colony of heaven," and had to obey God rather than man. They were small in number but big in commitment. They were too God-intoxicated to be "astronomically intimidated." They brought an end to such ancient evils as infanticide and gladiatorial contest.

Things are different now. The contemporary church is often a weak, ineffectual voice with an uncertain sound. It is so often the arch-supporter of the status quo. Far from being disturbed by the presence of the church, the power structure of the average community is consoled by the church's silent and often vocal sanction of things as they are.

But the judgment of God is upon the church as never before. If the church of today does not recapture the sacrificial spirit of the early church, it will lose its authentic ring, forfeit the loyalty of millions, and be dismissed as an irrelevant social club with no meaning for the twentieth century. I am meeting young people every day whose disappointment with the church has risen to outright disgust.

Maybe again, I have been too optimistic. Is organized religion too inextricably bound to the status quo to save our nation and the world? Maybe I must turn my faith to the inner spiritual church, the church within the church, as the true *ecclesia* and the hope of the world. But again I am thankful to God that some noble souls from the ranks of organized religion have broken loose from the paralyzing chains of conformity and joined us as active partners in the struggle for freedom. They have left their secure congregations and walked the streets of Albany, Georgia, with us. They have gone through the highways of the South on tortuous rides for freedom. Yes, they have gone to jail with us. Some have been kicked out of their churches, and lost support of their bishops and fellow ministers. But they have gone with the faith that right defeated is stronger than evil triumphant. These men have been the leaven in the lump of the race. Their witness has been the spiritual salt that has preserved the true meaning of the gospel in these troubled times. They have carved a tunnel of hope through the dark mountain of disappointment.

I hope the church as a whole will meet the challenge of this decisive hour. But even if the church does not come to the aid of justice, I have no despair about the future. I have no fear about the outcome of our struggle in Birmingham, even if our motives are presently misunderstood. We will reach the goal of freedom in Birmingham and all over the nation, because the goal of America is freedom. Abused and scorned though we may be, our destiny is tied up with the destiny of America. Before the Pilgrims landed at Plymouth we were here. Before the pen of Jefferson etched across the pages of history the majestic words of the Declaration of Independence, we were here. For more than two centuries our foreparents labored in this country without wages; they made cotton king; and they built the homes of their masters in the midst of brutal injustice and shameful humiliation—and yet out of a bottomless vitality they continued to thrive and develop. If the inexpressible cruelties of slavery could not stop us, the opposition we now face will surely fail. We will win our freedom because the sacred heritage of our nation and the eternal will of God are embodied in our echoing demands.

I must close now. But before closing I am impelled to mention one other point in your statement that troubled me profoundly. You warmly commended the Birmingham police force for keeping "order" and "preventing violence." I don't believe you would have so warmly commended the police force if you had seen its angry violent dogs literally biting six unarmed, nonviolent Negroes. I don't believe you would so quickly commend the policemen if you would observe their ugly and inhuman treatment of Negroes here in the city jail; if you would watch them push and curse old Negro women and young Negro girls; if you would see them slap and kick old Negro men and young boys; if you will observe them, as they did on two occasions, refuse to give us food because we wanted to sing our grace together. I'm sorry that I can't join you in your praise for the police department.

It is true that they have been rather disciplined in their public handling of the demonstrators. In this sense they have been rather publicly "nonviolent." But for what purpose? To preserve the evil system of segregation. Over the last few years I have consistently preached that nonviolence demands that the means we use must be as pure as the ends we seek. So I have tried to make it clear that it is wrong to use immoral means to attain moral ends. But now I must affirm that it is just as wrong, or even more so, to use moral means to preserve immoral ends. Maybe Mr. Connor and his policemen have been rather publicly nonviolent, as Chief Pritchett was in Albany, Georgia, but they have used the moral means of nonviolence to maintain the immoral end of flagrant racial injustice. T. S. Eliot has said that there is no greater treason than to do the right deed for the wrong reason.

I wish you had commended the Negro sit-inners and demonstrators of Birmingham for their sublime courage, their willingness to suffer and their amazing discipline in the midst of the most inhuman provocation.

One day the South will recognize its real heroes. They wil be the James Merediths, courageously and with a majestic sense of purpose facing jeering and hostile mobs and the agonizing loneliness that characterizes the life of the pioneer. They will be old, oppressed, battered Negro women, symbolized in a seventy-two-year-old woman of Montgomery, Alabama, who rose up with a sense of dignity and with her people decided not to ride the segregated buses, and responded to one who inquired about her tiredness with ungrammatical profundity: "My feet is tired, but my soul is rested." They will be the young high school and college students, young ministers of the gospel and a host of their elders courageously and nonviolently sitting-in at lunch counters and willingly going to jail for conscience's sake. One day the South will know that when these disinherited children of God sat down at lunch counters they were in reality standing up for the best in the American dream and the most sacred values in our Judeo-Christian heritage, and thusly, carrying our whole nation back to those great wells of democracy which were dug deep by the Founding Fathers in the formulation of the Constitution and the Declaration of Independence.

Never before have I written a letter this long (or should I say a book?). I'm afraid that it is much too long to take your precious time. I can assure you that it would have been much shorter if I had been writing from a comfortable desk, but what else is there to do when you are alone for days in the dull monotony of a narrow jail cell other than write long letters, think strange thoughts, and pray long prayers?

If I have said anything in this letter that is an overstatement of the truth and is indicative of an unreasonable impatience, I beg you to forgive me. If I have said anything in this letter that is an understatement of the truth and is indicative of my having a patience that makes me patient with anything less than brotherhood, I beg God to forgive me.

I hope this letter finds you strong in the faith. I also hope that circumstances will soon make it possible for me to meet each of you, not as an integrationist or a civil rights leader, but as a fellow clergyman and a Christian brother. Let us all hope that the dark clouds of racial prejudice will soon pass away and the deep fog of misunderstanding will be lifted from our fear-drenched communities and in some not too distant tomorrow the radiant stars of love and brotherhood will shine over our great nation with all of their scintillating beauty.

Yours for the cause of Peace and Brotherhood,
Martin Luther King, Jr.

Martin Luther King, Jr., *Why We Can't Wait* (New York: Harper & Row, 1963, 1964). The American Friends Committee first published this essay as a pamphlet. It has probably been reprinted more than anything else Dr. King wrote.

[17]
Martin Luther King, Jr.: Charismatic Leadership in a Mass Struggle

Clayborne Carson

The legislation to establish Martin Luther King, Jr.'s birthday as a federal holiday provided official recognition of King's greatness, but it remains the responsibility of those of us who study and carry on King's work to define his historical significance. Rather than engaging in officially approved nostalgia, our rememberance of King should reflect the reality of his complex and multifaceted life. Biographers, theologians, political scientists, sociologists, social psychologists, and historians have given us a sizable literature of King's place in the Afro-American protest tradition, his role in the modern black freedom struggle, and his eclectic ideas regarding nonviolent activism. Although King scholars may benefit from and may stimulate the popular interest in King generated by the national holiday, many will find themselves uneasy participants in annual observances to honor an innocuous, carefully cultivated image of King as a black heroic figure.

The King depicted in serious scholarly works is far too interesting to be encased in such a didactic legend. King was a controversial leader who challenged authority and who once applauded what he called "creative maladjusted nonconformity."[1] He should not be transformed into a simplistic image designed to offend no one—a black counterpart to the static, heroic myths that have embalmed George Washington as the Father of His Country and Abraham Lincoln as the Great Emancipator.

One aspect of the emerging King myth has been the depiction of him in the mass media, not only as the preeminent leader of the civil rights movement, but also as the initiator and sole indispensible element in the southern black struggles of the 1950s and 1960s. As in other historical myths, a Great Man is seen as the decisive factor in the process of social change, and the unique qualities of a leader are used to explain major historical events. The King myth departs from historical reality because it attributes too much to King's exceptional qualities as a leader and too little to the impersonal, large-scale social factors that made it possible for King to display

---

Clayborne Carson is associate professor of history, Stanford University, and senior editor and director of the Martin Luther King, Jr., Papers Project, Martin Luther King, Jr., Center for Nonviolent Social Change and Stanford University. He wishes to thank Penny Russell, Rachel Bagby, Susan Carson, and other project staff members for their assistance.

[1] Martin Luther King, Jr., speech at the University of California, Berkeley, tape recording, May 17, 1967, Martin Luther King, Jr., Papers Project (Stanford University, Stanford, Calif.).

his singular abilities on a national stage. Because the myth emphasizes the individual at the expense of the black movement, it not only exaggerates King's historical importance but also distorts his actual, considerable contribution to the movement.

A major example of this distortion has been the tendency to see King as a charismatic figure who single-handedly directed the course of the civil rights movement through the force of his oratory. The charismatic label, however, does not adequately define King's role in the southern black struggle. The term *charisma* has traditionally been used to describe the godlike, magical qualities possessed by certain leaders. Connotations of the term have changed, of course, over the years. In our more secular age, it has lost many of its religious connotations and now refers to a wide range of leadership styles that involve the capacity to inspire—usually through oratory—emotional bonds between leaders and followers. Arguing that King was not a charismatic leader, in the broadest sense of the term, becomes somewhat akin to arguing that he was not a Christian, but emphasis on King's charisma obscures other important aspects of his role in the black movement. To be sure, King's oratory was exceptional and many people saw King as a divinely inspired leader, but King did not receive and did not want the kind of unquestioning support that is often associated with charismatic leaders. Movement activists instead saw him as the most prominent among many outstanding movement strategists, tacticians, ideologues, and institutional leaders.

King undoubtedly recognized that charisma was one of many leadership qualities at his disposal, but he also recognized that charisma was not a sufficient basis for leadership in a modern political movement enlisting numerous self-reliant leaders. Moreover, he rejected aspects of the charismatic model that conflicted with his sense of his own limitations. Rather than exhibiting unwavering confidence in his power and wisdom, King was a leader full of self-doubts, keenly aware of his own limitations and human weaknesses. He was at times reluctant to take on the responsibilities suddenly and unexpectedly thrust upon him. During the Montgomery bus boycott, for example, when he worried about threats to his life and to the lives of his wife and child, he was overcome with fear rather than confident and secure in his leadership role. He was able to carry on only after acquiring an enduring understanding of his dependence on a personal God who promised never to leave him alone.[2]

Moreover, emphasis on King's charisma conveys the misleading notion of a movement held together by spellbinding speeches and blind faith rather than by a complex blend of rational and emotional bonds. King's charisma did not place him above criticism. Indeed, he was never able to gain mass support for his notion of nonviolent struggle as a way of life, rather than simply a tactic. Instead of viewing

---

[2] Martin Luther King, Jr., described this episode, which occurred on the evening of January 27, 1956, in a remarkable speech delivered in September 1966. It is available on a phonograph record; "Dr. King's Entrance into the Civil Rights Movement," *Martin Luther King, Jr.: In Search of Freedom* (Mercury SR 61170).

himself as the embodiment of widely held Afro-American racial values, he willingly risked his popularity among blacks through his steadfast advocacy of nonviolent strategies to achieve radical social change.

He was a profound and provocative public speaker as well as an emotionally powerful one. Only those unfamiliar with the Afro-American clergy would assume that his oratorical skills were unique, but King set himself apart from other black preachers through his use of traditional black Christian idiom to advocate unconventional political ideas. Early in his life King became disillusioned with the unbridled emotionalism associated with his father's religious fundamentalism, and, as a thirteen year old, he questioned the bodily resurrection of Jesus in his Sunday school class.[3] His subsequent search for an intellectually satisfying religious faith conflicted with the emphasis on emotional expressiveness that pervades evangelical religion. His preaching manner was rooted in the traditions of the black church, while his subject matter, which often reflected his wide-ranging philosophical interests, distinguished him from other preachers who relied on rhetorical devices that manipulated the emotions of listeners. King used charisma as a tool for mobilizing black communities, but he always used it in the context of other forms of intellectual and political leadership suited to a movement containing many strong leaders.

Recently, scholars have begun to examine the black struggle as a locally based mass movement, rather than simply a reform movement led by national civil rights leaders.[4] The new orientation in scholarship indicates that King's role was different from that suggested in King-centered biographies and journalistic accounts.[5] King was certainly not the only significant leader of the civil rights movement, for sustained protest movements arose in many southern communities in which King had little or no direct involvement.

In Montgomery, for example, local black leaders such as E. D. Nixon, Rosa Parks, and Jo Ann Robinson started the bus boycott before King became the leader of the Montgomery Improvement Association. Thus, although King inspired blacks in Montgomery and black residents recognized that they were fortunate to have such a spokesperson, talented local leaders other than King played decisive roles in initiating and sustaining the boycott movement.

---

[3] Martin Luther King, Jr., "An Autobiography of Religious Development," [c. 1950], Martin Luther King, Jr., Papers (Mugar Library, Boston University). In this paper, written for a college class, King commented: "I guess I accepted Biblical studies uncritically until I was about twelve years old. But this uncritical attitude could not last long, for it was contrary to the very nature of my being."

[4] The new orientation is evident in William H. Chafe, *Civilities and Civil Rights: Greensboro, North Carolina, and the Black Struggle for Equality* (New York, 1980); David R. Colburn, *Racial Change and Community Crisis: St. Augustine, Florida, 1877-1980* (New York, 1985); Robert J. Norrell, *Reaping the Whirlwind: The Civil Rights Movement in Tuskegee* (New York, 1985); and John R. Salter, *Jackson, Mississippi: An American Chronicle of Struggle and Schism* (Hicksville, N.Y. 1979).

[5] The tendency to view the struggle from King's perspective is evident in the most thoroughly researched of the King biographies, despite the fact that the book concludes with Ella Baker's assessment: "The movement made Martin rather than Martin making the movement." See David J. Garrow, *Bearing the Cross: Martin Luther King, Jr., and the Southern Christian Leadership Conference* (New York, 1986), esp. 625. See also David L. Lewis, *King: A Biography* (Urbana, 1978); Stephen B. Oates, *Let the Trumpet Sound* (New York, 1982); and Adam Fairclough, *To Redeem the Soul of America: The Southern Christian Leadership Conference and Martin Luther King, Jr.* (Athens, 1987).

Black voters in Marion, Ala., wait to cast their ballots in a state primary, 1966.
© *Flip Schulke*.
All Rights Reserved.

Similarly, the black students who initiated the 1960 lunch counter sit-ins admired King, but they did not wait for him to act before launching their own movement. The sit-in leaders who founded the Student Nonviolent Coordinating Committee (SNCC) became increasingly critical of King's leadership style, linking it to the feelings of dependency that often characterize the followers of charismatic leaders.[6] The essense of SNCC's approach to community organizing was to instill in local residents the confidence that they could lead their own struggles. A SNCC organizer failed if local residents became dependent on his or her presence; as the organizers put it, their job was to work themselves out of a job. Though King influenced the struggles that took place in the Black Belt regions of Mississippi, Alabama, and Georgia, those movements were also guided by self-reliant local leaders who occasionally called on King's oratorical skills to galvanize black protestors at mass meetings while refusing to depend on his presence.

If King had never lived, the black struggle would have followed a course of development similar to the one it did. The Montgomery bus boycott would have occurred, because King did not initiate it. Black students probably would have

---

[6] See Clayborne Carson, *In Struggle: SNCC and the Black Awakening of the 1960s* (Cambridge, Mass., 1981); and Howard Zinn, *SNCC: The New Abolitionists* (Boston, 1965).

rebelled—even without King as a role model—for they had sources of tactical and ideological inspiration besides King. Mass activism in southern cities and voting rights efforts in the deep South were outgrowths of large-scale social and political forces, rather than simply consequences of the actions of a single leader. Though perhaps not as quickly and certainly not as peacefully nor with as universal a significance, the black movement would probably have achieved its major legislative victories without King's leadership, for the southern Jim Crow system was a regional anachronism, and the forces that undermined it were inexorable.

To what extent, then, did King's presence affect the movement? Answering that question requires us to look beyond the usual portrayal of the black struggle. Rather than seeing an amorphous mass of discontented blacks acting out strategies determined by a small group of leaders, we would recognize King as a major example of the local black leadership that emerged as black communities mobilized for sustained struggles. If not as dominant a figure as sometimes portrayed, the historical King was nevertheless a remarkable leader who acquired the respect and support of self-confident, grass-roots leaders, some of whom possessed charismatic qualities of their own. Directing attention to the other leaders who initiated and emerged from those struggles should not detract from our conception of King's historical significance; such movement-oriented research reveals King as a leader who stood out in a forest of tall trees.

King's major public speeches—particularly the "I Have a Dream" speech—have received much attention, but his exemplary qualities were also displayed in countless strategy sessions with other activists and in meetings with government officials. King's success as a leader was based on his intellectual and moral cogency and his skill as a conciliator among movement activists who refused to be simply King's "followers" or "lieutenants."

The success of the black movement required the mobilization of black communities as well as the transformation of attitudes in the surrounding society, and King's wide range of skills and attributes prepared him to meet the internal as well as the external demands of the movement. King understood the black world from a privileged position, having grown up in a stable family within a major black urban community; yet he also learned how to speak persuasively to the surrounding white world. Alone among the major civil rights leaders of his time, King could not only articulate black concerns to white audiences, but could also mobilize blacks through his day-to-day involvement in black community institutions and through his access to the regional institutional network of the black church. His advocacy of nonviolent activism gave the black movement invaluable positive press coverage, but his effectiveness as a protest leader derived mainly from his ability to mobilize black community resources.

Analyses of the southern movement that emphasize its nonrational aspects and expressive functions over its political character explain the black struggle as an emotional outburst by discontented blacks, rather than recognizing that the movement's strength and durability came from its mobilization of black community institutions, financial resources, and grass-roots leaders.[7] The values of southern blacks were profoundly and permanently transformed not only by King, but also by involvement in sustained protest activity and community-organizing efforts, through thousands of mass meetings, workshops, citizenship classes, freedom schools, and informal discussions. Rather than merely accepting guidance from above, southern blacks were resocialized as a result of their movement experiences.

Although the literature of the black struggle has traditionally paid little attention to the intellectual content of black politics, movement activists of the 1960s made a profound, though often ignored, contribution to political thinking. King may have been born with rare potential, but his most significant leadership attributes were related to his immersion in, and contribution to, the intellectual ferment that has always been an essential part of Afro-American freedom struggles. Those who have written about King have too often assumed that his most important ideas were derived from outside the black struggle — from his academic training, his philosophical readings, or his acquaintance with Gandhian ideas. Scholars are only beginning to recognize the extent to which his attitudes and those of many other activists, white and black, were transformed through their involvement in a movement in which ideas disseminated from the bottom up as well as from the top down.

Although my assessment of King's role in the black struggles of his time reduces him to human scale, it also increases the possibility that others may recognize his qualities in themselves. Idolizing King lessens one's ability to exhibit some of his best attributes or, worse, encourages one to become a debunker, emphasizing King's flaws in order to lessen the inclination to exhibit his virtues. King himself undoubtedly feared that some who admired him would place too much faith in his ability to offer guidance and to overcome resistance, for he often publicly acknowledged his own limitations and mortality. Near the end of his life, King expressed his certainty that black people would reach the Promised Land whether or not he was with them. His faith was based on an awareness of the qualities that he knew he shared with all people. When he suggested his own epitaph, he asked not to be remembered for his exceptional achievements — his Nobel Prize and other awards, his academic accomplishments; instead, he wanted to be remembered for giving his life to serve others, for trying to be right on the war question, for trying to feed the hungry and clothe the naked, for trying to love and serve humanity. "I want you to say that I tried to love and serve humanity."[8] Those aspects of King's life did not require charisma or other superhuman abilities.

If King were alive today, he would doubtless encourage those who celebrate his life to recognize their responsibility to struggle as he did for a more just and peaceful

---

[7] For incisive critiques of traditional psychological and sociological analyses of the modern black struggle, see Doug McAdam, *Political Process and the Development of Black Insurgency, 1930–1970* (Chicago, 1982); and Aldon D. Morris, *Origins of the Civil Rights Movement: Black Communities Organizing for Change* (New York, 1984).

[8] James M. Washington, ed., *A Testament of Hope: The Essential Writings of Martin Luther King, Jr.* (San Francisco, 1986), 267.

world. He would prefer that the black movment be remembered not only as the scene of his own achievements, but also as a setting that brought out extraordinary qualities in many people. If he were to return, his oratory would be unsettling and intellectually challenging rather than remembered diction and cadences. He would probably be the unpopular social critic he was on the eve of the Poor People's Campaign rather than the object of national homage he became after his death. His basic message would be the same as it was when he was alive, for he did not bend with the changing political winds. He would talk of ending poverty and war and of building a just social order that would avoid the pitfalls of competitive capitalism and repressive communism. He would give scant comfort to those who condition their activism upon the appearance of another King, for he recognized the extent to which he was a product of the movement that called him to leadership.

The notion that appearances by Great Men (or Great Women) are necessary preconditions for the emergence of major movements for social changes reflects not only a poor understanding of history, but also a pessimistic view of the possibilities for future social change. Waiting for the Messiah is a human weakness that is unlikely to be rewarded more than once in a millennium. Studies of King's life offer support for an alternative optimistic belief that ordinary people can collectively improve their lives. Such studies demonstrate the capacity of social movements to transform participants for the better and to create leaders worthy of their followers.

[18]

While the problem of humanization has always, from an axiological point of view, been humankind's central problem, it now takes on the character of an inescapable concern.[1] Concern for humanization leads at once to the recognition of dehumanization, not only as an ontological possibility but as an historical reality. And as an individual perceives the extent of dehumanization, he or she may ask if humanization is a viable possibility. Within history, in concrete, objective contexts, both humanization and dehumanization are possibilities for a person as an uncompleted being conscious of their incompletion.

But while both humanization and dehumanization are real alternatives, only the first is the people's vocation. This vocation is constantly negated, yet it is affirmed by that very negation. It is

---

1. The current movements of rebellion, especially those of youth, while they necessarily reflect the peculiarities of their respective settings, manifest in their essence this preoccupation with people as beings in the world and with the world—preoccupation with *what* and *how* they are "being." As they place consumer civilization in judgment, denounce bureaucracies of all types, demand the transformation of the universities (changing the rigid nature of the teacher-student relationship and placing that relationship within the context of reality), propose the transformation of reality itself so that universities can be renewed, attack old orders and established institutions in the attempt to affirm human beings as the Subjects of decision, all these movements reflect the style of our age, which is more anthropological than anthropocentric.

44 · PAULO FREIRE

thwarted by injustice, exploitation, oppression, and the violence of the oppressors; it is affirmed by the yearning of the oppressed for freedom and justice, and by their struggle to recover their lost humanity.

Dehumanization, which marks not only those whose humanity has been stolen, but also (though in a different way) those who have stolen it, is a *distortion* of the vocation of becoming more fully human. This distortion occurs within history; but it is not an historical vocation. Indeed, to admit of dehumanization as an historical vocation would lead either to cynicism or total despair. The struggle for humanization, for the emancipation of labor, for the overcoming of alienation, for the affirmation of men and women as persons would be meaningless. This struggle is possible only because dehumanization, although a concrete historical fact, is *not* a given destiny but the result of an unjust order that engenders violence in the oppressors, which in turn dehumanizes the oppressed.

Because it is a distortion of being more fully human, sooner or later being less human leads the oppressed to struggle against those who made them so. In order for this struggle to have meaning, the oppressed must not, in seeking to regain their humanity (which is a way to create it), become in turn oppressors of the oppressors, but rather restorers of the humanity of both.

This, then, is the great humanistic and historical task of the oppressed: to liberate themselves and their oppressors as well. The oppressors, who oppress, exploit, and rape by virtue of their power, cannot find in this power the strength to liberate either the oppressed or themselves. Only power that springs from the weakness of the oppressed will be sufficiently strong to free both. Any attempt to "soften" the power of the oppressor in deference to the weakness of the oppressed almost always manifests itself in the form of false generosity; indeed, the attempt never goes beyond this. In order to have the continued opportunity to express their "generosity," the oppressors must perpetuate injustice as well. An unjust social order is the permanent fount of this "generosity," which is nourished by death, despair, and poverty. That is why the dispensers of false generosity become desperate at the slightest threat to its source.

True generosity consists precisely in fighting to destroy the causes which nourish false charity. False charity constrains the fearful and subdued, the "rejects of life," to extend their trembling hands. True generosity lies in striving so that these hands—whether of individuals or entire peoples—need be extended less and less in supplication, so that more and more they become human hands which work and, working, transform the world.

This lesson and this apprenticeship must come, however, from the oppressed themselves and from those who are truly solidary with them. As individuals or as peoples, by fighting for the restoration of their humanity they will be attempting the restoration of true generosity. Who are better prepared than the oppressed to understand the terrible significance of an oppressive society? Who suffer the effects of oppression more than the oppressed? Who can better understand the necessity of liberation? They will not gain this liberation by chance but through the praxis of their quest for it, through their recognition of the necessity to fight for it. And this fight, because of the purpose given it by the oppressed, will actually constitute an act of love opposing the lovelessness which lies at the heart of the oppressors' violence, lovelessness even when clothed in false generosity.

But almost always, during the initial stage of the struggle, the oppressed, instead of striving for liberation, tend themselves to become oppressors, or "sub-oppressors." The very structure of their thought has been conditioned by the contradictions of the concrete, existential situation by which they were shaped. Their ideal is to be men; but for them, to be men is to be oppressors. This is their model of humanity. This phenomenon derives from the fact that the oppressed, at a certain moment of their existential experience, adopt an attitude of "adhesion" to the oppressor. Under these circumstances they cannot "consider" him sufficiently clearly to objectivize him—to discover him "outside" themselves. This does not necessarily mean that the oppressed are unaware that they are downtrodden. But their perception of themselves as oppressed is impaired by their submersion in the reality of oppression. At this level, their perception of themselves as opposites of the oppressor does not yet

46 · PAULO FREIRE

signify engagement in a struggle to overcome the contradiction;[2] the one pole aspires not to liberation, but to identification with its opposite pole.

In this situation the oppressed do not see the "new man" as the person to be born from the resolution of this contradiction, as oppression gives way to liberation. For them, the new man or woman themselves become oppressors. Their vision of the new man or woman is individualistic; because of their identification with the oppressor, they have no consciousness of themselves as persons or as members of an oppressed class. It is not to become free that they want agrarian reform, but in order to acquire land and thus become landowners—or, more precisely, bosses over other workers. It is a rare peasant who, once "promoted" to overseer, does not become more of a tyrant towards his former comrades than the owner himself. This is because the context of the peasant's situation, that is, oppression, remains unchanged. In this example, the overseer, in order to make sure of his job, must be as tough as the owner—and more so. Thus is illustrated our previous assertion that during the initial stage of their struggle the oppressed find in the oppressor their model of "manhood."

Even revolution, which transforms a concrete situation of oppression by establishing the process of liberation, must confront this phenomenon. Many of the oppressed who directly or indirectly participate in revolution intend—conditioned by the myths of the old order—to make it their private revolution. The shadow of their former oppressor is still cast over them.

The "fear of freedom" which afflicts the oppressed,[3] a fear which may equally well lead them to desire the role of oppressor or bind them to the role of oppressed, should be examined. One of the basic elements of the relationship between oppressor and oppressed is

---

2. As used throughout this book, the term "contradiction" denotes the dialectical conflict between opposing social forces.—Translator's note.

3. This fear of freedom is also to be found in the oppressors, though, obviously, in a different form. The oppressed are afraid to embrace freedom; the oppressors are afraid of losing the "freedom" to oppress.

prescription. Every prescription represents the imposition of one individual's choice upon another, transforming the consciousness of the person prescribed to into one that conforms with the prescriber's consciousness. Thus, the behavior of the oppressed is a prescribed behavior, following as it does the guidelines of the oppressor.

The oppressed, having internalized the image of the oppressor and adopted his guidelines, are fearful of freedom. Freedom would require them to eject this image and replace it with autonomy and responsibility. Freedom is acquired by conquest, not by gift. It must be pursued constantly and responsibly. Freedom is not an ideal located outside of man; nor is it an idea which becomes myth. It is rather the indispensable condition for the quest for human completion.

To surmount the situation of oppression, people must first critically recognize its causes, so that through transforming action they can create a new situation, one which makes possible the pursuit of a fuller humanity. But the struggle to be more fully human has already begun in the authentic struggle to transform the situation. Although the situation of oppression is a dehumanized and dehumanizing totality affecting both the oppressors and those whom they oppress, it is the latter who must, from their stifled humanity, wage for both the struggle for a fuller humanity; the oppressor, who is himself dehumanized because he dehumanizes others, is unable to lead this struggle.

However, the oppressed, who have adapted to the structure of domination in which they are immersed, and have become resigned to it, are inhibited from waging the struggle for freedom so long as they feel incapable of running the risks it requires. Moreover, their struggle for freedom threatens not only the oppressor, but also their own oppressed comrades who are fearful of still greater repression. When they discover within themselves the yearning to be free, they perceive that this yearning can be transformed into reality only when the same yearning is aroused in their comrades. But while dominated by the fear of freedom they refuse to appeal to others,

48 · PAULO FREIRE

or to listen to the appeals of others, or even to the appeals of their own conscience. They prefer gregariousness to authentic comradeship; they prefer the security of conformity with their state of unfreedom to the creative communion produced by freedom and even the very pursuit of freedom.

The oppressed suffer from the duality which has established itself in their innermost being. They discover that without freedom they cannot exist authentically. Yet, although they desire authentic existence, they fear it. They are at one and the same time themselves and the oppressor whose consciousness they have internalized. The conflict lies in the choice between being wholly themselves or being divided; between ejecting the oppressor within or not ejecting them; between human solidarity or alienation; between following prescriptions or having choices; between being spectators or actors; between acting or having the illusion of acting through the action of the oppressors; between speaking out or being silent, castrated in their power to create and re-create, in their power to transform the world. This is the tragic dilemma of the oppressed which their education must take into account.

This book will present some aspects of what the writer has termed the pedagogy of the oppressed, a pedagogy which must be forged *with*, not *for*, the oppressed (whether individuals or peoples) in the incessant struggle to regain their humanity. This pedagogy makes oppression and its causes objects of reflection by the oppressed, and from that reflection will come their necessary engagement in the struggle for their liberation. And in the struggle this pedagogy will be made and remade.

The central problem is this: How can the oppressed, as divided, unauthentic beings, participate in developing the pedagogy of their liberation? Only as they discover themselves to be "hosts" of the oppressor can they contribute to the midwifery of their liberating pedagogy. As long as they live in the duality in which *to be is to be like*, and *to be like* is *to be like the oppressor*, this contribution is impossible. The pedagogy of the oppressed is an instrument for their critical discovery that both they and their oppressors are manifestations of dehumanization.

PEDAGOGY OF THE OPPRESSED · 49

Liberation is thus a childbirth, and a painful one. The man or woman who emerges is a new person, viable only as the oppressor-oppressed contradiction is superseded by the humanization of all people. Or to put it another way, the solution of this contradiction is born in the labor which brings into the world this new being: no longer oppressor nor longer oppressed, but human in the process of achieving freedom.

This solution cannot be achieved in idealistic terms. In order for the oppressed to be able to wage the struggle for their liberation, they must perceive the reality of oppression not as a closed world from which there is no exit, but as a limiting situation which they can transform. This perception is a necessary but not a sufficient condition for liberation; it must become the motivating force for liberating action. Nor does the discovery by the oppressed that they exist in dialectical relationship to the oppressor, as his antithesis—that without them the oppressor could not exist[4]—in itself constitute liberation. The oppressed can overcome the contradiction in which they are caught only when this perception enlists them in the struggle to free themselves.

The same is true with respect to the individual oppressor as a person. Discovering himself to be an oppressor may cause considerable anguish, but it does not necessarily lead to solidarity with the oppressed. Rationalizing his guilt through paternalistic treatment of the oppressed, all the while holding them fast in a position of dependence, will not do. Solidarity requires that one enter into the situation of those with whom one is solidary; it is a radical posture. If what characterizes the oppressed is their subordination to the consciousness of the master, as Hegel affirms,[5] true solidarity with the oppressed means fighting at their side to transform the objective reality which has made them these "beings for another." The oppres-

---

4. See Hegel, *op. cit.*, pp. 236–237.
5. Analyzing the dialectical relationship between the consciousness of the master and the consciousness of the oppressed, Hegel states: "The one is independent, and its essential nature is to be for itself; the other is dependent, and its essence is life or existence for another. The former is the Master, or Lord, the latter the Bondsman." *Ibid.*, p. 234.

50 · PAULO FREIRE

sor is solidary with the oppressed only when he stops regarding the oppressed as an abstract category and sees them as persons who have been unjustly dealt with, deprived of their voice, cheated in the sale of their labor—when he stops making pious, sentimental, and individualistic gestures and risks an act of love. True solidarity is found only in the plenitude of this act of love, in its existentiality, in its praxis. To affirm that men and women are persons and as persons should be free, and yet to do nothing tangible to make this affirmation a reality, is a farce.

Since it is a concrete situation that the oppressor-oppressed contradiction is established, the resolution of this contradiction must be *objectively* verifiable. Hence, the radical requirement—both for the individual who discovers himself or herself to be an oppressor and for the oppressed—that the concrete situation which begets oppression must be transformed.

To present this radical demand for the objective transformation of reality, to combat subjectivist immobility which would divert the recognition of oppression into patient waiting for oppression to disappear by itself, is not to dismiss the role of subjectivity in the struggle to change structures. On the contrary, one cannot conceive of objectivity without subjectivity. Neither can exist without the other, nor can they be dichotomized. The separation of objectivity from subjectivity, the denial of the latter when analyzing reality or acting upon it, is objectivism. On the other hand, the denial of objectivity in analysis or action, resulting in a subjectivism which leads to solipsistic positions, denies action itself by denying objective reality. Neither objectivism nor subjectivism, nor yet psychologism is propounded here, but rather subjectivity and objectivity in constant dialectical relationship.

To deny the importance of subjectivity in the process of transforming the world and history is naïve and simplistic. It is to admit the impossible: a world without people. This objectivistic position is as ingenuous as that of subjectivism, which postulates people without a world. World and human beings do not exist apart from each other, they exist in constant interaction. Marx does not espouse such a dichotomy, nor does any other critical, realistic thinker. What Marx criticized and scientifically destroyed was not subjectivity, but subjectivism and psychologism. Just as objective social reality exists not by chance, but as the product of human action, so it is not transformed by chance. If humankind produce social reality (which in the "inversion of the praxis" turns back upon them and conditions them), then transforming that reality is an historical task, a task for humanity.

Reality which becomes oppressive results in the contradistinction of men as oppressors and oppressed. The latter, whose task it is to struggle for their liberation together with those who show true solidarity, must acquire a critical awareness of oppression through the praxis of this struggle. One of the gravest obstacles to the achievement of liberation is that oppressive reality absorbs those within it and thereby acts to submerge human beings' consiousness.[6] Functionally, oppression is domesticating. To no longer be prey to its force, one must emerge from it and turn upon it. This can be done only by means of the praxis: reflection and action upon the world in order to transform it.

> Hay que hacer al opresión real todavía mas opresiva añadiendo a aquella la *conciéncia* de la opresión haciendo la infamia todavía mas infamante, al pregonarla.[7]

Making "real oppression more oppressive still by adding to it the realization of oppression" corresponds to the dialectical relation between the subjective and the objective. Only in this interdependence is an authentic praxis possible, without which it is impossible

---

6. "Liberating action necessarily involves a moment of perception and volition. This action both precedes and follows that moment, to which it first acts as a prologue and which it subsequently serves to effect and continue within history. The action of domination, however, does not necessarily imply this dimension; for the structure of domination is maintained by its own mechanical and unconscious functionality." From an unpublished work by José Luiz Fiori, who has kindly granted permission to quote him.

7. Karl Marx and Friedrich Engels, *La Sagrada Familia y otros Escritos* (Mexico, 1962), p. 6. Emphasis added.

52 · PAULO FREIRE

to resolve the oppressor-oppressed contradiction. To achieve this goal, the oppressed must confront reality critically, simultaneously objectifying and acting upon that reality. A mere perception of reality not followed by this critical intervention will not lead to a transformation of objective reality—precisely because it is not a true perception. This is the case of a purely subjectivist perception by someone who forsakes objective reality and creates a false substitute.

A different type of false perception occurs when a change in objective reality would threaten the individual or class interests of the perceiver. In the first instance, there is no critical intervention in reality because that reality is fictitious; there is none in the second instance because intervention would contradict the class interests of the perceiver. In the latter case the tendency of the perceiver is to behave "neurotically." The fact exists; but both the fact and what may result from it may be prejudicial to the person. Thus it becomes necessary, not precisely to deny the fact, but to "see it differently." This rationalization as a defense mechanism coincides in the end with subjectivism. A fact which is not denied but whose truths are rationalized loses its objective base. It ceases to be concrete and becomes a myth created in defense of the class of the perceiver.

Herein lies one of the reasons for the prohibitions and the difficulties (to be discussed at length in Chapter 4) designed to dissuade the people from critical intervention in reality. The oppressor knows full well that this intervention would not be to his interest. What *is* to his interest is for the people to continue in a state of submersion, impotent in the face of oppressive reality. Of relevance here is Lukács' warning to the revolutionary party:

> ... il doit, pour employer les mots de Marx, expliquer aux masses leur propre action non seulement afin d'assurer la continuité des expériences révolutionnaires du prolétariat, mais aussi d'activer consciemment le développement ultérieur de ces expériences.[8]

In affirming this necessity, Lukács is unquestionably posing the

---

8. Georg Lukács, *Lénine* (Paris, 1965), p. 62.

problem of critical intervention. "To explain to the masses their own action" is to clarify and illuminate that action, both regarding its relationship to the objective facts by which it was prompted, and regarding its purposes. The more the people unveil this challenging reality which is to be the object of their transforming action, the more critically they enter that reality. In this way they are "consciously activating the subsequent development of their experiences." There would be no human action if there were no objective reality, no world to be the "not I" of the person and to challenge them; just as there would be no human action if humankind were not a "project," if he or she were not able to transcend himself or herself, if one were not able to perceive reality and understand it in order to transform it.

In dialectical thought, world and action are intimately interdependent. But action is human only when it is not merely an occupation but also a preoccupation, that is, when it is not dichotomized from reflection. Reflection, which is essential to action, is implicit in Lukács' requirement of "explaining to the masses their own action," just as it is implicit in the purpose he attributes to this explanation: that of "consciously activating the subsequent development of experience."

For us, however, the requirement is seen not in terms of explaining to, but rather dialoguing with the people about their actions. In any event, no reality transforms itself,[9] and the duty which Lukács ascribes to the revolutionary party of "explaining to the masses their own action" coincides with our affirmation of the need for the critical intervention of the people in reality through the praxis. The pedagogy of the oppressed, which is the pedagogy of people engaged in the fight for their own liberation, has its roots here. And those who recognize, or begin to recognize, themselves

---

9. "The materialist doctrine that men are products of circumstances and upbringing, and that, therefore, changed men are products of other circumstances and changed upbringing, forgets that it is men that change circumstances and that the educator himself needs educating." Karl Marx and Friedrich Engels, *Selected Works* (New York, 1968), p. 28.

54 · PAULO FREIRE

as oppressed must be among the developers of this pedagogy. No pedagogy which is truly liberating can remain distant from the oppressed by treating them as unfortunates and by presenting for their emulation models from among the oppressors. The oppressed must be their own example in the struggle for their redemption.

The pedagogy of the oppressed, animated by authentic, humanist (not humanitarian) generosity, presents itself as a pedagogy of humankind. Pedagogy which begins with the egoistic interests of the oppressors (an egoism cloaked in the false generosity of paternalism) and makes of the oppressed the objects of its humanitarianism, itself maintains and embodies oppression. It is an instrument of dehumanization. This is why, as we affirmed earlier, the pedagogy of the oppressed cannot be developed or practiced by the oppressors. It would be a contradiction in terms if the oppressors not only defended but actually implemented a liberating education.

But if the implementation of a liberating education requires political power and the oppressed have none, how then is it possible to carry out the pedagogy of the oppressed prior to the revolution? This is a question of the greatest importance, the reply to which is at least tentatively outlined in Chapter 4. One aspect of the reply is to be found in the distinction between *systematic education*, which can only be changed by political power, and *educational projects*, which should be carried out *with* the oppressed in the process of organizing them.

The pedagogy of the oppressed, as a humanist and libertarian pedagogy, has two distinct stages. In the first, the oppressed unveil the world of oppression and through the praxis commit themselves to its transformation. In the second stage, in which the reality of oppression has already been transformed, this pedagogy ceases to belong to the oppressed and becomes a pedagogy of all people in the process of permanent liberation. In both stages, it is always through action in depth that the culture of domination is culturally confronted.[10] In the first stage this confrontation occurs through the

---

10. This appears to be the fundamental aspect of Mao's Cultural Revolution.

change in the way the oppressed perceive the world of oppression; in the second stage, through the expulsion of the myths created and developed in the old order, which like specters haunt the new structure emerging from the revolutionary transformation.

The pedagogy of the first stage must deal with the problem of the oppressed consciousness and the oppressor consciousness, the problem of men and women who oppress and men and women who suffer oppression. It must take into account their behavior, their view of the world, and their ethics. A particular problem is the duality of the oppressed: they are contradictory, divided beings, shaped by and existing in a concrete situation of oppression and violence.

Any situation in which "A" objectively exploits "B" or hinders his and her pursuit of self-affirmation as a responsible person is one of oppression. Such a situation in itself constitutes violence, even when sweetened by false generosity, because it interferes with the individual's ontological and historical vocation to be more fully human. With the establishment of a relationship of oppression, violence has *already* begun. Never in history has violence been initiated by the oppressed. How could they be the initiators, if they themselves are the result of violence? How could they be the sponsors of something whose objective inauguration called forth their existence as oppressed? There would be no oppressed had there been no prior situation of violence to establish their subjugation.

Violence is initiated by those who oppress, who exploit, who fail to recognize others as persons—not by those who are oppressed, exploited, and unrecognized. It is not the unloved who initiate disaffection, but those who cannot love because they love only themselves. It is not the helpless, subject to terror, who initiate terror, but the violent, who with their power create the concrete situation which begets the "rejects of life." It is not the tyrannized who initiate despotism, but the tyrants. It is not the despised who initiate hatred, but those who despise. It is not those whose humanity is denied them who negate humankind, but those who denied that humanity (thus negating their own as well). Force is used not by those who

56 · PAULO FREIRE

have become weak under the preponderance of the strong, but by the strong who have emasculated them.

For the oppressors, however, it is always the oppressed (whom they obviously never call "the oppressed" but—depending on whether they are fellow countrymen or not—"those people" or "the blind and envious masses" or "savages" or "natives" or "subversives") who are disaffected, who are "violent," "barbaric," "wicked," or "ferocious" when they react to the violence of the oppressors.

Yet it is—paradoxical though it may seem—precisely in the response of the oppressed to the violence of their oppressors that a gesture of love may be found. Consciously or unconsciously, the act of rebellion by the oppressed (an act which is always, or nearly always, as violent as the initial violence of the oppressors) can initiate love. Whereas the violence of the oppressors prevents the oppressed from being fully human, the response of the latter to this violence is grounded in the desire to pursue the right to be human. As the oppressors dehumanize others and violate their rights, they themselves also become dehumanized. As the oppressed, fighting to be human, take away the oppressors' power to dominate and suppress, they restore to the oppressors the humanity they had lost in the exercise of oppression.

It is only the oppressed who, by freeing themselves, can free their oppressors. The latter, as an oppressive class, can free neither others nor themselves. It is therefore essential that the oppressed wage the struggle to resolve the contradiction in which they are caught; and the contradiction will be resolved by the appearance of the new man: neither oppressor nor oppressed, but man in the process of liberation. If the goal of the oppressed is to become fully human, they will not achieve their goal by merely reversing the terms of the contradiction, by simply changing poles.

This may seem simplistic; it is not. Resolution of the oppressor-oppressed contradiction indeed implies the disappearance of the oppressors as a dominant class. However, the restraints imposed by the former oppressed on their oppressors, so that the latter cannot reassume their former position, do not constitute *oppression*. An act is oppressive only when it prevents people from being more fully human. Accordingly, these necessary restraints do not *in themselves* signify that yesterday's oppressed have become today's oppressors. Acts which prevent the restoration of the oppressive regime cannot be compared with those which create and maintain it, cannot be compared with those by which a few men and women deny the majority their right to be human.

However, the moment the new regime hardens into a dominating "bureaucracy"[11] the humanist dimension of the struggle is lost and it is no longer possible to speak of liberation. Hence our insistence that the authentic solution of the oppressor-oppressed contradiction does not lie in a mere reversal of position, in moving from one pole to the other. Nor does it lie in the replacement of the former oppressors with new ones who continue to subjugate the oppressed—all in the name of their liberation.

But even when the contradiction is resolved authentically by a new situation established by the liberated laborers, the former oppressors do not feel liberated. On the contrary, they genuinely consider themselves to be oppressed. Conditioned by the experience of oppressing others, any situation other than their former seems to them like oppression. Formerly, they could eat, dress, wear shoes, be educated, travel, and hear Beethoven; while millions did not eat, had no clothes or shoes, neither studied nor traveled, much less listened to Beethoven. Any restriction on this way of life, in the name of the rights of the community, appears to the former oppressors as a profound violation of their individual rights—although they had no respect for the millions who suffered and died of hunger, pain, sorrow, and despair. For the oppressors, "human beings" refers only to themselves; other people are "things." For the oppressors, there exists only one right: their right to live in peace, over against

---

11. This rigidity should not be identified with the restraints that must be imposed on the former oppressors so they cannot restore the oppressive order. Rather, it refers to the revolution which becomes stagnant and turns against the people using the old repressive, bureaucratic State apparatus (which should have been drastically suppressed, as Marx so often emphasized).

58 · PAULO FREIRE

the right, not always even recognized, but simply conceded, of the oppressed to survival. And they make this concession only because the existence of the oppressed is necessary to their own existence.

This behavior, this way of understanding the world and people (which necessarily makes the oppressors resist the installation of a new regime) is explained by their experience as a dominant class. Once a situation of violence and oppression has been established, it engenders an entire way of life and behavior for those caught up in it—oppressors and oppressed alike. Both are submerged in this situation, and both bear the marks of oppression. Analysis of existential situations of oppression reveals that their inception lay in an act of violence—initiated by those with power. This violence, as a process, is perpetuated from generation to generation of oppressors, who become its heirs and are shaped in its climate. This climate creates in the oppressor a strongly possessive consciousness—possessive of the world and of men and women. Apart from direct, concrete, material possession of the world and of people, the oppressor consciousness could not understand itself—could not even exist. Fromm said of this consciousness that, without such possession, "it would lose contact with the world." The oppressor consciousness tends to transform everything surrounding it into an object of its domination. The earth, property, production, the creations of people, people themselves, time—everything is reduced to the status of objects at its disposal.

In their unrestrained eagerness to possess, the oppressors develop the conviction that it is possible for them to transform everything into objects of their purchasing power; hence their strictly materialistic concept of existence. Money is the measure of all things, and profit the primary goal. For the oppressors, what is worthwhile is to have more—always more—even at the cost of the oppressed having less or having nothing. For them, *to be is to have* and to be the class of the "haves."

As beneficiaries of a situation of oppression, the oppressors cannot perceive that if *having* is a condition of *being*, it is a necessary condition for all women and men. This is why their generosity is false. Humanity is a "thing," and they possess it as an exclusive right, as inherited property. To the oppressor consciousness, the humanization of the "others," of the people, appears not as the pursuit of full humanity, but as subversion.

The oppressors do not perceive their monopoly on *having more* as a privilege which dehumanizes others and themselves. They cannot see that, in the egoistic pursuit of *having* as a possessing class, they suffocate in their own possessions and no longer *are;* they merely *have*. For them, *having more* is an inalienable right, a right they acquired through their own "effort," with their "courage to take risks." If others do not have more, it is because they are incompetent and lazy, and worst of all is their unjustifiable ingratitude towards the "generous gestures" of the dominant class. Precisely because they are "ungrateful" and "envious," the oppressed are regarded as potential enemies who must be watched.

It could not be otherwise. If the humanization of the oppressed signifies subversion, so also does their freedom; hence the necessity for constant control. And the more the oppressors control the oppressed, the more they change them into apparently inanimate "things." This tendency of the oppressor consciousness to "in-animate" everything and everyone it encounters, in its eagerness to possess, unquestionably corresponds with a tendency to sadism.

> The pleasure in complete domination over another person (or other animate creature) is the very essence of the sadistic drive. Another way of formulating the same thought is to say that the aim of sadism is to transform a man into a thing, something animate into something inanimate, since by complete and absolute control the living loses one essential quality of life—freedom.[12]

Sadistic love is a perverted love—a love of death, not of life. One of the characteristics of the oppressor consciousness and its necrophilic view of the world is thus sadism. As the oppressor consciousness,

---

12. Erich Fromm, *The Heart of Man* (New York, 1966), p. 32.

60 · PAULO FREIRE

in order to dominate, tries to deter the drive to search, the restlessness, and the creative power which characterize life, it kills life. More and more, the oppressors are using science and technology as unquestionably powerful instruments for their purpose: the maintenance of the oppressive order through manipulation and repression.[13] The oppressed, as objects, as "things," have no purposes except those their oppressors prescribe for them.

Given the preceding context, another issue of indubitable importance arises: the fact that certain members of the oppressor class join the oppressed in their struggle for liberation, thus moving from one pole of the contradiction to the other. Theirs is a fundamental role, and has been so throughout the history of this struggle. It happens, however, that as they cease to be exploiters or indifferent spectators or simply the heirs of exploitation and move to the side of the exploited, they almost always bring with them the marks of their origin: their prejudices and their deformations, which include a lack of confidence in the people's ability to think, to want, and to know. Accordingly, these adherents to the people's cause constantly run the risk of falling into a type of generosity as malefic as that of the oppressors. The generosity of the oppressors is nourished by an unjust order, which must be maintained in order to justify that generosity. Our converts, on the other hand, truly desire to transform the unjust order; but because of their background they believe that they must be the executors of the transformation. They talk about the people, but they do not trust them; and trusting the people is the indispensable precondition for revolutionary change. A real humanist can be identified more by his trust in the people, which engages him in their struggle, than by a thousand actions in their favor without that trust.

Those who authentically commit themselves to the people must re-examine themselves constantly. This conversion is so radical as not to allow of ambiguous behavior. To affirm this commitment but to consider oneself the proprietor of revolutionary wisdom—which

---

13. Regarding the "dominant forms of social control," see Herbert Marcuse, *One-Dimensional Man* (Boston, 1964) and *Eros and Civilization* (Boston, 1955).

must then be given to (or imposed on) the people—is to retain the old ways. The man or woman who proclaims devotion to the cause of liberation yet is unable to enter into *communion* with the people, whom he or she continues to regard as totally ignorant, is grievously self-deceived. The convert who approaches the people but feels alarm at each step they take, each doubt they express, and each suggestion they offer, and attempts to impose his "status," remains nostalgic towards his origins.

Conversion to the people requires a profound rebirth. Those who undergo it must take on a new form of existence; they can no longer remain as they were. Only through comradeship with the oppressed can the converts understand their characteristic ways of living and behaving, which in diverse moments reflect the structure of domination. One of these characteristics is the previously mentioned existential duality of the oppressed, who are at the same time themselves and the oppressor whose image they have internalized. Accordingly, until they concretely "discover" their oppressor and in turn their own consciousness, they nearly always express fatalistic attitudes towards their situation.

> The peasant begins to get courage to overcome his dependence when he realizes that he is dependent. Until then, he goes along with the boss and says "What can I do? I'm only a peasant."[14]

When superficially analyzed, this fatalism is sometimes interpreted as a docility that is a trait of national character. Fatalism in the guise of docility is the fruit of an historical and sociological situation, not an essential characteristic of a people's behavior. It almost always is related to the power of destiny or fate or fortune—inevitable forces—or to a distorted view of God. Under the sway of magic and myth, the oppressed (especially the peasants, who are almost submerged in nature)[15] see their suffering, the fruit of exploitation,

---

14. Words of a peasant during an interview with the author.
15. See Candido Mendes, *Memento dos vivos—A Esquerda católica no Brasil* (Rio, 1966).

62 · PAULO FREIRE

as the will of God—as if God were the creator of this "organized disorder."

Submerged in reality, the oppressed cannot perceive clearly the "order" which serves the interests of the oppressors whose image they have internalized. Chafing under the restrictions of this order, they often manifest a type of horizontal violence, striking out at their own comrades for the pettiest reasons.

> The colonized man will first manifest this aggressiveness which has been deposited in his bones against his own people. This is the period when the niggers beat each other up, and the police and magistrates do not know which way to turn when faced with the astonishing waves of crime in North Africa. . . . While the settler or the policeman has the right the livelong day to strike the native, to insult him and to make him crawl to them, you will see the native reaching for his knife at the slightest hostile or aggressive glance cast on him by another native; for the last resort of the native is to defend his personality vis-à-vis his brother.[16]

It is possible that in this behavior they are once more manifesting their duality. Because the oppressor exists within their oppressed comrades, when they attack those comrades they are indirectly attacking the oppressor as well.

On the other hand, at a certain point in their existential experience the oppressed feel an irresistible attraction towards the oppressors and their way of life. Sharing this way of life becomes an overpowering aspiration. In their alienation, the oppressed want at any cost to resemble the oppressors, to imitate them, to follow them. This phenomenon is especially prevalent in the middle-class oppressed, who yearn to be equal to the "eminent" men and women of the upper class. Albert Memmi, in an exceptional analysis of the "colonized mentality," refers to the contempt he felt towards the colonizer, mixed with "passionate" attraction towards him.

---

16. Frantz Fanon, *The Wretched of the Earth* (New York, 1968), p. 52.

> How could the colonizer look after his workers while periodically gunning down a crowd of colonized? How could the colonized deny himself so cruelly yet make such excessive demands? How could he hate the colonizers and yet admire them so passionately? (I too felt this admiration in spite of myself.)[17]

Self-depreciation is another characteristic of the oppressed, which derives from their internalization of the opinion the oppressors hold of them. So often do they hear that they are good for nothing, know nothing and are incapable of learning anything—that they are sick, lazy, and unproductive—that in the end they become convinced of their own unfitness.

> The peasant feels inferior to the boss because the boss seems to be the only one who knows things and is able to run things.[18]

They call themselves ignorant and say the "professor" is the one who has knowledge and to whom they should listen. The criteria of knowledge imposed upon them are the conventional ones. "Why don't you," said a peasant participating in a culture circle,[19] "explain the pictures first? That way it'll take less time and won't give us a headache."

Almost never do they realize that they, too, "know things" they have learned in their relations with the world and with other women and men. Given the circumstances which have produced their duality, it is only natural that they distrust themselves.

Not infrequently, peasants in educational projects begin to discuss a generative theme in a lively manner, then stop suddenly and say to the educator: "Excuse us, we ought to keep quiet and let you talk. You are the one who knows, we don't know anything." They often insist that there is no difference between them and the animals; when they do admit a difference, it favors the animals. "They are freer than we are."

---

17. *The Colonizer and the Colonized* (Boston, 1967), p. x.
18. Words of a peasant during an interview with the author.
19. See chapter 3, p. 113 ff.—Translator's note.

64 · PAULO FREIRE

It is striking, however, to observe how this self-depreciation changes with the first changes in the situation of oppression. I heard a peasant leader say in an *asentamiento*[20] meeting, "They used to say we were unproductive because we were lazy and drunkards. All lies. Now that we are respected as men, we're going to show everyone that we were never drunkards or lazy. We were exploited!"

As long as their ambiguity persists, the oppressed are reluctant to resist, and totally lack confidence in themselves. They have a diffuse, magical belief in the invulnerability and power of the oppressor.[21] The magical force of the landowner's power holds particular sway in the rural areas. A sociologist friend of mine tells of a group of armed peasants in a Latin American country who recently took over a latifundium. For tactical reasons, they planned to hold the landowner as a hostage. But not one peasant had the courage to guard him; his very presence was terrifying. It is also possible that the act of opposing the boss provoked guilt feelings. In truth, the boss was "inside" them.

The oppressed must see examples of the vulnerability of the oppressor so that a contrary conviction can begin to grow within them. Until this occurs, they will continue disheartened, fearful, and beaten.[22] As long as the oppressed remain unaware of the causes of their condition, they fatalistically "accept" their exploitation. Further, they are apt to react in a passive and alienated manner when confronted with the necessity to struggle for their freedom and self-affirmation. Little by little, however, they tend to try out forms of rebellious action. In working towards liberation, one must neither lose sight of this passivity nor overlook the moment of awakening.

Within their unauthentic view of the world and of themselves, the oppressed feel like "things" owned by the oppressor. For the latter, *to be* is *to have*, almost always at the expense of those who have

---

20. *Asentamiento* refers to a production unit of the Chilean agrarian reform experiment.—Translator's note.
21. "The peasant has an almost instinctive fear of the boss." Interview with a peasant.
22. See Regis Debray, *Revolution in the Revolution?* (New York, 1967).

nothing. For the oppressed, at a certain point in their existential experience, *to be* is not to resemble the oppressor, but *to be under him*, to depend on him. Accordingly, the oppressed are emotionally dependent.

> The peasant is a dependent. He can't say what he wants. Before he discovers his dependence, he suffers. He lets off steam at home, where he shouts at his children, beats them, and despairs. He complains about his wife and thinks everything is dreadful. He doesn't let off steam with the boss because he thinks the boss is a superior being. Lots of times, the peasant gives vent to his sorrows by drinking.[23]

This total emotional dependence can lead the oppressed to what Fromm calls necrophilic behavior: the destruction of life—their own or that of their oppressed fellows.

It is only when the oppressed find the oppressor out and become involved in the organized struggle for their liberation that they begin to believe in themselves. This discovery cannot be purely intellectual but must involve action; nor can it be limited to mere activism, but must include serious reflection: only then will it be a praxis.

Critical and liberating dialogue, which presupposes action, must be carried on with the oppressed at whatever the stage of their struggle for liberation.[24] The content of that dialogue can and should vary in accordance with historical conditions and the level at which the oppressed perceive reality. But to substitute monologue, slogans, and communiqués for dialogue is to attempt to liberate the oppressed with the instruments of domestication. Attempting to liberate the oppressed without their reflective participation in the act of liberation is to treat them as objects which must be saved from a burning building; it is to lead them into the populist pitfall and transform them into masses which can be manipulated.

At all stages of their liberation, the oppressed must see them-

---

23. Interview with a peasant.
24. Not in the open, of course; that would only provoke the fury of the oppressor and lead to still greater repression.

66 · PAULO FREIRE

selves as women and men engaged in the ontological and historical vocation of becoming more fully human. Reflection and action become imperative when one does not erroneously attempt to dichotomize the content of humanity from its historical forms.

The insistence that the oppressed engage in reflection on their concrete situation is not a call to armchair revolution. On the contrary, reflection—true reflection—leads to action. On the other hand, when the situation calls for action, that action will constitute an authentic praxis only if its consequences become the object of critical reflection. In this sense, the praxis is the new *raison d'être* of the oppressed; and the revolution, which inaugurates the historical moment of this *raison d'être*, is not viable apart from their concomitant conscious involvement. Otherwise, action is pure activism.

To achieve this praxis, however, it is necessary to trust in the oppressed and in their ability to reason. Whoever lacks this trust will fail to initiate (or will abandon) dialogue, reflection, and communication, and will fall into using slogans, communiqués, monologues, and instructions. Superficial conversions to the cause of liberation carry this danger.

Political action on the side of the oppressed must be pedagogical action in the authentic sense of the word, and, therefore, action *with* the oppressed. Those who work for liberation must not take advantage of the emotional dependence of the oppressed—dependence that is the fruit of the concrete situation of domination which surrounds them and which engendered their unauthentic view of the world. Using their dependence to create still greater dependence is an oppressor tactic.

Libertarian action must recognize this dependence as a weak point and must attempt through reflection and action to transform it into independence. However, not even the best-intentioned leadership can bestow independence as a gift. The liberation of the oppressed is a liberation of women and men, not things. Accordingly, while no one liberates himself by his own efforts alone, neither is he liberated by others. Liberation, a human phenomenon, cannot be achieved by semihumans. Any attempt to treat people as semihumans only dehumanizes them. When people are already dehumanized, due to the oppression they suffer, the process of their liberation must not employ the methods of dehumanization.

The correct method for a revolutionary leadership to employ in the task of liberation is, therefore, *not* "libertarian propaganda." Nor can the leadership merely "implant" in the oppressed a belief in freedom, thus thinking to win their trust. The correct method lies in dialogue. The conviction of the oppressed that they must fight for their liberation is not a gift bestowed by the revolutionary leadership, but the result of their own *conscientização.*

The revolutionary leaders must realize that their own conviction of the necessity for struggle (an indispensable dimension of revolutionary wisdom) was not given to them by anyone else—if it is authentic. This conviction cannot be packaged and sold; it is reached, rather, by means of a totality of reflection and action. Only the leaders' own involvement in reality, within an historical situation, led them to criticize this situation and to wish to change it.

Likewise, the oppressed (who do not commit themselves to the struggle unless they are convinced, and who, if they do not make such a commitment, withhold the indispensable conditions for this struggle) must reach this conviction as Subjects, not as objects. They also must intervene critically in the situation which surrounds them and whose mark they bear; propaganda cannot achieve this. While the conviction of the necessity for struggle (without which the struggle is unfeasible) is indispensable to the revolutionary leadership (indeed, it was this conviction which constituted that leadership), it is also necessary for the oppressed. It is necessary, that is, unless one intends to carry out the transformation *for* the oppressed rather than *with* them. It is my belief that only the latter form of transformation is valid.[25]

The object in presenting these considerations is to defend the eminently pedagogical character of the revolution. The revolutionary leaders of every epoch who have affirmed that the oppressed must

---

25. These points will be discussed at length in chapter 4.

68 · PAULO FREIRE

accept the struggle for their liberation—an obvious point—have also thereby implicitly recognized the pedagogical aspect of this struggle. Many of these leaders, however (perhaps due to natural and understandable biases against pedagogy), have ended up using the "educational" methods employed by the oppressor. They deny pedagogical action in the liberation process, but they use propaganda to convince.

It is essential for the oppressed to realize that when they accept the struggle for humanization they also accept, from that moment, their total responsibility for the struggle. They must realize that they are fighting not merely for freedom from hunger, but for

> . . . freedom to create and to construct, to wonder and to venture. Such freedom requires that the individual be active and responsible, not a slave or a well-fed cog in the machine. . . . It is not enough that men are not slaves; if social conditions further the existence of automatons, the result will not be love of life, but love of death.[26]

The oppressed, who have been shaped by the death-affirming climate of oppression, must find through their struggle the way to life-affirming humanization, which does not lie *simply* in having more to eat (although it does involve having more to eat and cannot fail to include this aspect). The oppressed have been destroyed precisely because their situation has reduced them to things. In order to regain their humanity they must cease to be things and fight as men and women. This is a radical requirement. They cannot enter the struggle as objects in order *later* to become human beings.

The struggle begins with men's recognition that they have been destroyed. Propaganda, management, manipulation—all arms of domination—cannot be the instruments of their rehumanization. The only effective instrument is a humanizing pedagogy in which the revolutionary leadership establishes a permanent relationship of dialogue with the oppressed. In a humanizing pedagogy the method

---

26. Fromm, *op. cit.*, pp. 52–53.

ceases to be an instrument by which the teachers (in this instance, the revolutionary leadership) can manipulate the students (in this instance, the oppressed), because it expresses the consciousness of the students themselves.

> The method is, in fact, the external form of consciousness manifest in acts, which takes on the fundamental property of consciousness—its intentionality. The essence of consciousness is being with the world, and this behavior is permanent and unavoidable. Accordingly, consciousness is in essence a 'way towards' something apart from itself, outside itself, which surrounds it and which it apprehends by means of its ideational capacity. Consciousness is thus by definition a method, in the most general sense of the word.[27]

A revolutionary leadership must accordingly practice *co-intentional* education. Teachers and students (leadership and people), co-intent on reality, are both Subjects, not only in the task of unveiling that reality, and thereby coming to know it critically, but in the task of re-creating that knowledge. As they attain this knowledge of reality through common reflection and action, they discover themselves as its permanent re-creators. In this way, the presence of the oppressed in the struggle for their liberation will be what it should be: not pseudo-participation, but committed involvement.

---

27. Alvaro Vieira Pinto, from a work in preparation on the philosophy of science. I consider the quoted portion of great importance for the understanding of a problem-posing pedagogy (to be presented in chapter 2), and wish to thank Professor Vieira Pinto for permission to cite his work prior to publication.

[19]
Narrative, Free Space, and Political Leadership in Social Movements

Richard A. Couto
University of Richmond

Interviews with leaders of civil rights efforts in four rural communities in the South suggest how narratives nurture political resistance among repressed and subordinated groups. Narratives provide group members historical precedents of individual and collective resistance, an alternative explanation of the group's condition, and an exposition of the virtues of a group that others consider virtueless. This discussion of narratives permits us to understand them as a formative element of local leadership and as an explicitly political element of social movements. This discussion also permits us to interpret social movements as a set of related local efforts of resistance and in terms of the spaces in which narratives occur.

Recent studies of the civil rights movement have emphasized its nature as a set of related local community struggles, each of which has its own history (Carson 1986; Chafe 1980; Norell 1985; Robinson 1987). As the number of these studies increase, a gap in the literature of political science becomes more obvious. Political studies of community power offer little insight to relate local community struggles to social movements of which they are a part. Moreover, political studies of community power do little to explain what makes local or large-scale social movements necessary or possible. Instead the community power studies of most political scientists suggest that pluralist democracy provides opportunity for every group to improve its condition incrementally. Consequently, we may infer that American politics has no apparent need of social movements or radical political change (Dahl 1956, 1961; Polsby 1963). Critiques of pluralism, on the other hand, emphasize the ability of the powerful to repress the powerless and to stymie democratic processes (Gaventa 1980, 5–32). The analysis of repressive mechanisms of the powerful, however, does not explain the capacity of repressed people to act to change their condition as they do in social movements. Thus, the civil rights movement confounds both pluralists and their critics. The civil rights movement suggests that social movements are a necessary means for some groups to acquire a place within the pluralist paradigm of incremental politics. It also suggests that social movements, as a myriad set of related local political conflicts, are possible despite powerful systems of domination and repression. Perhaps it is because social movements are anomalies for political scientists that we pay little attention to the politics of social movements, in general, and to what makes them possible as local resistance efforts to repression and subordination, in particular.

To understand a social movement as local politics of oppressed people, a condition that pluralism does not envision, we have to shift our attention from those who prevent social movements, the focus of pluralist critiques, to those who lead movements for change at the local level. This attention shift is from national leaders of a social movement to the "heroic courage and contributions of thousands of largely unsung heroes" in what David Garrow describes as a "plural pantheon" (Garrow 1990). In broader but analogous terms, James MacGregor Burns has urged us to examine anonymous secondary and tertiary leaders behind those whom are widely known. He lauded these leaders as a crucial component of leadership (Burns 1978, 289).

This article deals with the people in these less visible tiers of leadership. In particular, it focuses on the ways in which apparently powerless people preserve the ability to resist political repression and subordination. This article details narratives acquired in four rural, southern, African-American communities all of which had local movements for civil rights. It suggests that narratives preserved resistance among sets of oppressed people and prepared them for leadership in local social movements for civil rights. The article offers narrative as an analytical tool to explain the politics that make social movements necessary and possible precisely as a set of related, local struggles for change. It also offers narratives and free spaces as factors with which to measure social movements.

Narratives within Free Spaces

Works in several different fields help relate narrative to social movements. Albert O. Hirschman, for example, discusses voice as a process of change and organization renewal. Voice attempts to change an objectionable state of affairs unlike exit that provides individual escape from them (Hirschman 1970, 30). Hirschman, like the pluralists, assumes that individuals or groups have some economic or political power to exercise exit. Indeed, his central lament is the decline of voice because exit is readily available (Hirschman 1970, 43). Thus, Hirschman skirts those instances where there is no exit or where it is severely limited; for example, when political repression reinforces economic subordination. His concern with the diminution of voice because of the ubiquitousness of exit offers less insight into voice within situations where exit is not readily available. On the other hand, Hirschman does refer to the black power movement of the 1960s as an unusual combination of voice and exit, "because of its open advocacy of the group process . . . and because it spurned and castigated a supreme value of American society—success via exit from one's group" (Hirschman 1970, 112). The unique form of voice in this social movement of African-Americans for group, and not merely individual, improvement is less significant, in terms of our analysis, than the continuation of any voice at all among African-Americans in the rural South during the era of Jim Crow. Voice continued despite the conditions that Hirschman did not examine, poor prospects for exit. This continuation of voice suggests a corollary, if not an antithesis, to Hirschman's theses of the ubiquitousness of exit and the atrophy of voice: voice survives despite the lack of exit.

The work of Sara Evans and Harry Boyte and several others suggest the accuracy and importance of this postulate of voice despite exit. Tracing several social movements over the past century, they find that groups restricted by race, gender, and class discrimination regularly develop and express voice in free spaces. Free spaces are "environments in which people are able to learn a new self-respect, a deeper and more assertive group identity, public skills, and values of cooperation and civic virtue" (Evans and Boyte 1986, 17). The voice found in Evans and Boyte's free spaces speaks of democratic reform for group benefit not exit for individual gain, just as Hirschman found in the black power movement. Aldon Morris (1984) portrayed a set of free spaces in his discussion of "halfway houses" of the civil rights movement where voice survived. Similarly, Doug McAdam emphasized the civil rights movement as an insurgency with a context that extended back to Reconstruction. During this time, according to McAdam some African-Americans maintained "cognitive liberation" within their organizations despite their oppressed condition (McAdam 1985, 1, 48–51).

These treatments of voice in social movements in general and the civil rights movement in particular have two common characteristics. First, they suggest that social movements express a need for broad forms of political change in a voice fostered in organizations but carried by individuals, who are concerned with the welfare of groups. Second, these studies suggest that the dominant approaches to the study of social movements ordinarily underestimate the political nature of social movements. Although this later criticism takes various shades and hues, it is far more united in criticizing political science for its inability to explain or understand social movements as a political process.[1] This criticism does more than challenge the methods and paradigms of political science. It invites political scientists to take

---

[1] Evans and Boyte (1986, viii) criticized resource mobilization studies, the domain of sociologists, for overlooking the political content and democratic character of social movements. Charles Perrow (1979, 199–205) qualifies this criticism by distinguishing "a commodious view" of some sociologists, which includes many resources and many means of mobilization, from the more narrow economic analysis of other sociologists. From this point, critics shift to political science and become more severe. Hirschman (1970) finds political scientists so enamored with exit as a fundamental and beneficial social mechanism that they ignore the study of voice as a political form of change (19). He explains this paradoxical inattention to voice, and hence political phenomenon, as an application of economists' methods and assumptions to politics. This, of course, is reminiscent of the criticism by others of resource mobilization theory. Hirschman offered his essay as an effort to liberate his colonized colleagues in political science. McAdam takes this criticism one step further to include what political scientists have done in the study of social movements as well as what they have not done. According to McAdam (1985, 14–19), pluralistic studies transform social movements into apolitical, psychological phenomena because social movements will not fit into the pluralistic assumptions of ordinary, "rational" politics as incremental, self-interested group action.

up two explicitly political questions that their critics leave unanswered. How does the political transformation of people in free spaces occur? How is voice preserved so that it may emerge at times of overt insurgency or political protest?

James C. Scott, a political scientist, addresses a portion of the research agenda these critics imply. He suggests that repressed groups maintain "hidden transcripts" and an infrastructure of political resistance even when oppressed. Scott describes domination and resistance as matters of degree. When resistance is manifest, as in a social movement, hidden transcripts become public. When domination prevails, voice is expressed further and further from public view and within safe and free spaces of the oppressed. At the height of repression, these spaces may be restricted to the memory of an individual or perhaps the family (Scott 1990, 3, 65, 92, 148). Scott thus suggests that free spaces preserve voice even at times when there are no social movements that overtly resist domination, the cases with which Evans and Boyte, Morris, and McAdam are dealing. If we accept Scott's conclusion, we may look at the family and other realms as spaces with a political function to preserve voice despite domination and repression. If we enter these realms as free spaces, we are still left with the questions: what is the content of the "hidden transcripts"; how do they support resistance; and how are oppressed people transformed by them.

Robert Bellah and his associates examine these latter questions in their discussion of the community of memory. This concept, in terms we employ here, combines voice and free spaces. Bellah et al. suggest that the community of memory nurtures individuals by carrying on a moral tradition that reinforces the aspirations of their group (Bellah et al. 1985, 286). The test of this community is its sense of a common past. The telling and retelling of stories establishes that past and offers "examples of the men and women who have embodied and exemplified the meaning of the community." In addition, there are stories of suffering "that sometimes creates deeper identities than success." These stories approximate a moral tradition and turn community of memory members "toward the future as communities of hope." Such communities of hope sponsor transforming social movements, exemplified for Bellah and his associates, as for many others, in the civil rights movement (Bellah et al. 1985, 153).

Bellah and his associates borrow heavily from the philosopher Alasdair MacIntyre and his views on tradition and virtue to develop their own idea of the community of memory. We may infer from MacIntyre's work that narratives shared within free spaces make two contributions to social movements. First, they transmit and continue a belief in the virtue of the oppressed. This virtue is "the kind of capacity for judgment which the agent possesses in knowing how to select among the relevant stack of maxims and how to apply them in particular situations." Virtue is illustrated in the narratives (MacIntyre 1981, 207) the continuation of which is itself virtuous. Virtue enables its possessors "to pursue both their own good and the good of the tradition of which they are bearers even in situations defined by the necessity of tragic, dilemmatic choice" (MacIntyre 1981, 208).

Second, narratives may support social movements because they assert a social life or at least better understanding of a group's social condition than that which prevails in the dominant culture. When the values and human worth of social groups are marginal to the larger and dominant culture of which they are a part, then the more central MacIntyre's concept of virtue becomes for these groups. Without their own narratives within their own free space, marginal groups become the virtueless groups of the dominant culture (MacIntyre 1981, 209). The awareness of economic subordination and political repression of a group by its members reminds them constantly of the inaccuracies of the prevailing explanations of these inequalities and explanations of other parts of American life. The continuation of virtue among such marginal groups helps them preserve self-esteem. It also assists group members to explain the dominant assumptions of their society in terms of power relations rather than the shortcomings and inferiority of their group.[2]

For political scientists, narratives have theoretical significance as a means and a measure of social movements. Narratives mobilize a group to attempt political change. They do not mobilize people to take action directly, as a speech might enthuse a crowd. Rather narratives provide deep and lasting insights into the need and methods of change to individuals who lead social movements or support them despite risks to themselves. Narratives may inspire social movements but, more precisely, the dissemination and expression of narratives measure the extent and political success of social movement participants. At times of great danger of reprisal for overt resistance, narratives are told in carefully guarded free spaces such as the family. As the danger of reprisal diminishes, group members extend their narratives to new free spaces—schools, work places, churches, and organizations specifically formed to support the group's efforts at change. Leadership of covert resistance continues the narratives of a community of memory that may later inspire the leadership of social movements. This latter leadership acts publicly upon the narratives of the community and extends them to new places. Thus, one measure of the political strength of a social movement is the access its leaders acquire to relate the narratives of a group to an attentive audience who has not heard

---

[2]Christopher Nash (1990) provides a synthesis of the controversy and alternative that narrative presents to philosophy as well as social sciences. For other discussions, see Paul Robinson and William M. Sullivan (eds.) *Interpretative Social Science: A Second Look* (Berkeley: University of California Press, 1987); Calvin O. Schrag, *Radical Reflection and the Origin of the Human Sciences* (West Lafayette, IN: Purdue University Press, 1980), esp. chapter 5, "Understanding and Reason: Towards a Hermeneutic of Everyday Life," 97–130; Arthur C. Danto, *Narration and Knowledge* (New York: Columbia University Press, 1985); Bryan Fay, Eugene O. Golob, and Richard R. Vann, eds., *Louis O. Mink: Historical Understanding* (Ithaca: Cornell University Press, 1987), 106–17 and 182–203; and Sheldon S. Wolin, "Paradigm and Political Theories" in *Paradigms and Revolutions: Appraisals and Applications of Kuhn's Philosophy of Science,* ed. Gary Gutting (Notre Dame: University of Notre Dame Press, 1980), 160–91. For a compelling discussion of another community of memory that illustrates the points of Bellah and his colleagues as well as MacIntyre's discussion, see Lawrence L. Langer, *Holocaust Testimonies: The Ruins of Memory* (New Haven: Yale University Press, 1991).

them before because they were proscribed in the places where narratives may now be told. This theoretical significance of narratives as a support of social movements opens up a field for political psychology. Narrative as a measure of social movements opens up new possibilities for theories of political communication.

METHOD AND BACKGROUND

Narratives taken from interviews conducted from 1978 to 1988 with more than 50 local leaders provide the data of this study. In addition, some narratives taken from related written accounts are included. The leaders interviewed range in age, at the time of their interviews, from their mid-thirties to their mid-seventies. They are male and female and although some white people were interviewed, all the narratives used here come from interviews with African-Americans. People interviewed were selected because of their part in establishing federally funded health centers in their communities. These centers were part of the civil rights movement both locally and nationally. Printed information and preliminary interviews determined key informants about the effort to establish the community health center in each place. Fifteen of the people interviewed have been elected or appointed to public office since 1970, as a consequence of local and national changes in the civil and voting rights of African-Americans. In most instances, these 15 people were the first African-Americans in this century in their communities to reach the public office they held.

The civil rights movement in three of these four communities had profound effects on their states, the South and the nation. For example, citizenship schools, a free space of the civil rights movement mentioned by Evans and Boyte, developed on Johns Island, spread throughout the South from 1956 to 1964, and provided training for tens of thousands of African-American southerners who had been blocked by the literacy requirement in their efforts to register to vote (Evans and Boyte 1986, 64–66; Glen 1988, 155–72; Morris 1984, 149–55). The first major effort to register African-Americans in a rural area of Tennessee occurred in Haywood and Fayette Counties in 1959 and 1960 (Couto 1993). Reactions to this effort set precedents of repression and resistance in the South (Lewis 1964, 137–40; Hamilton 1973, 30–31, 185–87). The tent cities established in these counties sheltered sharecroppers evicted from their land. These settlements, and the stories of their residents, made clear for a new generation of African-American leaders the juxtaposition of political repression and economic subordination that marked sharecropping (Forman 1972, 116–45). Local leaders organized an independent political party in Lowndes County in the aftermath of the Selma march in 1965. Their action and their party's symbol, the black panther, were formative elements in the black power movement (Carmichael and Hamilton 1967). Events in these three places earn frequent mention in studies of the civil rights movement. Organized African-American efforts for change occurred later in Lee County, Arkansas, but captured headlines of nationally circulated newspapers when they happened

(Reed 1971a; Maxwell 1972; Terry 1972). Events elsewhere may have inspired the civil rights activity in Lee County but Lee County, as much as any other place, showed how to promote racial equality through federal programs (Schwartz 1988). Thus, the events in the communities suggest, in various ways, the reflexive and symbiotic relation of local and national social movements. This, in turn, underscores the role of narrative in nurturing local leadership of social movements and the dissemination of narrative as a measure of social movements.

Most of all, interviews with leaders in these four communities contain stories that support local movements for change. The stories tell about the evil of oppressors and the wrongdoing of employers and officials. They warn about the violence and deceit dominant community members might use against the members of the community of memory. Other stories relate the resistance of some members of the community of memory in the face of this evil and deceit and the forms of resistance. These stories impart a wisdom of choosing a time and a means to resist oppression. They extol nonviolent, healing remedies for wrongs. They offer the means of comparing the community of memory and the dominant community and of excluding some people from the community of memory who might be mistaken as members. These stories also offer measures of change and progress for the community of memory. Table 1 provides a taxonomy of the narratives found in the interviews and suggestions of their relation to social movements. Needless to say, this is not an exhaustive categorization of narrative. Nor is it meant to suggest a mechanistic relationship of narratives to social movements. Table 1 is merely a summary of some narratives found in one set of interviews that suggest how narratives may nurture leadership of local movements for political change.

NARRATIVES AND FREE SPACES AS SOCIAL MOVEMENTS

Creation of free spaces, beyond the family, wherein narratives extol the virtues of community members is itself a political act. Because of this, some narratives express the restrictions on association as well as the struggle and success of asserting a space as free. Ned Cobb, in describing the repression of an organization of Alabama sharecroppers in the 1930s, succinctly stated the politics of free space at that time.

> White folks in this country didn't allow niggers to have no organization, no secret meetins. They kept up with you and watched you, didn't allow you to associate in a crowd, unless it was your family or your church. It just worked in a way that the nigger wasn't allowed to have nothin but church services and, O, they liked to see you goin to church, too (Rosengarten 1984, 797-98).

This limit on free spaces prevailed until and, to a lesser extent, during the time of the civil rights movement when people began to claim new spaces as free. Narratives from the interviews tell of heroic efforts to create those new free spaces and to withstand the reprisals that followed. For instance, providing food and shelter for civil rights workers and a place in which to conduct meetings brought warnings and threats to two of the women interviewed. Mattie Lee Holcombe Moorer,

TABLE 1
TAXONOMY OF NARRATIVES, RELATED VIRTUES, AND LESSONS FOR MOVEMENT POLITICS

Narrative Type	Content and Virtues Extolled	Lessons for Movement Politics
I. Acquisition, Preservation, and Function of Free Spaces	• Schools and the example of teachers • Landowners and economic independence • Family and examples of parents' resistance to subordination • Virtuous expression of self-esteem within community • Reprisals against free spaces	• Pride in the accomplishments of the past • Obligation to continue the example of others and to make meaningful the sacrifices of others • The importance of space within which to disseminate narratives
II. Climate of Fear and Repression	• Harm done by officials and authorities • Inaction of officials and authorities to redress wrongs • Harm done by officials and authorities to community members in their custody • Cheating in wages • Cheating in politics	• The suffering and vulnerability of community members that could occur again without political change and organization
III. Precedents of Resistance	• Overt resistance • Covert resistance • Use of ambiguity and error • Use of the illogic in subordination • Use of the assumptions and language of prejudice	• Virtues of the past to continue • Wisdom of the past to continue • Choice of tactics and strategies • Self-control • Knowledge of the limits of adversaries which are imposed by their prejudice

- Virtues of resistance
- Courage and intelligence
- Timing of resistance
- Knowledge of the foibles and excesses of an adversary
- Vision and imagination for changes of mutual benefit
- Awareness of difference among people in the appeal of imagined changes

IV. Comparisons between and within Communities

- The strength of prejudice
- Denying resources
- Curtailing rather than sharing resources
- The contradictions of prejudice
- Trust for the provision of vital services but petty subordination and humiliation
- Common bonds and plights of black and white people
- Good members of the white community
- Class and caste distinctions
- White-made black leaders and subordination
- Black leaders who cast aside dependency
- White control of opportunities for blacks

V. On Change and Progress

- Less violence and intimidation
- More resources
- Remaining inequalities
- The possibility of losing ground
- Pride in changes that have occurred
- Reasons for continued efforts

one of those women, recalled the stakes of free spaces in stories that are now part of the community of memory of the movement in Lowndes County.

> I remember when a white man come on me. He said, "Mattie Lee quit going to these mass meetings." He did me a favor once, and I did one. He lent me some money and I paid him exactly what I owed him and 25 cents on the dollar. And I did not borrow the money but for a month. I ain't talking about no year. So I looked at him and I said, "Let me tell you something," I said, "I may be dead when I leave Lowndes County but I am going to be the last one alive." He found out to get me from Lowndes County he was going to have to get me killed, 'Cause, you see, this is my home. I never lived nowhere but here.

The central role of free spaces in a social movement and the risk entailed in establishing them is evidenced by the reprisals taken against them. African-Americans families in Haywood and Lowndes Counties were evicted after family members registered to vote. Local movement leaders responded by creating tent cities that sheltered the evicted families and, of course, served movement leaders as a mechanism to disseminate narratives and material from which to create new ones. Narratives from Johns Island describe the efforts to conceal and thus to protect a printing press, which was used to produce newsletters, from arson and destruction. Narratives from Lee County describe the arson that destroyed the offices of the Lee County Concerned Citizens and the determined opposition of white political leaders to a federal grant to construct a building from which to provide health and other services apart from their control.

The Economic Base of Free Space and Covert Resistance

Establishing and preserving an economic base independent from white authorities and landlords is part of the ongoing struggle of resistance that members of the community of memory preserve in narratives. Likewise, narratives recount sacrifices of parents for the education of their children to illustrate the determination of community members to preserve free spaces, as fundamental as the family or as extensive as educational opportunities, as mechanisms to disseminate the narratives of the community of memory and thus to preserve its voice.

The narratives in the interviews identify free spaces, schools, or centers of training, that were important sources of leadership preparation and training. The Penn Center and the Calhoun Colored School served the Sea Islands and Lowndes County respectively. In Haywood County, the Douglas School not only replaced dilapidated buildings that served the African-American children of tenant farmers, it also attracted a cadre of talented African-Americans as teachers. In these spaces, African-American farmers and their children could better express themselves and maintain their alternative understanding of their history and current conditions. All of these schools attempted to increase landownership among African-American farmers.

The efforts to acquire land make clear the strong relationship of economic independence and the expression of narrative in free spaces. Landowning was an extremely important factor in providing economic security which supported the expression of voice. Tom Rice recalled that land ownership meant first of all better educational opportunities for his children in Haywood County. Land ownership gave Rice and other African-American farmers more control over the time their children spent in school.

> I really can't explain how important it was to own the land. It meant a whole lot to me. First, I could keep my children in school and train them the best I knew how to train them. When I was working other land, I didn't have time to train them and I didn't have money enough to send them to school. It meant a lot to me in many ways.

The freedom to use time and property, which land ownership brought, became important again during the civil rights movement. African-American landowners could demonstrate and protest during the day and work their fields at another time unlike other tenant farmers. Likewise, landowners were free to house civil rights workers unlike tenants who were subject to retaliation for their actions from their landlords like the tenant farmers in Lowndes and Haywood Counties. The tent cities they moved to were possible only because some African-Americans owned land for others to pitch tents on. The increased economic security that landownership imparted was essential to the political expression of resistance to oppressive forms of inequality among sharecroppers.[3]

The African-American church also illustrated the economic base of free spaces. The church was the only organization under the control of local African-Americans for most of the time since emancipation. It provided a space for decision making and leadership training. It was a space for recounting Biblical narratives of suffering and deliverance that obviously inspired leaders and participants in the movement for civil rights. On the other hand, the economic dependence of local African-American clergymen on white bankers for mortgages or the white community for support and reputation muted their voice in local movements for civil rights. Narrators recount manipulating clergymen to gain their symbolic support of the local movement. Others recount criticizing them severely for their otherworldliness. It was the officers of the local churches, and not their pastors, that ordinarily led the first efforts at organizing and voter registration that made the core of the civil rights movement (Carmichael and Hamilton 1977, 101). The narrators recognized that when a church or its pastor was economically dependent on white officials, it did not offer a free space for narratives of overt resistance.

---

[3]The relation of economic security and the expression of voice is clear in the era of the civil rights movement and it is a consistent element of movements for civil rights dating back to Reconstruction (Couto 1991). The most serious land redistribution effort of the Freedmen's Bureau took place on the Sea Islands. It was the remnant of the landowners created by this reform, concentrated around Penn Center at Frogmore, SC, that elected Leroy Brown to the county commission. He was the first African-American in South Carolina to be elected to public office in the civil rights movement (Jackson et al. 1974). The Resettlement Administration of the New Deal modestly replicated the work of the Freedmen's Bureau in instances like Haywood County. Once again, the work of this federal agency had impacts on the civil rights movement later (Salamon 1979).

CLIMATE OF FEAR AND REPRESSION

The narrators detailed violent and corrupt dealings of members of the dominant group toward the members of the community of memory. The police and law officials are central to these stories. The characters of the story include deputies and sheriffs who killed African-American men with slight or no provocation and no accountability. The most vicious of these law officers had reputations that caused African-American men and women to cross the street rather than pass them on the sidewalk. The stories recount verbal abuse as standard practice. There are also stories of violence by mobs led by police officers or which assume that the police were part of mobs or part of Ku Klux Klan action that might threaten members of the community.

Members of the community could get very little protection from law officers and could never assume their protection. Instead, they devised alternatives to police protection or countered police inaction with a suggestion of a show of their own force. For example, Leroy Brown recounted one of his first actions as a Beaufort County commissioner. He discussed with law officers the need to prevent violence at a scheduled demonstration by the Ku Klux Klan. One of them, a white man, assured him that he and his deputies would be there. Brown recounted how he thought, "Yes, under your white robes," but told them only that he thought he could get some of the African-American marine recruits at nearby Paris Island to help out also in an unofficial way.

Without police protection, members of the community suffered violent retaliations from whites on trivial matters such as arguments over the behavior of dogs (Carawan and Carawan 1966, 163–64). When they resisted the force of the dominant group with force of their own, they were often beaten, shot, or killed. For example, Jesse Cannon, a resident in Haywood County, can recall three incidents in the space of 20 years in which African-American men resisted the unlawful violence of sheriffs or mobs of deputies. Each of the men were either lynched or arrested and convicted of murder in local courts. Others in Haywood County remember the violence surrounding the first effort of the local chapter of the NAACP to register to vote in 1940. A mob, led by the night sheriff, on four nights in the course of a week, took leaders of the NAACP from their homes, threatened them, and banished them from the county. The mob members beat one man, Elbert Williams, to death (Couto 1993).

The stories assured members of the community that they could depend on little justice from the police or the courts. Crimes of blacks against whites were severely punished, often without trial or any consideration beyond a charge of wrongdoing. Even when in jail, the injustice continued in the form of leased and forced labor. Experiences in Haywood County found their way into a blues song of Sleepy John (Allen) Estes that warned,

> If you hobo through Brownsville,
> Don't be peekin' out.

Billy Whitten [police officer] will get you
And Mr. Guy Harold [county prison farm superintendent] will wear you out.

Crimes of whites against blacks, on the other hand, went unpunished and were often justified by the behavior of the members of the community of memory. This could apply to whites who supported blacks as well. For example, in Lowndes County the murderers of both Viola Liuzzo and Jonathan Daniels were acquitted in state courts. In the latter case, Daniels was alleged to have drawn a switchblade knife on his murderer (Mendelsohn 1966, 214–15).

The stories of community members being cheated as tenant farmers are legendary and began with the courts of the Freedmen's Bureau immediately with the onset of Reconstruction. Landowners settled their accounts with tenant farmers in such a way to ensure that their tenants, especially the more industrious ones and those whom they wanted to maintain in their employment, came out without cash or in debt. Studies of sharecropping in the 1930s often included the story of one extraordinary settlement.

> A tenant offering five bales of cotton was told, after some owleyed figuring, that this cotton exactly balanced his debt.
> Delighted at the prospect of a profit this year, the tenant reported that he had one more bale which he hadn't yet brought in. "Shucks," shouted the boss, "why didn't you tell me before? Now I'll have to figure the account all over again to make it come out even" (Johnson 1935, 9).

These experiences found their way into another set of lyrics:

Ought's an ought an' figger's a figger,
All fer de white man an' none for de nigger (Nixon 1938, 21).

Cheating, according to the narratives, continued after African-Americans began voting. Community members told stories of ballot boxes from heavily African-American precincts being lost, thrown away, or discarded. Even when an African-American candidate won at the polls, white officials, the stories go, cheated with the absentee ballot process to gain majorities for white candidates. These stories are told with resignation to illustrate the difficulty of acquiring equity. There is far less emphasis on fear once widespread political participation began.

These stories specify the marginal status of the community's members by recounting the considerable injustice done to the community's members. They also measure the change in the conditions of the community by recalling terrible conditions that are ended. Perhaps the worst part of these bygone conditions was the wrongdoing, inaction, and indifference of people in authority who had responsibility for public order. This lack of redress caused great fear. The degree of that fear measures the courage of the community members who resisted the conditions of violence and terror. Their courage was subtle, a community member looked a white man in the eye, or heroic, a community member challenged a white man's account of a debt (Carawan and Carawan 1966, 162). Esau Jenkins, cofounder of the Citizenship Schools on Johns Island, had both types of courage, according to stories told about him. Jenkins' picture now hangs in the courthouse in Charleston, an unimaginable space of honor at the time of the stories depicting his courage.

PRECEDENTS OF RESISTANCE

Most of the local leaders interviewed had stories that offered models of resistance; most often someone within the person's family. These heroes and heroines were most often ordinary people like the narrator and listeners of the stories. The stories thus express the extraordinary characteristics and capacities of ordinary people. The modes of resistance recounted may vary but they expressed a lifetime's attitude and not a single act. There are important common elements in the stories such as a member of the community looking at a dominant person in the eye and the art of challenging a dominant person without incurring retaliation. These stories imparted a sense of virtue of community members in two ways: they described the virtuous intelligence, determination, and courage of specific people in the stories, and they asserted the capacity for such virtue in each member of the community.

The traditions of virtue in these narratives went back to slavery. When she was 70 years of age, Mattie Lee Holcombe Moorer, who supported early efforts of the Student Nonviolent Coordinating Committee (SNCC) in Lowndes County, as we mentioned, recounted her youthful fascination with stories of slavery. "There were plenty of slavery time people living then and that is where you would find me. I would always go and hear their stories. About how they come and how they were sold. I just loved to hear it." In particular, there were stories about the determined and overt resistance to slavery of her great-grandmother, Melinda. "She was sold three times. They say they never could make a slave out of her. Never could."

In times like slavery and legal segregation, there was virtue in resisting petty subordination without reprisal. Some narratives recount instances when community of memory members trap members of the dominant group in the latter's own illogical and exploitative assertions. One such story, which was spread around the South by theater groups, involved Mr. Charlie, Mr. Charlie's cow, and Uncle Tom. Uncle Tom is a black man, envious of Mr. Charlie, a white man, and his cow. In the story, Uncle Tom expresses interest in having a cow like Mr. Charlie's or buying half of it. Mr. Charlie eventually sells Uncle Tom half of the cow, the front half. Uncle Tom pays to feed his half and Mr. Charlie keeps all the revenue from the milk and cream from his half. Uncle Tom realizes, when he is penniless, that he has entered an unequal arrangement. Uncle Tom decides to have his half of the cow for food. He takes a 2×4, hits the cow over the head, and kills it. When Mr. Charlie complains and protests this action taken against "his cow," Uncle Tom explains that he didn't do anything to Mr. Charlie's part. "I just knocked the hell out of mine."

Other stories of preceding resistance illustrate how individuals protected themselves from reprisals by acceding to the misinterpretation of their actions. In one such story, Thelma Shell Price recalled that her mother worked for a white woman.

> She did cooking and cleaning. The white lady made her come in the back door even though she swept the front porch as well as the rest of the house.
>
> There was a rooster in the backyard and every time my mother came to the house, that rooster would come and spur my mother's heel. So she complained to the white woman. But all she said was, "Don't worry, he'll get used to you." And my mother thought, "When? When is that rooster going to get used to me?" And she couldn't quit her job, so she had to stay there and keep going through that yard with that big rooster chasing her, spurring at her heel.
>
> But one day, that rooster was about to spur her but she had grabbed a piece of stove wood and hit him on the side of the head. He fell on his back with his legs sticking straight in the air. And she thought, "Is he dead?" She thought he was dead. That rooster laid for half-a-day on the ground with his feet up in the air.
>
> So the next day, when my mother came to the yard, that rooster was up and it ran to the other side of the yard. He had no thought of spurring that day. And the white woman looked out and said to my mother, "Well, what's got into that rooster?" And my mother looked over at him and said, "I don't know." And the white woman said, "I guess he got used to you." And my mother said, "I guess so. I guess he got used to me."
>
> You see, my mother let him know that nothing that small would have control over her.

Other stories offer examples of resistance by using the bias of others toward community members to extricate themselves from problems. Such stories illustrate the intelligence of the community members and the ignorance that prejudice fosters in some members of the dominant community. Bill Saunders of Johns Island tells a story of an old man.

> I forget his name but his memory stays with me like the memory of Esau Jenkins. He was smart and he knew how to get things and get things done, even when he didn't have power.
>
> One day, right here in Charleston, this old man ran a red light. Drove right through the intersection on red. And this cop, white cop of course, pulls him over. He tells him to get out of the car and begins to tell him off and curse him and call him all kinds of names. You know.
>
> Well, the old black man, he just stands there and takes it. Finally the cop says, "Boy, didn't you see that light was red?" And the old black man, with his hat in his hand—you never spoke to a white person with your hat on—says, "Well officer, of course I did, sir." And the cop stares at him, amazed. You know. He says, "Then why the hell did you drive right through it?"
>
> This time the old black man looks at the cop amazed. Finally, he says, real surprised, "Well officer, sir, I thought green meant go for you and red meant go for us."
>
> The cop didn't know what to do and called him some more names and let him drive off.
>
> If that happened today, a young black man would start cursing the cop back and argue that the light wasn't red and probably end up with a fine and under arrest. You see, we have to keep alive the wisdom of measuring a situation and getting what we want.

Similarly, Olly Neal, Jr., in Lowndes County, Arkansas, learned to express self-respect and assertive resistance from the example of his mother.

> She never allowed us to talk back to older whites but that didn't stop her from talking strong. I remember in 1949, my daddy and momma bought a blue Chevrolet truck. Momma brought the truck over to what was at that time called Busby Chevrolet, I believe. Now white folks were in the habit of referring to older black men as uncle and the white man at the Chevrolet place called her, "Auntie."

She turned to him and said very calmly, "How is my sister doing?" He said, "What?" And she said, "Well, you must be my sister's son because I only have one sister and if I'm your aunt, you must be her son."⁴

Neal learned, again from his mother, that the expression of self-respect is an art that requires timing.

> But I remember one later occasion when I took the truck over to Busby's and they asked me, "This Uncle Olly's truck?" And I replied, "Hell, no! It's *Mr.* Neal's!" Of course, they went straight and told momma and daddy and when I got home momma whipped my tail for doing the same thing she had done. She was just fearful of us getting killed.

A great deal of merit is imputed to anyone who has coped in the repressive atmosphere of race relations as the community of memory understands them. Because of that people are seen as heroic even if stories indicate their fear. Annie Hrabowski, another elderly women and early supporter of SNCC in Lowndes County, recalls that her father had no fear. However, she also tells a story of his panic when one day, when she was about six years old and Jim Crow was reigning as king of race relations, she walked with him to the courthouse. They were walking past the front door. She pointed to it and protested the door was right there and asked impatiently why didn't they enter by it. Her innocent suggestion stimulated a stern lecture on her need to learn some things and not to talk so much. Yet her father remained fearless in her memory. Likewise, Bill Saunders estimates that any African-American who came of age in segregation and still walks the streets of Charleston has earned the equivalent of a masters degree in psychology by merely surviving.

Saunders recalled his use of paradox in his narratives. In particular, at the height of the civil rights movement he expressed admiration for "Uncle Toms." This admiration contrasted sharply with his reputation as a radical, black leader in Charleston. He identified with SNCC rather than the SCLC and led the one hundred-day Charleston hospital workers strike in 1969. His reputation accentuated the paradox of his stories and drove his point home. He assumed that "Uncle Toms" did not ascribe to white authorities' views but manipulated them. Thus his stories imparted virtue to another set of African-Americans and offered another set of virtues for members of the community of memory to emulate.

COMPARISONS BETWEEN AND WITHIN COMMUNITIES

Saunders' explanation of "Uncle Toms" suggests the manner in which allowance is made for individuals and the climate of fear in which community members lived

---

⁴Evans and Boyte cite a very similar story involving Martin Luther King, Jr.

> One day, when Martin was a child, a policeman stopped the car driven by his father, "Daddy" King. "Boy, show me your license," the officer ordered brusquely. "Do you see this child here?" . . . asked King, pointing to Martin Luther. "That's a *boy* there. I'm a *man*. I'm Reverend King." "When I stand up," Daddy King told his son, "I want everybody to know that a *man* is standing up. Nobody can make a slave out of you if you don't think like a slave" (Evans and Boyte 1986, 53).

and which they had to regulate, often by themselves. In more than 50 interviews, no member of the community of memory ever referred to another as an "Uncle Tom." When the term was used, community members explained that members of the dominant community used it to divide the community of memory. This is not to say that members of the community of memory accept everyone as equal within it. Some stories distinguish white-made black leaders who often had wealth and/or authority but were not trusted within free spaces. Two weeks of terror in Haywood County were touched off after a local chapter of the NAACP would not admit a prominent African-American businessman to its meeting for fear he would report on their dealings to white officials. Teachers were also often distinguished within the community of memory because their incomes were greater than most other members and directly dependent on white authorities. Dependence or allegiance to white authorities clearly separated some African-American persons from other members of the community.

This separation provided dilemmas for entry into the free spaces of the local civil rights movements for some African-American professionals. In 1965, at the time of the Selma March, Uralee Haynes and her husband were both school teachers. Their employer, the school superintendent, had intimidated them and deterred them from their intention to register to vote after World War II. In light of that, they were slow to join the movement in Lowndes County in 1965, as Haynes recalled:

> I did not go to the meetings at first. I certainly did not. My husband and I did do things like giving advice and making contributions as much as we possibly could. We really just could not openly work with them.
>
> When the ice was broken and people begin to register we realized that if we didn't go then that we would be cursed by these people here as people not interested in any improvement at all. So we thought, it would be best that we would go over and register and the two of us went at the same time. Before any other professional went to register. My husband and I went up and registered and I think that was the thing that made them know that we were really with them. We went to the old jail and took the test and registered.

Another set of narratives offer distinctions between community of memory members and members of the dominant community. These stories provide instruction about the virtue of the community and its goal of mutual benefit for members of both groups. The stories also express skepticism about the ability of some white and black people to deal with change. This skepticism is grounded in the poor response of most white people to opportunities to conduct change before local movements for civil rights started.

These stories also expressed disbelief and hurt about the values and attitudes of the dominant community members. They recounted how narrators or their family members had to go to the backdoors of white homes although they cleaned every part of them including the front porch. Especially upsetting were the lengths to which dominant community members would go not to share what they had with community of memory members. Stories told of local white officials and groups who closed formerly all-white swimming pools and athletic facilities rather than integrate them. African-American parents could not understand why white parents would keep their children from such facilities rather than share them with African-American children. These actions by members of the dominant community were all the more disconcerting because stories in the community of memory, like that of Mr. Charlie's cow, made clear that blacks and whites had common interests and bonds and could not deny them without injury to one another. Narrators go beyond hurt to anger when recalling the dominant community's tolerance of deprivation, especially the deplorable conditions and limited school year of three months in segregated schools for African-American children.

When change did come, stories explain efforts by whites to control the access to the opportunities these changes meant, such as integrated schools. One resident of Lee County recalled:

> When school desegregation occurred here, the white communities would select the black families in their communities whose children they considered to be "good enough" to go to school with their children and these were the ones that went to white schools. And this was how it was done throughout the county.

On the other hand, the stories also preserve the memory of the few individual white persons who expressed characteristics different from those of the dominant community. For example, a white landowner set aside a portion of the earnings of his black tenant farmer until there was enough money saved to sell the land to him. Other white farmers set aside race to unite with black farmers in organizing efforts. Some wealthy whites used their money and influence to support organized efforts of African-Americans for change. The stories also recount white officials, like John Doar of the Justice Department, who assisted community members in federal court to win injunctions and assert their rights. These dominant community members had special merit because they recognized the virtue of members of the community of memory; the common bond they had with them; and the injustice of others' action toward them. In other words, they believed and valued the narratives of the community.

On Change and Progress

Narratives within free spaces also offer members of the community of memory measures of progress and change. Older members of the community of memory acknowledge that there is change. Jesse Cannon knew in 1959 that times had changed when a black man was arrested for killing a white sheriff and brought to trial. Just those two steps, arrest and trial, instead of a lynching, gave him a measure of change.

Others in the community point out there are "black faces in high places," that is to say there are African-American elected officials in counties where there were no African-American voters 30 years ago. An African-American teacher, Uralee Haynes, intimidated by her school superintendent from attempting to register to vote succeeded her as superintendent. An African-American man in Haywood

County, Earl Rice, became an assistant principal and science department head in a school that he could not attend as a boy because it was for white children only. He is now principal of a middle school. Bill Saunders headed the Democratic party in Charleston County 30 years after African-Americans began slowly to regain the right to vote.

In terms of an ideal of equality, African-Americans, on average, still lag behind whites in every measure of life conditions and chances—employment, income, housing, education, and health—in each of these counties. In recent years the gaps between the races on these measures have increased. Consequently, there is an ambivalence among the people with whom we spoke about the amount and nature of change they have seen. John Hulett, sheriff of Lowndes County and the first African-American elected official in the county in this century, believes there has been progress but that it is not permanent. Continued organizing and effort are necessary to preserve what has been achieved.

Moreover, Hulett believes, "It is possible we could go backward and that bothers me." He is hopeful that will not occur but his realization of the possibility of going backward in terms of the political, social, and economic gains that African-Americans have made is part of the alternative history of the community of memory members. It is rooted in their understanding of Reconstruction as progressive, political measures taken on behalf of African-Americans in the 1860s, compromised in the 1870s and gradually eliminated until the 1890s brought on the era of legal racial segregation and subordination that lasted for 60 years.

Bill Saunders talks of the hundred-year cycle which African-Americans see in American history. He understands that the 1990s may be a decade in which the legislation of the 1960s is eliminated and when legal and extralegal means reinforce the economic subordination of African-Americans. The possibility of this happening now is directly related to his understanding of what happened between 1865 and 1900 when Reconstruction melded into legal segregation. Saunders doubts that there will be a recurrence because African-Americans have made too many gains in too many fields and have more economic and political power now than they had then.

Apart from politics, Moorer is sure that Lowndes County has "been blessed" with change on at least two counts: John Hulett and the health center that began shortly after the local voter registration drive and with federal support. Hulett in Moorer's estimation "is the best high sheriff I have ever known anywhere from Lowndes County because he does not kill, he does not shoot, he doesn't beat prisoners up" as former sheriffs had done. This increased protection from violence, legal and extralegal, is the most common measure of progress in the community of memory. On the other hand, the health center represents increased social services for members of the community and as such it is also a sign of progress. The clinic cares for women and children in a manner far superior than what Ms. Moorer remembers as past standards. Her first child died in a breech birth that endangered her own life.

The older narrators remember going without resources and services. Some items, like textbooks, reached them only after white school officials considered them inadequate for white school children. These narrators contrast early experiences, like their schooling, with their current opportunity, which the civil rights movement brought, to claim a fairer portion of new public resources. Moorer can remember selling eggs she could not eat because their sale provided scarce cash income. Septima Clark could remember farm workers on Johns Island who harvested vegetable crops but suffered from malnutrition. Clark came to Johns Island as a teenager to teach in segregated school. She died in a nursing home begun and operated by an African-American nonprofit organization on Johns Island with federal funds. Both women's lives span a time when African-Americans can make new and increased claims to a greater share of the resources they produce.

Likewise, there are fewer obvious life and death consequences to the disparities of wealth such as Rev. Willis Goodwin recounted on Johns Island. People died in his car during his efforts to transport them to Charleston hospitals because he was stopped by bridges drawn to permit luxury boats to pass under. There are still measures of disparity to be sure and fatal consequences such as infant mortality.

This progress in social services, according to the narratives, is not without some troublesome aspects. African-Americans are in a better position to gain a fair portion of resources. The resources for education, health care, housing, and other services, however, are not adequate. In addition, resources that are acquired at one time may be lost at another. For example, the clinic in Haywood County was closed by federal officials. Federal authorities took control of the clinic on Johns Island from the original board and placed it in the hands of local political and medical officials, former opponents of the clinic. The clinic in Lowndes County also underwent a political struggle for control. In other words, the stories of these clinics repeat the history familiar to members of the community of memory. "That's the way you know" is how Betty Douglas in Haywood County summed up her alternative history. "You get something good going. And they won't let you have it. They take it away."

Conclusion

As political phenomena, narratives offer a link between local struggles and social movements and suggest grounds upon which political scientists may approach the study of social movements. Social movements are possible, in part, because narratives within free spaces preserve an understanding of why they are necessary. Specifically, these narratives preserve a sense of dignity and worth—virtue—among some oppressed people despite their marginal status and efforts to discredit them and their group. The stories taken from these interviews illustrate the narratives of which MacIntyre writes and suggest the bonds of a community of memory. They also illustrate the content of the hidden transcripts of Scott's analysis and the preservation of an alternative voice within free spaces despite repression.

Covert resistance becomes a social movement when previously proscribed places, segregated institutions, the media, public hearings, or electoral politics, become spaces for the exposition of the community of memory's narratives. When the conditions of repression are paramount and the possibility of overt resistance is small, narratives are preserved in the most private of free spaces, the family or even the memory of a few individuals. As the conditions of repression diminish and prospects for successful overt resistance increase, people take initial steps of resistance, part of which involves claiming new space, schools, and work for example, as free. The degree of freedom of these spaces is precisely the possibility of sharing narratives of the community of memory without fear of reprisals. The expression of narratives in new free spaces permits an ever increasing number of individuals to recognize their ties to a community of memory. In the words of James C. Scott, community members learn "the full extent to which their claims, their dreams, their anger is shared by other subordinates with whom they have not been in direct touch" (1991, 223). If this interplay of free space and narrative takes place in enough local places, eventually leaders emerge to coordinate efforts on a larger scale. Thus, the profound leadership of Martin Luther King, Jr. within the civil rights movement sprang, in largest measure, from his extraordinary ability to render the voice and narratives of African-Americans in the South in spaces where they had not been heard before.

Narratives and free spaces are not only political mechanisms of social movements, they are also measures of the political success of a movement. At root, a movement entails efforts to claim new spaces, like the Birmingham jail or the Lincoln Memorial, from which to tell an increasingly articulate narrative to a newly attentive audience. King obviously was a leader in the movement for civil rights. In another sense, however, he was led by the pantheon of second and third tier leaders for whom narratives had preserved the ability to claim spaces like the bus seats in Montgomery as free.

Manuscript submitted 21 May 1991
Final manuscript received 16 March 1992

REFERENCES

Bellah, Robert N., Richard Madsen, William M. Sullivan, Ann Swidler, and Steven M. Tipton. 1985. *Habits of the Heart: Individualism and Commitment in American Life.* Berkeley: University of California Press.
Burns, James MacGregor. 1978. *Leadership.* New York: Harper & Row.
Carawan, Guy, and Candie Carawan. 1966. *"Ain't You Got a Right to the Tree of Life?": The People of Johns Island, South Carolina.* New York: Simon & Schuster.
Carson, Clayborne. 1986. "Civil Rights Reform and the Black Freedom Struggle." In *The Civil Rights Movement in America*, ed. Charles W. Eagles. Jackson: University Press of Mississippi.
Carmichael, Stokely, and Charles V. Hamilton. 1967. *Black Power: The Politics of Liberation in America.* New York: Random House.

Chafe, William Henry. 1980. *Civilities and Civil Rights: Greensboro, North Carolina and the Black Struggle for Equality.* New York: Oxford University Press.

Couto, Richard A. 1991. *Ain't' Gonna Let Nobody Turn Me Round: The Pursuit of Racial Justice in the Rural South.* Philadelphia: Temple University Press.

Couto, Richard A. 1993. *Lifting the Veil: A Century of Struggles for Civil Rights.* Knoxville: The University of Tennessee Press.

Dahl, Robert A. 1956. *A Preface to Democratic Theory.* Chicago: The University of Chicago Press.

Dahl, Robert A. 1961. *Who Governs? Democracy and Power in an American City.* New Haven: Yale University Press.

Evans, Sara M., and Harry C. Boyte. 1986. *Free Spaces: The Sources of Democratic Change in America.* New York: Harper & Row.

Forman, James. 1972. *The Making of Black Revolutionaries: A Personal Account.* New York: Macmillan.

Garrow, David, J., "How King Borrowed: Reading the Truth between Sermons and Footnotes," *The Washington Post,* 18 November 1990.

Gaventa, John. 1980. *Power and Powerlessness: Quiescence and Rebellion in an Appalachian Valley.* Urbana, IL: University of Illinois Press.

Glen, John. 1988. *Highlander: No Ordinary School, 1932–1962.* Lexington: University Press of Kentucky.

Hamilton, Charles V. 1973. *The Bench and the Ballot: Southern Federal Judges and Black Voters.* New York: Oxford University Press.

Hirschman, Albert O. 1970. *Exit, Voice, and Loyalty: Response to Decline in Firms, Organizations, and States.* Cambridge: Harvard University Press.

Jackson, Juanita, Sabra Slaughter, and J. Herman Blake. 1974. "The Sea Islands as a Cultural Resource." *The Black Scholar* 5:32–39.

Johnson, Charles, Edwin R. Embree, and W. W. Alexander. 1935. *The Collapse of Cotton Tenancy: Summary of Field Studies and Statistical Surveys, 1933-5.* Chapel Hill, NC: University of North Carolina Press.

Lewis, Anthony. 1964. *Portrait of a Decade: The Second American Revolution.* New York: Random House.

MacIntyre, Alasdair. 1981. *After Virtue: A Study in Moral Theory.* Notre Dame, IN: University of Notre Dame Press.

Maxwell, Neil, "Black vs. White: A Boycott Devastates Little Southern Town Bypassed by the 60s." *Wall Street Journal,* 24 February 1972.

McAdam, Doug. 1985. *Political Process and the Development of Black Insurgency 1930–1970.* Chicago: University of Chicago Press.

Mendelsohn, Jack. 1966. *The Martyrs: Sixteen Who Gave Their Lives for Racial Justice.* New York: Harper & Row.

Morris, Aldon D. 1984. *The Origins of the Civil Rights Movement: Black Communities Organizing for Change.* New York: Free Press.

Nash, Christopher, ed. 1990. *Narrative in Culture: The Uses of Storytelling in the Sciences, Philosophy, and Literature.* New York: Routledge.

Nixon, Herman C. 1938. *Forty Acres and Steel Mules.* Chapel Hill, NC: University of North Carolina Press.

Norell, Robert J. 1985. *Reaping the Whirlwind: The Civil Rights Movement in Tuskegee.* New York: Knopf.

Perrow, Charles. 1979. "The Sixties Observed." In *The Dynamics of Social Movements: Resource Mobilization, Social Control, and Tactics,* ed. Mayer N. Zald and John D. McCarthy. Cambridge, MA: Winthrop.

Polsby, Nelson. 1963. *Community Power and Political Theory.* New Haven: Yale University Press.

Reed, Roy, "Arkansas Blacks Halt Year-Old Boycott," *New York Times,* 27 July 1971.

Reed, Roy, "Widespread Racial Violence Persists in Eastern Arkansas Farming Area," *New York Times,* 10 October 1971.

Robinson, Jo Anne Gibson. 1987. *The Montgomery Bus Boycott and the Women Who Started It: Memoir of Jo Anne Gibson Robinson.* Ed. David J. Garrow. Knoxville: University of Tennessee Press.

Rosengarten, Theodore. 1984. *All God's Dangers: The Life of Nate Shaw.* New York: Vintage Books.

Salamon, Lester M. 1979. "The Time Dimension in Policy Evaluation: The Case of the New Deal Land-Reform Experiments." *Public Policy* 27:129–83.

Schwartz, Marvin. 1988. *In-Service to America: A History of VISTA in America, 1965–1985.* Fayetteville, AR: University of Arkansas Press.

Scott, James C. 1990. *Domination and the Arts of Resistance: Hidden Transcripts.* New Haven: Yale University Press.

Terry, Bill, "Marianna—A Town Torn By Race," *The Washington Post,* 14 February 1971.

Woofter, Thomas J., Jr. 1930. *Black Yeomanry: Life on St. Helena Island.* New York: Henry Holt.

Richard A. Couto is professor of Leadership Studies, Jepson School of Leadership Studies, University of Richmond, Richmond, VA 23173.

Part V
Inclusion and Democratic Leadership

[20]

Strong Democracy: Politics as a Way of Living

> *Democracy is not an alternative to other principles of associated life. It is the idea of community life itself. . . . [It is] a name for a life of free and enriching communion.*
>
> (John Dewey)

> *We have in mind men whose state of virtue does not rise above that of ordinary people . . . who seek not an ideally perfect constitution, but first a way of living.*
>
> (Aristotle)

Strong democracy is a distinctively modern form of participatory democracy. It rests on the idea of a self-governing community of citizens who are united less by homogeneous interests than by civic education and who are made capable of common purpose and mutual action by virtue of their civic attitudes and participatory institutions rather than their altruism or their good nature. Strong democracy is consonant with—indeed it depends upon—the politics of conflict, the sociology of pluralism, and the separation of private and public realms of action. It is not intrinsically inimical to either the size or the technology of modern society and is therefore wedded neither to antiquarian republicanism nor to face-to-face parochialism. Yet it challenges the politics of elites and masses that masquerades as democracy in the West and in doing so offers a relevant alternative to what we have called thin democracy—that is, to instrumental, representative, liberal democracy in its three dispositions.

The Argument for Citizenship

Strong democracy has a good deal in common with the classical democratic theory of the ancient Greek polis, but it is in no sense identical with that theory. It also shares much with its cousin liberal democracy, and in practical terms it is sometimes complementary to rather than a radical alternative to the liberal argument. Yet it is distinctive in a number of crucial ways and is a powerful foil for American democratic practice.

It is a much less total, less unitary theory of public life than the advocates of ancient republicanism might wish, but it is more complete and positive than contemporary liberalism. It incorporates a Madisonian wariness about actual human nature into a more hopeful, Jeffersonian outlook on human potentialities. As portrayed here, it is a new theory drawn from a variety of established practices and nourished by classical theories of community, civic education, and participation.

The theory of strong democracy does not quite envision politics in the ancient sense of a "way of life," and it is explicitly hostile to the still more extravagant claim that politics is *the* way of life. It has no share in the republican nostalgia of such commentators as Hannah Arendt or Leo Strauss. Modern men and women know too well the dangers of a unitary politics that lays claim to all the human soul and affects to express man's "higher nature." "How small of all that human hearts endure / That part which laws or kings can cause or cure," wrote Samuel Johnson, in what should be the epigraph of every tract urging greater democracy.

Yet while recognizing the dangers of totalism, we need not accept the wan residualism of liberal democratic pluralism, which depicts politics as nothing more than the chambermaid of private interests. The history of the twentieth century should have taught us that when democracy cannot respond to the need for community with anything more than a pusillanimous privatism, other, more oppressive political ideologies will step in. That, indeed, was the theme of the previous chapter of this book.

The theory of strong democracy offers a different and more vigorous response: it envisions politics not as a way of life but as a way of living—as, namely, the way that human beings with variable but malleable natures and with competing but overlapping interests can contrive to live together communally not only to their mutual advantage but also to the advantage of their mutuality.

Because democratic politics makes possible cooperation and an approximation of concord where they do not exist by nature, it is potentially a realm of unique openness, flexibility, and promise. It is in fact the quintessential realm of change that, while it is occasioned by conflict and by the inadequacy of man's higher nature, becomes the occasion for mutualism and the superseding of his lower nature. This is perhaps why John Dewey was moved to call democracy not a form of associated life but "the idea of community life itself."[1]

There is an element of hubris in Dewey's almost Periclean vision of political life, but there is moderation as well. Neither the solitary, nearly divine philosopher nor the solitary Hobbesian predator fully embodies that odd creature *Homo politicus* who inhabits both the ancient and modern worlds of democracy: dependent, yet under democracy self-determining; insufficient and ignorant, yet under democracy teachable; selfish, yet under democracy cooperative; stubborn and solipsistic, yet under democracy creative and capable of genuine self-transformation.

The stress on transformation is at the heart of the strong democratic conception of politics. Every politics confronts the competition of private interests and the conflict that competition engenders. But where liberal democracy understands politics as a means of eliminating conflict (the anarchist disposition), repressing it (the realist disposition), or tolerating it (the minimalist disposition), strong democracy also aspires to transform conflict through a politics of distinctive inventiveness and discovery. It seeks to create a public language that will help reformulate private interests in terms susceptible to public accommodation (see Chapter 8); and it aims at understanding individuals not as abstract persons but as citizens, so that commonality and equality rather than separateness are the defining traits of human society (see Chapter 9).

Open to change and hospitable to the idea of individual and social transformation, strong democracy can overcome the pessimism and cynicism, the negativity and passivity that, while they immunize liberalism against naïve utopianism and the tyranny of idealism, also undermine its cautious hopes and leave its theory thin and threadbare and its practice vulnerable to skepticism and dogmatism. Under strong democracy, politics is given the power of human promise. For the first time the possibilities of transforming private into public, dependency into interdependency, conflict into coop-

1. John Dewey, *The Public and Its Problems* (New York: Holt, 1927), p. 148.

eration, license into self-legislation, need into love, and bondage into citizenship are placed in a context of participation. There they are secure from the manipulation of those bogus communitarians who appeal to the human need for communion and for a purpose higher than private, material interests only in order to enslave humankind.

Strong democratic politics is finally not so different from the political condition depicted by Michael Oakeshott when he wrote of sailors on "a boundless sea [where] there is neither harbor nor shelter nor floor for anchorage, neither starting-point nor appointed destination, [and where] the enterprise is to keep afloat on an even keel."[2] This imagery speaks not only to conservatives, for it depicts a politics free of crass instrumentalism, a politics that is to a degree an end in itself rather than one that only has ends. Where democracy is end as well as means, its politics take on the sense of a journey in which the going is as important as the getting there and in which the relations among travelers are as vital as the destinations they may think they are seeking.

Yet though strong democracy can be made to sound attractive, rhetoric alone is an insufficient argument for it. Having introduced the idea in a very general way, I must now try to give it a more formal expression. I have suggested that strong democracy is the only form of democracy that can provide an adequate response to the dilemmas of modern politics. I want now to go further and argue that among democratic regime forms, it alone accounts for and responds to what we may call the basic conditions of politics—i.e., the circumstances that give rise to politics in the first place. This argument must begin by stipulating the conditions of politics. Then it will be possible to give a formal definition of strong democracy (and of several other competing forms) in terms of these conditions.

Defining the Conditions of Politics

One can understand the realm of politics as being circumscribed by conditions that impose *a necessity for public action, and thus for reasonable public choice, in the presence of conflict and in the absence of private or independent grounds for judgment.*

A political question thus takes the form: "What shall we do when something has to be done that affects us all, we wish to be reason-

---

2. Michael Oakeshott, *Rationalism in Politics* (New York: Basic Books, 1962), p. 127.

able, yet we disagree on means and ends and are without independent grounds for making the choice?" This formulation suggests that the ultimate political problem is one of action, not Truth or even Justice in the abstract. The vital advantage of this viewpoint, which Machiavelli recognized and Burke celebrated, is that it eschews metaphysics and circumvents philosophical issues of Final Truth and Absolute Morals. It requires a proximate solution for real problems that will persist whether or not an ultimate measure of judgment is available. The disadvantage, which such pure philosophers as Kant and Rawls have found it difficult to overcome, is that *some* reasonable answer must be found, even where none can be philosophically warranted. For when one is confronted by the logic of consequences (see "Necessity" below), making no decision at all becomes a decision. This means that the political actor, unlike the speculative philosopher, can afford neither the luxury of agnosticism nor the Olympian nonchalance of skepticism. To be political is to *have* to choose—and, what is worse, to have to choose under the worst possible circumstances, when the grounds of choice are not given a priori or by fiat or by pure knowledge (*epistemē*). To be political is thus to be free with a vengeance—to be free in the unwelcome sense of being without guiding standards or determining norms yet under an ineluctable pressure to act, and to act with deliberation and responsibility as well.

This is the true dilemma of Plato's Cave, the problem that philosophers have called Right Opinion, where we are without final truth and absolute knowledge yet wish to act in a manner that conforms to right. We hope our choice to be something more than arbitrary or impulsive or merely self-interested yet we must choose without the guidance of impartial truth. Under these conditions, the cave can hardly be a tidy place.[3] No wonder it is so disdained by the philosopher. It is grimy with the muddled activity of reluctant doers who must nonetheless do as best they can. It is dark and confused and tumultuous because it is peopled by creatures who are defined by

---

3. Montaigne captures perfectly the untidy, practical spirit of politics when he writes:

> The virtue assigned to the affairs of the world is a virtue with many bends, angles, and elbows, so as to join and adapt itself to human weakness; mixed and artificial, not straight, clean, constant, or purely innocent. . . . [H]e who walks in a crowd must step aside, keep his elbows in, step back or advance, even leave the straight way, according to what he encounters. (*On Vanity*, in *The Complete Essays of Montaigne*, trans. Donald M. Frame [Stanford: Stanford University Press, 1958], p. 758)

what they do rather than by how they think, by the search for proximate good rather than for immutable certainty, and by the need to discover a reasonable basis for their commonality rather than an unimpeachable foundation for their individuality. Enshrouded in ambivalence, it is a world constrained to reject Thrasymachean ideologies of pure interest without being able to achieve Socratic philosophies of pure right.

These points may be more readily acknowledged if we isolate the several key constituents of this definition of the political condition and examine them individually. The definition can be rephrased in a fashion that highlights its crucial constituent elements (in italics), as follows: the need for politics arises when some *action* of *public* consequence becomes *necessary* and when men must thus make a *public choice* that is *reasonable* in the face of *conflict* despite the *absence of an independent ground* of judgment. The key concepts in need of elaboration are then *action, publicness, necessity, choice, reasonableness, conflict*, and the *absence of an independent ground*.

Action. The realm of politics is first and foremost a realm of human action. While there is a sense in which every human thought, every event, every utterance (called "speech acts" by certain philosophers) can be regarded as an action, our definition intends a somewhat narrower and more common usage. *Action* here suggests building or closing a hospital, starting or concluding a war, taxing or exempting a corporation, initiating or deferring a welfare plan—in other words, doing (or not doing), making (or not making) something in the physical world that limits human behavior, changes the environment, or affects the world in some material way. Where there is no action (or no nonaction of consequence), there is no politics.

This assimilation of politics to action may seem obvious enough, but at least within the liberal democratic tradition there has been a tendency to see politics as a thing or a place or a set of institutions—as, at best, something done by others (politicians, bureaucrats, party workers, voters)—and to undervalue the degree to which action entails activity, energy, work, and participation. Thus, when Hannah Arendt defined politics as the active life (*vita activa*) in her book *The Human Condition*, what was curious was not the definition itself but the degree to which her colleagues received it as a radical antiquarian critique of modern liberal democracy, as if action had nothing to do with modern politics. Liberal democrats have too often permitted their concern with accountability, representation, passively maintained individual rights, and abstract autonomy to suffuse their conception of the political with torpor. Nonetheless, politics remains something we do, not something (such as power, for example) that we possess or use or watch or think about. Politics is action and is about action. In states defined by watching rather than doing—in "watchdog" or "watchman" states—citizens, like spectators everywhere, may find themselves falling asleep.

Publicness. Politics describes a realm of action, but not all action is political. We may more properly restrict politics to *public* action: i.e., to action that is both undertaken by a public and intended to have public consequences. Politics describes the realm of *we*. Determining whether gold makes a useful filling for cavities is a private choice (action) undertaken by a special group of authorities, in this case dentists, and is of concern only to individual dental patients. Determining whether gold is a useful monetary standard is a public choice (action) with clearly public consequences and must be decided by duly constituted public authorities. Matters of taste, to take another example, may be both contentious and of consequence, but unless they have public results (such as a public mural or a national anthem) they are not, strictly speaking, political matters.[4]

Some apparently private actions and choices, such as tobacco smoking, turn out to have public consequences, such as polluting the common air. Other actions are private when examined one at a time but have public consequences when taken in the aggregate: for example, siting private homes where they can have the greatest solitude and the widest vistas, at the expense of destroying solitude and vistas for everyone else.[5]

The failure of such philosophers as Robert Nozick to distinguish between private and public acts is a major reason why they have been unable to develop a convincing concept of the political. Of course the thin line between public and private is often obscured or controversial. Indeed, it is one primary function of political activity

4. The recent half-hearted but earnest proposals that songs by John Lennon and Bruce Springsteen be adopted as, respectively, the American national anthem and the official state song of New Jersey illustrate how questions of private esthetics can become questions of public policy.

5. Fred Hirsch, in *Social Limits to Growth* (Cambridge, Mass.: Harvard University Press, 1978), calls this the problem of "positional goods." The theme is at the heart of his powerfully argued case for a *public* interpretation of the dilemmas of growth.

to provide a continuing forum for the discussion and definition of these terms. Conditions change, and along with them the notion of the public. A flexible politics demands that we be sensitive to such change and constantly willing to reformulate what is and what is not public. "What is political?" is always a fundamental question of politics.

If what affects the public is political, then much more obviously what the public does as a whole community is political. If all actions with public consequences are political, then all public (common or community) actions are necessarily so. When *I* act, the publicness of the act can only be measured by the publicness (or privacy) of its consequences; when *we*—the community, the people, the nation—act, the act is public regardless of its consequences.

Necessity. Politics encompasses the realm not simply of action but of necessary action. It is enmeshed in events that are part of a train of cause and effect already at work in the world. This engagement guarantees that even the choice not to make some political decision will have public consequences. Recent political science has given the odd name "nondecision" to this behavior. A nondecision is still a species of decision because as a passive component of ongoing events it has specifiable public consequences: it reinforces a status quo or permits a train of action already in process to gain momentum.

Nondecisions are thus part of the logic produced by what we may call the first law of inertial politics: that events set in motion in the public realm will continue to their logical conclusion (their inertial terminus) if there are no contrary inputs from conscious political actors. "Nonactors" thereby bear responsibility for whatever results their nondecisions have allowed the momentum of events to produce.

There is little that is startling in the first law of inertial politics. It is the political analogue of consequentialism, which is the moral posture that evaluates conduct on the basis of the actual effects it has in the world rather than on the basis of its intentions or the good (or bad) will motivating it—and as such it has had a long history in the Western political tradition. Its most illustrious, or notorious, modern proponent was perhaps Machiavelli, who in *The Prince* warned princely nonactors that their failure to take timely action might permit the unfolding of an untoward chain of events with grave consequences for themselves and their principalities. In his most vivid example, Machiavelli chides the overly scrupulous prince who in his shortsighted mercy abstains from executing the children of enemies who have betrayed him and his principality; for once, owing to this small act (or nonact) of Christian mercy, the children mature into men, they will transform the wrongs of their childhood into a sword of vengeance and provoke civil war and renewed fratricide. And will not these consequences, Machiavelli concludes, be far more devastating than any that a timely infanticide might have occasioned?[6] Cruel as their conduct seems when measured by the deontological standards of private moral conduct, public actors are always necessarily weighing the benefits of short-term noninterference against its long-term costs. "It is a fearsome thing to kill," confesses a shuddering character in Brecht's *Man Is Man*, "but it is not granted to us not to kill."[7]

In recent times, market liberals have insisted that to do nothing (laisser faire) is to eschew both action and its costs. But in fact market forces produce all kinds of outcomes, including many that are unfair, many that are unintended, and many that reflect the working of specifiable historical forces that are skewed, or Darwinian, or otherwise inequitable.[8] Liberals thus often remain oblivious to realities

---

6. In chap. 17 of *The Prince*, Machiavelli states the general principle as follows:

> A Prince, therefore, must not mind incurring the charge of cruelty for the purpose of keeping his subjects united and faithful; for, with a very few examples, he will be more merciful than those who, from excess of tenderness, allow disorders to arise, from whence spring bloodshed and rapine; for these as a rule injure the whole community, while the executions carried out by the Prince injure only the individual.

At issue is the contest between deontological and consequentialist morals: Machiavelli's point (and ours) would seem to be that in politics, where the fate of living communities rather than the souls of individual women and men is at stake, consequentialist reasoning is unavoidable.

7. Like Machiavelli, Brecht here pursues a consequentialist logic that sees men as confronted with a choice between actual evils that are distinguished only by degree, rather than between an ideal good and an ideal evil.

8. Markets are many things, but they are never free. The sociological critique of market liberalism is too well known to require rehearsing here, but this passage from John Ruskin suggests the tone of all subsequent critiques:

> In the community regulated only by laws of demand and supply, but protected from open violence, the persons who become rich are, generally speaking, industrious, resolute, proud, covetous, prompt, methodical, sensible, unimaginative, insensitive, and ignorant. The persons who remain poor are the entirely foolish, the entirely wise, the idle, the reckless, the humble, the thoughtful, the dull, the imaginative, the sensitive, the well-informed, the improvident, the irregularly and impulsively wicked, the clumsy knave, the open thief, and the entirely merciful, just, and Godly person. (*Unto This Last*, ed. L. J. Hubenka [Lincoln: University of Nebraska Press, 1967], pp. 74–75)

that statesmen cannot fail to grasp. A country suffering invasion can decide to resist or not to resist, but it cannot abstain from deciding, for that would be tantamount to deciding not to resist. A government facing runaway inflation can impose wage-price controls or not impose them, but it cannot defer to the market and pretend that it has not acted at all, for deference to a market that has itself produced inflation clearly amounts to a decision to permit or even to encourage inflation. Policy-makers understand this well enough. They often choose not to act precisely as part of a conscious political strategy aimed at getting inertial forces already at work to play themselves out. They may for example permit prices to "float" upward, in the hope of controlling demand, or permit profits to soar, in the hope of expanding the base for economic productivity and thus increasing national and individual wealth (the Kemp-Roth Supply-Side strategy suggesting that all boats rise on a rising tide).

The logic of consequences is thus always a public logic and is always an element in the conditions that underlie politics. The inertial momentum of history makes political decision inevitable.

Choice. In the political arena, to speak about doing is to speak about choosing—about deliberating, determining, and deciding. Action that is impulsive, arbitrary, or unconsidered is not yet political action. Just as we would not understand a sleepwalker to be a human agent or a hysteric to be a human actor, so a rabble is not an electorate and a mob is not a citizenry. If action is to be political, it must ensue from forethought and deliberation, from free and conscious choice. Anyone can be an actor. Only a citizen can be a *political* actor.

The political condition thus requires that we have some working notion of citizenship, one that incorporates both autonomy and volition. To speak of those who choose with deliberation and act with responsibility is in the political realm to speak of citizens. In a monarchy, as Hegel notes, only a despot or a king may be a citizen (i.e., a responsible political actor), whereas in a democracy the entire adult population may qualify; but in both cases, only free choosers count as political actors. "Masses" would by these measures seem not to count—not even when they "vote." Freedom is integral to politics, and for there to be politics there must be a living notion of the free, choosing will. It is thus hardly an accident that positivist social science, having liberated itself from the messy idea of freedom, finds itself incapable of comprehending politics.

This is not to argue that all actors in a political community are free (are citizens) or that there cannot be a real politics when choices of public consequence are made by a minority of citizens or by a single ruler. The question is not *who* chooses (for that issue is a feature of political regimes, not of the political condition to which regimes respond) but whether those who choose do so freely. Political actors are always citizens, although this fact forces every actual polity to confront the vital problem of defining the class of citizens (the class of free choosers—see Chapter 9).

Reasonableness. This criterion is to a degree already implicit in the idea of deliberate choice. Citizens construed as free choosers are by definition reasonable—nonimpulsive, thoughtful, and fair. But reasonableness is not simply a characteristic of deliberate choosers and actors but a distinguishing mark of political choices and actions, and as such it requires independent elaboration.

To say that politics is the search for reasonable choices, which must be made in the face of conflict and in the absence of independent grounds for judgment, is to say that politics seeks choices that are something less than arbitrary even though they cannot be perfectly Right or True or Scientific. Abstract rationality is not at stake, for that concept suggests some prepolitical standard of truth, some agreement on at least formal norms, of the sort that Rawls proposes or that Habermas would seem to have in mind. Yet in reality it is precisely the absence of such norms that gives rise to politics. Reasonableness as used here is a rather more commonsensical notion, whose color is practical rather than metaphysical. A reasonable choice or a reasonable settlement is not necessarily rational at all, but it will be seen as deliberate, nonrandom, uncoercive, and in a practical sense fair.

The word *reasonable* bespeaks practicality. It suggests that persons in conflict have consented to resolve their differences in the absence of mediating common standards, to reformulate their problems in a way that encompasses their interests (newly and more broadly conceived) even while it represents the community at large in a new way. "Well, I guess that's reasonable," admits an adversary who has not gotten his way but has been neither coerced nor cajoled into the agreement he has consented to. He is neither victor nor loser; rather, he has reformulated his view of what constitutes his interests and can now "see" things in a new manner.

Reasonable choices are generally public choices. That is to say, they are choices informed by an extension of perspective and by the reformulation of private interests in the setting of potential public goals. To be reasonable is therefore not to deny Self, but to place Self in the context of Other and to inform it with a sense of its dependence on the civic polity.

Conflict. It is not news to liberal democrats that politics arises out of conflict and takes place in a realm defined by (inter alia) power and interest. The entire tradition of liberal thought from Hobbes to Laswell supports the idea that politics is conflict resolution. Yet the paradox of consensus remains: if one claims that the condition of unanimity and consensus that politics wishes to achieve by art already exists by nature, then politics loses its purpose and becomes superfluous.

Rousseau makes the point with his customary incisiveness in the *Social Contract*. He anticipates and remonstrates with enthusiasts who would imagine that the General Will not only achieves an artificial community but is engendered by and acts as a mirror to a natural consensus. "If there were no different interests," he writes, "the common interest would be barely felt, as it would encounter no obstacle; all would go on of its own accord, and politics would cease to be an art."[9] Where there is natural consensus there cannot be conflict or power or need for reasonableness. Angels need not be reasonable (they are angelic); mutualists need not learn to think communally (they are defined by their communality). The garden where there is no discord makes politics unnecessary; just as the jungle where there is no reasonableness makes politics impossible.

Conflict, of course, must have limits in any political setting; otherwise, the war of all against all would preclude society in toto. Theorists have traditionally distinguished substantive, quotidian conflict (the raison d'être of politics) from procedural, long-term consensus (the sine qua non of politics). The latter, in the form of basic law, a constitution, the social contract itself, makes the former tolerable.

Formal consensus is sometimes described as "agreeing to disagree," but a more accurate description would be "agreeing on *how*

---

9. Jean-Jacques Rousseau, footnote to chap. 3, book 2 of *The Social Contract*. The paradox noted here (and clarified in the next chapter) is evident, for example, in Jane J. Mansbridge's otherwise excellent study of participation in a Vermont town and in an urban crisis center (*Beyond Adversary Democracy* [New York: Basic Books, 1980]).

to disagree": on whether, that is, to deal with conflict by suppressing it, ameliorating it, tolerating it, resolving it, or transforming it. It is around these political modes and the institutions connected with them that the several versions of democracy laid out in the next chapter revolve.

Absence of an Independent Ground. Among the several components proposed here for the political condition, the absence of an independent ground for judgment is probably the most novel and the most central. It certainly is a crucial criterion in distinguishing strong democracy from its competing regime types. Yet it has been litttle considered in previous discussions of democratic theory.

As we have seen, to choose and act politically is to choose and act responsibly, reasonably, and publicly yet without the guidance of independent consensual norms. Where there is certain knowledge, true science, or absolute right, there is no conflict that cannot be resolved by reference to the unity of truth, and thus there is no necessity for politics.[10]

Politics concerns itself only with those realms where truth is not— or is not *yet*—known. We do not vote for the best polio vaccine or conduct surveys on the ideal space shuttle, nor has Boolean algebra been subjected to electoral testing. But Laetrile and genetic engineering, while they belong formally to the domain of science, have aroused sufficient conflict among scientists to throw them into the political domain—and rightly so. Where consensus stops, politics starts.[11]

Liberal political theorists have always been afflicted by paradox

---

10. A lunatic may insist that lightning is a manifestation of Zeus's spitefulness and fire a cannon into the clouds to wreak vengeance; but the *political* question here is not the physical nature of lightning but only the erratic behavior of the lunatic, inasmuch as such behavior has public consequences.

11. There is of course a lively debate about whether scientific communities are themselves ultimately political. Thomas Kuhn has advanced the well-known argument that scientific debates within such communities are settled by power (by means of the position and prestige enjoyed by scientific elites and the inertia of their theories) rather than by scientific judgment. See Thomas S. Kuhn, *The Structure of Scientific Revolutions* (Chicago: University of Chicago Press, 1962).

But whether scientific communities are political has no effect on the claim made here, which is that political communities are never scientific (i.e., rooted in objective consensus). Indeed, a good illustration of this point is that the failure of scientists to reach consensus can take a controversy out of the domain of science and place it in the domain of politics. Thus genetic engineering, the possible effects of which are currently a matter of fundamental and seemingly irresolvable scientific debate, has become a legitimate concern of public policy makers—with respect not just to the possible public consequences but to the very course of inquiry and experiment.

when they consider the role of independent "natural" norms in politics. Although they understand that uncertainty and conflict are the occasion for politics, they share the human aspiration to certainty and find themselves drawn to putative absolutes of one kind or another that might facilitate "scientific" or "rational" or "natural" solutions to political questions. They look hopefully to theoretical reason (Kant's categorical imperative or Rawls's principles of justice, for example); or to natural law (John Locke and the American tradition of judicial review, for example); or to a naturalistically grounded theory of absolute right (Hobbes or Robert Nozick); or to some notion of communicative rationality (Habermas); or to true knowledge (Plato's *epistemē*). In each case, philosophy is required to provide norms external to the political process with which political problems can then be resolved. The consequences for the political process are, however, paralytic. In conflating epistemology and action, the liberal can no longer distinguish the needs of the reasonable actor from those of the speculative metaphysician. The tendency in recent American jurisprudence to substitute formal reasoning and the abstract principles it yields for political processes is a perfect illustration.[12]

The seductiveness of abstract principle in the face of uncertainty is perfectly understandable given the muddy ambiguities typical of the actual political realm. Even when he has lost the metaphysical ladder on which he hoped to ascend out of the cave, the philosopher is loath to say with Yeats,

> Now that my ladder's gone
> I must lie down where all the ladders start
> In the foul rag and bone shop of the heart.[13]

But politics is a rag and bone shop of the practical and the concrete, the everyday and the ambiguous, the malleable and the evanescent. There is no firm stairway to nature or to some higher realm from which one can borrow shaping norms and fixed standards to lend abstract order to inchoate experience. If there is political truth, it can only be the kind of truth that, in William James's phrase, "is made in the course of experience."

It is, similarly, not so much Burke's conservatism as his sense of

---

12. For an excellent critical discussion see John Hart Ely, *Democracy and Distrust* (Cambridge, Mass.: Harvard University Press, 1980).
13. William Butler Yeats, "The Circus Animals' Parade."

the concreteness of politics that leads him to the conviction that "the science of constructing a commonwealth, or renovating it, or reforming it, is, like every other experimental science, not to be taught a priori."[14] In speaking thus, Burke merely echoes the traditional republican wariness of universal principles and abstract reasoning. He speaks for Machiavelli, for Montesquieu, and even for his nemesis Rousseau when he warns of the "multitude of misfortunes" that can be traced to "considering certain general maxims without attending to circumstances, to time, to places, to conjectures and to actors"; for, he concludes, "if we do not attend scrupulously to these, the medicine of today becomes the poison of tomorrow."[15]

The political condition is engendered by history, circumstance, and context. Real political actors, confronted with controversies and dilemmas issuing out of fundamental conflicts of interest and value in a changing society, are required to make responsible and reasonable choices. The philosopher, like Minerva's owl, comes too late to help. Or, if he has somehow arrived promptly, the dilemmas are superseded by virtue of his arrival and the need for politics disappears. The citizen wishes in any case only to act rightly, not to know for certain; only to choose reasonably, not to reason scientifically; only to overcome conflict and secure transient peace, not to discover eternity; only to cooperate with others, not to achieve moral oneness; only to formulate common causes, not to obliterate all differences. Politics is what men do when metaphysics fails; it is not metaphysics reified as a constitution.

STRONG DEMOCRACY AS A RESPONSE TO THE POLITICAL CONDITION

Every political regime, even those that are ultimately politics-denying, can be characterized as arising out of a response to the seven components of the political condition elucidated above. I will offer a typology of democratic regime types in the next chapter, but here I want to introduce strong democracy—a regime form that has the particular virtue of responding directly to the dilemmas posed by

---

14. Edmund Burke, *Reflections on the Revolution in France* (London: Dent, 1910), p. 58.
15. Ibid., p. 277. It is ironic that Burke contemns Rousseau along with the other Philosophes for an attachment to metaphysics that Rousseau himself despises. Indeed, in books 3 and 4 of *The Social Contract*, as well as in the essays on Poland and Corsica, Rousseau exhibits an almost Burkean concern with time, place, and circumstance.

the political condition. This condition obtains, it will be recalled, when there is *a necessity for public action, and thus for reasonable public choice, in the presence of conflict and in the absence of private or independent grounds for judgment.*

The response to these conditions is strong democracy, which can be formally defined as *politics in the participatory mode where conflict is resolved in the absence of an independent ground through a participatory process of ongoing, proximate self-legislation and the creation of a political community capable of transforming dependent, private individuals into free citizens and partial and private interests into public goods.*

We shall see in the next chapter how this definition distinguishes strong democracy from its rival forms, and in subsequent chapters we shall examine what strong democracy entails for common talk and action, citizenship, and community and for the institutions these things require. This chapter can thus be ended with only some brief remarks on strong democracy's aptness as a response to the seven conditions of politics.

Action. Aristotle was persuaded in the *Eudaimonian Ethics* that man was defined above all by action. Voltaire and Rousseau, who agreed on little else, might have written with a single pen this thought (actually Voltaire's): "Man is born for action as the sparks fly upward. Not to do anything is the same for man as not to exist."[16] Or this (Rousseau's): "Man is born to act and to think, not to reflect."[17] Yet in recent centuries, as C. B. Macpherson has noted, "the notion that activity itself is pleasurable, is a utility, has sunk almost without a trace under [the] utilitarian vision of life."[18] Hannah Arendt spent much of her productive career deploring the disappearance of the *vita activa* as a central element in political life. Indeed, the thin conception of democracy depends so much on a passive and inarticulate citizenry that Bernard Berelson and his colleagues have asked, "How could a mass democracy work if all the people were deeply involved in politics?"[19]

The centrality of process, transformation, and creation to the idea

16. Voltaire, *Philosophical Letters*, no. 23 (Indianapolis: Bobbs-Merrill, 1961).
17. Jean-Jacques Rousseau, "Preface to Narcisse," trans. Benjamin R. Barber and Janis Forman, *Political Theory* 6, 4 (November 1978): 13.
18. C. B. Macpherson, *The Real World of Democracy* (Oxford: Oxford University Press, 1966), p. 38.
19. B. R. Berelson et al., *Voting* (Chicago: University of Chicago Press, 1954), p. 318.

of action in the strong democratic definition of democracy is not, then, a standard feature of democratic thinking. In strong democracy, politics is something done by, not to, citizens. Activity is its chief virtue, and involvement, commitment, obligation, and service—common deliberation, common decision, and common work—are its hallmarks.

Publicness. Strong democracy creates a public capable of reasonable public deliberation and decision and therefore rejects traditional reductionism and the fiction of atomic individuals creating social bonds ex nihilo.[20] But it also rejects the myth of corporatism and collectivism that posits an abstract community prior to individuals and from which individuals derive their significance and purpose. Strong democracy is thus hostile to that reductive historical sociology that makes an individual's class or race or social movement the sole determinant of his actions and that tries to reconstruct conscious human beings as pure species beings. Far from positing community a priori, strong democratic theory understands the creation of community as one of the chief tasks of political activity in the participatory mode. Far from positing historical identity as the condition of politics, it posits politics as the conditioner of given historical identities—as the means by which men are emancipated from determinative historical forces.

With John Dewey, strong democracy recognizes that "the public has no hands except those of individual human beings"; yet it also recognizes "that the essential problem is that of transforming the action of such hands so that it will be animated by regard for social ends." It thus focuses attention on the question, "How can a public be organized?"[21] Or in our language, how can a civic community be created? The creation of community here becomes a concomitant of the creation of public goods and public ends. Conversely, the creation of public ends depends on the creation of a community of citizens who regard themselves as comrades and who are endowed with an enlarging empathy. Community, public goods, and citizen-

---

20. Bruce Ackerman alludes to (and to some extent represents) this tradition of atomism when he refers to the liberal definition of women and men as "asocial monads" (*Social Justice and the Liberal State* [New Haven: Yale University Press, 1980], p. 100).

21. John Dewey, *The Public*, pp. 82 and 14.

134   *The Argument for Citizenship*

ship thus ultimately become three interdependent parts of a single democratic circle whose compass grows to describe a true public.[22]

Necessity. Because it is rooted in participatory action and in a keen sense of the public character of politics, strong democracy is particularly sensitive to the element of necessity in public choice. Its concrete sense of the interconnectedness of events and of the embeddedness of citizens in a changing polity safeguard it from that dangerous innocence with which liberals disclaim responsibility for historical laws and events not of their own making. Like the realist, the participationist sees power as inevitable—as a presence with which every politics must reckon. But he also recognizes that power legitimized and power used are what make social freedom and political equality possible.

In sum, strong democracy not only places agency and responsibility at the center of political activity, it understands them as an indispensable response to man's need to act in the face of conflict—which is the precipitating condition of politics itself.

Choice. Participation as a political mode obviously presupposes citizens capable of meaningful and autonomous choice, as do all coherent theories of democracy. Consent without autonomy is not consent. But participation enhances volition in that it lends to choice the direct engagement of the deliberating mind and the choosing will. While clients or voters or constituents or masses may be characterized in ways that omit their free agency, participants cannot: individual volition is the heart of the idea of self-legislation through participation. In this emphasis, strong democracy may be said to go beyond the simple idea of free agency shared by all democratic theories.[23]

---

22. Gandhi employs the metaphor of the democratic circle with poetic if extravagant effect:

> Life will not be a pyramid with the apex sustained by the bottom. But it will be an oceanic circle whose centre will be the individual always ready to perish for the village, the latter ready to perish for the circle of villages, till at last the whole becomes one life composed of individuals, never aggressive in their arrogance but ever humble, sharing the majesty of the oceanic circle of which they are integral units. (M. K. Gandhi, *Democracy: Real and Deceptive*, compiled by R. K. Prabhu [Ahmedabad: Navajivan, 1942], pp. 73–74)

23. Since every democratic theory requires a commitment to the reality of human agency—of meaningful volition in a world of choice that is not (*pace* B. F. Skinner) beyond freedom and dignity—the only legitimate debate concerns the degree and

Reasonableness. I have suggested that public choices and actions, which must be more than arbitrary or merely self-interested yet cannot be expected to be scientific or certifiable by the standards of abstract philosophy, must at least be "reasonable." The way in which participatory processes of ongoing, proximate self-legislation meet this criterion goes to the heart of the strong democratic project. Much of Chapter 8 is devoted to specifying what *reasonable* means from the perspective of strong democratic talk and action. Here it should be noted only that reasonableness is not an abstract precondition of politics but an attitude that strong democratic politics itself engenders.

Conflict. Every form of pluralist democracy perceives conflict as central to politics, but pluralists have often charged that participatory and communitarian theories slight conflict in favor of consensualism. Consensual democracy resolves conflict by defining it out of the political picture from the outset. Strong democracy is different. It is unique among nonrepresentative forms in that it acknowledges (and indeed uses) the centrality of conflict in the political process. This recognition differentiates it radically from "unitary" modes of democracy and insulates it from collectivist and unitary abuses of communitarianism.

At the same time, strong democracy resists the liberal idea that conflict is intractable and at best vulnerable only to adjudication or toleration. Instead, it develops a politics that can transform conflict into cooperation through citizen participation, public deliberation, and civic education. Strong democratic theory begins but does not end with conflict: it acknowledges conflict but ultimately transforms rather than accommodates or minimizes it.

Absence of an Independent Ground. It is perhaps the greatest virtue of strong democracy, and certainly the one that makes it unique, that it yields a truly autonomous politics. The procedures of self-legislation and community-building on which it relies are self-contained and self-correcting and thus are genuinely independent of external norms, prepolitical truths, or natural rights. Strong democratic politics, it would be foolish to deny, does operate in a world of

---

character of volition under various social circumstances. See for example Christian Bay's *The Structure of Freedom* (Stanford: Stanford University Press, 1958). In the end, however, as John Stuart Mill noted long ago, the philosophical debate about free will simply does not bear on the political debate about free choice.

values and truth claims, and participants in the political process naturally have their own ideas about right and interest and truth. This form of politics is anything but "value-free" in the sense attributed to politics by the positivists. But the autonomy of the democratic process under strong democracy equalizes value inputs. It gives to each individual's convictions and beliefs an equal starting place and associates legitimacy with what happens to convictions and beliefs in the course of public talk and action rather than with their prior epistemological status. The legitimacy of a value is thus a feature of its publicness, of how it is refined, changed, or transformed when confronted with a public and the public norms which that public has already legitimized through its politics. Politics in the participatory mode does not choose between or merely ratify values whose legitimacy is a matter of prior record. It makes preferences and opinions earn legitimacy by forcing them to run the gauntlet of public deliberation and public judgment. They emerge not simply legitimized but transformed by the processes to which they have been subjected.

The basic difference between the politics of bargaining and exchange and the politics of transformation is that in the former, choice is a matter of selecting among options and giving the winner the legitimacy of consent, whereas in the latter, choice is superseded by judgment and leads men and women to modify and enlarge options as a consequence of seeing them in new, public ways. For this reason, decision without common talk always falls short of judgment and cannot be the basis of strong democratic politics. The test of legitimacy is whether an individual value has been changed in some significant way to accommodate larger—that is, more common or public—concerns. If a value emerges from the political process entirely unchanged by that process, then either it remains a private value masquerading as a public norm or it denotes a prior consensus that has been revealed by the political process. In neither case has participatory politics accomplished its task of legitimation.

For this reason, there can be no strong democratic legitimacy without ongoing talk. Where voting is a static act of expressing one's preference, participation is a dynamic act of imagination that requires participants to change how they see the world. Voting suggests a group of men in a cafeteria bargaining about what they can buy as a group that will suit their individual tastes. Strong democratic politics suggests a group of men in a cafeteria contriving new menus, inventing new recipes, and experimenting with new diets in the effort to create a public taste that they can all share and that will supersede the conflicting private tastes about which they once tried to strike bargains. Voting, in the bargaining model, often fixes choices and thereby stultifies the imagination; judging, in the model of strong democracy, activates imagination by demanding that participants reexamine their values and interests in light of all the inescapable others—the public.

The rightness of public acts depends then neither on a prepolitical notion of abstract right nor on a simple conception of popular will or popular consent.[24] For what is crucial is not consent pure and simple but the active consent of participating citizens who have imaginatively reconstructed their own values as public norms through the process of identifying and empathizing with the values of others. This perspective enables strong democratic theory to substitute for the usual discussion of Abstract Right versus Popular Will a more concrete and institutionally pertinent discussion of the character of citizenship and of its implementation as political judgment. How this discussion evolves is examined in Chapters 8 and 9.

This brief review was meant to show that at least on first analysis strong democracy would seem to meet the conditions of politics with particular aptness (although this is not to claim that it is the sole appropriate response).[25] To extend and deepen our understanding of the theory of strong democracy, we now need to place it in the context of the rival forms of democracy—that is, to place it within a formal typology of democratic regime forms that includes

---

24. Michael Walzer, a sensitive and incisive radical democrat, portrays the problem as a "tension between philosophy and democracy," between Rational Right as purveyed by philosophy and legitimate will as exhibited in popular choice ("Philosophy and Democracy," *Political Theory* 9, 3 [August 1981]: 379–99). But the problem is not Right versus Opinion but achieving right opinion. What is required is a self-regulating will, not a will subordinated to abstract reason.

25. Were strong democracy the *only* possible response to the seven conditions of politics enumerated here, critics could say that those conditions were analytically indistinguishable from it—that I had loaded the definition of politics so as to preclude any outcome other than the desired (strong democratic) one. A problem of this sort afflicts the relationship between Rawls's two principles of justice and the conditions of the "original position" to which they are supposedly a response. I have charged Rawls with this error in my "Justifying Justice: Problems of Psychology, Measurement, and Politics in Rawls," *American Political Science Review* 69, 2 (June 1975), and am thus naturally anxious to avoid committing it here myself.

138   *The Argument for Citizenship*

representative democracy and its constituent variations as well as "unitary" democracy as a competing form of participatory politics. The next chapter thus concludes the effort to give strong democracy an ideal formal definition. The subsequent chapters will attempt to give substance to the ideal.

[21]
On a Razor's Edge

In spite of the resources that come with it, authority is also a strait jacket.[1] Constituents confer resources in exchange for services. Power is received in the promise of fulfilling expectations—people in authority, we insist, must provide direction, protection, and order. These expectations often make good sense. In technical situations, adequate preparations for the current problem have been made already. Procedures, lines of authority, role placements, and norms of operation have been established. People have a sufficiently clear idea about what needs to be done and how to go about doing it. Creativity and ingenuity may be needed, but only to devise variations on known themes, not new themes altogether.

Our expectations of authority figures become counterproductive when our organizations and communities face an adaptive challenge—when the application of known methods and procedures will not suffice. We continue to expect our authorities to restore equilibrium with dispatch. If they do not act quickly to reduce our feelings of urgency, we bring them down. Sometimes, we kill them.

That we sometimes call these situations "crises in leadership" is symptomatic of the problem of habitually blaming authority. Stymied by our expectation that authorities should provide in adaptive situations what they can and do provide routinely, we blame them for the persistence of frustrating problems that demand our own adaptive work. And so, predictably, our authorities supply us with fake remedies and diversions. We ask for it. If they want to maintain

126 / LEADING WITH AUTHORITY

the authorization we give them, they have to deliver, or provide *promises* of deliverance. When we discover that our authorities have failed, too frequently we expiate our failures by scapegoating them and looking for someone with fresh promises.

When authorities do provide the quick fixes we repeatedly demand, they may be setting a course for crisis, both for themselves and their people. Maybe the storm that's brewing will hit on someone else's watch, and they will escape unscathed; maybe not. Many heads of state have fallen as problems fester into crises—recently: Duvalier in Haiti, Marcos in the Philippines, Ortega in Nicaragua, Honecker in East Germany, Ceauscescu in Romania, to name a few. Many heads of American businesses went the same route during the last decade by failing to mobilize adaptive responses to foreign competition.

Exercising leadership from a position of authority in adaptive situations means going against the grain. Rather than fulfilling the expectation for answers, one provides questions; rather than protecting people from outside threat, one lets people feel the threat in order to stimulate adaptation; instead of orienting people to their current roles, one disorients people so that new role relationships develop; rather than quelling conflict, one generates it; instead of maintaining norms, one challenges them.

Of course, real life is fluid. An authority figure, even in adaptive situations, will have to act differently to fulfill each of these social functions depending on several factors, as just mentioned: the severity of the problem, the resilience of the social system, the ripeness of the issue, and time. For example, in an organization one may have to act firmly to maintain norms and restore clear role assignments, while challenging people with questions and raising conflict about direction. But to make tactical decisions to move between technical and adaptive modes along each of these five dimensions, one first needs a clear conception of the differences. Table 2 outlines the shifts that adaptive situations require of authorities.

In adaptive situations, fulfilling the social functions of authority requires walking a razor's edge. Challenge people too fast, and they will push the authority figure over for failing their expectations for stability. But challenge people too slowly, and they will throw him down when they discover that no progress has been made. Ultimately, they will blame him for lack of progress. To stay balanced on the edge, one needs a strategic understanding of the specific tools and constraints that come with one's authority.

Yet in either case, an authority figure cuts his feet. When he is the focus of hopes and pains that are beyond his magic, or any magic, some people are bound to attack, at least in words. Even the most agile cannot dodge these attacks completely, nor shield himself, mentally and physically, from an assortment of wounds.

Leadership is a razor's edge because one has to oversee a sustained period of social disequilibrium during which people confront the contradictions in their lives and communities and adjust their values

Table 2. Leadership with Authority in Adaptive Situations

Social function	Situational type	
	Technical	Adaptive
Direction	Authority provides problem definition and solution	Authority identifies the adaptive challenge, provides diagnosis of condition, and produces questions about problem definitions and solutions
Protection	Authority protects from external threat	Authority discloses external threat
Role orientation	Authority orients	Authority disorients current roles, or resists pressure to orient people in new roles too quickly
Controlling conflict	Authority restores order	Authority exposes conflict, or lets it emerge
Norm maintenance	Authority maintains norms	Authority challenges norms, or allows them to be challenged

128 / LEADING WITH AUTHORITY

and behavior to accommodate new realities. We have begun to explore the resources that authority brings to directing this process. These tools can be organized according to five strategic principles of leadership:

1. *Identify the adaptive challenge.* Diagnose the situation in light of the values at stake, and unbundle the issues that come with it.
2. *Keep the level of distress within a tolerable range for doing adaptive work.* To use the pressure cooker analogy, keep the heat up without blowing up the vessel.
3. *Focus attention on ripening issues and not on stress-reducing distractions.* Identify which issues can currently engage attention; and while directing attention to them, counteract work avoidance mechanisms like denial, scapegoating, externalizing the enemy, pretending the problem is technical, or attacking individuals rather than issues.
4. *Give the work back to people, but at a rate they can stand.* Place and develop responsibility by putting the pressure on the people with the problem.
5. *Protect voices of leadership without authority.* Give cover to those who raise hard questions and generate distress—people who point to the internal contradictions of the society. These individuals often will have latitude to provoke rethinking that authorities do not have.

I have suggested that authority, formal and informal, is a key component of the holding environment—the containing vessel—for the stresses of change. In the short run, people in authority must regulate the stresses directly. They have to work within the vessel's current carrying capacity. In the medium term, the authority figure can reinforce his contribution to the holding environment by strengthening his own authority relationships within the community, and thus increase the community's resilience during his tenure.

For the long term, the vessel can be given enduring resilience so that it can tolerate the higher pressures that tougher issues generate, somewhat independent of the personal presence and power of the authority figure. People in authority can spur the development of civic associations that generate social networks of identification.[2]

They can increase the trustworthiness of authority structures and institutions.[3] They can create rituals that embody and strengthen shared orienting values. They can model norms of collaboration, responsibility-taking, and effective conflict resolution. They can authorize broadly.[4] And they can promote an ethos of learning and creativity. Over time, a community can become familiar with adaptive work, its pain and its profit.

The primary focus of this book is on the short-run task of making progress on an adaptive challenge. The long-term task of leadership—developing adaptive capacity—is largely beyond our current scope, although to some extent the long term is served by accumulating progress and capturing lessons from individual successes. In focusing on immediate problems, a person intent on leading must ask four practical and related questions: How can he identify an adaptive challenge, keep attention focused on the ripening issue, regulate stress to keep it within a productive range, and take action to promote social learning so that a new equilibrium is reached? The efforts in 1965 to secure voting rights for black Americans provides a testing ground for these questions; in this chapter, we focus on President Lyndon Johnson's strategy of leading from a position of authority.[5]

Prelude: The Ripening of the Issue

When Johnson assumed the presidency, he moved immediately to repair the containing vessel that had been weakened by Kennedy's assassination. He acted to reduce the public's disorientation and fear of being aboard a rudderless ship. In his first address to the nation, the new President sounded a clear and direct call to Congress for action. He introduced few, if any, of his personal ideas; instead he promised to carry on the work of his predecessor. By so doing, he reduced the distress of transition and established trust.

> And now the ideas and the ideals which [Kennedy] so nobly represented must and will be translated into effective action . . . In this critical moment, it is our duty, yours and mine, to do away with uncertainty and delay and doubt and to show that we are capable of decisive action; that from the brutal loss of our leader we will derive

130 / LEADING WITH AUTHORITY

not weakness but strength, that we can and will act and act now . . . John Kennedy's death commands what his life conveyed—that America must move forward.

Presidents usually bring their own people into their administrations. Yet in 1963, with only eleven months to prove himself before the next presidential election, Johnson relied on Kennedy's Cabinet and White House. Through continuity in personnel, Johnson again buttressed the holding environment at the same time that he avoided drawing attention to himself. With major initiatives ahead, he could not afford to isolate himself on the point and increase his vulnerability to attack. "I constantly had before me the picture that Kennedy had selected me as executor of his will, it was my duty to carry on and this meant his people as well as his programs. They were part of his legacy. I simply couldn't let the country think that I was all alone."[6]

Even after he was elected President in his own right, Johnson kept Kennedy men around him. Not only did he value their talent, but he needed the ongoing support of their constituencies: media, Easterners, and intellectuals.[7] Thus, he continued to borrow Kennedy's authority, shield his program with Kennedy's name, and deflect public attention from his own person. He had to strengthen the holding environment to contain the pressures he planned to generate with his policies.

Of his many initiatives, perhaps Johnson's most successful were in civil rights.[8] At his best, Lyndon Johnson built for himself the opportunity for leadership by listening intently to the nation, identifying its internal contradictions, and transforming the dialogue of competing interests into legislation and programs. He encouraged Martin Luther King Jr.'s civil rights vision, and he encouraged what he viewed as George Wallace's populist vision of economic justice.[9] Progress would be made by pushing people to engage with one another to adjust their views or reach compromises. The parties would be made to do the work.

Indeed, in his legislative program Johnson routinely put the pressure on the people who asked him for help. Thus, Johnson put the pressure on black leaders to persuade reluctant conservatives. The key to success on civil rights, in Johnson's opinion, lay in the hands of the minority party, the Republicans headed by Senator Everett Dirksen. Without their support, no new legislation could get past Senator Richard Russell and the block of Southern Democratic senators committed to its defeat. They would filibuster it to death, as they had done with nearly every civil rights bill for nearly a century.[10] Yet Johnson was not going to do the lobbying work alone. To win the Republicans over, Johnson called on Roy Wilkins, head of the National Association for the Advancement of Colored People (NAACP), as prelude to introducing the Civil Rights Act of that year. He placed the call on January 6, 1964, six weeks after assuming the presidency.

> Johnson: "When are you going to get down here and start civil righting?"
> Wilkins: "As soon as I get rid of my board of directors annual meeting."
> Johnson: "Well you tell them that I think they've got a mighty good man. I don't know of a better, fairer, or abler man in the United States. What I want you to do though is to get on this bill now. Because unless you get twenty-five Republicans you're not going to get cloture [to stop a filibuster]. Now you can't quote me on this, but Russell says he's already got enough commitments to prevent cloture. I think you are going to have to sit down with Dirksen and persuade him this is in the interest of the Republican party, and you think that if the Republicans go along with you on cloture, why you'll go along with them at elections. And let them know that you're going with the presidential candidate that offers you the best hope and the best chance of dignity and decency in this country, and you're going with a senatorial man who does the same thing. *I'm no magician.* Now I want to be with you, and I'm going to help you any way I can. But you're going to have to get these folks in here, and the quicker you get them the better. If we lose this fight we're going back ten years."

Indeed, the Senate went through seventy-five days of filibuster over the Civil Rights bill—the longest in its history. But on June 10, 1964, it was ready to vote on cloture. The key, as Johnson had said, was Dirksen. In response to Russell's protest that "the bill simply involves a political question and not a moral issue," Dirksen finally took his stand. Declaring "civil rights is an idea whose time has come . . . we are confronted with a moral issue," he had turned around.[11] Dirksen's priorities had shifted in the course of his conversations with Wilkins and others. The issue had been made to ripen. As Johnson later described the problem to his biographer Doris Kearns: "The challenge was to learn what it was that mattered to each of these men, understand which issues were critical to whom and why. Without that understanding nothing is possible. Knowing the leaders and understanding their organizational needs let me shape my legislative program to fit both their needs and mine." In pursuing domestic policies in general, Johnson sought to induce the relevant parties—business leaders, educators, labor, the media—to get involved with one another. Some authorities might concentrate on getting people to acquiesce to their commands. Johnson sought to educate people to cooperate with one another, respecting one another's goals. He corraled people into collaborative work. As he described it, "I wanted each of these men to participate in my administration in a dozen different ways. The key was to get men from different groups so involved with each other on so many committees and delegations covering so many issues that no one could afford to be uncompromising on any one issue alone."[12]

Johnson intended to mobilize the nation as a whole to work on issues that had been avoided for nearly two hundred years. Yet mobilizing the society to tackle hard problems and learn new ways required far more than fashioning deals in the legislature; it required public leadership. Johnson had to identify the adaptive challenges facing the nation, regulate the level of distress, counteract work-avoiding distractions, place responsibility where it belonged, and protect voices of leadership in the community. Nowhere did he illustrate this strategy of leadership better than during events in Selma, Alabama.

Selma—Eight Days in 1965

On Sunday, March 7, 1965, black Americans set out to march from Selma to the state capital at Montgomery in an all-out drive for voting rights. Selma, a city of about 29,000, had slightly more black people than white, but only 3 percent of the people on its voting rolls were black. Out of 15,000 black citizens, 325 were registered to vote.[13] The county had used time-worn methods to prevent black citizens from registering to vote, including lengthy written examinations and tricky oral questions like: Recite the Thirteenth Amendment to the Constitution, and what two rights does a citizen have after indictment by a grand jury? Governor Wallace of Alabama had declared during his campaign in 1962: "From this cradle of the Confederacy, this very heart of the great Anglo-Saxon Southland . . . , segregation now! Segregation tomorrow! Segregation forever!"[14]

In response to the voting rights march, Governor Wallace sent the state police against the 600 unarmed black people as they reached the city limits.[15] Americans throughout the country witnessed with shock and fury the televised scenes of black men, women, and children being beaten with billy clubs, stricken with tear gas, and bullwhipped by troopers on horseback. As loud as the screaming was the yelling of white onlookers, "Git 'em! Git 'em!"[16] In reaction, spontaneous demonstrations sprang up across the land as massive pressure focused on President Johnson to mobilize the national guard.[17]

Johnson, however, refused to move. In fact, he faced contrary pressures from Sunday's bloodshed, each with its own long history. On one hand, the outraged public called on the President to act forcefully at once to protect the marchers in Selma. People marched and sat-in at the White House; they marched and sat-in at the Justice Department; they berated him in the press nationwide. Dr. Martin Luther King Jr., "dismayed and discouraged," accused the federal government of "timidity."[18] On the other hand, many others wanted Johnson to keep out of the matter. They expressed great fear of federal interference in their own state affairs. White Southerners, among others in the nation, were tired of federal government intervention into their way of life and wanted to maintain local norms and control. Johnson was faced with a conflict between two different constituencies with two opposing values: states' rights, which represented white supremacy, and voting rights.

This conflict was nothing new. It dated back to the Civil War era. What should be the balance of power between local and central government in determining civil rights? No one knew better than Johnson, a long-time Texas politician, how sensitive this question

134 / LEADING WITH AUTHORITY

remained in the South. And no one knew better than Johnson, as former Senate Majority Leader and Vice-President, that the balance of power between local and central governments had been shifting on the rights issue. The Supreme Court ruled in 1954 that segregated schools were illegal.[19] President Eisenhower felt obliged to back up that ruling in 1957 when he sent federal troops to Little Rock, Arkansas, to integrate Central High School. Five years later, in 1962, John F. Kennedy sent federal troops to protect James Meredith as he enrolled at the University of Mississippi. Just months before the march in Selma, Johnson and Congress had passed the historic Civil Rights Act of 1964, which further strengthened the power of the central government over local affairs. Black people could no longer be discriminated against in most places of public accommodation, like hotels, restaurants, and bathrooms. Employers and unions had to provide equal employment opportunities for minorities. Schools were given financial and technical assistance to speed desegregation.

The country had spent years deliberating and testing the issue and, by and large, had come down on the side of protecting civil rights against local transgression. But not fully. The previous year, Congress had been unable to agree on a voting rights provision for the 1964 Civil Rights Act. Johnson had floated the idea, but Congress rejected it. Too many white people found it hard enough to integrate restaurants and schools. They refused to give blacks political power. The Congressional stalemate on voting rights indicated that the country as a whole was not yet ready to enfranchise minorities. Urgency over the issue was far from widespread; voting rights had not yet fastened in people's minds. The steps taken in 1964 toward guaranteeing civil rights were as large as the public seemed able to take at that moment.

Legislators were not about to take pains unless constituents demanded it. Taking pains for a legislator meant making costly bargains with other legislators, giving in on one issue in exchange for support on another, and paying the price back home. These bargains were least painful and risky if the legislator had multiple goals with varying importance to his or her district. A minor goal could be traded away for an urgent one, particularly if other legislators had complementary priorities, without much cost. Such was the case with civil rights legislation. Until Selma, white citizens across the nation generally gave voting rights low priority. For instance, during the

Senate debate over the Civil Rights Bill of 1957, four liberal Western senators—Wayne Morse, Warren Magnuson, Mike Mansfield, and Jim Murray—agreed to support a greatly weakened bill in exchange for Southern support to finance the construction of the Hells Canyon Dam in Idaho. The dam would generate electrical power for the region. Although these Western senators would normally back civil rights, they were compelled to make trades because their districts cared more about the dam.[20]

In private meetings in early 1965, Johnson, knowing the constraints of his role, encouraged King in his plans to ripen the voting rights issue. Although he hoped there would be no violence, he thought public pressure might set the stage for legislative action.[21] As did King. By generating nationwide urgency, the civil rights movement aimed to change the public's priorities and throw Congress into motion. King and his strategists had learned through decades of effort that the federal government would protect the rights of black Americans when public pressure forced it to.[22] So the civil rights movement would turn up the heat. Through the carefully scripted presence of television reporters, the brutality of racism would be transmitted into living rooms throughout the land. Demonstrations would force the nation to pay attention. On Sunday, March 7, after the televised beatings in Selma, Dr. King announced:

> In the vicious maltreatment of defenseless citizens of Selma, where old women and young children were gassed and clubbed at random, we have witnessed an eruption of the disease of racism which seeks to destroy all of America . . . The people of Selma will struggle for the soul of the Nation, but it is fitting that all Americans help to bear the burden. I call, therefore, on clergy of all faiths, representative of every part of the country to join me in Selma for a minister's march on Montgomery Tuesday morning.[23]

In anticipation of Tuesday's march, the pressure on Johnson grew enormously. Marches and demonstrations proliferated across the country. Busloads and planeloads of priests, ministers, rabbis, nuns, and lay people descended on Selma.[24] In Washington, D.C., sit-ins at the Justice Department continued to block Attorney General Katzenbach's office. The White House was deluged with telegrams and calls to take action. A group of demonstrators sat-in during a White

136 / LEADING WITH AUTHORITY

House tour, yelling angry epithets at whoever passed by. Clearly, the public did not relish the prospect of more televised beatings, this time with King and the nation's clergy at the forefront. The public looked to President Johnson to restore order. As he described it, "Everywhere I looked I was being denounced for my 'unbelievable lack of action.'"[25]

On Monday afternoon, King's lawyers appealed to the federal court in Montgomery for an injunction forbidding local and state authorities from interfering with Tuesday's march.[26] Instead, Judge Frank Johnson issued a restraining order to delay the march entirely for a few days until proper safety precautions could be made. In light of this order, President Johnson felt compelled to step in. He quietly sent LeRoy Collins from the Justice Department aboard Air Force One to negotiate a middle path with King that would keep the public pressure on without going farther than any President could legally allow. At the very last minute, on Tuesday morning as the march itself was moving, they made a deal. King avoided clashing with local and State police, and with the federal court, and turned the march back after a dramatic moment of prayer at the site of Sunday's violence.[27] The nation held its breath as it lived through the encounter on television. And though momentarily relieved, the acute level of tension remained very high. Dr. King insisted that the full three-day march to Montgomery still lay ahead.

Johnson continued to hold steady. He neither quelled nor inflamed the situation. Rather than take dramatic public action or a clear stand, Johnson issued a luke-warm statement Tuesday afternoon deploring the brutality in Selma and urging leaders on all sides to "approach this tense situation with calmness, reasonableness, and respect for law and order."[28] He added that he would be sending a voting rights bill to Congress by the weekend. Privately, however, after seeing the televised beatings and judging their public impact, he called in the Justice Department and asked them to draft the strongest bill that would have any chance of surviving a constitutional challenge.[29]

On Tuesday night, Reverend James J. Reeb, a white Unitarian minister from Boston, was beaten badly by a group of white people in Selma; he died two days later. His was the second death. Jimmy Lee Jackson, a seventeen year-old black man, had been shot by state troopers two weeks before while marching in nearby Marion, Alabama.[30] Reverend Reeb's fatal beating added more fuel to the demonstrations and the urgency. "But," as Kearns described it, "Johnson refused to be pushed. Pickets surrounded the White House, carrying placards calculated to shame him into action: 'LBJ, open your eyes, see the sickness of the South, see the horrors of your homeland.' Telegrams and letters demanding action streamed into the President's office."[31] Still, Johnson held steady through Tuesday night, Wednesday, Thursday, and Friday. At one point, a presidential aide interjected, "We have to do something." Johnson replied, "We will. Keep the pressure on. Make it clear we're not going to give an inch. Now that Wallace . . . it's his ox that's in the ditch, let's see how he gets him out."[32]

Finally, on Friday, Wallace asked to meet with the President, and Johnson granted the request at once. As Johnson understood the situation, Wallace had national aspirations. He had run briefly for President in 1964. He could ill afford more bloodshed broadcast nationwide from his state. As much as he hated to give in on civil rights, Wallace also had to maintain law and order. Thus, Johnson had something Wallace needed. He could help Wallace back out of his corner because he, Johnson, had refused to back into one himself. "On Saturday, in the Oval Office, they discussed the question of troops. Johnson appealed to the large ambition and the populist strain that he perceived in Wallace: How could there be any fixed limits, he suggested, to the political career of the first Southern governor to combine economic and social reform with racial harmony? Why not Wallace?"[33]

The meeting resulted in an arrangement. Johnson would rescue Wallace from his obligations to maintain the law and protect innocent black people, for which he would have paid dearly with his own white constituents, but Wallace would have to ask Johnson publicly to mobilize the national guard.[34] Following the meeting, Johnson took Wallace into a prearranged press conference where he made sure that Wallace was still publicly on the hook, that is, accountable for protecting all citizens, black and white. Johnson announced: "If local authorities are unable to function, the federal government will completely meet its responsibilities."[35]

The next day, Sunday, while 15,000 demonstrators outside the

138 / LEADING WITH AUTHORITY

White House sang "We shall overcome," and chanted: "LBJ, just you wait, See what happens in '68," Johnson solicited an invitation to appear before a joint session of Congress the next evening, Monday, March 15, and he began to prepare for his now historic speech.[36]

Principles of Leadership

Before reviewing the speech that served as the climax to these events, we should analyze Johnson's strategy of leadership. As events in Selma unfolded, Johnson would have had to ask himself several questions in making his assessment. Of course, one cannot say with any certainty how Lyndon Johnson thought his way through this crisis or whether his leadership actions were reflective or instinctive. Even Johnson himself could not tell us completely because our human minds work faster than we can recall, and many of our calculations are made unconsciously. Also, Johnson was very good at telling history the way he wanted it told. Nevertheless, we can pose the strategic questions without knowing the extent to which Johnson may have done so himself. This analysis may not explain Johnson as much as it illustrates a conception of leadership.

Identifying the Adaptive Challenge. Johnson immediately confronted two questions already familiar to him: (1) What issues were represented by this conflict—what were people really fighting about? and (2) Did the issues constitute a technical problem for which an authoritative response would suffice, or did the situation require adaptive change? In many situations, the answers to these questions are not obvious, but in this situation they were readily apparent. The country had been working on these questions for years. The issue was a conflict over values: Would the values of freedom and equality or the values of traditional, local white cultures prevail? Stated simply, either white people had to make room, or black people had to accept their place. Johnson could not solve this dilemma. No authoritative presidential decision would "fix" this kind of problem. This problem existed in the minds and hearts of citizens, and only adjustments *there* would resolve the value conflict. What the President could do was animate and prod people across the nation to address the internal contradiction between the values of freedom and equality they espoused and the mode of suppression they lived or permitted. Although laws, political stands, and programs could not mandate adaptive change, they could fix attention on the need for adjustment. They could begin to change institutions to create new norms and set new limits on behavior.[37] As Johnson commented after passage the previous year of the Civil Rights Act, "I understand that a law doesn't change people's feeling. But it's a beginning. It shows the way."[38]

Johnson wanted to know, given the limits and constraints of his authority, how he could make it possible for people to learn new attitudes and habits of behavior. How could he change people's feelings at least sufficiently to generate the political will for legislation that would then set a new standard and norm for the society? These questions are the kind that politicians and activists need to keep asking throughout their careers. Johnson did not have the final answers. But his responses to Selma illustrate at least four conditions for stimulating adaptive change after the challenge has been identified: *managed stress,* disciplined by *attention to the issues,* with *pressure* on those who need to take responsibility for the changes in their midst, and *protective cover* for threatened leadership voices.

Regulating Distress. In the midst of crisis, the first priority is to evaluate the level of social distress, and, if it is too high, take action to bring it into a productive range. Confronted by overwhelming distress, a society and its factions may fall back on extreme measures to restore direction, protection, and order: authoritarian rule, suppression of dissent, fragmentation into smaller identity groups (ethnic, religious, regional), and war (civil and otherwise). Thus, Johnson had to assess the level of disequilibrium in the society in order to determine whether or not emergency actions were called for, like sending in the National Guard. Could the nation sustain the storm without breaking apart? Were the bonds that held people together (political and civic institutions, economic interdependencies, cultural norms, shared values, patriotic identifications) sufficiently resilient to withstand the stresses?[39] Was the nation overwhelmed for other reasons (a depressed economy or war)?

These questions defined the upper limits of tolerance, and Johnson's answers were clear: The nation *as a whole* could take it.

140 / LEADING WITH AUTHORITY

Americans had withstood much more. The bonds holding the nation together were not breaking. Political institutions were operating. Particular cultural and political norms were being challenged, as were critical values, but many of society's other norms and values were functioning as before to provide meaning, orientation, and structure to people's lives. People were still going about their business. The Vietnam build-up was not capturing very much attention. The economy was functioning smoothly. Many people questioned deeply the contradictions within the nation, but relatively few seemed to give up their patriotism. To be sure, civil rights activists were being brutally injured and killed, and that might itself be cause for immediate action, but the nation itself was not apparently at risk—as it had been one hundred years before. Johnson could afford to hold steady for a time.

Crises provide authority figures with more power because people look to them to provide resolution. Distress enhances their visibility and impact. Thus, in times of distress, people around the country scrutinize a President's every response—precisely because he is the nation's central figure of authority. They search for indications of how worried *they* should be about the situation. If *he* appears alarmed, then their fears will rise.

Hence, a President's immediate mechanism to contain distress during a crisis is to contain himself. If he indicates through his calm demeanor that the situation, serious as it is, is no cause for panic, he reduces the possibility of one. He can regulate the level of disequilibrium in the society by the cues he gives, even by the pitch and tone of his voice. Of course, he can go too far; when he denies for too long the difficulty people experience, they will get angry.

However, people look to authority not only for cues but also for action. Action itself can reduce the experience of disequilibrium because it shifts the appearance of responsibility for the problem onto the shoulders of the one taking action. Action suggests that "*He* will show us the way." People can relax their attention because someone in authority is paying attention. Thus, authoritative action will tend to reduce stress, while inaction will increase it. This may be true regardless of the content of the action. Action itself communicates. For example, it is quite conceivable that what mattered most in reducing the sense of crisis during Franklin Roosevelt's first one hundred days was not his specific actions but his activism.[40]

How did Johnson regulate the level of distress? In this case, events beyond his own immediate doing had provoked the distress. Southern blacks and Southern whites had caused it, albeit with Johnson's tacit encouragement. As the central authority figure for the nation, Johnson had the presence of mind, or the instincts, to use it as opportunity. King and his organizers turned up the heat, but Johnson let the stew simmer. By his calm demeanor and lukewarm statements, Johnson communicated that the crisis was no emergency. But by inaction, Johnson raised the level of tension so that people could no longer ignore their own responsibility for the harsh reality of black people being beaten for requesting an equal right to vote.

Directing Disciplined Attention to the Issues. By having waited over a week to make a move, Johnson allowed television images of racial brutality to settle into the public consciousness. He prevented premature closure. When he finally announced during his press conference with Wallace that, if necessary, he would take decisive action, he merely relieved the immediate source of distress. The underlying issue had now fastened in people's minds, where it would continue to generate dissonance. Dissonance would call for more action. The issue would ripen: people would come to see the issue as a public priority. And therein lay the opportunity. Johnson waited to seize that moment when he could address the issue of racial justice rather than merely diffuse the dissonance. He took the event and gave it meaning that would have been lost before.

Had Johnson intervened as the nation demanded, by mobilizing the National Guard, he would surely have reduced the public's distress over police brutality against black Americans. Johnson's action would have directed the nation's attention to a side issue: protecting the marchers' right to express their demands. Yet as Johnson unbundled the issues, the point was not the right to march; the point was the right to vote. Had Johnson intervened immediately, the issue might have been understood the wrong way—the easy way.

Worse, his intervention would also have diverted the nation's attention from the issue of racism to the issue of state's rights. Johnson, the Southern politician, knew better than to let that happen.

> If I just send in federal troops with their big black boots and rifles, it'll look like Reconstruction all over again. I'll lose every moderate,

142 / LEADING WITH AUTHORITY

and not just in Alabama but all over the South. Most southern people don't like this violence; they know, deep in their hearts, that things are going to change. And they'll accommodate. They may not like it, but they'll accommodate. But not if it looks like the Civil War all over again. That'll force them right into the arms of extremists, and make a martyr out of Wallace. And that's not going to help the Negroes . . . I may have to send in troops. But not until I have to, not until everyone can see I had no other choice.[41]

Had he intervened immediately, Johnson would probably have survived quite well, personally. As a Southerner intervening with federal troops to protect innocent black people, he would likely have gained considerable popularity throughout much of the nation. There were good precedents for federal interference into racial disturbances: Kennedy in Mississippi, Eisenhower in Arkansas. And *they* were Northerners.

Stepping in decisively to resolve the crisis, however, would have interrupted the work being done in the polity. By letting the distress persist for over a week, Johnson provided the nation with no choice but to face the issue of racism itself. The appalled public would not permit Southern whites to frame the issue as states' rights. Furthermore, voters throughout the nation had witnessed from their own living rooms that the marchers longed for the right to vote, not the right to march. The issue would not be mistaken as states' rights or the right of black people to march. By refusing to be pushed by the public, Johnson pushed people to face the internal contradictions of *their* society, embodied in the sights they could not avoid watching on television.

Giving the Work Back to People. Johnson's long experience taught him to be wary of the trap that Wallace had set—shifting all responsibility to the highest authority. By stepping in with troops, Johnson would have presented himself and his office as a receptacle for blame or credit. Either would be a diversion from working on the problem of equality. The solution to the crisis would have become "Johnson's solution," framed as federal interference in states' affairs, or federal protection of the right to march. Instead, Johnson did nothing to divert responsibility until the public's will had crystallized.[42] He let the people with the problem bear weight. He let blacks carry the major responsibility for provoking change. He waited for Wallace to request federal troops. And he waited until voters across the nation had done enough work to reveal to themselves, and to him, the outlines of a solution—their solution. As Kearns described it, "When Johnson finally sent troops to Alabama [two weeks after the crisis began], the act was generally regarded, not as an imperious imposition of federal power, but as a necessary measure to prevent further violence. By waiting out his critics and letting the TV clips make their own impression on the country, he had succeeded in persuading most of the country that he had acted reluctantly and out of necessity, not because he was anxious to use federal power against a guilty South."[43]

The civil rights movement had focused attention and ripened the issue. Johnson's task was to restrain himself from absorbing the attention and responsibility. The tactic of holding steady shifted the feeling of necessity to the public so that it would face the issue with its costs and its gains. The public and its representatives were made to do the work of changing their attitudes and priorities about justice.

Thus, by keeping the spotlight on the persons embodying the issues, Johnson gave the work of adjustment back to the people with the problem: the civil rights activists, George Wallace, Congress, and the general public. For example, he encouraged King in private meetings to arouse public attention. Animated constituents would generate the political will and leeway for legislative action. Moreover, he let Wallace stew for awhile, appealing to him at the White House in his moment of distress to adjust his own view of himself. To paraphrase Johnson: "Wallace could be a statesman, not just for Alabama, but for the nation. He could help his people adjust to the demands for economic and social reform. Social justice might make sense to a populist like Wallace in the context of economic justice."[44] Johnson's authority as President gave him a grip on Wallace, but only because he had refrained from stealing the limelight and shifting the responsibility for law and order away from the governor. When Wallace finally asked for federal assistance (on the grounds that Alabama could not afford the cost of protecting the marchers), Johnson let everyone know that he was acting on Wallace's initiative.[45] He made sure that the debate remained focused on civil rights and not on states' rights, and that Wallace had borne the burden. As

144 / LEADING WITH AUTHORITY

Johnson put it publicly, "It is not a welcome duty for the federal government to ever assume a state government's own responsibility for assuring the protection of citizens in the exercise of their constitutional rights."[46]

Protecting Voices of Leadership in the Community. Johnson provided protection to King and his colleagues in the form of encouragement, guidance, and warning. But this was not without its risks. For example, a police attack on Dr. King and his national entourage of clergy during Tuesday's march would have been a very big blow to his presidency. As a Southerner, how could he have recaptured the high ground? Who would believe that his was just a tactical error? When a federal court issued a restraining order to delay the march for a few days, Johnson knew that a limit had been reached. Although King had tactically violated local and state law previously to make his point, he relied on *national* values, politics, and opinion to hold the states and cities in a process of change. Breaching a federal court order would have violated the national structure of authority—the final containing vessel. And Johnson sat atop that structure. Neither Johnson nor King, nor the civil rights cause itself, could afford damaging a fundamental trust for legal process. To avoid a confrontation between King and the federal government, Johnson tried to dissuade King from marching that day; King insisted, however, and they reached a compromise. In essence, Johnson made clear to King the limits of the cover he could provide. The march went on in truncated form, and Johnson held steady through it.[47]

The pressure on Johnson to "take control of the situation" was enormous. Presidents are expected to control internal conflict, which often means supressing dissonant voices. But by and large, Johnson stayed out of King's way and let the tension grow. By so doing, he risked losing trust, and thus the basis of his authority. Yet by protecting King, Wilkins, and others, Johnson let the issues surface and ripen, and kept his hands free to orchestrate the ensuing debate.

The Speech

By waiting, Johnson raised the stakes, not only for the nation but for himself. If, as President, he failed to act decisively after what seemed so prolonged a time of crisis, the public would hold him accountable. Public expectations constrained him. As with any person in a position of senior authority, a President eventually has to provide a clear focal point to restore a sense of direction and order. Johnson did that eight days after the crisis in Selma had begun. By that time, the nation looked to Johnson with ever heightened anticipation. But by that time, the nation was ready to hear what it needed to hear, and not just what it wanted to hear. Johnson spoke before a joint session of Congress during prime evening television. The speech, excerpted at length, captures Johnson's strategy.

> I speak tonight for the dignity of man and the destiny of democracy ... At times history and fate meet at a single time in a single place to shape a turning point in man's unending search for freedom. So it was at Lexington and Concord. So it was at Appomattox. So it was last week in Selma, Alabama ... There is no cause for pride in what has happened in Selma. There is no cause for self-satisfaction in the long denial of equal rights of millions of Americans. But there is cause for hope and for faith in our democracy in what is happening here tonight.
>
> For the cries of pain, the hymns and protest of oppressed people, have summoned into convocation all the majesty of this great government ... In our time we have come to live with moments of great crisis ... But rarely in any time does an issue lay bare the secret heart of America itself ... a challenge, not to our growth or abundance, our welfare or our security, but to the values and the purposes and the meaning of our nation.
>
> The issue of equal rights for American Negroes is such an issue, and should we defeat every enemy, double our wealth, conquer the stars, and still be unequal to this issue, then we will have failed as a people and a nation. For with a country as with a person, "What shall it profit a man, if he shall gain the whole world, and lose his own soul?" ... There is no issue of states' rights or national rights. There is only the struggle for human rights ...
>
> Last time a President sent a civil rights bill to Congress it contained a provision to protect voting rights. That bill was passed after eight long months of debate. And when that bill came to my desk for signature, the heart of the voting provision had been eliminated. This time, on this issue, there must be no delay, no hesitation, no compro-

mise with our purpose . . . And we ought not, and we cannot, and we must not wait another eight months before we get a bill. We have already waited 100 years and more. And the time for waiting is gone.

So I ask you to join me in working long hours, nights and weekends if necessary to pass this bill. And I don't make the request lightly. For from the window where I sit with the problems of our country, I recognize that outside this chamber is the outraged conscience of the Nation, the grave concern of many nations—and the harsh judgment of history on our acts.

But even if we pass this bill, the battle will not be over. What happened in Selma is part of a far larger movement which reaches into every section and state of America. It is the effort of American Negroes to secure for themselves the full blessings of American life. Their cause must be our cause too. It is not just Negroes, but all of us, who must overcome the crippling legacy of bigotry and injustice. *And we shall overcome.* As a man whose roots go into Southern soil I know how agonizing racial feelings are. I know how difficult it is to reshape attitudes and the structure of society . . . I say to all of you here and to all in the Nation tonight, that those who ask you to hold on to the past do so at the cost of denying you your future.

This great, rich, restless country can offer opportunity and education to all—black and white, North and South, sharecropper and city dweller. These are the enemies—poverty and ignorance—and not our fellow man. And these too shall be overcome. Let no one, in any section, look with prideful righteousness on the troubles of his neighbors. There is no part of America where the promise of equality has been fully kept. In Buffalo as well as Birmingham, in Philadelphia as well as Selma, Americans are struggling for the fruits of freedom. This is one nation. What happens in Selma or in Cincinnati is a matter of legitimate concern to every citizen. But let each of us look within our own communities and our own hearts, and root out injustice there . . .

The real hero of this struggle is the American Negro. His actions and protests—his courage to risk safety and even life—have awakened the conscience of the Nation. His demonstrations have been designed to call attention to injustice, to provoke change and stir reform. He has called upon us to make good the promise of America. And who among us can say we would have made the same progress were it not for his persistent bravery, and his faith in American democracy. For at the heart of battle for equality is a belief in the democratic process.[48]

Historic in its sweep and claim, this speech inspired much of the country. It also demonstrates and helps summarize our principles of leadership. First, Johnson spoke clearly to the orienting values of the nation, the values that had made it one nation: freedom, equality, and democracy. The issue of civil rights was to be seen in that context. He identified the adaptive challenge by identifying the discrepancy between our values and behavior. Indeed, he identified the next adaptive challenge as well: poverty.

Second, by speaking in so dramatic a fashion—before a joint session of Congress—Johnson tried to maintain the level of urgency at the same time that he addressed its causes. Taking charge might have reduced the pressure had Johnson not demanded immediate Congressional action. Moreover, Johnson pointed out that Congress had failed to complete its work on voting rights in the earlier civil rights legislation. These acts kept the pressure on.

Third, Johnson kept attention focused on the issue by cautioning the public to stay clear of the likely work avoidance mechanisms that might arise: (1) viewing the events in Selma as an issue of states' rights rather than national values, (2) viewing voting rights legislation as a technical fix after which people could relax their attention, (3) holding onto the past, and (4) scapegoating the white people of Selma by a "prideful righteousness" that would deny the presence of racism throughout the land.

Fourth, Johnson told people that the challenge of civil rights would require adaptive and ongoing work: the attitudes and the structure of society would have to change. He acknowledged how difficult that would be. In large part, the work belonged to the general public. Voting rights legislation was no final remedy; it was simply a catalytic step. Yet Congress would not be off the hook either. By challenging its members so publicly to spend sleepless nights, he made them bear the weight as well. He put all of their names on the line (including his own) by expecting rapid passage of the bill he would submit in two days.[49]

Finally, Johnson exercised leadership in one of the few ways that authority figures can—by protecting the voices of those who lead with little authority, even though such voices often will be both deviant and annoying. He credited the civil rights movement for provoking the nation to face the large gap between what we stood for and the way we lived.

In exercising leadership on civil rights, was Johnson advancing his own vision for the country? Not really. As a Southern congressman since 1937 and senator since 1949, Johnson came out in favor of civil rights only in 1956 when he saw the issue ripening and saw himself as a national contender.[50] For nearly twenty years he had voted against every civil rights bill before Congress—laws to end the poll tax, segregation in the armed services, and lynching.[51] In 1960 he opposed liberal proposals for federal voting registrars in favor of the middle-of-the-road proposal for voting referees, which had not worked. As Vice-President, he had decided against liberalizing Senate rules, which distressed civil rights advocates.[52] During the debate over the Civil Rights Act of 1964, he backed a moderate conception for a voting rights clause. When Congress seemed unready even for that, he did not push it.

It seems then that the civil rights movement and the events in Selma had their impact on Johnson's conscience, as well as that of the nation. As he described in his memoirs, "Nothing makes a man come to grips more directly with his conscience than the Presidency. Sitting in that chair involves making decisions that draw out a man's fundamental commitments. The burden of his responsibility literally opens up his soul. No longer can he accept matters as given: no longer can he write off hopes and needs as impossible. In that house of decision, the White House, a man becomes his commitments. He understands who he really is. He learns what he genuinely wants to be."[53]

We often think that leadership means having a clear vision and the capacity to persuade people to make it real. In this case, Johnson had authored no vision. Events acted on him to shape the vision to which he then gave powerful articulation. He *identified the nation's vision* and put it into words. As the nation clarified its values, so did he. Johnson's leadership lay in his wherewithal to give meaning to the crisis and avoid the common pitfall of restoring order prematurely. He let the heat remain high. He kept people's attention on the issues generating the heat. He shifted responsibility to those with the problem. He let the dissident voices be heard. Along with the nation, he wrestled with its fundamental orienting values. He gave those values the power of his voice and his presence.[54] And he seized the moment to turn the nation's emerging values into potent legislation.[55]

Johnson signed the Voting Rights Act into law on August 6, 1965. Within one week, federal registrars set up shop; six months later, 9,000 black people were registered to vote in Selma.[56]

6. On a Razor's Edge

1. See "Leader or Clerk?" in Richard E. Neustadt, *Presidential Power and the Modern Presidents: The Politics of Leadership from Roosevelt to Reagan,* third edition (New York: Free Press, 1990), chap. 1; and Warren Bennis, *Why Leaders Can't Lead: The Unconscious Conspiracy Continues* (San Francisco: Jossey-Bass, 1989).
2. Robert D. Putnam's study, *Making Democracy Work: Civic Traditions in Modern Italy* (Princeton: Princeton University Press, 1993), shows a strong positive correlation between institutions of civic engagement (for example, soccer clubs, choral societies, and literary guilds) and community performance (for example, economic development, legislative innovation, and bureaucratic responsiveness).
3. For example, many scholars attribute the greatness of George Washington to his foresight and ability to strengthen the central government in its first years. Washington placed highest priority on increasing the federal government's credibility and prestige. He did so by staying out of "entangling alliances" (during the French Revolution), displaying overwhelming military power (the Whiskey Rebellion), and maintaining the financial solvency of the government (by supporting Hamilton's proposal to fund the debt). Richard Ellis and Aaron Wildavsky describe this as "substituting the appearance of power for the reality of power," which I think confuses the difference between formal powers and informal authority. The source of the government's informal authority lay in perceptions of credibility. That does not make it unreal; it simply suggests that trust is a major source of informal and ultimately formal authorization. In my terms, Washington aimed to strengthen the holding environment provided by central government, and this boosted critically the government's power to hold the nation together through its stage of infancy. See Richard Ellis and Aaron Wildavsky, "'Greatness' Revisited: Evaluating the Performance of Early American Presidents in Terms of Cultural Dilemmas," *Presidential Studies Quarterly,* vol. 21, winter 1991, pp. 18–22.

    Also see Chapters 4 and 5, above, for the example of Ruckelshaus and his efforts to restore the credibility of the EPA as a mediating institution in the society on environmental issues.
4. For a discussion of the relationship between empowerment and the dispersion of authority, see Herbert C. Kelman and V. Lee Hamilton, *Crimes of Obedience: Toward a Social Psychology of Authority and Responsibility* (New Haven: Yale University Press, 1989), pp. 322–327.
5. I use the term *black American* instead of the contemporary phrase *Afri-*

can-American because this case takes place in the 1960s, a time when the term *black American* was becoming an authentic expression of the demand for equality and respect.

6. Quotations from Doris Kearns, *Lyndon Johnson and the American Dream* (New York: New American Library, 1976), pp. 180–181.
7. Ibid., pp. 184–185.
8. It is, of course, hard to say which of Johnson's successes matters most. As Joseph Califano summarizes, "Johnson changed the country more than most of us realize. By the time he left office, he had pushed through Congress Medicare and Medicaid to provide health care for the aged and most of the poor; funds for preschool, elementary, secondary, and higher education; air, water, and noise pollution laws; measures to preserve land; civil rights legislation; food stamps for the needy; a massive housing bill, and a score of consumer-protection laws. He had articulated the concept of affirmative action, dramatized the blight of poverty amid unprecedented wealth, signed the Freedom of Information Act, and created the National Endowments for the Arts and Humanities, the John F. Kennedy Center for the Performing Arts, the Corporation for Public Broadcasting, several cabinet departments and agencies, and he changed the role of the federal government in American life." Joseph A. Califano Jr., *The Triumph and Tragedy of Lyndon Johnson: The White House Years* (New York: Simon and Schuster, 1991), p. 12.
9. Kearns, *Lyndon Johnson*, p. 239.
10. The exception was Eisenhower's 1957 Civil Rights Act which survived the Senate because Senate Majority Leader Lyndon Johnson, eyeing his 1960 run for the presidency, got it passed. See Robert Dallek, *Lone Star Rising: Lyndon Johnson and His Times: 1908–1960* (New York: Oxford University Press, 1991), pp. 517–528.
11. Quotations from Richard N. Goodwin, *Remembering America* (Boston: Little, Brown, 1988), pp. 313, 314, italics added.
12. Quotations from Kearns, *Lyndon Johnson*, p. 194.
13. Robert A. Caro, *The Years of Lyndon Johnson: Means of Ascent* (New York: Vintage Books, 1990), p. xvi.
14. Cited in Califano, *The Triumph and Tragedy of Lyndon Johnson*, p. 53.
15. "Troopers Rout Selma Marchers," *The Washington Post*, March 8, 1965, p. A1.
16. Caro, *Means of Ascent*, p. xv; and J. L. Chestnut Jr., and Julia Cass, *Black in Selma: The Uncommon Life of J. L. Chestnut, Jr.* (Farrar, Straus and Giroux, 1990), p. 207.
17. Kearns, *Lyndon Johnson*, p. 239. The National Guard consists of troops normally under the command of the various state governors. "Calling out the national guard" consists of federalizing these troops, which then fall under the President's command.

18. "King is Dismayed by U.S. 'Timidity,'" *The Washington Post,* March 8, 1965, p. A2.
19. *Brown v. Board of Education,* 347 U.S. 483 (1954) (Brown I). For a summary, see Laurence H. Tribe, *American Constitutional Law,* second edition (Mineola, NY: The Foundation Press, 1988), pp. 1474–1480.
20. Dallek, *Lone Star Rising,* pp. 521–522.
21. According to Califano, "On February 9, 1965, the President met with Martin Luther King at the White House to hear a report on King's campaign to register blacks to vote in Selma, the capital of Dallas County, Alabama. As a political leader preparing to persuade Congress to pass a voting rights bill, Johnson appreciated King's choice of Selma . . . Johnson told King that he would soon send voting-rights legislation to Congress. He thought that the public pressure of Selma would help and hoped there would be no violence." Califano, *The Triumph and Tragedy of Lyndon Johnson,* p. 55.
22. For example, in 1941 the civil rights movement threatened a massive march on Washington to demand equal opportunity for the jobs, both civilian and military, created as the country geared up for World War II. The threat of the march forced Roosevelt, two weeks before the target date, to issue an Executive Order promoting fair employment practices. The march was then called off. See Thomas R. Brooks, *Walls Come Tumbling Down: A History of the Civil Rights Movement 1940–1970* (Englewood Cliffs, NJ: Prentice-Hall, 1974).
23. "Trooper's Rout Selma Marchers with Tear Gas," *The Washington Post,* March 8, 1965, p. A3.
24. Chestnut and Cass, *Black in Selma,* p. 209.
25. Lyndon B. Johnson, *The Vantage Point: Perspectives of the Presidency 1963–1969* (New York: Holt, Rinehart and Winston, 1971), p. 162.
26. Ralph David Abernathy, *And the Walls Came Tumbling Down* (New York: Harper and Row, 1989), p. 334.
27. I discuss the events and tactics of this moment in greater depth in Chapter 9. I do not think Johnson intended to stop the Selma demonstrations altogether, but once the federal court order had been issued, he was obligated to slow King down. Had King broken the law, Johnson would have been forced to take action against King, and both Johnson's and King's strategies would have backfired. See Abernathy, *And the Walls Came Tumbling Down,* pp. 335–342.
28. "President's Statement," *The Washington Post,* March 10, 1965, p. A3.
29. See James Henderson, Philip B. Heymann, Richard E. Neustadt, Glenn Reichardt, and Mark H. Moore, "Voting Rights Act of 1965 (B): LBJ and the Department of Justice" (Cambridge: John F. Kennedy School of Government Case Program, Harvard University, 1975), Case #694–75–114.

30. "Cleric's Death Saddens Selma Crowd," *The Washington Post*, March 12, 1965, p. A8; Abernathy, *And the Walls Came Tumbling Down*, p. 325.
31. Kearns, *Lyndon Johnson*, p. 239.
32. Goodwin, *Remembering America*, p. 320.
33. Kearns, *Lyndon Johnson*, p. 239.
34. Goodwin, *Remembering America*, p. 323.
35. "Transcript of News Conference at the White House," *The Washington Post*, March 14, 1965, p. A12.
36. "Crowd of 15,000 at Lafayette Park Protests Federal Inaction in Selma," *The Washington Post*, March 15, 1965, p. A6; Caro, *Means of Ascent*, p. xviii; and Goodwin, *Remembering America*, p. 324.
37. Some of the consequences of federal initiatives in civil rights have now been studied a generation later. The consequences are impressive. For an analysis linking structural to attitudinal change, see Thomas F. Pettigrew, "Advancing Racial Justice: Past Lessons for Future Use," in Harry J. Knopke, Robert J. Norrell, and Ronald W. Rogers, eds., *Opening Doors: Perspectives on Race Relations in Contemporary America* (Tuscaloosa, AL: University of Alabama Press, 1991), pp. 165–178. For an in-depth case study of an integrated public middle school as a vehicle for attitudinal change, see Janet Ward Schofield, *Black and White in School: Trust, Tension, or Tolerance?* (New York: Praeger, 1982). As well, there are earlier case studies of institutional change leading to attitudinal change. For example, see Leo Bogart, ed., *Social Research and the Desegregation of the U.S. Army* (Chicago: Markham, 1969), pp. 1–41, for an analysis of the way authoritative action and structural change played a critical role in changing attitudes to desegregate the U.S. Army beginning in 1948.
38. Goodwin, *Remembering America*, p. 316.
39. In the terms of political economy, one could analyze the adaptive capacity and resilience of a community in terms of the concept "social capital," which can be understood as "the features of social organization, such as trust, norms, and networks, that can improve the efficiency of society by facilitating coordinated actions . . ." See Putnam, *Making Democracy Work*, p. 167. The more social capital, the stronger the holding environment of the community and thus the higher the limit of tolerance of stress the community can withstand without resorting to work avoidance.
40. Of course, not all action reduces the general level of stress. Urgent or extreme action in a situation that seems not to call for it will generate alarm. I describe one such example in Chapter 7: President Carter's mass firing of his cabinet in July 1979.
41. Goodwin, *Remembering America*, pp. 319–320.
42. As Senate Minority Leader, Johnson had used a similar strategy in the Senate's efforts to repudiate Joseph McCarthy. As he told Maury Maverick,

"You have got to realize that . . . the hysteria around the country and in the Government . . . can be dispelled only by letting it run its course so that people can see for themselves what is really behind all the noise." Johnson waited faithfully for McCarthy to alienate his conservative Senate colleagues and then the American people, both of which McCarthy eventually did. When McCarthy's own Republican colleagues were set to censure him, Johnson called a meeting of the Democratic Policy Committee and persuaded its members to refrain from taking a stand for fear "that it would play into McCarthy's hands and put him back in the good graces of the Republican Party." Instead, the committee recommended that each senator vote his own conscience. He then arranged for a bipartisan committee to investigate McCarthy, and selected meticulously a group of conservative Democrats and Republicans with indisputable credentials and reputations to condemn McCarthy, which it did. The Senate concurred in a vote of 67-to-22.

Issues have their own rate of ripening. The rate can be sped up, as the Selma events demonstrate, but ultimately the rate is determined by the speed at which people learn. I believe Johnson understood both the possibility of ripening issues, as he demonstrated by calling Roy Wilkins in January 1964, as well as the limits to which one could accelerate the process of ripening. Johnson spoke to these limits when he told Elizabeth Rowe after McCarthy had been censured, "You see, you always wanted me to hurry, to speed it up, but I kept telling you, you can't speed it up. You have got to know when the time has come." Dallek, *Lone Star Rising*, pp. 451–459.

43. Kearns, *Lyndon Johnson*, p. 239.
44. Ibid., p. 239. Wallace did run for President in 1968 on this platform.
45. See Goodwin, *Remembering America*, p. 323.
46. Charles E. Fager, *Selma: The March that Changed the South* (Boston: Beacon Press, 1985), pp. 148–149.
47. For a detailed account of the bargaining between King, Abernathy, and LeRoy Collins, Johnson's emissary, which led to turning the march around after reaching the spot where Sunday's beatings had taken place, see Abernathy, *And the Walls Came Tumbling Down*, pp. 337–341.
48. From "Text of Johnson Address to Joint Session of Congress," *The Washington Post*, March 16, 1965, p. A14.
49. Thomas Schelling describes this as a "commitment strategy." By committing himself publicly, Johnson communicated his resolve to Congress. Schelling used the term somewhat differently given the context in which he developed it: nuclear arms control, where commitment to retaliate made deterrent threat credible, and thereby *reduced* the probability of ever having to act on the commitment. Thomas C. Schelling, *The Strategy of Conflict* (Cambridge: Harvard University Press, 1960), p. 14.

50. Dallek, *Lone Star Rising*, pp. 496, 517–528.
51. Caro, *Means of Ascent*, p. xvii.
52. "President Seizes Rights Movement Leadership," *The Washington Post*, March 17, 1965, p. A14.
53. Johnson, *The Vantage Point*, p. 157.
54. Johnson's great speech to Congress was written by Richard Goodwin, one of Johnson's speechwriters. Johnson deliberately picked Goodwin for the job, and not another of his writers, because he felt Goodwin knew best how to put his values and sentiments into words. According to Goodwin, the speech would have been altogether different had it been written for another man. See Goodwin, *Remembering America*, p. 328.
55. The legislation was more powerful than any previously imagined to address the issue. By a double trigger mechanism, federal registrars would replace local officials in those states where discrimination was widely used, and the Attorney General would have virtual veto power over any state legislation on voter qualifications. See Henderson et al., "Voting Rights Act of 1965 (B): LBJ and the Department of Justice."
56. Chestnut and Cass, *Black in Selma*, pp. 233–235.

[22]
The New Cultural Politics of Difference

In these last few years of the twentieth century, there is emerging a significant shift in the sensibilities and outlooks of critics and artists. In fact, I would go so far as to claim that a new kind of cultural worker is in the making, associated with a new politics of difference. These new forms of intellectual consciousness advance reconceptions of the vocation of critic and artist, attempting to undermine the prevailing disciplinary divisions of labor in the academy, museum, mass media and gallery networks, while preserving modes of critique within the ubiquitous commodification of culture in the global village. Distinctive features of the new cultural politics of difference are to trash the monolithic and homogeneous in the name of diversity, multiplicity and heterogeneity; to reject the abstract, general and universal in light of the concrete, specific and particular; and to historicize, contextualize and pluralize by highlighting the contingent, provisional, variable, tentative, shifting and changing. Needless to say, these gestures are not new in the history of criticism or art, yet what makes them novel—along with the cultural politics they produce—is how and what constitutes difference, the weight and gravity it is given in representation, and the way in which highlighting issues like exterminism, empire, class, race, gender, sexual orientation, age, nation, nature and region at this historical moment acknowledges some discontinuity and disruption from previous forms of cultural critique. To put it bluntly, the new cultural politics of difference consists of creative responses

4   *Cultural Criticism and Race*

to the precise circumstances of our present moment—especially those of marginalized First World agents who shun degraded self-representations, articulating instead their sense of the flow of history in light of the contemporary terrors, anxieties and fears of highly commercialized North Atlantic capitalist cultures (with their escalating xenophobias against people of color, Jews, women, gays, lesbians and the elderly). The thawing, yet still rigid, Second World ex-communists cultures (with increasing nationalist revolts against the legacy of hegemonic party henchmen) and the diverse cultures of the majority of inhabitants on the globe smothered by international communication cartels and repressive postcolonial elites (sometimes in the name of communism, as was the case in Ethiopia) or starved by austere World Bank and IMF politics that subordinate them to the North (as in free-market capitalism in Chile) also locate vital areas of analysis in this new cultural terrain.

The new cultural politics of difference is neither simply oppositional in contesting the mainstream (or *male*stream) for inclusion, nor transgressive in the avant-gardist sense of shocking conventional bourgeois audiences. It embraces the distinct articulations of talented (and usually privileged) contributors to culture who desire to align themselves with demoralized, demobilized, depoliticized and disorganized people in order to empower and enable social action and, if possible, to enlist collective insurgency for the expansion of freedom, democracy and individuality. This perspective impels these cultural critics and artists to reveal, as an integral component of their production, the very operations of power within their immediate work contexts (academy, museum, gallery, mass media). This strategy, however, also puts them in an inescapable double bind—while linking their activities to the fundamental, structural overhaul of these institutions, they often remain financially dependent on them (so much for "independent" creation). For these critics of culture, theirs is a gesture that is simultaneously progressive and co-opted. Yet without social movement or political pressure from outside these institutions (extraparliamentary and extracurricular actions like the social movements of the recent past), transformation degenerates into mere accommodation or sheer stagnation, and the role of the "co-opted progressive"—no matter how fervent one's subversive rhetoric—is rendered more difficult. There can be no artistic breakthrough or social progress without some form of crisis in civilization—a crisis usually generated by organizations or collectivities that convince ordinary people to put their bodies and lives on the line. There is, of course, no guarantee that such pressure will yield the result one wants, but there is a guarantee that the status quo will remain or regress if no pressure is applied at all.

The new cultural politics of difference faces three basic challenges—intellectual, existential and political. The intellectual challenge—usually cast as methodological debate in these days in which academicist forms of expression have a monopoly on intellectual life—is how to think about representational practices in terms of history, culture and society. How does one understand, analyze and enact such practices today? An adequate answer to this question can be attempted only after one comes to terms with the insights and blindnesses of earlier attempts to grapple with the question in light of the evolving crisis in different histories, cultures and societies. I shall sketch a brief genealogy—a history that highlights the contingent origins and often ignoble outcomes—of exemplary critical responses to the question. This genealogy sets forth a historical framework that characterizes the rich yet deeply flawed Eurocentric traditions which the new cultural politics of difference builds upon yet goes beyond.

The Intellectual Challenge

An appropriate starting point is the ambiguous legacy of the Age of Europe. Between 1492 and 1945, European breakthroughs in oceanic transportation, agricultural production, state consolidation, bureaucratization, industrialization, urbanization and imperial dominion shaped the makings of the modern world. Precious ideals like

6   *Cultural Criticism and Race*

the dignity of persons (individuality) or the popular accountability of institutions (democracy) were unleashed around the world. Powerful critiques of illegitimate authorities—of the Protestant Reformation against the Roman Catholic Church, the Enlightenment against state churches, liberal movements against absolutist states and feudal guild constraints, workers against managerial subordination, women against sexist practices, people of color and Jews against white and gentile supremacist decrees, gays and lesbians against homophobic sanctions—were fanned and fueled by these precious ideals refined within the crucible of the Age of Europe. Yet the discrepancy between sterling rhetoric and lived reality, glowing principles and actual practices, loomed large.

By the last European century—the last epoch in which European domination of most of the globe was uncontested and unchallenged in a substantive way—a new world seemed to be stirring. At the height of England's reign as the major imperial European power, its exemplary cultural critic, Matthew Arnold, painfully observed in his "Stanzas from the Grand Chartreuse" that he felt some sense of "wandering between two worlds, one dead / the other powerless to be born." Following his Burkean sensibilities of cautious reform and fear of anarchy, Arnold acknowledged that the old glue—religion—that had tenuously and often unsuccessfully held together the ailing European regimes could not do so in the mid-nineteenth century. Like Alexis de Tocqueville in France, Arnold saw that the democratic temper was the wave of the future. So he proposed a new conception of culture—a secular, humanistic one—that could play an integrative role in cementing and stabilizing an emerging bourgeois civil society and imperial state. His famous castigation of the immobilizing materialism of the declining aristocracy, the vulgar philistinism of the emerging middle classes and the latent explosiveness of the working-class majority was motivated by a desire to create new forms of cultural legitimacy, authority and order in a rapidly changing moment in nineteenth-century Europe.

For Arnold (in *Culture and Anarchy*, 1869), this new conception of culture

> seeks to do away with classes; to make the best that has been thought and known in the world current everywhere; to make all men live in an atmosphere of sweetness and light. . . .
> This is the *social idea* and the men of culture are the true apostles of equality. The great men of culture are those who have had a passion for diffusing, for making prevail, for carrying from one end of society to the other, the best knowledge, the best ideas of their time, who have laboured to divest knowledge of all that was harsh, uncouth, difficult, abstract, professional, exclusive; to humanize it, to make it efficient outside the clique of the cultivated and learned, yet still remaining the best knowledge and thought of the time, and a true source, therefore, of sweetness and light.

As an organic intellectual of an emergent middle class—as the inspector of schools in an expanding educational bureaucracy, Professor of Poetry at Oxford (the first non-cleric and the first to lecture in English rather than Latin) and an active participant in a thriving magazine network—Arnold defined and defended a new secular culture of critical discourse. For him, this discursive strategy would be lodged in the educational and periodical apparatuses of modern societies as they contained and incorporated the frightening threats of an arrogant aristocracy and especially of an "anarchic" working-class majority. His ideals of disinterested, dispassionate and objective inquiry would regulate this new secular cultural production, and his justifications for the use of state power to quell any threats to the survival and security of this culture were widely accepted. He aptly noted, "Through culture seems to lie our way, not only to perfection, but even to safety."

This sentence is revealing in two ways. First, it refers to "our way" without explicitly acknowledging who constitutes the "we." This move is symptomatic among many bourgeois, male, Eurocentric critics whose universalizing gestures exclude (by guarding a

8   *Cultural Criticism and Race*

silence around) or explicitly degrade women and peoples of color. Second, the sentence links culture to safety—presumably the safety of the "we" against the barbaric threats of the "them," that is, those viewed as different in some debased manner. Needless to say, Arnold's negative attitudes toward British working-class people, women and especially Indians and Jamaicans in the Empire clarify why he conceives of culture as, in part, a weapon for bourgeois, male, European "safety."

For Arnold, the best of the Age of Europe—modeled on a mythological mélange of Periclean Athens, late Republican/early Imperial Rome and Elizabethan England—could be promoted only if there was an interlocking affiliation among the emerging middle classes, a homogenizing of cultural discourse in the educational and university networks, and a state advanced enough in its policing techniques to safeguard it. The candidates for participation and legitimation in this grand endeavor of cultural renewal and revision would be detached intellectuals willing to shed their parochialism, provincialism and class-bound identities for Arnold's middle-class-skewed project: ". . . Aliens, if we may so call them—persons who are mainly led, not by their class spirit, but by a general *humane* spirit, by the love of human perfection." Needless to say, this Arnoldian perspective still informs much of the academic practices and secular cultural attitudes today—dominant views about the canon, admission procedures and collective self-definitions of intellectuals. Yet Arnold's project was disrupted by the collapse of nineteenth-century Europe—World War I. This unprecedented war brought to the surface the crucial role and violent potential not of the masses Arnold feared but of the state he heralded. Upon the ashes of this wasteland of human carnage—some of it the civilian European population—T. S. Eliot emerged as the grand cultural spokesman.

Eliot's project of reconstituting and reconceiving European highbrow culture—and thereby regulating critical and artistic practices—after the internal collapse of imperial Europe can be viewed as a response to the probing question posed by Paul Valéry in "The Crisis of the Spirit" after World War I,

> This Europe, will it become *what it is in reality,* i.e., a little cape of the Asiatic continent? or will this Europe remain rather what it seems, i.e., the priceless part of the whole earth, the pearl of the globe, the brain of a vast body?

Eliot's image of Europe as a wasteland, a culture of fragments with no cementing center, predominated in postwar Europe. And though his early poetic practices were more radical, open and international than his Eurocentric criticism, Eliot posed a return to and revision of tradition as the only way of regaining European cultural order and political stability. For Eliot, contemporary history had become, as James Joyce's Stephen declared in *Ulysses* (1922), "a nightmare from which I am trying to awake"—"an immense panorama of futility and anarchy" as Eliot put it in his renowned review of Joyce's modernist masterpiece. In his influential essay "Tradition and the Individual Talent" (1919) Eliot stated:

> Yet if the only form of tradition, of handing down, consisted in following the ways of the immediate generation before us in a blind or timid adherence to its successes, "tradition" should positively be discouraged. We have seen many such simple currents soon lost in the sand; and novelty is better than repetition. Tradition is a matter of much wider significance. It cannot be inherited, and if you want it you must attain it by great labour.

Eliot's fecund notion of tradition is significant in that it promotes a historicist sensibility in artistic practice and cultural reflection. This historicist sensibility—regulated in Eliot's case by a reactionary politics—produced a powerful assault on existing literary canons (in which, for example, Romantic poets were displaced by the Metaphysical and Symbolist ones) and unrelenting attacks on modern Western civilization (such as the liberal ideas of democracy, equality and freedom). Like Arnold's notion of culture, Eliot's idea of tradition was part of his intellectual arsenal, to be used in the battles raging in European cultures and societies.

Eliot found this tradition in the Church of England, to which he converted in 1927. Here was a tradition that left room for his Catholic cast of mind. Calvinistic heritage, puritanical temperament and ebullient patriotism for the old American South (the place of his upbringing). Like Arnold, Eliot was obsessed with the idea of civilization and the horror of barbarism (echoes of Joseph Conrad's Kurtz in *Heart of Darkness*) or more pointedly the notion of the decline and decay of European civilization. With the advent of World War II, Eliot's obsession became a reality. Again unprecedented human carnage (fifty million dead)—including an undescribable genocidal attack on Jewish people—throughout Europe as well as around the globe, put the last nail in the coffin of the Age of Europe. After 1945, Europe consisted of a devastated and divided continent, crippled by a humiliating dependency on and deference to the USA and USSR.

The second historical coordinate of my genealogy is the emergence of the USA as *the* world power. The USA was unprepared for world power status. However, with the recovery of Stalin's Russia (after losing twenty million lives), the USA felt compelled to make its presence felt around the globe. Then with the Marshall Plan to strengthen Europe against Russian influence (and provide new markets for US products), the 1948 Russian takeover of Czechoslovakia, the 1948 Berlin blockade, the 1950 beginning of the Korean War and the 1952 establishment of NATO forces in Europe, it seemed clear that there was no escape from world power obligations.

The post–World War II era in the USA, or the first decades of what Henry Luce envisioned as "The American Century," was not only a period of incredible economic expansion but of active cultural ferment. In the classical Fordist formula, mass production required mass consumption. With unchallenged hegemony in the capitalist world, the USA took economic growth for granted. Next to exercising its crude, anticommunist, McCarthyist obsessions, buying commodities became the primary act of civic virtue for many American citizens at this time. The creation of a mass middle class—a prosperous working class with a bourgeois identity—was countered by the first major emergence of subcultures of American non-WASP intellectuals: the so-called New York intellectuals in criticism, the Abstract Expressionists in painting and the bebop artists in jazz music. This emergence signaled a vital challenge to an American, male, WASP elite loyal to an older and eroding European culture.

The first significant blow was dealt when assimilated Jewish Americans entered the higher echelons of the cultural apparatus (academy, museums, galleries, mass media). Lionel Trilling is an emblematic figure. This Jewish entrée into the anti-Semitic and patriarchal critical discourse of the exclusivistic institutions of American culture initiated the slow but sure undoing of the male WASP cultural hegemony and homogeneity. Lionel Trilling's project was to appropriate Matthew Arnold for his own political and cultural purposes—thereby unraveling the old male WASP consensus, while erecting a new post–World War II liberal academic consensus around cold-war, anticommunist renditions of the values of complexity, difficulty, variousness and modulation. In addition, the postwar boom laid the basis for intense professionalization and specialization in expanding institutions of higher education—especially in the natural sciences which were compelled to respond somehow to Russia's successful ventures in space. Humanistic scholars found themselves searching for new methodologies that could buttress self-images of rigor and scientific seriousness. For example, the close reading techniques of New Criticism (severed from their conservative, organicist, anti-industrialist ideological roots), the logical precision of reasoning in analytic philosophy, and the jargon of Parsonian structural-functionalism in sociology helped create such self-images. Yet towering cultural critics like C. Wright Mills, W. E. B. Du Bois, Richard Hofstadter, Margaret Mead and Dwight MacDonald bucked the tide. This suspicion of the academicization of knowledge

12   Cultural Criticism and Race

is expressed in Trilling's well-known essay "On the Teaching of Modern Literature":

> can we not say that, when modern literature is brought into the classroom, the subject being taught is betrayed by the pedagogy of the subject? We have to ask ourselves whether in our day too much does not come within the purview of the academy. More and more, as the universities liberalize themselves, turn their beneficent imperialistic gaze upon what is called life itself, the feeling grows among our educated classes that little can be experienced unless it is validated by some established intellectual discipline. . . .

Trilling laments the fact that university instruction often quiets and domesticates radical and subversive works of art, turning them into objects "of merely habitual regard." This process of "the socialization of the anti-social, or the acculturation of the anti-cultural, or the legitimization of the subversive" leads Trilling to "question whether in our culture the study of literature is any longer a suitable means for developing and refining the intelligence." Trilling asks this question not in the spirit of denigrating and devaluing the academy but rather in the spirit of highlighting the possible failure of an Arnoldian conception of culture to contain what he perceives as the philistine and anarchic alternatives becoming more and more available to students of the sixties—namely, mass culture and radical politics.

This threat is partly associated with the third historical coordinate of my genealogy—the decolonization of the Third World. It is crucial to recognize the importance of this world-historical process if one wants to grasp the significance of the end of the Age of Europe and the emergence of the USA as a world power. With the first defeat of a Western nation by a non-Western nation—in Japan's victory over Russia (1905)—and with revolutions in Persia (1905), Turkey (1908), China (1912), and Mexico (1911–12), and much later the independence of India (1947) and China (1949) and the triumph of Ghana (1957), the actuality of a decolonized globe loomed large. Born of violent struggle, consciousness-raising and the reconstruction of identities, decolonization simultaneously brings with it new perspectives on that long-festering underside of the Age of Europe (of which colonial domination represents the *costs* of "progress," "order" and "culture"), as well as requiring new readings of the economic boom in the USA (wherein the black, brown, yellow, red, female, elderly, gay, lesbian, and white working class live the same *costs* as cheap labor at home in addition to US-dominated Latin American and Pacific Rim markets).

The impetuous ferocity and moral outrage that motors the decolonization process is best captured by Frantz Fanon in *The Wretched of the Earth* (1961).

> Decolonization, which sets out to change the order of the world, is obviously a program of complete disorder. . . . Decolonization is the meeting of two forces, opposed to each other by their very nature, which in fact owe their originality to that sort of substantification which results from and is nourished by the situation in the colonies. Their first encounter was marked by violence and their existence together—that is to say the exploitation of the native by the settler—was carried on by dint of a great array of bayonets and cannons. . . .
>
> In decolonization, there is therefore the need of a complete calling in question of the colonial situation. If we wish to describe it precisely, we might find it in the well-known words: "The last shall be first and the first last." Decolonization is the putting into practice of this sentence.
>
> The naked truth of decolonization evokes for us the searing bullets and bloodstained knives which emanate from it. For if the last shall be first, this will only come to pass after a murderous and decisive struggle between the two protagonists.

Fanon's strong words, though excessively Manichaean, still describe the feelings and thoughts between the occupying British Army and colonized Irish in Northern Ireland, the occupying Israeli Army and subjugated Palestinians on the West Bank and Gaza Strip, the South African Army and oppressed black South Africans in the townships, the Japanese police and Koreans living in Japan. His

14   *Cultural Criticism and Race*

words also partly invoke the sense many black Americans have toward police departments in urban centers. In other words, Fanon is articulating century-long heartfelt human responses to being degraded and despised, hated and haunted, oppressed and exploited, marginalized and dehumanized at the hands of powerful, xenophobic, European, American, Russian and Japanese imperial countries.

During the late fifties, sixties and early seventies in the USA, these decolonized sensibilities fanned and fueled the Civil Rights and Black Power movements, as well as the student antiwar, feminist, gray, brown, gay and lesbian movements. In this period we witnessed the shattering of male, WASP, cultural homogeneity and the collapse of the short-lived liberal consensus. The inclusion of African Americans, Latino/a Americans, Asian Americans, Native Americans and American women into the culture of critical discourse yielded intense intellectual polemics and inescapable ideological polarization that focused principally on the exclusions, silences and blindnesses of male, WASP, cultural homogeneity and its concomitant Arnoldian notions of the canon.

In addition, these critiques promoted three crucial processes that affected intellectual life in the country. First is the appropriation of the theories of postwar Europe—especially the work of the Frankfurt school (Marcuse, Adorno, Horkheimer), French/Italian Marxisms (Sartre, Althusser, Lefebvre, Gramsci), structuralisms (Lévi-Strauss, Todorov) and poststructuralisms (Deleuze, Derrida, Foucault). These diverse and disparate theories—all preoccupied with keeping alive radical projects after the end of the Age of Europe—tend to fuse versions of transgressive European modernisms with Marxist or post-Marxist left politics and unanimously shun the term "postmodernism." Second, there is the recovery and revisioning of American history in light of the struggles of white male workers, women, African Americans, Native Americans, Latino/a Americans, gays and lesbians. Third is the impact of forms of popular culture, such as television, film, music videos and even sports, on highbrow literate culture. The black-based hip-hop culture of youth around the world is one grand example.

After 1973, with the crisis in the international world economy, America's slump in productivity, the challenge of OPEC nations to the North Atlantic monopoly of oil production, the increasing competition in hi-tech sectors of the economy from Japan and West Germany and the growing fragility of the international debt structure, the USA entered a period of waning self-confidence (compounded by Watergate) and a nearly contracting economy. As the standards of living for the middle classes declined, owing to runaway inflation, and the quality of living fell for most, due to escalating unemployment, underemployment and crime, religious and secular neoconservatism emerged with power and potency. This fusion of fervent neonationalism, traditional cultural values and "free market" policies served as the groundwork for the Reagan-Bush era.

The ambiguous legacies of the European Age, American preeminence and decolonization continue to haunt our postmodern moment as we come to terms with both the European, American, Japanese, Soviet and Third World *crimes against* and *contributions to* humanity. The plight of Africans in the New World can be instructive in this regard.

By 1914 European maritime empires had dominion over more than half of the land and a third of the peoples in the world—almost 72 million square kilometers of territory and more than 560 million people under colonial rule. Needless to say, this European control included brutal enslavement, institutional terrorism and cultural degradation of black diasporan people. The death of roughly seventy-five million Africans during the centuries-long transatlantic slave trade is but one reminder, among others, of the assault on black humanity. The black diasporan condition of New World servitude—in which they were viewed as mere commodities with production value, who had no proper legal status, social standing or public worth—can be characterized as, following Orlando Pat-

16   *Cultural Criticism and Race*

terson, natal alienation. This state of perpetual and inheritable domination that diasporan Africans had at birth produced the *modern black diasporan problematic of invisibility and namelessness*. White-supremacist practices—enacted under the auspices of the prestigious cultural authorities of the churches, printed media and scientific academics—promoted black inferiority and constituted the European background against which black diasporan struggles for identity, dignity (self-confidence, self-respect, self-esteem) and material resources took place.

An inescapable aspect of this struggle was that the black diasporan peoples' quest for validation and recognition occurred on the ideological, social and cultural terrains of other nonblack peoples. White-supremacist assaults on black intelligence, ability, beauty and character required persistent black efforts to hold self-doubt, self-contempt and even self-hatred at bay. Selective appropriation, incorporation and rearticulation of European ideologies, cultures and institutions alongside an African heritage—a heritage more or less confined to linguistic innovation in rhetorical practices, stylizations of the body in forms of occupying an alien social space (hairstyles, ways of walking, standing, hand expressions, talking) and means of constituting and sustaining camaraderie and community (e.g. antiphonal, call-and-response styles, rhythmic repetition, risk-ridden syncopation in spectacular modes in musical and rhetorical expressions)—were some of the strategies employed.

The modern black diasporan problematic of invisibility and namelessness can be understood as the condition of *relative lack of black power to represent themselves to themselves and others as complex human beings, and thereby to contest the bombardment of negative, degrading stereotypes put forward by white-supremacist ideologies*. The initial black response to being caught in this whirlwind of Europeanization was to resist the misrepresentation and caricature of the terms set by uncontested nonblack norms and models, and to fight for self-representation and recognition. Every modern black person, especially cultural disseminators, encounters this problematic of invisibility and namelessness. The initial black diasporan response was a mode of resistance that was *moralistic in content* and *communal in character*. That is, the fight for representation and recognition highlighted moral judgments regarding black "positive" images over and against white-supremacist stereotypes. These images "re-presented" monolithic and homogeneous black communities, in a way that could displace past misrepresentations of these communities. Stuart Hall has talked about these responses as attempts to change "the relations of representation."

These courageous yet limited black efforts to combat racist cultural practices uncritically accepted nonblack conventions and standards in two ways. First, they proceeded in an *assimilationist manner* that set out to show that black people were really like white people—thereby eliding differences (in history, culture) between whites and blacks. Black specificity and particularity was thus banished in order to gain white acceptance and approval. Second, these black responses rested upon a *homogenizing impulse* that assumed that all black people were really alike—hence obliterating differences (class, gender, region, sexual orientation) between black peoples. I submit that there are elements of truth in both claims, yet the conclusions are unwarranted owing to the basic fact that nonblack paradigms set the terms of the replies.

The insight in the first claim is that blacks and whites are in some important sense alike—that is, in their positive capacities for human sympathy, moral sacrifice, service to others, intelligence and beauty, or negatively, in their capacity for cruelty. Yet the common humanity they share is jettisoned when the claim is cast in an assimilationist manner that subordinates black particularity to a false universalism, that is, nonblack rubrics or prototypes. Similarly, the insight in the second claim is that all blacks are in some significant sense "in the same boat"—that is, subject to white-supremacist abuse. Yet this common condition is stretched too far when viewed

18   *Cultural Criticism and Race*

in a *homogenizing* way that overlooks how racist treatment vastly differs owing to class, gender, sexual orientation, nation, region, hue and age.

The moralistic and communal aspects of the initial black diasporan responses to social and psychic erasure were not simply cast into simplistic binary oppositions of positive-negative, good-bad images that privileged the first term in light of a white norm so that black efforts remained inscribed within the very logic that dehumanized them. They were further complicated by the fact that these responses were also advanced principally by anxiety-ridden, middle-class, black intellectuals (predominantly male and heterosexual), grappling with their sense of double-consciousness—namely their own crisis of identity, agency and audience—caught between a quest for white approval and acceptance and an endeavor to overcome the internalized association of blackness with inferiority. And I suggest that these complex anxieties of modern black diasporan intellectuals partly motivate the two major arguments that ground the assimilationist moralism and homogeneous communalism just outlined.

Kobena Mercer has talked about these two arguments as the *reflectionist* and the *social engineering* arguments. The reflectionist argument holds that the fight for black representation and recognition must reflect or mirror the real black community, not simply the negative and depressing representations of it. The social engineering argument claims that since any form of representation is constructed—that is, selective in light of broader aims—black representation (especially given the difficulty of blacks gaining access to positions of power to produce any black imagery) should offer positive images of themselves in order to inspire achievement among young black people, thereby countering racist stereotypes. The hidden assumption of both arguments is that we have unmediated access to what the "real black community" is and what "positive images" are. In short, these arguments presuppose the very phenomena to be interrogated, and thereby foreclose the very issues that should serve as the subject matter to be investigated.

Any notions of the "real black community" and "positive images" are value-laden, socially loaded and ideologically charged. To pursue this discussion is to call into question the possibility of such an uncontested consensus regarding them. Stuart Hall has rightly called this encounter "the end of innocence or the end of the innocent notion of the essential Black subject . . . the recognition that 'Black' is essentially a politically and culturally *constructed* category." This recognition—more and more pervasive among the postmodern black diasporan intelligentsia—is facilitated in part by the slow but sure dissolution of the European Age's maritime empires, and the unleashing of new political possibilities and cultural articulations among formerly colonialized peoples across the globe.

One crucial lesson of this decolonization process remains the manner in which most Third World, authoritarian, bureaucratic elites deploy essentialist rhetorics about "homogeneous national communities" and "positive images" in order to repress and regiment their diverse and heterogeneous populations. Yet in the diaspora, especially among First World countries, this critique has emerged not so much from the black male component of the left but rather from the black women's movement. The decisive push of postmodern black intellectuals toward a new cultural politics of difference has been made by the powerful critiques and constructive explorations of black diasporan women (for instance, Toni Morrison). The coffin used to bury the innocent notion of the essential black subject was nailed shut with the termination of the black male monopoly on the construction of the black subject. In this regard, the black diasporan womanist critique has had a greater impact than the critiques that highlight exclusively class, empire, age, sexual orientation or nature.

This decisive push toward the end of black innocence—though prefigured in various degrees in the best moments of W. E. B. Du

20   *Cultural Criticism and Race*

Bois, Anna Cooper, C. L. R. James, James Baldwin, Claudia Jones, the later Malcolm X, Frantz Fanon, Amiri Baraka and others—forces black diasporan cultural workers to encounter what Hall has called the "politics of representation." The main aim now is not simply access to representation in order to produce positive images of homogeneous communities—though broader access remains a practical and political problem. Nor is the primary goal here that of contesting stereotypes—though contestation remains a significant though limited venture. Following the model of the black diasporan traditions of music, athletics and rhetoric, black cultural workers must constitute and sustain discursive and institutional networks that deconstruct earlier modern black strategies for identity-formation, demystify power relations that incorporate class, patriarchal and homophobic biases, and construct more multivalent and multi-dimensional responses that articulate the complexity and diversity of black practices in the modern and postmodern world.

Furthermore, black cultural workers must investigate and interrogate the Other of blackness-whiteness. One cannot deconstruct the binary oppositional logic of images of blackness without extending it to the contrary condition of blackness-whiteness itself. However, a mere dismantling will not do—for the very notion of a deconstructive social theory is oxymoronic. Yet social theory is what is needed to examine and *explain* the historically specific ways in which "whiteness" is a politically constructed category parasitic on "blackness," and thereby to conceive of the profoundly hybrid character of what we mean by "race," "ethnicity" and "nationality." For instance, European immigrants arrived on American shores perceiving themselves as "Irish," "Sicilian," "Lithuanian" and so on. They had to learn that they were "white" principally by adopting an American discourse of positively valued whiteness and negatively charged blackness. This process by which people define themselves physically, socially, sexually and even politically in terms of whiteness or blackness has much bearing not only on constructed notions of race and ethnicity but also on how we understand the changing character of US nationalities.

And given the Americanization of the world, especially in the sphere of mass culture, such inquiries—encouraged by the new cultural politics of difference—raise critical issues of "hybridity," "exilic status" and "identity" on an international scale. Needless to say, these inquiries must traverse those of "male-female," "colonizer-colonized," "heterosexual-homosexual," and others, as well.

In light of this brief sketch of the emergence of our present crisis—and the turn toward history and difference in cultural work—four major historicist forms of theoretical activity provide resources for how we understand, analyze and enact our representational practices: Heideggerian *destruction* of the Western metaphysical tradition, Derridean *deconstruction* of the Western philosophical tradition, Rortian *demythologization* of the Western intellectual tradition and Marxist, Foucaultian, feminist, antiracist or antihomophobic *demystification* of Western cultural and artistic conventions.

Despite his abominable association with the Nazis, Martin Heidegger's project is useful in that it discloses the suppression of temporality and historicity in the dominant metaphysical systems of the West from Plato to Rudolf Carnap. This is noteworthy in that it forces one to understand philosophy's representational discourses as thoroughly historical phenomena. Hence, they should be viewed with skepticism as they are often flights from the specific, concrete, practical and particular. The major problem with Heidegger's project—as noted by his neo-Marxist student, Herbert Marcuse—is that he views history in terms of fate, heritage and destiny. He dramatizes the past and present as if it were a Greek tragedy with no tools of social analysis to relate cultural work to institutions and structures or antecedent forms and styles.

Jacques Derrida's version of deconstruction is one of the most influential schools of thought among young academic critics. It is salutary in that it focuses on the political power of rhetorical operations—of tropes and metaphors in binary oppositions like white/black, good/bad, male/female, machine/nature, ruler/ruled, reality/appearance—showing how these operations sustain hierarchal worldviews by devaluing the second terms as something subsumed under the first. Most of the controversy about Derrida's project revolves around this austere epistemic doubt that both unsettles binary oppositions while it undermines any determinate meaning of a text, that is, book, art object, performance, building. Yet, his views about skepticism are no more alarming than those of David Hume, Ludwig Wittgenstein or Stanley Cavell. He simply revels in it for transgressive purposes, whereas others provide us with ways to dissolve, sidestep or cope with skepticism. None, however, slide down the slippery, crypto-Nietzschean slope of sophomoric relativism as alleged by old-style humanists, be they Platonists, Kantians or Arnoldians.

The major shortcoming of Derrida's deconstructive project is that it puts a premium on a sophisticated ironic consciousness that tends to preclude and foreclose analyses that guide action with purpose. And given Derrida's own status as an Algerian-born, Jewish leftist marginalized by a hostile French academic establishment (quite different from his reception by the youth in the American academic establishment), the sense of political impotence and hesitation regarding the efficacy of moral action is understandable—but not justifiable. His works and those of his followers too often become rather monotonous, Johnny-one-note rhetorical readings that disassemble texts with little attention to the effects and consequences these dismantlings have in relation to the operations of military, economic and social powers.

Richard Rorty's neopragmatic project of demythologization is insightful in that it provides descriptive mappings of the transient metaphors—especially the ocular and specular ones—that regulate some of the fundamental dynamics in the construction of self-descriptions dominant in highbrow European and American philosophy. His perspective is instructive because it discloses the crucial role of narrative as the background for rational exchange and critical conversation. To put it crudely, Rorty shows why we should speak not of History, but histories, not of Reason, but historically constituted forms of rationality, not of Criticism or Art, but of socially constituted notions of criticism and art—all linked but not reducible to political purposes, material interests and cultural prejudices.

Rorty's project nonetheless leaves one wanting, owing to its distrust of social analytical explanation. Similar to the dazzling new historicism of Stephen Greenblatt, Louis Montrose and Catherine Gallagher—inspired by the subtle symbolic-cum-textual anthropology of Clifford Geertz and the powerful discursive materialism of Michel Foucault—Rorty's work gives us mappings and descriptions with no explanatory accounts for change and conflict. In this way, it gives us an aestheticized version of historicism in which the provisional and variable are celebrated at the expense of highlighting who gains, loses or bears what costs.

Demystification is the most illuminating mode of theoretical inquiry for those who promote the new cultural politics of difference. Social structural analyses of empire, exterminism, class, race, gender, nature, age, sexual orientation, nation and region are the springboards—though not landing grounds—for the most desirable forms of critical practice that take history (and herstory) seriously. Demystification tries to keep track of the complex dynamics of institutional and other related power structures in order to disclose options and alternatives for transformative praxis; it also attempts to grasp the way in which representational strategies are creative responses to novel circumstances and conditions. In this way, the central role of human agency (always enacted under circumstances not of one's choosing)—be it in the critic, artist or constituency and audience—is accented.

I call demystificatory criticism "prophetic criticism"—the approach appropriate for the new cultural politics of difference—because while it begins with social structural analyses it also makes explicit its moral and political aims. It is partisan, partial, engaged and crisis-centered, yet always keeps open a skeptical eye to avoid dogmatic traps, premature closures, formulaic formulations or rigid conclusions. In addition to social structural analyses, moral and political judgments, and sheer critical consciousness, there indeed is evaluation. Yet the aim of this evaluation is neither to pit art objects against one another like racehorses nor to create eternal canons that dull, discourage or even dwarf contemporary achievements. We listen to Ludwig van Beethoven, Charlie Parker, Luciano Pavarotti, Laurie Anderson, Sarah Vaughn, Stevie Wonder or Kathleen Battle, read William Shakespeare, Anton Chekhov, Ralph Ellison, Doris Lessing, Thomas Pynchon, Toni Morrison or Gabriel García Márquez, see works of Pablo Picasso, Ingmar Bergman, Le Corbusier, Martin Puryear, Barbara Kruger, Spike Lee, Frank Gehry or Howardena Pindell—not in order to undergird bureaucratic assents or enliven cocktail party conversations, but rather to be summoned by the styles they deploy for their profound insight, pleasures and challenges. Yet all evaluation—including a delight in Eliot's poetry despite his reactionary politics, or a love of Zora Neale Hurston's novels despite her Republican party affiliations—is inseparable from, though not identical or reducible to, social structural analyses, moral and political judgments and the workings of a curious critical consciousness.

The deadly traps of demystification—and any form of prophetic criticism—are those of reductionism, be it of the sociological, psychological or historical sort. By reductionism I mean either one factor analyses (that is, crude Marxisms, feminisms, racialisms, etc.) that yield a one-dimensional functionalism, or a hyper-subtle analytical perspective that loses touch with the specificity of an artwork's form and the context of its reception. Few cultural workers of whatever stripe can walk the tightrope between the Scylla of reductionism and the Charybdis of aestheticism—yet demystificatory (or prophetic) critics must.

The Existential Challenge

The existential challenge to the new cultural politics of difference can be stated simply: how does one acquire the resources to survive and the cultural capital to thrive as a critic or artist? By cultural capital (Pierre Bourdieu's term), I mean not only the high-quality skills required to engage in critical practices but, more important, the self-confidence, discipline and perseverance necessary for success without an undue reliance on the mainstream for approval and acceptance. This challenge holds for all prophetic critics, yet it is especially difficult for those of color. The widespread, modern, European denial of the intelligence, ability, beauty and character of people of color puts a tremendous burden on critics and artists of color to "prove" themselves in light of norms and models set by white elites whose own heritage devalued and dehumanized them. In short, in the court of criticism and art—or any matters regarding the life of the mind—people of color are guilty, that is, not expected to meet standards of intellectual achievement, until "proven" innocent, that is, acceptable to "us."

This is more a structural dilemma than a matter of personal attitudes. The profoundly racist and sexist heritage of the European Age has bequeathed to us a set of deeply ingrained perceptions about people of color, including, of course, the self-perceptions that people of color bring. It is not surprising that most intellectuals of color in the past exerted much of their energies and efforts to gain acceptance from and approval by "white normative gazes." The new cultural politics of difference advises critics and artists of color to put aside this mode of mental bondage, thereby freeing themselves to both interrogate the ways in which they are bound by certain conventions and to learn from and build on these very norms and models. One hallmark of wisdom in the context of any struggle is to avoid knee-jerk rejection and uncritical acceptance.

Self-confidence, discipline and perseverance are not ends in themselves. Rather they are the necessary stuff of which enabling criticism and self-criticism are made. Notwithstanding inescapable jealousies, insecurities and anxieties, one telling characteristic of critics and artists of color linked to the new prophetic criticism should be their capacity for and promotion of relentless criticism

26 Cultural Criticism and Race

and self-criticism—be it the normative paradigms of their white colleagues that tend to leave out considerations of empire, race, gender and sexual orientation, or the damaging dogmas about the homogeneous character of communities of color.

There are four basic options for people of color interested in representation—if they are to survive and thrive as serious practitioners of their craft. First, there is the Booker T. Temptation, namely the individual preoccupation with the mainstream and its legitimizing power. Most critics and artists of color try to bite this bait. It is nearly unavoidable, yet few succeed in a substantive manner. It is no accident that the most creative and profound among them—especially those with staying power beyond mere flashes in the pan to satisfy faddish tokenism—are usually marginal to the mainstream. Even the pervasive professionalization of cultural practitioners of color in the past few decades has not produced towering figures who reside within the established white patronage system that bestows the rewards and prestige for chosen contributions to American society.

It certainly helps to have some trustworthy allies within this system, yet most of those who enter and remain tend to lose much of their creativity, diffuse their prophetic energy and dilute their critiques. Still, it is unrealistic for creative people of color to think they can sidestep the white patronage system. And though there are indeed some white allies conscious of the tremendous need to rethink politics, it's naive to think that being comfortably nested within this very same system—even if one can be a patron to others—does not affect one's work, one's outlook and, most important, one's soul.

The second option is the Talented Tenth Seduction, namely, a move toward arrogant group insularity. This alternative has a limited function—to preserve one's sanity and sense of self as one copes with the mainstream. Yet it is, at best, a transitional and transient activity. If it becomes a permanent option it is self-defeating, in that it usually reinforces the very inferiority complexes promoted by the subtly racist mainstream. Hence it tends to revel in a parochialism and encourage a narrow racialist and chauvinistic outlook.

The third strategy is the Go It Alone Option. This is an extreme rejectionist perspective that shuns the mainstream and group insularity. Almost every critic and artist of color contemplates or enacts this option at some time in their pilgrimage. It is healthy in that it reflects the presence of independent, critical and skeptical sensibilities toward perceived constraints on one's creativity. Yet it is, in the end, difficult if not impossible to sustain if one is to grow, develop and mature intellectually, as some semblance of dialogue with a community is necessary for almost any creative practice.

The most desirable option for people of color who promote the new cultural politics of difference is to be a Critical Organic Catalyst. By this I mean a person who stays attuned to the best of what the mainstream has to offer—its paradigms, viewpoints and methods—yet maintains a grounding in affirming and enabling subcultures of criticism. Prophetic critics and artists of color should be exemplars of what it means to be intellectual freedom fighters, that is, cultural workers who simultaneously position themselves within (or alongside) the mainstream while clearly aligned with groups who vow to keep alive potent traditions of critique and resistance. In this regard, one can take clues from the great musicians or preachers of color who are open to the best of what other traditions offer yet are rooted in nourishing subcultures that build on the grand achievements of a vital heritage. Openness to others—including the mainstream—does not entail wholesale cooptation, and group autonomy is not group insularity. Louis Armstrong, W. E. B. Du Bois, Ella Baker, Jose Carlos Mariategui, M. M. Thomas, Wynton Marsalis, Martin Luther King, Jr., and Ronald Takaki have understood this well.

The new cultural politics of difference can thrive only if there are communities, groups, organizations, institutions, subcultures and networks of people of color who cultivate critical sensibilities and personal accountability—without inhibiting individual expres-

28 *Cultural Criticism and Race*

sions, curiosities and idiosyncrasies. This is especially needed given the escalating racial hostility, violence and polarization in the USA. Yet this critical coming together must not be a narrow closing ranks. Rather it is a strengthening and nurturing endeavor that can forge more solid alliances and coalitions. In this way, prophetic criticism—with its stress on historical specificity and artistic complexity—directly addresses the intellectual challenge. The cultural capital of people of color—with its emphasis on self-confidence, discipline, perseverance and subcultures of criticism—also tries to meet the existential requirement. Both are mutually reinforcing. Both are motivated by a deep commitment to individuality and democracy—the moral and political ideals that guide the creative response to the political challenge.

The Political Challenge

Adequate rejoinders to intellectual and existential challenges equip the practitioners of the new cultural politics of difference to meet the political ones. This challenge principally consists of forging solid and reliable alliances of people of color and white progressives guided by a moral and political vision of greater democracy and individual freedom in communities, states and transnational enterprises, for instance, corporations, and information and communications conglomerates.

Jesse Jackson's Rainbow Coalition is a gallant yet flawed effort in this regard—gallant due to the tremendous energy, vision and courage of its leader and followers, yet flawed because of its failure to take seriously critical and democratic sensibilities within its own operations. In fact, Jackson's attempt to gain power at the national level is a symptom of the weakness of US progressive politics, and a sign that the capacity to generate extraparliamentary social motion or movements has waned. Yet given the present organizational weakness and intellectual timidity of left politics in the USA, the major option is that of multiracial grass-roots citizens' participation in credible projects in which people see that their efforts can make a difference. The salutary revolutionary developments in Eastern Europe are encouraging and inspiring in this regard. Ordinary people organized can change societies.

The most significant theme of the new cultural politics of difference is the agency, capacity and ability of human beings who have been culturally degraded, politically oppressed and economically exploited by bourgeois liberal and communist illiberal status quos. This theme neither romanticizes nor idealizes marginalized peoples. Rather it accentuates their humanity and tries to attenuate the institutional constraints on their life-chances for surviving and thriving. In this way, the new cultural politics of difference shuns narrow particularisms, parochialisms and separatisms, just as it rejects false universalisms and homogeneous totalisms. Instead, the new cultural politics of difference affirms the perennial quest for the precious ideals of individuality and democracy by digging deep in the depths of human particularities and social specificities in order to construct new kinds of connections, affinities and communities across empire, nation, region, race, gender, age and sexual orientation.

The major impediments of the radical libertarian and democratic projects of the new cultural politics are threefold: the pervasive processes of objectification, rationalization and commodification throughout the world. The first process—best highlighted in Georg Simmel's *The Philosophy of Money* (1900)—consists of transforming human beings into manipulable objects. It promotes the notion that people's actions have no impact on the world, that we are but spectators not participants in making and remaking ourselves and the larger society. The second process—initially examined in the seminal works of Max Weber—expands bureaucratic hierarchies that impose impersonal rules and regulations in order to increase efficiency, be they defined in terms of better service or better surveillance. This process leads to disenchantment with past mythologies of deadening, flat, banal ways of life. The third and most important process—best examined in the works of Karl Marx,

Georg Lukács and Walter Benjamin—augments market forces in the form of oligopolies and monopolies that centralize resources and powers and promote cultures of consumption that view people as mere spectatorial consumers and passive citizens.

These processes cannot be eliminated, but their pernicious effects can be substantially alleviated. The audacious attempt to lessen their impact—to preserve people's agency, increase the scope of their freedom and expand the operations of democracy—is the fundamental aim of the new cultural politics of difference. This is why the crucial questions become: What is the moral content of one's cultural identity? And what are the political consequences of this moral content and cultural identity?

In the recent past, the dominant cultural identities have been circumscribed by immoral patriarchal, imperial, jingoistic and xenophobic constraints. The political consequences have been principally a public sphere regulated by and for well-to-do, white males in the name of freedom and democracy. The new cultural criticism exposes and explodes the exclusions, blindnesses and silences of this past, calling from it radical libertarian and democratic projects that will create a better present and future. The new cultural politics of difference is neither an ahistorical Jacobin program that discards tradition and ushers in new self-righteous authoritarianisms, nor a guilt-ridden, leveling, anti-imperialist liberalism that celebrates token pluralism for smooth inclusion. Rather, it acknowledges the uphill struggle of fundamentally transforming highly objectified, rationalized and commodified societies and cultures in the name of individuality and democracy. This means locating the structural causes of unnecessary forms of social misery (without reducing all such human suffering to historical causes), depicting the plight and predicaments of demoralized and depoliticized citizens caught in market-driven cycles of therapeutic release—drugs, alcoholism, consumerism—and projecting alternative visions, analyses and actions that proceed from particularities and arrive at moral and political connectedness. This connectedness does not signal a homogeneous unity or monolithic totality but rather a contingent, fragile coalition building in an effort to pursue common radical libertarian and democratic goals that overlap.

In a world in which most of the resources, wealth and power are centered in huge corporations and supportive political elites, the new cultural politics of difference may appear to be solely visionary, utopian and fanciful. The recent cutbacks of social service programs, business takebacks at the negotiation tables of workers and management, speedups at the workplace and buildups of military budgets reinforce this perception. And surely the growing disintegration and decomposition of civil society—of shattered families, neighborhoods and schools—adds to this perception. Can a civilization that evolves more and more around market activity, more and more around the buying and selling of commodities, expand the scope of freedom and democracy? Can we simply bear witness to its slow decay and doom—a painful denouement prefigured already in many poor black and brown communities and rapidly embracing all of us? These haunting questions remain unanswered yet the challenge they pose must not remain unmet. The new cultural politics of difference tries to confront these enormous and urgent challenges. It will require all the imagination, intelligence, courage, sacrifice, care and laughter we can muster.

The time has come for critics and artists of the new cultural politics of difference to cast their nets widely, flex their muscles broadly and thereby refuse to limit their visions, analyses and praxis to their particular terrains. The aim is to dare to recast, redefine and revise the very notions of "modernity," "mainstream," "margins," "difference," "otherness." We have now reached a new stage in the perennial struggle for freedom and dignity. And while much of the First World intelligentsia adopts retrospective and conservative outlooks that defend the crisis-ridden present, we promote a prospective and prophetic vision with a sense of possibility and potential, especially for those who bear the social costs of the present. We look to the past for strength, not solace; we look at the present

Cultural Criticism and Race

and see people perishing, not profits mounting; we look toward the future and vow to make it different and better.

To put it boldly, the new kind of critic and artist associated with the new cultural politics of difference consists of an energetic breed of New World *bricoleurs* with improvisational and flexible sensibilities that sidestep mere opportunism and mindless eclecticism; persons from all countries, cultures, genders, sexual orientations, ages and regions with protean identities who avoid ethnic chauvinism and faceless universalism; intellectual and political freedom fighters with partisan passion, international perspectives and, thank God, a sense of humor that combats the ever-present absurdity that forever threatens our democratic and libertarian projects and dampens the fire that fuels our will to struggle. Yet we will struggle and stay, as those brothers and sisters on the block say, "out there"—with intellectual rigor, existential dignity, moral vision, political courage and soulful style.

[23]
Must Feminists Give up on Liberal Democracy?

Feminism has often found itself at odds with liberal democracy: indeed feminist judgements in this area have usually been harsher than our judgements on liberalism *per se*. Despite many and much rehearsed limitations, liberalism can at least claim credit in the historical development of the feminist tradition, and it enjoys today its double legacy as founding inspiration and favourite target of attack. Liberal *democracy*, by contrast, does not even inspire us. The prolonged exclusion of women from the most basic right to vote turned out to be the merest tip of the iceberg: a discouraging hint at deeper structures that keep women politically unequal. Whatever its claims in other fields of endeavour, liberal democracy has not served women well.[1]

Within this generally damning perspective, there are nonetheless two discernible strands.[2] The first stems from the politics of the contemporary women's movement, which emerged out of a period of widespread dissatisfaction with the banalities of liberal democracy, and shared with virtually all radical groupings of the 1960s and 1970s a vision of a more active, participatory democracy. In the practices of most women's groups, this translated into a distrust of hierarchy and leadership, a concern with sharing expertise and influence and time, and a preference for the direct democracy of the meeting rather than the anonymity of the vote. The relationship between these principles of self-organization and the principles that should govern the polity as a whole were hardly a matter of urgent concern, but, under the broad slogan of 'the personal is political', feminists developed an analysis of power as all-pervasive and democracy as everywhere significant. The women's movement then became associated with the values of local, decentralized democracy, with the idea that democracy matters wherever there are relations of power, and with the importance of organizational forms as prefiguring ultimate goals.

The theorization of feminist perspectives on democracy lagged considerably behind, and as these developed (largely in the course of the 1980s) they moved onto what might seem the more respectable ground of citizenship and political equality.[3] Where the first moment in feminist thinking had coincided with an explosion in participatory democracy, the second occurred at a time of growing disdain for the 'fetish of direct democracy'[4] and resurgent confidence in the procedures of liberal democracy. This confidence has not on the whole been shared by feminists, but the transition from participation towards citizenship nonetheless mirrors the movement in radical thought as a whole. In the first phase, feminists concerned themselves with what we might call the micro-level of democracy inside a movement and democracy in everyday life. In the second phase, we have turned to the macro-level of women's membership in the political community: exploring questions of inclusion and exclusion, and dampening down the universalizing pretensions of modern political thought.[5] The first moment almost sidelined more conventional democratic debates. Perhaps the second will in its turn be sidelined, but, in associating itself with the language of citizenship, it occupies more central ground.

There are reasons behind this shift that are distinctive to feminism, but it also reproduces a division that has characterized all the critical literature on liberal democracy. For many democrats, the decisive weakness of liberal democracy is the way it has restricted the scope and intensity of citizen engagement, retreating so far from classical ideals of democracy as to cast some doubt on the use of the term. The more ambitious practices of active and equal involvement in decision-making have given way to a minimalist or, in Benjamin Barber's term, a 'weak' democracy[6] that offers little more than protection against the excesses of what governments might do. The central principle of contemporary democracy is that governments must subject themselves to periodic recall: there must be enough freedom of association and information to promote the organization of a variety of political parties and there must be regular elections in which all adults are permitted to vote. Those who query the limits of this typically argue for more democracy and democracy in more places. The earlier practices of the women's movement fell broadly within this school.

The second major line of attack focuses on the failure to deliver on the promise of political equality. Liberal democracy tends to regard this as adequately met by the equal rights to vote and to stand for election; and in doing so it abstracts from the social and economic conditions that would make this equality effective. Even setting aside issues of gender and race, our unequal access to economic resources combines with our unequal access to knowledge, information and political skills to render us politically (not just socially) unequal. Robert Dahl clearly acknowledges this in his recent magisterial restatement of his views on democracy, and goes so far as to question whether political equality is compatible with the market economy.[7] But as this very example indicates, the promise of political equality has provoked an extensive literature on the obstacles that might stand in its path; and many defenders of 'actually existing democracy' will admit at least some part of the problem. Certainly, since the post-war development of the welfare state, most of those societies that would appear in the roll-call of liberal democracies have come to address various social or economic rights that may be necessary to make citizenship effectively equal. This poses important questions to the current analyses of women and citizenship. Is the differential political treatment of women and men part of the sorry history of liberal democracies, or built into their very foundations? Does liberal democracy have to turn itself into something *other* – an alternative to liberal democracy – in order to deal with sexual inequality? Or can the inadequacies and inequalities be redressed within some future, but still *liberal* democracy?

I explore here the powerful critiques that feminists have developed under the three broad headings of citizenship, participation and heterogeneity; under each heading, I query whether the arguments add up to a case against liberal democracy. The preoccupation with liberal democracy as a totalizing system we must be either 'for' or 'against' proves relatively unhelpful, for it attributes to liberal democracy a greater theoretical fixity than is confirmed by its subsequent history.[8] The 'democratization' of liberal democracy has already moved it a long way from its founding moments: so far indeed that the neo-liberals and neo-conservatives of the 1970s and 1980s cried out against what they saw as an all-too successful democratic subversion.[9] If the precise character of liberal democracy can be formed and re-formed in a process of political contestation, then feminists may have quite enough on their hands in engendering democracy without also worrying about whether the results are still 'liberal democracy'.

Democracy and Difference

Citizenship

Recent explorations of women and citizenship share considerable common ground with other critiques of liberal democracy, in that they address the substantive conditions that would make political equality more than a nice choice of words. The most obvious point of entry here is the extraordinary under-representation of women in the world's political assemblies. All versions of liberal democracy link the right to vote with the right to stand for election – and few are as cavalier as Joseph Schumpeter, who noted in a brief footnote that we are free to compete for political leadership 'in the same sense in which everyone is free to start another textile mill'.[10] It is, however, in considering the imbalance between the proportion of women in the citizen body and the proportion elected to power that the vacuous nature of this particular right is most starkly revealed.[11] The caring responsibilities that most women carry in relation to the young, the sick and the old – not to mention the able-bodied men – act as a powerful practical barrier to their political involvement, while the cultural constructions of politics as a matter primarily for men work to disadvantage those women who still put themselves forward. The results are entirely predictable: with the important exception of the Nordic countries, the women elected to the world's national assemblies make up between 2 and 12 per cent of the whole.

The solutions to this fall roughly into three categories. Some of the problems relate to the sexual division of labour in production and reproduction, and will only finally be resolved when men and women share equally in the full range of paid and unpaid work. Others are associated with the working conditions of politicians, and require major modification to accommodate people who are active parents as well. Others again relate to the 'boy's club' prejudices of party selectorates or voters, which require affirmative action (such as quotas) to boost the election of women. The importance feminists currently attach to the third reflects our sadly realistic assessment of the time it will take to alter the first two, though this may be a case of dealing with the symptoms rather than tackling the underlying cause. It is worth noting, meanwhile, that the literature on women's (under-) representation rarely addresses it as something intrinsic to the nature of liberal democracy.

The more unique move made by recent theorists is to consider the broader collection of rights and responsibilities that *already* underpin liberal democratic notions of citizenship, and the ways in which these have been gendered. Feminists have drawn attention, for example, to the relationship between citizenship and the defence of one's nation, or between citizenship and the work that one does, noting that in both instances the status of women as citizens appears profoundly ambiguous. In much of the late nineteenth- and early twentieth-century battle for women's suffrage, the fact that women did not fight to defend the realm was regarded as a definitive argument. Carole Pateman has noted that part of the counter-argument for extending the vote to women was that, in their role as mothers and educators, they too were performing a public service: that the women who died in childbirth were sacrificing their lives to the nation just as much as the men who died in battle; that the women who devoted their lives to bearing and rearing children were performing tasks without which no society could survive; that this seemingly private activity was as much a qualification for citizenship as going out to work or defending the nation.[12] The troubling legacy from this, she argues, is that men and women were then incorporated into citizenship in decisively different ways: men primarily as soldiers and workers, women primarily as mothers.

Similar points have been made in relation to the development of the welfare state. In most post-war liberal democracies, the meaning of citizenship was expanded to embrace what are classed as 'social rights', such that a citizen could legitimately expect to be provided with access to education and employment, and, failing that, a living income. Yet the welfare state that supposedly encapsulated this wider citizenship was typically founded around a model of the male as breadwinner responsible for dependent wife and children, and social security provision in Britain, for example, was organized around this conception. Despite subsequent – in my view, largely trivial – changes, the household remains as the unit for calculating social entitlement, and within this household there is a primary/secondary divide. Such practices reflect and help sustain a profoundly gendered division of labour.

The novelty of this argument lies not so much in what is being said about the sexual division of labour, as in the links being forged between the gendered distribution of paid and unpaid labour and the gendered distribution of political status and power. Under the rubric of citizenship, feminists are now exploring issues that used to be dealt with as economic or social policy, and the strategic significance of this is that it lifts the arguments over sexual equality from the private to the public realm. Part of the traditional critique of liberal democracy is that it concedes only the formality of political equality, while ignoring or indeed condoning the social inequalities that are associated with the market economy. The standard riposte is that any of the measures that might be proposed to deal with these 'other' inequalities will come into conflict with liberties that are also part of the democratic tradition: that there is a tension between freedom and equality, and that a balance must be struck between the two.[13] Political equality may not meet all the requirements of an egalitarian society – but then half a cake is always better than none. The more challenging point made in recent feminist explorations is that membership of the political community is itself profoundly gendered. It is not a matter of political equality being *inadequate* – as if this equality has been won, but should now be extended from the political to the social realm – but that our 'political' status as citizens is premised on arrangements of sexual inequality. If men 'earnt' their citizenship as soldiers and workers, while women 'earnt' their citizenship as mothers and educators of their children, then the political settlement has already legitimated the sexual division of labour. The inequalities are intrinsic to the politics, not an extraneous, additional concern.

When equality in the household or at work is conceived as an 'additional' question, then the staunchest supporter of liberal democracy can feel justified in refusing to consider the case. Political equality is one thing; all these other kinds of equality are quite another. No right-thinking democrat would now argue for inequalities in political rights, but democrats can take any position they fancy on what are seen as a range of additional concerns. The demarcation line helps close down discussion of more substantial notions of equality – and, as those following events in East Central Europe have noted, this has particularly disastrous consequences for women. The 1989 revolutions created or restored the rights of citizens to elect their governments; but this has been associated with a reinstatement of women as primarily mothers, with moves to criminalize abortion, shut down child-care facilities, or encourage women out of their full-time jobs.[14] The differential basis on which men and women are incorporated into citizenship is not some historical oddity, but all too alive and well.

These are powerful arguments, but they leave open the question as to how far they challenge the basic principles of liberal democracy. They shift the boundaries between what are public and what are private concerns, and they query the particular point at which this division has been drawn. But while liberal democracies insist on some such boundary (otherwise what does it mean to put 'liberal' in front?), they have proved reasonably flexible in their definitions of where this boundary should lie. Partly under the impact of labour and social democratic parties, liberal democracies have extended the legitimate scope of government interference to include extensive regulation of the workings of the market. And partly under the impact of feminism, they have entered more decisively into the regulation of sexual violence, as in the growing recognition of rape within marriage as a crime. Meanwhile the work of Scandinavian feminists suggests the scope for a new 'social citizenship' that builds care work into the responsibilities of the state.[15] The analysis of unequal citizenship remains as a major and urgent task for anyone concerned with sexual equality. But unless it can be demonstrated that liberal democracy is founded – and not just historically, but in some sense in its very logic – on the differential treatment of women and men, then the work of dealing with this difference may not alter its basic parameters. To argue otherwise would be to establish some central and defining principle that cannot be made compatible with sexual equality. This case is not yet established, and remains an important, but open, question.[16]

Participation

The second major ground for feminist dissatisfaction lies in the critique of liberal democratic minimalism, and the contrast drawn between this and more active participation. Here too there are problems in considering whether the criticisms add up to a case *against* liberal democracy, or more modestly compute as an argument for more democracy within broadly liberal democratic norms. There is an additional difficulty, for women's experience provides evidence on both sides of the argument. While I regard the positive case as stronger, this has to be considered within a balance sheet that moderates the enthusiasm of earlier years.

Let me start with the downside. In a recent overview of feminist writing on citizenship, Kathleen Jones notes that 'feminist ideas about political institutions stress participation almost to the point of obsession':[17] the very phrasing reveals ambivalence towards this kind of obsession. In the course of a powerful argument for a more actively participatory democracy, Iris Marion Young nonetheless warns against the uncritical retention of 'an anarchist, participatory democratic communitarianism to express our vision of the ideal society',[18] and notes the almost overwhelming pressures towards homogeneity that such a politics can bring in its train. As these and other comments indicate, the early practices of direct democracy in the women's movement lent themselves to an overly consensual – indeed illiberal – politics, which made it peculiarly difficult for feminists to agree to disagree. The emphasis on face-to-face meetings encouraged more active and equal participation, but women's groups found it hard to develop the mechanisms for coping with conflict, and particularly in the early years (much less so later on) expected women to discover how fundamentally their interests were shared. The false unities of 'sisterhood' imposed tremendous pressure towards reaching a common consensus, while the almost familial model of political activity exacted 'a toll that is not always consistent with the feminist stress on autonomy and self-development'.[19] Sceptics will recognize this as one of the standard points made in contrasts between liberal and participatory democracy, for liberalism will accept disagreement as inevitable – and certainly not anyone's fault. The more active engagement of participatory democracy often tends towards the opposite, for, instead of taking people and their interests as given, it looks forward to a process of discussion, transformation and change. This is not to say that participatory democracy necessarily anticipates convergence on some 'general will', but in the early years of the contemporary movement such tendencies were undoubtedly strong.

This is one problem feminists have encountered in developing a more active and engaged democracy, serving not so much as a reason for dropping all such ambitions but as a reminder of the problems that direct democracy can bring. The second arises from female rather than feminist experience, and relates to the pressures on women's time. The founding inspiration for all visions of democracy lies back in the fifth century BC, when the citizens of Athens (and other Greek city states) participated in an extraordinarily rich and engaged political life. Citizens did indeed rule, sharing, in however minor a way, in the administrative responsibilities of the city and deciding central matters of legislation and policy in the frequent citizen assemblies. The very intensity of the engagement was, however, at odds with political equality, and the citizen body was severely restricted in size. The most fervent admirer of classical democracy can hardly ignore the premise on which it was founded: the citizens were 'freed' for politics by a vast army of women and foreigners and slaves.

The obvious point made by any contemporary democrat is that citizen assemblies and rotation of duties work only in the context of tiny communities, and do not translate easily to the modern nation state which counts its citizens by the million. In feminist literature, the issue is posed even more starkly, for the very notion of the active citizen presumes someone else is taking care of the children and doing the necessary maintenance of everyday life. In one of the earliest contributions to the now substantial body of feminist political theory, Susan Moller Okin notes that, 'if women were to be politically equal, they, too, would have to spend a considerable amount of time in political meetings and other public activities', which would mean either revising downwards what could be expected of any active citizen, or else substantially socializing the conditions under which child rearing takes place.[20] Current feminist preferences have veered away from purely socialized solutions towards a mixture of increased social provision and equal parenting between women and men. Though this would significantly reduce the burdens on women's time, it is hard to see how anyone would then be 'freed' for citizenship in its grander sense.

Set in this context, the alliance between feminism and participatory democracy looks strained, and, considering the intense pressures on women's time, it is remarkable that feminists have been so wedded to a politics of meetings. We might more readily expect male politicos to warm to a politics of continuous meetings and discussion and debate, all of them held conveniently outside the home and away from the noise of the children. But most women have been so grounded by responsibilities for children and parents and husbands and house that they could well have settled for the less arduous democracy of casting the occasional vote. From Oscar Wilde through to Michael Walzer, people have recurrently worried that activism involves too many meetings: that, whatever the excitements of politics, people also want to 'take long walks, play with their children, paint pictures, make love, and watch television'.[21] Add onto to this rather delightful list the more mundane maintenance that swallows up so much of women's time, and it is astonishing that early feminists sought out the most demanding of democratic forms.

The point can be made more generally to stress the potentially inegalitarian implications of a politics that relies on meetings. Once reformed to include genuinely universal suffrage (and let us not forget how recently this was accomplished), liberal democracy claims to weight all its citizens as equals. In the moment of voting each of us counts only as one. As Philip Green has so acutely observed, this then serves as the definitive answer to any pretensions to greater democracy, for each reference to direct action, to mass protest, to more substantial meeting-based participation exposes itself to the thorny question: who elected *you* to decide?[22] The higher the demands placed on participation, the more inevitable that it will be unevenly spread around; the more active the democratic engagement, the more likely it is to be carried by only a few. The two forms of political participation that are most equally distributed across the populations of contemporary democracies are voting in elections and signing petitions: the two activities, significantly, that demand the least of our time. All other moments of democratic engagement involve groups that are largely self-selecting and were not authorized to speak for the rest. In considering what counts as fair and equal representation, the very weakness of liberal democracy then turns into its strength. Precisely because it sets its demands so low, asking only that we turn up at the polling booth to register an occasional vote, it can anticipate majority involvement. 'In this way the liberal pluralist tradition tends to make elections into virtually absolute trumps: the only legitimate method of ascertaining the will of the only definable cast of characters known as "the People".'[23] All further extensions of democracy can be criticized as unrepresentative.

This is where we must turn to the counter-arguments that press feminism to a more participatory engagement. Liberal democracy takes the high ground of requiring the sanction of the popular vote, but in doing so it fails to engage with the inadequacies of voting as an expression of our interests or needs. Through centuries of contestation, democrats have pointed out that voting once every five years hardly counts as a substantial expression of popular control, that choosing between alternatives that may vary only in detail does not give citizens much of a choice, that choosing between vaguely expressed and all too frequently abandoned programmes leaves the decisions to the political elites. The further problem relates to the vote as an expression of interests. In the analysis of female identity and interests, feminism adds considerable weight to those who have queried this connection.

One of the defining characteristics of women's movement politics was the importance attached to 'consciousness-raising', and the widely shared sense that women were grappling with a contradictory identity they had in some sense been forced to assume. In Simone de Beauvoir's classic statement, 'one is not born a woman, one becomes one', and part of this social construction is precisely a culture of passivity and self-denial.

Women have felt the need to 'unlearn' the lessons of their past: hence the otherwise odd experience of having to 'discover' that women were oppressed. What made this possible was of course the contradictory nature of women's experiences and consciousness, the feeling that things did not fit. But the political problem that flows from this is not so much that women know what they want and have been unable to make themselves heard; even more pervasive and damaging are the difficulties in articulating one's needs. A key implication in terms of democracy is the transformative significance of meetings, discussion, talk. Interests are not already 'there', pre-given or fixed. Democracy is not just about registering (however occasionally) one's existing preferences and views. For women in particular, there is a prior and continuing process of creating one's identity, constructing one's interests and forming one's political views.

Feminists have built on such arguments to query the very notion of a 'women's interest' that can be simply mobilized and expressed;[24] and, if in the earlier years there was a common perception of stripping away the accretions of centuries to find the 'real' person beneath, contemporary theory speaks almost with one voice in regarding female identity as multiple, unstable, something to be created and re-created, rather than simply uncovered. The further one goes in this direction, the more crucial is that vision of wider participation that informs critics of liberal democracy. The inadequacy of the vote is not just that it occurs so infrequently and provides no substantial popular control. As important is its presumption that interests are pre-given, and the way this works to sustain the status quo.[25] The social construction of femininity (by implication, masculinity as well) is such that we cannot simply accept initial positions as expressions of people's interests and needs. The opinions that are registered through elections, referendums or the seemingly endless plethora of opinion polls and attitude surveys are not to be taken as the first and last word, for, when gender so profoundly structures our sense of our selves and our interests, these original positions are ambiguous and suspect.

This first part of the argument for a more active democracy combines with the second point: that feminist analysis of oppression goes beyond material inequalities of income or occupation to focus on women's marginality and lack of power. If sexual inequality reduced itself to the distribution of income and work (too little of the first and far too much of the second) it would in principle lay itself open to remedies from above. Armed with the crucial democratic weapon of the vote, women could work to elect a government more responsive to women's poverty, one committed to a fuller programme of equal pay for equal work, combined with a set of welfare policies that would cater for women's needs. But the problems of oppression are not resolved through redistribution alone, for they involve not merely an unequal end-state in the distribution of goodies, but an institutional context that limits our ability to participate and the development of our own capacities.[26] The kind of autonomy and self-respect that feminism seeks to develop can be arrived at only when women shake off their status as dependants, and this in turn happens only through the activity of women themselves.

For both these reasons, feminism remains committed to a politics of participation, to women's more active involvement in making decisions for themselves. But, once again, the question arises: is this an argument against the principles of liberal democracy, or for further democratization within the framework of liberal democracy? Women's acute sensitivity to the pressures of time joins with feminist experience of pitfalls of direct democracy to block too polarized an alternative between more meetings and just going out to vote, encouraging us to combine the strengths of both traditions rather than setting up one as superior to the other. The problem with liberal democracy may then lie not so much in its being intrinsically incapable of extending forms of citizen participation, as in the complacency with which it claims to have met all legitimate democratic aspirations. Not that this makes it so much easier to deal with. The closure may be historically contingent rather than logically determined, but at a period in history when liberal democrats feel they have won all the political battles, this complacency is a powerful obstacle to further democratization.

Heterogeneity and group difference

The final area of contention may prove the most difficult for liberal democracy to swallow, for it takes issue with the individual as the basic unit in democratic life. If we consider liberal democracy as an amalgam of certain key principles from the liberal and democratic traditions, what it takes from liberalism is an abstract individualism which may note the differences between us, but says these differences should not count. At its best, this is a statement of profound egalitarianism that offers all citizens the same legal and political rights, regardless of their wealth, status, race or sex. At its worst, it refuses the pertinence of continuing difference and inequality, pretending for the purposes of argument that we are all of us basically the same. Feminists working on issues of legal or economic equality have noted how difficult this can make it for women to press for any differential treatment that may be necessary for significant equality. Feminists working on issues of democratic representation have come up against the same kind of problems, most notably in arguing that the sex of our representatives matters.

As recent experience in the Nordic countries has shown, the under-representation of women is entirely open to remedy – and even without that much needed upheaval that would redistribute work more equally between women and men. With sufficient political will, aided by formal party quotas to ensure a 40 per cent minimum for either sex, the numbers of women elected as political representatives can be dramatically raised. That political will materializes, however, only when gender is acknowledged as a salient political factor. The abstract individualism of liberal democracy is a powerful impediment to this, for it encourages a notion of the 'individual' and 'citizen' as a character of indifferent sex. In societies that are thoroughly saturated by gender, such indifference to sex can only reinforce the position of men.

Recent feminist work has pushed this insight further, building on the analysis of sexual difference to develop far-reaching arguments that deal with the multiple group differences of heterogeneous societies, and the ways these can be represented and expressed. The starting point, for example, of Iris Young's critique of existing democracy is that it fails to admit the pertinence of group differentiation.[27] Liberal democracy presumes a continuing plurality of opinions and beliefs (as its insistence on multi-party competition confirms), but, with the exception of what have come to be known as consociational democracies, it does not see this plurality as relating to different, and unequal, social groups. Political parties address us as people with varying opinions on the major national issues of the day, and, though these parties will frequently draw their support from distinct class groupings, the aggregate has to be broad enough (and vague enough) to contest a national election. Pressure groups can of course mobilize on a more particular social basis (black parents for better schools, students for higher grants, farmers for larger subsidies) but then the very particularity works against them, for they are only one among many competing interests. The question raised in Iris Young's work is whether political equality can be meaningful without formal mechanisms for representing group difference.

Democracy and Difference

The vitality of democracy, she argues, cannot wait on us to settle whether such group differentiation is desirable or inevitable (though she herself believes it is both of these things). 'Our political problem is that some of our groups are privileged and others are oppressed.'[28] Existing mechanisms deliver effective power to the dominant groups, and, while their dominance may be dressed up in the trappings of an impartial general perspective or presented as just the majority decision mobilized through a national vote, the consequence is the continued suppression of any marginalized, disadvantaged voice. Democracy cannot continue to proceed on the assumption of an undifferentiated humanity, or the complacent assertion that voices are equally weighted by their equal right to participate in the vote.

The alternative agenda Young proposes would provide for public funding to promote the self-organization of oppressed groups; establish a requirement on policy-makers that they take into consideration the policy proposals that then emanate from such groups; and, most controversial of all, supply a veto power over specific policies that most directly affect any of these groups. I do not present this as a blueprint for the future – the debate on it has barely commenced – and indeed have several reservations on the notion of group representation. These include the difficult problems of group closure (people coming to define themselves politically through what is only one frozen single aspect of their lives); the question of who is to legislate on which groups qualify for additional group representation; and the almost insuperable obstacles to establishing what any group wants. I have dealt with these at greater length elsewhere;[29] the most pertinent in this context is how to develop acceptably democratic procedures for mobilizing any group voice. After centuries of experimentation, we have only two tried and tested procedures. People can cast their votes in some anonymous ballot, or can turn up at meetings in order to express their views. The first seems particularly inappropriate to the development of a hitherto marginalized perspective, for how are we to identify all the relevant constituents, and how make sure they are voting with that particular part of their identity in mind? (One could feasibly organize all women onto a women's register, but could not expect them all to be voting *as women*, rather than as Catholics or as socialists or as people with some other axe to grind. With smaller, and less visible, sub-groupings, it is hard even to know who makes up the group.) The alternative is to rely on the meeting, which has the double advantage of leaving it to the group members to identify themselves, and enabling them to develop a group perspective. But the slightest acquaintance with studies of political participation confirms what most of us know already from personal experience of meetings: that those who go to meetings are a tiny proportion of the potential group.

The issue of group inequality is far too serious to be brushed aside by any such reservations as these. The questions of democracy and difference are ones that lie at the heart of contemporary dilemmas in democracy – and, on an international scale, have their counterpart in the fragmentation of older empires into smaller nationalities and the rising threat to national minorities. People do not define themselves just as citizens of a nation but, either through choice or necessity, often identify with some smaller sub-group. Where this reflects a history of systematic ill-treatment for particular minorities, it cannot be summarily dismissed as an irrelevant basis for democratic organization. But the mechanisms we are offered to deal with systemic group difference and inequality often look like the old interest-group politics dressed up in more radical guise. Iris Young's vision of an active and grass-roots representation for oppressed groups looks a good deal more promising than the elitist practices of consociational democracies – but still does not resolve all problems. As those who speak in the older language of civic republicanism rightly remind us, democracy also includes a vision of people coming to perceive the limits of their own specific interests and concerns, learning to recognize the potential conflicts between their own position and that adopted by others, and acknowledging the wider community to which we all ultimately belong. This vision has usually failed – it has never proved comprehensive enough to embrace all specific group interests or articulate all grassroots concerns – but this is not enough to dislodge it from its place in the democratic tradition. Perhaps the worst legacy of the Thatcherite years in Britain has been the way they legitimated a politics of individual and narrow group interest, scorning the idealism of all those who contributed to the more generous visions of the modern welfare state. And while this lays itself open to a powerful critique in terms of the *other* interests that have been discarded or denied – primarily those in the lowest income brackets in society – it is even more fundamentally at odds with any notion that there might be common concerns.

Feminists have their own experience of this, which surfaces in exasperation that we must continue to articulate 'the women's point of view' when this is only one of many burning concerns. What inspires this is not just a fear of being kept on the sidelines (the fear expressed by many women politicians throughout this century who have resisted association with 'women's issues' as something that would keep them from the centres of power) but a more profound sense that politics is about a whole range of issues and visions which do not reduce to group interest or need. In this sense, one of the major problems in developing a feminist vision of democracy is how to resist the pressures towards subsuming women under the supposedly gender-neutral 'man' without thereby capitulating to the narrowness of merely group interest or need. Or, to put it the other way round, how to retain a vision of human beings working democratically together in pursuit of their shared concerns, without falling into the complacency that dismisses the systematic inequalities between groups?

What is important here is that liberal democracy as currently practised makes it hard even to address this dilemma, for it recurrently returns us to the individual as the basic unit in political life, blocking serious consideration of the empowerment of disadvantaged *groups*. This is perhaps the point of most marked divergence between feminist and liberal democratic perspectives, and, as feminist theorists pursue the complex and difficult implications of a 'politics of difference', we can anticipate considerable resistance from those who see democracy in relentlessly individual terms. The question then is whether these hardy individualists exhaust the possibilities of liberal democracy, whether such individualism is intrinsic to its nature? It is hard to give a definitive 'yes'. Michael Walzer has recently reformulated the communitarian critiques of liberalism as a debate *within* liberalism;[30] Will Kymlicka has set out an impeccably liberal case for recognizing group rights;[31] while the current practices of consociational democracies already provide institutionalized representation for communities as well as individuals. Unless we define these theoretical and political initiatives as outside the scope of liberal democracy, then liberal democracy has already made gestures towards recognizing the pertinence of the group.

Feminism and liberal democracy

These three areas indicate both the extent of feminist dissatisfaction with existing liberal democracy and the problems in resolving whether this adds up to an alternative view. Feminist explorations of citizenship raise major questions about the basis on which women have been included in the political community, and consider the substantive conditions that have to be met in order to qualify for political equality. The weight feminism attaches to women being able to transform their identity and sense of themselves highlights the continuing importance of active involvement in collective discussion and action. The critique of dependency as a crucial part of sexual inequality puts feminism firmly in the camp of a strong democracy, where what matters is empowerment as well as the ultimate policy results. The analysis of systemic inequalities – not only between women and men, but more generally between oppressed and dominant social groups – raises important questions about empowering people not only as individuals but also as members of specific groups.

Each of these pinpoints what has been a recurrent feature of liberal democracy, and the arguments combine in an enduring and radical critique of the limits of existing democracy. Yet none of them can be presented as a decisive alternative to liberal democracy, partly because of the difficulties in disentangling what are historical origins from what is defining essence. Origins do not shape all subsequent developments, and establishing either the historical – or, as feminists are well able to do, the contemporary – associations between liberal democracy and sexual inequality does not prove a necessary or intrinsic connection. A richer and more equal democracy may still be possible within the broad framework liberal democracy implies.

When the world is littered with the skeletons of 'alternatives' to liberal democracy, it is particularly difficult to present one's critique as leading to a qualitatively different political form. Thus feminists may – I believe should – associate themselves with the impetus towards a more active and engaged democracy; but we cannot afford to present this as an alternative to holding elections. Feminists have always challenged – and will continue to challenge – the way that particular divisions between the public and private secure the exclusion and oppression of women; but few would want to build on this to argue for dissolving all such distinctions. Feminists are rightly extending the analysis of sexual difference into a wider consideration of the systematic differences between unequal social groups; but the requirements of democratic accountability combine with the reservations over 'merely' group interest and need to set some cautionary limits to this.

Caution is of course the watchword of the moment, and the more likely danger for the immediate future lies less in the risk of non-democratic alternatives to liberal democracy than in the complacency of those who feel they have reclaimed the political agenda. In both its theory and its practice, liberal democracy has largely failed to engage with sexual equality, and it would be a sorry outcome for democracy in general if the extraordinary political events of the 1980s and 1990s ushered in a period of unquestioning celebration of the limited democracy we currently enjoy. It is indeed against this background that I worry about the shift in emphasis from participation towards citizenship. However shaky the democracy of the meeting, however exposed to the taunt that too few people will go, the more active and engaged democracy that was practised in the early years of the women's movement cannot be dislodged from feminist notions of a better and fuller democracy. The trump card of elections, of guaranteeing the numerical equality that gives each individual an equal weight, has to be seen in this context. It serves as a crucial reminder of the founding and abiding principle of democracy – that in democracy we are meant to be equals – and introduces a necessary caution into all our discussions about developing and deepening democracy. But premised as it still is on a notion that interests or preferences are unproblematic, and working as it always does to discourage more radical innovation, it cannot be taken as the simple last word. It does not help to discuss these issues in terms of an 'alternative' to liberal democracy, but, for all the reasons outlined above, feminism will continue to inspire a more substantial democracy than that which is currently on offer.

Notes

1 Among the critical literature, see Carole Pateman, 'Feminism and democracy' (1983), repr. in Pateman, *The Disorder of Women* (Cambridge: Polity, 1990); Sheila Rowbotham, 'Feminism and democracy', in *New Forms of Democracy*, ed. D. Held and C. Pollitt (Milton Keynes: Open University Press: London: Sage, 1986); Anne Phillips, *Engendering Democracy* (Cambridge: Polity, 1991).
2 I restrict myself here to feminist engagement with liberal democracy over the twenty-five years since the contemporary women's movement was born. Other stories can be told of earlier feminist engagements.
3 For an overview of more recent literature, see Kathleen B. Jones, 'Citizenship in a woman-friendly polity', *Signs*, 15, 4 (1990).
4 Norberto Bobbio, *Which Socialism?* (Cambridge: Polity, 1986), p. 78.
5 For feminist critiques of universalizing theory, see Carole Pateman, *The Sexual Contract* (Cambridge: Polity, 1988); essays in Linda Nicholson (ed.), *Feminism/Postmodernism* (London Routledge, 1990); and ch. 3.

6 Benjamin Barber, *Strong Democracy: Participatory Politics for a New Age* (Berkeley: University of California Press, 1984).
7 'If democracy is to exist and citizens are to be political equals, then will democracy not require something other than a market-oriented, private enterprise economy, or at the very least a pretty drastic modification of it?' Robert Dahl, *Democracy and its Critics* (New Haven, CT: Yale University Press, 1989), p. 326.
8 I am indebted to David Beetham for the remarks that finally liberated me from this preoccupation.
9 This is argued in Ernesto Laclau and Chantal Mouffe, *Hegemony and Socialist Strategy* (London: Verso, 1985), ch. 4.
10 Joseph A. Schumpeter, *Capitalism, Socialism and Democracy* (London: Allen & Unwin, 1954), p. 272n.
11 For a recent overview of conditions throughout the world, see Vicky Randall, *Women and Politics* (2nd edn, London: Macmillan, 1987). For a fuller discussion of the issues of representation, see Phillips, *Engendering Democracy*, ch. 3.
12 Carole Pateman, talk on work in progress, Gender Group, London School of Economics, 26 April 1991. See also her 'Equality, difference, subordination: the politics of motherhood and women's citizenship', in *Beyond Equality and Difference*, ed. G. Bock and S. James (London: Routledge, 1992).
13 Steven Lukes has argued persuasively that this formulation is inadequate: that the trade-offs are not between equality on the one hand and liberty on the other, but between different combinations or interpetations of both. See 'Equality and liberty: must they conflict?', in *Political Theory Today*, ed. David Held (Cambridge: Polity, 1991).
14 See, for example, Barbara Einhorn, 'Where have all the women gone? Women and the women's movement in East Central Europe', *Feminist Review*, 39 (1991).
15 See Birte Siim, 'Towards a feminist rethinking of the welfare state', in *The Political Interests of Gender*, in ed. K. B. Jones and A. G. Jonasdottir (London: Sage, 1988).
16 This parallels that other major question that must be put to liberal democracy: what is the relationship between democracy and the market? Is the market historically contingent or a condition without which liberal democracy cannot possibly thrive? See Christopher Pierson, 'Democracy, markets and capital: are there necessary economic limits to democracy?', *Political Studies*, 40 (1992).
17 Jones, 'Citizenship in a woman-friendly polity', p. 788.
18 Iris Marion Young, 'The ideal of community and the politics of difference', in *Feminism/Postmodernism*, ed. Linda Nicolson (London: Routledge, 1990), p. 301.
19 Jones, 'Citizenship in a woman-friendly polity', p. 808.

20 Susan Moller Okin, *Women in Western Political Thought* (London: Virago, 1980), p. 278.
21 Michael Walzer, 'A day in the life of a socialist citizen', in *Obligations: Essays on Disobedience, War and Citizenship* (Cambridge, MA: Harvard University Press, 1970), p. 234.
22 Philip Green, 'A review essay of Robert A. Dahl *Democracy and Its Critics*', *Social Theory and Practice*, 16, 2 (1990).
23 Ibid., p. 238.
24 See Rosemary Pringle and Sophie Watson, ' "Women's interests" and the post-structuralist state', in *Destabilizing Theory: Contemporary Feminist Debates*, ed. Michèle Barrett and Anne Phillips (Cambridge: Polity, 1992).
25 There is a parallel here with the arguments developed in Benjamin Barber's *Strong Democracy*, which similarly emphasizes the transformative significance of active participation through meetings. Note, however, that aspects of his argument have been roundly criticized from a feminist perspective by Iris Young in her essay on 'Polity and group difference'.
26 Iris Marion Young, *Justice and the Politics of Difference* (Princeton, NJ: Princeton University Press, 1990).
27 Young, *Justice and the Politics of Difference*; see also 'Polity and group difference: a critique of the ideal of universal citizenship', *Ethics*, 99 (1989).
28 Young, 'Polity and group difference', p. 261.
29 Chapter 5.
30 Michael Walzer, 'The communitarian critique of liberalism', *Political Theory*, 18, 1 (1990).
31 Will Kymlicka, *Liberalism, Community and Culture* (Oxford: Clarendon Press, 1989).

CONNECTIVE LEADERSHIP:
Female Leadership Styles in the 21st-Century Workplace

JEAN LIPMAN-BLUMEN
Claremont Graduate School

> **ABSTRACT:** *This paper describes an integrative leadership model, "connective leadership," which combines the traditional masculine American ego-ideal with additional female role behaviors more appropriate for an interdependent world. Based on the L-BL Achieving Styles Model, connective leadership emphasizes connecting individuals to their own, as well as others', tasks and ego drives. Achieving styles are defined as the characteristic behaviors individuals use to achieve their goals. The Achieving Styles Model includes three sets of achieving styles (direct, instrumental, and relational), each subsuming three individual styles, resulting in a full complement of nine distinct achieving styles. Gender differences in achieving styles are reported and related to the connective leadership paradigm.*

American cultural traditions define personality, achievement, and the purpose of human life in ways that leave the individual suspended in glorious, but terrifying, isolation.
        Bellah, Madsen, Sullivan, Swidler, and Tipton 1985:6

CONNECTIVE LEADERSHIP: AN INTEGRATIVE MODEL FOR THE 21st CENTURY

Contrary to traditional beliefs, female leadership is no longer an oxymoron. Viewed from the perspective of global interdependence, it contains the seeds of connective leadership, a new, integrative model of leadership more suited to the dramatically changing workplace of the twenty-first century. Inevitably, the workplace will reflect the increasingly interdependent, external environment, shaped by new realities and demands emanating from global political and economic trends (Starr 1988; Drucker 1989). Internally, the backgrounds, talents, and interests of a highly diverse work force will foster additional, yet consonant,

---

Direct all correspondence to: Jean Lipman-Blumen, Peter F. Drucker Graduate Management Center, Claremont Graduate School, Jagels 205, Claremont, CA 91711. e-mail: lipmanj@clargrad.bitnet

transformations in the workplace (Pfeffer 1983; Gutek, Larwood, and Stromberg 1986). To address the complex demands of the twenty-first-century workplace, organizational and political leadership will need to reflect certain behaviors to which females traditionally have been socialized, but which many women are being urged to abandon to ensure their occupational success.

"Connective leadership" derives its label from its character of connecting individuals not only to their own tasks and ego drives, but also to those of the group and community that depend upon the accomplishment of mutual goals. It is leadership that connects individuals to others and *others'* goals, using a broad spectrum of behavioral strategies. It is leadership that "proceed(s) from a premise of connection" (Gilligan 1982:38) and a recognition of networks of relationships that bind society in a web of mutual responsibilities. It shares responsibility, takes unthreatened pride in the accomplishments of colleagues and protégés, and experiences success without the compulsion to outdo others.

Connective leadership reaches out beyond its own traditional constituencies to presumed adversaries, using mutual goals, rather than mutual enemies, to create group cohesion and community membership (Gardner 1990). It is leadership able to resolve the tension between agency and communion (Bakan 1966), comfortable in integrating others' diverse needs, able to take pride in others' success that may even surpass one's own. This new, integrative form of leadership not only encompasses both transactional and transformational behaviors (Burns 1978; Tichy and Devanna 1986; Doig and Hargrove 1987; Bass 1990; Gardner 1990), but also stretches its practitioners beyond individualism and charisma (Gerth and Mills 1946; Kouzes and Posner 1987; Conger 1989), even beyond competition and collaboration (Gray 1989; Badaracco 1991).

THE PSYCHOLOGICAL ROOTS: GENDER DIFFERENCES

The components of connective leadership are familiar to women, but more worrisome to men. Gilligan (1982), Miller (1976), and Chodorow (1974) concur that the psychosocial trajectories of women and men are differentially characterized by their respective needs for connection and separation. For males, separation from the maternal figure is the path to individuation and maturity. Competitively moving out beyond others, in ways delineated by rule-bound, hierarchical structures, becomes the mark of mature male success. According to post-Freudian interpretations, only under highly structured conditions can adult males feel comfortable acknowledging their connections to others. According to Gilligan (1982:44), "Rule-bound competitive achievement situations, which for women threaten the web of connection, for men provide a mode of connection that establishes clear boundaries and limits aggression, and thus appears comparatively safe."

For many females, connecting to, caring for, and taking responsibility for mediating the conflicting needs of others indicate adult success and provide a sense of safety. Females commonly interpret the various stages in structural hierarchies as problematical way stations of separation, positions dangerously poised at the far reaches of the social web (Chodorow 1974; Miller 1976; Gilligan 1982). Females' definition of self involves altruistically helping and caring for others (Fowlkes 1983), a self-definition historically reflected in traditional female occupations.[1]

The traditional American concept of leadership is a pastiche based upon a masculine ego-ideal glorifying the competitive, combative, controlling, creative, aggressive, self-reliant individualist. It describes a leadership form better suited to a frontier society than to the interdependent global and organizational environments that will characterize the twenty-first century. This standard leadership image is dominated by behaviors focussed on task mastery, competition, and power, and encapsulated in a limited set of achieving styles, labeled "direct achieving styles."

THE AMERICAN EGO-IDEAL AND ACHIEVING STYLES

"Achieving styles,"[2] central to this discussion, are simply the characteristic ways in which individuals go about getting things done—the learned behaviors people use for achieving goals regardless of their substantive nature. One might conceptualize achieving styles as personal technologies or methods of attacking problems, or even implementation strategies. Achieving styles are divided into three sets, "direct," "instrumental," and "relational," each with three associated styles, which are described in detail below. Each individual uses a unique combination of these learned behaviors, ordinarily relying on styles associated with previous success, perhaps shifting emphases, to accomplish his or her current goals (Lipman-Blumen 1991). Occasionally, under crisis conditions, individuals may move to a somewhat different configuration; however, if the crisis is easily circumscribed and resolved, individuals subsequently revert to their former achieving styles.

The central argument of this paper presents five main points, in which achieving styles play a key role.

- First, American leadership images represent a masculine ego-ideal, that is, an ideal image of what we all would be, if only we could.
- Second, that ego-ideal draws on a very limited set of achieving styles, which we shall call "direct" styles, that emphasize individualism, self-reliance, and belief in one's own abilities, as well as power, competition, and creativity.
- Third, we reject two other sets of learned behaviors—"instrumental" and "relational" achieving styles—ordinarily associated with more traditional female behavior.

The set we dismiss as weak are the "relational" achieving styles, which focus on collaborating with, contributing to, and deriving a vicarious sense of accomplishment from others' success. They are the helpful, nurturant, vicarious role be-

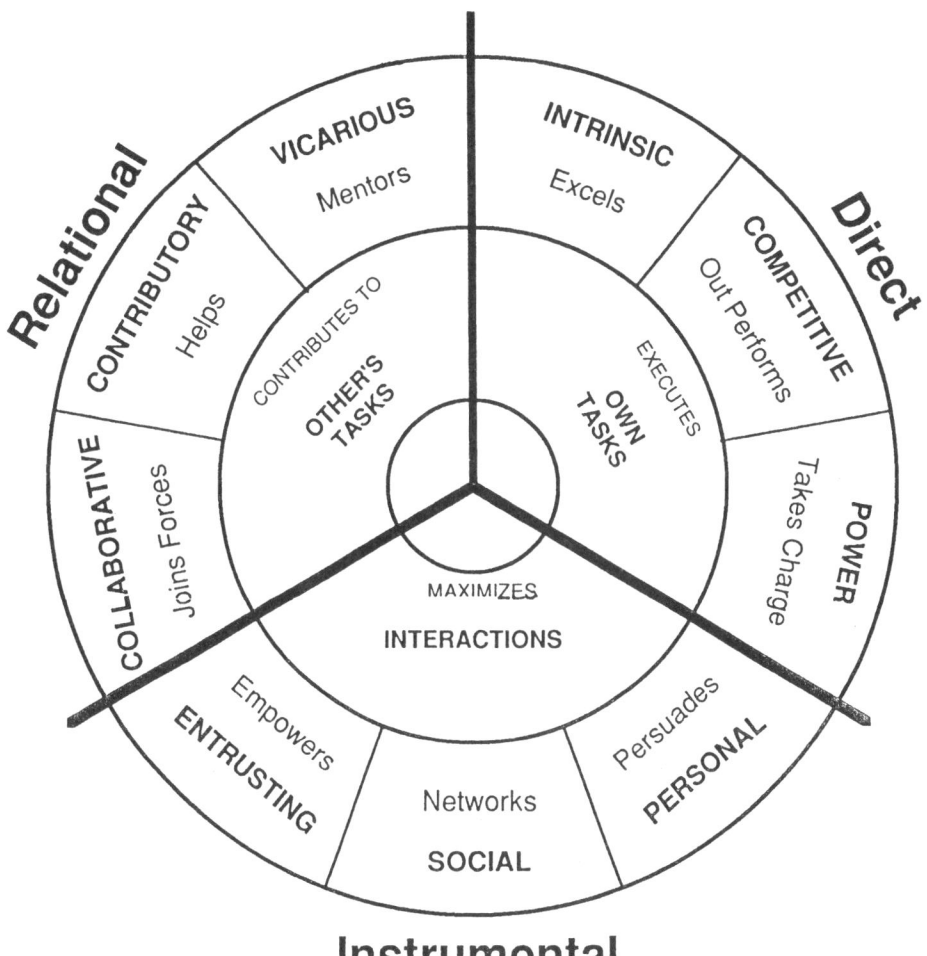

Figure 1
L-BL Achieving Styles Model

haviors associated with the traditional female role. An ongoing study of achieving styles (Lipman-Blumen, Handley-Isaksen, and Leavitt 1983; Lipman-Blumen 1991) confirms that women engaged in full-time homemaker roles favor these achieving styles above all others. So do many women in the workplace, although they experience difficulty maintaining these styles in the absence of a critical mass of like-minded, usually female, coworkers.

Americans also reject a second set of learned achievement behaviors, the "instrumental" achieving styles, which, until recently, they perceived as manipulative and slightly unsavory behaviors. The instrumental styles take their name from the propensity to use the self and others as instruments for accomplishment.

Instrumental styles involve complex, subtle strategies. Individuals who prefer the instrumental styles use many aspects of the self, including intelligence, skill, wit, charm, family background, and previous accomplishments, to engage others in their tasks. They enjoy attracting followers by projecting and dramatizing themselves and their goals, through symbols and dramatic behavior, as well as counterintuitive, and therefore unexpected and unforgettable, gestures. For example, Indian independence leader Mohandas Gandhi was much enamored of instrumental styles, which also emphasize human interaction, group process, and informal systems (more recently understood as "networks"). Instrumental achieving styles involve accomplishing tasks through networks of relationships, believing in and entrusting one's vision to others, and thereby empowering others through one's confidence in them.

From pre-Biblical days, these styles have been attributed to women; however, the denigration associated with these styles generally prompts American women, not to mention men, to deny them. Earlier research (Lipman-Blumen et al. 1983) suggests that American women tend to rank two styles in the instrumental set much lower than the remaining seven achieving styles that complete the achieving styles spectrum.

- Fourth, the networked world in which all nations now live calls for new forms of leadership that connect people to each other, to their own and others' tasks and dreams, to their families, colleagues, institutions, and networks, as well as to their nations and global neighbors. The two rejected sets of behavior—"relational" and "instrumental" achieving styles—one accepted by, the other attributed to women—provide these important aspects of connective leadership.

To meet the leadership challenge of the 1990s and beyond, it will be necessary to integrate these two underutilized sets of achieving styles with our currently faltering masculine ego-ideal. In fact, to meet this need, female achieving styles—both actual and attributed—probably must predominate. Connective leadership, which connects individuals creatively to their tasks and visions, to one another, to the immediate group and the larger network, empowering others and instilling confidence, represents a crucial set of strategies for success, not only in the workplace, but in our interdependent world community.

- Fifth, connective leadership also integrates and creatively revitalizes individualism with a crucial female perspective, that is, seeing the world as a total system of interconnected, uniquely important parts, rather than as independent, competitive, isolated, and unequal entities. This perspective leads to an emphasis on external goals that all human groups can unite to accomplish, rather than on more internal objectives that set individuals, groups, and nations apart and often against one another.

Connective leadership repudiates the traditional use of external enemies to unite constituents behind their own parochial leaders. It also deconstructs hierarchies in which workers are urged to compete for the pinnacle positions, where many ostensibly successful individuals find themselves "suspended in glorious, but terrifying, isolation" (Bellah et al. 1985:6).

THE AMERICAN EGO-IDEAL: THE DIRECT ACHIEVER IN RUGGED INDIVIDUALIST'S CLOTHING

From our earliest national origins, the rugged individualist has served as the ultimate emblem of American leadership. This essentially masculine symbol melds the images, sounds, and smells of the early Western frontier (Taylor 1972): the cowboy's corral, the battlefield, the mine, the factory, the political back room, and the corporate boardroom.

The fierce individualist personifies the manner in which Americans are taught to achieve their goals, as well as define themselves, their most cherished dreams, and their values. These individualistic qualities also characterize the most admired American leaders. Because they confront tasks directly through their own efforts, we shall call these leaders "direct achievers." As direct achievers, they tend to use three "direct" styles, all of which focus on realizing their own visions, whether through individualistic ("intrinsic direct"), competitive ("competitive direct"), or controlling ("power direct") behaviors.

Individuals who prefer the first "direct" style—the "intrinsic direct"— determinedly seek challenges and measure their visionary goals against personal, internalized standards of excellence that demand an exacting performance— perhaps a performance one can only count on oneself to deliver. Their stubborn pursuit of a dream is often associated with self-reliant creativity. Intrinsic direct achievers' passionate devotion to the vision or goal *they* have identified seeks only one reward: the intrinsic satisfaction derived from doing something well (much like McClelland's [1961] high-need achiever). Earlier research (Lipman-Blumen et al. 1983; Lipman-Blumen 1991) indicates that women, as well as men, endorse this behavior.

The second "direct" achieving style—the "competitive direct"—characterizes the rugged individualist who competes unrelentingly, determined to overcome all contenders, monumental odds, and immeasurable hardships. Perhaps, the most robust gender-linked finding in the achieving styles literature is the consistently lower valuation that women assign to competitive behavior (Axline, Billings, and VanderHorst 1991). Across virtually all age, occupational, and cultural groups, women consistently are less likely than men of their own group to report that they use competitive strategies to accomplish their goals.

The third "direct" style—the "power direct" achieving style—describes the "take charge" behavior of traditional American heroes. These independent heroes strive to be in total control of all resources, from people and situations to institutions and global events. Although leaders who prefer the "power direct" achieving style may delegate tasks to others, they retain strict control over both the targeted goals and the means to their accomplishment.

The second, but less pronounced, gender difference our research (Lipman-Blumen 1991) reveals is the predilection for power. According to these data, men also tend to prefer power more intensely than women. With respect to power, however, many female executives are beginning to imitate their male colleagues, a strategy that threatens to undermine their connective leadership advantage.

These three "direct" achieving styles are the hallmarks of the self-reliant American hero. Americans perceive the "direct" achieving styles as the wellsprings of their unique admixture of pragmatism, innovation, creativity, and vision. Americans also associate these styles with determination and masculinity. That John Wayne's image is alive and well, not only in TV reruns and commercials, but also in the American psyche, is evidence from popular culture of "direct" achievers' enduring appeal.

"Direct" achieving leaders do not attract and unite their followers simply by the creativity and worthiness of their own dreams and goals. They also commonly draw constituents or followers to their cause by defining an external enemy, sometimes exaggerating that enemy's potential threat, and even creating enemies when none exist. This strategy brings internal cohesion to the leader's group, inflating both the leader's strength and the group's need for the leader's protection and guidance. Identifying an external enemy is an important strategy for the power-oriented, competitive leader.

Although many Western societies share this individualistic ideal, the American scene has provided the quintessential historical stage for the exploits of the rugged solo hero, the "direct achiever." For example, George Washington, Henry David Thoreau, Andrew Carnegie, Theodore and Franklin D. Roosevelt, John Wayne, Steve Jobs, Lee Iacocca, and Ronald Reagan all share to some degree this characteristic stance. Their examples encourage us to believe that we, as individuals, can make an important difference, should "go for it," can compete fiercely and win. These heroes embody the American ego-ideal: rugged individuals, with creative, visionary dreams, taking control, pitting themselves against impossible odds and winning.

American history texts depict archetypal American characters as individualistic, "direct" achievers, doing it all by themselves. Still, a healthy skepticism is warranted lest these allegedly "individual" exploits are taken as the whole, rather than the tip, of the human collaboration iceberg.

Despite historical accounts, the scope of their accomplishments suggests that these industrial and military leaders did not accomplish their feats single-handedly. Nevertheless, American mythology bathes them in an isolating spotlight, obscuring the many others whose contributions helped create their astounding successes—their aides-de-camp, their coaches or mentors, their assistants, their teammates, their parents, their wives and children. This misperception only encourages us to believe leaders succeed single-handedly, powerfully, and competitively.

If the heroes who exemplify the American ego-ideal appear larger than life or accomplish tasks that seem beyond the capabilities of a single individual, that is probably exactly the case. These are the makings of mythical figures, embodying cultural myths and images. Mythologized heroes serve as ego-ideals precisely because they inspire—and even goad—believers to reach beyond themselves to almost superhuman goals.

The cultural heroes Americans understand best speak to them of individual dreams, individual efforts, individual rights, individual property, individual problems. American culture encourages a profound, if irrational, faith that a nation of rugged individuals, working *separately*, often competing against one another, can produce a totality that miraculously will result in a successful *collective* effort.

The recent resurgence of the American entrepreneur (Gevirtz 1984; Drucker 1985) is consistent with this ego-ideal. The daring entrepreneur who starts a new business in his garage and takes on the industrial megagiants is the late-20th-century American hero. Still, that hero inevitably falters when success enlarges the task beyond the capabilities of one even larger-than-life individual. At that point, these self-reliant individuals have trouble sharing the challenge with peers, entrusting others with their dream, believing others can do it as well as they, collaborating, getting others to feel the task belongs to them, negotiating, helping others to fulfill their own dreams, making the group work synergistically, avoiding the pitfalls of team activities, and taking pride in others' success.

Individualistic leaders rarely embody these important aspects of connective leadership. More often than not, they fail to unite people and nations through their mutual needs. In fact, they commonly tend to set people in opposition to one another. They lack the skills of connective leaders who draw people to one another's goals, reach out to bring others into the process, and experience a sense of accomplishment when colleagues and protégés succeed. Connective leadership replaces egocentrism with mutuality.

When the task grows patently beyond the capabilities of one larger-than-life leader, the hero leaves, or is driven out, and starts again, as the lone hero. The "Lone Ranger rides again," or maybe now it is the *lonely* ranger—American images, all.

A SCHIZOID LOVE AFFAIR WITH TEAMWORK

American culture partially tempers its devotion to individualism with a schizoid love affair with teamwork. Americans experience a deep-seated tension between the pursuit of individualism and a reflexive response to teamwork. Teamwork is a national shibboleth, deeply embedded in the core of democracy. In theory, at least, the team has an apparent leveling or democratizing effect. Everyone can try out for the team. All team members are equal. Still, Americans confront an abiding ambivalence that hobbles their unequivocal commitment to team effort. Even within teams, individualism remains their true love.

It is no accident that Americans anoint baseball the "all-American" sport. Baseball also serves as national metaphor. As the late Baseball Commissioner A. Bartlett Giamatti (1985) suggested,

> Baseball fits America so well because it embodies the interplay of individual and group that we so love, and because it expresses our longing for the rule of law while licensing our resentment of law givers . . . What each individual must do (is) obvious to all, and each player's initiative, poise, and skill are highlighted.

Baseball permits us the illusion of promoting teamwork, while simultaneously keeping a detailed scorecard on each player's hits, runs, and errors. The player's scorecard is tallied without acknowledging his teammates' contributions to that performance.

Periodically, of course, the "communal choreography" of the team takes over, fusing the individual players into a cohesive group, muting the loneliness, terror, and ecstasy of stardom (Giamatti 1985). Moreover, baseball enables team members to cooperate with one another while simultaneously competing with another team.

MISMATCH BETWEEN EGO-IDEAL AND INSTITUTIONAL NEEDS

To complicate matters, there is a growing lack of fit among (1) the American ego-ideal, (2) the needs of our increasingly large and complex institutions, and (3) the demands of an interdependent world. As previously noted, the American ego-ideal reifies individualistic, competitive, controlling behavior. Yet, as organizations grow in size and complexity, the tasks involved outstrip the capabilities of single-handed action. They require cooperation and coordination. Paradoxically, as the world shrinks through interdependence, that need increases. Still, the formal structure of large-scale institutions, from corporations to governments, makes it difficult to ensure quick and easy cooperation. Bureaucratic rules, reflecting an individualistic ego-ideal, present serious barriers.

According to Weber (Gerth and Mills 1946), formal hierarchies are designed to facilitate the coordination of complex tasks. In reality, however, the formal structure frequently inhibits goal attainment. As Weber (Gerth and Mills 1946) indicated, the informal system arises in the service of the formal structure. It offsets the barriers to cooperation within formal organizations and bureaucracies. One example of the informal system, the traditional "old boy network," stretched within and across institutions. It functioned as an uncharted, largely invisible, homosocial system (Lipman-Blumen 1976), excluding from membership less-powerful males and women. Non-isometric with the formal system, the "old boy network," nonetheless, ironically grafted the competition, power, and internal status differentials learned in the formal structure onto friendship patterns and alliances within the informal system. Within "the old boy network," resources moved to valued members in an efficient distribution system, reinforcing a system of obligations and reciprocations.

More recently, to offset their isolation, professional women have developed their own "old girl networks." It is my impression, based on observation, that these female networks commonly feature open, visible membership, even dues, with explicit criteria revolving around professional background and interests. As such, they are less like the traditional, covert, male informal networks and more reminiscent of the open, formal, but casual, associations described by de Toqueville ([1835] 1959) that included members from a broad range of backgrounds. Here, too, resources are distributed, but with seemingly less attention to power, competition, and internal status differentials. With some notable exceptions, these female professional networks thrive on inclusion and connection, potential models for the twenty-first-century workplace.

At its best, the informal system is a world of relationships and emotionality; familiar territory to women, but rather uncomfortable terrain for many male leaders. Through human interaction composed of friendships, understandings, and mutual help, members distribute various resources, particularly those essential to goal attainment. To partake of these resources, one must demonstrate political, social, and organizational "savvy." At its best, the system operates through inclusiveness and connection, rather than by exclusiveness and separation.

In the coming decades, the navigational skills required by the informal system will be increasingly distinguishable from the individualism, competitiveness, and power that currently permeate the byways of male networks. The new informal systems will call for a revised understanding of "connections"—connections between the self and others, as well as between the self and task, be it one's own or another's. They will require expertise in dealing with connections among people within and between groups, from small teams to far-flung networks, sometimes even networks of nations. The informal system will necessitate knowledge of relationships, human interaction, emotionality, and group processes.

NEW ACHIEVING STYLES FOR AN INTERDEPENDENT GLOBAL ORDER

Global interdependence increases the urgency of America's leadership problem. Fostering connective leadership demanded by the global environment requires integrating two other, more appropriate sets of achieving styles—more feminine behaviors—with the traditional American "direct" styles.

Instrumental Styles: Personal, Social, and Entrusting

The first additional set of achieving styles required for success in an interdependent order is the "instrumental" set, whose label reflects the characteristic use of (1) the self, (2) the system, and (3) others as instruments for goal attainment. Like the other achieving styles sets, this one also includes three styles: "personal," "social," and "entrusting."

Personal Instrumental

The "personal instrumental" style is evident in the action of leaders skilled in projecting and utilizing all aspects of their persona. Leaders who prefer the "personal instrumental" style utilize their intelligence, wit, compassion, humor, family background, previous accomplishments and defeats, courage, physical appearance, and sexual appeal to connect themselves to those whose commitment and help they seek to engage. The admiration and affection of followers may serve as both motive and sustenance for "personal instrumental" achievers. They unabashedly pursue an emotional connection with their followers, relationships based on compassion and inspiration, rather than competition and power. In 1987, a group of children attending an international women's peace conference in Moscow presented flowers to General Secretary Gorbachev. Touched by this gesture, Gorbachev turned his back to the audience to wipe his tears. Two thousand women in that audience wept openly in empathy.

Demonstrating and evoking compassion, even to the point of self-sacrifice (Miller 1976; Gilligan 1982), are traditional female behaviors. Connective leadership also draws on these instrumental strategies. Some examples include the following: (1) Mohandas Gandhi fasting to near-death to persuade Muslims and Hindus to work and live together in peace; (2) Corazon Aquino leading a national revolution without guns and bloodshed; (3) Gorbachev transforming traditional concepts of weakness into strength, by daring to unilaterally dismantle powerful weapons of war; (4) Martin Luther King linking arms with other activists marching for civil rights. Each of these leaders, however, raised doubts and fears among both followers and adversaries still attuned to traditional power-driven, competitive images of leadership. Moreover, Aquino and Gorbachev have been pushed back repeatedly to more traditional "direct" leadership forms by both constituents and other contenders for power.

Leaders who dare step beyond the limits of their own followers to reach out to a broader, even a global constituency, risk the ire of their traditional constituents while simultaneously stirring fear and confusion in the hearts of outsiders. They draw upon their own "personal instrumental" skills as negotiators and persuaders to bridge interpersonal schisms. They use their gifts of persuasion and negotiation, rather than aggression, power, and competition, to accomplish their goals. They display a keen sense of symbolism and dramatic gestures, often creating counterintuitive gestures and symbols whose surprise and simplicity engrave their message upon the constituents' consciousness. For example, on his initial visit to Washington, Gorbachev unexpectedly stepped from his guarded limousine to shake the hands and touch the hearts of ordinary American citizens.

Leaders skilled in "personal instrumental" behavior understand the meaning, as well as the denial, of ritual and costume. Assuming the presidency in the wake of a dictatorship, Corazon Aquino symbolized her quest for a modest, democratic government by wearing a plain yellow dress and refusing the trappings of palaces and limousines. Her deliberately simple gestures and costume symbolized reconciliation and equality. Gandhi's rejection of Western, custom-tailored suits for a homespun *dhoti* symbolized his rejection of English rule, as well as his dedication to effecting Indian independence (Collins and Lapierre 1975).

With real genius, Gandhi could use a broad range of achieving styles in his nascent form of connective leadership (Gandhi 1957). Here, however, let us focus on Gandhi's use of the "personal instrumental" style. The Indian independence leader used dramatic, counterintuitive symbolism to draw people to his cause. He chose the spinning wheel, reflecting female and rural images, as a counterintuitive symbol of India's political independence through industrial self-reliance. This unforgettable symbol ignited an emotional connection between Gandhi and his followers. Commonplace now because his example has been followed by so many, Gandhi's "personal instrumental" fasts electrified the world, compelling both supporters and opponents to join hands, if only temporarily.

Charismatic leaders rely heavily on "personal instrumental" action. The drama of their behavior, from counterintuitive, symbolic gestures to their use of ritual, costume, and timing, telegraphs a magnetic message to potential followers. This "personal instrumental" style is part of the leadership repertoire exercised by many effective leaders, from Gandhi to Winnie Mandela at the height of her power.

Social Instrumental

Leadership behaviors that characterize the second "instrumental "style—the "social instrumental"—involve a heightened appreciation for process, for how human relationships offset the rigidity of structure and task. Leaders who use the "social instrumental" style demonstrate system or political "savvy." They are comfortable with informal processes. They appreciate institutions based on relationships. More specifically, leaders who use "social instrumental" strategies understand relationships and networks as vital and legitimate conduits for accomplishing their ends within and between institutions. They do things through other people, selecting specific individuals for specific tasks. "Social instrumental" actors first draw upon certain segments of their network for one task, then reshuffle the group, replacing some members with other, more relevant parties from the larger network for the next task.

"Social instrumental" actors build and draw upon networks of parties who, themselves, may not be congenial to one another. Since the alliances they string together are not necessarily intended as permanent structures, "social instrumental" achievers rely on their own "social" and "personal instrumental" skills to maintain the alliance for the endurance of the task. During the Gulf War, George Bush's masterful construction of an alliance of Gulf states, many of whom nursed long-standing enmities toward one another, was an exercise in "social instrumental" action.

Entrusting Instrumental

Connective leaders who use the third "instrumental" style—the "entrusting instrumental"—comfortably rely on everyone, not just specifically chosen individuals, to accomplish their tasks. "Entrusting instrumental" actors are adept at attracting others over whom they have no formal authority to help them realize their goals. By contrast to the "power direct" style, which involves command, delegation, and control over implementation, the "entrusting instrumental" style is used by leaders who believe in and rely on others, and simply expect others to help perform their tasks. Relinquishing their control over execution, "social instrumental" leaders entrust others with their vision, expecting others to implement their goals as well as, maybe better than, they could themselves. This expressed confidence empowers those in whom it is placed to meet the "entrusting instrumental" leader's expectations. In the Gulf War, George Bush's use of the "entrusting instrumental" style with parties over whom he had no formal control offered a new model for international action.

THE REPOSITORIES OF INSTRUMENTAL KNOWLEDGE AND SKILLS

Where are the repositories of instrumental knowledge and skill? Who, by training and circumstance, already understands instrumental action? Who knows how to make things happen without formal authority?

From necessity, those denied access to the penthouses of institutional power—those who cannot simply command others to comply—become expert in the byways of the informal interpersonal system (Janeway 1980). Those without formal power learn to interpret nuance, to negotiate and persuade. The informal system demands understanding the processes that occur in all social systems, particularly the subtle processes of human interaction. The less powerful become adept at micromanipulation (Lipman-Blumen 1984), the art of influence at the interpersonal level. From necessity, the powerless use micromanipulation, while the powerful engage in macromanipulation (Lipman-Blumen 1984), the process of influence at the societal or social-policy level.

Those without direct access to resources learn to rely on, rather than command, others to carry out tasks. Women's socialization to the complexities of human interaction, their social and emotional roles within all groups, as well as their resource-poor historical position, have taught them a special expertise, well-suited to this difficult arena. From early on, females are trained in "instrumental" achieving styles.

Still, these three "instrumental" styles that allow us to accomplish our tasks through relationships or by projecting our persona remain suspect in American culture. They offend our traditional, self-reliant ego-ideal. Traditionally, we have maligned such leadership strategies as "manipulative social climbing" or "weak dependence." We have deeply mistrusted the motives of leaders, such as President Lyndon Johnson, who demonstrated such skills (Caro 1983), regardless of the results they achieved.

In traditional American culture, those who overwhelm followers with their persona find their intentions questioned. We suspect dishonesty, incompetence, and possibly malevolence in those who use personal relationships, invoking family or group membership. We criticize as weak those who depend upon others to accomplish their ends.

In many other traditional societies, however, "social instrumental" behavior, particularly, is stitched into the cultural fabric. In countries as diverse as Japan, China, and Italy, the relationships that form one's social network represent an important part of a person's identity. Rather than stirring suspicion and distrust, these behaviors assure others that the individual can be held to his/her group's norms. Relationships offer the keys to success in all aspects of life. Instrumental achieving styles strengthen not only individuals, but the groups and institutions to which they belong.

Discomfort with "instrumental" styles forces individuals to deny these abilities within themselves and to disguise them from others. In fact, despite women's early training and reputation for instrumentality, research on achieving styles (Lipman-Blumen et al. 1983; Lipman-Blumen 1991) indicates that females, just like males, tend to reject these instrumental styles as self-descriptors. Driven under cover, these sensitivities and skills inevitably become one-sided, fail to evoke reciprocity, and, consequently, meet a dead end. Without the nutrients of openness and legitimacy, these processes cannot blossom into productive reciprocity, which, as Axelrod's (1984) research suggests, is a basic ingredient in stable cooperative systems.

Perhaps, in an earlier era, when survival depended upon an aggressive ability to wrest one's sustenance from a strange and hostile environment, self-reliance shielded individuals against those who would use, parasitize, or otherwise abuse relationships to accomplish their goals. The stark frontier society is gone. In its place, we have a different, complex environment, transformed by technology and the threat of mutual annihilation into a global community, where all actions affect and are visible to all.

Intricate institutional arrangements link groups separated by continents into interdependent economic, industrial, and political networks. These new conditions demand a greater sensitivity to organizational and human processes. Without the instrumental component of connective leadership, which incorporates such understanding, we shall have a difficult time adjusting to this new world community.

There is some indication that cultural attitudes are gradually changing. A new vocabulary is emerging to polish the image of these previously maligned styles. The positive connotations of "networking," "negotiating," and "consulting," provide preliminary lexical evidence of a budding awareness of "instrumental" behaviors' importance for the work environment of the 1990s and beyond.

Relational Achieving Styles: Contributory, Collaborative, and Vicarious

The final connective leadership component required by an interdependent environment involves an orientation toward others and their special goals. The third, or "relational," set of achieving styles contains three styles— "contributory," "collaborative," and "vicarious"—that encompass such inclinations. Complex alliances and institutions within a global community necessitate authentic teamwork toward common goals. They also call for helping others to accomplish their goals, for "mentoring" successors, and altruistically taking pride in others' achievements. We immediately recognize the relational styles as part of the traditional female milieu.

Individuals who prefer the three styles of the "relational" achieving styles set approach their goals by (1) collaborating on group goals, (2) contributing to others' objectives, and/or (3) deriving a vicarious sense of achievement from the success of others with whom they identify. Societies trapped in the thrall of individualism historically disdained and undervalued these "relational styles," while simultaneously offering them lip service, perhaps because of their association with women and children. "Relational" achievers receive public accolades for their altruistic contributions and collaboration, along with private suspicion that they do so more out of weakness than of will.

Cultural definitions portray women and children as weak partly because they achieve respectively through helping others and seeking help to accomplish their ends, rather than acting independently. We do not hail them as our heroes and leaders, even if they kindle a sentimental glow in our hearts. These conflicts between disdaining and commending "relational" styles present serious obstacles for leaders in an interdependent environment. What remedies, if any, exist for resolving these draining conflicts?

COOPERATION/COLLABORATION "WRONGLY UNDERSTOOD"

Organizational experts recommend cooperation and teamwork, but still have considerable difficulty explaining how to encourage these behaviors. The results from a recent study (Lefton and Buzzotta 1987) of 26 American executive teams, composed of 275 CEOs, company presidents and vice presidents, many from the *Fortune* 500 companies, are instructive.

The researchers report that "while these teams came much closer to the ideal than most, the members of the teams themselves acknowledged that less than 40 percent of their interaction could be called teamwork." (Lefton and Buzzotta 1987:8). The rest of the time, these top executives reported, their interaction was marked by internal conflict and competition at worst, and non-listening and hypocritical agreement at best.

Although cooperation in organizations has become a semantic touchstone, all our norms, as well as our child-rearing practices, even our adult socialization methods, still shape people into self-reliant, independent (rather than strong *inter*dependent) individuals. Collaboration remains suspect. Even when people do successfully collaborate, society tends to single out a "leader," sometimes merely the most visible member of the group, and anoint that person the hero.

Most American leaders, like others worldwide, achieved their success with the help of others. Nonetheless, our cultural achieving styles spectacles only permit a vision of the leader, not the collaborators, nor the ones who relinquished their own dreams to help the leader succeed. The contributors are eclipsed in the shadow of the leader. For example, Chrysler CEO Lee Iacocca is crowned the "Corporate Messiah," while the workers whose labor and sacrifice were midwife to the Chrysler miracle are ignored, or even worse, blamed as the root of the problem.

Despite repeated calls for teamwork, the reward structure of American institutions favors primarily individual achievers, that is, stars, not their helpers. Professional baseball provides a useful example. Star players receive multimillion-dollar salaries, while their teammates must be satisfied with far less. In industry and government, reward systems offer assistants and collaborators less recognition, including lower salaries, smaller offices, and shorter vacations. Individuals, more often than groups, still receive the bonuses and awards, organizational slogans and academic treatises on teamwork notwithstanding. American organizations are caught in a circular dilemma. Because they prize individual achievement above all, American organizations barely reward cooperation and teamwork. Because rewards are lacking for cooperation and collaboration, it becomes virtually impossible to stimulate them in the workplace. This creates the classic case of "the Folly of Rewarding A, While Hoping for B" (Kerr 1989).

CREATING AND SUSTAINING COOPERATIVE SYSTEMS

Some relevant work from game theory casts new light on cooperation. Axelrod (1984) examined the conditions under which individuals or nations should cooperate, as well as the optimal strategies for eliciting cooperation rather than hostile acts and retaliation from others.

Axelrod invited various game theorists to write programs for a Computerized Prisoner's Dilemma Tournament. The Prisoner's Dilemma, a well-known laboratory game, allows players to seek their own self-interest or that of the group. Pursuing one's self-interest involves the risk of winning or losing "big" versus achieving slightly lower, but more dependable, mutual gains through cooperation. The game, rather than forcing cooperation, permits players to exploit or mutually resist cooperating with one another. The game also recognizes that, as in real life, players do not have totally opposing interests.

Game theorists in economics, psychology, sociology, political science, and mathematics submitted fourteen entries, which were run against each other in a round-robin tournament. Unexpectedly, the simplest program of all, Tit for Tat, was the clear winner. Tit for Tat offers a simple strategy in which a player starts by cooperating and subsequently merely mimics the other player's behavior on the last move. A second round-robin, this one with 62 entries representing as many different strategies, yielded the same result: Tit for Tat won again.

This led Axelrod to ask three questions. Limitations of space permit only the following oversimplified summary:

> First, how can a potentially cooperative strategy get an initial foothold in an environment which is predominantly noncooperative? [Translation: how can a female leadership perspective emerge in an essentially masculine environment?] Second, what type of strategy can thrive in a complex environment composed of other individuals using a wide diversity of more or less sophisticated strategies? Third, under what conditions can such a strategy, once fully established among a group of people, resist invasion by a less cooperative strategy? (1984:viii-ix).

First, "when there actually is a sufficiently high probability of continuing interaction between two individuals" (as in real life, long-term relationships within families, work groups and communities), cooperation is likely to emerge. The first tendrils of cooperative behavior are nourished by reciprocal cooperation on the second player's part. The expectation that cooperation will continue is important; however, so is the recognition that noncooperation breeds more noncooperation, to the detriment of all. (So, women, too, must also learn to use "direct" styles under certain conditions.)

Through a variety of computer simulations using all the submitted strategies, Axelrod (1984) demonstrated that, once established, cooperative efforts of a group can withstand the attack of a hostile, noncooperative group. A single individual trying to cooperate with a noncooperative party, however, has very little chance. Thus, for cooperation to take root, it is crucial to assemble a critical mass of individuals with cooperative, collaborative, and contributory skills.

Axelrod's (1984) work sheds light on why female leaders isolated in a male leadership environment may find that their "relational" styles are ineffective, commonly meeting serious resistance. Faced with serious opposition, solo female leaders are forced to forego "relational" action and resort to more typically masculine leadership strategies. Corazon Aquino is just one example. Separated from other collaborative, contributory, and vicarious colleagues, aspiring female leaders make a disheartening discovery. Only "direct" achieving, masculine leadership strategies, marked by controlling, authoritarian, competitive, and strictly independent behavior, win their male colleagues' grudging respect. Female leaders, forced back into the classical male leadership model, find themselves in a Catch-22 situation: they now risk being seen as "aggressive" and unfeminine.

The second condition for fostering ongoing cooperation occurs when each party has a reputation for toughness, that is, noncooperation will be responded to in kind. "Direct" achieving styles are useful here. In fact, the combination of tough and tender, "direct" and "relational" achieving styles is important.

The third condition critical to sustaining cooperative systems involves an understanding of group processes, a willingness to rely on others, and a predilection to allow relationships to develop into a stable system of reciprocity. Here "instrumental" achieving styles play an important role, emphasizing group process, human interaction, system savvy, reliance on others, and action through relationships that blossom into enduring networks.

A FINAL NOTE ABOUT WOMEN AND CONNECTIVE LEADERSHIP

The psychological literature (Miller 1976; Gilligan 1982) suggests that women take responsibility for keeping the group together, whether the group is the family or the work team. Females' need for connection, expressed in finely-tuned interpersonal skills, are legendary, although recent manuals on executive leadership warn women with serious leadership aspirations to steer clear of roles demanding such "instrumental," as well as "relational," styles.

Despite abundant mythology about women's competitiveness vis-à-vis one another, there is convincing evidence that women excel in collaborative, contributory, and mentoring behavior, all important aspects of connective leadership. Collaborating, contributing to others' tasks, taking vicarious pride in others' accomplishments, of course, are central to traditional female role behavior. Women have been ridiculed for taking pride in their children's and spouse's achievements, even though most societies socialize females to sacrifice themselves, first for their brothers, next for their husbands, and then for their children. The association between female behavior and powerlessness undoubtedly stirs fears, making these "female" styles suspect in societies dedicated to take-charge, competitive individualism.

Research data confirm women's greater propensity for putting the needs of others above their own. Laboratory studies of men and women playing the Prisoner's Dilemma (Axelrod 1984) and the Pollution Game (Dana and Rubenstein 1970) have demonstrated that, on average, women are significantly more likely than men to set aside their narrow self-interests for the sake of others. They exhibit vicarious or altruistic behavior. Women's socialization has taught them the importance of contributing to the goals of others, of collaborating in a group. They nurture others, basking vicariously and altruistically in the success of those they value and love (Gilligan 1982). Gilligan's (1982) work suggests that women often experience guilt and depression when their behavior violates these norms.

In other research (Lipman-Blumen et al. 1983; Lipman-Blumen 1991), full-time homemakers rank collaborative, contributory, and mentoring behavior (i.e., "relational" achieving styles) higher than men do. As indicated above, women across the entire occupational spectrum consistently rank competitiveness lower than do males matched in age, education, and occupation. Women's reluctance to act competitively holds up across cultures with differing levels of competitiveness. More specifically, Taiwanese subjects of both sexes had substantially higher competitive scores than American subjects, from high school students to senior executives. For example, Taiwanese housewives had competitive scores commensurate with those of American male senior executives. Still, compared to Taiwanese men of their own age and educational level, Taiwanese women produced significantly lower competitive achieving scores (Lipman-Blumen 1988).

One male group that consistently approximates this female pattern of moderated competition and elevated contributory, collaborative, or mentoring behavior is senior executives. They are significantly less competitive and more "relational" than mid-level male managers, still vying for promotion. This leads to a special paradox commonly observed in many American firms: "less competitive" females are bypassed for promotion to senior managerial positions, to which their "more aggressive" male colleagues are appointed. Once promoted to senior positions, male senior executives confront an ironic reality of top management: the need to moderate their competitiveness and increase their relational skills. A second paradox is also noticeable in American corporations: many women are succumbing to advice that urges them to eliminate their "instrumental" and "relational" styles, instead of integrating them with "direct" leadership skills. In doing so, these women may be depriving themselves of their advantage as connective leaders.

Earlier researchers (Hennig and Jardim 1977) suggested women experienced difficulty achieving in organizations because, as children, they had not played on teams. A clearer understanding of women's psychosocial development (Chodorow 1974; Miller 1976; and Gilligan 1982), not to mention baseball, prompts us to reconsider that assessment. Perhaps, a clarification of institutional processes and the conditions of cooperation and altruism will further legitimate both "instrumental" and "relational" achieving styles to which women traditionally were socialized. In turn, a revised interpretation of "relational" and "instrumental" styles will foster their dynamic integration with "direct" achieving styles that, together, provide the basis for connective leadership. Further research is needed to resolve a central paradox of the twenty-first-century American workplace: to regain their competitive edge in world markets, American organizations confront the necessity of de-emphasizing competition and developing connective leaders who can give them the connective edge.

Acknowledgments: Prepared for a panel, "Women in the Workplace: Critical Issues for the 1990s and Beyond," annual meeting of the Pacific Sociological Association, Irvine, California, April 11–14, 1991. An earlier version of this paper was presented as an invited address, American Psychological Association, Division 35, Atlanta, Georgia, August 13, 1988.

NOTES

1. Fowlkes (1983) reminds us that the professionalization of these caretaking be-

haviors, however, commonly reduces and transforms them into impersonal, "interpersonal support" (Fowlkes 1983). We might speculate that this transformation from personal to impersonal is designed to demonstrate that these traditional female occupations genuinely meet the "affective neutrality" and "functional specificity" standards (Parsons 1951, 1968) embedded in the traditional/masculine definition of "professions."

2. Achieving styles described in this paper are based on the L-BL Achieving Styles Model (1983, 1991). Individual achieving styles are measured by the L-BL Achieving Styles Inventory (ASI), a 45-item Likert-style instrument. Organizational achieving styles, the achieving styles that a particular organization rewards, as perceived by knowledgeable observers or participants, are measured by the L-BL Organizational Achieving Styles Inventory (OASI).

REFERENCES

Axelrod, Robert. 1984. *The Evolution of Cooperation*. New York: Basic Books.

Axline, Sheryl, Jeanne Billings, and Nicole VanderHorst. 1991. "A Review of Gender-Linked Findings in the Achieving Styles Literature." Claremont, CA: Claremont Graduate School. Photocopy.

Badaracco, Joseph L., Jr. 1991. *The Knowledge Link: How Firms Compete through Strategic Alliances*. Cambridge: Harvard Business School.

Bakan, David. 1966. *The Duality of Human Existence*. Boston: Beacon Press.

Bass, Bernard M. 1990. *Bass and Stogdill's Handbook of Leadership: Theory, Research, and Managerial Applications*, 3d. ed. New York: Free Press.

Bellah, Robert N., Richard Madsen, William M. Sullivan, Ann Swidler, and Steven M Tipton. 1985. *Habits of the Heart*. Berkeley: University of California Press.

Burns, James MacGregor. 1978. *Leadership*. New York: Harper and Row.

Caro, Robert A. 1983. *The Path to Power: The Years of Lyndon Johnson*. New York: Vintage.

Chodorow, Nancy. 1974. "Family Structure and Feminine Personality," Pp. 43–66 in *Women, Culture, and Society*, edited by Michelle Zimbalist Rosaldo and Louise Lamphere. Stanford, CA: Stanford University Press.

Collins, Larry, and Dominique Lapierre. 1975. *Freedom at Midnight*. New York: Simon and Schuster.

Conger, Jay A. 1989. *The Charismatic Leader: Behind the Mystique of Exceptional Leadership*. San Francisco: Jossey-Bass.

Dana, Jonathan, and Franklin D. Rubenstein. 1970. "The Psychology of Pollution and Other Externalities." Stanford, CA: Stanford Graduate School of Business. Photocopy.

de Toqueville, Alexis. [1835] 1959. *Democracy in America*. Translated by Henry Reeve, revised by Francis Bowen, and edited by Phillips Bradley. New York: Vintage Books.

Doig, Jameson W. and Erwin C. Hargrove, eds. 1987. *Leadership and Innovation: A Biographical Perspective on Entrepreneurs in Government*. Baltimore, MD: Johns Hopkins University Press.

Drucker, Peter F. 1985. *Innovation and Entrepreneurship: Practice and Principles*. New York: Harper and Row.

———. 1989. *The New Realities*. New York: Harper and Row.

Fowlkes, Martha R. 1983. "Katie's Place: Women's Work, Professional Work, and Social Reform." Pp. 143–159 in *Research in the Interweave of Social Roles: Families and Jobs*, Vol. 3, edited by Helena Z. Lopata and Joseph H. Pleck. Greenwich, CT: JAI.

Gandhi, Mohandas K. 1957. *Gandhi: An Autobiography*. Boston: Beacon Press.

Gardner, John W. 1990. *On Leadership*. New York: Free Press.

Gerth, H.H. and C. Wright Mills, eds.

1946. *From Max Weber: Essays in Sociology*. New York: Oxford University Press.
Gevirtz, Don. 1984. *The New Entrepreneurs: Innovation in American Business*. New York: Penguin.
Giamatti, A. Bartlett. 1985. Speech before the Massachusetts Historical Society.
Gilligan, Carol. 1982. *In a Different Voice: Psychological Theory and Women's Development*. Cambridge: Harvard University Press.
Gray, Barbara. 1989. *Collaborating: Finding Common Ground for Multiparty Problems*. San Francisco: Jossey-Bass.
Gutek, Barbara, Laurie Larwood, and Ann Stromberg. 1986. "Women at Work." Pp. 217–234 in *International Review of Industrial and Organizational Psychology*, edited by C. L. Cooper and I. Robertson. New York: Wiley.
Hennig, Margaret and Anne Jardim. 1977. *The Managerial Woman*. Garden City, NY: Anchor Press/Doubleday.
Janeway, Elizabeth. 1980. *Powers of the Weak*. New York: Knopf.
Kerr, Steven. 1989. "On the Folly of Rewarding A, While Hoping for B," Pp. 72–87 in *Readings in Managerial Psychology*, fourth edition, edited by Harold J. Leavitt, Louis R. Pondy, and David M. Boje. Chicago: University of Chicago Press.
Kouzes, James M. and Barry Z. Posner. 1987. *The Leadership Challenge: How to Get Extraordinary Things Done in Organizations*. San Francisco: Jossey-Bass.
Lefton, Robert E. and V. R. Buzzotta. 1987–1988. "Teams and Teamwork: A Study of Executive Level Teams." *National Productivity Review*. 7:7–19.
Lipman-Blumen, Jean. 1976. "Toward a Homosocial Theory of Sex Roles: An Explanation of the Sex Segregation of Social Institutions." Pp. 15–31 in *Women and the Workplace: The Implications of Occupational Segregation*, edited by Martha Blaxall and Barbara Reagan. Chicago: University of Chicago Press.
———. 1984. *Gender Roles and Power*. Englewood Cliffs, NJ: Prentice-Hall.
———. 1991. *Individual and Organizational Achieving Styles: A Conceptual Handbook for Researchers and Human Resource Professionals*, 4th. ed. Claremont, CA: The Achieving Styles Institute.
———. 1988. *Individual and Organizational Achieving Styles: A Technical Manual for Researchers and Human Resource Professionals*. Claremont, CA: The Achieving Styles Institute.
Lipman-Blumen, Jean, Alice Handley-Isaksen, and Harold J. Leavitt. 1983. "Achieving Styles in Men and Women: A Model, An Instrument, and Some Findings." Pp. 147–204 in *Achievement and Achievement Motives: Psychological and Sociological Approaches*, edited by Janet T. Spence. San Francisco: W.H. Freeman.
McClelland, D. 1961. *The Achieving Society*. New York: Van Nostrand Reinhold.
Miller, Jean Baker. 1976. *Toward a New Psychology of Women*. Boston: Beacon Press.
Parsons, Talcott. 1951. *The Social System*. New York: Free Press.
———. 1968. "Professions." Pp. 536–547 in *International Encyclopedia of the Social Sciences*, Vol 12, edited by David L. Sills. New York: Macmillan.
Pfeffer, Jeffrey. 1987. "Organizational Demography." *Research in Organizational Behavior* 5:299–357. Greenwich, CT: JAI.
Starr, Martin K., ed. 1988. *Global Competitiveness: Getting the U.S. Back on Track*. New York: W.W. Norton.
Taylor, George Rogers. 1972. *The Turner Thesis: Concerning the Role of the Frontier in American History*. Lexington, MA: D.C. Heath.
Tichy, Noel and Mary Anne Devanna. 1986. *The Transformational Leader*. New York: Wiley.

Part VI
International Leadership

Many of the differences in employee motivation, management styles, and organizational structures of companies throughout the world can be traced to differences in the collective mental programming of people in different national cultures.

Motivation, Leadership, and Organization: Do American Theories Apply Abroad?

Geert Hofstede

A well-known experiment used in organizational behavior courses involves showing the class an ambiguous picture—one that can be interpreted in two different ways. One such picture represents either an attractive young girl or an ugly old woman, depending on the way you look at it. Some of my colleagues and I use the experiment, which demonstrates how different people in the same situation may perceive quite different things. We start by asking half of the class to close their eyes while we show the other half a slightly altered version of the picture—one in which only the young girl can be seen—for only five seconds. Then we ask those who just saw the young girl's picture to close their eyes while we give the other half of the class a five-second look at a version in which only the old woman can be seen. After this preparation we show the ambiguous picture to everyone at the same time.

The results are amazing—most of those "conditioned" by seeing the young girl first see only the young girl in the ambiguous

Organizational Dynamics, Summer 1980. © 1980, AMACOM, a division of American Management Associations. All rights reserved. 0090-2616/80/0014-0042/$02.00/0

picture, and those "conditioned" by seeing the old woman tend to see only the old woman. We then ask one of those who perceive the old woman to explain to one of those who perceive the young girl what he or she sees, and vice versa, until everyone finally sees both images in the picture. Each group usually finds it very difficult to get its views across to the other one and sometimes there's considerable irritation at how "stupid" the other group is.

CULTURAL CONDITIONING

I use this experiment to introduce a discussion on cultural conditioning. Basically, it shows that in five seconds I can condition half a class to see something different from what the other half sees. If this is so in the simple classroom situation, how much stronger should differences in perception of the same reality be between people who have been conditioned by different education and life experience—not for five seconds, but for twenty, thirty, or forty years?

I define culture as the collective mental programming of the people in an environment. Culture is not a characteristic of individuals; it encompasses a number of people who were conditioned by the same education and life experience. When we speak of the culture of a group, a tribe, a geographical region, a national minority, or a nation, culture refers to the collective mental programming that these people have in common; the programming that is different from that of other groups, tribes, regions, minorities or majorities, or nations.

Culture, in this sense of collective mental programming, is often difficult to change; if it changes at all, it does so slowly. This is so not only because it exists in the minds of the people but, if it is shared by a number of people, because it has become crystallized in the institutions these people have built together: their family structures, educational structures, religious organizations, associations, forms of government, work organizations, law, literature, settlement patterns, buildings and even, as I hope to show, scientific theories. All of these reflect common beliefs that derive from the common culture.

Although we are all conditioned by cultural influences at many different levels—family, social, group, geographical region, professional environment—this article deals specifically with the influence of our national environment: that is, our country. Most countries' inhabitants share a national character that's more clearly apparent to foreigners than to the nationals themselves; it represents the cultural mental programming that the nationals tend to have in common.

NATIONAL CULTURE IN FOUR DIMENSIONS

The concept of national culture or national character has suffered from vagueness. There has been little consensus on what represents the national culture of, for example, Americans, Mexicans, French, or Japanese. We seem to lack even the terminology to describe it. Over a period of six years, I have been involved in a large research project on national cultures. For a set of 40 independent nations, I have tried to determine empirically the main criteria by which their national cultures differed. I found four such criteria, which I label dimensions; these are Power Distance, Uncertainty Avoidance, Individualism–Collectivism, and Masculinity–Femininity. To understand the dimensions of national culture, we can compare it with the dimensions of personality we use when we describe individuals' behavior. In recruiting, an organization often tries to get an impression of a candidate's dimensions of personality, such as intelligence (high-low); energy

THE RESEARCH DATA

The four dimensions of national culture were found through a combination of theoretical reasoning and massive statistical analysis, in what is most likely the largest survey material ever obtained with a single questionnaire. This survey material was collected between 1967 and 1973 among employees of subsidiaries of one large U.S.-based multinational corporation (MNC) in 40 countries around the globe. The total data bank contains more than 116,000 questionnaires collected from virtually everyone in the corporation, from unskilled workers to research Ph.D.s and top managers. Moreover, data were collected twice—first during a period from 1967 to 1969 and a repeat survey during 1971 to 1973. Out of a total of about 150 different survey questions (of the precoded answer type), about 60 deal with the respondents' beliefs and values; these were analyzed for the present study. The questionnaire was administered in the language of each country; a total of 20 language versions had to be made. On the basis of these data, each of the 40 countries could be given an index score for each of the four dimensions.

I was wondering at first whether differences found among employees of one single corporation could be used to detect truly national culture differences. I also wondered what effect the translation of the questionnaire could have had. With this in mind, I administered a number of the same questions in 1971-1973 to an international group of about 400 managers from different public and private organizations following management development courses in Lausanne, Switzerland. This time, all received the questionnaire in English. In spite of the different mix of respondents and the different language used, I found largely the same differences between countries in the manager group that I found among the multinational personnel. Then I started looking for other studies, comparing aspects of national character across a number of countries on the basis of surveys using other questions and other respondents (such as students) or on representative public opinion polls. I found 13 such studies; these compared between 5 and 19 countries at a time. The results of these studies showed a statistically significant similarity (correlation) with one or more of the four dimensions. Finally, I also looked for national indicators (such as per capita national income, inequality of income distribution, and government spending on development aid) that could logically be supposed to be related to one or more of the dimensions. I found 31 such indicators—of which the values were available for between 5 and 40 countries—that were correlated in a statistically significant way with at least one of the dimensions. All these additional studies (for which the data were collected by other people, not by me) helped make the picture of the four dimensions more complete. Interestingly, very few of these studies had even been related to each other before, but the four dimensions provide a framework that shows how they can be fit together like pieces of a huge puzzle. The fact that data obtained within a single MNC have the power to uncover the secrets of entire national cultures can be understood when it's known that the respondents form well-matched samples from their nations: They are employed by the same firm (or its subsidiary); their jobs are similar (I consistently compared the same occupations across the different countries); and their age categories and sex composition were similar—only their nationalities differed. Therefore, if we look at the differences in survey answers between multinational employees in countries A, B, C, and so on, the general factor that can account for the differences in the answers is national culture.

---

level (active-passive); and emotional stability (stable-unstable). These distinctions can be refined through the use of certain tests, but it's essential to have a set of criteria whereby the characteristics of individuals can be meaningfully described. The dimensions of national culture I use represent a corresponding set of criteria for describing national cultures.

Characterizing a national culture does not, of course, mean that every person in the nation has all the characteristics assigned to that culture. Therefore, in describing national cultures we refer to the common elements within each nation—the national norm—but we are not describing individuals. This should be kept in mind when interpreting the four dimensions explained in the following paragraphs.

Power distance

The first dimension of national culture is called *Power Distance*. It indicates the extent to which a society accepts the fact that power in institutions and organizations is distributed unequally. It's reflected in the values of the less powerful members of society as well as in those of the more powerful ones. A fuller picture of the difference between small Power Distance and large Power Distance societies is shown in Figure 1. Of course, this shows only the extremes; most countries fall somewhere in between.

Uncertainty avoidance

The second dimension, *Uncertainty Avoidance*, indicates the extent to which a society feels threatened by uncertain and ambiguous situations and tries to avoid these situations by providing greater career stability, establishing more formal rules, not tolerating deviant ideas and behaviors, and believing in absolute truths and the attainment of expertise. Nevertheless, societies in which uncertainty avoidance is strong are also characterized by a higher level of anxiety and aggressiveness that creates, among other things, a strong inner urge in people to work hard. (See Figure 2.)

Geert Hofstede is Director, Human Resources, of Fasson Europe at Leyden, the Netherlands, and vice-president, International Research and Program Development, Management Decisions Systems, Inc., Darien, Connecticut. He has been a professor of organizational behavior and his earlier work experience includes ten years in his native Holland as an industrial worker, foreman, and department manager; six years of behavioral research on the international staff of a multinational corporation; and teaching at IMEDE (Lausanne, Switzerland) and INSEAD (Fontainebleau, France). He holds a master's-level degree in mechanical engineering from Delft Institute of Technology, Holland, and a doctorate in social psychology from Groningen University, also in Holland. An earlier article by Hofstede, "Alienation at the Top," appeared in Organizational Dynamics, Winter 1976.

Individualism–Collectivism

The third dimension encompasses *Individualism* and its opposite, *Collectivism*. Individualism implies a loosely knit social framework in which people are supposed to take care of themselves and of their immediate families only, while collectivism is characterized by a tight social framework in which people distinguish between in-groups and out-groups; they expect their in-group (relatives, clan, organizations) to look after them, and in exchange for that they feel they owe absolute loyalty to it. A fuller picture of

Figure 1
THE POWER DISTANCE DIMENSION

Small Power Distance	Large Power Distance
Inequality in society should be minimized.	There should be an order of inequality in this world in which everybody has a rightful place; high and low are protected by this order.
All people should be interdependent.	A few people should be independent; most should be dependent.
Hierarchy means an inequality of roles, established for convenience.	Hierarchy means existential inequality.
Superiors consider subordinates to be "people like me."	Superiors consider subordinates to be a different kind of people.
Subordinates consider superiors to be "people like me."	Subordinates consider superiors as a different kind of people.
Superiors are accessible.	Superiors are inaccessible.
The use of power should be legitimate and is subject to the judgment as to whether it is good or evil.	Power is a basic fact of society that antedates good or evil. Its legitimacy is irrelevant.
All should have equal rights.	Power-holders are entitled to privileges.
Those in power should try to look less powerful than they are.	Those in power should try to look as powerful as possible.
The system is to blame.	The underdog is to blame.
The way to change a social system is to redistribute power.	The way to change a social system is to dethrone those in power.
People at various power levels feel less threatened and more prepared to trust people.	Other people are a potential threat to one's power and can rarely be trusted.
Latent harmony exists between the powerful and the powerless.	Latent conflict exists between the powerful and the powerless.
Cooperation among the powerless can be based on solidarity.	Cooperation among the powerless is difficult to attain because of their low-faith-in-people norm.

this dimension is presented in Figure 3.

Masculinity

The fourth dimension is called *Masculinity* even though, in concept, it encompasses its opposite pole, *Femininity*. Measurements in terms of this dimension express the extent to which the dominant values in society are "masculine"—that is, assertiveness, the acquisition of money and things, and *not* caring for others, the quality of life, or people. These values were labeled "masculine" because, *within* nearly all societies, men scored higher in terms of the values' positive sense than of their negative sense (in terms of assertiveness, for example, rather than its lack)—even though the society as a whole might veer toward the "feminine" pole. Interestingly, the more an entire society scores

Figure 2
THE UNCERTAINTY AVOIDANCE DIMENSION

Weak Uncertainty Avoidance	Strong Uncertainty Avoidance
The uncertainty inherent in life is more easily accepted and each day is taken as it comes.	The uncertainty inherent in life is felt as a continuous threat that must be fought.
Ease and lower stress are experienced.	Higher anxiety and stress are experienced.
Time is free.	Time is money.
Hard work, as such, is not a virtue.	There is an inner urge to work hard.
Aggressive behavior is frowned upon.	Aggressive behavior of self and others is accepted.
Less showing of emotions is preferred.	More showing of emotions is preferred.
Conflict and competition can be contained on the level of fair play and used constructively.	Conflict and competition can unleash aggression and should therefore be avoided.
More acceptance of dissent is entailed.	A strong need for consensus is involved.
Deviation is not considered threatening; greater tolerance is shown.	Deviant persons and ideas are dangerous; intolerance holds sway.
The ambiance is one of less nationalism.	Nationalism is pervasive.
More positive feelings toward younger people are seen.	Younger people are suspect.
There is more willingness to take risks in life.	There is great concern with security in life.
The accent is on relativism, empiricism.	The search is for ultimate, absolute truths and values.
There should be as few rules as possible.	There is a need for written rules and regulations.
If rules cannot be kept, we should change them.	If rules cannot be kept, we are sinners and should repent.
Belief is placed in generalists and common sense.	Belief is placed in experts and their knowledge.
The authorities are there to serve the citizens.	Ordinary citizens are incompetent compared with the authorities.

to the masculine side, the wider the gap between its "men's" and "women's" values (see Figure 4).

A SET OF CULTURAL MAPS OF THE WORLD

Research data were obtained by comparing the beliefs and values of employees within the subsidiaries of one large multinational corporation in 40 countries around the world. These countries represent the wealthy countries of the West and the larger, more prosperous of the Third World countries. The Socialist block countries are missing, but data are available for Yugoslavia (where the corporation is represented by a local, self-managed company under Yugoslavian

Figure 3
THE INDIVIDUALISM DIMENSION

Collectivist	Individualist
In society, people are born into extended families or clans who protect them in exchange for loyalty.	In society, everybody is supposed to take care of himself/herself and his/her immediate family.
"We" consciousness holds sway.	"I" consciousness holds sway.
Identity is based in the social system.	Identity is based in the individual.
There is emotional dependence of individual on organizations and institutions.	There is emotional independence of individual from organizations or institutions.
The involvement with organizations is moral.	The involvement with organizations is calculative.
The emphasis is on belonging to organizations; membership is the ideal.	The emphasis is on individual initiative and achievement; leadership is the ideal.
Private life is invaded by organizations and clans to which one belongs; opinions are predetermined.	Everybody has a right to a private life and opinion.
Expertise, order, duty, and security are provided by organization or clan.	Autonomy, variety, pleasure, and individual financial security are sought in the system.
Friendships are predetermined by stable social relationships, but there is need for prestige within these relationships.	The need is for specific friendships.
Belief is placed in group decisions.	Belief is placed in individual decisions.
Value standards differ for in-groups and out-groups (particularism).	Value standards should apply to all (universalism).

law). It was possible, on the basis of mean answers of employees on a number of key questions, to assign an index value to each country on each dimension. As described in the box on page 44, these index values appear to be related in a statistically significant way to a vast amount of other data about these countries, including both research results from other samples and national indicator figures.

Because of the difficulty of representing four dimensions in a single diagram, the position of the countries of the dimensions is shown in Figures 5, 6, and 7 for two dimensions at a time. The vertical and horizontal axes and the circles around clusters of countries have been drawn subjectively, in order to show the degree of proximity of geographically or historically related countries. The three diagrams thus represent a composite set of cultural maps of the world.

Of the three "maps," those in Figure 5 (Power Distance × Uncertainty Avoidance) and Figure 7 (Masculinity × Uncertainty Avoidance) show a scattering of countries in all corners—that is, all combinations of index values occur. Figure 6 (Power Distance × Individualism), however, shows one empty corner: The combination of Small Power Distance and Collectivism does not occur. In fact, there is a tendency for Large Power Distance to be associated with Collectivism and for Small Power Distance with Individualism. However, there is a third

Figure 4
THE MASCULINITY DIMENSION

Feminine	Masculine
Men needn't be assertive, but can also assume nurturing roles.	Men should be assertive. Women should be nurturing.
Sex roles in society are more fluid.	Sex roles in society are clearly differentiated.
There should be equality between the sexes.	Men should dominate in society.
Quality of life is important.	Performance is what counts.
You work in order to live.	You live in order to work.
People and environment are important.	Money and things are important.
Interdependence is the ideal.	Independence is the ideal.
Service provides the motivation.	Ambition provides the drive.
One sympathizes with the unfortunate.	One admires the successful achiever.
Small and slow are beautiful.	Big and fast are beautiful.
Unisex and androgyny are ideal.	Ostentatious manliness ("machismo") is appreciated.

factor that should be taken into account here: national wealth. Both Small Power Distance and Individualism go together with greater national wealth (per capita gross national product). The relationship between Individualism and Wealth is quite strong, as Figure 6 shows. In the upper part (Collectivist) we find only the poorer countries, with Japan as a borderline exception. In the lower part (Individualism), we find only the wealthier countries. If we look at the poorer and the wealthier countries separately, there is no longer any relationship between Power Distance and Individualism.

THE CULTURAL RELATIVITY OF MANAGEMENT THEORIES

Of particular interest in the context of this discussion is the relative position of the United States on the four dimensions. Here is how the United States rates:

• On *Power Distance* at rank 15 out of the 40 countries (measured from below), it is below average but it is not as low as a number of other wealthy countries.
• On *Uncertainty Avoidance* at rank 9 out of 40, it is well below average.
• On *Individualism* at rank 40 out of 40, the United States is the single most individualist country of the entire set (followed closely by Australia and Great Britain).
• On *Masculinity* at rank 28 out of 40, it is well above average.

For about 60 years, the United States has been the world's largest producer and exporter of management theories covering such key areas as motivation, leadership, and organization. Before that, the centers of theorizing about what we now call "management" lay in the Old World. We can trace the history of management thought as far back as we want—at least to parts of the Old Testament of the Bible, and to ancient Greece (Plato's *The Laws* and *The Republic*, 350 B.C.). Sixteenth-century European "management" theorists include Niccolò Machiavelli (Italy) and Thomas More (Great Britain); early twentieth-century theorists include Max Weber (Germany) and Henri Fayol (France).

49

THE 40 COUNTRIES							
(Showing Abbreviations used in Figures 5, 6, and 7.)							
ARG	Argentina	FRA	France	JAP	Japan	SIN	Singapore
AUL	Australia	GBR	Great Britain	MEX	Mexico	SPA	Spain
AUT	Austria	GER	Germany (West)	NET	Netherlands	SWE	Sweden
BEL	Belgium	GRE	Greece	NOR	Norway	SWI	Switzerland
BRA	Brazil	HOK	Hong Kong	NZL	New Zealand	TAI	Taiwan
CAN	Canada	IND	India	PAK	Pakistan	THA	Thailand
CHL	Chile	IRA	Iran	PER	Peru	TUR	Turkey
COL	Colombia	IRE	Ireland	PHI	Philippines	USA	United States
DEN	Denmark	ISR	Israel	POR	Portugal	VEN	Venezuela
FIN	Finland	ITA	Italy	SAF	South Africa	YUG	Yugoslavia

Today we are all culturally conditioned. We see the world in the way we have learned to see it. Only to a limited extent can we, in our thinking, step out of the boundaries imposed by our cultural conditioning. This applies to the author of a theory as much as it does to the ordinary citizen: Theories reflect the cultural environment in which they were written. If this is true, Italian, British, German, and French theories reflect the culture of Italy, Britain, Germany, and France of their day, and American theories reflect the culture of the United States of its day. Since most present-day theorists are middle-class intellectuals, their theories reflect a national intellectual middle-class culture background.

Now we ask the question: To what extent do theories developed in one country and reflecting the cultural boundaries of that country apply to other countries? Do American management theories apply in Japan? In India? No management theorist, to my knowledge, has ever explicitly addressed himself or herself to this issue. Most probably assume that their theories are universally valid. The availability of a conceptual framework built on four dimensions of national culture, in conjunction with the cultural maps of the world, makes it possible to see more clearly where and to what extent theories developed in one country are likely to apply elsewhere. In the remaining sections of this article I shall look from this viewpoint at most popular American theories of management in the areas of motivation, leadership, and organization.

MOTIVATION

Why do people behave as they do? There is a great variety of theories of human motivation. According to Sigmund Freud, we are impelled to act by unconscious forces within us, which he called our id. Our conscious conception of ourselves—our ego—tries to control these forces, and an equally unconscious internal pilot—our superego—criticizes the thoughts and acts of our ego and causes feelings of guilt and anxiety when the ego seems to be giving in to the id. The superego is the product of early socialization, mainly learned from our parents when we were young children.

Freud's work has been extremely influential in psychology, but he is rarely quoted in the context of management theories. The latter almost exclusively refer to motivation theories developed later in the United States, particularly those of David McClelland, Abraham Maslow, Frederick

Figure 5
THE POSITION OF THE 40 COUNTRIES
ON THE POWER DISTANCE AND UNCERTAINTY AVOIDANCE SCALES

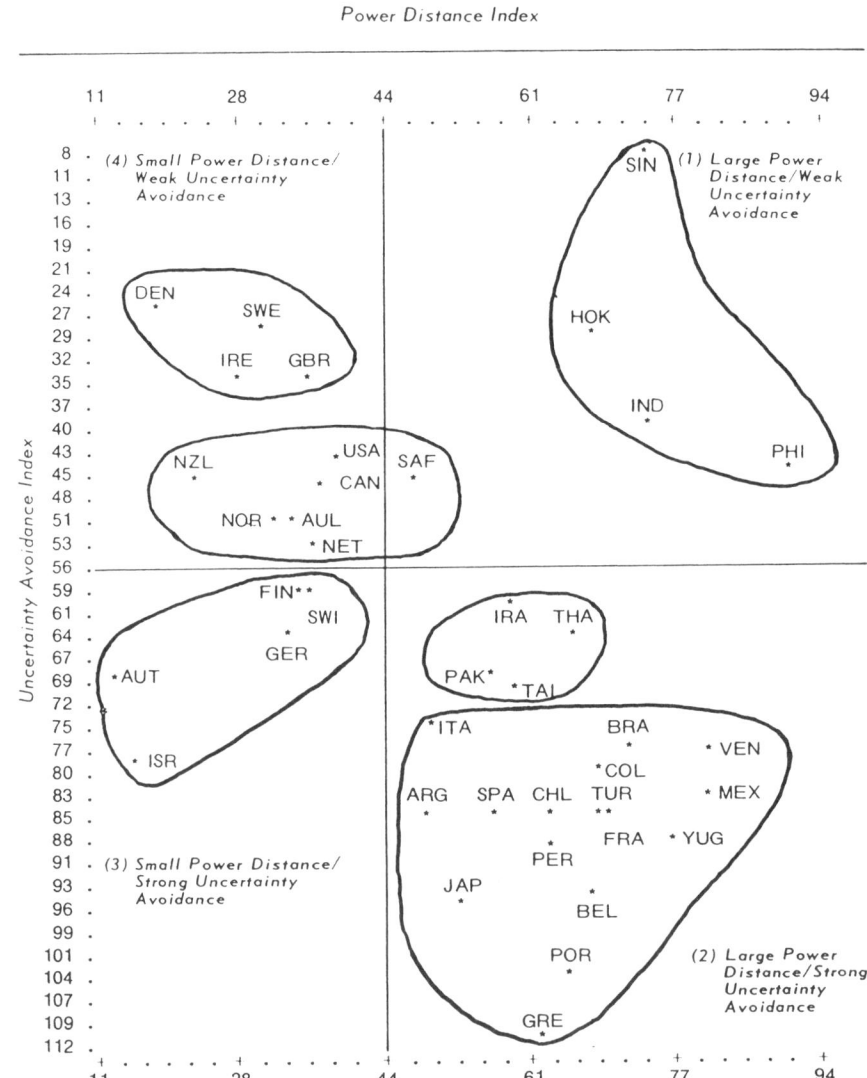

Figure 6
THE POSITION OF THE 40 COUNTRIES
ON THE POWER DISTANCE AND INDIVIDUALISM SCALES

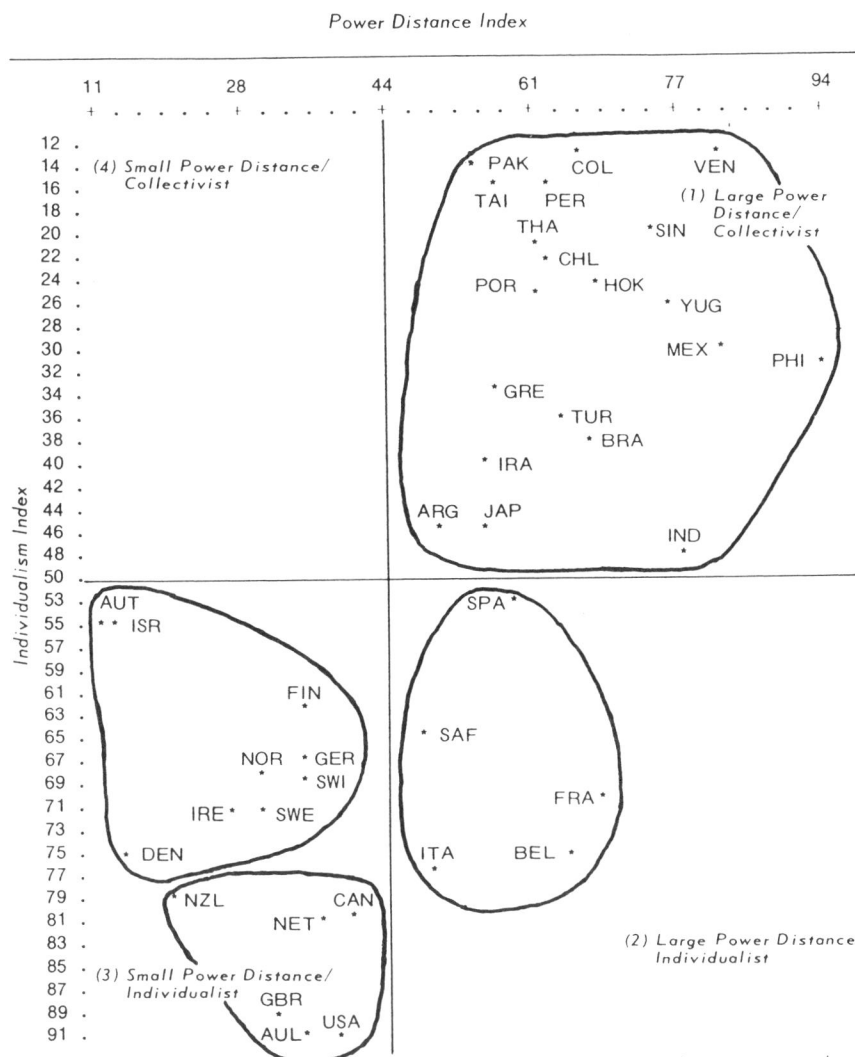

Herzberg, and Victor Vroom. According to McClelland, we perform because we have a need to achieve (the achievement motive). More recently, McClelland has also paid a lot of attention to the power motive. Maslow has postulated a hierarchy of human needs, from more "basic" to "higher": most basic are physiological needs, followed by security, social needs, esteem needs and, finally, a need for "self-actualization." The latter incorporates McClelland's theory of achievement, but is defined in broader terms. Maslow's theory of the hierarchy of needs postulates that a higher need will become active only if the lower needs are sufficiently satisfied. Our acting is basically a rational activity by which we expect to fulfill successive levels of needs. Herzberg's two-factor theory of motivation distinguishes between hygienic factors (largely corresponding to Maslow's lower needs—physiological, security, social) and motivators (Maslow's higher needs—esteem, self-actualization); the hygienic factors have only the potential to motivate negatively (demotivate—they are necessary but not sufficient conditions), while only the motivators have the potential to motivate positively. Vroom has formalized the role of "expectancy" in motivation; he opposes "expectancy" theories and "drive" theories. The former see people as being *pulled* by the expectancy of some kind of result from their acts, mostly consciously. The latter (in accordance with Freud's theories) see people as *pushed* by inside forces—often unconscious ones.

Let us now look at these theories through culture-conscious glasses. Why has Freudian thinking never become popular in U.S. management theory, as has the thinking of McClelland, Maslow, Herzberg, and Vroom? To what extent do these theories reflect different cultural patterns? Freud was part of an Austrian middle-class culture at the turn of the century. If we compare present-day Austria and the United States on our cultural maps, we find the following:

- Austria scores considerably lower on Power Distance.
- Austria scores considerably higher on Uncertainty Avoidance.
- Austria scores considerably lower on Individualism.
- Austria scores considerably higher on Masculinity.

We do not know to what extent Austrian culture has changed since Freud's time, but evidence suggests that cultural patterns change very slowly. It is, therefore, not likely to have been much different from today's culture. The most striking thing about present-day Austrian culture is that it combines a fairly high Uncertainty Avoidance with a very low Power Distance (see Figure 5). Somehow the combination of high Uncertainty Avoidance with high Power Distance is more comfortable (we find this in Japan and in all Latin and Mediterranean countries—see Figure 5). Having a powerful superior whom we can both praise and blame is one way of satisfying a strong need for avoiding uncertainty. The Austrian culture, however (together with the German, Swiss, Israeli, and Finnish cultures) cannot

---

"For strong Uncertainty Avoidance countries like Austria, working hard is caused by an inner urge—it is a way of relieving stress."

Figure 7
THE POSITION OF THE 40 COUNTRIES
ON THE UNCERTAINTY AVOIDANCE AND MASCULINITY SCALES

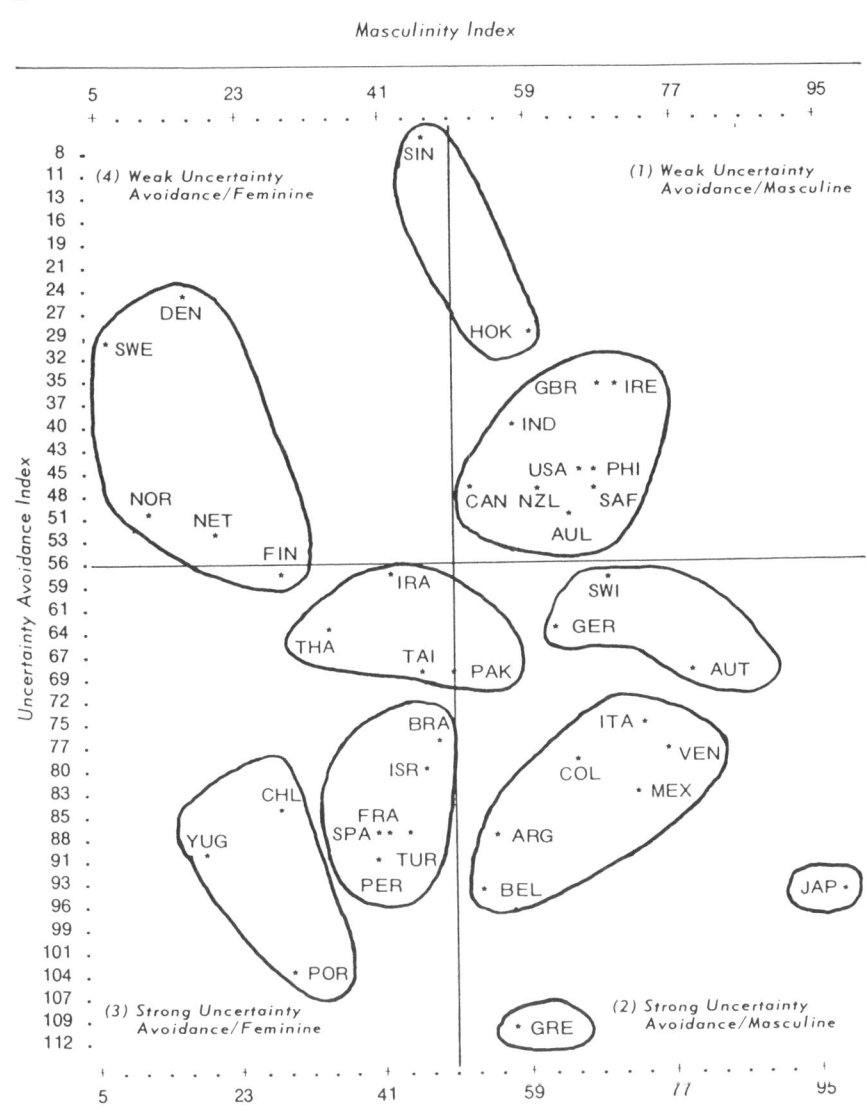

rely on an external boss to absorb its uncertainty. Thus Freud's superego acts naturally as an inner uncertainty-absorbing device, an internalized boss. For strong Uncertainty Avoidance countries like Austria, working hard is caused by an inner urge—it is a way of relieving stress. (See Figure 2.) The Austrian superego is reinforced by the country's relatively low level of Individualism (see Figure 6). The inner feeling of obligation to society plays a much stronger role in Austria than in the United States. The ultrahigh Individualism of the United States leads to a need to explain every act in terms of self-interest, and expectancy theories of motivation do provide this explanation—we always do something *because* we expect to obtain the satisfaction of some need.

The comparison between Austrian and U.S. culture has so far justified the popularity of expectancy theories of motivation in the United States. The combination in the United States of weak Uncertainty Avoidance and relatively high Masculinity can tell us more about why the achievement motive has become so popular in that country. David McClelland, in his book *The Achieving Society*, sets up scores reflecting how strong achievement need is in many countries by analyzing the content of children's stories used in those countries to teach the young to read. It now appears that there is a strong relationship between McClelland's need for achievement country scores and the combination of weak Uncertainty Avoidance and strong Masculinity charted in Figure 7. (McClelland's data were collected for two historic years—1925 and 1950—but only his 1925 data relate to the cultural map in Figure 7. It is likely that the 1925 stories were more traditional, reflecting deep underlying cultural currents; the choice of stories in 1950 in most countries may have been affected by modernization currents in education, often imported from abroad.) Countries in the upper righthand corner of Figure 7 received mostly high scores on achievement need in McClelland's book; countries in the lower lefthand corner of Figure 7 received low scores. This leads us to the conclusion that the concept of the achievement motive presupposes two cultural choices—a willingness to accept risk (equivalent to weak Uncertainty Avoidance; see Figure 2) and a concern with performance (equivalent to strong Masculinity; see Figure 4). This combination is found exclusively in countries in the Anglo-American group and in some of their former colonies (Figure 7). One striking thing about the concept of achievement is that the word itself is hardly translatable into any language other than English; for this reason, the word could not be used in the questionnaire of the multinational corporation used in my research. The English-speaking countries all appear in the upper righthand corner of Figure 7.

If this is so, there is reason to reconsider Maslow's hierarchy of human needs in the light of the map shown in Figure 7. Quadrant 1 (upper righthand corner) in Figure 7 stands for *achievement motivation*, as we have seen (performance plus risk). Quadrant 2 distinguishes itself from quadrant 1 by strong Uncertainty Avoidance, which means *security motivation* (performance plus security). The countries on the feminine side of Figure 7 distinguish themselves by a focusing on quality of life rather than on performance and on relationships between people rather than on money and things (see Figure 4). This means *social motivation*: quality of life plus security in quadrant 3, and quality of life plus risk in quadrant 4. Now, Maslow's hierarchy puts self-actualization (achievement) plus esteem above social needs above security needs. This, however, is not the description of a universal human motivation process—it is the description of a value system, the value system of the U.S. middle class to which the author belonged. I suggest that if we want to continue thinking in terms of a hierarchy for countries in the lower righthand corner of Figure 7 (quadrant 2), security needs should rank at the top; for countries in the upper lefthand corner (quadrant 4), social needs should rank at the top, and for countries in the lower lefthand corner (quadrant 3) *both* security and social needs should rank at the top.

One practical outcome of presenting motivation theories is the movement toward humanization of work—an attempt to make work more intrinsically interesting to the workers. There are two main currents in humanization of work—one, developed in the United States and called *job enrichment*, aims at restructuring individual jobs. A chief proponent of job enrichment is Frederick Herzberg. The other current, developed in Europe and applied mainly in Sweden and Norway, aims at restructuring work into group work—forming, for example, such semiautonomous teams as those seen in the experiments at Volvo. Why the difference in approaches? What is seen as a "human" job depends on a society's prevailing model of humankind. In a more masculine society like the United States, humanization takes the form of masculinization, allowing individual performance. In the more feminine societies of Sweden and Norway, humanization takes the form of femininization—it is a means toward more wholesome interpersonal relationships in its deemphasis of interindividual competition.

Leadership

One of the oldest theorists of leadership in world literature is Machiavelli (1468-1527). He described certain effective techniques for manipulation and remaining in power (including deceit, bribery, and murder) that gave him a bad reputation in later centuries. Machiavelli wrote in the context of the Italy of his day, and what he described is clearly a large Power Distance situation. We still find Italy on the larger Power Distance side of Figure 5 (with all other Latin and Mediterranean countries), and we can assume from historical evidence that Power Distances in Italy during the sixteenth century were considerably larger than they are now. When we compare Machiavelli's work with that of his contemporary, Sir Thomas More (1478-1535), we find cultural differences between ways of thinking in different countries even in the sixteenth century. The British More described in *Utopia* a state based on consensus as a "model" to criticize the political situation of his day. But practice did not always follow theory, of course: More, deemed too critical, was beheaded by order of King Henry VIII, while Machiavelli the realist managed to die peacefully in his bed. The difference in theories is nonetheless remarkable.

In the United States a current of leadership theories has developed. Some of the best known were put forth by the late Douglas McGregor (Theory X versus Theory Y), Rensis Likert (System 4 management), and Robert R. Blake with Jane S. Mouton (the Managerial Grid®). What these theories have in common is that they all advocate participation in the manager's decisions by his/her subordinates (participative management); however, the initiative toward participation is supposed to be taken by the manager. In a worldwide perspective (Figure 5), we can understand these theories from the middle position of the United States on the Power Distance side (rank 15 out of 40 countries). Had the culture been one of larger Power Distance, we could have expected more "Machiavellian" theories of leadership. In fact, in the management literature of another country with a larger Power Distance index score, France, there is little concern with participative management American style, but great concern with who has the power. However, in countries with smaller Power Distances than the United States (Sweden, Norway, Germany, Israel), there is considerable sympathy for models of management in which even the initiatives are taken by the subordinates (forms of industrial democracy) and with which there's little sympathy in the United States. In the approaches toward "industrial democracy" taken in these countries, we notice their differences on the second dimension, Uncertainty Avoidance. In weak Uncertainty Avoidance countries like Sweden, industrial democracy was started in the form of local experiments and only later was given a legislative framework. In strong Uncertainty Avoidance countries like Germany, industrial democracy was brought about by legislation first and then had to be brought alive in the organizations ("Mitbestimmung").

The crucial fact about leadership in any culture is that it is a complement to subordinateship. The Power Distance Index scores in Figure 5 are, in fact, based on the values of people as *subordinates*, not on the values of superiors. Whatever a naïve literature on leadership may give us to understand, leaders cannot choose their styles at will; what is feasible depends to a large extent on the cultural conditioning of a leader's subordinates. Along these lines, Figure 8 describes the type of subordinateship that, other things being equal, a leader can expect to meet in societies at three different levels of Power Distance—subordinateship to which a leader must respond. The middle level represents what is most likely found in the United States.

Neither McGregor, nor Likert, nor Blake and Mouton allow for this type of cultural proviso—all three tend to be prescriptive with regard to a leadership style that, at best, will work with U.S. subordinates and with those in cultures—such as Canada or Australia—that have not too different Power Distance levels (Figure 5). In fact, my research shows that subordinates in larger Power Distance countries tend to agree more frequently with Theory Y.

A U.S. theory of leadership that allows for a certain amount of cultural relativity, although indirectly, is Fred Fiedler's contingency theory of leadership. Fiedler states that different leader personalities are needed for "difficult" and "easy" situations, and that a cultural gap between superior and subordinates is one of the factors that makes a situation "difficult." However, this theory does not address the kind of cultural gap in question.

In practice, the adaptation of managers to higher Power Distance environments does not seem to present too many problems. Although this is an unpopular message—one seldom professed in management development courses—managers moving to a larger Power Distance culture soon learn that they have to behave more autocratically in order to be effective, and tend to do so; this is borne out by the colonial history of most Western countries. But it is interesting that the Western ex-colonial power with the highest Power Distance norm—France—seems to be most appreciated by its former colonies and seems to maintain the best postcolonial relationships with most of them. This suggests that subordinates in a large Power Distance culture feel even more comfortable with superiors who are real autocrats than with those whose assumed autocratic stance is out of national character.

The operation of a manager in an environment with a Power Distance norm lower than his or her own is more problematic. U.S. managers tend to find it difficult to collaborate wholeheartedly in the "industrial democracy" processes of such countries as Sweden, Germany, and even the Netherlands. U.S. citizens tend to consider their country as the example of democracy, and find it difficult to accept that other countries might wish to develop forms of democracy for which they feel no need and that make major inroads upon managers' (or leaders') prerogatives. However, the very idea of management prerogatives is not accepted in very low Power Distance countries. This is, perhaps, best illustrated by a remark a Scandinavian social scientist is supposed to have made to Herzberg in a seminar: "You are against participation for the very reason we are in favour of it—one doesn't know where it will stop. We think that is good."

One way in which the U.S. approach to leadership has been packaged and formalized is management by objectives (MBO), first advocated by Peter Drucker in 1955 in *The Practice of Management*. In the United States, MBO has been used to spread a pragmatic results orientation throughout the organization. It has been considerably more successful where results are objectively measurable than where they can only be interpreted subjectively, and, even in the United States, it has been criticized heavily. Still, it has been perhaps the single most popular management technique "made in U.S.A." Therefore, it can be accepted as fitting U.S. culture. MBO presupposes:

- That subordinates are sufficiently independent to negotiate meaningfully with the boss (not-too-large Power Distance).
- That both are willing to take risks (weak Uncertainty Avoidance).
- That performance is seen as important by both (high Masculinity).

Let us now take the case of Germany, a below-average Power Distance country. Here, the dialogue element in MBO should present no problem. However, since Germany scores considerably higher on Uncertainty Avoidance, the tendency toward accepting risk and ambiguity will not exist to the same extent. The idea of replacing the arbitrary authority of the boss with the impersonal authority of mutually agreed-upon objectives, however, fits the small Power Distance/strong Uncertainty Avoidance cultural cluster very well. The objectives become the subordinates' "superego." In a book of case studies about MBO in Germany, Ian R. G. Ferguson states that "MBO has acquired a different flavour in the German-speaking area, not least because in these countries the societal and political pressure towards increasing the value of man in the organization on the right to co-determination has become quite clear. Thence, MBO has been transliterated into Management by Joint Goal Setting (Führung durch Zielvereinbarung)." Ferguson's view of MBO fits the ideological needs of the German-speaking countries of the moment. The case studies in his book show elaborate formal systems with extensive ideological justification; the stress on *team* objectives is quite strong, which is in line with the lower individualism in these countries.

The other area in which specific information on MBO is available is France. MBO was first introduced in France in the early 1960s, but it became extremely popular for a time after the 1968 student revolt. People expected that this new technique would lead to the long-overdue democratization of organizations. Instead of DPO (Direction par Objectifs), the French name for MBO became DPPO (Direction *Participative* par Objectifs). So in France, too, societal developments affected the MBO system. However, DPPO remained, in general, as much a vain slogan as did Liberté, Egalité, Fraternité (Freedom, Equality, Brotherhood) after the 1789 revolt. G. Franck wrote in 1973 ". . . I think that the career of DPPO is terminated, or rather that it has never started, and it won't ever start as long as we continue in France our tendency to confound ideology and reality. . . ." In a postscript to Franck's article, the editors of *Le Management* write: "French blue- and white-collar workers, lower-level and higher-level managers, and 'patrons' all belong to the same cultural system which maintains dependency relations from level to level. Only the deviants really dislike this system. The hierarchical structure protects against anxiety; DPO, however, generates anxiety. . . ." The reason for the anxiety in the French cultural context is that MBO presupposes a depersonalized authority in the form of internalized objectives; but French people, from their early childhood onward, are accustomed to large Power Distances, to an authority that is highly personalized. And in spite of all attempts to introduce Anglo-Saxon management methods, French superiors do not easily decentralize and do not stop short-circuiting intermediate hierarchical levels, nor do French subordinates expect them to. The developments of the 1970s have severely discredited DPPO, which probably does injustice to the cases in which individual French organizations or units, starting from less exaggerated expectations, have benefited from it.

In the examples used thus far in this section, the cultural context of leadership may look rather obvious to the reader. But it also works in more subtle, less obvious ways. Here's an example from the area of management decision making: A prestigious U.S. consulting firm was asked to analyze the decision-making processes in a large Scandinavian "XYZ" corporation. Their report criticized the corporation's decision-making style, which they characterized as being, among other things, "intuitive" and "consensus based." They compared "observations of traditional XYZ practices" with "selected examples of practices in other companies." These "selected examples," offered as a model, were evidently taken from their U.S. clients and reflect the U.S. textbook norm—"fact based" rather than intuitive management, and "fast decisions based on clear responsibilities" rather than the use of informal, personal contacts and the concern for consensus.

Is this consulting firm doing its Scandinavian clients a service? It follows from Figure 7 that where the United States and the Scandinavian culture are wide apart is on the Masculinity dimension. The use of intuition and the concern for consensus in Scandinavia are "feminine" characteristics of the culture, well embedded in the total texture of these societies. Stressing "facts" and "clear responsibilities" fits the "masculine" U.S. culture. From a neutral viewpoint, the reasons for criticizing the U.S. decision-making style are as good as those for criticizing the Scandinavian style. In complex decision-making situations, "facts" no longer exist independently from the people who define them, so "fact-based management" becomes a misleading slogan. Intuition may not be a bad method of deciding in such cases at all. And if the implementation of decisions requires the commitment of many people, even a consensus process that takes more time is an asset rather than a liability. But the essential element overlooked by the consultant is that decisions have to be made in a way that corresponds to the values of the environment in which they have to be effective. People in this consulting firm lacked insight into their own cultural biases. This does not mean that the Scandinavian corporation's management need not improve its decision making and could not learn from the consultant's experience. But this can be done only through a mutual recognition of cultural differences, not by ignoring them.

ORGANIZATION

The Power Distance × Uncertainty Avoidance map (Figure 5) is of vital importance for structuring organizations that will work best in different countries. For example, one U.S.-based multinational corporation has a worldwide policy that salary-increase proposals should be initiated by the employee's direct superior. However, the French management of its French subsidiary interpreted this policy in such a way that the superior's superior's superior—three levels above—was the one to initiate salary proposals. This way of working was regarded as quite natural by both superiors and subordinates in France. Other factors being equal, people in large Power Distance cultures prefer that decisions be centralized because even superiors have strong dependency needs in relation to their superiors; this tends to move decisions up as far as they can go (see Figure 8). People in small Power Distance cultures want decisions to be decentralized.

While Power Distance relates to centralization, Uncertainty Avoidance relates to formalization—the need for formal rules and specialization, the assignment of tasks to experts. My former colleague O. J. Stevens at INSEAD has done an interesting research project (as yet unpublished) with M.B.A. students from Germany, Great Britain, and France. He asked them to write their own diagnosis and solution for a small case study of an organizational problem—a conflict in one company between the sales and product development departments. The majority of the French referred the problem to the next higher authority (the president of the company); the Germans attributed it to the lack of a written policy, and proposed establishing one; the British attributed it to a lack of interpersonal communication, to be cured by some kind of group training.

Stevens concludes that the "implicit model" of the organization for most French was a pyramid (both centralized and formal); for most Germans, a well-oiled machine (formalized but not centralized); and for most British, a village market (neither formalized nor centralized). This covers three quadrants (2, 3, and 4) in Figure 5. What is missing is an "implicit model" for quadrant 1, which contains four Asian countries, including India. A discussion with an Indian colleague leads me to place the family (centralized, but not formalized) in this quadrant as the "implicit model" of the organization. In fact, Indian organizations tend to be formalized as far as relationships between people go (this is related to Power Distance), but not as far as workflow goes (this is Uncertainty Avoidance).

The "well-oiled machine" model for Germany reminds us of the fact that Max Weber, author of the first theory of bureaucracy, was a German. Weber pictures bureaucracy as a highly formalized system (strong Uncertainty Avoidance), in which, however, the rules protect the lower-ranking members against abuse of power by their superiors. The superiors have no power by themselves, only the power that their bureaucratic roles have given them as incumbents of the roles—the power is in the role, not in the person (small Power Distance).

The United States is found fairly close to the center of the map in Figure 5, taking an intermediate position between the "pyramid," "machine," and "market" implicit models—a position that may help explain the success of U.S. business operations in very different cultures. However, according to the common U.S. conception of organization, we might say that *hierarchy is not a goal by itself* (as it is in France) and that *rules are not a goal by themselves*. Both are means toward obtaining results, to be changed if needed. A breaking away from hierarchic and bureaucratic traditions is found in the development toward matrix organizations and similar temporary or flexible organization systems.

Another INSEAD colleague, André Laurent, has shown that French managers strongly disbelieve in the feasibility of matrix organizations, because they see them as violating the "holy" principle of unit of command. However, in the French subsidiary of a multinational corporation that has a long history of successful matrix management, the French managers were quite positive

Figure 8
SUBORDINATESHIP FOR THREE LEVELS OF POWER DISTANCE

Small Power Distance	Medium Power Distance (United States)	Large Power Distance
Subordinates have weak dependence needs.	Subordinates have medium dependence needs.	Subordinates have strong dependence needs.
Superiors have weak dependence needs toward their superiors.	Superiors have medium dependence needs toward their superiors.	Superiors have strong dependence needs toward their superiors.
Subordinates expect superiors to consult them and may rebel or strike if superiors are not seen as staying within their legitimate role.	Subordinates expect superiors to consult them but will accept autocratic behavior as well.	Subordinates expect superiors to act autocratically.
Ideal superior to most is a loyal democrat.	Ideal superior to most is a resourceful democrat.	Ideal superior to most is a benevolent autocrat or paternalist.
Laws and rules apply to all and privileges for superiors are not considered acceptable.	Laws and rules apply to all, but a certain level of privileges for superiors is considered normal.	Everybody expects superiors to enjoy privileges; laws and rules differ for superiors and subordinates.
Status symbols are frowned upon and will easily come under attack from subordinates.	Status symbols for superiors contribute moderately to their authority and will be accepted by subordinates.	Status symbols are very important and contribute strongly to the superior's authority with the subordinates.

toward it; obviously, then, cultural barriers to organizational innovation can be overcome. German managers are not too favorably disposed toward matrix organizations either, feeling that they tend to frustrate their need for organizational clarity. This means that matrix organizations will be accepted *if* the roles of individuals within the organization can be defined without ambiguity.

The extreme position of the United States on the Individualism scale leads to other potential conflicts between the U.S. way of thinking about organizations and the values dominant in other parts of the world. In the U.S. Individualist conception, the relationship between the individual and the organization is essentially calculative, being based on enlightened self-interest. In fact, there is a strong historical and cultural link between Individualism and Capitalism. The capitalist system—based on self-interest and the market mechanism—was "invented" in Great Britain, which is still among the top three most Individualist countries in the world. In more Collectivist societies, however, the link between individuals and their traditional organizations is not calculative, but moral: It is based not on self-interest, but on the individual's loyalty toward the clan, organization, or society—which is supposedly the best guarantee of that individual's ultimate interest. "Collectivism" is a bad word in the United States, but "individualism" is as much a bad word in the writings of Mao Tse-tung, who writes from a strongly Collectivist cultural tradition (see Figure 6 for the Collectivist scores of the Chinese majority countries Taiwan, Hong Kong, and Singapore). This means that U.S. organizations may get themselves into considerable trouble in more Collectivist environments if they do not recognize their local employees' needs for ties of mutual loyalty between company and employee. "Hire and fire" is very ill perceived in these countries, if firing isn't prohibited by law altogether. Given the value position of people in more Collectivist cultures, it should not be seen as surprising if they prefer other types of economic order to capitalism—if capitalism cannot get rid of its Individualist image.

CONSEQUENCES FOR POLICY

So far we have seriously questioned the universal validity of management theories developed in one country—in most instances here, the United States.

On a practical level, this has the least consequence for organizations operating entirely within the country in which the theories were born. As long as the theories apply within the United States, U.S. organizations can base their policies for motivating employees, leadership, and organization development on these policies. Still, some caution is due. If differences in environmental culture can be shown to exist between countries, and if these constrain the validity of management theories, what about the subcultures and countercultures within the country? To what extent do the familiar theories apply when the organization employs people for whom the theories were not, in the first instance, conceived—such as members of minority groups with a different educational level, or belonging to a different generation? If culture matters, an organization's policies can lose their effectiveness when its cultural environment changes.

No doubt, however, the consequences of the cultural relativity of management theories are more serious for the multinational organization. The cultural maps in Figures 5, 6, and 7 can help predict the kind of culture difference between subsidiaries and mother company that will need to be met. An important implication is that identical personnel policies may have very different effects in different countries—and within countries for different subgroups of employees. This is not only a matter of different employee values; there are also, of course, differences in government policies and legislation (which usually reflect quite clearly the country's different cultural position). And there are differences in labor market situations and labor union power positions. These differences—tangible as well as intangible—may have consequences for performance, attention to quality, cost, labor turnover, and absenteeism. Typical universal policies that may work out quite differently in different countries are those dealing with financial incentives, promotion paths, and grievance channels.

The dilemma for the organization operating abroad is whether to adapt to the local culture or try to change it. There are examples of companies that have successfully changed local habits, such as in the earlier mention of the introduction of matrix organization in France. Many Third World countries want to transfer new technologies from more economically advanced countries. If they are to work at all, these technologies must presuppose values that may run counter to local traditions, such as a certain discretion of subordinates toward superiors (lower Power Distance) or of individuals toward in-groups (more Individualism). In such a case, the local culture has to be changed; this is a difficult task that should not be taken lightly. Since it calls for a conscious strategy based on insight into the local culture, it's logical to involve acculturated locals in strategy formulations. Often, the original policy will have to be adapted to fit local culture and lead to the desired effect. We saw earlier how, in the case of MBO, this has succeeded in Germany, but generally failed in France.

A final area in which the cultural boundaries of home-country management theories are important is the training of managers for assignments abroad. For managers who have to operate in an unfamiliar culture, training based on home-country theories is of very limited use and may even do more harm than good. Of more importance is a thorough familiarization with the other culture, for which the organization can use the services of specialized crosscultural training institutes—or it can develop its own program by using host-country personnel as teachers.

Acknowledgments

This article is based on research carried out in the period 1973-78 at the European Institute for Advanced Studies in Management, Brussels. The article itself was sponsored by executive search consultants Berndtson International S.A., Brussels. The author acknowledges the helpful comments of Mark Cantley, André Laurent, Ernest C. Miller, and Jennifer Robinson on an earlier version of it.

Selected Bibliography

The first U.S. book about the cultural relativity of U.S. management theories is still to be written, I believe—which lack in itself indicates how difficult it is to recognize one's own cultural biases. One of the few U.S. books describing the process of cultural conditioning for a management readership is Edward T. Hall's *The Silent Language* (Fawcett, 1959, but reprinted since). Good reading also is Hall's article "The Silent Language in Overseas Business" (*Harvard Business Review*, May-June 1960). Hall is an anthropologist and therefore a specialist in the study of culture. Very readable on the same subject are two books by the British anthropologist Mary Douglas, *Natural Symbols: Exploration in Cosmology* (Vintage, 1973) and the reader *Rules and Meanings: The Anthropology of Everyday Knowledge* (Penguin, 1973). Another excellent reader is Theodore D. Weinshall's *Culture and Management* (Penguin, 1977).

On the concept of national character, some well-written professional literature is Margaret Mead's "National Character," in the reader by Sol Tax, *Anthropology Today* (University of Chicago Press, 1962), and Alex Inkeles and D. J. Levinson's, "National Character," in Lindzey and Aronson's *Handbook of Social Psychology*, second edition, volume 4, (Addison-Wesley, 1969). Critique on the implicit claims of universal validity of management theories comes from some foreign authors: An important article is Michel Brossard and Marc Maurice's "Is There a Universal Model of Organization Structure?" (*International Studies of Management and Organization*, Fall 1976). This journal is a journal of translations from non-American literature, based in New York, that often contains important articles on management issues by non-U.S. authors that take issue with the dominant theories. Another article is Gunnar Hjelholt's "Europe Is Different," in Geert Hofstede and M. Sami Kassem's reader, *European Contributions to Organization Theory* (Assen Netherlands: Von Gorcum, 1976).

Some other references of interest: Ian R. G. Ferguson's *Management by Objectives in Deutschland*, (Herder und Herder, 1973) (in German); G. Franck's "Epitaphe pour la DPO," in *Le Management*, November 1973 (in French); and D. Jenkins's *Blue- and White-Collar Democracy*, (Doubleday, 1973).

Note: Details of Geert Hofstede's study of national cultures has been published in his book, *Culture's Consequences: International Differences in Work-Related Values* (Beverly Hills: Sage Publications, 1980).

[26]
GLOBAL WOMEN POLITICAL LEADERS:
An Invisible History, An Increasingly Important Future

Nancy J. Adler*
McGill University

No one doubts that we need different approaches than we have used in the past to guide the global community into the twenty-first century. Yet, while many people continue to review men's historic patterns of leadership, few have even begun to appreciate the equivalent patterns of historic and potential success in global women leaders. This article identifies the set of 25 global women leaders who have led modern countries and governments. Within the investigation, it contrasts the expected similarity of context with the reality of diversity among both the women leaders themselves and the naions they govern. The article reviews the women's paths to power, as well as their records of leadership and personal achievement.

"Studies of political leadership have been remarkably non-gender specific. This is due primarily to a tacit assumption...that leaders are men! Historically, there is of course a good deal of validity to this assumption—almost all political leaders *have been* men. To refer to a generic head of state as "him" may thus be understandable, if inaccurate" (Genovese, 1993b, p. ix).

INTRODUCTION

No one doubts that the world needs wise and insightful leaders to guide the global community into the twenty-first century—that we need different approaches than we have used in the twentieth century if the planet and humanity are to survive, let alone prosper. Similarly, everyone agrees that tomorrow's world leaders will need to challenge and to transcend the more parochial and limited leadership styles of the past. Yet, while many people continue to review men's historic patterns of success in search of models for

---

* Direct all correspondence to: Nancy J. Adler, Faculty of Management, McGill University, 1001 rue Sherbrooke ouest, Montreal, Quebec, Canada H3A 1G5. *e-mail:* adler@management.mcgill.ca

twenty-first-century global leadership, few have even begun to appreciate the equivalent patterns of historic and potential success in global women leaders.

This article identifies the set of global women leaders who have led modern countries and governments. It investigates the myth that only certain types of women, along with particular political and socioeconomic contexts, give rise to global women leaders. Within this investigation, it contrasts the expected similarity of context with the reality of diversity among both the women leaders themselves and the nations they govern. It appears that societies that provide more favorable conditions for women's private and professional lives, including facilitating progress into the lower and middle levels of management, do not seem to disproportionately favor their success in assuming the highest levels of societal leadership.

The article reviews the women leaders' paths to power, including both their ascriptive characteristics—such as membership in politically prominent or extremely well-to-do families—as well as their records of personal achievement. The analysis documents a pattern of grassroots populism that goes beyond the more structural support traditionally given to aspirants of a nation's highest political office. In addition, the analysis highlights the societal symbolism of being a woman along with its distinct relevance for being elected to the office of president or prime minister.

Definitions of success in the political sphere are always elusive; subject, among other factors, to the political perspective of the assessor. Given that the vast majority of the women leaders are either still in office or have held office so recently that sufficient time has yet to pass to gain an appropriate perspective on their accomplishments, the article concludes with a necessarily limited discussion of the potential contribution of increasing numbers of women leaders to the governance of society.

AN APPROACH TO UNDERSTANDING: META-ETHNOGRAPHIC ANALYSIS

Given the paucity of analyses of global women leaders, the variance in published descriptions based on the political perspective of particular authors, and the need to avoid prematurely concluding that extant leadership models whose development was based almost exclusively on male leaders are appropriate for understanding the patterns of women's leadership, a comprehensive grounded-theory approach has been taken to this study. Meta-ethnographic analysis was selected as a methodology. Meta-ethnography involves procedures for synthesizing existing qualitative research to make second-level inferences (Noblit & Hare, 1988).[1] The database in meta-ethnography includes "multivocal literatures...[based on] accessible writings on a common, often contemporary topic" (Ogawa & Malen, 1991, p. 265, as quoted in Bartholomew, 1996, p. 71). In this study, the database on global women leaders was drawn from academic books and articles, journalistic newspaper and magazine reports, and literature from each countries' respective embassy, as well as archival documentary film footage and news reports from the British Broadcasting Corporation (BBC) and U.S. television networks. Sources include both autobiographical and second-party reports by people from both within and outside each focal country. In most cases, sources are limited to the English-based literature.

GLOBAL WOMEN LEADERS: NUMBERS INCREASING

The myth, of course, is that there are few global women leaders and that their assumption of power is not only rare but also a sporadic occurrence. One international survey, for example, concluded that less than .005% of the world's political leaders are women (Blondel, 1987, pp. 116-117). While still rare, 25 women have held the most senior positions of political leadership in their country. Eleven women currently lead their countries, serving as either prime minister or president in Bangladesh, Dominica, Iceland, Ireland, Nicaragua, Norway, Pakistan, Turkey, and Sri Lanka—where both the prime minister and president are women—and in Switzerland as a State Councillor, that country's highest elected leadership position. Only slightly more, 14 women, have held equivalent elite leadership positions in the entire history of modern political states (Argentina, Great Britain, Canada, the Central African Republic, France, Haiti, India, Israel, Lithuania, Netherlands-Antilles, the Philippines, Poland, Portugal, and the former Yugoslavia). While five stayed in office less than a year (Canada, France, Haiti, Lithuania, and Portugal), six remained in office for more than a decade (Dominica, Great Britain, Iceland, India, Norway, and Sri Lanka).[2] Given the current numbers, just over 5% of all nations currently have a woman as head of state and/or government.

While the public knows all too little about these women political leaders as a group, it is evident that the salient question is no longer "Can a woman be a global leader?" Clearly, these 25 women presidents and prime ministers, along with their economic counterparts, have already definitively answered that question.[3]

As shown in Table 1, not only do global women leaders already exist, but the number who hold the highest political office in their country is rapidly increasing. The first elected prime minister, Sirimavo Bandaranaike of Sri Lanka, took office is 1960.[4] She was followed by just two other woman in the 1960s—Indira Gandhi, who was elected prime minister of India in 1966,[5] and Golda Meir, who became Israel's prime minister in 1969.[6] Another four women assumed senior leadership positions in their countries in the 1970s: Isabel Perón in Argentina in 1974,[7] Elizabeth Domitien in the Central African Republic in 1975,[8] and Portugal's Maria de Lourdes Pintasilgo[9] and Great Britain's Margaret Thatcher,[10] both in 1979. Thus, no particular geographic region dominated, as Asia, the Middle East, the Americas, Africa, and Europe each gained a global woman leader among these first seven women presidents and prime ministers.

The 1980s brought seven additional women to power. In 1980, Iceland's Vigdís Finnbógadottir became the first woman in the world elected as a constitutional head of state.[11] In the same year, Dominica's Eugenia Charles[12] was elected the first woman prime minister of a Caribbean country. In 1981, Norway elected Gro Harlem Brundtland as its first and youngest prime minister.[13] In 1982, Yugoslavia's Milka Planinc became Eastern Europe's first woman prime minister.[14] In 1984, the Netherlands-Antilles elected Maria Liberia-Peters as its first woman prime minister.[15] Similarly in 1986, the Philippines elected Corazon Aquino as its first woman president.[16] In 1988, at the age of 35, Pakistan's Benazir Bhutto was elected prime minister, thus becoming the first woman to head a modern Islamic state.[17] As shown in Figure 1, four of the seven women who came to office in the 1980s—Finnbógadottir, Charles, Brundtland, and Bhutto—remain in office today.

Table 1
Global Women Leaders: A Chronology

Country	Name	Office	Date
Sri Lanka	*Sirimavo Bandaranaike	Prime Minister	1960-1965; 1970-1977, 1994—*
India	(Indira Gandhi)	Prime Minister	1966-1977, 1980-1984
Israel	(Golda Meir)	Prime Minister	1969-1975
Argentina	(María Estela [Isabel] Martínez de Perón)	President	1974-1976
Central African Rep.	Elizabeth Domitien	Prime Minister	1975-1976
Portugal	Maria de Lourdes Pintasilgo	Prime Minister	1979
Great Britain	Margaret Thatcher	Prime Minister	1979-1990
Dominica	*Mary Eugenia Charles	Prime Minister	1980-1995*
Iceland	*Vigdís Finnbógadottir	President	1980—*
Norway	*Gro Harlem Brundtland	Prime Minister	1981; 1986-1989; 1990—*
Yugoslavia	Milka Planinc	Prime Minister	1982-1986
Netherland-Antilles	Mary Liberia-Peters	Prime Minister	1984; 1989-1994
The Philippines	Corazon Aquino	President	1986-1992
Pakistan	*Benazir Bhutto	Prime Minister	1988-1990; 1993—*
Lithuania	Kazimiera-Danute Prunskiene	Prime Minister	1990-1991
Haiti	Ertha Pascal-Trouillot	President	1990-1991
Myanmar (Burma)	Aung San Suu Kyi	Opposition Leader**	1990—**
Ireland	*Mary Robinson	President	1990—*
Nicaragua	*Violeta Barrios de Chamorro	President	1990—*
Bangladesh	*Khaleda Zia	Prime Minister	1991—*
France	Edith Cresson	Prime Minister	1991-1992
Poland	Hanna Suchocka	Prime Minister	1992-1993
Canada	Kim Campbell	Prime Minister	1993
Turkey	*Tansu Çiller	Prime Minister	1993—*
Sri Lanka	*Chandrika Bandaranaike Kumaratunga	Executive President and former Prime Minister	1994—*
Switzerland	*Ruth Dreifuss	State Councillor***	1995—*

Notes: ( ) = No longer living.
  * Currently in office, as of 1995.
  ** Party won 1990 election but prevented by military from taking office; Nobel Prize laureate.
  *** Switzerland is governed by a Council of (7) Ministers, rather than an elected president or prime minister.

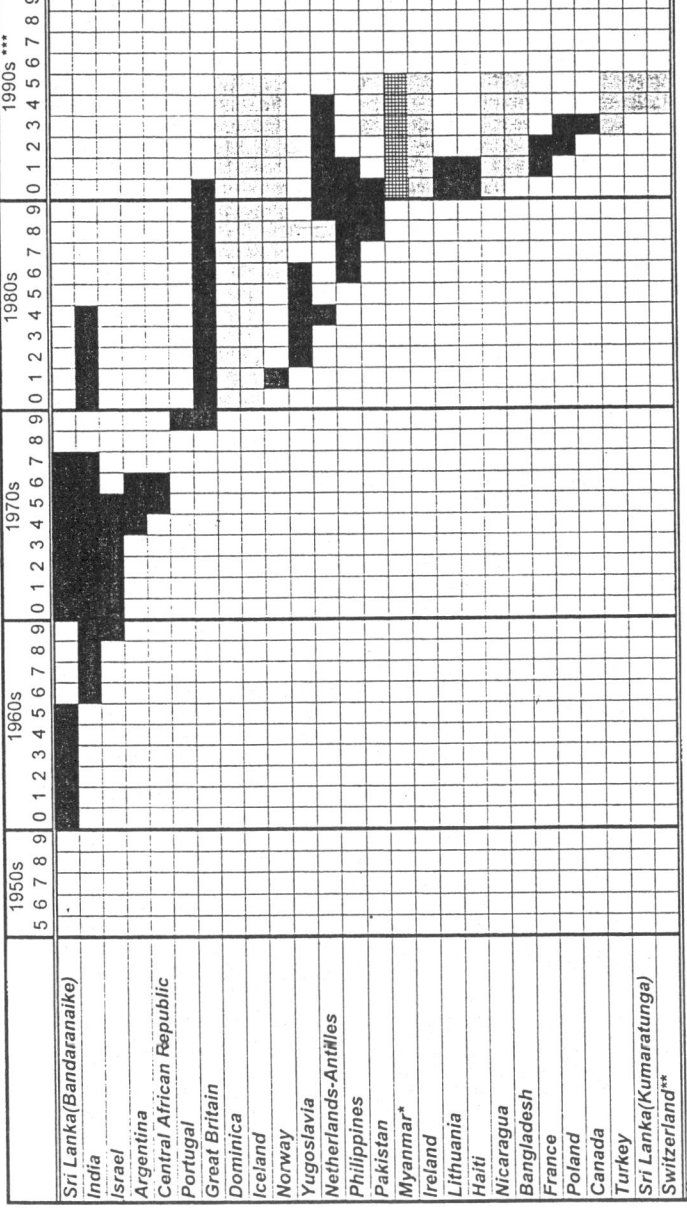

Figure 1
Women Prime Ministers and Presidents: A Chronology

Notes: * Party won 1990 election but Aung San Suu Kyi prevented by military from taking office.
** Switzerland is governed by a Council of (7) Ministers, rather than an elected president or prime minister.
*** 1990s through mid-decade 1995.

Although the decade of the 1990s is not yet half over, already 11 women have become president or prime minister of their countries.[18] Thus, in the last five years, the number of women who have attained high office has nearly doubled over that of the past. In 1990 alone, four women came to office: Kazimiera Prunskiene became the first woman prime minister of Lithuania;[19] Nicaragua's Violeta Chamorro became the first woman elected president in Central America;[20] and Ireland's Mary Robinson[21] and Haiti's Ertha Pascal-Trouillot[22] each became her country's first woman president. In 1991, France's Edith Cresson[23] and Bangladesh's Khaleda Zia[24] each became her country's first woman prime minister. In 1992, Hanna Suchocka began her term as Poland's prime minister.[25] By 1993, Kim Campbell became prime minister of Canada and, thus, North America's first woman head of government.[26] On the same day, Turkey elected Tansu Çiller as its first female prime minister.[27] 1994 brought Chandrika Bandaranaike Kumaratunga, daughter of the world's and Sri Lanka's first female prime minister, to power, initially as Sri Lanka's prime minister and immediately thereafter as the country's first elected executive president. The decade of the 1990s reached its midpoint with Switzerland's 1995 election of Ruth Dreifuss as State Councillor, the highest elected leadership position in that country. (The Swiss are governed by a seven-member Council of Ministers, rather than by a popularly elected president or prime minister.)

Sri Lanka's Kumaratunga is the only woman ever to follow another woman into office; all of the other women are "firsts," with many being not only the first woman political leader in her country but also the first woman leader in her region. Few of the women leaders have ever met their counterparts in other countries, and even then, their national and political contexts are not similar.[28] Pakistan's Benazir Bhutto describes the press's assumption of similarity when the reality is, in fact, differences:

> Members of the American press were intrigued by the similarities between my upcoming battle with [then Pakistani Prime Minister] Zia and Corazon Aquino's challenge to [former President of the Philippines] Ferdinand Marcos. Their views of the similarities between Mrs. Aquino and me were a bit romantic, however. Yes, we were both women from well-known landowning families who had been educated in the United States. Both of us had lost loved members of our families to dictators, Mrs. Aquino, her husband, and I, my father and brother. Mrs. Aquino had fought Marcos with "people power" to orchestrate a peaceful revolution just as I was hoping to do. But the similarities between us ended there....Corazon Aquino had enjoyed the support of both the military and the church.... I had neither. The generals opposed me because I threatened the corrupt system by which they received discounts on land, free cars, and exemptions in customs duties. And while some of the religious establishment was with me, the fundamentalist mullahs supported Zia's dictatorship.
>
> Most important of all, the Americans had served notice on Marcos, even providing transportation out of the country for him, his family, and entourage. The Reagan administration was solidly behind Zia. I could expect little real help from America, save for the good wishes and moral support of various members of the United States government and the press (Benazir Bhutto, as quoted in Opfell, 1993, p. 149).

Thus, these 25 women political leaders have no role models beyond those provided by the men in their country. Therefore, while leading their respective countries, they are also both creating their roles and acting as role models for future leaders, both women and men.

WHO ARE THE GLOBAL WOMEN LEADERS?

What do we know about the 25 women presidents and prime ministers? Are there commonalities in their personal backgrounds? Are there particular national contexts that favor women political leaders? How did the women reach their positions of leadership—by moving up from the lower ranks of the political hierarchy or through alternative routes? How important is it that they are women? Are they today's heroines of global leadership or something less illustrious? What might they potentially bring to leadership in the twenty-first century?

Background: Preparing for Leadership

Unfortunately, we know considerably less than we would like to about the group of global women leaders. However, it appears that diversity, rather than any pattern or consistency, defines them. No apparent pattern emerges that either insures or precludes women's success in rising to the highest level of leadership in their society.

Diverse Socioeconomic Backgrounds

The majority of the global women leaders come from economically advantaged families. However, some grew up in poverty, such as Elizabeth Domitien in the Central African Republic, Haiti's Ertha Pascal-Trouillot, and Israel's Golda Meir, who came first to the United States as a Russian immigrant and later emigrated to Israel. Others grew up in modest circumstances, such as Argentina's Isabel Perón and Britain's Margaret Thatcher, who as a child lived above the family-owned grocery store. Among the others, many—such as Nicaragua's Violeta Chamorro, Pakistan's Benazir Bhutto, the Philippines' Corazon Aquino, Turkey's Tansu Çiller, and Sri Lanka's Bandaranaike—come from families with all the advantages of wealth.

Diverse Religious Backgrounds

As a group, the women leaders represent most of the world's major religious traditions, including Buddhism, Catholicism, Hinduism, Islam, Judaism, and various Protestant faiths. With more than 40% of the women leaders being Catholic and three current prime ministers leading modern Islamic states—Bangladesh, Pakistan, and Turkey—the myth must be dispelled that certain religions are so prejudiced against women that no woman could achieve the highest level of power. While many of the world's religions do not make it easy for a woman to reach the elite levels of societal leadership, none seems to make it impossible. Moreover, it appears that the dynamics of women's elite leadership may not replicate either the societal experience of the majority of women, who face obstacles in entering the labor force, or the experience of most professional women, whose progress up through the ranks of management is either impeded or blocked altogether.

Highly Educated Internationally

Most of the women leaders are highly educated, with only a few of those who were appointed rather than elected, such as Argentina's Isabel Perón and Elizabeth Domitien in the Central African Republic, never having gone to university (Weir, 1993). Their academic backgrounds vary, with 12 having earned predictable degrees, such as law (Great Britain's Margaret Thatcher, Canada's Kim Campbell, Dominica's Eugenia Charles, Haiti's Ertha

Pascal-Trouillot, Ireland's Mary Robinson, the Philippines' Corazon Aquino,[29] and Poland's Hanna Suchocka), business or economics (France's Edith Cresson, Lithuania's Kazimiera Prunskiene, Sri Lanka's Kumaratunga, and Turkey's Tansu Çiller), and political science (Sri Lanka's Kumaratunga and Pakistan's Benazir Bhutto). However, as a group they studied a much broader range of fields than just law, economics, and political science, including medicine (Norway's Brundtland); chemistry (Great Britain's Thatcher); demography (France's Cresson); chemical engineering (Portugal's Pintasilgo); history (India's Indira Gandhi); French, literature, and theatre (Iceland's Finnbógadottir); and teaching (Bangladesh's Khaleda Zia and the Netherlands-Antilles' Maria Liberia-Peters). Portugal's Maria de Lourdes Pintasilgo demonstrated her vision and leadership early when she chose as a student to acquire a degree in chemical engineering, explaining that:

> she wanted to demonstrate that Portuguese women could succeed as chemical engineers because too many women had lost heart in the beginning stages of their training (Pintasilgo, as quoted in Opfell, 1993, p. 82).

Given the importance of global understanding for twenty-first century leadership, it is noteworthy that two-thirds of the women leaders were educated internationally; fifteen received at least part of their education outside of their home country. Perhaps Iceland's Finnbógadottir best symbolizes this cosmopolitan education, having finished high school in Iceland and then studied French, literature, and theatre in France, followed by theatre studies in Denmark, French philosophy in Sweden, and finally English literature and education again in Iceland.

Before agreeing to run for office, Corazon Aquino once questioned, "What do I know about the presidency?" to which an advisor responded, "What does anyone know—there's no school for presidents" (Conason, 1986, p. 11). During the campaign, when Aquino's opponent, Ferdinand Marcos repeatedly and:

> invidiously taunted Cory with...being totally inexperienced, [Aquino invariably answered] "Sure, I don't know anything about stealing or cheating, and definitely I don't know anything about killing my opponents" (Opfell, 1993, p. 135).

The breadth of educational experience is visible in various of the women's approaches to leadership. For example, Norway's Gro Harlem Brundtland, who has become a world leader on environmental issues, responded to a critique that, as a medical doctor, she did not have sufficient experience to hold political office, explaining:

> There is a very close connection between being a physician and being a politician. The doctor first tries to prevent illness, then tries to treat it if it comes. It is exactly the same as what you try to do as a politician, but with regard to society (Brundtland, as quoted in Opfell, 1993, p. 104).

Given the problems facing global society at the close of the twentieth century, one must ask if the traditional, historical paths to leadership are what will be most helpful for twenty-first century leaders. If not, society must learn to recognize and begin to use the appropriate dimensions of breadth.

Diverse Family Backgrounds

A review of their family backgrounds reveals that most women leaders are married and have children. Only one in five is single—a proportion distinctly higher than that of the general population but quite similar to that of senior professional women worldwide. Among them, the 25 women leaders represent a full range of lifestyles. For example, Israel's Golda Meir separated from her husband and raised their two children on her own; India's Indira Gandhi, while married and also raising two children, lived at her prime minister father's home in a different city from her husband; Canada's Kim Campbell and Dominica's Eugenia Charles both were elected as single women; while Iceland's Finnbógadottir adopted a child after her divorce, thus raising her daughter as a single mother. To date, Pakistan's Benazir Bhutto is the only prime minister to have given birth while in office. During her pregnancy, Bhutto had to disguise her baby's publicly announced expected birthdate to keep her political opponents from using the baby's birth against her (Lamb, 1991).

Although almost all of the women leaders are mothers, most of their children were grown up before the women assumed power. By the time the women leaders reach their country's highest political office, most no longer face the time-consuming balancing act confronting many younger professional women who are still raising small children at home while continuing to meet the demands of highly challenging careers. Senior global leadership, whether in the political or economic sphere, is often sequential to—rather than consecutive with—raising a family. Corazon Aquino, for example, agreed to become a presidential candidate in the Philippines "only because...[my] children are now grown" (Conason, 1986, p. 11). In addition, earlier in their careers, many of the women leaders had the advantage of household help, nannies, extended families, and/or boarding schools to help balance the time demands of their professional and private lives. Being a mother, however, was by no means politically inconsequential. For example, early in Margaret Thatcher's career, the Conservative party's "selection committee turned her down [for a parliament seat to contest], saying she should stay home and rear [her twin babies]" (Opfell, 1993, p. 72). The Conservative party did not allow Thatcher to campaign for a seat until her twins had reached age six.

THE CONTEXT OF POWER[30]

Studies of women entering the workforce and moving into and up through the professional and managerial ranks have suggested, and often demonstrated, that general societal factors can either help or hinder women's progress (Adler & Izraeli, 1994). Factors cited often include general measures of economic well-being (such as per capita GNP), educational level (such as literacy rates), and physical well-being (such as life expectancy), as well as the legal, social, cultural, and religious climate of the country (including such indicators as laws and socio-religious traditions supporting, or failing to support, women's equal rights and participation in society). While it would be logical to assume that those countries with the most advantageous conditions would also produce a majority of the world's women leaders, such a pattern does not seem to emerge and, therefore, fails to explain women's success, and lack thereof, in obtaining the highest levels of political leadership within a country. The countries led by women presidents and prime ministers are as diverse as the women themselves, with few of the countries that are frequently cited as being most progressive in advancing women at lower levels (such as the United States and the Scandinavian countries) being represented among those that have elected global women leaders.

The women lead or have led countries that are among both the economically most advantaged (including Canada, France, Great Britain, Iceland, Norway, and Switzerland) and least advantaged (including Bangladesh, the Central African Republic, Haiti, Pakistan, and Sri Lanka). They have led countries that are both among the largest in the world in population (India, Bangladesh, and Pakistan) and geography (Canada and Argentina) and among the smallest, again both in population (Dominica, Iceland, and the Netherlands-Antilles) and geography (Dominica and the Netherlands-Antilles). Similarly, they have led countries with long traditions of democracy as well as those with almost no democratic tradition whatsoever.

The pattern of diversity continues with such social indicators as literacy. Women have led six of the 25 countries in the world that have literacy rates between 99% and 100% (Iceland, France, Norway, Poland, Switzerland, and Great Britain) along with three that are among the 25 countries with the world's lowest literacy rates (Central African Republic: 18%; Haiti: 21%; and Bangladesh: 24%). Similarly, women have led five of the countries that rank in the world's top ten on life expectancy (Iceland, Norway, Switzerland, Israel, and Canada) and one of the 25 countries with the world's lowest life expectancy (Central African Republic).

Whereas the dominant pattern is a lack of pattern (that is, a pattern of diversity), the set of countries that the women have led is slightly skewed toward those that are more advantaged and more important. For example, as suggested above, women lead or have led four of the world's top 20 countries as measured by GNP per capita (Switzerland, Canada, Norway, and Iceland) and only one of the bottom 20 (Bangladesh). In contrast to the fact that only just over 5% of countries today have women leaders, women lead or have led 50% of countries with the highest life expectancy, 36% of the most populous countries, 33% of both the geographically largest and the most urban countries, 25% of those with the highest literacy rates, and 20% of those with the world's highest GNP per capita.

PATHS TO POWER: DYNASTY AND DEMOCRACY

The women leaders' political philosophies and parties represent the full spectrum from communism (e.g., Yugoslavia's Planinc and Lithuania's Prunskiene), to socialism (e.g., Sri Lanka's Kumaratunga), to liberal labor party traditions (e.g., Ireland's Mary Robinson and Norway's Gro Harlem Brundtland), to conservatism (e.g., Britain's Margaret Thatcher, Canada's Kim Campbell, and Turkey's Tansu Çiller), to non-party affiliation (e.g. Portugal's Pintasligo and Iceland's Finnbógadottir). In 1993, when Kim Campbell became prime minister of Canada, women headed two of the three major Canadian political parties, both the left-of-center New Democratic Party and Campbell's own right-of-center Progressive Conservative Party. Similarly, in Bangladesh, Prime Minister Zia faced an opposition party headed by a woman. In 1991, commentators referred to "modern history's [first] political matriarchy in Norway...three women led the parties which commanded the allegiance of about 70% of the electorate" (Opfell, 1993, p. 109). Clearly, neither women in general nor women leaders in particular represent one political persuasion.

The press, however, tends to present women leaders as more similar than they, in fact, are. For example, the press labeled former communist party member Kazimiera

Prunskiene as "Lithuania's Thatcher...The Iron Lady of the East" (Opfell, 1993, p. 166). Prunskiene did not like the comparison to Britain's conservative prime minister:

> If I had been made of iron...I'd have been broken a long time ago. Lithuania needs a firm hand, but not one made of iron....Mrs. Thatcher is Mrs. Thatcher. My name is Prunskiene (Opfell, 1993, p. 166).

Similarly, when the former Yugoslavia's prime minister and communist party member, Milka Planinc, met with Margaret Thatcher in 1983, the press referred to Planinc as "another Iron Lady" (Opfell, 1993, p. 118). Similarly to Prunskiene, Planinc quickly rejected the title (Opfell, 1993, p. 118). Margaret Thatcher herself challenged the Iron Lady label that the press had given her, saying:

> I stand here in my red chiffon gown, my face softly made up, my hair gently waved— the Iron Lady of the western world (Opfell, 1993, p. 76).

Political Dynasty and Leadership

"The ascent of any person to power within a society is, almost by definition, a rare and extraordinary event" (Genovese & Thompson, 1993, p. 3). While most women leaders come to power without family connections, a third were strongly advantaged by membership—either by birth or marriage—in highly prominent, political families— including in Argentina, Bangladesh, India, Nicaragua, Pakistan, the Philippines, and Sri Lanka. Of the eight women leaders from politically prominent families, all except Indira Gandhi saw their father or husband assassinated prior to assuming office themselves. However, contrary to popular belief, such family ties, while extremely influential, are not strong enough to allow the widowed wife or daughter to automatically inherit national leadership. Only one woman, Isabel Perón, who had been serving as Argentina's vice president, inherited her position; Argentina appointed her to the presidency immediately upon the death of her husband, President Juan Perón. All of the other women from dynastic families had to campaign, often for years, before they were personally elected as either president or prime minister of their countries. None of the other five women leaders who were appointed, rather than elected, to office, came from a politically dynastic family.

Pakistanis, for example, elected Benazir Bhutto prime minister following her return from exile nine years after her father, former Prime Minister Aulfiqar Ali Bhutto, had been hanged. Similarly, Bangladesh elected Khaleda Zia prime minister only after she had campaigned for a decade following the assassination of her husband, President Zia-ur Rahman, who years earlier had declared Bangladesh's independence. Likewise, Nicaraguans elected Violeta Chamorro president more than 12 years after the assassination of her politically prominent journalist husband. The people of the Philippines, while immediately uniting behind Corazon Aquino, widow of the slain opposition leader Benigno Aquino, only elected her president two-and-a-half years later. Sri Lanka's Bandaranaike became the world's first woman prime minister in 1960, a year after her prime minister husband's murder. Her daughter, Sri Lanka's current Executive President, Chandrika Kumaratunga, lost both her prime minister father and her politically active actor husband to murder—39 years and 6 years, respectively, prior to assuming her country's highest leadership position. Although Indira Gandhi is the only woman leader from a politically dynastic family whose father and husband were not murdered, she is also the only woman prime minister to have been assassinated.

In reviewing the pattern from a geographic perspective, it is evident that in Asian and Latin American countries that have had women leaders, membership in a politically dynastic family is an extremely important, and perhaps even necessary, precondition for societal leadership. However, in only one case—that of Argentina's Isabel Perón—was it a sufficient precondition. In all other cases, the women had to demonstrate leadership skills beyond family membership to gain sufficient popular and/or party support to be successfully elected. Whereas some women from politically dynastic families had not formally prepared for leadership, having assumed the primary role of mother and homemaker prior to their husband's assassinations, this alternative route to power is not completely dissimilar to that of a number of the non-dynastic women leaders, who spent their early careers in professions not directly associated with politics, such as medicine, teaching, chemical engineering, and theatre. For women, the path to the most senior level of societal leadership does not appear to be limited to traditional career progress up through the political party system or public bureaucracy.

Moreover, it is important to recognize that, where a particular woman eventually emerged as her country's national leader, other members from the same dynastic family could conceivably have assumed the mantle of national leadership. The most visible current example of this, of course, is in Pakistan, where Benazir Bhutto's mother and brother have both been highly active and ambitious in politics for years. Similarly, in Nicaragua, Violeta Chamorro's four children have been politically prominent for years through the family's role in journalism. Beyond being a member of a politically dynastic family, a woman must distinguish herself before her country will recognize and elect her as its national leader.

Symbols of Legacy and Unity

Most women leaders who come to office following the assassination of their father or husband become symbols for carrying on the legacy of the slain former leader or for national unity, or both. In terms of creating a powerful vision—one of the key aspects of leadership—both legacy and unity are compelling. As the daughter of a slain martyr, and as captured in the title of her autobiography, *Daughter of Destiny* (Bhutto, 1989), there is no question that Benazir Bhutto's political vision for Pakistan is to carry on the nation-building legacy of her slain father (Anderson, 1993). Similarly, in Sri Lanka (the former Ceylon):

> Wanting to perpetuate [her husband, slain prime minister] Solomon's memory, [Bandaranaike] travelled tirelessly through Ceylon...she believed she must work for the welfare of the millions who had loved Solomon (Opfell, 1993, p. 6).

Likewise, there is equally no question that Khaleda Zia's initial vision for Bangladesh was to carry on the nation-building legacy of her slain husband, who had earlier declared Bangladesh independence.

Both Nicaragua's Chamorro and the Philippines' Aquino became symbols of national unity following their husband's murders. Chamorro "claims to have no ideology beyond 'national reconciliation,'" saying "I don't have a party. I'm no politician. I just love my country" (Benn, 1995). Of Chamorro's four adult children, two are prominent Sandanistas and the other two, equally prominently, oppose the Sandanistas, not an unusual split in war-torn Nicaragua (Saint-Germain, 1993, p. 80). Chamorro's ability to bring all the members of her family together for Sunday dinner each week has achieved nearly legendary status in Nicaragua (Saint-Germain, 1993, p. 80). As "the grieving matriarch who can still hold the family together" (Saint-Germain, 1993, p. 80), Chamorro gives symbolic hope to the nation that it, too, can find peace based on a unity that brings together all Nicaraguans. That a national symbol for a woman leader is family unity is neither surprising nor coincidental. Based on similar dynamics in the Philippines, Aquino, as widow of the slain opposition leader, was seen as the only person who could credibly unify the people of the Philippines following Benigno Aquino's death.

ELECTED LEADERS: POPULAR SUPPORT

Most women leaders do not gain power through membership in politically dynastic families nor following the death of a family member. Most achieve their elite leadership roles in highly competitive elections. Of the 25 women presidents and prime ministers, only six were appointed (Isabel Perón in Argentina, Elizabeth Domitien in the Central African Republic, Edith Cresson in France, Ertha Pascal-Trouillot of Haiti, Kazimiera Prunskiene of Lithuania, and Maria de Lourdes Pintasilgo in Portugal), with the others all winning popular and/or party-based elections.[31]

While the women from politically dynastic families do not automatically inherit their leadership positions, those who are not members of such families are often given extremely slim chances of winning election. For example, bookies in Ireland gave 1,000 to 1 odds against victory for Mary Robinson, yet she ultimately received 53% of the vote (O'Neill, 1994, p. B3) and today enjoys the support of more than 90% of the Irish population—a popularity rating that is the envy of politicians around the world.

Popular Support: The Basis of Democracy

One reason that women are perceived as having such a low probability of winning is that, in contrast to the experience of most men who run for political office, the official political party structure—including both the woman's own party as well as opposition parties—often fails to either initially support or even recognize the woman's candidacy or her potential to win. For example, in Israel, the ruling Labor Alignment called the then-72-year-old Golda Meir out of retirement following the sudden fatal heart attack of Prime Minister Levi Eshkol and asked her to accept appointment as an *interim* prime minister until the party could solidify its coalition to elect a new permanent prime minister. However, while the Labor Party assumed that she would be "merely a caretaker," Golda took charge (Thompson, 1993, p. 148). Seven months after being appointed prime minister:

> She was no longer an interim figure selected by party leaders and slated to return to retirement as soon as the major contenders sorted things out; she was the prime minister and the unquestioned choice to lead her party into the elections....[Although] Golda's party fell 5 seats short of an absolute majority in the 120-member Knesset,...her personal popularity and prominence [combined with]...the size of her parliamentary bloc...[made it] obvious that she would form the next government (Thompson, 1993, p. 148).

While Golda's own party did not consider her as a potential prime minister, her own actions and her broad-based personal popularity became the basis on which she built her success and gained Israel's highest leadership position.

In Ireland, Mary Robinson visited more small communities than any other politician before her own party took her candidacy seriously. Similarly, the opposition admits that by the time it recognized Mary Robinson as a serious presidential candidate, she was already unbeatable. In assessing her campaign, experts agree that "by the time the other parties realised the strategic role being played by women, it was too late" (Finlay, 1990, p. 62). In Mary Robinson's own victory speech, she stated:

> There was nothing rational or reasonable about the campaign which developed into a barnstorming, no-holds-barred battle between my ad hoc assembly of political activists, amateurs, idealists and romantic realists against the might, money and merciless onslaught of the greatest political party on this island. And we beat them! (Robinson, RDS, Dublin, November 9, 1990, victory speech as quoted in Finlay, 1990, p. 8).

Whereas the lack of political party support certainly often works to the women candidates' detriment, the opposition's failure to take them seriously until late in the campaign often gives the women a strategic advantage.

Similar to Ireland, Iceland elected Vigdís Finnbógadottir president with the explicit, broad-based support of women from throughout the country:

> Finnbógadottir's ... initial election was made possible by the enormous influence of a one-day "women's strike" in 1975. Shops, offices, banks, schools, newspapers, restaurants and theatres closed for the day and men had to look after the children, to prove how much society depended on women. According to Finnbógadottir, "The atmosphere created by the strike certainly helped me to be elected. It gave people the idea that a woman as leader would be a valuable thing" (Finnbógadottir, as quoted in Benn, 1995, p. A6).

This pattern of popular support preceding, and in some cases completely replacing, support from the traditional political party structure also holds for many of the women from dynastic families. In the Philippines, for example, "Aquino insisted that she preferred not to be a candidate, but would relent in the face of popular demand....When more than a million signatures were obtained...Aquino declared her candidacy" (Col, 1993, pp. 20-21). Following her decision to run for the presidency, "Aquino personally visited 68 of 73 provinces and held more than a thousand rallies" (Col, 1993, p. 25). By contrast, Marcos, her opponent, visited only "22 provinces and held only 34 rallies" (Col, 1993, p. 25). Filipinos refer to Aquino's victory as the "People's Revolution."

Similarly, the Pakistan People's Party in London "had trouble accepting the leadership of [Benazir Bhutto,] a young woman whom they had known as a child" (Gupta, 1986 as quoted in Anderson, 1993, p. 49). While they did choose Benazir to lead the Party "largely because of the mystique of her family name and her own suffering under [the ruling military dictator] Zia," they assumed that her leadership would be primarily symbolic (Anderson, 1993, p. 49). Bhutto's own popular support first became evident when "an immense crowd turned out peacefully to cheer their loyalty ... to Benazir" (Weisman, 1986) in April 1986 on her return to Pakistan from exile:

> [F]ar more people [turned out] ... than anyone—politicians, diplomats, or other analysts—had foreseen. Many people had doubted that Benazir Bhutto would find the kind of support

among the people that her father had, but her triumphant return proved them wrong (Anderson, 1993, p. 52).

As history has shown, the Party was also wrong; Bhutto went on to be elected Prime Minister.

Bangladesh presents one of the least subtle expressions of political parties' failure to take women candidates seriously until after they have gained sufficient popular support. Immediately prior to Khaleda Zia's election as Prime Minister of Bangladesh:

> The worldwide press noted that two dead men [appeared to be] ... locked in electoral battle ... [in Bangladesh. The two leading political parties] displayed only the portraits of Mujib-ur Rahman [slain father of candidate Hasina Wajed] and Zia-ur Rahman [slain husband of candidate Khaleda Zia] on their campaign posters, and campaign speeches dwelt only on the qualities of the two charismatic but departed [male] leaders....[The two women candidates for prime minister] Zia's widow and Mujib's daughter were ignored (Opfell, 1993, p. 197).

Bangladesh elected Khaleda Zia prime minister in 1991 and she has remained in power ever since.

This pattern of party reticence is echoed in the behavior of the Indian Congress Party when it initially chose Indira Gandhi as its leader while at the same time assuming that she would serve primarily as a symbol:

> The Congress [Party] President Kamaraj orchestrated Mrs. Gandhi's selection as prime minister because he perceived her to be weak enough that he and the other regional party bosses (known as the Syndicate) could control her, and yet strong enough to beat Desai [the opposition] in a party election because of the high regard for her father (Everett, 1993, p. 110). Kamaraj felt that a woman would be an ideal tool for the Syndicate, especially Nehru's daughter...and once she was properly in power the Syndicate could switch professions: from queenmakers to puppet masters (Moraes, 1980, p. 123).

According to Bhutto, the Indian Congress Party called Indira "a dumb doll behind her back. But this silk-and-steel woman...outmaneuvered them all" (Bhutto, 1989, p. 72, as quoted in Anderson, 1993, p. 49). After coming to power, "Mrs. Gandhi pursued a populist style [including rhetorically championing the needs of the poor] to establish a personal relationship with the electorate unmediated by institutions" (Everett, 1993, p. 113).

The party structure's discounting of women's leadership potential and its replacement with the women's own broad-based popular support is a pattern across countries that goes beyond initial unity to support both democracy and societal change.

Symbolism: Change is Possible

The combination of being an outsider—a woman at a senior leadership level previously completely controlled by men—and beating the electoral odds produces powerful public imagery around the possibility of change for an entire nation: if a woman can win when no one thought she could and when no other woman has ever won before, then other national changes become believably possible. Mary Robinson's presidential acceptance speech captures the coupling of a woman being elected to high office with the possibility of national change:

> I was elected by men and women of all parties and none, by many with great moral courage who stepped out from the faded flags of the Civil War and voted for a new Ireland. And above all by the women of Ireland—Mna na hEireann—who instead of rocking the cradle rocked the system, and who came out massively to make their mark on the ballot paper, and on a new Ireland (RDS, Dublin, November 9, 1990, as reported in Finlay, 1990, p. 1).

People saw Robinson "as a representative of a changing Ireland" (Opfell, 1993, p. 186).

Similarly, commentators view Çiller's election as prime minister of Turkey as a sign and a confirmation of change:

> As Çiller called out, "I'm your mother and your soul sister" to the mass of men packing Ankara Sports Hall, instead of laughing her off stage, they roared approval.... It was the moment that signalled Turkish politics had changed forever (Benn, 1995, p. A3).

"Because few women have played a major role in Turkish politics, Çiller's ascendancy was welcomed as a sign of Turkey's modernity" (Lazerges, 1993, p. 1)—as a sign of change. This was particularly important at the time of Çiller's election, when Turkey, a predominantly Muslim country, was trying to communicate its modernity to the Christian countries of Europe in its bid to gain acceptance into the European Union.

A woman gaining the highest office symbolizes change simply because women have never held high office before; that is, simply because it is new. Corazon Aquino, for example, campaigned in the Philippines stating "Let's try a change. I'm not here for revenge. What's important is that what happened to my husband will never happen again" (Sheehy, 1986, p. 19). It is perhaps not coincidental that a disproportionate number—16 of 25—of the women have led countries that were experiencing major change. Nine were struggling to establish independence (Bangladesh, Dominica, India, Israel, Lithuania, Netherlands-Antilles, Poland, Sri Lanka, and Yugoslavia) and another seven were either attempting to reunite the country following a civil war or experiencing other major societal changes, often including instituting a new form of government (Central African Republic, Haiti, Ireland, Nicaragua, Pakistan, the Philippines, and Portugal). In considering the role of women leaders in the twenty-first century, the symbolism surrounding the possibility of change, and the hope for unity, is both important and attractive.

WOMEN AS LEADERS

While advocating, or choosing not to advocate, traditional women's issues varies among the women leaders, the fact that they are women always remains salient. Few, therefore, attempt to hide the fact that they are women or fail to leverage its symbolic meaning in the political process.

The Visibility of Being a Woman

Because women are new to the elite levels of leadership, they have the advantage of visibility.[32] President François Mitterrand, for example, admittedly created a worldwide media event by appointing Edith Cresson as France's first woman prime minister (Belmont, 1991). Similarly, following Mary Robinson's election to the presidency of Ireland:

Newspapers and magazines in virtually every country in the world carried the story....
[T]he rest of the world understood Ireland to have made a huge leap forward.... Mary
Robinson had joined a very small number of women ... who had been elected to their
country's highest office. It was, quite properly, seen as historic (Finlay, 1990, pp. 149-
150).

Likewise, observers commented that for Turkey's Tansu Çiller, who has not acted as a particular advocate of women's issues, "perhaps her triumph lies in the fact of her being a woman" (Lazerges, 1993, p. 1).

Leveraging Visibility

Çiller highlights a strategy used by many of the women leaders, that of leveraging the symbolic meaning of being a woman in the political process:

During the campaign [Çiller] captivated many people with words proper to a housewife
little accustomed to talking in public, she made use of the traditional and familiar
vocabulary Anatolian people are used to. She repeatedly insisted that she would be a
"mother" for the youth, a "sister" for the middle-aged and a "daughter" for the elderly.
She would "embrace them all with motherly care" (Lazerges, 1993, p. 1).

Rather than attempting to minimize or negate the reality that they are women, the women leaders use the positive imagery surrounding women's family roles of daughter, sister, mother, and grandmother to enhance their position. For example, while Çiller refers to herself as mother, sister, and daughter to the Turkish people, Bhutto refers to herself as a sister to the Pakistani people (Bhutto, 1988; Anderson, 1993); Dominica's Eugenia Charles refers to herself as "mother of the people" (Opfell, 1993, p. 90); and Israel's Golda Meir "built on her grandmotherly image and charmed the nation" (Opfell, 1993, p. 45). Indira Gandhi "sometimes identified herself as mother of her country, as in a 1967 campaign speech to villagers: 'My burden is manifold because scores of my family members are poverty stricken and I have to look after them'" (in Malhotra, 1989, p. 104, as quoted in Everett, 1993, p. 128). With both Aquino and Chamorro being elected in predominantly Catholic countries, each was symbolically positioned as reflecting the Madonna (Col, 1993; Saint-Germain, 1993).

Using these familiar roles positively and powerfully connects the women leaders directly to the people of their respective countries, without relying on the traditional mediating influence of political party hierarchy. In addition, using the familiar imagery of grandmother, mother, sister, and daughter negates many of the sexual connotations often associated with women that tend to undermine women leaders' efficacy—connotations associated primarily with such sexually explicit roles as mistress and seductress. Given the concern at lower and middle management levels about potentially inappropriate sexual relations between men and women in the workplace and the heightened contemporary concern over sexual harassment, it is important to observe that these dynamics and concerns are considerably less relevant in understanding the dynamics of power for the most senior women leaders. Whereas the question the press most frequently asked Margaret Thatcher underscored her visibility as a woman: "What was it like being a woman prime minister?" (to which Thatcher (1993) generally responded that she couldn't answer because she hadn't tried the alternative), neither the press nor the public ever stopped Thatcher from attending a G-7, Commonwealth, or other international conference for fear that she would be sexually harassed.

The reality is not that the women leaders are invisible as women; they are highly visible. However, the equally powerful reality is that the women leaders skillfully use their visibility to their advantage, rather than allowing it to negate the possibility of their success.

Inconsistent Support for Women

Not surprisingly, being a woman leader and concern for traditional women's issues are not synonymous. Similar to all leaders, the women set their political visions and agendas according to the complex set of issues affecting their particular society, not strictly relative to a circumscribed list of concerns that are of primary importance only to one group, in this case, women. Of the women leaders, some supported other women directly by nominating or appointing them to powerful leadership roles both within their cabinet and more broadly within society. Similarly, some of the woman leaders supported a range of issues that most women in their countries considered to be of primary importance to them as women. However, while some supported both women and women's issues, others supported neither.

At one extreme, Britain's Margaret Thatcher promoted "what many referred to as policies that were hostile to women's interests" (Genovese, 1993c, p. 215; see also Genovese, 1993a; Thatcher, 1993, 1995). Similarly, Bangladesh's Khaleda Zia, who is described as "no feminist" (Benn, 1995, p. A3), recently stated that:

> There are no other women in the cabinet. I simply will not appoint an unqualified woman, even to the Ministry of Social and Women's Affairs, just as a token (Zia, as quoted in Benn, 1995, p. A3).

Likewise, Golda Meir, with her overriding focus on establishing the new state of Israel, did not advocate issues of particular concern to women.

India's Indira Gandhi "supported female emancipation...but with less fervour than did her mother" (Opfell, 1993, p. 18). Indira "initiated a birth control program and made contraceptives available in distribution clinics throughout India" (Opfell, 1993, p. 27); however, this was primarily an effort to control India's population. Similarly, Bandaranaike supported political rights and education for women along with family planning in Sri Lanka (Opfell, 1993, p. 5). By contrast, Dominica's Eugenia Charles "has never been interested in being thought of as a 'woman's politician' and few women have advanced far in electoral politics under her leadership" (Benn, 1995, p. A6).

Distinct from many of the women leaders, the Irish elected Mary Robinson on a feminist platform. Robinson describes women's issues as one of the most important reasons that she chose to run for the presidency of Ireland:

> [Robinson]...found that she was [attracted]...to the powerful symbolism inherent in the notion of a woman running for—and winning—the highest office in the land. In a country that had never had a woman in the Supreme Court, or in the highest constitutional offices, and where women had been damaged over the years by the subservience of their position, the election of a woman to the presidency would represent an enormous breakthrough (Finlay, 1990, p. 19).

Similarly, Norway's Gro Harlem Brundtland has consistently supported women and women's concerns, including promoting many women politicians. By selecting eight women for her initial 18-member cabinet, "Brundtland formed the world's first gender-balanced cabinet" (Opfell, 1993, p. 107). According to Brundtland:

> A natural balance of men and women makes prejudiced decisions less likely and gives the greatest possible breadth of experience (Brundtland, as quoted in Opfell, 1993, p. 107).

In stark contrast to most countries, women hold more than a third of the parliamentary seats in Norway (Genovese & Thompson, 1993, p. 2).[33] According to Brundtland:

> The participation of women at the highest levels of Norwegian politics has transformed the country, with the emphasis on environment, employment, children and youth (Benn, 1995, p. A4).

In addition, backed by the strength of her own medical training, Brundtland:

> shocked and delighted world opinion by staunchly defending the right to abortion at the Cairo Conference on World Population, declaring "Morality becomes hypocrisy if it means accepting mothers dying in connection with unwanted pregnancies and illegal abortion and unwanted children living in misery" (Benn, 1995, p. A4).

In addition to Brundtland and Robinson, Iceland's Vigdis Finnbógadottir is well-known as a strong supporter of women and their rights.

In a more limited sense than Brundtland, Robinson, and Finnbógadottir, Isabel Perón "championed the cause of Argentinean women," as had Evita Perón before her (Opfell, 1993, p. 59). Portugal's Pintasilgo, who publicly refers to herself as a feminist, chaired the National Commission on the Status of Women and has written numerous articles and a book on the status of women (Opfell, 1993, pp. 84-87). However, whereas she invited several women to join her government, they all turned her down (Opfell, 1993, p. 86). As Pintasilgo explained:

> Women who are very competent in their fields feel that political life is less pure, that they're going to have to make compromises on an intellectual or moral level (Pintasilgo, as quoted in Opfell, 1993, p. 86).

rance's Edith Cresson succeeded in naming "three women to cabinet posts" and invited other women "to serve as deputy ministers and undersecretaries" (Opfell, 1993, p. 209). By contrast, Poland's Hanna Suchocka explained that her cabinet included no women because:

> None of the coalition parties presented a woman candidate. If I could, I would propose a few women because it is easier to work with women. They are reliable and conscientious (Suckocka, as quoted in Opfell, 1993, pp. 221-222).

Similarly to Pintasilgo, Ertha Pascal-Trouillot wrote several books, including one on *The Judicial Status of the Haitian Women in Social Legislation* (Opfell, 1993, p. 157). Pascal-Trouillot "said she accepted the 'heavy task' [of becoming Haiti's provisional president following the ouster of the former president] in the name of Haitian women" (Opfell, 1993, p. 159). Benazir Bhutto is also a champion of women's rights, although she is highly constrained by the current political and religious environment in Pakistan.

With three strong advocates of both women and their rights currently in office, and a number of their predecessors and contemporaries having taken individual stands in support of women, perhaps an alternative agenda will begin to emerge by the end of the decade. It may take until the early years of the twenty-first century before enough women leaders are in office for a clear women's voice to emerge.

The Process of Leading: Democracy, Consensus, and Unity

Given the small number of global women leaders along with the fact that almost half are currently in office, it is too early to assess whether global women leaders use distinct leadership styles, and if so, if they differ from those of their male counterparts. However, while too early to determine definitive patterns, certain incidents suggest that the global women leaders' approaches to leading may be consistent with those described in prior research on women's leadership styles. In the most comprehensive review of leadership styles of women and men at all levels of organizations, Eagly and Johnson (1990) found that:

> The strongest evidence...for a sex difference in leadership style occurred on the tendency for women to adopt a more democratic or participative style and for men to adopt a more autocratic or directive style....[Of the 370 studies reviewed comparing male and female leaders' behavior] 92% of the comparisons went in the direction of more democratic behaviour from women than men (Eagly & Johnson, 1990, as quoted in Vinnicombe & Colwill, 1995, p. 32).

Whereas these prior studies have not focused on elite levels of leadership nor included many non-American or non-Western women, some parallels appear worth investigating. Of the 25 global women leaders, some also appear to use more democratic approaches, including attempting to minimize hierarchy, using more inclusive processes to build consensus, and actively seeking international and national unity. Some examples follow.

Minimizing Hierarchy

Filipino President Corazon Aquino, for example, chose not to live in the Presidential Malacanang Palace, as her predecessor Marcos had done, but rather worked out of a "small office" (Opfell, 1993, p. 136). Similarly indicative of minimizing hierarchy, Israelis joked that as prime minister, Golda Meir ran committees and legations "like a kibbutz, with everybody on equal terms and on an equal work basis" (Opfell, 1993, p. 43).

Likewise, Lithuania's Prunskiene used her hierarchy-minimizing interpersonal skills to attempt to put Lithuania and the U.S.S.R. on an equal footing and, thus, to alleviate crisis. When Gorbachev demanded that Lithuania rescind its declaration of independence, Prime Minister Prunskiene "remained cool...and brushed away fears":

> "Gorbachev is always saying that he and I are such good friends," she confided, with a smile, "so I am writing a letter to my dear friend saying, 'Mikhail Sergeievich, will you attend to your dear Kazimiera Prunskiene with tanks?'" (Prunskiene, as quoted in Opfell, 1993, p. 164).

Unfortunately, her strategy failed: Gorbachev sent in tanks.

Using Inclusive Processes to Build Consensus

Maria Liberia-Peters of the Netherlands-Antilles, for example, was frequently "complimented for her ability to reach consensus among the ministers" (Opfell, 1993, p. 124). Liberia-Peters continually "reached out, having more meetings with business and community leaders than had any previous prime minister" (Opfell, 1993, p. 125). Similarly, Poland's Suchocka was described as "a politician who wants to reconcile and unify, not antagonize" (Opfell, 1993, p. 222). Immediately after President Lech Walesa met with Suchoka to ask her to consider becoming a candidate for prime minister, Suchocka told the press:

> I think that as a woman I had a better chance of forming a government because women often eliminate conflicts. I agreed to become a candidate for prime minister because I believe that after all these conflicts and arguments, we need a government of national agreement (Opfell, 1993, p. 221).

Likewise, Bangladesh's Khaleda Zia included her constituents by:

> crisscross[ing] the country to talk with people....Thursday evenings she reserved for listening to public grievances....[S]ome nights she walks through the city streets, even in the slums, to listen and learn (Opfell, 1993, p. 199).

Similarly, Mary Robinson keeps the door to president's house open to the people of Ireland, while Iceland's Finnbógadottir, after being elected president "continued to be friendly and accessible. Her office door was open to whomever wanted to talk to her" (Opfell, 1993, p. 99).

Portugal's Pintasilgo underscored the importance she placed on maintaining an inclusive process, stating that: "it heartened her when women felt free to speak up at meetings. To her, their coming forward was more important than the passage of legislative measures" (Opfell, 1993, p. 86).

Creating Unity

Norway's Brundtland is attempting to unify not only Norway, but all the nations of the world. For example, at the opening session of the United Nations' World Commission on the Environment, Brundtland urged:

> There is an urgent need to fashion a long-term integrated global strategy for survival on this planet. We need a strategy for common survival and common security, a strategy for a common future (Brundtland, as quoted in Opfell, 1993, p. 106).

Brundtland urged: "We must learn to think globally and in a long-term perspective. No single region or nation can isolate itself from the rest of the world" (Brundtland, as quoted in Opfell, 1993, p. 108).

In an attempt at creating national unity in the strife torn Philippines, Aquino "as a gesture of reconciliation...freed four Communist leaders....By summer she succeeded in getting the leaders to the negotiating table" (Opfell, 1993, p. 136). Early in her presidency, Aquino announced that:

> There would be general amnesty for all political crimes, including those of her husband's assassins. All partisan banners would be removed from public buildings and monuments (Opfell, 1993, p. 178).

"Aquino placed overriding importance on her fixed conviction that the people [of the Philippines] must relearn the principles of democracy" (Opfell, 1993, p. 136).

As Chamarro began her term, Nicaraguans saw her as "the 'great conciliator,' as a symbol of new hope" (Opfell, 1993, p. 178). By the June following her April inauguration, Chamarro:

> had disarmed the last of the 17,000 member Contra force and persuaded the Sandinista army, Central America's largest, to trim its ranks to 28,000. In September, she staged a ceremonial farewell to arms. After watching 15,000 automatic rifles being dumped from giant trucks into a pit, she tossed red flowers over the guns, then stood back as hoses poured concrete on the tomb (Opfell, 1993, p. 178).

Unfortunately, "Her symbolism...did not bring political peace" (Opfell, 1993, p. 178).

Similarly attempting to bring peace through internal unity, Ireland's Mary Robinson gave her commitment: "I will seek to encourage mutual understanding and tolerance between the different communities on this island" (Opfell, 1993, p. 186). Robinson actively worked for respect and peace among Ireland's Protestants and Catholics, using her own Protestant/Catholic marriage as a symbol for the possibility of national respect, unity, and peace.

HOW IMPORTANT ARE GLOBAL WOMEN LEADERS?

Could women be the answer, at least in part, to the world's needs for new leadership in the twenty-first century? Will bringing people from groups that have previously been severely underrepresented, such as women, into senior leadership positions alter the nature of organizations and the very society in which we live? Not necessarily. Change depends on the type of leadership that women bring to power, not on the mere fact that they are women. If women lead in ways essentially similar to those of contemporary male leaders, then the answer is an unequivocal "no": the ascension of women to positions of power can be predicted to bring equity but not other substantial changes. By increasing their numbers, women will strictly replace men; they will not fundamentally alter either leadership styles or the vision of the global society in which we live. However, at the very minimum, by drawing on both women and men for global leadership positions rather than restricting selection almost exclusively to men, the overall quality of leadership in the world should improve. As *Fortune* magazine accurately observed in the early 1990s:

> The best reason for believing that more women will be in charge before long is that in a ferociously competitive global economy, no company [or country] can afford to waste valuable brainpower simply because it's wearing a skirt (Fisher, 1992, p. 44).

If women's leadership visions and styles do, in fact, differ substantially from those of their male counterparts, then raising the question of women's ability to bring meaningful change to twenty-first century leadership becomes more interesting, and the answer to the question of their ability to bring change becomes a cautious "yes." However, the caveat to be cautious is imperative for several reasons. First, as suggested in the discussion above, it is not yet clear that women currently lead in ways substantially different from those of their male counterparts nor that their future leadership styles will deviate from those of historic male leaders. Second, even if women leaders' approaches are unique, the question is yet to be resolved if they will be congruent with the needs of the twenty-first century. And third, the women leaders may or may not be successful in effecting the changes in process and in outcome that they envision. As Pakistan's Prime Minister Benazir Bhutto recently commented to the United States' First Lady Hillary Rodham Clinton, whom Bhutto referred to as "both tough and a great leader":

> Women who take on tough issues and stake out new territory are often on the receiving end of ignorance. I can personally attest to that (Bhutto in Islamabad, Pakistan, March 26, 1995, as quoted in Dahlburg, 1995, p. A4).

Only as we approach the twenty-first century, and more women leaders have a chance to govern, will we be able to begin to assess the efficacy and impact of global women leaders, both for their individual countries and for the world community. Until that time, perhaps it would be wise to keep the remarks in mind of Burmese opposition leader, Aung San Suu Kyi, as she opened the U.N. Conference on Women in Beijing, China (via videotape):

> For millennia women have dedicated themselves almost exclusively to the task of nurturing, protecting and caring for the young and the old, striving for the conditions of peace that favor life as a whole....It is time to apply in the arena of the world the wisdom and experience that women have gained. Insecure people tend to be intolerant, and their intolerance unleashes forces that threaten the security of others (Suu Kyi, as quoted in Tyler, 1995, p. A9). Without tolerance, the foundation for democracy and respect for human rights cannot be strengthened, and the achievement of peace will remain elusive (Suu Kyi, as quoted in Tempest & Farley, 1995, p. A27).

Acknowledgments: The author would like to express her appreciation to the Social Sciences and Humanities Research Council of Canada for their support of her research. She would also like to thank Pernille Tvaergaard for her assistance in the research and Laura A. Liswood for her insightful comments on the global women leaders.

NOTES

1. Such meta-ethnographic synthesis "constitutes much more than a traditional literature review and therefore represents a form of original research" (Bartholomew, 1995, p. 71, based on Ogawa & Malen, 1991).
2. Of the five who were in office for less than a year, all except Kim Campbell in Canada were appointed, whereas all of the women leaders with long tenures were elected. Kim Campbell was elected by her party, but her party was defeated in the national elections.
3. Whereas the focus of this article is on the most senior global political leaders, a similar number of women have emerged at the most senior levels of economic leadership, including, for example, Britain's Anita Roddick, the founder and CEO of the Body Shop, Italy's Wanda Ferragamo, and American Katherine Graham of the Washington Post Company.
4. For background on Sri Lanka's Sirimavo Bandaranaike, who is both the former and the current Prime Minister of Sri Lanka, see Manor (1989) and Seneviratne (1975), among others.
5. For background on Indira Ghandi, the former Prime Minister of India, see Abbas (1966, 1973), Alexander (1969), Ali (1983), Bhatia (1974), Birla (1987), Brecher (1966), Carras (1979), Indira Gandhi (1973, 1981, 1983, 1986), Sonia Gandhi (1989), Gupte (1985, 1992), Hutheesing (1969), Hutheesing and Hatch (1967), Kalhan (1990), Malhotra (1989), Masani (1974), Masani (1976), Mohan (1967), Sahgal (1978), Vatudeo (1974), and Willcoxen (1969), among others.

6. For background on Golda Meir, the former Prime Minister of Israel, see Agress (1969), Mann (1971), Martin (1988), Golda Meir (1962, 1973, 1975), Menahem Meir (1983), Shenker and Shenker (1970), Slater (1979), and Syrkin (1963, 1969), among others.
7. For background on Isabel Perón, the former President of Argentina, see Alexander (1979), Crasweller (1987), Page (1983), and Weir (1993), among others.
8. For background on Elizabeth Domitien, the former Prime Minister of the Central African Republic, see Opfell (1993).
9. For background on Maria de Lourdes Pintasilgo, the former Prime Minister of Portugal, see Pintasilgo (1980a, 1980b, 1985a, 1985b) and Opfell (1993), among others.
10. For background on Margaret Thatcher, the former Prime Minister of the United Kingdom of Great Britain and Northern Ireland, see Bruce-Gardyne (1984), Cole (1987), Donoughe (1987), Gardiner (1975), Genovese (1993a), Harris (1988), Jenkins (1988), Junor (1983), Kavanaugh (1987), Kavanagh and Seldon (1989), Lewis (1975), Mayer (1979), McFadyeen and Renn (1984), Minogue and Biddess (1987), Murray (1980), Odgen (1990), Opfell (1993), Pearce (1987), Riddel (1983), Smith (1991), Thatcher (1986, 1995), and Young (1989), among others.
11. For background on Vigdís Finnebógadottir, the President of Iceland, see Liswood (1995) and Opfell (1993), among others.
12. For background on the Prime Minister of Dominica, Eugenia Charles, see Liswood (1995) and Opfell (1993), among others.
13. For background on the Prime Minister of Norway, Gro Harlem Brundtland, see Hirsti (1989), Johanssen and Brunvanc (1981), Liswood (1995), Opfell (1993), and *Our Common Future* (1989), among others.
14. For background on the former Prime Minister of Yugoslavia, Milka Planinc, see Opfell (1993), among others.
15. For background on the former Prime Minister of the Netherlands-Antilles, Maria Liberia-Peters, see Liswood (1995) and Opfell (1993), among others.
16. For background on the former President of the Philippines Corazon Aquino, see Burton (1989), Buss (1987), Chrisotomo (1986), Col (1993), Komisar (1987), Liswood (1995), Mercado (1986), Nadel (1987), and Opfell (1993), among others.
17. For background on the Prime Minister of Pakistan, Benazir Bhutto, see Anderson (1993), Bhutto (1989), Liswood (1995), and Opfell (1993), among others.
18. The 11 include Switzerland, which elects a Council of (7) Ministers rather than a president or prime minister. However, the 11 do not include the opposition leader in Myanmar (formerly Burma), Aung San Suu Kyi—daughter of Burmese nationalist leader U Aung San and Nobel laureate—whose party won the 1990 election but who was prevented from taking office by the military (see Everett, 1993, p. 112).
19. For background on the former Prime Minister of Lithuania, Kazimiera Prunskiene, see Liswood (1995) and Opfell (1993), among others.
20. For background on the President of Nicaragua, Violeta Chamorro, see Edmister (1990), Liswood (1995), Opfell (1993), and Saint-Germain (1993), among others.
21. For background on the President of Ireland, Mary Robinson, see Finlay (1990), McQuillon (1994), Liswood (1995), O'Neill (1994), and Opfell (1993), among others.
22. For background on the former President of Haiti, Ertha Pascal-Trouillot, see Opfell (1993), among others.
23. For background on the former Prime Minister of France, Edith Cresson, see Cresson (1976), Liswood (1995), and Opfell (1993), among others.
24. For background on the Prime Minister of Bangladesh, Khaleda Zia, see Liswood (1995) and Opfell (1993), among others.
25. For background on Poland's former Prime Minister, Hanna Suchocka, see Liswood (1995) and Opfell (1993), among others.
26. For background on Canada's former Prime Minister, Kim Campbell, see her forthcoming autobiography.
27. For background on Turkey's Prime Minister, Tansu Çiller, see Liswood (1995), among others.
28. The Women's Leadership Project in conjunction with the Center for Strategic International Studies will hold the first forum for global women leaders in Stockholm in May 1996.

29. After graduating from college in the United States, Corazon Aquino returned to the Philippines to study law but did not finish her degree after getting married.
30. The statistics and country listings used in this section are taken from *Traveler's World Atlas and Guide,* published by Rand McNally & Company, Chicago, 1989. A midpoint year, 1989, was selected for comparable data among the various years that the women have held the office of president or prime minister.
31. Given the range in types of government, the process for selecting a president or prime minister varies from country to country. The majority of the 25 women come from republics with a parliamentary form of government, meaning that the party is elected in the popular election and then the winning party's leader either becomes the national leader or forms a coalition that then governs nationally.
32. Visibility is also consistently named as an advantage among the women expatriate managers and executives who are sent abroad on assignment by their companies. In comparison to their male counterparts, they describe having easier access to clients, receiving more time with clients at meetings, being noticed at receptions, and being remembered better following even brief meetings—all of which are advantages of the visibility that comes from uniqueness (see Adler, 1994).
33. Norway's 36% women in parliament contrasts with 5% in the U.S. House of Representatives, 2% in the U.S. Senate, 7% in the British Parliament, and 10% in Germany's Parliament in the same year (Genovese, 1993, p. 2).

REFERENCES

Abbas, Khwaja Ahmed. (1966). *Indira Gandhi: Return of the red rose.* Bombay, India: Popular Prakashan.
Abbas, Khwaja Ahmed. (1973). *That woman.* Delhi, India: Indian Book Co.
Adler, Nancy J. (1994). Competitive frontiers: Women managing across borders. In Nancy J. Adler & Dafna N. Izraeli (Eds.), *Competitive frontiers: Women managers in a global economy* (pp. 22-40). Cambridge, MA: Blackwell.
Adler, Nancy J., & Izraeli, Dafna N. (Eds.). (1994). *Competitive frontiers: Women managers in a global economy.* Cambridge, MA: Blackwell.
Agress, Eliahu. (1969). *Golda Meir: Portrait of a prime minister.* New York: Sabra Books.
Alexander, M.K. (1969) *Madame Gandhi: A political biography.* North Quincy, MA: Christopher Publishing House.
Alexander, Robert J. (1979) *Juan Domingo Perón: A history.* Boulder, CO: Westview.
Ali, Tarig. (1983). *An Indian dynasty: The story of the Nehru-Gandhi family.* New York: G.P. Putnam's Sons.
Anderson, Nancy Fix. (1993). Benazir Bhutto and dynastic politics: Her father's daughter, her people's sister. In Michael A. Genovese (Ed.), *Women as national leaders* (pp. 41-69). Newbury Park, CA: Sage.
Bartholomew, Susan. (1996). *National institutional context and technological advantage in biotechnology: A comparative analysis of the United States, Great Britain, Germany, and Japan.* Ph.D. dissertation, Faculty of Management, McGill University, Montreal, Canada.
Belmont, Jacques. (1991). Edith Cresson: Pour la premiere fois en France une femme premier ministre [Edith Cresson: France's First Woman Prime Minister]. *L'Actualite en France (Anglais),* (May 16), 7-8.
Benn, Melissa. (1995). The women who rule the world. *Cosmopolitan,* (February).
Bhatia, Krishna. (1974). *Indira: A biography.* New York: Praeger.
Bhutto, Benazir. (1989). *Daughter of destiny: An autobiography.* New York: Simon & Shuster.
Birla, K.K. (1987). *Indira Gandhi: Reminiscences.* Delhi, India: Vikas.
Blondel, Jean. (1987). *Political leadership: Towards a general analysis.* London: Sage.

Brecher, Michael (1966). *Nehru's mantle: The politics of succession*. New York: Praeger.
Bruce-Gardyne, Jock. (1984). *Mrs. Thatcher's first administration: The prophets confounded*. London: Macmillan.
Burton, Sandra. (1989). *Impossible dream: The Marcoses, the Aquinios, and the unfinished revolution*. New York: Warner Books.
Buss, Claude A. (1987). *Corazon Aquino and the people of the Philippines*: Stanford, CA: Portable Stanford.
Carras, Mary. (1979). *Indira Gandhi in the crucible of leadership*. Boston: Beacon.
Chrisotomo, Isabelo T. (1986). *Cory: Profile of a president*. Quezon City, Philippines: J. Kriz.
Col, Jeanne-Marie. (1993). Managing softly in turbulent times: Corazon C. Aquino, president of the Philippines. In Michael A. Genovese (Ed.), *Women as national leaders* (pp. 13-40). Newbury Park, CA: Sage.
Cole, John. (1987). *The Thatcher years*. London: BBC Books.
Conason, Joe (1986). How did an unprepossessing woman undo one of Asia's most durable despots—and emerge as the Philippines' Joan of Arc. *The Village Voice*, 10-13.
Crasweller, Robert D. (1987). *Perón and the enigmas of Argentina*. New York: W.W. Norton & Company.
Cresson, Edith. (1976). *Avec le Soleil* [With the Sun]. Paris: J.C. Larres.
Dahlburg, John-Thor. (1995). Pakistan's Bhutto finds kindred spirit in Mrs. Clinton. *The Los Angeles Times*, (March 27), A4.
Donoughé, Bernard. (1987). *Prime Minister*. London: Jonathon Cape.
Eagly, Alice H., & Johnson, Blair T. (1990). Gender and leadership style: A meta-analysis. *Psychological Bulletin, 108*(2), pp 233-256.
Edminster, Patricia Taylor. (1990). *Nicaragua divided: La Prensa and the Chamorro legacy*. Pensacola, FL: University of West Florida Press.
Everett, Jana. (1993). Indira Gandhi and the exercise of power. In Michael A. Genovese (Ed.), *Women as national leaders* (pp. 103-134). Newbury Park, CA: Sage.
Finlay, Fergus. (1990). *Mary Robinson: A president with a purpose*. Dublin, Ireland: The O'Brien Press.
Fisher, Anne B. (1992). When will women get to the top? *Fortune*, (September 21), 44-56.
Gandhi, Indira. (1986). *Letters to a friend, 1950-1984* (Selected with commentary from correspondence with Dorothy Norman). London: Weidenfeld & Nicolson.
Gandhi, Indira. (1981). *My truth*. Delhi, India: Vikas.
Gandhi, Indira. (1983). *On people & problems*. London: Hodder & Stoughton.
Gandhi, Indira. (1973). *Speeches and writing*. New York: Harper & Row.
Gandhi, Sonia (Ed.). (1989). *Freedom's daughter: Letters between Indira Gandhi and Jawaharlal Nehru*. London: Hodder & Stoughton.
Gardiner, George. (1975). *Margaret Thatcher: From childhood to leadership*. London: Kimber.
Genovese, Michael A. (1993a). Margaret Thatcher and the politics of conviction leadership. In Michael A. Genovese (Ed.), *Women as national leaders* (pp. 177-210). Newbury Park, CA: Sage.
Genovese, Michael A. (Ed.). (1993b). *Women as national leaders*. Newbury Park, California: Sage.
Genovese, Michael A. (Ed.). (1993c). Women as national leaders: What do we know? In Michael A. Genovese (Ed.), *Women as national leaders* (pp. 211-218). Newbury Park, CA: Sage.
Genovese, Michael A., & Thompson, Seth. (1993). Women as chief executives: Does gender matter? In Michael A. Genovese (Ed.), *Women as national leaders* (pp. 1-12). Newbury Park, CA: Sage.
Gupta, S. (1986). Interview with Benazir Bhutto. *India Today* (International Edition), (May 15), 14-15.
Gupte, Pranay. (1992). *Mother India: A political biography of Indira Gandhi*. Charles Scriber's Sons.

Gupte, Pranay. (1985). *Vengence: India after the assassination of Indira Gandhi*. New York: W.W. Norton.
Hall, Stuart, & Jacques, Martin. (1983). *The politics of Thatcherism*. London: Lawrence & Wishart.
Harris, Kenneth. (1988). *Thatcher*. Boston, MA: Little, Brown & Company.
Hirsti, Reidar (Ed.). (1989). *Gro—midt i live t [Gro—In the Middle of Life]*. Oslo, Norway: Tiden Norsk Forlag.
Hutheesing, Krishna. (1969). *Dear to behold: An intimate portrait of Indira Gandhi*. New York: Macmillan.
Hutheesing, Krishna, & Hatch, Alden. (1967). *We Nehrus*. New York: Holt, Rinehart & Winston.
Jenkins, Peter. (1988). *Mrs. Thatcher's revolution: The ending of the socialist era*. Cambridge, MA: Harvard University Press.
Johanssen, Kjell Chr., & Brunvand, Per. (1981). *Gro Norges forste kvinnelige statsminister [Gro: Norway's First Woman Prime Minister]*. Oslo, Norway: Tiden Norsk Forlag.
Junor, Penny. (1983). *Margaret Thatcher*. London: Sidgwick & Jackson.
Kalhan, Promilla. (1990). *Kamala Nehru: An intimate biography*. Delhi, India: NIB Publishers.
Kanter, Rosabeth Moss. (1977). *Men and women of the corporation*. New York: Basic Books.
Kavanagh, Dennis. (1987). *Thatcherism and British politics: The end of consensus*. Oxford, UK: Oxford University Press.
Kavanagh, Dennis, & Seldon, Anthony (Eds.). (1989). *The Thatcher effect: A decade of change*. Oxford, UK: Oxford University Press.
Komisar, Lucy. (1987). *Corazon Aquino: The story of a revolution*. New York: George Braziller.
Lamb, Christina. (1991). *Waiting for Allah: Benazir Bhutto and Pakistan*. London: Penguin Books.
Lazerges, Antoine. (1993). Tansu Çiller/Turkish "Mama." *Diario, 16*(June 15), 2.
Lewis, Russell (1975). *Margaret Thatcher: A personal and political biography*. London: Routledge & Kegan Paul.
Liswood, Laura A. (1995). *Women world leaders*. London: Harper Collins.
Malhotra, I. (1989). *Indira Gandhi: A personal and political biography*. Boston, MA: Northeastern University Press.
Mann, Peggy. (1971). *Golda: The life of Israel's prime minister*. New York: Coward, McMann, Geoghegan.
Manor, James. (1989). *The expedient Utopian: Bandaranaike and Ceylon*. New York: Cambridge University Press.
Martin, Ralph G.(1988). *Golda Meir, the romantic years*. New York: Charles Scribner's Sons.
Masani, Shakuntala. (1974). *The story of India*. Delhi, India: Vikas.
Masani, Zareer. (1976). *Indira Gandhi: A biography*. New York: T.Y. Crowell.
Mayer, Allen J. (1979). *Madame prime minister: Margaret Thatcher and her rise to power*. New York: Newsweek Books.
McFadyeen, Melanie, & Renn, Margaret (1984). *Thatcher's reign*. London: Chatto & Windus.
McQuillon, Deirdre. (1994). *Mary Robinson: A president in progress*. Dublin, Ireland: Gill & Macmillan.
Meir, Golda. (1973). *A land of our own: An oral autobiography*, edited by Marie Syrkin. New York: G.P. Putnam's Sons.
Meir, Golda. (1975). *My life*. New York: Dell.
Meir, Golda. (1962). *This is our strength*, edited by Henry M. Cristman. New York: Macmillan Co.
Meir, Menahem. (1983). *My mother Golda Meir: A son's evocation of life with Golda Meir*. New York: Arbor House.
Mercado, Monina Allerey (Ed.). (1986). *People power: An eyewitness history: The Philippine revolution of 1986*. Manila, Philippines: James B. Reuter, S.J. Foundation.
Minogue, Kenneth, & Biddess, Michael. (1987). *Thatcherism: Personality and politics*. New York: St. Martin's Press.

Mohan, Anand. (1967). *Indira Gandhi: A biography*. New York: Meredith.
Moraes, D. (1980). *Indira Gandhi*. Boston: Little Brown.
Morrison, Ann, White, Randall P., Van Velsor, Ellen, & The Center for Creative Leadership. (1992). *Breaking the glass ceiling: Can women reach the top of America's largest corporations*. Updated edition. Reading, MA: Addison-Wesley.
Murray, Patricia. (1980). *Margaret Thatcher*. London: W.H. Allen.
Nadel, Laura (1987). *Corazon Aquino: Journey to power*. New York: Julian Messner.
Noblit, G.W., & Hare, R.D. (1988). *Meta-ethnography: Synthesizing qualitative studies*. Beverly Hills, CA: Sage.
Ogawa, R.T., & Malen, B. (1991). Towards rigor in reviews of multivocal literatures: Applying the exploratory case study method. *Review of Educational Research, 61(3)*, 265-286.
Ogden, Chris. (1990). Maggie, an intimate portrait of a woman in power. New York: Simon & Shuster.
O'Neill, Juliet. (1994). Here's to you, Mrs. Robinson. *The Montreal Gazette*, (July), B3.
Opfell, Olga S. (1993). *Women prime ministers and presidents*. Jefferson, NC: McFarland & Company.
O'Sullivan, Michael. (1993). *Mary Robinson: A president with a purpose*. Dublin, Ireland: Blackwater Press.
Our Common Future (Brundtland Report). (1989). New York: Oxford University Press.
Page, Joseph A. (1983). *Perón, a biography*. New York: Random House.
Pearce, Edward. (1987). *Looking down on Margaret Thatcher*. London: Hamish Hamilton.
Pintasilgo, Maria de Lourdes. (1985a). *As Minhas Respostas [My Answer]*. Lisbon, Portugal: Dom Quixote.
Pintasilgo, Maria de Lourdes. (1985b). Dimensoes da mudanca [Dimensions of Change]. Lisbon, Portugal: Afrontamento.
Pintasilgo, Maria de Lourdes. (1980a). Les Nouveaux Feminismes: Question pour les chrétians? [The New Feminists: Questions for Christians]. Paris: Editions du Cerf.
Pintasilgo, Maria de Lourdes. (1980b). *Sulcos do nosso querer commun [Furrows of Our Common Ground]*. Lisbon, Portugal: Afrontamento.
Riddell, Peter. (1983). The Thatcher government. London: Robertson.
Sahgal, Nayantara. (1978). *Indira Gandhi: Her rise to power*. New York: Unger.
Saint-Germain, Michelle A. (1993). Women in power in Nicaragua: Myth and reality. In Michael A. Genovese (Ed.), *Women as national leaders* (pp. 70-102). Newbury Park, CA: Sage.
Seneviratne, Maureen. (1975). *Sirimavo Bandaranaike: The world's first woman prime minister*. Colombo, Sri Lanka: Hanta Publisher, in association with Laklooms.
Shenkar, Israel, & Shenkar, Mary (Eds.). (1970). *As good as Golda: The warmth and wisdom of Israel's prime minister*. New York: McCall.
Slater, Robert. (1979). *Golda, the unnamed queen of Israel: A pictorial biography*. Middle Village, NY: Jonathon David.
Smith, Geoffrey. (1991). *Reagan and Thatcher*. New York: W.W. Norton & Company.
Syrkin, Marie. (1969). *Golda Meir, Israel's leader*. New York: G.P. Putnam's Sons.
Syrkin, Marie. (1963). *Golda Meir, woman with a cause*. New York: G.P. Putnam's Sons.
Sheehy, Gail. (1986). The passage of Corazon Aquino. *Washington Post Parade*, (June 24), 14-20.
Skyes, Patricia Lee. (1993). Women as national leaders: Patterns and prospects. In Michael A. Genovese (Ed.), *Women as national leaders* (pp. 219-220). Newbury Park, CA: Sage.
Tempest, Rone, & Farley, Maggie. (1995). Women open forum with protests. *The Los Angeles Times*, (September 1), A1, A27.
Thatcher, Margaret. (1993). *The Downing Street years*. New York: Harper Collins.
Thatcher, Margaret. (1995). *The path to power*. New York: Harper Collins.
Thatcher, Margaret. (1986). *In defense of freedom*. London: Autumn Press.

Thompson, Seth. (1993). Golda Meir: A very public life. In Michael A. Genovese (Ed.), *Women as national leaders* (pp. 135-160). Newbury Park, CA: Sage.

Traveler's World Atlas and Guide. (1989). Chicago: Rand McNally & Company.

Turner, Frederick C., & Miguens, Jose (Eds.). (1983). *Juan Perón and the reshaping of Argentina.* Pittsburg, PA: University of Pittsburg.

Tyler, Patrick E. (1995). U.N. forum hears speech by Burmese. *The New York Times,* (September 1), A9.

Vatudeo, Uma. (1974). *Indira Gandhi: Revolution in restraint.* Delhi, India: Vikas.

Vinnicombe, Susan, & Colwill, Nina L. (1995). *The essence of women in management.* London: Prentice Hall.

Weir, Sara J. (1993). Peronisma: Isabel Perón and the politics of Argentina. In Michael A. Genovese (Ed.), *Women as national leaders* (pp. 161-178). Newbury Park, CA: Sage.

Weisman, S.R. (1986). A daughter returns to Pakistan to cry for victory. *New York Times,* (April 11), 2.

Willcoxen, Harriet. (1969). *First lady of India: The story of Indira Gandhi.* Garden City, NY: Doubleday.

Young, Hugo. (1989). *The iron lady: A biography of Margaret Thatcher.* New York: Farrar, Straus, Giroux.

[27]
CULTURAL INFLUENCES ON LEADERSHIP AND ORGANIZATIONS
PROJECT GLOBE

ABSTRACT

GLOBE is both a research program and a social entity. The GLOBE social entity is a network of 170 social scientists and management scholars from 62 cultures throughout the world, working in a coordinated long-term effort to examine the interrelationships between societal culture, organizational culture and practices, and organizational leadership. The meta-goal of the Global Leadership and Organizational Effectiveness (GLOBE) Research Program is to develop an empirically based theory to describe, understand, and predict the impact of cultural variables on leadership and organizational processes and the effectiveness of these processes.

This monograph presents a description of the GLOBE research program and some initial empirical findings resulting from GLOBE research. A central question in this part of the research concerns the extent to which specific leadership attributes and behaviors are universally endorsed as contributing to effective leadership and the extent to which the endorsement of leader attributes and behaviors is culturally contingent.

We identified six global leadership dimensions of culturally endorsed implicit theories of leadership (CLTs). Preliminary evidence indicates that these dimensions are significantly correlated with isomorphic dimensions of societal and organizational culture. These findings are consistent with the hypothesis that selected cultural differences strongly influence important ways in which people think about leaders as well as societal norms concerning the status, influence, and privileges granted to leaders.

The hypothesis that charismatic/value-based leadership would be universally endorsed is strongly supported. Team-oriented leadership is strongly correlated with charismatic/value-based leadership, and also universally endorsed. Humane and participative leadership dimensions are nearly universally endorsed. The endorsement of the remaining global leadership dimensions—self-protective and autonomous leadership—varies by culture.

We identified 21 specific leader attributes and behaviors that are universally viewed as contributing to leadership effectiveness. Eleven of the specific leader characteristics composing the global charismatic/value-based leadership dimension were among these 21 attributes. Eight specific leader characteristics were universally viewed as impediments to leader effectiveness. We also identified 35 specific leader characteristics that are viewed as contributors in some cultures and impediments in other cultures. We present these, as well as other findings, in more detail in this monograph.

A particular strength of the GLOBE research design is the combination of quantitative and qualitative data. Elimination of common method and common source variance is also a strength of the design strategy. Future directions, research strategies, and anticipated contributions are presented in anticipation of continued GLOBE efforts.

Robert J. House
University of Pennsylvania
Principal Investigator

Paul J. Hanges
University of Maryland
Principal Investigator;

S. Antonio Ruiz-Quintanilla
Cornell University
GLOBE Coordinating Team

Peter W. Dorfman
New Mexico State University
GLOBE Coordinating Team and representing Mexico

Mansour Javidan
University of Calgary
GLOBE Coordinating Team and representing Iran

Marcus Dickson
Wayne State University
Principal Investigator

Vipin Gupta
Fordham University
Senior Globe Research Associate

and

Ikhlas A. Abdalla, Arab Fund for Economic & Social Development, representing Qatar

Babajide Samuel Adetoun, Appropriate Development Associates, representing Nigeria

Ram N. Aditya, Louisiana Tech University, Senior GLOBE Research Associate

Hafid Agourram, University of Quebec—Montreal, representing Morocco

Adebowale Akande, Potchefstroom University, representing South Africa

Bolanle Elizabeth Akande, Center for Sustainable Development and Gender Issues, representing Nigeria

Staffan Akerblom, Stockholm School of Economics, representing Sweden and member of the GLOBE Coordinating Team

Carlos Altschul, Universidad de Buenos Aires, representing Argentina

Eden Alvarez-Backus, Sony Electronics, representing the Philippines

Julian Andrews, University of Alberta, representing Canada

Maria Eugenia Arias, independent consultant, representing Costa Rica

Mirian Sofyan Arif, University of Indonesia, representing Indonesia

Neal M. Ashkanasy, University of Queensland, representing Australia

Arben Asllani, Bellevue University, representing Albania

Guiseppe Audia, London Business School, representing Italy

Gyula Bakacsi, Budapest University of Economic Sciences, representing Hungary

Helena Bendova, Jihoceske Univerzit, representing the Czech Republic

David Beveridge, Western Illinois University, representing Bolivia

Rabi S. Bhagat, University of Memphis, representing the U.S.A.

Alejandro Blacutt, Universidad Catolica Bolivian, representing Bolivia

Jiming Bao, Fudan University, representing China

Domenico Bodega, University of Luigi Bocconi, representing Italy

Muzaffer Bodur, Bogazici University, representing Turkey

Simon Booth, University of Reading, representing England

Annie E. Booysen, University of South Africa, representing South Africa

Dimitrios Bourantas, Athens University of Economics and Business, representing Greece

Klas Brenk, Univerziti Ljubljana, representing Slovenia

Felix Brodbeck, University of Munich, representing Germany and member of the GLOBE Coordinating Team

Dale Everton Carl, University of Calgary, representing Canada

Philippe Castel, Universite de Bourgogne, representing France

Chieh-Chen Chang, National Sun Yat-Sen University, representing Taiwan

Sandy Chau, Lingnam College, representing Hong Kong

Frenda Cheung, Hong Kong Polytechnic University, representing Hong Kong

Jagdeep Chhokar, Indian Institute of Management—Ahmedabad, representing India and member of the GLOBE Coordinating Team

Jimmy Chiu, City University of Hong Kong, representing Hong Kong

Peter Cosgriff, Lincoln University, representing New Zealand

Ali Dastmalchian, University of Lethbridge, representing Iran

Jose Augusto Dela Coleta, Centro Universitario do Triangulo, representing Brazil

Marilia Ferreira Dela Coleta, Universidade Federal de Uberlandia, representing Brazil

Deanne N. den Hartog, Vrije Universiteit—Amsterdam, representing the Netherlands

Marc Deneire, University of Nancy 2, representing France

Gemma Donnelly-Cox, University of Dublin—Trinity College, representing Ireland

Christopher Earley, University of Indiana, representing China

Mahmoud A. E. Elgamal, Kuwait University, representing Kuwait

Miriam Erez, Israel Institute of Technology, representing Israel
Sarah Falkus, University of Queensland, representing Australia
Mark Fearing, Lincoln University, representing New Zealand
Richard H. G. Field, University of Alberta, representing Canada
Carol Fimmen, Western Illinois University, representing Bolivia
Michael Frese, University of Giessen, representing Germany
Pingping Fu, Chinese University of Hong Kong, representing China
Mikhail V. Gratchev, Institute of World Economy and International Relations, representing Russia
Celia Gutierrez, Complutense University, representing Spain
Mohamed Abou Hhashha, Alexandria University, representing Egypt
Frans Marti Hartanto, Institut Technologi Bandung, representing Indonesia
Markus Hauser, University of Pennsylania, Senior Globe Research Associate
Ingalill Holmberg, Stockholm School of Economics, representing Sweden
Marina Holzer, Altschul Consultores, representing Argentina
Michael Hoppe, Center for Creative Leadership, representing the U.S.A.
Jon P. Howell, New Mexico State University, representing Mexico
Elena Ibrieva, University of Nebraska—Lincoln, representing Kazakhstan
John C. Ickis, INCAE, representing Costa Rica
Zakaria Ismail, Universiti Kebangsaan Malaysia, representing Malaysia
Slawomir Jarmuz, University of Opole, representing Poland
Jorge Correia Jesuino, Instituto Superior de Sciencias do Trabalho e da Empresa, representing Portugal
Li Ji, Hong Kong Baptist University, representing Singapore
Kuen-Yung Jone, Kaohsiung Medical College, representing Taiwan
Geoffrey Jones, University of Reading, representing England
Revaz Jorbenadse, Tbilisi State University, representing Georgia
Hayat Kabasakal, Bogazici University, representing Turkey
Mary Keating, University of Dublin—Trinity College, representing Ireland
Jeffrey C. Kennedy, Lincoln University, representing New Zealand
Jay S. Kim, Ohio State University, representing South Korea
Giorgi Kipiani, Georgian Academy of Sciences, representing Georgia
Matthias Kipping, University of Reading, representing England
Edvard Konrad, Universiti Ljubljana, representing Slovenia
Paul L. Koopman, Vrije Universiteit-Amsterdam, representing the Netherlands
Fuh-Yeong Kuan, Shu-Te Institute of Technology, representing Taiwan
Alexandre Kurc, University of Nancy 2, representing France
Marie-Francoise Lacassagne, Universite de Bourgogne, representing France
Sang M. Lee, University of Nebraska—Lincoln, representing Albania and Kazakhstan

Christopher Leeds, University of Nancy 2, representing France

Francisco Leguizamon, INCAE, representing Costa Rica

Martin Lindell, Swedish School of Economics and Business Administration, representing Finland

Jean Lobell, AcXEL International, representing the Philippines

Fred Luthans, University of Nebraska—Lincoln, representing Albania and Kazakhstan

Jerzy Maczynski, University of Wroclaw, representing Poland

Norma Mansor, University of Malaysia, representing Malaysia

Gillian Martin, University of Dublin—Trinity College, representing Ireland

Michael Martin, University of Nebraska—Lincoln, representing Albania

Sandra M. Martinez, New Mexico State University, representing Mexico

Cecilia McMillen, University of San Francisco de Quito, representing Costa Rica

Emiko Misumi, Institute for Group Dynamics, representing Japan

Jyuji Misumi, Institute for Group Dynamics, representing Japan

Moudi al-Homoud, Kuwait University, representing Kuwait

Nabil M. Morsi, Alexandria University, representing Egypt

Phyllisis M. Ngin, Melbourne Business School, representing Singapore

Jeremiah O'Connell, Bentley College, representing Spain

Enrique Ogliastri, Universidad de los Andes, representing Colombia and member of the GLOBE Coordinating Team

Nancy Papalexandris, Athens University of Economics and Business, representing Greece

T. K. Peng, I-Shou University, representing Taiwan

Maria Marta Preziosa, Instituto para el Desarrollo de Ejecutivos en la Argentina, representing Argentina

Jose M. Prieto, Complutense University, representing Spain

Boris Rakitsky, Institute of Perspectives and Problems of the Country, representing Russia

Gerhard Reber, Johannes Kepler University, representing Austria

Nikolai Rogovsky, International Labor Organization; representing Russia

Joydeep Roy-Bhattacharya, Independent literary author, GLOBE Project Manager (1994-1998)

Amir Rozen, Israel Institute of Technology, representing Israel

Argio Sabadin, Universiti Ljubljana, representing Slovenia

Majhoub Sahaba, Groupe EFET, representing Morocco

Colombia Salom de Bustamante, Universidad de los Andes, representing Venezuela

Carmen Santana-Melgoza, Smith College, representing Mexico

Daniel Alan Sauers, Lincoln University, representing New Zealand

Jette Schramm-Nielsen, Copenhagen Business School, representing Denmark;

Majken Schultz, Copenhagen Business School, representing Denmark

Zuqi Shi, Fudan University, representing China

Camilla Sigfrids, Swedish School of Economics and Business Administration, representing Finland

Ahamed Sleem, Alexandria University, representing Egypt

Kye-Chung Song, Chungnam National University, representing South Korea

Erna Szabo, Johannes Kepler University, representing Austria

Albert C. Teo, National University of Singapore, representing Singapore

Henk Thierry, University of Tilburg, representing the Netherlands

Jann Hidayat Tjakranegara, Institut Technologi Bandung, representing Indonesia

Sylvana Trimi, University of Nebraska—Lincoln, representing Albania

Anne S. Tsui, Hong Kong University of Science and Technology, representing China

Pavakanum Ubolwanna, Thammasat University, representing Thailand

Marius W. van Wyk, University of South Africa, representing South Africa and member of the GLOBE Coordinating Team

Marie Vondrysova, University of South Bohemia, representing the Czech Republic

Jürgen Weibler, University of Hagen, representing Switzerland

Celeste Wilderom, Tilburg University, representing the Netherlands

Rongxian Wu, Suzhou University, representing China

Rolf Wunderer, University of St. Gallen, representing Switzerland

Nik Rahiman Nik Yakob, Universiti Kebangsaan Malaysia, representing Malaysia

Yongkang Yang, Fudan University, representing China

Zuoqiu Yin, Fudan University, representing China

Michio Yoshida, Kumamoto University, representing Japan

Jian Zhou, Fudan University, representing China[1]

INTRODUCTION

To what extent is leadership culturally contingent? The Global Leadership and Organizational Behavior Effectiveness Research Program (GLOBE), as well as a substantial amount of other empirical research (House, Wright, & Aditya, 1997), has demonstrated that what is expected of leaders, what leaders may and may not do, and the status and influence bestowed on leaders vary considerably as a result of the cultural forces in the countries or regions in which the leaders function. For instance, Americans, Arabs, Asians, English, Eastern Europeans, French, Germans, Latin Americans, and Russians tend to glorify the concept of leadership and consider it reasonable to discuss leadership in the context of both the political and the organizational arenas. People of the Netherlands, Scandinavia, and Germanic Switzerland often have distinctly different views of leadership. Consider the following statements taken from interviews with managers from various countries:

- Americans appreciate two kinds of leaders. They seek empowerment from leaders who grant autonomy and delegate authority to subordinates. They also respect the bold, forceful, confident, and risk-taking leader, as personified by John Wayne.
- The Dutch place emphasis on egalitarianism and are skeptical about the value of leadership. Terms like *leader* and *manager* carry a stigma. If a father is employed as a manager, Dutch children will not admit it to their schoolmates.
- Arabs worship their leaders—*as long as they are in power!*
- Iranians seek power and strength in their leaders.
- Malaysians expect their leaders to behave in a manner that is humble, modest, and dignified.
- The French expect leaders to be "cultivated"—highly educated in the arts and in mathematics.

Does extant empirical research literature confirm the expectations that are implied in the preceding statements? Because we are just beginning to understand how the role of culture influences leadership and organizational processes, numerous research questions remain unanswered. What characteristics of a society make it more or less susceptible to leadership influence? To what extent do cultural forces influence the expectations that individuals have with respect to the role of leaders and their behavior? To what extent will leadership styles vary in accordance with culturally specific values and expectations? To what extent does culture moderate relationships between organizational processes, organizational form, and organizational effectiveness? What principles or laws of leadership and organizational processes transcend cultures?

We do not have comprehensive answers to these questions, but progress has been made in a number of areas (see House et al. [1997] for an extensive review of relevant leadership literature). This chapter describes a programmatic effort undertaken to explore the fascinating and complex effects of culture on leadership and organizational processes

THE NEED FOR CROSS-CULTURAL LEADERSHIP THEORY AND RESEARCH

Given the increased globalization of industrial organizations and increased interdependencies among nations, the need for better understanding of cultural influences on leadership and organizational practices has never been greater. Situations that leaders and would-be leaders must face are highly complex, constantly changing, and difficult to interpret. More than ever before, managers of international firms face fierce and rapidly changing international competition. The trend toward the global economic village is clear, and the twenty-first century may very well become known as the century of the "global world" (McFarland, Senen, & Childress, 1993). Since effective organizational leadership is critical to the success of international operations, this globalization of industrial organizations presents numerous organizational and leadership challenges. For instance, the cultural diversity of employees found in worldwide multinational organizations presents a substantial challenge with respect to the design of multinational organizations and their leadership. What practical knowledge and advice does the management literature provide to assist leaders in adapting to cultural constraints? Unfortunately, though the need for such information clearly exists, little if any help is available at this time (House & Aditya, 1997; House et al., 1997). Cross-cultural research and the development of cross-cultural theory are needed to fill this knowledge gap.

From a scientific and theoretical perspective, compelling reasons exist for considering the role of societal and organizational culture in influencing leadership and organizational processes. Because the goal of science is to develop universally valid theories, laws, and principles, there is a need for leadership and organizational theories that transcend cultures. There are inherent limitations in transferring theories across cultures. What works in one culture may not work in another culture. As Triandis (1993) suggests, leadership researchers will be able to "finetune" theories by investigating cultural variations as parameters of those theories. In addition, a focus on cross-cultural issues can help researchers uncover new relationships by forcing investigators to include a much broader range of variables often not considered in contemporary theories, such as the importance of religion, language, ethnic background, history, or political systems (Dorfman, 1996). Thus, cross-cultural research may also help to develop new theories of leadership and organizational processes and effectiveness, as well as to fine-tune existing theories

Table 1. GLOBE-Participating Countries

Albania	France	Kazakhstan	(Caucasian sample)
Argentina	Georgia	Kuwait	South Africa
Australia	Germany	Malaysia	(Indigenous sample)
Austria	(former FRG)	Mexico	South Korea
Bolivia	Germany	Morocco	Spain
Brazil	(former GDR)	Namibie	Sweden
Canada	Greece	Netherlands	Switzerland
China	Guatemala	New Zealand	(French speaking)
Colombia	Hong Kong	Nigeria	Switzerland
Costa Rica	Hungary	Philippines	(German speaking)
Czech Republic	India	Poland	Taiwan
Denmark	Indonesia	Portugal	Thailand
Ecuador	Iran	Qatar	Turkey
Egypt	Ireland	Russia	United States
El Salvador	Israel	Singapore	Venezuela
England	Italy	Slovenia	Zambia
Finland	Japan	South Africa	Zimbabwe

by incorporating cultural variables as antecedents and moderators within existing theoretical frameworks.

While the research literature on cross-cultural leadership has blossomed in the last 15 years (House et al., 1997), it is often atheoretical, fraught with methodological problems, and fragmented across a wide variety of publication outlets (Dorfman, 1996). More important, far more questions than answers exist regarding the culturally contingent aspects of leadership. Project GLOBE is intended to contribute theoretical developments and empirical findings to fill this knowledge deficiency.

THE GLOBE RESEARCH PROGRAM

The idea of a global research program concerned with leadership and organization practices (form and processes) was conceived in the summer of 1991. In the spring of 1993, a grant proposal was written that followed a substantial literature review and development of a pool of 753 questionnaire items. GLOBE was funded in October 1993, and the recruiting of GLOBE Country Co-Investigators (referred to hereafter as CCIs) began.[2] In this section, we present an overview of Project GLOBE.

GLOBE is a multi-phase, multi-method project in which investigators spanning the world are examining the interrelationships between societal culture, organizational culture, and organizational leadership. One hundred seventy social scientists and management scholars from 62 cultures representing all major regions of the world are engaged in this long-term programmatic series of cross-cultural leadership studies. Table 1 lists the countries in which cultures are being studied as part of the GLOBE research.[3]

GLOBE was conceived and initially designed by the first author of this monograph as the Principal Investigator. He was later joined by Michael Agar, Marcus Dickson, Paul Hanges, and S. Antonio Ruiz-Quintanilla as Co-Principal Investigators. Because cross-cultural research requires knowledge of all the cultures being studied, we have developed a network of approximately 170 Country Co-Investigators (CCIs) who are social scientists or management scholars from around the world. The CCIs, together with the Principal Investigators and Research Associates, constitute the members of the GLOBE community.

The CCIs are responsible for leadership of the project in a specific culture in which they have expertise. Their activities include collecting quantitative and qualitative data, ensuring the accuracy of questionnaire translations, writing country-specific descriptions of their cultures in which they interpret the results of the quantitative data analyses in their own cultural context, and contributing insights from their unique cultural perspectives to the ongoing GLOBE research. In most cases, CCIs are natives of the cultures from which they are collecting data, and in most cases, they reside in that culture. Some of the CCIs are persons with extensive experience in more than one culture. Most cultures have a research team of between two and five CCIs working on the project. The GLOBE Coordinating Team (GCT) coordinates the activities of the project as a whole.[4] The GCT is also responsible for designing quantitative measures and qualitative methods, performing cross-cultural statistical analyses, and coordinating efforts to present results of the project to the scholarly community. To date, CCIs have made over 90 presentations at professional meetings and over 30 papers and book chapters have been written.

An initial goal of the GLOBE Project was to develop societal and organizational measures of culture and leader attributes that are appropriate to use across all cultures. We have accomplished this in the first phase of the research project. Items were analyzed by conventional psychometric procedures (e.g., item analysis, factor analysis, generalizability analysis) to establish nine dimensions of societal culture and nine isomorphic dimensions of organizational culture. In addition, as part of the first phase of the project, we were able to identify six underlying dimensions of global leadership patterns that are viewed by managers as contributors or impediments to outstanding leadership. The psychometric properties of these scales exceed conventional standards (Hanges, House, Dickson, Ruiz-Quintanilla, Dorfman & 103 coauthors, 1997, under review).

One of the major questions addressed by GLOBE research concerns the dimensions by which societal and organizational cultures can be measured. We identified nine dimensions of cultures that differentiate societies and organizations. That is, with respect to these dimensions, there is high within-culture and within-organization agreement and high between-culture and between-organization differentiation.

A second major question addressed by GLOBE concerns the extent to which specific leader attributes and behaviors are universally endorsed as contributing to effective leadership, and the extent to which attributes and behaviors are linked to cultural characteristics. We found that cultures can be differentiated on the basis of the leader behaviors and attributes that their members endorse. We also found high within-culture agreement with respect to leader attributes and behaviors that are viewed as contributors or impediments to effective leadership. These leader behaviors and attributes constitute *C*ulturally endorsed implicit *L*eadership *T*heories (CLTs).

Of the six global leader behavior dimensions of CLTs, two of these dimensions are universally viewed as contributors to effective leadership, one is nearly universally endorsed as a contributor, and one is nearly universally perceived as an impediment to outstanding leadership. The endorsement of the remaining two dimensions varies by culture. In addition, we identified 21 specific leader attributes or behaviors that are universally viewed as contributors to leadership effectiveness and 8 that are universally viewed as impediments to leader effectiveness. Further, 35 specific leader attributes or behaviors are viewed as contributors in some cultures and impediments in other cultures. We present these, as well as other findings, in more detail on the following pages.

Project GLOBE also addresses questions relevant to how societal cultural forces influence organizational form and effectiveness. We describe the research questions, hypotheses, and research design relevant to both leadership and organizational aspects of GLOBE in some detail further on.

Project GLOBE employs both quantitative and qualitative methods to provide richly descriptive, yet scientifically valid, accounts of cultural influences on leadership and organizational processes. Quantitative aspects include measurement of societal culture, organizational culture, and leadership attributes and behaviors. Contemporaneous with the quantitative analysis, qualitative culture-specific research is being conducted in the same cultures. Qualitative culture-specific interpretations of local behaviors, norms, and practices are being developed through content analysis of data derived from interviews, focus groups, and published media.

The planned GLOBE research program consists of four phases. GLOBE Phase 1 was devoted to the development of research instruments. Phase 2 is devoted to assessment of nine dimensions of societal and organizational cultures and tests of hypotheses relevant to the relationships among these cultural dimensions and cultural-level implicit theories of leadership. Phase 2 also concerns relationships between organizational contingencies (size, technology, environment), organizational strategy, organizational form and processes, and organizational effectiveness. Phase 2 data collection has been completed. A projected third phase of the research project will investigate the impact and effectiveness of specific leader behaviors and styles on subordinates' attitudes and job performances and on leader and organizational effectiveness. Phase 3 will also be directed toward the identification of emic (culture-specific) aspects of leadership and organizational practices, as well as the longitudinal effects of leadership and organizational practices and organizational form on organizational effectiveness. A projected fourth phase will employ field and laboratory experiments to confirm, establish causality, and extend previous findings.

GLOBE Objectives

The meta-goal of GLOBE is to develop an empirically based theory to describe, understand, and predict the impact of specific cultural variables on leadership and organizational processes and the effectiveness of these processes. Specific objectives include answering the following fundamental questions:

1. Are there leader behaviors, attributes, and organizational practices that are universally accepted and effective across cultures?
2. Are there leader behaviors, attributes, and organizational practices that are accepted and effective in only some cultures?
3. How do attributes of societal and organizational cultures affect the kinds of leader behaviors and organizational practices that are accepted and effective?
4. What is the effect of violating cultural norms relevant to leadership and organizational practices?
5. What is the relative standing of each of the cultures studied on each of the nine core dimensions of culture?
6. Can the universal and culture-specific aspects of leader behaviors, attributes, and organizational practices be explained in terms of an underlying theory that accounts for systematic differences across cultures?

Construct Definitions of Leadership and Culture

Leadership has been a topic of study for social scientists for much of the twentieth century (Yukl, 1994), yet there is no consensually agreed-upon definition of leadership (Bass, 1990). A seemingly endless variety of definitions have been developed, but almost all have at their core the concept of influence—leaders influence others to help accomplish group or organizational objectives. The variety of definitions is appropriate, as the degree of specificity of the definition of leadership should be driven by the purposes of the research. Smith and Bond (1993) specifically note: "If we wish to make statements about universal or etic aspects of social behavior, they need to be phrased in highly abstract ways. Conversely, if we wish to highlight the meaning of these generalizations in specific or emic ways, then we need to refer to more precisely specified events or behaviors" (p. 58). The GLOBE goals are both etic (investigating aspects of leadership and organizational practices that are comparable across cultures) and emic (examining and describing culture-specific differences in leadership and organizational practices and their effectiveness). We recognize and expect that the evaluative and semantic interpretation of the term *leadership,* and the ways in which leadership and organizational processes are enacted, are likely to vary across cultures, but we also expect that some aspects of leadership will be universally endorsed.

In August 1994 the first GLOBE research conference was held at the University of Calgary in Canada. Fifty-four researchers from 38 countries gathered to develop a collective understanding of the project and to initiate its implementation. In this meeting considerable time was spent generating a working definition of *leadership* that reflected the diverse viewpoints held by GLOBE researchers. A consensus with respect to a universal definition of organizational leadership emerged: *the ability of an individual to influence, motivate, and enable others to contribute toward the effectiveness and success of the organizations of which they are members.* Note that this is a definition of *organizational* leadership, not leadership in general. Simonton (1994, p. 411), speaking of leadership in general, defines a leader as a "group member whose influence on group attitudes, performance, or decision making greatly exceeds that of the average member of the group." The GLOBE project concerns the phenomenon of organizational leadership, not leadership in general.

As with *leadership,* there is no consensually agreed upon definition among social scientists for the term *culture.* Generally speaking, *culture* is used by social scientists to refer to a set of parameters of collectives that differentiate the collectives from each other in meaningful ways. The focus is on the "sharedness" of cultural indicators among members of the collective. The specific criteria used to differentiate cultures usually depend on the preferences of the investigator and the issues under investigation, and tend to reflect the discipline of the investigator. For the GLOBE research program, we theoretically define *culture* as shared motives, values, beliefs, identities, and interpretations or meanings of significant events that result from common experiences of members of collectives and are transmitted across age generations. Note that these are *psychological* attributes and that this definition can be applied at both the societal and the organizational levels of analysis.

GLOBE Operational Definition of Culture

The most parsimonious operationalizations of *societal* culture consist of commonly experienced language, ideological belief systems (including religion and political belief systems), ethnic heritage, and history. Parallel to this, the most parsimonious operationalizations of *organizational* culture consist of commonly used nomenclature within an organization, shared organizational values, and organizational history. For purposes of GLOBE research, therefore, culture is operationally defined by the use of measures reflecting two kinds of cultural manifestations: (1) the commonality (agreement) among members of collectives with respect to the psychological *attributes* specified earlier; and (2) the commonality of observed and reported *practices* of entities such as families, schools, work organizations, economic and legal systems, and political institutions.

The common cultural attributes we have chosen to measure are indicators of shared modal values of collectives. These values are expressed in response to questionnaire items in the form of judgments of *What Should Be*. Emphasis on values grows out of an anthropological tradition of culture assessment (Kluckhohn & Strodtbeck, 1961). Another measure of culture, modal practices, is measured by indicators assessing *What Is*, or *What Are*, common behaviors, institutional practices, proscriptions and prescriptions. This approach to the assessment of culture grows out of a psychological/behavioral tradition, in which it is assumed that shared values are enacted in behaviors, policies, and practices. This assumption will be tested as part of Project GLOBE.

The GLOBE Conceptual Model

The theoretical base that guides the GLOBE research program is an integration of implicit leadership theory (Lord & Maher, 1991), value/belief theory of culture (Hofstede, 1980), implicit motivation theory (McClelland, 1985), and structural contingency theory of organizational form and effectiveness (Donaldson, 1993; Hickson, Hinings, McMillan, & Schwitter, 1974). The relevant and essential features of each of these theories are briefly described in the following paragraphs. The integrated theory is then described. For a more detailed description of the integrated theory, see House et al. (1997).

Implicit Leadership Theory

According to this theory individuals have implicit theories (beliefs, convictions, and assumptions) about the attributes and behaviors that distinguish leaders from others, effective leaders from ineffective ones, and moral leaders from evil ones. Implicit leadership theories influence the values that individuals place on selected leader behaviors and attributes, and their motives relevant to acceptance and enactment of leader behavior. The following propositions express the major assertions of implicit leadership theory.

1. Leadership qualities are attributed to individuals, and those persons are accepted as leaders, on the basis of the degree of fit, or congruence, between the leader behaviors they enact and the implicit leadership theory held by the attributers.
2. Implicit leadership theories constrain, moderate, and guide the exercise of leadership, the acceptance of leaders, the perception of leaders as influential, acceptable, and effective, and the degree to which leaders are granted status and privileges.

There is substantial experimental evidence in support of this theory (Hanges, Braverman, & Rentsch, 1991; Hanges, Lord, Day, Sipe, Smith, & Brown, 1997; Lord & Maher, 1991; Sipe & Hanges, 1997).

Value/Belief Theory

Hofstede (1980) and Triandis (1995) assert that the values and beliefs held by members of cultures influence the degree to which the behaviors of individuals, groups, and institutions within cultures are enacted, and the degree to which they are viewed as legitimate, acceptable, and effective. Hofstede's version of value/ *belief* theory includes four dimensions of cultural values and beliefs: Individualism versus Collectivism, Masculinity versus Femininity, Tolerance versus Intolerance of Uncertainty, and Power Distance (Stratification) versus Power Equalization. We have substituted two cultural dimensions labeled Gender Egalitarianism and Assertiveness for Hofstede's Masculinity dimension. As explained later, we also measured Collectivism with two, rather than one, scale. Finally, we have added three additional dimensions: Humanistic, Performance, and Future Orientation. Collectively, the nine dimensions reflect not only the dimensions of Hofstede's theory but also David McClelland's theories of national economic development (McClelland, 1961) and human motivation (McClelland, 1985). The humanism, power distance, and performance orientation of cultures, when measured with operant (behavioral) indicators, are conceptually analogous to the affiliative, power, and achievement motives in McClelland's implicit motivation theory. We believe that the nine core GLOBE dimensions reflect important aspects of the human condition.

Implicit Motivation Theory

Implicit motivation theory is the theory of non-conscious motives originally advanced by McClelland, Atkinson, Clark, and Lowell (1953). In its most general form the theory asserts that the essential nature of human motivation can be understood in terms of three implicit (non-conscious) motives: achievement, affiliation, and power (social influence). In contrast to behavioral intentions and conscious values, which are predictive of discrete task behaviors for short periods of time under constant situational forces (Ajzen & Fishbein, 1970), implicit motives are predictive of (1) motive arousal in the presence of selected stimuli, (2) spontaneous behavior in the absence of motive-arousal stimuli, and (3) long-term (as long as 20 years) individual *global behavior patterns*, such as social relationship patterns, citizenship behavior, child-rearing practices, and leadership styles. While McClelland's theory is an individual theory of non-conscious motivation, the GLOBE theory is a theory of motivation resulting from cultural forces.

Structural Contingency Theory

The central proposition of this theory is that there is a set of demands that are imposed on organizations that must be met if organizations are to survive and be effective. These demands are referred to as organizational contingencies. It is

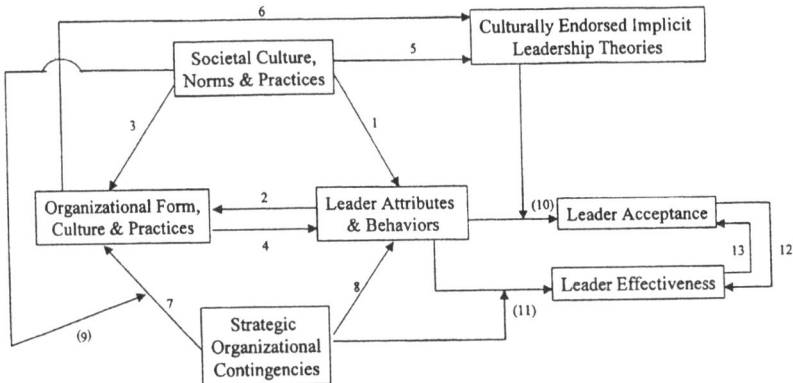

Note: Numbers in parentheses indicate an interaction among two adjoining arrows.

Figure 1. The Globe Theoretical Model

asserted that these contingencies influence organizational form and practice and that congruence between the demands of the contingencies and organizational form and practice is associated with organizational effectiveness. While this is a popular theoretical perspective, its empirical verification is mostly limited to small sample studies of organizations in industrialized countries (Child, 1981). Hickson and colleagues (1974) have asserted that the propositions of structural contingency theory are universal and culture-free. This assertion rests on the assumption that organizational contingencies impose demands on organizations that are so strong that it is imperative for all organizations to respond to them in essentially the same way in order to perform effectively and survive in competitive environments. We refer to this assertion as the *task environment imperative*. Child (1981) has presented a serious challenge to this assertion.

The Integrated Theory

A diagram of the integrated theory is presented in Figure 1.

The central theoretical proposition. The central theoretical proposition of the integrated theory is that the attributes and entities that distinguish a given culture from other cultures are predictive of the practices of organizations and leader attributes and behaviors that are most frequently enacted, acceptable, and effective in that culture. The integrated theory consists of the following propositions, which are also shown in the system diagram in Figure 1:

1. *Societal cultural values and practices affect what leaders do.* Substantial empirical evidence supports this assertion (House et al., 1997). First, founders of organizations—the organizations' original leaders—are immersed in their own societal culture, and they are most likely to enact the global leader behavior patterns that are favored in that culture. Founders influence the behavior of subordinate leaders and subsequent leaders by use of selective management selection criteria, role modeling, and socialization. Further, the dominant cultural norms endorsed by societal cultures induce global leader behavior patterns and organizational practices that are differentially expected and viewed as legitimate among cultures. Thus, the attributes and behaviors of leaders are, in part, a reflection of the organizational practices, which in turn are a reflection of societal cultures (e.g., Kopelman, Brief, & Guzzo, 1990).
2. *Leadership affects organizational form, culture, and practices.* Founders of organizations establish the initial culture of their organizations (e.g., Schein, 1992; Schneider, 1987; Schneider, Goldstein, & Smith, 1995), and founders and subsequent leaders continue to influence the organizational culture (e.g., Bass, 1985; Miller & Droge, 1986; Schein, 1992; Thompson & Luthans, 1990; Yukl, 1994).
3. *Societal cultural values and practices also affect organizational form, culture and practices.* Societal culture has a direct influence on organizational culture, as the shared meaning that results from the dominant cultural values, beliefs, assumptions, and implicit motives endorsed by culture results in common implicit leadership theories and implicit organization theories held by members of the culture (e.g., Lord and Maher, 1991; House et al., 1997).
4. *Organizational form, culture, and practices also affect what leaders do.* Over time, founders and subsequent leaders in organizations respond to the organizational culture and alter their behaviors and leader styles (e.g., Lombardo, 1983; Schein, 1992; Trice and Beyer, 1984).
5 and 6. *Societal culture and organizational form, culture, and practices influence the process by which people come to share implicit theories of leadership.* Over time, CLTs are developed in each culture in response to both societal and organizational culture and practices (e.g., Lord & Maher, 1991). CLTs thus differentiate cultures.
7. *Strategic organizational contingencies affect organizational form, culture and practices.* Organizational contingencies (size, technology, environment) impose requirements that organizations must meet in order to perform effectively, compete, and survive. Organizational practices are largely directed toward meeting the requirements imposed on organizations by organizational contingencies (Burns & Stalker, 1961; Donaldson, 1993; Lawrence & Lorsch, 1967; Tushman, Newman, & Nadler, 1988).

8. *Strategic organizational contingencies affect leader attributes and behavior.* Leaders are selected and adjust their behaviors to meet the requirements of organizational contingencies.
9. *Relationships between strategic organizational contingencies and organizational form, culture, and practices will be moderated by cultural forces.* For example, in low uncertainty avoidance cultures we expect that forces toward formalization will be weaker, and therefore the relationship between such forces and organizational formalization practices will be lower. In low power distance cultures we expect that forces toward centralization of decision making will be weaker, and therefore the relationship between such forces and decentralization and delegation practices will be lower. We specify such moderating effects in detail below when we discuss Phase 2 and 3 hypotheses.
10. *Leader acceptance is a function of the interaction between CLTs and leader attributes and behaviors.* Accordingly, leader attributes and behaviors that are congruent with CLTs will be more accepted than leader attributes and behaviors that are not congruent with CLTs.
11. *Leader effectiveness is a function of the interaction between leader attributes and behaviors and organizational contingencies.* Leaders who effectively address organizational contingencies will be more effective than leaders who do not.
12. *Leader acceptance influences leader effectiveness.* Leaders who are not accepted will find it more difficult to influence subordinates than those who are accepted. Thus, leader acceptance facilitates leader effectiveness.
13. *Leader effectiveness influences leader acceptance.* Leaders who are effective will, in the long run, come to be accepted by all or most subordinates. Subordinates will either be dismissed or voluntarily leave the organization led by leaders they do not accept.

In summary, the attributes and practices that distinguish cultures from each other, as well as strategic organizational contingencies, are predictive of the leader attributes and behaviors, and organizational practices, that are most frequently perceived as acceptable, are most frequently enacted, and are most effective.

Cultural change. Thus far, the theory does not accommodate or account for cultural change. For example, exposure to international media, cross-border commerce, international political and economic competition, or other forms of cross-cultural interaction may introduce new competitive forces and new common experiences, which may result in changes in any of the culture or leadership variables previously described.

Further, when strategic organizational contingencies change as a result of new technological developments or changes in the economic or political environment, new leader behaviors and organizational practices that violate cultural norms may be required. These new behaviors and practices, when enacted, will constitute new common experiences, which can in turn result in changes in psychological commonalties and consequently changes in any of the cultural variables previously described.

Although cultural change can be stimulated by external events and forces, the process of change is hypothesized to be governed by the set of relationships described in the preceding propositions. There will almost certainly be resistance to new leadership and organizational practices when such practices violate existing collectively shared norms and expectations for leaders (Gagliardi, 1986). Recent work by Hanges and colleagues on person perception confirms this hypothesis by demonstrating that people resist new leaders when the new leader initially behaves in a manner inconsistent with perceivers' expectations or stereotypes (Hanges et al., 1991; Hanges et al., 1997; Sipe & Hanges, 1997). These laboratory studies have shown that the resistance to acceptance of a new leader is so strong that the functional relationship between leadership perceptions and other variables is non-linear and discontinuous. Various individual difference variables (e.g., personality, stereotypical attitudes), as well as situational factors (e.g., mental workload, job-context), have been found to increase or diminish this resistance to accept new leaders (Hanges et al., 1997; Sipe & Hanges, 1997). This research suggests that newly introduced practices will often be modified to accommodate existing norms in an emic (culture specific) manner, and there may be substantial lags in the rate at which changes in the variables of the theory take place.

Substantial additional theoretical development is required to reach a better description of the forces of resistance, the likely resulting conflicts within cultural entities, the time lags and the feedback processes that will occur among the relationships, and the functional form of the relationships depicted in Figure 1. Nevertheless, we advance the theory presented here as a framework to guide investigation of the major relationships and variables relevant to cultural influences on leadership and organizational practices and effectiveness. The theory is depicted in Figure 1 in the form of a systems model. The complexity of the model, however, mitigates against its being tested in its entirety. Rather, individual linkages or subsets of linkages can be tested, and the validity of the model can be inferred from such tests. For a more detailed, fine-grained elaboration of the relationships depicted in Figure 1, see House et al. (1997).

TWO FUNDAMENTAL CROSS-CULTURAL ISSUES

Two central aspects of cultures are frequently discussed in the cross-cultural literature: etic aspects and emic aspects. For Project GLOBE, we employ multiple methodologies to assess etic and emic issues.

Etic phenomena are common to all cultures, or at least to all cultures studied to date. A phenomenon is etic if all cultures can be assessed in terms of a common metric with respect to the phenomena. Thus, cultures can be compared in terms of etic phenomena. In contrast to etic phenomena, emic phenomena are culture-specific phenomena that occur in only a subset of cultures.

Etic Issues: Cross-cultural Comparisons and Relationships

Project GLOBE employs a number of different methods to make etic comparisons among the cultures studied. The primary method will be latent constructs that measure the nine core GLOBE dimensions. These constructs are developed from questionnaire responses obtained from middle managers and unobtrusive measures of the dimensions. The industries studied are food processing, financial services, and telecommunications services. Our sampling strategy for the collection of questionnaire data controls for nation, industry, occupation broadly defined (managers), and organizational level broadly defined (middle management). The samples for Phase 2, in which hypotheses are tested, are described later on.

Sampling from middle managers permits us to generalize to the subcultures of middle managers in the countries and the three industries studied. This sampling strategy increases the internal validity of the study by ensuring that the units of analysis are well defined and internally homogeneous. We expect the findings to reflect some aspects of the national cultures of the countries represented. Strictly speaking, we are studying the cultures of middle managers in 62 cultures. Thus, we must be cautious when making generalizations about national cultures or differences among them because of the specific nature of our sample. As we show later, however, the use of latent constructs each composed of two indicators to measure the nine core GLOBE *As Is* dimensions at the societal level, increases the generalizability of our findings beyond the culture of middle managers alone. And, cross-industry analysis will enable us to assess the relative impact of strategic imperatives imposed by industry constraints as well as cultural influences.

Emic Issues: Country-specific Information

While the GLOBE quantitative data allow comparisons and contrasts among cultures, they do not allow for emic, or culture-specific, descriptions of the cultures studied. CCIs will describe selected emic attributes and entities of the national setting in which the middle management informants are embedded. The attributes and entities are those that the CCIs judge to have non-trivial influences on the interpretation and practice of leadership and organizational practices of the cultures studied.

CCIs have collected unobtrusive measures and conducted participant observations. They also collected and content-analyzed media and focus group interview transcripts. With these data CCIs are able to describe and interpret selected emic characteristics of their national cultures. Such interpretations will give cognizance to gender, ethnic, and religious diversity, generational differences, and other relevant complexities of the cultures. Thus, the complexity and variability of complex cultures with two or more subcultures will be described. These qualitative interpretive analyses will be reported as chapters of a number of anthologies resulting from the GLOBE research program. The local CCI teams will author these chapters.

CONSTRUCT DEFINITIONS

The major constructs investigated in the GLOBE research program are nine attributes of cultures, which are operationalized as quantitative dimensions: (1) Uncertainty Avoidance, (2) Power Distance, (3) Collectivism I: Societal Emphasis on Collectivism, (4) Collectivism II: Family Organizational Collectivistic Practices, (5) Gender Egalitarianism, (6) Assertiveness, (7) Future Orientation, (8) Performance Orientation, and (9) Humane Orientation. These dimensions were selected on the basis of a review of the literature relevant to the measurement of culture in previous large-sample studies and on the basis of existing cross-culture theory.

Uncertainty Avoidance is defined as the extent to which members of an organization or society strive to avoid uncertainty by reliance on social norms, rituals, and bureaucratic practices to alleviate the unpredictability of future events.

Power Distance is defined as the degree to which members of an organization or society expect and agree that power should be unequally shared.

Collectivism I reflects the degree to which organizational and societal institutional norms and practices encourage and reward collective distribution of resources and collective action.

Collectivism II reflects the degree to which individuals express pride, loyalty, and cohesiveness in their organizations or families.[5]

Gender Egalitarianism is the extent to which an organization or a society minimizes gender role differences.

Assertiveness is the degree to which individuals in organizations or societies are assertive, confrontational, and aggressive in social relationships.

Future Orientation is the degree to which individuals in organizations or societies engage in future-oriented behaviors such as planning, investing in the future, and delaying gratification.

Performance Orientation refers to the extent to which an organization or society encourages and rewards group members for performance improvement and excellence. This dimension is similar to the dimension called Confucian Dynamism by Hofstede and Bond (1988). It reflects achievement-oriented behavior described by McClelland (1980).

Finally, *Humane Orientation* is the degree to which individuals in organizations or societies encourage and reward individuals for being fair, altruistic, friendly, generous, caring, and kind to others. This dimension is similar to the dimension labeled Kind Heartedness by Hofstede and Bond (1988). It reflects affiliative-oriented behavior described by McClelland (1980). These definitions and examples of questionnaire items for each dimension are presented in Table 2.

The first six culture dimensions had their origins in the dimensions of culture identified by Hofstede (1980). The first three scales are intended to reflect the same constructs as Hofstede's dimensions labeled Uncertainty Avoidance, Power Distance, and Individualism. The Collectivism I dimension measures organizational and societal emphasis on collectivism, with low scores reflecting individualistic emphasis and high scores reflecting collectivistic emphasis by means of norms, policies, rules, procedures, laws, social programs, or institutional practices. The Collectivism II dimension measures group (family and/or organization) collectivism—pride in and loyalty to family and/or organization and family and/or organizational cohesiveness. In lieu of Hofstede's Masculinity dimension, we

Table 2. Culture Construct Definitions and Sample Questionnaire Items

Culture Construct Definitions	Specific Questionnaire Item
Power Distance: The degree to which members of a collective expect power to be distributed equally.	Followers are (should be) expected to obey their leaders without question.
Uncertainty Avoidance: The extent to which a society, organization, or group relies on social norms, rules, and procedures to alleviate unpredictability of future events.	Most people lead (should lead) highly structured lives with few unexpected events.
Humane Orientation: The degree to which a collective encourages and rewards individuals for being fair, altruistic, generous, caring, and kind to others.	People are generally (should be generally) very tolerant of mistakes.
Collectivism I: The degree to which organizational and societal institutional practices encourage and reward collective distribution of resources and collective action	Leaders encourage (should encourage) group loyalty even if individual goals suffer.
Collectivism II: The degree to which individuals express pride, loyalty, and cohesiveness in their organizations or families.	Employees feel (should feel) great loyalty toward this organization
Assertiveness: The degree to which individuals are assertive, confrontational and aggressive in their relationships with others.	People are (should be) generally dominant in their relationships with each other.
Gender Egalitarianism: The degree to which a collective minimizes gender inequality.	Boys are encouraged (should be encouraged) more than girls to attain a higher education. (Scored inversely.)
Future Orientation: The extent to which individuals engage in future-oriented behaviors such as delaying gratification, planning, and investing in the future.	More people live (should live) for the present rather than for the future. (Scored inversely.)
Performance Orientation: The degree to which a collective encourages and rewards group members for performance improvement and excellence.	Students are encouraged (should be encouraged) to strive for continuously improved performance.

developed two dimensions labeled Gender Egalitarianism and Assertiveness. Future Orientation is derived from Kluckhohn and Strodtbeck's (1961) Past, Present, Future Orientation dimension, which focuses on the temporal mode of a society. Performance Orientation was derived from McClelland's work on need for achievement. Humane Orientation has its roots in Kluckhohn and Strodtbeck's (1961) work on the Human Nature Is Good versus Human Nature Is Bad dimension, as well as Putnam's (1993) work on the Civic Society and McClelland's (1985) conceptualization of the affiliative motive.

THE FOUR PHASES OF GLOBE

Four phases of empirical research are planned as part of Project GLOBE. Phase 1 has been completed and reported in a monograph by Hanges and colleagues (1998, under review). Phase 2 questionnaire data collection has also been completed. The analysis of scale properties of the questionnaire administered to approximately 17,000 middle managers in Phase 2 is also completed. Unobtrusive measures for the nine dimensions have also been developed.

Phase 1: Scale Development and Validation

In this section, we describe Phases 1 and 2 in modest detail. Phase 1 of GLOBE concerned the development and validation of the GLOBE questionnaire scales designed to measure societal and organizational culture variables as well as CLTs. The GLOBE scales have sound psychometric properties, and findings indicate justification for the use of the scales as aggregate measures of cultural phenomena. All 54 GLOBE scales demonstrated significant and non-trivial within-culture response agreement, between-culture differences, and respectable item reliability of response consistency. Generalizability coefficients, which are joint measures of these psychometric properties, exceed .85 for all scales. These coefficients indicate that the scales can be meaningfully used to measure differences between cultures in terms of societal, organizational, and leadership phenomena. In this section, we provide a brief description of the questionnaire development process. Detailed descriptions of scale development and validation can be found in Hanges and colleagues (1998, under review).

Item Generation

The first author of this monograph accomplished item generation for the culture scales with substantial help from Paul Koopman, Henk Thierry, and Celeste Wilderom of the Netherlands. The original item pool contained 753 items, of which 382 were leadership items and 371 were societal and organizational culture items.

Table 3. Sample CLT Questionnaire Items and Response Alternatives

Definition of Leadership	Ability to influence, motivate, and enable others to contribute to success of their organization.
Sample CLT Items	Sensitive: Aware of slight changes in moods of others.
	Motivator: Mobilizes, activates followers.
	Evasive: Refrains from making negative comments to maintain good relationships and save face.
	Diplomatic: Skilled at interpersonal relations, tactful.
	Self-interested: Pursues own best interests.
Response Alternatives	Impedes or facilitates unusually effective leadership
	1. Substantially impedes
	2. Moderately impedes
	3. Slightly impedes
	4. Neither impedes nor facilitates
	5. Slightly facilitates
	6. Moderately facilitates
	7. Substantially facilitates

Note: CLT, culturally endorsed implicit leaderships theory.

In generating leadership items, our focus was on developing a comprehensive list of leader attributes and behaviors rather than on developing a priori leadership scales. The initial pool of leadership items was based on leader behaviors and attributes described in several extant leadership theories. The theories are described in House and Aditya (1997). These leadership items consisted of behavioral and attribute descriptors and their definitions. Examples of these items are presented in Table 3. Items were rated on a 7-point Likert-type scale that ranged from a low of "This behavior or characteristic greatly inhibits a person from being an outstanding leader" to a high of "This behavior or characteristic contributes greatly to a person being an outstanding leader."

Organizational and societal culture items were written for the nine core GLOBE dimensions, previously described, at both the societal and the organizational levels. We also wrote the items to reflect two culture manifestations: institutional practices reported "*As Is*" and values reported in terms of what "*Should Be*." The items were written as "quartets" having isomorphic structures across the two levels of analysis (societal and organizational) and across the two culture manifestations (*As Is* and *Should Be*). Note that the should be items reflect specific and concrete contextualized values rather than general and abstract values such as love, peace, order of freedom.

The basic structure of the items comprising quartets is identical, but the frame of reference is varied according to the particular cultural manifestation and levels of analysis being assessed. Table 4 contains an example of a quartet of parallel culture items, showing essentially the same question in four forms: Organization *As Is*; Organization *Should Be*; Society *As Is*; and Society *Should Be*. Items were derived from a review of relevant literature and interviews and focus groups held in several countries, as well as from extant organizational and culture theory. Psy-

Table 4. Example of Parallel Items for the Culture Scales

			Organization *As Is*			
\multicolumn{7}{l}{The pay and bonus system in this organization is designed to maximize:}						
1	2	3	4	5	6	7
Individual Interests						Collective Interests
			Organization *Should Be*			
\multicolumn{7}{l}{In this organization, the pay and bonus system *should* be designed to maximize:}						
1	2	3	4	5	6	7
Individual Interests						Collective Interests
			Society *As Is*			
\multicolumn{7}{l}{The economic system in this society is designed to maximize:}						
1	2	3	4	5	6	7
Individual Interests						Collective Interests
			Society *Should be*			
\multicolumn{7}{l}{I believe that the economic system in this society should be designed to maximize:}						
1	2	3	4	5	6	7
Individual Interests						Collective Interests

chometric analyses indicated justification for grouping the items into scales relevant to the nine core GLOBE dimensions of societies and organizations.

Item Screening

Societal and organizational culture questionnaire items were screened for appropriateness by use of three procedures: Q sorting, item evaluation, and translation/back-translation. Leadership items were screened by item evaluation and conceptual equivalence of the back translation. The Q sorting procedure consisted of sorting the culture items into theoretical categories represented by the a priori dimensions of culture described above, first by seven Ph.D. students in the Department of Psychology at the University of Maryland and subsequently by CCIs representing 38 countries. The sorters were not informed of the theoretical dimensions for which the items were intended. Items that were sorted by 80% of the sorters into the categories for which they were theoretically intended were retained for further analysis. There were no dimensions of societal or organizational culture for which a majority of items failed to meet this criterion. Thus, a sufficient number of items was retained for the measurement of each dimension.

The ability of the sorters to agree on the allocation of items to dimensions indicates that the sorters were sorting according to common interpretations of both the theoretical dimensions and the items that they sorted into these dimensions. This level of agreement indicates that the scales comprising the retained items were interpreted to have the same meaning in all of the cultures represented by the CCIs. This is an especially important result because it strongly suggests commonalty of meaning of the questionnaire scales across cultures.

In addition to this sorting task, CCIs provided Item Evaluation Reports, in which they noted any items containing words or phrases that were ambiguous or could not be adequately translated in the target country's native language. CCIs also identified questions that might be culturally inappropriate. Most of the items that were problematic were dropped from further consideration. In a few cases, we were able to rewrite items to eliminate potential problems but retain the intent and dimensionality of the original item.

In order to avoid any systematic bias that may be present when respondents complete a survey that is not in their native language (Brislin, 1986), CCIs were responsible for having the survey translated from English into their native language. This was done by the CCI, by some other person fluent in both languages, or by a professional translator. The translation was then independently translated again, from the native language of the culture back to English. This back-translation was then sent to the GLOBE Coordinating Team (GCT), where it was compared to the original English version of the survey to verify the veridicality of the translation. Through the process of deleting items based on sorting, item evaluation, and translation, the item pool was reduced to a total of 379 items, which were retained for further evaluation.

Pilot Studies

Two pilot studies were then conducted to assess the psychometric properties of the resulting a priori culture scales and to empirically develop leadership scales.

Pilot study 1. The CCIs in 28 countries distributed the survey of retained items to individuals in their respective countries who had full-time working experience as a white-collar employee or manager. Because the survey was lengthy, it was divided into two parallel versions, A and B. Each version contained approximately half of the leadership items and half of the organizational and societal culture items. A total of 877 individuals completed the first pilot study survey.

Several different statistical analyses were performed to assess the psychometric properties of the scales. Specifically, we conducted a series of exploratory factor analyses, reliability analyses, and aggregability analyses (r_{wg} analyses, intraclass correlations [ICC-1], one-way analyses of variance), and generalizability analyses (ICC-2) of the scales. These analyses were performed at the *ecological* level of analysis; that is, on the means of the country item responses for each scale. We refined our scales on the basis of these analyses while trying to maintain, whenever possible, the isomorphic quartet structure of the culture scales described above and illustrated in Table 4. These statistical analyses, when considered together, provide evidence of the construct validity of the culture scales.

A separate factor analysis of each of the culture scales indicated that they were all unidimensional. A first-order exploratory factor analysis of the leader attributes items yielded 16 unidimensional factors that describe *specific* leader attributes and behaviors.

The r_{wg} analyses (James, Demaree, & Wolf, 1984) demonstrated that the scales could be aggregated to either the organizational or the societal levels of analysis (average $r_{wg} = .73$, n = 54). Intraclass correlation coefficients (ICC-1) and one-way analyses of variance for each of the scales indicated statistically significant within-culture agreement and between-culture differences. The societal culture scales exhibited low to moderate correlations with each other. Thus, they provide independent and unique information about societal cultures. The leadership scales substantially differed in their relationship to one another. The absolute correlation among the first-order leadership scales ranged from a low of .00 (Status-Conscious with Calmness) to a high of .86 (Status-Conscious with Procedural). Thus, the leadership scales exhibited acceptable levels of unidimensionality and internal consistency. Overall, 20 percent of the interrelationships were statistically significant. A second-order factor analysis of the 16 leadership factors yielded four unidimensional factors that describe *classes* of leader behaviors that represent *global* leader behavior patterns.

It is interesting to note that some of the same culture dimensions were highly inversely correlated across the two *As Is* and *Should Be* scale orientations for particular dimensions of culture. The findings indicate that there are substantial differences in people's perceptions of how things *should be* as opposed to how things *are perceived to be*. This raises an interesting and very important question: Are the most meaningful indicators of the cultures of collectives' current practices reflected by *As Is* scales or values reflected by *Should Be* scales? We shall assess the relationship between (1) societal *As Is* and *Should Be* scores, and (2) organizational *As Is* scores. The findings from this analysis will indicate which of the two ways of measuring cultural variation is most strongly associated with organizational practices as measured by the organizational *As Is* scores.

We ended Pilot Study 1 with 16 first-order factorially derived leadership scales that represent specific leader behaviors, four second-order factorially derived leadership dimensions that represent global leader behavior patterns, nine organizational culture *As Is* scales, nine organizational culture *Should Be* scales. The factor analyses conducted as part of Pilot Study 1 also demonstrated that the themes in all of the scales could be meaningfully identified and labeled.

Pilot study 2. The purpose of the second pilot study was to replicate the psychometric analyses of the scales in a different sample to assess sampling robustness. Data for this study came from 15 countries that did not participate in the previous pilot study. In general, the psychometric properties of all of the scales were confirmed by replication. We replicated the ecological analyses conducted in Pilot Study 1 at the *individual level of analysis*. We used this level of analysis because there were too few countries in the replication sample to conduct an ecological-factor analysis. A total of 1,066 individuals completed one of the two versions of the pilot study questionnaires. Using an individual-level analysis to replicate an ecological-level analysis is a conservative approach. If this analysis is found to correspond to the ecological analysis, the findings constitute strong evidence for the generality of the factor structure and evidence of *strong etic* phenomena (Leung & Bond, 1989). Pilot Study 2 confirmatory factor analyses yielded acceptable fit for the first- and second-order CLT factor structures and replicated the unidimensionality of the societal culture scales.

In summary, we developed 16 unidimensional leadership scales and 36 societal scales that exhibit acceptable levels of internal consistency. The aggregation tests indicated that we are justified in aggregating these scales to the societal level of analysis. Correlational analysis indicated that the leadership scales substantially differed in their relationship to one another. The leadership scales also exhibited acceptable levels of unidimensionality and internal consistency. We found sufficient agreement within societies and sufficient differences between societies to aggregate the scales to the society level of analysis. Further, the shared themes in all of the scales were replicated by the Pilot Study 2 factor analyses.

Phase 2: Measurement and Hypothesis Testing

Phase 2 consists of further assessment of scale properties and measurement of (1) the core societal and organizational *As Is* and *Should Be* dimensions, (2) the CLT dimensions, (3) the organizational contingencies and strategic processes of firms reported by high-level executives, and (4) respondent demographic variables. Phase 2 also consists of tests of theoretical hypotheses presented below. Data collection for these aspects of Phase 2 is complete. In addition, Phase 2 involves further development of unobtrusive measurement scales to assess the societal-level cultural dimensions. These scales are described on the following pages.

The questionnaire data collected in GLOBE Phase 2 consist of (1) responses to approximately 17,000 questionnaires relevant to societal and organizational dimensions of culture, from middle managers of approximately 825 organizations in 62 cultures, and (2) unobtrusive measures of the societal dimensions (Table 5) and responses to four different executive questionnaires administered to separate top-level executives in the organizations from which the middle management data were collected. The executive questionnaires, described in the paragraphs that follow, elicited responses relevant to organizational attributes, organization strategic processes, organizational contingencies, and performance. These responses will be used in Phase 2 to test hypotheses relevant to structural contingency theory of organizational form and effectiveness.

Questionnaire data collection for Phase 2 is complete. Table 6 provides a summary and overview of the latent constructs used to test the GLOBE hypotheses and their indicators.

Based on the pilot studies and on focus groups and interviews conducted by CCIs, which were ongoing during the pilot studies, several additional CLT items were added to the middle manager questionnaires. These new items were written to ensure that including only Western leadership behaviors did not bias the 16 leadership scales. Further, we wrote several items that described autocratic, narcissistic, manipulative, and punitive behaviors, because it was suggested in interviews and focus groups that in some societies such behaviors would enhance leader effectiveness.

Finally, we added several new items to the survey to develop a second measure of collectivist cultural orientation, because the collectivistic scale derived from the pilot studies did not include items relevant to family or organizational collectivism. The new items were adopted from Triandis's work on collectivism (Triandis, 1995) and concerned several descriptors of organizational and family practices

Table 5. Sample Unobtrusive Measures*

Avoidance of uncertainty	High number of information processing equipment items (e.g., fax machines, cell phones) per 1,000 people, indicating high emphasis on information availability.
Power distance	Limited number of scientists per gross national product (GNP), indicating suppression of intellectual inquiry.
Societal emphasis on collectivism	Early time zone, indicating eastern and southeastern location where societal collectivism is predominant.
Family collectivism	Low divorce rates per marriage, indicating pressure for sustaining intimate relationships.
Gender egalitarianism	High proportion of females with earned income, indicating low discrimination against females and females' contribution to workforce.
Future orientation	High proportion of public education expenditure devoted to higher education, indicating public investment for future opportunities and future economic performance.
Performance orientation	Low share of government-funded research and development (R and D), indicating free market competition and low government intervention.
Humane orientation	Few retail outlets per capita, indicating low emphasis on economic amenities and high emphasis on relationship orientation.

Note: *There is no effect of GNP, per capita income, population size of country, or year of independence on the correlations between the unobtrusive measures and their isomorphic questionnaire based measures, for the total sample of 54 cultures. However, selected subsamples such as more or less wealthy countries, indicated differences in correlations suggesting boundary conditions for some of the unobtrusive measures. These boundary conditions are being further investigated.

usually associated with collectivistic cultures: organizational and family pride, loyalty and cohesiveness. We confirmed the two Collectivism scales by factor analytically deriving two dimensions of Collectivism: Societal Emphasis on Collective Behavior and Organizational and Family Collectivism (see note 5). Thus, there were 18 scales to measure the nine culture *As Is* and nine *Should Be* culture dimensions—one scale for each of the dimensions except Collectivism, which had two scales.

Measurement of Organizational Attributes

The executive questionnaires to which we previously referred were designed to measure several attributes and processes of the organizations from which middle manager data were collected. The questionnaires included scales to measure attributes of strategies, perceived organizational effectiveness, and three organizational strategic contingency variables: size in terms of number of employees; the dominant technology of each organization in terms of the degree to which the work is repetitive, well understood, and controllable; and environments in terms of competitiveness, hostility, and predictability/uncertainty. Organizational strategy was assessed in terms of strong versus weak customer orientation, incremental versus comprehensiveness of strategic decision making, consensus versus individual formulation, formality versus informality, and adaptability versus rigidity and

Table 6. Latent Constructs and Manifest and Qualitative Indicators

Latent Constructs	Manifest Indicators	Qualitative Indicators
Societal cultural norms: nine core dimensions (Phase 2)	Questionnaires Unobtrusive measures	Interviews Media analysis Focus groups CCI participant observation
Organizational practices: nine core dimensions (Phase 2)	Questionnaires by middle managers	
Organizational contingencies: technology, environment, size (Phase 2)	Questionnaires by top executives	
Societal culturally endorsed implicit leadership theories (CLTs)	Middle manager questionnaire ratings	Interviews and media analysis Focus groups CCI participant observation
Leader behavior (Phase 3)	Questionnaires	Interviews Media analysis
Leader acceptance (Phase 3)	Questionnaires	CCI participant observation Interviews, media, and analysis
Leader effectiveness (Phase 4)	Lab/field experiments	Interviews with subjects

Note: Country Co-Investigator (CCI).

entrepreneurial/risk orientation. The strategic contingency scales were adapted from questionnaires used in several previous studies in which their construct validity was established (Khandwalla, 1977; Lumpkin & Dess, 1996). The executives reported the level of their firms' performance, relative to major competitors, during the previous 3 years with respect to sales and pretax profit. The executives also provided information relevant to the general market and economic conditions of the firms, frequency of organizational changes, degree of government regulation of firm's activities, and demographic variables relevant to the firm and to themselves. The psychometric properties of these scales and the impact of the strategic contingency variables on organizational practices and effectiveness is currently being assessed as part of the Phase 2 research.

Phase 2 Hypotheses

The results of Pilot Studies 1 and 2 set the stage for Phase 2 by providing the necessary questionnaire scales to test hypotheses. Hypotheses will be tested, concerning (1) relationships between societal culture dimensions, organizational culture dimensions, and CLTs; (2) relationships specified by structural contingency theory of organizational form and effectiveness; and (3) the moderating effects of societal culture dimensions on relationships specified by structural contingency theory. Tests of the first two GLOBE hypotheses are reported below. Although we do not report tests of the remaining GLOBE hypotheses, we present these hypotheses here.

Hypotheses concerning relationships between societal culture dimensions, organizational culture dimensions, and CLTs.

Hypothesis 1. The global CLT dimension charismatic/value-based leadership will be universally endorsed.

The component subscales that constitute the global (second-order factor) charismatic/value-based leadership dimension are visionary, inspirational, self-sacrifice, integrity, decisive, and performance orientation. We expect charismatic/value-based leader behavior to be universally endorsed because the visions articulated by, and the integrity enacted by, value-based leaders stress values that have universal appeal (House et al., 1997). Charismatic/value-based leaders articulate and emphasize end-values. Examples of end-values are dignity, peace, order, beauty, and freedom. End-values are values that are intrinsically motivating, self-sufficient, and need not be linked to other values. Also, end-values are not exchangeable for other values and have universal appeal (Rokeach, 1973). Thus, the values stressed by charismatic/value-based leaders are more likely to be universally accepted and endorsed. Consequently the visions of charismatic/value-based leaders usually stress end-values that are congruent with the values stressed in the culture (House & Aditya, 1997). Similarly, we expect leader integrity to be universally endorsed because integrity is an end-value that is also universally held in all cultures (Rokeach, 1973).

We recognize that Hypothesis 1 is controversial. Bass (1997) argues that transformational leadership, a form of charismatic/value-based leadership, is universally acceptable and effective. In contrast, it may be argued that some cultures may more highly value leaders who can find pragmatic accommodations with all influential parties. In such cultures, value-based leadership may be far less important than ability to achieve pragmatic effects, regardless of the means by which such effects are attained.

Regardless of whether it is supported or not, the test of Hypothesis 1 is of both theoretical and practical interest. Failure to support this hypothesis would result in identification of the specific cultures in which value-based leadership is and is not endorsed. The issue of universal endorsement of leadership dimensions, of necessity, needs to be answered on the basis of empirical evidence. The test of Hypothesis 1 is intended to contribute to clarification of that issue. The discovery of both universally endorsed and culture-specific leadership dimensions is of major importance to the development of cross-cultural leadership theory and of practical importance to individuals whose work involves cross-cultural interaction.

Hypothesis 2. There will be positive correlations between societal dimensions and isomorphic CLT dimensions.

The rationale for this hypothesis is that the dimensions of societal culture will influence the legitimacy and acceptance of leader behaviors. More specifically, societal culture will influence the kind of attributes and behaviors that are reported to be expected, acceptable, and effective. Correlations between these dimensions constitute a test of the *cultural influence proposition* (Hofstede, 1980; Kluckhohn & Strodtbeck, 1961; Triandis, 1995), which asserts that societal culture has a pervasive influence on the values, expectations, and behavior of its members. Therefore, societal culture is expected to influence organizational values (*Should Be* measures) and practices (*As Is* measures), as well as expectations for leader behaviors that are expressed as CLTs in the form of questionnaire item responses.

Hypothesis 3. There will be positive correlations between organizational culture dimensions and isomorphic CLTs.

Dimensions of organizational culture are also expected to influence the legitimacy and acceptance of leader attributes and behaviors.

The rationale for this hypothesis is that shared organizational values and practices will influence the legitimacy and acceptance of leader attributes and behaviors.

Hypothesis 4. The magnitude of relationships between organizational cultural dimensions and isomorphic CLT dimensions will be greater than the magnitude of relationships between societal culture dimensions and isomorphic CLT dimensions.

The rationale for this hypothesis is that organizational variables are more salient, more proximate, and more relevant to the tasks and behaviors of managers than societal cultural variables. Therefore, organizational cultural variables will have a stronger influence on CLTs than societal cultural variables. Correlations between organizational culture dimensions and CLT dimensions constitute a test of the *organizational influence proposition.*

The *cultural influence proposition* asserts that societal culture has a pervasive influence on values, expectations, and behavior and will therefore influence CLTs. Correlations between societal culture dimensions and CLT dimensions constitute a test of the *cultural influence proposition.* Thus, comparisons of the regression coefficients of the relationships between societal culture dimensions and CLTs with the regression coefficients of the relationships between organizational culture dimensions and CLTs constitute competitive tests of the cultural influence and the organizational influence propositions.

Hypothesis 5. Relative to organizations in the food-processing industry, organizations in the financial-services industry will have higher scores on the organizational cultural dimensions of gender egalitarianism, humanism, and future orientation, and lower scores on power distance practices.[6]

The rationale for this hypothesis is that financial institutions need to be employee- and customer-service–oriented, future-oriented, and flexible in order to compete. Customer satisfaction depends on the degree to which financial institutions treat customers individually, design their services to meet customer preferences, and make investments that protect or enhance the future value of client and organizational assets. Financial institutions also need to adopt a more humane orientation toward their employees, more future orientation toward their clients, and less centralization of decision making in comparison with the food processing organizations. Such practices require employees with relatively high levels of education. Thus, financial institutions need to (1) minimize employee turnover to retain well-educated employees who would be costly to replace, and (2) maintain stability with clients.

Hypotheses Concerning Relationships Specified by Structural Contingency Theory and the Moderating Effects of Societal Cultural Dimensions

In addition to the research described in the preceding paragraphs, we will also conduct tests of structural contingency theory of organizational form and effectiveness (Donaldson, 1993; Hickson et al., 1974), and tests relevant to the effects of culture on relationships between organizational contingencies, organizational practices, strategy formulation processes (Hauser, House, & Puranam, 1999), and effectiveness.

Hypothesis 6. Organizational contingency variables will be associated with relevant organizational practices as specified by Structural Contingency Theory (Hickson et al., 1974). However, societal dimensions of culture that are isomorphic with the organizational practices will moderate these correlations.

The rationale for this hypothesis is that organizations are expected to have a tendency to align their practices with both strategic contingency variables and the cultural forces of the society in which they function. More specifically, structural contingency theory asserts that organizations become more formalized with size. This theory also asserts that under conditions of technological and environmental uncertainty organizations will engage in less formalization in order to maintain flexibility and thus adaptability to uncertain environmental demands.

The GLOBE data set includes a measure of organizational uncertainty avoidance practices. Organizational uncertainty avoidance practices take the form of formalization of rules, procedures, and policies. The GLOBE data set also includes a measure of the degree to which the strategy planning process is formalized. Using these measures we will test the following hypotheses which are operationalizations of this proposition.

Hypothesis 6a. Organizational size will be positively correlated with formalization of strategic planning processes.

Hypothesis 6b. Organizational size will be positively correlated with degree of uncertainty avoidance practices.

We expect managers in high uncertainty avoidance cultures to be more receptive to organizational uncertainty avoidance practices and formalization of strategic planning processes. Therefore,

Hypothesis 6c. The relationships specified in hypotheses 6a and 6b will be more strongly supported in high uncertainty avoidance cultures.

Hypothesis 6d. Technological uncertainty will be negatively correlated with organizational uncertainty avoidance practices.

Hypothesis 6e. Environmental uncertainty will be negatively correlated organizational uncertainty avoidance practices.

We expect managers in low uncertainty avoidance cultures to be less receptive to organizational uncertainty avoidance practices. Therefore,

Hypothesis 7. The relationships specified in hypotheses 6c and 6d will be more strongly supported in low uncertainty cultures.

Under conditions of environmental hostility, high-level managers are expected to be under substantial stress. We expect managers in high stress enviornments to increase control over organizational operations and therefore to centralize and closely control decision making (Aldrich, 1979; Staw, Sandelands, & Dutton, 1981). Consequently centralization and control are expected to be manifested in increased power distance practice. Therefore,

Hypothesis 8. Environmental hostility will be positively correlated with degree of organizational uncertainty avoidance and power distance practices and degree of formalization of strategic planning processes.

Hypothesis 9. The relationships specified in hypothesis 8 will be stronger for organizations in high power distance and high uncertainty avoidance cultures.

In addition to the above hypotheses we will also test hypotheses relevant to strategic alignment of strategic and structural organizational practices, CLT dimensions, and societal cultural forces. Specifically we will test the following hypotheses:

Hypothesis 10. Future-oriented organizational strategies will be positively correlated with future orientation of organizational cultures and the future-oriented CLT dimension.

Hypothesis 10a. Hypothesis 10 will be more strongly supported in future-oriented societies.

Hypothesis 11. Entrepreneurial orientation of organizational strategies will be positively correlated with the assertiveness and performance orientation dimensions of organizational cultures and the performance-oriented CLT dimension.

Hypothesis 11a. Hypothesis 11 will be more strongly supported in assertive and performance-oriented societies.

Hypothesis 12. Consensually based strategy formulation practices will be positively correlated with middle manager endorsement of participative leadership and negatively correlated with organizational power distance practices.

Hypothesis 12a. Hypothesis 12 will be more strongly supported in low power distance societies.

Hypothesis 13. Flexible strategy formulation practices will be associated with organic organizational cultures.

Organic organizational cultures are manifested by low organizational power distance and low uncertainly avoidance practices (Dickson, 1997).

Hypothesis 13a. Hypothesis 13 will be more strongly supported in low power distance and low uncertainty avoidance societies.

Hypothesis 14. The higher the correspondence between structural contingencies, societal culture dimensions, organizational culture dimensions, and CLTs specified in Hypotheses 6 through 13a, the higher the economic performance of the organizations studied.

The rationale for this hypothesis is that organizations that have strong alignment of CLTs, strategic processes, organizational practices, with societal culture will be most effective. However, we caution that some societal culture dimensions might be detrimental to the competitive and technological environment of business organizations. For example, in societies with a low future and performance orientation, low assertiveness and high uncertainty avoidance and humane orientation, an organizational misfit with societal practices is likely positively correlated with economic performance of organizations. This proposition will also be tested as part of Phase 2.

Samples

National borders may not be an adequate way to demarcate cultural boundaries, since many countries have large subcultures. It is impossible to obtain representative samples of such multicultural nations as China, India, or the United States. Nonetheless, the samples drawn from such countries need to be comparable with respect to the dominant forces that shape cultures, such as ecological factors, history, language, and religion. The country samples also need to be relatively homogeneous within cultures. For multicultural countries, whenever possible we sampled the subculture in which there is the greatest amount of commercial activity. When possible we also sampled more than one subculture (indigenous and Caucasian subcultures in South Africa, French and German subcultures in Switzerland, and East and West subcultures in Germany).

The units of analysis for the GLOBE project consisted of cultural level aggregated responses of samples of typical middle managers in three industries: food processing, financial services, and telecommunications services. The food-processing industry is a relatively stable industry. The telecommunications and financial industries may be stable or unstable, depending on country and economic conditions. By including these industries, we have obtained a fair number of dynamic industries and high-technology industries in the overall sample. Cultures in at least three countries in each of the following geographical regions are represented in the GLOBE sample: Africa, Asia, Europe (eastern, central, and northern), Latin America, North America, North Africa, Middle East, and the Pacific Rim, as indicated in Table 1.

Middle managers in these industries were asked to use a 7-point scale to describe leader attributes and behaviors that they perceive to enhance or impede outstanding leadership. They were also asked to give their perceptions of the practices and values (in the form of *As Is* and *Should Be* responses, respectively) in the society in which they live, and of the organizations in which they are employed, using 7-point scales as illustrated in Table 4. Independent samples of middle managers completed one of two questionnaires. Half of the respondents in each culture completed the societal culture questionnaire (Sample 1), and the other half completed the organizational culture questionnaire (Sample 2). All respondents completed the Leadership Attributes Questionnaire. Thus, the societal culture and the organizational culture questionnaires were completed by independent samples of respondents.

In addition, CCIs collected qualitative information about their societies and organizations in the industries they studied with respect to etic and emic dimensions of their cultures. Middle managers participated in interviews and focus groups and completed questionnaires. CCIs have also recorded archival information and participant observations, and collected unobtrusive measures to be used to describe and interpret the cultures studied. CCIs also conducted content analyses of the dominant general and business media in their cultures. In this capacity, they provided both etic and emic information concerning the study dimensions previously described.

Our design strategy consisted of obtaining responses of middle managers in two of the three target industries in each country studied.[7] This yielded samples from approximately 40 countries in each of the target industries. As stated earlier, data relevant to 54 countries were available at the time this chapter was written.

The sample design also permitted us to relate the within-culture mean dimension responses to the societal and organizational questionnaires to the within-culture mean dimension responses to the Leader Attribute Questionnaire. The means of the leadership item responses of Sample 1 and Sample 2 within each country were not significantly different. Thus, the individual leadership scale scores for the two samples were averaged to produce means on the leadership scales for all cultures. As a result of the independent assessment of the organizational and societal variables, and because the mean CLT responses in each sample in each culture were not different, the responses are free of common source response bias.

Unobtrusive Measures[8]

All instruments are subject to potential unknown biases. One procedure for minimizing response bias contamination is to use multiple methodologies to measure the same constructs. Measuring a construct with multiple methodologies permits verification of the measurement of cultures on the latent construct of interest by triangulation. Latent construct measurement based on two or more manifest indicators allows one to reduce, if not eliminate, potential response bias associated with questionnaire responses. The latent constructs used to measure societal level responses consist of questionnaire responses and unobtrusive measures. As previously noted, examples of unobtrusive measures are shown in Table 5.

The intercorrelations of the unobtrusive measures and the core *As Is* questionnaire scale scores for each dimension are all above .5 (all significant, $p < .05$). These intercorrelations indicate validity of the GLOBE societal *As Is* questionnaire measures. They also indicate that the middle manager responses to the societal questionnaire reflect the broader society in which the managers are embedded and not a more narrowly defined culture of middle managers.

Questionnaire Response Bias

Triandis (1995) has noted that the various cultures have different response patterns when responding to questionnaires. The presence of these different response patterns can bias cross-cultural comparisons. Thus several different statistical techniques have been developed to eliminate the contamination of survey responses. Following Triandis's (1995) suggestion, individual responses to all questions were standardized before aggregation to the societal and organizational levels of analysis. This procedure minimizes the effects of individual response bias. Using latent constructs composed of aggregated within-person standardized questionnaire response scores and unobtrusive measurement scales further lessens the effects of questionnaire response bias on the between-country comparisons.

Phase 2 CLT Scales

One of the objectives of GLOBE is to determine whether there are dimensions of CLTs that are universally endorsed and dimensions that are differentially endorsed across cultures. Recall that CLTs are culturally endorsed profiles of perceived effective or ineffective leader attributes or behaviors about which members within each culture agree. Profiles of CLT dimensions reflect what is commonly referred to as "leadership styles" in the leadership literature.

Shaw (1990) suggests that much of the cross-national literature indicating differences in managerial beliefs, values, and styles can be interpreted as showing culturally influenced differences in leader prototypes, which are analogous to

CLTs as conceptualized for Project GLOBE. A study by O'Connell, Lord, and O'Connell (1990) supports the argument that culture plays a strong role in influencing the content of leader attributes and behaviors perceived as desirable and effective. Their study specifically examined the similarities and differences between Japanese and American CLTs. For the Japanese, the traits of being fair, flexible, a good listener, outgoing, and responsible were highly rated in many domains, such as business, media, and education. For Americans, traits of intelligence, honesty, understanding, verbal skills, and determination were strongly endorsed as facilitating leader effectiveness in numerous domains. A study by Gerstner and Day (1994) also provides additional evidence that ratings of leadership attributes and behaviors vary across cultures. These investigators identified three dimensions relevant to distinct CLTs as expressed by university students from eight nations. These dimensions had rank order correlations with Hofstede's (1980) measures of power distance, uncertainty avoidance, and individualism of .81, 1.00, and .70, respectively and thus can be interpreted to measure these constructs. The GLOBE research project follows in the tradition of these studies. Following is a brief description of the development of the final Leader Attribute Questionnaire to identify CLTs.

Using the means of Phase 2 Leader Attribute Questionnaire subscales from 54 countries, we performed multilevel confirmatory factor analysis to confirm the 16-dimension factor structure of the leadership scales developed in the two pilot studies. This factor structure was confirmed. However, Phase 2 research included several additional items not included in the pilot study questionnaires that reflected the findings from ongoing interview and focus group research. We conducted a maximum likelihood exploratory factor analysis with a varimax rotation of these CLT items. This analysis resulted in five additional CLT subscales which exhibited sound psychometric properties. Thus, we have a total of 21 leadership subscales for Phase 2 analysis. These subscales and sample items are presented in Table 7.

As with the pilot data, our analysis revealed significant interrelationships among the factors, hence the need to create a second-order factor structure. A second-order factor analysis produced four factors: (1) Charismatic/Value-Based Leadership that is Team-Oriented, (2) Autonomous Leadership, (3) Humane Leadership, and (4) Non-Participative Self-Protective Leadership. Guided by prevailing theory, we divided Factor 1 into Charismatic/Value-Based Leadership and Team-Oriented Leadership to create two dimensions. We also divided Factor 4 into two dimensions: Self-Protective Leadership and Participative Leadership (the scores of the non-participative subscales were reversed to reflect participative leadership). These divisions of the empirically derived second-order factors were made to preserve conceptual clarity and to have dimensions that can be related to prevailing leadership theory and previous empirical studies.

The 21 subscales are grouped into six higher order leader behavior/attribute dimensions, which are presented in Table 8. As previously stated, we refer to the higher order dimensions as *global* CLT dimensions because they represent *classes*

Table 7. Leadership Prototype Scales: First-order Factors and Leader Attribute Items

- **Administratively Competent**
  - orderly
  - administratively skilled
  - organized
  - good administrator
- **Autocratic**
  - autocratic
  - dictatorial
  - bossy
  - elitist
- **Autonomous**
  - individualistic
  - independent
  - autonomous
  - unique
- **Charismatic I: Visionary**
  - foresight
  - prepared
  - anticipatory
  - plans ahead
- **Charismatic II: Inspirational**
  - enthusiastic
  - positive
  - morale booster
  - motive arouser
- **Charismatic III: Self-sacrificial**
  - risk taker
  - self-sacrificial
  - convincing
- **Conflict Inducer**
  - normative
  - secretive
  - intra-group competitor

- **Decisive**
  - willful
  - decisive
  - logical
  - intuitive
- **Diplomatic**
  - diplomatic
  - worldly
  - win/win problem solver
  - effective bargainer
- **Face Saver**
  - indirect
  - avoids negatives
  - evasive
- **Humane Orientation**
  - generous
  - compassionate
- **Integrity**
  - honest
  - sincere
  - just
  - trustworthy
- **Malevolent**
  - hostile
  - dishonest
  - vindictive
  - irritable
  - noncooperative
  - intelligent (reverse scored)
- **Modesty**
  - modest
  - self-effacing
  - patient

- **Non-participative**
  - non-delegator
  - micro-manager
  - non-egalitarian
  - individually oriented
- **Performance Oriented**
  - improvement oriented
  - excellence oriented
  - performance oriented
- **Procedural**
  - ritualistic
  - formal
  - habitual
  - procedural
- **Self-protective**
  - self-centered
  - non-participative
  - loner
  - asocial
- **Status Consciousness**
  - status-conscious
  - class conscious
- **Team 1: Collaborative Team Orientation**
  - group oriented
  - collaborative
  - loyal
  - consultative
- **Team II: Team Integrator**
  - communicative
  - team-builder
  - informed
  - integrator

Table 8. Global Culturally Endorsed Implicit Leadership Theory (CLT) Dimensions

1. *Charismatic/Value Based, 4.5–6.5*	2. *Team Oriented, 4.7–6.2*
*Charismatic 1: Visionary	*Team 1: Collaborative Team Orientation
*Charismatic 2: Inspirational	*Team 2: Team Integrator
*Charismatic 3: Self-sacrifice	*Diplomatic
*Integrity	*Malevolent (reverse scored)
*Decisive	*Administratively competent
*Performance oriented	
3. *Self-Protective, 2.5–4.6*	4. *Participative, 4.5–6.1*
*Self-centered	*Autocratic (reverse scored)
*Status conscious	*Non-participative (reverse scored)
*Conflict inducer	*Delegator[a]
*Face saver	
*Procedural	
5. *Humane, 3.8–5.6*	6. *Autonomous, 2.3–4.7*
*Modesty	*Individualistic
*Humane orientation	*Independent
	*Autonomous
	*Unique

Note: The numbered, italicized topics are Global CLT Dimensions. They are composed of CLT subscales. The only exception is Topic 6 (Autonomous) which is composed of questionnaire items, not subscales, and the item delegator ([a]) which is included in the participative dimension since it had a .81 correlation with the sum of the two subscales: autocratic and non-participative (scores revised). Numbers represent worldwide mean values on a 7-point scale ranging from 1 (substantially impedes) to 7 (substantially facilitates) effective leadership.

of leader behavior rather than specific leader behaviors. We refer to the 21 first-order factors as CLT subscales. These subscales measure more specific leader attributes and behaviors. Composite profiles of the six CLT dimensions represent what is generally referred to as leadership styles.

Universally Endorsed Leader Attributes

Hypothesis 1 states that charismatic/value-based leadership and integrity attributes will be universally endorsed as contributors to outstanding leadership. From Table 8, it can be seen that the global CLT charismatic/value-based leadership dimension had culture scores ranging from 4.5 to 6.5 on the 7-point response scale, thus indicating positive endorsement by all cultures.

To test Hypothesis 1 more rigorously, we established the following criteria for Leader Attribute Questionnaire items to be considered universally endorsed as contributors to outstanding leadership: (1) 95 percent of country scores had to exceed a mean of 6 on a 7-point scale for that attribute, and (2) the worldwide grand mean score for all countries had to exceed 6 for the attribute. The results of

Table 9. Universal Positive Leader Attributes

Questionnaire Items	Corresponding Leadership Scale (First-order Factors)
Trustworthy	Integrity
Just	Integrity
Honest	Integrity
Foresight	Charisma 1: visionary
Plans ahead	Charisma 1: visionary
Encouraging	Charisma 2: inspirational
Positive	Charisma 2: inspirational
Dynamic	Charisma 2: inspirational
Motive arouser	Charisma 2: inspirational
Confidence builder	Charisma 2: inspirational
Motivational	Charisma 2: inspirational
Dependable*	
Intelligent	Malevolent (reverse score)
Decisive	Decisiveness
Effective bargainer	Diplomatic
Win-win problem solver	Diplomatic
Administratively skilled	Administratively competent
Communicative	Team 2: team integrator
Informed	Team 2: team integrator
Coordinator	Team 2: team integrator
Team builder	Team 2: team integrator
Excellence oriented	Performance oriented

Note: *This item did not load on any factor.

this analysis are presented in Table 9. Three of the positively endorsed items concern aspects of integrity. Note that most of the other universal positively endorsed items are components of the first-order Charismatic/Value-Based Leadership and Team-Oriented dimensions. The portrait of a leader who is universally viewed as effective is clear: the person should exhibit the integrity and charismatic qualities listed in Table 9 and build effective teams. Thus, Hypothesis 1 is strongly supported.

Table 10. Universal Negative Leader Attributes

Questionnaire Attributes	Corresponding Leadership Scale (First-order Factors)
Loner	Self-protective
Asocial	Self-protective
Noncooperative	Malevolent
Irritable	Malevolent
Nonexplicit	Face saver
Egocentric	*
Ruthless	*
Dictatorial	Autocratic

Note: *These items did not load on any factor.

Universal Impediments to Leadership Effectiveness

The criteria for specific attributes, measured at the item level, to be considered universally viewed as impediments to effective leadership required that (1) an item grand mean for all countries be less than 3, and (2) 95 percent of country scores on the item be less than 3. These combined criteria indicate that the attribute was universally perceived as inhibiting outstanding leadership. Results are presented in Table 10.

Culturally Contingent Endorsement of Leader Attributes

Most interesting, from a cross-cultural viewpoint, are the attributes that in some countries were considered to enhance outstanding leadership and in other countries were considered to impede outstanding leadership. We present in Table 11 those attributes (items) that yielded scores above and below the scale midpoint of 4, contingent on country-specific responses. For instance, while the attribute Individualistic had a grand country mean of 3.11 (slightly inhibits outstanding leadership), individual country scores ranged from a low of 1.67 (moderately impedes) to a high of 5.10 (moderately contributes). Similarly, the item Status Conscious ranged in value from a low of 1.92 (moderately impedes) to a high of 5.77 (moderately contributes). Even more striking was the Risk Take item, which is a com-

Table 11. Culturally Contingent CLT Items

Anticipatory (3.84–6.51)	Intuitive (3.72–6.47)
Ambitious (2.85–6.73)*	Logical (3.89–6.58)
Autonomous (1.63–5.17)	Micro-manager (1.60–5.00)*
Cautious (2.17–5.78)*	Orderly (3.81–6.34)*
Class conscious (2.53–6.09)	Procedural (3.03–6.10)
Compassionate (2.69–5.56)	Provocateur (1.38–6.00)*
Cunning (1.26–6.38)*	Risk taker (2.14–5.96)
Domineering (1.60–5.14)*	Ruler (1.66–5.20)*
Elitist (1.61–5.00)*	Self-effacing (1.85–5.23)*
Enthusiastic (3.72–6.44)	Self-sacrificial (3.00–5.96)
Evasive (1.52–5.67)	Sensitive (1.96–6.35)*
Formal (2.12–5.43)	Sincere (3.99–6.55)*
Habitual (1.93–5.38)	Status-conscious (1.92–5.77)
Independent (1.67–5.32)	Subdued (1.32–6.18)*
Indirect (2.16–4.86)	Unique (3.47–6.06)
Individualistic (1.67–5.10)	Willful (3.06–6.48)
Intra-group competitor (3.00–6.49)*	Worldly (3.48–6.18)*
Intra-group conflict avoider (1.84–5.69)*	

Notes: CLT, culturally endorsed implicit leadership theory.
Numbers represent worldwide minimum and maximum values on a 7-point scale ranging from 1 (substantially impedes) to 7 (substantially facilitates) effective leadership.
*These items did not load on any factor.

ponent of the Charismatic/Value-Based second-order factor. Risk Taken ranges in value from a 2.14 (moderately impedes) to a 5.96 (moderately contributes).

These findings raise several important questions. For instance, if some attributes (items) and some global CLT dimensions are differentially endorsed among nations, as indicated by our analyses thus far, are they equally compelling and influential? What psychological and sociological processes link the CLT dimensions to dominant cultural values? Are CLT dimensions more rigidly set for homogeneous societies, such as Japan, than for culturally diverse societies, such as the United States?

Test of Hypothesis 2 and 3

The sine qua non of the GLOBE project concerns the link between culture and leadership. While all of the analyses addressing this issue have not been completed, we do have positive preliminary findings. Hypotheses 2 and 3 states that there will be significant positive relationships between CLT dimensions and their isomorphic societal and organizational culture dimensions and organizational.

Table 12 shows our predictions concerning the specific cultural dimensions that should predict cross-cultural differences in the second-order global CLT dimensions. We generated these hypotheses by examining each first-order leadership

Table 12. A Priori Hypotheses Predicting Effective Leadership Style from Societal and Organizational Culture

Second-Order Leadership Factor	Predicted Culture Dimension
Charismatic/Value Based	1. Performance Orientation
	2. Future Orientation
	3. Humane Orientation
Team Oriented	1. Collectivism I
	2. Collectivism II
	3. Humane Orientation
	4. Assertiveness*
	5. Uncertainty Avoidance*
Participative	1. Assertiveness*
	2. Power Distance*
	3. Humane Orientation
Humane Orientation	1. Humane Orientation
	2. Gender Egalitarianism
Autonomous	1. Collectivism I*
	2. Collectivism II*
Self-protective	1. Humane Orientation
	2. Power Distance
	3. Uncertainty Avoidance

Note: Dimensions followed by asterisks hypothesized to be inversly related to leadership factors.

scale and identifying the societal and organizational cultural dimensions that are isomorphic with each second-order leadership dimension (e.g., perceived effectiveness of Charismatic/Value-Based leadership was expected to be associated with the societal and organizational dimensions entitled Performance, Future, and Humane Orientation). Table 12 shows these hypotheses.

Table 13. Results for Hierarchical Linear Modeling Analyses Predicting Leadership Dimensions from Organizational and Societal Culture

Dependent Variable: Team-oriented Leadership	
	Coefficient
Constant	5.89**
Organizational Level	
Collectivism Should Be	.28**
Societal Level	
Humane Orientation Should Be	−.13*
Collectivism Should Be	.40**
Organizational Variance Explained:	37.4%
Societal Variance Explained:	32.7%
Total Variance Explained:	10.8%

Dependent Variable: Participative Leadership	
	Coefficient
Constant	4.79**
Organizational Level	
Power Distance Should Be	−.16**
Uncertainty Avoidance Should Be	−.13**
Societal Level	
Uncertainty Avoidance Should Be	−.46**
Power Distance Should Be	−.35**
Humane Orientation Should Be	.25*
Assertiveness Should Be	.12*
Organizational Variance Explained:	29.7%
Societal Variance Explained:	82.2%
Total Variance Explained:	26.9%

Dependent Variable: Humane Orientation	
	Coefficient
Constant	4.83**
Organizational Level	
Humane Orientation Should Be	.37**
Societal Level	
Humane Orientation Should Be	.41**
Organizational Variance Explained:	20.7%
Societal Variance Explained:	31.6%
Total Variance Explained:	7.0%

(continued)

Table 13. (Continued)

Dependent Variable: Charisma	
	Coefficient
Constant	5.88**
Organizational Level	
Performance Orientation Should Be	.22**
Societal Level	
Performance Orientation Should Be	.35**
Organizational Variance Explained:	41.6%
Societal Variance Explained:	14.2%
Total Variance Explained:	11.9%

Notes: *$p < .05$; **$p < .01$; ***$p < .0001$.
The unit of measurement for these regressions is the organization. The number of organizations is 391. The degrees of freedom are 390. All organizations existed in societies from which three or more organizations provided data.
Organizational variance explained is calculated by dividing the total variance accounted for by the organizational predictors by the total amount of variance occurring at the organizational level of analysis. Societal variance explained is calculated by dividing the total variance accounted for by the society predictors by the total amount of variance occurring at the society level of analysis.

We tested Hypotheses 2 and 3 by using hierarchical linear modeling, a procedure that allows one to identify the amount of variance in a dependent variable that is accounted for by organizations as well as the societies in which the organizations function. The total amount of variance of CLTs accounted for is thus a joint function of the societal-level variables and the organizational-level variables in the societies in which the organizations are nested. Table 13 reveals that the endorsement of CLT global leader behavior dimensions are associated only with respondent value orientation (i.e., *Should Be* responses), and not with observed practices (i.e., *As Is* responses). The statistically significant relationships between societal and organizational culture dimensions and CLT dimensions presented in Table 13 are as follows:

1. Approximately 11 percent of the total variance in team-oriented leadership endorsement is accounted for by organizational collective value orientation and by the humane and collective value orientations of societies in which these organizations reside. It is important to realize, however, that some of the variance in team-oriented leadership is likely attributable to levels of analysis in which we are not presently interested (e.g., industry, individual levels). When only the portions of variance that are of direct interest were examined, the organizational variable accounted for 37 percent of the variance in endorsement of all team-oriented leadership that occurred at the organizational level of analysis. The two society variables accounted for 32 percent of the endorsement of team-oriented leadership variance that occurred at the society level of analysis.

2. Approximately 27 percent of the total variance in participative leadership endorsement is accounted for by organizational-level power distance and uncertainty avoidance value orientation and by four societal-level variables: uncertainty avoidance, power distance, humane orientation, and assertiveness value orientations. The two organizational-level variables accounted for approximately 30 percent, and the societal-level variables accounted for approximately 82 percent of the variance in endorsement of participative leadership that occurred at their respective levels.
3. Approximately 7 percent of the total variance in endorsement of humane-oriented leadership is accounted for by organizational-level and societal-level humane value orientation. The organizational-level variable accounted for approximately 21 percent, and the societal-level variable accounted for approximately 32 percent, respectively, of the variance in endorsement of humane-oriented leadership that occurred at their respective levels.
4. Approximately 12 percent of the total variance in endorsement of charismatic/value-based leadership is accounted for by organizational-level and societal-level value placed on performance orientation. The organizational-level variable accounted for approximately 41 percent, and the societal-level variable accounted for approximately 14 percent, of the variance in endorsement of charismatic/value-based leadership that occurred at their respective levels.
5. The variance in endorsement of self-protective and autonomous leadership accounted for by organizational-level and societal-level variables is negligible and not reported in Table 13. This finding indicates that the variance in these two types of CLT endorsement is likely attributable to industry or individual differences, or other unmeasured situational variables.

Hypotheses 2 and 3 are supported with respect to endorsement of the above four global leader dimensions. These findings show that both societal and organizational cultural variables have non-trivial influences on CLTs and explain, in part, why there is variance across cultures with respect to what is expected of leaders and the influence and privileges they are granted.

Country-Level Uses of the Middle Manager Data

A profile shall be constructed for each nation consisting of the societal, organizational, and global CLT scores. In essence, for each culture CCIs shall construct a quantitative description of the attributes perceived as facilitating or impeding outstanding leadership, the culturally endorsed values (*Should Be* responses), and the common practices (*As Is* responses) in the societies and organizations studied. The CCIs can then interpret the results and compare the data from their culture to the data relevant to all other cultures. Fourteen of these interpretations have been included as part of the culture-specific chapters of the first of several GLOBE anthologies. The content of the anthologies is described in the following paragraphs. Upon completion of Phase 2, we shall have profiles of the dominantly endorsed leader behaviors and attributes and of the societal and organizational dimensions of each culture. We shall also have substantially greater knowledge concerning cultural and organizational influences on endorsed leader attributes in the dominant cultures or subcultures of the 62 cultures studied. This information shall be based on both the quantitative and the qualitative findings, and when published, it shall have substantial practical value for leaders who practice management in the cultures studied or deal with individuals of these cultures.

In-Depth Country-specific Descriptions of Cultures

Country-specific qualitative research by the CCIs has been ongoing from the beginning of Phase 1 and will continue to the final phase of the project. Many of the CCI teams will write a qualitative description of the major cultural variables that are relevant to leadership and organizational practices in their particular culture. The in-depth description of each culture will incorporate the following topics: (1) an overall description of the culture in terms of its political and economic system and the major historical forces and leaders that have shaped that system; (2) a brief description of prevailing organizational practices in the industries and organizations studied by the CCIs in terms of the constructs that underlie the core study dimension; (3) a description of the emic (culture-specific) manifestations of the core dimensions of the study at the societal, organizational, and leader levels of analysis; (4) a description of other emic characteristics of the society, industries studied, and leadership practices within these industries that have nontrivial implications for the practice of leadership and organizations; (5) the culture-specific semantic interpretation of the concept of leadership—what it means, the role and status of leaders in the culture, leadership functions, privileges, responsibilities, and the like; (6) identification of qualitative unobtrusive indicators of the importance assigned to leadership or leaders based on CCI participant observation; (7) an interpretation of the quantitative dimensions relevant to their cultures and in relation to other cultures; (8) an interpretative discussion of the kinds of leadership behavior required for effective leadership in the industries under investigation; and (9) prescriptive implications.

In essence, the CCIs will write a qualitative analysis of major variables relevant to leadership and organizational practices in the industries studied. The qualitative description and interpretation will be based on CCI participant observation, unobtrusive measures, and content analyses of media, interviews, and focus group discussions. CCIs have been provided with a set of self-instruction guides to ensure at least a moderate level of uniformity and quality of the qualitative research.

The completed chapters will be based on the combination of the quantitative survey data and the qualitative research findings produced by CCIs. An interpretive analysis of all of the findings will then be possible. It is hoped that this interpretation will lead to the development of a cross-cultural theory of leadership and organizational practices.

Projected Phase 3: Prediction of Leader Behavior, Organizational Practices, and Their Effectiveness

Phase 3 will consist of longitudinal tests of the following hypotheses:

Hypothesis 14a. Societal culture dimensions assessed in Phase 2 will predict isomorphic organizational practices and leader behavior dimensions assessed in Phase 3.

The rationales for Hypotheses 8 and 9 are specified following Hypotheses 2 and 3, earlier.

Hypothesis 15. The stronger the alignment among strategic organizational contingencies, societal culture dimensions, and organizational culture dimensions measured in Phase 2, as specified in Hypotheses 6a through 13a, the higher the economic performance of the organizations studied. The rationale for this hypothesis is specified following Hypothesis 14, earlier.

In addition, armed with Phase 2 measures of CLTs and the nine core GLOBE societal dimensions for 62 cultures, we will be able to test the following hypotheses with regard to leadership:

Hypothesis 16. CLTs measured in Phase 2 will predict observed leader behaviors in Phase 3.

Hypothesis 17. The more congruent the individual leader behaviors are with the CLTs, (1) the more readily leadership attempts by such individuals will be accepted and effective, (2) the more the individuals will be perceived as legitimate leaders, (3) the more highly motivated will be their subordinates/followers, (4) the more committed will be their subordinates/followers, and (5) the higher will be the leaders' performance and that of their subordinates.

Hypothesis 18. For purposes of introducing substantial organizational change, charismatic/value-oriented leadership will be the most effective leader behavior.

Phase 3 Method

The data collection for Phase 3 has begun. Based on the findings of Phase 2, a Multi-Culture Leader Behavior Description Questionnaire (MCLQ) designed to capture respondents' perceptions of leaders with whom they are familiar, was developed. The samples to be investigated will be CEOs from a variety of industries in approximately 25 cultures. In countries in which it is not a violation of cultural norms, respondents will be asked to describe the leader behavior of their immediate supervisor.[9] Independent measures of the immediate supervisor's performance and work units will also be collected.

The MCLQ was developed to reflect the leader behaviors identified in Phase 2, described earlier, and listed in Table 7. For example, since leader integrity is identified as a specific leadership attribute, the MCLQ includes several items describing behaviors that reflect leader integrity. Leader integrity items of the MCLQ will take the form, "The leader is ethical, follows a moral code, practices what he or she preaches."

Respondents will also be asked to express their emotional and evaluative responses to the leaders, their willingness to support the leaders, their willingness to go above and beyond the call of duty in the interest of the leaders' vision and direction, their confidence in the leaders, and their commitment to the leaders' goals. Measures of leadership and work-unit effectiveness shall also be collected. As in Phase 2, high-level executives shall be asked to complete the organizational practices and structural contingency scales developed in Phase 1.

Search for Emic Leader Behaviors and Emic Manifestations of Etic Dimensions of Cultures

In addition to the etic research previously described, we are interested in identifying the specific behavioral manifestations and mannerisms employed in enacting CLTs. Since respondents in all countries could describe the degree to which the leader attributes included in Table 7 contribute to or impede leader effectiveness, these dimensions are etic. They represent universal continua, along which leader behavior or attributes in all countries can be scaled. As mentioned above, the second-order CLT dimensions describe global etic leader behavior *patterns*. However, some important *specific behaviors* or attitudes by which these global etic dimensions are enacted will likely vary among cultures. For example, Smith, Misumi, Tayeb, Peterson, and Bond (1989) found that American managers are more likely to provide directions to subordinates on a face-to-face basis, whereas Japanese managers are likely to use written memos. In the United States, subordinates are usually provided negative feedback directly from their supervisors in face-to-face interactions. In Japan, such feedback is usually channeled through a peer of the subordinate. Thus, Smith and colleagues (1989) concluded that the global etic behavior dimension referred to as "performance-oriented leadership" is enacted with different specific emic behaviors in Japan and the United States. These differences in behaviors reflect the U.S. individualistic norm of "brute honesty" and the Japanese collectivistic norm of "face saving."

We expect to find emic organizational practices as well as emic organizational forms in several cultures. Family-founded and -managed firms in Hong Kong, and post-Soviet entrepreneurial firms managed by the "New Russians" in Russia are examples of such emic organizational practices. For each culture, emic organizational practices as well as emic leader behaviors will be described in the country specific chapters of the GLOBE anthologies.

Summary: Projected Phase 3 Results

In summary, respondents will describe their organizational cultures and their immediate superiors. Measures of leader and work-unit effectiveness and individual emotional and cognitive evaluative responses to leader behaviors will also be obtained. These measures will be used to test Phase 3 hypotheses and to determine the performance effectiveness of the leader behaviors described by the dimensions of the CLTs identified in Phase 2. Measures of organizational culture, structural contingencies, and effectiveness of organizations will also be collected. These measures will be used to conduct longitudinal tests of structural contingency theory. Measures of emic leader behaviors and organizational practices shall also be obtained to gain culture-specific knowledge about leadership in each of the cultures studied. We shall eliminate the possibility of common source bias by collecting measures of organizational cultures and leader behavior from different subsamples within each culture studied.

Projected Phase 4: Laboratory and Field Experiments

The research through Phase 3 will allow us to determine: (1) those leader behaviors that are universally *perceived* as facilitators of or impediments to outstanding leadership; (2) whether there are any universally *practiced* leader behaviors and universal organizational practices; (3) leader behaviors and organizational practices that have positive or negative cognitive, affective, and performance consequences; (4) leader behaviors and organizational practices that are culture specific; that is, those that are practiced in only some cultures and have positive or negative effects in only some cultures; (5) the effects of culture on the frequency, acceptability, and effectiveness of organizational practices; (6) whether the associations among organizational contingencies, organizational practices, and organizational effectiveness predicted by structural contingency theory hold longitudinally; (7) the moderating effects of societal culture on the associations predicted by structural contingency theory, (8) the moderating effect of CLTs on CEO leader behavior and leader and organizational effectiveness relationships, and (9) relationships between CEO leader behaviors and the introduction of strategic organizational change.

Phase 4 of the program will be designed to determine *experimentally* the effects of the various leader behaviors by cultures and thus determine *causal* relationships among leader behaviors and outcomes. Here we describe the conceptual fundamentals of the projected Phase 4 research. An operational research design will be specified when the results of Phase 3 are available.

Phase 4 Hypotheses

Hypotheses 17 and 18 of Phase 3 concerning the moderating effect of CLTs on leader behavior-outcome relationships and charismatic/value-based leadership to stimulate organizational change will be tested experimentally as Hypotheses 19 and 20 to determine the *causal effect* of leader behaviors and CLTs on the dependent variables.

> **Hypothesis 19.** Leader behaviors that are consistent with CLTs measured in Phase 2 will be more accepted and will have more positive cognitive, affective, behavioral, and performance effects on followers than leader behaviors that are inconsistent with CLTs measured in Phase 2.
>
> **Hypothesis 20.** For purposes of introducing substantial organizational change in organizational practices, charismatic/value-based leadership will be the most effective leader behavior.

Phase 4 Method

Using the culture-specific endorsed leader profiles obtained in Phase 2 as guides, we shall conduct controlled field and laboratory experiments in at least two cultures in each major region of the world. The leader behaviors to be studied will be those that were found in Phase 3 to be most relevant to leader effectiveness, either positively or negatively, in the 62 cultures studied. The experiments will be designed so that we will be able to assess the effects of various leader behaviors on follower affective responses, behavior, and effectiveness. The cultures to be selected for the experiments will be those with well-defined and consensually agreed CLT profiles as indicated by low within-country variance of responses to Phase 2 CLT scales. The experiments will be designed so that we shall be able to assess the effects of various leader behaviors on follower affective responses, behavior, and effectiveness.

The laboratory setting in which Hypothesis 19 will be tested will be a realistic simulation of an organization. The independent variables will be three kinds of leader behaviors. Confederate leaders will enact the leader behaviors. The dependent variables will be the affective responses, behavior, and performance effectiveness of individual followers and groups of followers.

In Treatment Condition 1, the effects of the leader behaviors endorsed by each culture will be assessed. That is, the experimental treatment will consist of leader behaviors endorsed by the CLT of the country in which the experiment is conducted.

In Treatment Condition 2, the effects of those leader behaviors found in Phase 3 to have the most consistent positive effects on follower cognitions, affect, and performance across cultures will be assessed. Thus this treatment will consist of universally or near universally endorsed leader behaviors enacted by confederate leaders.

In Treatment Condition 3, confederates will enact leader behaviors that are in conflict with the CLT profiles of each culture.

The outcome of these experiments will be substantially increased knowledge concerning the following questions:

1. Are there any universally effective leader behaviors?
2. What is the effect of violating strongly held culturally endorsed preferences for selected leader behaviors?
3. Are behaviors that are consistent with culture specific preferences more effective than a select set of other behaviors that have been found in Phase 3 to be the most consistently positively endorsed leader behaviors across cultures? The answer to the latter question will tell us whether the behaviors specified in CLTs are also the behaviors that are more effective and will indicate whether leaders can make a difference by being different. More specifically, we will be able to determine whether a select set of behaviors can consistently have more positive effects than a set of culturally endorsed behaviors, even if the former behaviors are in conflict with culturally endorsed norms.

Hypotheses 19 and 20 will also be tested by using a field experimental design. As one possible example, we may ask university business school students to respond to a proposed change in the system by which they are graded in their educational program. It will be proposed that the grading system be changed to grade subjects on the basis of their relative standing and a forced curve distribution. It will be explained that this system is consistent with competitive schools, will enhance the reputation of their school, and will enhance the amount of learning achieved by students.

In the first experimental treatment, the confederate leader, acting as a representative of the school's curriculum committee or in another relevant official capacity, will introduce and advocate the proposed change by enacting the leader behaviors most strongly endorsed by the CLT of the culture.

In the second treatment, the leader will introduce and advocate the proposed change by linking it to a vision that emphasizes increased international status and competitiveness of the school and appeals to the patriotism and to the values endorsed in the culture. The leader will also express high performance standards and strong confidence in the students and appeal to country loyalty by stressing international competition among business schools. These behaviors are part of the Charismatic/Value-Based Leadership global dimension.

In sum, in Phase 4 we hope to make a substantial contribution to knowledge concerning the behavioral and performance effects of leader behaviors as well as their cognitive and affective effects. The results of Phase 4 will be reported in a monograph or book.

UNIQUE STRENGTHS OF THE GLOBE RESEARCH DESIGN

Project GLOBE differs from previous cross-cultural research in several ways. The primary strength of this research is that we have not made assumptions about how best to measure cultural phenomena. Rather, we use multiple measurement methods in order to empirically test which methods are most meaningful. This is most evident in the development of three sets of measures assessing culture: (1) those based on shared values of organizational or society members, (2) those based on current organizational and societal *practices*, and (3) unobtrusive measures. In addition, we developed measures of leader attributes that differentiate cultures in terms of perceived effectiveness, as well as leader attributes that are *universally* endorsed (or rejected) across cultures. Further, we have collected data relevant to organizational contingency variables and organizational effectiveness.

We developed new measures and collected original data for our hypotheses and research questions, rather than collecting data on only some variables and relying on measures developed at other times in other places from other samples for the other variables. Since the organizational culture, societal culture, and leadership measures employed in Phase 2 were completed by different people, we were able to eliminate the frequently encountered problem of common source bias. By use of multiple indicators of societal culture, we were able to eliminate common method variance. The psychometric properties of the GLOBE scales and tests of their validity exceed normal empirical research standards and are described in the previously mentioned monograph (Hanges et al., 1998, under review).

CONTRIBUTIONS

The GLOBE research program is directed toward filling a substantial knowledge gap concerning the cross-cultural forces relevant to effective leadership and organizational practices. The research findings will be useful for resolving several important theoretical social science issues and for a wide variety of practical purposes. In this section, we briefly describe the various contributions we expect to result from the GLOBE research.

Practical Relevance

The final product of the GLOBE research program, the books and articles in which the various cultures will be described and interpreted, will include practically useful information about the cultures studied.

It is expected that the quantitative findings resulting from the GLOBE research program will provide substantial enlightenment concerning the processes by which culture influences leadership and organizational practices. In the GLOBE anthologies consisting of culture-specific chapters, cultures will be described in terms of the nine core dimensions as well as their unique (emic) attributes. A description will be provided concerning universal and culturally contingent leader attributes and behaviors, the commonly enacted and most favored leader behavior patterns and organizational practices found in the cultures studied, and the cultural influences on the effectiveness of leader behaviors and organizational practices. In addition, leader behaviors that are culturally offensive will be identified and described. As mentioned previously, 14 chapters, which will comprise the first anthology, have been completed.

The qualitative research chapters in the GLOBE anthologies describe the most critical leader behaviors and organizational practices in each culture studied, the constraints imposed on leaders by cultural prescriptions and proscriptions, and unique norms of the cultures studied relevant to leadership and organizational practices. This information will be useful as case content for leadership training and career development programs and for the design of management and leadership education programs intended to prepare individuals who will manage and lead others in cultures other than their home cultures.

The descriptions of cultural prescriptions and proscriptions will be useful for the adjustment and effective interaction of individuals who work with others from the cultures studied. More specifically, this information will be useful to expatriates assigned to other than their native cultures, managers of diverse cultural and ethnic groups both domestic and abroad, individuals involved in the management of public and private international affairs, and those who conduct negotiations with commercial and political organizations in other cultures.

Knowledge of the culturally endorsed implicit theories of leadership in each culture, and most and least effective leader attributes and behaviors, will be useful for selecting, counseling, and training individuals who are to be assigned to, or who work with, members of the cultures studied. The resulting findings will be useful for informing potential managers of the kinds of behaviors and organizational practices that are acceptable and effective and unacceptable and ineffective in the cultures studied.

Information concerning the constraints imposed on leaders by cultural norms will be useful to decision makers who need to anticipate and respond to the actions of leaders of other cultures. Knowledge about cultural and organizational norms and practices in the cultures studied can inform the formulation of meaningful prescriptions for managing in other cultures—for strategy and policy formulation, organizational improvement interventions, human resource management practices, and the design of organization structures and incentive and control systems.

The industries studied are subjected to a wide variety of organizational contingencies. Many of the findings relevant to the effects of organizational contingencies on organizational practices and effectiveness in these industries are thus likely to be relevant to other industries and, therefore, useful to managers whose industries face similar organizational contingencies.

In sum, the findings of the study will provide a wide variety of information about 62 cultures, representing all major regions of the world, that can help managers and leaders in their adjustment, strategy and policy formulation, human resource management practices, and organizational practices.

Beneficial Social and Economic Applications

The research program is expected to have several additional beneficial social and economic applications. Within regions, countries that share similar regional resources and backgrounds can make comparisons to determine similarities and differences among themselves and share ways to improve inter-country relationships, economic productivity, and quality of life for their citizens. The research program is also expected to lead to increased intercultural communication among educators who normally would not have contact with each other, and thus it will result in greater intercultural awareness and cooperation among scholars. CCIs have been extremely active in practicing cross-cultural communications. GLOBE-related research has been presented in over 90 conference papers, chapters of books, or journal publications.

Many of the Country Co-Investigators, being indigenous to their cultures, are influence and change agents within those cultures, at least with respect to those with whom they have contact in their roles as university faculty members, social scientists, and consultants. The intra-country social influence of the CCIs will most likely be substantially enhanced by participating in the GLOBE research. These CCIs, in turn, will serve as country boundary spanners and will facilitate importation and transfer of knowledge within their countries. Forty scholarly papers based on GLOBE data have been presented at national or regional conferences thus far.

CCIs in several nations have begun to translate the products of the research (which will be several books and scholarly articles) into other languages and thus increase the dissemination of this information to a wider number of countries. The chapters of the books will make reports on each of the cultures studied available in the public domain.

Ancillary Social Science Contributions

The resulting data can be used for multiple purposes beyond the hypotheses of the study. For example, the worldwide Phase 2 data can be used to compare countries with their trading partners or their major competitors with respect to cultural, organizational, or leadership practices that are relevant to improving trade between them or with respect to practices that facilitate harmonious and productive trade. We have already witnessed over 50 research projects and papers presented at scholarly conferences in which cultural and managerial practices have been compared among subsets of the GLOBE participating nations. An entire issue of the *Polish Psychological Bulletin* has been devoted to this research (Maczynski, 1997).

Relationships between the variables under study and economic practices and outcomes can also be subjected to analysis. The societal-level data can be used in econometric or sociological models and related to firm-level practices such as forms of production systems and organization, transfer of technology, pricing, risk taking with respect to entry into new markets, investment with respect to research and development, and foreign investment practices. With the exception of four studies we were able to locate concerning economic growth, little attention is given to cultural influences on economic practices and output. The four studies to which we refer are those authored by Hofstede and Bond (1988); Franke (1997); House et al. (1977), and McClelland (1961).

The measures of culture can also be related to national levels of saving, distribution of wealth and social privileges, consumption levels and patterns, issues of economic growth and development, regulatory practices, and national productivity and efficiency. To date, cultural influences on such variables have gone largely ignored.

Indices of economic practices, adherence to norms of human rights, safety, and quality of life, by country, are either available in published form or can be collected by CCIs, other scholars, or interested government agencies or foundations. The GLOBE Phase 2 worldwide data can be analyzed in relation to these indices. Thus, it will be possible to determine concurrent or predictive relationships between the GLOBE dimensions and such indices.

The worldwide data can also be analyzed to determine relationships between the variables under study and many indices of social and physical well-being. For example, the GLOBE societal culture dimensions can be related to such outcomes as mortality rates, life expectancy rates, hygiene practices, preventive or remedial medical practices, stress levels, suicide rates, frequency of ethnic and border conflicts, indicators of social unrest, and violations of human rights. Following are some examples of expected relationships between GLOBE societal dimensions and socially and practically relevant variables:

- Cultural tendencies toward power stratification and assertiveness are likely positively related to tendencies toward intra-country conflict among labor and management and possibly even to tendencies of nations to enter into aggressive ethnic border conflicts and military actions.
- Humane orientation is likely inversely related to the frequency and severity of hostile actions within cultures. Humane orientation is also likely positively related to such practices as the establishment and enforcement of human rights norms and laws, and inversely related to their violations.
- Assertiveness is likely positively related to the frequency and severity of hostile actions within cultures.
- Performance and future orientation are likely positively related to national competitiveness and economic development.
- Gender equalization is likely inversely related to female abuse and positively related to female literacy, education, and labor market participation.

Following are four examples of findings that show how some of the cultural variables under study have been shown to relate to, or predict, important behavior. In *The Achieving Society,* David McClelland (1961) demonstrated rather convincingly that cultural indicators of achievement motivation were predictive of subsequent economic development in developing countries over a 25-year period. Hofstede and Bond (1988) found that a measure of cultural future orientation and delay of gratification referred to as the Confucian Dynamic was positively related to the economic growth of the Asian tigers from 1965 to 1985. Kogut and Singh (1986) have shown that the level of cultural uncertainty avoidance is inversely related to the level of risk taken by organizations when entering markets in foreign nations. Finally, one of the unobtrusive measures that correlates with the GLOBE measure of gender equalization is the United Nations index of female participation in labor markets.

OUTCOMES

The outcomes of Phases 1 and 2 of the GLOBE project will consist of several books and a series of articles. The first book will report the comparative quantitative cross-cultural results and hypothesis tests of GLOBE Phase 2 research. Another book or article will report the research findings relevant to the tests of structural contingency theory of organizational form and effectiveness as well as other findings relevant to organizational culture and practices enacted cross-culturally. The remaining books will be the anthologies described earlier, consisting of country-specific descriptions of cultures and interpretations of the Phase 2 quantitative data. Two or more methodological monographs or articles will illustrate new quantitative methods of cross-cultural research and also illustrate how recently developed sophisticated cross-level statistical procedures can be applied in cross-cultural research. One such monograph is currently under review (Hanges et al., 1998). Measurement papers will present the development and validation of questionnaires, unobtrusive measurement, and participant observation scales.

Phase 3 will test relationships found in Phase 2 longitudinally and will investigate emic as well as etic phenomena. Phase 3 results will appear in at least one additional book and several articles. Phase 4 will also result in at least one book or monograph that will report the results of the laboratory and field experiments.

CONCLUSION AND FUTURE ACTIVITIES

In summary, the GLOBE research is designed to contribute to the development of empirically based cross-cultural leadership and organizational theory by investigating the roles of societal and organizational values and institutionalized practices, organizational contingency variables, and implicit leadership theories as antecedents to cross-cultural variance in leader behavior, leader influence, leader effectiveness, and organizational practices and performance. GLOBE research is also designed to contribute to organizational theory and practice by exploring relationships between societal and organizational cultural variables and organizational effectiveness and by conducting cross-cultural tests of structural contingency theory. Based on the preliminary findings reported in this monograph, we are encouraged to believe that the GLOBE project has the potential of making a noteworthy contribution to the cross-cultural leadership and organizational literature.

ACKNOWLEDGMENT

The authors are indebted to Markus Hauser for his thoughtful comments and suggestions relevant to this monograph.

NOTES

1. The first seven authors participated in the statistical analyses and the writing of this monograph. The Senior Research Associates provided general research support to the Principal Investigator and the GLOBE Coordinating Team, assisted country representatives in translation and back-translations of instruments and in data collection, and assisted in the coordination of the GLOBE data collection. The remaining authors represented their cultures as Country Co-Investigators, made suggestions concerning the design and execution of the GLOBE program, collected the data on which this monograph is based, and provided interpretations of research findings in their respective cultures.

2. Phases I and II of the GLOBE research program were funded by the Dwight D. Eisenhower Leadership Education Program of the Department of Education of the United States.

3. While there are 62 cultures in the full Project GLOBE sample, the findings reported here are based on only 54 countries. The data for the remaining countries were not yet entered into the computer files at the time this monograph was finalized. The remaining cultures are Albania, China, Denmark, France, French-speaking Switzerland, Japan, Kazakhstan, and the United States.

4. Current members of the GCT are: Staffan Akerblom, Stockholm School of Economics, Sweden; Felix Brodbeck, University of Munich, Germany; Jagdeep S. Chhokar, Indian Institute of Management, Ahmedabad, India; Marcus W. Dickson, Wayne State University, United States; Peter W. Dorfman, New Mexico State University, United States; Paul J. Hanges, University of Maryland, United States; Robert J. House, University of Pennsylvania, United States; Mansour Javidan, University of Calgary, Canada; Enrique Ogliastri, University of Los Andes, Colombia; Antonio Ruiz-Quintanilla, Cornell University, United States; Marius van Wyk, University of South Africa, South Africa.

5. Data relevant to organizational practices were collected using the organizational level questions. Data relevant to families and societal practices were collected using the societal level questions.

6. This hypothesis was suggested by Celeste Wilderom, Tilburg University, The Netherlands.

7. CCIs were asked to collect data from organizations in only two industries per country because it was believed that CCIs would find collection of data from three industries to be excessively burdensome. In fact, approximately two-thirds of the CCI teams collected data from all three target industries.

8. Vipin Gupta identified the specific unobtrusive measures based on a literature survey of information published by the United Nations and the World Bank and other relevant published information. Gupta also conducted the statistical analyses to develop and validate the unobtrusive measures.

9. Interviews and focus groups revealed that, in several of the cultures studied, it would be a violation of cultural norms for subordinates to complete a questionnaire or answer interview questions that might be construed as evaluative with respect to individuals in positions of authority.

REFERENCES

Ajzen, L., & Fishbein, M. (1970). *Understanding attitudes and predicting social behavior.* Englewood Cliffs, NJ: Prentice-Hall.

Aldrich, H. E. (1979). *Organizations and environments.* Englewood Cliffs, NJ: Prentice-Hall.

Bass, B. M. (1985). *Leadership and performance beyond expectations.* New York: Free Press.

Bass, B. M. (1990). *Bass & Stogdill's handbook of leadership: Theory, research, and managerial applications* (3rd ed.). New York: Free Press.

Bass, B. M. (1997). Does the transactional-transformational leadership paradigm transcend organizational and national boundaries? *American Psychologist, 52*(2), 130-139.

Brislin, R. W. (1986). The wording and translation of research instruments. In W. J. Lohner & J. W. Berry (Eds.), *Field methods in cross-cultural research* (pp. 137-164). Beverly Hills, CA: Sage Publications.

Burns, T., & Stalker, G. M. (1961). *The management of innovation.* London: Tavistock Publications, Tavistock Centre.

Child, J. (1981). Culture, contingency, and capitalism in the cross-national study of organization. In L. L. Cummings (Ed.), *Research in organizational behavior* (pp. 303-356). Greenwich, CT: JAI Press.

Dickson, M. (1997). *Universality and variation in organizationally cognitive prototypes of effective leadership.* Unpublished doctoral dissertation, Department of Psychology, University of Maryland, College Park.

Donaldson, L. (1993). *Anti-management theories of organization: A critique of paradigm proliferation.* Cambridge: Cambridge University Press.

Dorfman, P. W. (1996). International and cross-cultural leadership research. In B. J. Punnett & O. Shenkar (Eds.), *Handbook for international management research* (pp. 267-349). Oxford, UK: Blackwell.

Franke, R.H. (1997). Industrial democracy and convergence in economic performance: Comparative analysis of industrial nations in the 1970s and 1980s. In R. Hodson (Ed.), *Research in the sociology of work.* Greenwich, CT: JAI Press.

Gagliardi, P. (1986). The creation and change of organizational cultures: A conceptual framework. *Organization Studies, 7*(2), 117-134.

Gerstner, C. R., & Day, D. V. (1994). Cross-cultural comparison of leadership prototypes. *Leadership Quarterly, 5*(2), 121-134.

Hanges, P. J., Braverman, E. P., & Rentsch, J. R. (1991). Changes in raters' impressions of subordinates: A catastrophe model. *Journal of Applied Psychology, 76,* 878-888.

Hanges, P. J., Lord, R. G., Day, D. V., Sipe, W. P., Smith, W. C., & Brown, D. J. (1997). Leadership and gender bias: Dynamic measures and nonlinear modeling. In R. G. Lord (Chair), *Dynamic systems, leadership perceptions, and gender effects*. Symposium presented at the Twelfth Annual Conference of the Society of Industrial and Organizational Psychology, St. Louis, MO.

Hanges, P., House, R. J., Ruiz-Quintanilla, S. A., Dickson, M. W., Dorfman, P. W., & 109 co-authors. (1998). The development and validation of scales to measure societal and organizational culture. Under review.

Hauser, M., House, R.J., & Puranman, P. (1999). *Strategy process: Cultures consequences*. Academy of Management Conference, Chicago, IL.

Hickson, D. J., Hinings, C. R., McMillan, J., & Schwitter. (1974). The culture-free context of organization structure: A tri-national comparison. *Sociology 8,* 59-80.

Hofstede, G. (1980). *Culture's consequences: International differences in work-related values*. London: Sage.

Hofstede, G., & Bond, M. H. (1988). The Confucius connection. From cultural roots to economic growth. *Organizational Dynamics, 16,* 4-21.

House, R.J. (1997). GLOBE: The Global Leadership and Organizational Behavior Effectiveness research program. *Polish Psychological Bulletin, 28*(3), 215-254.

House, R. J., & Aditya, R. N. (1997). The social scientific study of leadership: Quo vadis? *Journal of Management, 23*(3), 409-473.

House, R. J., Wright, N. S., & Aditya, R. N. (1997). Cross-cultural research on organizational leadership: A critical analysis and a proposed theory. In P. C. Earley & M. Erez (Eds.), *New perspectives in international industrial organizational psychology* (pp. 535-625). San Francisco: New Lexington.

James, L. R., Demaree, R. G., & Wolf, G. (1984). Estimating within-group interrater reliability with and without response bias. *Journal of Applied Psychology, 69*(1), 85-98.

Khandwalla, P. N. (1977). *The design of organizations*. New York: Harcourt Brace Jovanovich.

Kluckhohn, F. R., & Strodtbeck, F. L. (1961). *Variations in value orientations*. New York: HarperCollins.

Kogut, B., & Singh, H. (1988). The effect of national culture on the choice of entry mode. *Journal of Informational Business, 19,* 411-432.

Kopelman, R. E., Brief, A. P., & Guzzo, R. A. (1990). The role of climate and culture in productivity. In B. Schneider (Ed.), *Organizational climate and culture* (pp. 282-318). San Francisco: Jossey-Bass.

Lawrence, P. R., & Lorsch, J. W. (1967). *Organization and environment*. Cambridge, MA: Harvard University Press.

Leung, K., & Bond, M. H. (1989). On the empirical identification of dimensions for cross-cultural comparisons. *Journal of Cross-Cultural Psychology, 20,* 133-151.

Lombardo, M. M. (1983). I felt it as soon as I walked in. *Issues and Observations, 3*(4), 7-8.

Lord, R., & Maher, K. J. (1991). *Leadership and information processing: Linking perceptions and performance*. Boston: Unwin-Everyman.

Lumpkin, G. T., & Dess, G. G. (1996). Clarifying the entrepreneurial orientation construct and linking it to performance. *Academy of Management Review, 21* (1), 135-172.

McClelland, D. C. (1961). *The achieving society*. Princeton, NJ: Van Nostrand.

McClelland, D. C. (1985). *Human motivation*. Glenview, IL: Scott, Foresman.

McClelland, D. C., Atkinson, J. W., Clark, R. A., & Lowell, E. L. (Eds.). (1953). *The achievement motive.* New York: Appleton-Century-Crofts.

McFarland, L. J., Senen, S., & Childress, J. R. (1993). *Twenty-first-century leadership.* New York: Leadership Press.

Miller, D., & Droge, C. (1986). Psychological and traditional determinants of structure. *Administrative Science Quarterly, 31*(4), 539-560.

Misumi, J. (1985). *The behavioral science of leadership: An interdisciplinary Japanese research program.* Ann Arbor, MI: University of Michigan Press.

O'Connell, M. S., Lord, R. G., & O'Connell, M. K. (1990, August). *Differences in Japanese and American leadership prototypes: Implications for cross-cultural training.* Paper presented at the meeting of the Academy of Management, San Francisco.

Putnam, R. D. (1993). *Making democracy work.* Princeton, NJ: Princeton University Press.

Rokeach, M. (1973). *The nature of human values.* New York: Free Press.

Schein, E. H. (1992). *Organizational culture and leadership: A dynamic view* (2nd ed.). San Francisco: Jossey-Bass.

Schneider, B. (1987). The people make the place. *Personnel Psychology, 40,* 437-454.

Schneider, B., Goldstein, H. W., & Smith, D. B. (1995). The ASA Framework: An update. *Personnel Psychology, 48,* 747-783.

Shaw, J. B. (1990). A cognitive categorization model for the study of intercultural management. *Academy of Management Review, 15*(4), 626-645.

Simonton, D. K. (1994). *Greatness: Who makes history and why.* New York: Guilford Press.

Sipe, W. P., & Hanges, P. J. (1997). Reframing the glass ceiling: A catastrophe model of changes in the perception of women as leaders. In R. G. Lord (Chair), *Dynamic systems, leadership perceptions, and gender effects.* Symposium presented at the Twelfth Annual Conference of the Society of Industrial and Organizational Psychology, St. Louis, MO.

Smith, P. B., & Bond, M. H. (1993). *Social psychology across cultures: Analysis and perspectives.* London: Harvester Wheatsheaf.

Smith, P. B., Misumi, J., Tayeb, M. H., Peterson, M., & Bond, M. H. (1989). On the generality of leadership style across cultures. *Journal of Occupational Psychology, 30,* 526-537.

Staw, B. M., Sandelands, L. E., & Dutton, J. E. (1981). Threat-rigidity effects in organizational behavior: A multilevel analysis. *Administrative Science Quarterly, 26*(4), 501-524.

Thompson, K. R., & Luthans, F. (1990). Organizational culture: A behavioral perspective. In B. Schneider (Ed.), *Organizational climate and culture* (pp. 319-344). San Francisco: Jossey-Bass.

Triandis, H. C. (1993). The contingency model in cross-cultural perspective. In M. M. Chemers & R. Ayman (Eds.), *Leadership theory and research: Perspectives and directions* (pp. 167-188). San Diego: Academic Press.

Triandis, H. C. (1995). *Individualism and collectivism.* Boulder, CO: Westview Press.

Trice, H. M., & Beyer, J. M. (1984). *The cultures of work organizations.* Englewood Cliffs, NJ: Prentice-Hall.

Tushman, M. L., Newman, W. H., & Nadler, D. A. (1988). Executive leadership and organizational evolution: Managing incremental and discontinuous change. In R. H. Kilman & T. J. Covin (Eds.), *Corporate transformation: Revitalizing organizations for a competitive world* (pp. 102-130). San Francisco: Jossey-Bass.

Yukl, G. A. (1994). *Leadership in organizations* (3rd ed.). Englewood Cliffs, NJ: Prentice-Hall.

[28]

Martha C. Nussbaum

Compassion & terror

The name of our land has been wiped out.

– Euripides, *Trojan Women*

Not to be a fan of the Greens or Blues at the races, or the light-armed or heavy-armed gladiators at the Circus.

– Marcus Aurelius, *Meditations*

1

The towers of Troy are burning. All that is left of the once-proud city is a group of ragged women, bound for slavery, their husbands dead in battle, their sons murdered by the conquering Greeks, their daughters raped. Hecuba their queen invokes the king of the gods, using, remarkably, the language of democratic citizenship: "Son of Kronus, Council-President [*prytanis*] of Troy, father who gave us birth, do you see these undeserved sufferings that your Trojan people bear?" The Chorus answers grimly, "He sees, and yet the great city is no city. It has perished, and Troy exists no longer." Hecuba and the Chorus conclude that the gods are not worth calling on, and that the very name of their land has been wiped out.

This ending is as bleak as any in the history of tragic drama – death, rape, slavery, fire destroying the towers, the city's very name effaced from the record of history by the acts of rapacious and murderous Greeks. And yet, of course, it did not happen that way, not exactly: this story of Troy's fall is being enacted, some six hundred years after the event, by a company of Greek actors, in the Greek language of a Greek poet, in the presence of the citizens of Athens, most powerful of Greek cities. Hecuba's cry to the gods even casts Zeus as a peculiarly Athenian official – president of the city council.

So the name of Troy wasn't wiped out after all. The imagination of its con-

---

Martha C. Nussbaum, Ernst Freund Distinguished Service Professor of Law and Ethics at the University of Chicago, is appointed in the philosophy department, Law School, and Divinity School. A Fellow of the American Academy since 1988, Nussbaum is the author of numerous books, including "The Fragility of Goodness: Luck and Ethics in Greek Tragedy and Philosophy" (1986), "The Therapy of Desire: Theory and Practice in Hellenistic Ethics" (1994), and "Upheavals of Thought: The Intelligence of Emotions"(2001). This essay was originally delivered as the first Kristeller Memorial Lecture at Columbia University in April of 2002. Nussbaum writes, "Although I am sure Paul Kristeller would have taken issue with some aspects of its approach to classical texts, it is offered as a sincere tribute to his life of committed scholarship, which did so much to keep these texts alive in and for our time."

querors was haunted by it, transmitted it, and mourned it. Obsessively the Greek poets returned to this scene of destruction, typically inviting, as here, the audience's compassion for the women of Troy and blame for their assailants. In its very structure the play makes a claim for the moral value of compassionate imagining, as it asks its audience to partake in the terror of a burning city, of murder and rape and slavery. Insofar as members of the audience are engaged by this drama, feeling fear and grief for the conquered city, they demonstrate the ability of compassion to cross lines of time, place, and nation – and also, in the case of many audience members, the line of sex, perhaps more difficult yet to cross.

Nor was the play a purely aesthetic event divorced from political reality. The dramatic festivals of Athens were sacred celebrations strongly connected to the idea of democratic deliberation, and the plays of Euripides were particularly well-known for their engagement with contemporary events. *The Trojan Women*'s first audience had recently voted to put to death the men of the rebellious colony of Melos and to enslave its women and children. Euripides invited this audience to contemplate the real human meaning of its actions. Compassion for the women of Troy should at least cause moral unease, reminding Athenians of the full and equal humanity of people who live in distant places, their fully human capacity for suffering.

But did those imaginations really cross those lines? Think again of that invocation of Zeus. Trojans, if they worshipped Zeus as king of gods at all, surely did not refer to him as the president of the city council; *prytanis* is strictly an Athenian legal term. So it would appear that Hecuba is not a Trojan but a Greek. And her imagination is a Greek democratic (and, we might add, mostly male) imagination. Maybe that's a good thing, in the sense that the audience is surely invited to view her as their fellow and equal. But it still should give us pause.

Did compassion really enable those Greeks to comprehend the real humanity of others, or did it stop short, allowing them to reaffirm the essential Greekness of everything that's human? Of course compassion required making the Trojans somehow familiar, so that Greeks could see their own vulnerability in them, and feel terror and pity, as for their own relations. But it's easy for the familiarization to go too far: they are just us, and we are the ones who suffer humanly. Not those other ones, over there in Melos.

America's towers, too, have burned. Compassion and terror now inform the fabric of our lives. And in those lives we see evidence of the good work of compassion, as Americans make real to themselves the sufferings of so many people whom they never would otherwise have thought about: New York firefighters, that gay rugby player who helped bring down the fourth plane, bereaved families of so many national and ethnic origins. More rarely our compassion even crosses national boundaries: the tragedy led an unprecedented number of Americans to sympathize with the plight of Afghan women under the Taliban.

Yet at the same time, we also see evidence of how narrow and self-serving our sense of compassion can sometimes be. Some of us may notice with new appreciation the lives of Arab Americans among us – but others regard the Muslims in our midst with increasing wariness and mistrust. I am reminded of a Sikh taxi driver describing how often he was told to go home to 'his own country' – even though he came to the United

States as a political refugee from the miseries of police repression in the Punjab. And while our leaders have preached the virtues of tolerance, they have also resorted to the polarizing language of 'us' versus 'them,' as they marshal popular opinion to pursue a war on terrorism.

Indeed, the events of September 11 make vivid a philosophical problem that has been debated from the time of Euripides through much of the history of the Western philosophical tradition. This is the question of what to do about compassion, given its obvious importance in shaping the civic imagination, but given, too, its obvious propensity for self-serving narrowness. Is compassion, with all its limits, our best hope as we try to educate citizens to think well about human relations both inside the nation and across national boundaries? So some thinkers have suggested. I count Euripides among them, and would also include in this category Aristotle, Rousseau, Hume, and Adam Smith. Or is compassion a threat to good political thinking and the foundations of a truly just world community? So the Greek and Roman Stoics thought, and before them Plato, and after them Spinoza and (again) Adam Smith.

The enemies of compassion hold that we cannot build a stable and lasting concern for humanity on the basis of such a slippery and uneven motive; impartial motives based on ideas of dignity and respect should take its place. The friends of compassion reply that without building political morality on what we know and on what has deep roots in our childhood attachments, we will be left with a morality that is empty of urgency – a 'watery' concern, as Aristotle put it.

This debate continues in contemporary political and legal thought. In a recent exchange about animal rights, J. M. Coetzee invented a character who argues that the capacity for sympathetic imagination is our best hope for moral goodness in this area. Peter Singer replies, with much plausibility, that the sympathetic imagination is all too anthropocentric and we had better not rely on it to win rights for creatures whose lives are very different from our own.[1]

I shall not trace the history of the debate in this essay. Instead, I shall focus on its central philosophical ideas and try to sort them out, offering a limited defense of compassion and the tragic imagination, and then making some suggestions about how its pernicious tendencies can best be countered – with particular reference throughout to our current political situation.

2

Let me set the stage for the analysis to follow by turning to Smith, who, as you will have noticed, turns up in my taxonomy on both sides of the debate. Smith offers one of the best accounts we have of compassion, and of the ethical achievements of which this moral sentiment is capable. But later, in a section of *The Theory of Moral Sentiments* entitled "Of the Sense of Duty," he solemnly warns against trusting this imperfect sentiment too far when duty is what we are trying to get clear.

Smith's concern, like mine, is with our difficulty keeping our minds fixed on the sufferings of people who live on the other side of the world:

> Let us suppose that the great empire of China, with all its myriads of inhabitants, was suddenly swallowed up by an earthquake, and let us consider how a man of humanity in Europe, who had no sort of

[1] J. M. Coetzee, *The Lives of Animals*, ed. Amy Gutmann (Princeton, N.J.: Princeton University Press, 1999).

connexion with that part of the world, would be affected upon receiving intelligence of this dreadful calamity. He would, I imagine, first of all, express very strongly his sorrow for the misfortune of that unhappy people, he would make many melancholy reflections upon the precariousness of human life, and the vanity of all the labours of man, which could thus be annihilated in a moment.... And when all this fine philosophy was over, when all these humane sentiments had been once fairly expressed, he would pursue his business or his pleasure, take his repose or his diversion, with the same ease and tranquility, as if no such accident had happened. The most frivolous disaster which could befal himself would occasion a more real disturbance. If he was to lose his little finger to-morrow, he would not sleep tonight; but, provided he never saw them, he will snore with the more profound security over the ruin of a hundred millions of his brethren, and the destruction of that immense multitude seems plainly an object less interesting to him, than this paltry misfortune of his own.

That's just the issue that should trouble us as we think about American reactions to September 11. We see a lot of 'humane sentiments' around us, and extensions of sympathy beyond people's usual sphere of concern. But more often than not, those sentiments stop short at the national boundary.

We think the events of September 11 are bad because they involved *us* and *our* nation. Not just human lives, but *American* lives. The world came to a stop – in a way that it rarely has for Americans when disaster has befallen human beings in other places. The genocide in Rwanda didn't even work up enough emotion in us to prompt humanitarian intervention. The plight of innocent civilians in Iraq never made it onto our national radar screen. Floods, earthquakes, cyclones, the daily deaths of thousands from preventable malnutrition and disease – none of these makes the American world come to a standstill, none elicits a tremendous outpouring of grief and compassion. At most we get what Smith so trenchantly described: a momentary flicker of feeling, quickly dissipated by more pressing concerns close to home.

Frequently, however, we get a compassion that is not only narrow, failing to include the distant, but also polarizing, dividing the world into an 'us' and a 'them.' Compassion for our own children can so easily slip over into a desire to promote the well-being of our children at the expense of other people's children. Similarly, compassion for our fellow Americans can all too easily slip over into a desire to make America come out *on top* and to subordinate other nations.

One vivid example of this slip took place at a baseball game I went to at Comiskey Park, the first game played in Chicago after September 11 – and a game against the Yankees, so there was heightened awareness of the situation of New York and its people. Things began well, with a moving ceremony commemorating the firefighters who had lost their lives and honoring local firefighters who had gone to New York afterwards to help out. There was even a lot of cheering when the Yankees took the field, a highly unusual transcendence of local attachments. But as the game went on and the beer began flowing, one heard, increasingly, the chant "U-S-A. U-S-A," a chant first heard in 1980 during an Olympic hockey match in which the United States defeated Russia. In that context, the chant had expressed a wish for America to humiliate its Cold War enemy; as time passed, it became a general way of expressing the desire to crush an

Compassion & terror

opponent, whoever it might be. When the umpire made a bad call against the Sox, a group in the bleachers turned on him, chanting "U-S-A." From 'humane sentiments' we had turned back to the pain in our little finger.

With such examples before us, how can we trust compassion and the imagination of the other that it contains? But if we don't trust that, what else can we plausibly rely on to transform horror into a shared sense of ethical responsibility?

I shall proceed as follows. First, I shall offer an analysis of the emotion of compassion, focusing on the thoughts and imaginings on which it is based. This will give us a clearer perspective on how and where it is likely to go wrong. Second, I shall examine the countertradition's proposal that we can base political morality on respect for dignity, doing away with appeals to compassion. This proposal, at first attractive, contains, on closer inspection, some deep difficulties. Third, I will return to compassion, asking how, if we feel we need it as a public motive, we might educate it so as to overcome, as far as we can, the problem that Smith identified.

More than a warm feeling in the gut, compassion involves a set of thoughts, often quite complex.[2] We need to dissect them, if we are to make progress in understanding how it goes wrong and how it may be steered aright. There is a good deal of agreement about this among philosophers as otherwise diverse as Aristotle and Rousseau, and also among contemporary psychologists and sociologists who have done empirical work on the emotion.[3]

Compassion is an emotion directed at another person's suffering or lack of well-being. It requires the thought that the other person is in a bad way, and a pretty seriously bad way. (Thus we don't feel compassion for people's loss of trivial items like toothbrushes and paper clips.) It contains within itself an appraisal of the seriousness of various predicaments. Let us call this *the judgment of seriousness*.

Notice that this assessment is made from the point of view of the person who has the emotion. It does not neglect the actual suffering of the other, which certainly should be estimated in taking the measure of the person's predicament. And yet it does not necessarily take at face value the estimate of the predicament this person will be able to form. As Smith emphasized, we frequently have great compassion for people whose predicament is that they have lost their powers of thought; even if they seem like happy children, we regard this as a terrible catastrophe. On the other side, when people moan and groan about something, we don't necessarily have compassion for them: for we may think that they are not really in a bad predicament. Thus when very rich people grumble about taxes, many of us don't have the slightest compassion for them: for

---

2 I am drawing on an analysis of compassion for which I argue at greater length in Nussbaum, *Upheavals of Thought: The Intelligence of Emotions* (New York: Cambridge University Press, 2001), chaps. 6 – 8.

3 C. Daniel Batson of the University of Kansas should be mentioned with honor here, because he has not only done remarkable empirical work, but has also combined it with a conceptual and analytic clarity that is rare in social science research of this type. See in particular *The Altruism Question* (Hillsdale, N.J.: Lawrence Erlbaum, 1991). Candace Clark's sociological study is also exemplary: *Misery and Company: Sympathy in Everyday Life* (Chicago: University of Chicago Press, 1997).

we judge that it is only right and proper that they should pay what they are paying – and probably a lot more than that. So the judgment of seriousness already involves quite a complex feat of imagination: it involves both trying to look out at the situation from the suffering person's own viewpoint and then assessing the person's own assessment. Complex though the feat is, young children easily learn it, feeling sympathy with the suffering of animals and other children, but soon learning, as well, to withhold sympathy if they judge that the person is just a crybaby, or spoiled – and, of course, to have sympathy for the predicament of an animal who is dead or unconscious, even if it is not actually suffering.

Next comes *the judgment of nondesert*. Hecuba asked Zeus to witness the undeserved sufferings of the Trojan women, using the Greek word *anaxia*, which appears in Aristotle's definition of tragic compassion. Hecuba's plea, like Aristotle's definition, implies that we will not have compassion if we believe the person fully deserves the suffering. There may be a measure of blame, but then in our compassion we typically register the thought that the suffering exceeds the measure of the fault. The Trojan women are an unusually clear case, because, more than most tragic figures, they endure the consequences of events in which they had no active part at all. But we can see that nondesert is a salient part of our compassion even when we do also blame the person: typically we feel compassion at the punishment of criminal offenders, to the extent that we think circumstances beyond their control are at least in good measure responsible for their becoming the bad people they are. People who have the idea that the poor brought their poverty upon themselves by laziness fail, for that reason, to have compassion for them.[4]

Next there is a thought much stressed in the tradition that I shall call *the judgment of similar possibilities*: Aristotle, Rousseau, and others suggest that we have compassion only insofar as we believe that the suffering person shares vulnerabilities and possibilities with us. I think we can clearly see that this judgment is not strictly necessary for the emotion, as the other two seem to be. We have compassion for nonhuman animals, without basing it on any imagined similarity – although, of course, we need somehow to make sense of their predicament as serious and bad. We also imagine that an invulnerable god can have compassion for mortals, and it doesn't seem that this idea is conceptually confused. For the finite imaginations of human beings, however, the thought of similar possibilities is a very important psychological mechanism through which we get clear about the seriousness of another person's plight. This thought is often accompanied by empathetic imagining, in which we put ourselves in the suffering person's place, imagine their predicament as our own.

Finally, there is one thing more, not mentioned in the tradition, which I believe must be added in order to make the account complete. This is what, in writing on the emotions, I have called *the eudaimonistic judgment*, namely, a judgment that places the suffering person or persons among the important parts of the life of the person who feels the emotion. In my more general analysis of emotions, I argue that they are always eudaimonistic, meaning focused on the agent's most important goals and proj-

4 Clark's empirical survey of American attitudes finds this a prominent reason for the refusal of compassion for the poor.

ects. Thus we feel fear about damages that we see as significant for our own well-being and our other goals; we feel grief at the loss of someone who is already invested with a certain importance in our scheme of things. Eudaimonism is not egoism. I am not claiming that emotions always view events and people merely as means to the agent's own satisfaction or happiness. But I do mean that the things that occasion a strong emotion in us are things that correspond to what we have invested with importance in our account to ourselves of what is worth pursuing in life.

Compassion can evidently go wrong in several different ways. It can get the judgment of nondesert wrong, sympathizing with people who actually don't deserve sympathy and withholding sympathy from those who do. Even more frequently, it can get the judgment of seriousness wrong, ascribing too much importance to the wrong things or too little to things that have great weight. Notice that this problem is closely connected to obtuseness about social justice, in the sense, for example, that if we don't think a social order unjust for denying women the vote, or subordinating African Americans, then we won't see the predicament of women and African Americans as bad, and we won't have compassion for them. We'll think that things are just as they ought to be. Again, if we think it's unjust to require rich people to pay capital gains tax, we will have a misplaced compassion toward them. Finally, and obviously, compassion can get the eudaimonistic judgment wrong, putting too few people into the circle of concern. By my account, then, we won't have compassion without a moral achievement that is at least coeval with it.

My account, I think, is able to explain the unevenness of compassion better than other more standard accounts. Compassion begins from where we are, from the circle of our cares and concerns. It will be felt only toward those things and persons we see as important, and of course most of us most of the time ascribe importance in a very uneven and inconstant way. Empathetic imagining can sometimes extend the circle of concern. Thus Batson has shown experimentally that when the story of another person's plight is vividly told, subjects will tend to experience compassion toward the person and form projects of helping. This is why I say that the moral achievement of extending concern to others needn't antedate compassion, but can be coeval with it. Still, there is a recalcitrance in our emotions, given their link to our daily scheme of goals and ends. Smith is right: thinking that the poor victims of the disaster in China are important is easy to do for a short time, but hard to sustain in the fabric of our daily life; there are so many things closer to home to distract us, and these things are likely to be so much more thoroughly woven into our scheme of goals.

Let us return to September 11 armed with this analysis. The astonishing events made many Americans recognize with a new vividness the nation itself as part of their circle of concern. Most Americans rely on the safety of our institutions and our cities, and don't really notice how much they value them until they prove vulnerable – in just the way that lovers often don't see how much they love until their loved one is ill or threatened. So our antecedent concern emerged with a new clarity in the emotions we experienced. At the same time, we actually extended concern, in many cases, to people in America who had not previously been part of our circle of concern at all: the New York firefighters, the victims of the disasters. We extended concern to them both because we heard their stories and also, especially, because we were encouraged to see them as a part of the America we already loved and for which we now intensely feared. When disaster struck in Rwanda, we did not similarly extend concern, or not stably, because there was no antecedent basis for it: suffering Rwandans could not be seen as part of the larger 'us' for whose fate we trembled. Vivid stories can create a temporary sense of community, but they are unlikely to sustain concern for long, if there is no pattern of interaction that would make the sense of an 'us' an ongoing part of our daily lives.

Things are of course still worse with any group that figures in our imaginations as a 'them' against the 'us.' Such groups are not only by definition non-us, they are also, by threatening the safety of the 'us,' implicitly bad, deserving of any misfortune that might strike them. This accounts for the sports-fan mentality so neatly depicted in my baseball story. Compassion for a member of the opposing team? You've got to be kidding. "U-S-A" just means kill the ump.

3

In light of these difficulties, it is easy to see why much of the philosophical tradition has wanted to do away with compassion as a basis for public choice and to turn, instead, to detached moral principles whose evenhandedness can be relied on. The main candidate for a central moral notion has been the idea of human worth and dignity, a principle that has been put to work from the Stoics and Cicero on through Kant and beyond. We are to recognize that all humans have dignity, and that this dignity is both inalienable and equal, not affected by differences of class, caste, wealth, honor, status, or even sex. The recognition of human dignity is supposed to impose obligations on all moral agents, whether the humans in question are conationals or foreigners. In general, it enjoins us to refrain from all aggression and fraud, since both are seen as violations of human dignity, ways of fashioning human beings into tools for one's own ends. Out of this basic idea Cicero developed much of the basis for modern international law in the areas of war, punishment, and hospitality.[5] Other Stoics used it to criticize conventional norms of patriarchal marriage, the physical abuse of servants, and many other aspects of Roman social life.

This Stoic tradition was quite clear that respect for human dignity could move us to appropriate action, both personal and social, without our having to rely at all on the messier and more inconstant motive of compassion. Indeed, for separate reasons, which I shall get to shortly, Stoics thought compassion was never appropriate, so they could not rely on it.

What I now want to ask is whether this countertradition was correct. Respect for human dignity looks like the right thing to focus on, something that can plausibly be seen as of boundless worth, constraining all actions in pursuit of well-being, and also as equal, creating a kingdom of ends in which humans are ranked horizontally, so to speak, rather than vertically. Why should we not follow the countertradition, as in many respects we do already – as when constitutions make the notion of human dignity central to the analysis of constitutional

[5] See my "Duties of Justice, Duties of Material Aid: Cicero's Problematic Legacy," *Journal of Political Philosophy* 7 (1999): 1–31.

rights,[6] as when international human rights documents apply similar notions.

Now it must be admitted that human dignity is not an altogether clear notion. In what does it consist? Why should we think that all human life has it? The minute the Stoic tradition tries to answer such questions, problems arise. In particular, the answer almost always takes the form of saying, Look at how far we are above the beasts. Reason, language, moral capacity – all these are seen as worthy of respect and awe at least in part because the beasts, so-called, don't have them, because they make us better than others. Of course they wouldn't seem to make us better if they didn't have some attraction in themselves. But the claim that this dignity resides equally in all humanity all too often relies on the better-than-the-beasts idea. No matter how we humans vary in our rational and moral capacities, the idea seems to be, the weakest among us is light-years beyond those beasts down there, so the differences that exist among us in basic powers become not worth adverting to at all, not sources of differential worth at all. Dignity thus comes to look not like a scalar matter but like an all-or-nothing matter. You either have it, or, bestially, you don't.

This view has its moral problems, clearly. Richard Sorabji has shown how it was linked with a tendency to denigrate the intelligence of animals;[7] and of course it has been used, too, not only by the Stoics but also by Kant and modern contractarians to deny that we have any obligations of justice toward nonhuman forms of life. Compassion, if slippery, is at least not dichotomous in this way; it is capable of reaching sympathetically into multiple directions simultaneously, capable, as Coetzee said, of imagining the sufferings of animals in the squalid conditions we create for them.

There is another more subtle problem with the dignity idea. It was crucial, according to the Stoics, to make dignity radically independent of fortune: all humans have it, no matter where they are born and how they are treated. It exerts its claim everywhere, and it can never be lost. If dignity went up or down with fortune, it would create ranks of human beings: the well-born and healthy will be worth more than the ill-born and hungry. So the Stoics understood their project of making dignity self-sufficient as essential for the notion of equal respect and regard.

But this move leads to a problem: how can we give a sufficiently important place to the goods of fortune for political purposes once we admit that the truly important thing, the thing that lies at the core of our humanity, doesn't need the goods of fortune at all? How can we provide sufficient incentive for political planners to arrange for an adequate distribution of food and shelter and even political rights and liberties if we say that dignity is undiminished by the lack of such things?[8] Stoic texts thus look oddly quietistic: respect human dignity, they say. But it doesn't matter at all what

---

6 Germany is one salient example. In a forthcoming book, James Whitman describes the way this central notion has constrained legal practices in Europe generally, especially in the area of criminal punishment. Dignity, he argues, is a nonhierarchical notion that has replaced hierarchical orders of rank.

7 Richard Sorabji, *Animal Minds and Human Morals: The Origins of the Western Debate* (Ithaca, N.Y.: Cornell University Press, 1993).

8 I deal with this question at greater length in "Duties of Justice," and also in "The Worth of Human Dignity: Two Tensions in Stoic Cosmopolitanism," in *Philosophy and Power in the Graeco-Roman World: Essays in Honour of Miriam Griffin*, ed. Gillian Clark and Tessa Rajak (Oxford: Oxford University Press, 2002), 31–49.

conditions we give people to live in, since dignity is complete and immutable anyway. Seneca, for example, gives masters stern instructions not to beat slaves or use them as sexual tools (*Moral Epistle* 47). But as for the institution of slavery itself? Well, this does not really matter so much, for the only thing that matters is the free soul within, and that cannot be touched by any contingency. Thus, having begun his letter on slavery on an apparently radical note, Seneca slides into quietism in the end, when his master scornfully says, "He is a slave," and Seneca calmly replies, "Will this do him any harm? [*Hoc illi nocebit?*]"

Things are actually even worse than this. For the minute we start examining this reasoning closely, we see that it is not only quietistic – it is actually incoherent. Either people need external things or they do not. But if they do not, if dignity is utterly unaffected by rape and physical abuse, then it is not very easy, after all, to say what the harm of beating or raping a slave is. If these things are no harm to the victim, why is it wrong to do them? They seem not different from the institution of slavery itself: will they really do him any harm, if one maintains that dignity is sufficient for eudaimonia, and that dignity is totally independent of fortune? So Seneca lacks not only a basis for criticizing the institution of slavery, but also for the criticism his letter actually makes, of cruel and inhumane practices toward slaves.

Kant had a way of confronting this question, and it is a plausible one, within the confines of what I have called the countertradition. Kant grants that humanity itself, or human worth, is independent of fortune: under the blows of "step-motherly nature" goodwill still shines like a jewel for its own sake. But external goods such as money, health, and social position are still required for happiness, which we all reasonably pursue. So there are still very weighty moral reasons for promoting the happiness of others, reasons that can supply both individuals and states with a basis for good thoughts about the distribution of goods.

The Stoics notoriously deny this, holding that virtue is sufficient for eudaimonia. What I want to suggest now is that their position on human dignity pushes them strongly in this direction. Think of the person who suffers poverty and hardship. Now either this person has something that is beyond price, by comparison to which all the money and health and shelter in the world is as nothing – or she does not have something that is beyond price. Her dignity is just one part of her happiness – a piece of it that can itself be victimized and held hostage to fortune; her human dignity is being weighed in the balance with other goods and it no longer looks like the thing of surpassing, even infinite worth, that we took it to be. There are, after all, ranks and orders of human beings; slavery and abuse can actually change people's situation with regard to their most important and inclusive end, eudaimonia itself.

Because the Stoics do not want to be forced to that conclusion, they insist that external goods are not required for eudaimonia: virtue is sufficient. And basic human dignity, in turn, is sufficient for becoming virtuous, if one applies oneself in the right way. It is for this deep reason that the Stoics reject compassion as a basic social motive, not just because it is slippery and uneven. Compassion gets the world wrong, because it is always wrong to think that a person who has been hit by misfortune is in a bad or even tragic predicament. "Behold how tragedy comes about," writes Epictetus, "when chance events befall fools." In other words, only a fool would mind the events depicted in Euripides' play, and only fools in the audience would view these events as tragic.

So there is a real problem in how, and how far, the appeal to equal human dignity motivates. Looked at superficially, the idea of respect for human dignity appears to provide a principled, evenhanded motive for good treatment of all human beings, no matter where they are placed. Looked at more deeply, it seems to license quietism and indifference to things in the world, on the grounds that nothing that merely happens to people is really bad.

We have now seen two grave problems with the countertradition: what I shall call *the animal problem* and what I shall call *the external goods problem*. Neither of these problems is easy to solve within the countertradition. By contrast, the Euripidean tradition of focusing on compassion as a basic social motive has no such problems. Compassion can and does cross the species boundary, and whatever good there may be in our current treatment of animals is likely to be its work; we are able to extend our imaginations to understand the sufferings of animals who are cruelly treated and to see that suffering as significant, as undeserved, and to see its potential termination as part of our scheme of goals and projects.[9]

As for the problem of external goods, compassion has no such problem, for it is intrinsically focused on the damages of fortune: its most common objects, as

[9] See Coetzee, *The Lives of Animals*, 35: "There are people who have the capacity to imagine themselves as someone else, there are people who have no such capacity (when the lack is extreme, we call them psychopaths), and there are people who have the capacity but choose not to exercise it."

Aristotle listed them in the *Rhetoric*, are the classic tragic predicaments: loss of country, loss of friends, old age, illness, and so on.

But let us suppose that the countertradition can solve these two problems, providing people with adequate motives to address the tragic predicaments. Kant makes a good start on the external goods problem, at least. So let us imagine that we have a reliable way of motivating conduct that addresses human predicaments, without the uneven partiality that so often characterizes compassion. A third problem now awaits us. I shall call it *the problem of watery motivation*, though we might well call it *the problem of death within life*.

The term 'watery motivation' comes from Aristotle's criticism of Plato's ideal city. Plato tried to remove partiality by removing family ties and asking all citizens to care equally for all other citizens. Aristotle says that the difficulty with this strategy is that "there are two things above all that make people love and care for something, the thought that it is all theirs, and the thought that it is the only one they have. Neither of these will be present in that city" (*Pol.* 1262b22-3). Because nobody will think of a child that it is all theirs, entirely their own responsibility, the city will, he says, resemble a household in which there are too many servants so nobody takes responsibility for any task. Because nobody will think of any child or children that they are the only ones they have, the intensity of care that characterizes real families will simply not materialize, and we will have instead, he says, a 'watery' kind of care all round (*Pol.* 1262b15).

If we now examine the nature of Stoic motivation, I think we will see that Aristotle is very likely to be correct. I shall focus here on Marcus Aurelius, in many ways the most psychologically profound of Stoic thinkers. Marcus tells us that the first lesson he learned from his tutor was "not to be a fan of the Greens or Blues at the races, or the light-armed or heavy-armed gladiators at the Circus" (I.5). His imagination had to unlearn its intense partiality and localism; his tutor apparently assumed that already as young children we have learned narrow sectarian types of loyalty. And it is significant, I think, that the paradigmatic negative image for the moral imagination is that of sports fandom: for in all ages, perhaps, such fandom has been a natural way for human beings to express vicariously their sectarian loyalties to family, city, and nation. It was no accident that those White Sox fans invoked the hockey chant to express their distress about the fate of the nation.

The question is whether this negative lesson leaves the personality enough resources to motivate intense concern for people anywhere. For Marcus, unlearning partiality requires an elaborate and systematic program of uprooting concern for all people and things in this world. He tells us of the meditative exercises that he regularly performs in order to get himself to the point at which the things that divide people from one another no longer matter. One side of this training looks benign and helpful: we tell ourselves that our enemies are really not enemies, but part of a common human project:

> Say to yourself in the morning: I shall meet people who are interfering, ungracious, insolent, full of guile, deceitful and antisocial.... But I, ... who know that the nature of the wrongdoer is of one kin with mine – not indeed of the same blood or seed but sharing the same kind, the same portion of the divine – I cannot be harmed by any one of them, and no one can involve me in shame. I cannot feel anger against him who is of my kin, nor hate

Compassion & terror

him. We were born to labor together, like the feet, the hands, the eyes, and the rows of upper and lower teeth. To work against one another is therefore contrary to nature, and to be angry against a man or turn one's back on him is to work against him.[10]

Notice how close these thoughts are to the thought-content of a greatly extended sort of compassion. Passages such as these suggest that a strong kind of evenhanded concern can be meted out to all human beings, without divisive jealousy and partiality; that we should see ourselves not as team players, not as family members, not as loyal citizens of a nation, but, most essentially, as members of the humankind with the advancement of our kind as our highest goal.

Now even in this good case problems are lurking: for we notice that this exercise relies on the thoughts that give rise to the animal problem and the external goods problem. We are asked to imagine human solidarity and community by thinking of a 'portion of the divine' that resides in all and only humans: we look like we have a lot in common because we are so sharply divided from the rest of nature. And the idea that we have a common work relies, to at least some extent, on Marcus's prior denigration of external goods: for if we ascribed value to external goods we would be in principle competing with one another, and it would be difficult to conceive of the common enterprise without running into that competition.

But I have resolved to waive those two difficulties, so let me do so. Even then, the good example is actually very complex. For getting to the point where we can give such concern evenhandedly to all human beings requires, as Marcus

10 II.1, trans. G. Grube (Hackett edition). Cf. also VI.6: "The best method of defense is not to become like your enemy."

makes abundantly clear, the systematic extirpation of intense cares and attachments directed at the local: one's family, one's city, the objects of one's love and desire. Thus Marcus needs to learn not only not to be a sports fan, but also not to be a lover. Consider the following extraordinary passage:

> How important it is to represent to oneself, when it comes to fancy dishes and other such foods, "This is the corpse of a fish, this other thing the corpse of a bird or a pig." Similarly, "This Falernian wine is just some grape juice," and "This purple vestment is some sheep's hair moistened in the blood of some shellfish." When it comes to sexual intercourse, we must say, "This is the rubbing together of membranes, accompanied by the spasmodic ejaculation of a sticky liquid." How important are these representations, which reach the thing itself and penetrate right through it, so that one can see what it is in reality. (VI.13)[11]

Now, of course, these exercises are addressed to the problem of external goods. Here as elsewhere, Marcus is determined to unlearn the unwise attachments to externals that he has learned from his culture. This project is closely connected to the question of partiality, because learning not to be a sports fan is greatly aided by learning not to care about the things over which people typically fight. (Indeed, it is a little hard to see how a Kantian project can be stable, insofar as it teaches equal respect for human dignity while at the same time teaching intense concern for the externals that go to produce happiness, externals that strongly motivate people not to treat all human beings equally.) In the Marcus passage, however, the link to partiality seems even more direct: for learning to think of sex as just the rubbing of membranes really is learning not to find special value or delight in a particular, and this extirpation of eroticism really does seem to be required by a regime of impartiality.

But getting rid of our erotic investment, not just in bodies, but in families, nations, sports teams – all this leads us into a strange world, a world that is gentle and unaggressive, but also strangely lonely and hollow. To unlearn the habits of the sports fan we must unlearn our erotic investment in the world, our attachments to our own team, our own love, our own children, our own life.

Marcus suggests that we have two choices only: the world of real-life Rome, which resembles a large gladiatorial contest (see Seneca *De Ira* 2.8), each person striving to outdo others in vain competition for externals, a world exploding with rage and poisoned by malice; or the world of Marcus's gentle sympathy, in which we respect all human beings and view all as our partners in a common project whose terms don't seem to matter very much, thus rendering the whole point of living in the world increasingly unclear.[12]

And this means something like a death within life. For only in a condition close to death, in effect, is moral rectitude possible. Marcus repeatedly casts life as a kind of death already, a procession of meaningless occurrences:

> The vain solemnity of a procession; dramas played out on the stage; troops of

---

[11] Based on the translation in Pierre Hadot, *The Inner Citadel: The Meditations of Marcus Aurelius*, trans. Michael Chase (Cambridge, Mass.: Harvard University Press, 1998), with some modifications.

[12] It is significant that this adopted emperor did not, as the movie *Gladiator* shows us, make a principled rational choice of the best man to run the empire. In real life, Marcus chose his worthless son Commodus, tripped up yet once more by the love of the near.

sheep or goats; fights with spears; a little bone thrown to dogs; a chunk of bread thrown into a fish-pond; the exhausting labor and heavy burdens under which ants must bear up; crazed mice running for shelter; puppets pulled by strings.... (VII.3)[13]

(This, by an emperor who was at that very time on campaign in Parthia, leading the fight for his nation.) And the best consolation for his bleak conclusion also originates in his contemplation of death:

Think all the time about how human beings of all sorts, and from all walks of life and all peoples, are dead.... We must arrive at the same condition where so many clever orators have ended up, so many grave philosophers, Heraclitus, Pythagoras, Socrates; so many heroes of the old days, so many recent generals and tyrants. And besides these, Eudoxus, Hipparchus, Archimedes, other highly intelligent minds, thinkers of large thoughts, hard workers, versatile in ability, daring people, even mockers of the perishable and transitory character of human life, like Menippus. Think about all of these that they are long since in the ground.... And what of those whose very names are forgotten? So: one thing is worth a lot, to live out one's life with truth and justice, and with kindliness toward liars and wrongdoers. (VI.47)

Because we shall die, we must recognize that everything particular about us will eventually be wiped out: family, city, sex, children – all will pass into oblivion. So really, giving up those attachments is not such a big deal. What remains, and all that remains, is truth and justice, the moral order of the world. So only the true city should claim our allegiance.

Marcus is alarming because he has gone deep into the foundations of cosmopolitan moral principle. What he has seen is that impartiality, fully and consistently cultivated, requires the extirpation of the eroticism that makes life the life we know – unfair, uneven, full of war, full of me-first nationalism and divided loyalty.[14] So, if that ordinary erotic humanity is unjust, get rid of it. But can we live like this, once we see the goal with Marcus's naked clarity? Isn't justice something that must be about and for the living?

Compassion & terror

4

Let me proceed on the hypothesis that Marcus is correct: extirpating attachments to the local and the particular delivers us to a death within life. Let me also proceed on the hypothesis that we will reject this course as an unacceptable route to the goal of justice, or even as one that makes the very idea of justice a hollow fantasy. (This is Adam Smith's conclusion as well: enamored as he is of Stoic doctrine, he thinks we must reject it when it tells us not to love our own families.) Where are we then?

It looks as if we are back where Aristotle and Adam Smith leave us: with the unreliability of compassion, and yet the need to rely on it, since we have no more perfect motive.

This does not mean that we need give up on the idea of equal human dignity, or respect for it. But insofar as we retain, as well, our local erotic attachments, our relation to that motive must always remain complex and dialectical, a difficult conversation within ourselves as we ask how much humanity requires of us, and how much we are entitled to give to our

13 Translation from Hadot/Chase.

14 One might compare the imagery of ancient Greek skepticism. Pyrrho, frightened by a dog (and thus betraying a residual human attachment to his own safety) says, "How difficult it is entirely to divest oneself of the human being." Elsewhere he speaks of the skeptic as a eunuch, because he lacks the very source of disturbance.

own. Any such difficult conversation will require, for its success, the work of the imagination. If we don't have exceptionless principles, if, instead, we need to negotiate our lives with a complex combination of moral reverence and erotic attachment, we need to have a keen imaginative and emotional understanding of what our choices mean for people in many different conditions, and the ability to move resourcefully back and forth from the perspective of our personal loves and cares to the perspective of the distant. Not the extirpation of compassion, then, but its extension and education. Compassion within the limits of respect.

The philosophical tradition helps us identify places where compassion goes wrong: by making errors of fault, seriousness, and the circle of concern. But the ancient tradition, not being very interested in childhood, does not help us see clearly how and why it goes especially wrong. So to begin the task of educating compassion as best we can, we need to ask how and why local loyalties and attachments come to take in some instances an especially virulent and aggressive form, militating against a more general sympathy. To answer this question we need a level of psychological understanding that was not available in the ancient Greek and Roman world, or not completely. I would suggest (and have argued elsewhere) that one problem we particularly need to watch out for is a type of pathological narcissism in which the person demands complete control over all the sources of good, and a complete self-sufficiency in consequence.

Nancy Chodorow long ago argued that this narcissism colors the development of males in many cultures in the world.[15] Recent studies of teenage boys in America, particularly the impressive work of Dan Kindlon and Michael Thompson in their book *Raising Cain*, have given strong local support to this idea.[16] The boys that Kindlon and Thompson study have learned from their cultures that men should be self-sufficient, controlling, dominant. They should never have, and certainly never admit to, fear and weakness. The consequence of this deformed expectation, Kindlon and Thompson show, is that these boys come to lack an understanding of their own vulnerabilities, needs, and fears – weaknesses that all human beings share. They don't have the language to describe their own inner worlds and are by the same token clumsy interpreters of the emotions and inner lives of others. This emotional illiteracy is closely connected to aggression, as fear is turned outward, with little understanding of the implications of aggressive words and actions for others. Kindlon and Thompson's boys become the sports fans who chant "U-S-A" at the ump, who think of all obstacles to American supremacy and self-sufficiency as opponents to be humiliated.

So the first recommendation I would make for a culture of respectful compassion is a Rousseauian one: it is, that an education in common human weakness and vulnerability should be a very profound part of the education of all children. Children should learn to be tragic spectators and to understand with subtlety and responsiveness the predicaments to which human life is prone. Through stories and dramas, they should learn to decode the suffering of others, and this decoding should deliberately lead them into lives both near and far, including the lives of distant humans and the lives of animals.

15 Nancy Chodorow, *The Reproduction of Mothering* (Berkeley, Calif.: University of California Press, 1978).

16 Dan Kindlon and Michael Thompson, *Raising Cain: Protecting the Emotional Life of Boys* (New York: Ballentine Books, 1999).

As children learn to imagine the emotions of another, they should at the same time learn the many obstacles to such understanding, the many pitfalls of the self-centered imagination as it attempts to be just. Thus, one should not suppose that one can understand a family member, without confronting and continually criticizing the envy and jealousy in oneself that pose powerful obstacles to that understanding. One should not imagine that one can understand the life of a person in an ethnic or racial group different from one's own, or a sex different from one's own, or a nation, without confronting and continually criticizing the fear and greed and the demand for power that make such interactions so likely to produce misunderstanding and worse. What I am suggesting, then, is that the education of emotion, to succeed at all, needs to take place in a culture of ethical criticism, and especially self-criticism, in which ideas of equal respect for humanity will be active players in the effort to curtail the excesses of the greedy self.

At the same time, we can also see that the chances of success in this enterprise will be greater if the society in question does not overvalue external goods of the sort that cause envy and competition. The Stoics are correct when they suggest that overvaluation of external goods is a major source of destructive aggression in society. If we criticize the overvaluation of money, honor, status, and fame that Seneca saw at Rome and that we see in America now, then we may encourage people to pursue other, less problematic external goods, including love of family, of friends, of work, even, to a certain extent, of country. If people care primarily for friendship, good work, and – let's even hope – social justice, then they are less likely to see everything in terms of the hockey match and more likely to use Marcus's image of the common project. Because my vision is not a Stoic one, there will still be important sources of good to be protected from harm, and there will still be justified anger at damage to those good things. But a lot of occasions for anger in real life are not good or just, and we can do a lot as a society to prune away the greedy attachments that underpin them.

Compassion & terror

After *Raising Cain*, Kindlon wrote a book on rich teenagers in America.[17] It is an alarming portrait of the greed and overvaluations of a certain class in our nation, and its tales of children who humiliate others because they don't go on the same expensive ski vacations or have the same expensive designer clothes are a chilling illustration of how overvaluation is connected to destructive violence. There is a great deal to say about how education could address such problems, but I shall not go into that here.

Instead, I want to turn back to Euripides, reflecting, in concluding, on the role of tragic spectatorship, and tragic art generally, in promoting good citizenship of the sort I have been advocating here. Tragedies are not Stoic: they start with us 'fools' and the chance events that befall us. At the same time, they tend to get their priorities straight.

Thus, the overvaluations I have just mentioned are usually not validated in tragic works of art. The great Athenian tragic dramas, for example, revolve around attachments that seem essentially reasonable: to one's children, city, loved ones, bodily integrity, health, freedom from pain, status as a free person rather than a slave, ability to speak and persuade others, the very friendship and company of others. The loss of any of

17 Dan Kindlon, *Too Much of a Good Thing: Raising Children of Character in an Indulgent Age* (New York: Miramax, 2001).

these is worthy of lamentation, and the tragic dramas encourage us to understand the depth of such loss and, with the protagonists, to fear it. In exercising compassion the audience is learning its own possibilities and vulnerabilities – what Aristotle called "things such as might happen" – and learning that people different in sex, race, age, and nation experience suffering in a way that is like our way, and that suffering is as crippling for them as it would be for us.

Such recognitions have their pitfalls, and I have identified some of them in talking about *The Trojan Women*. We always risk error in bringing the distant person close to us; we ignore differences of language and of cultural context, and the manifold ways in which these differences shape one's inner world. But there are dangers in any act of imagining, and we should not let these particular dangers cause us to admit defeat prematurely, surrendering before an allegedly insuperable barrier of otherness.

When I was out in the rural areas of Rajasthan, visiting an education project for girls, I asked the Indian woman who ran the project (herself an urban woman with a Ph.D.) how she would answer the frequent complaint that a foreigner can never understand the situation of a person in another nation. She thought for a while and said finally, "I have the greatest difficulty understanding my own sister."

There are barriers to understanding in any human relationship. As Proust said, any real person imposes on us a "dead weight" that our "sensitivity cannot remove." The obstacles to understanding a sister may in some instances be greater than those to understanding a stranger. At least they are different. All we can do is trust our imaginations, and then criticize them (listening if possible to the critical voices of those we are trying to understand), and then trust them again. Perhaps out of this dialectic between criticism and trust something like understanding may eventually grow. At least the product will very likely be better than the obtuseness that so generally reigns in international relations.

As Euripides knew, terror has this good thing about it: it makes us sit up and take notice. Tragic dramas can't precisely teach anything new, since they will be moving only to people who at some level already understand how bad these predicaments are. But they can awaken the sleepers by reminding them of human realities they are neglecting in their daily political lives.

The experience of terror and grief for our towers might be just that – an experience of terror and grief for our towers. One step worse, it could be a stimulus for blind rage and aggression against all the opposing hockey teams and bad umpires in the world. But if we cultivate a culture of critical compassion, such an event may, like Hecuba's Trojan cry, possibly awaken a larger sense of the humanity of suffering, a patriotism constrained by respect for human dignity and by a vivid sense of the real losses and needs of others.

And in that case, it really would turn out that Euripides was right and Hecuba was wrong: the name of the Trojan land was not wiped out. It lives, in a work of the imagination to which we can challenge ourselves, again and again.

Name Index

Abednego 334
Abel, L. 260
Abernathy, R.D. 452
Ackerman, B. 419
Adam 224
Adams, J. 240
Aditya, R.N. 587–8, 604, 612
Adler, A. 9, 167, 316
Adler, N.J. xxiii, 559, 575
Adorno 467
Agar, M. 590
Ajzen, L. 595
Aldrich, H.E. 615
Alexander the Great 170
Allen, P. 214
Althusser 467
Amos 337
Anaxagoras 222
Anderson, L. 477
Anderson, N.F. 562, 564–5, 567
Anthony 28
Antigone 231
Antony 171, 174
Aquinas, Saint Thomas 333
Aquino, B. 561, 563
Aquino, C. 516, 522, 553–4, 556–9, 561–4, 566–7, 570–72, 575
Archimedes 117, 656
Arendt, H. xvii, 197–200, 206, 210–11, 404, 408, 418
Aristotle xiii, 324, 326, 403, 418, 645, 647–8, 653, 656, 659
Armstrong, L. 480
Arnold, M. 459–64
Athena 229
Atkinson, J.W. 595
Attila 169
Augustine, Saint 68, 266, 333
Aurelius, Marcus 643, 653–6, 658
Austin, J.L. 269
Axelrod, R. 519, 521–3
Axline, S. 511

Bach 227
Badaracco, J.L. 507
Bainton, R.H. 266
Bakan, D. 507

Baker, E. 345, 480
Baldwin, J. 473
Bandaranaike, S. 553–5, 557, 561–2, 568
Baraka, A. 473
Barber, B. xxii, 418, 487, 505
Barker 194
Barnett 339
Barnevik, P. 301–2
Barrios de Chamorro, V. 554, 556–7, 561–3, 567, 572
Barry, B. 210, 212
Bartholomew, S. 552, 573
Basil The Great 266
Bass, B.M. 48, 307–8, 310, 315, 318, 321–2, 507, 592, 597, 612
Bates 173
Batson, C.D. 647, 649
Battle, K. 477
Bay, C. 421
Bayer, E. 148, 152
Baynes 136, 140
Beck, L.W. 288
Beetham, D. 504
Beethoven 227, 364, 477
Beitz, C. 203
Bell, D. 35, 76
Bellah, R.N. 50–53, 306, 321, 380–81, 506, 511
Belmont, J. 566
Benhabib, S. 211
Benjamin, W. 483
Benn, M. 562, 564, 566, 568–9
Bennis, W. 297, 302, 314, 324
Bentham, J. xvii, 184–94
Berelson, B. 418
Berger, P. 23
Bergman, I. 477
Berle 172
Berlin, I. xviii, 23, 202, 274
Best, W. 160
Beyer, J.M. 597
Bhutto, A.A. 561
Bhutto, B. 553–4, 556–9, 561–2, 564–5, 567, 569, 573
Billings, J. 511
Bishop of Caesarea *see* Basil The Great
Blake, R.R. 543–4
Blanchard 302

Blanchard, K. 40, 315
Blank, R.M. 138
Blondel, J. 553
Bohm, D. 107
Bollier, D. 302
Bond, M.H. 592, 601, 608, 630, 637–8
Bonhard, O. 135
Bord, G. 139
Borkenau, F. 149, 165
Bormann, M. 127, 158
Bourdieu, P. 478
Boutwell 332
Bowie, N. xix, xx
Boyte, H.C. 379–80, 382, 392
Brandt, R.B. 259, 268
Braverman, E.P. 594
Brecht, B. 239, 270, 411
Brief, A.P. 597
Brislin, R.W. 606
Brooks, T.R. 452
Brown, D.J. 594
Brown, L. 387–8
Brundtland, G.H. 553–4, 558, 560, 569, 571
Buber, M. 333
Bukharin 156
Bull, J. 6
Bunyan, J. 337
Burke, E. 132, 407, 416–17
Burns, J.M. xv, xix, xx, 31–2, 36, 43–53, 55, 57, 298–9, 307, 309–10, 316–18, 321, 323, 325–6, 378, 507
Burns, T. 597
Bush, G. 76, 468, 517–18
Buzzotta, V.R. 520
Byron 227

Caesar 171
Calas, M. 308–9
Califano, J.A. 451–2
Campbell, K. 554, 556–7, 559–60, 573
Camus, A. 104–5, 277–9
Cannon, J. 388, 394
Cantril, H. 12
Carawan, C. 388–9
Carawan, G. 388–9
Carlzon, J. 301–2
Carmichael, S. 382, 387
Carnap, R. 474
Carnegie, A. 512
Caro, R.A. 519
Carritt, E.F. 272
Carson, C. xx, 343, 346, 377
Carter, J. 453
Cavell, S. 475

Ceausescu 36, 426
Chafe, W.H. 345, 377
Chamberlin, W.H. 144
Chamorro *see* Barrios de Chamorro
Charles, M.E. 553–4, 557, 559, 567–8
Charlie, Mr. 390, 394
Chase, M. 655–6
Chekhov, A. 477
Chernyshevsky 235
Chevalier de Malet 139
Chiang, K. 5
Child, J. 596
Childress, J.R. 588
Childs, H.L. 144
Chodorow, N. 507–8, 524, 657
Churchill, W. 5, 60, 67
Cicero 650
Ciliga, A. 123, 157, 159
Çiller, T. 554, 556–8, 560, 566–7
Ciulla, J. xx, 296–7
Clark, C. 647–8
Clark, G. 651
Clark, R.A. 595
Clark, S. 396
Clinton, B. 63
Clinton, H.R. 573
Cobb, N. 383
Coetzee, J.M. 645, 651, 653
Col, J.-M. 564, 567
Colburn, D.R. 345
Collingwood, R. 226
Collins, J. 295
Collins, L. 436, 517
Colwill, N.L. 570
Commodus 655
Comte 128
Conason, J. 558–9
Condorcet 223–4
Confucius 77, 227
Conger, J. 318, 507
Connolly, W. 196
Connor 331–2, 341
Conrad, J. 463
Cooper, A. 473
Couto, R.A. xxi, 382, 387–8, 399
Cresson, E. 554, 556, 558, 563, 566, 569
Croce 226
Cromwell, O. 169–70
Crow, J. 379, 392
Curtiss, J.S. 138

Dabbs, J. 338
Dahl, R. 201, 212–13, 377, 488, 504
Dahlburg, J.-T. 573

Dallek, R. 451, 454
D'Alquen, G. 130, 147, 154, 163
Dana, J. 523
Daniels, J. 389
Danto, A.C. 381
Day, D.V. 594, 619
De Beauvoir, S. 495
De Gaulle, C. 5, 63, 67
De Geus, A. 108, 112
De Pizan, C. xiii
De Tocqueville, A. 127, 459, 515
Debray, R. 371
Deleuze 467
Demai, E. 131
Demaree, R.G. 607
DePree, M. 297, 302
Derrida, J. 467, 474–5
Desai 565
Dess, G.G. 611
Deutscher, I. 124, 151, 153
Devanna, M.A. 507
Dewey, J. 403, 405, 419
Dickson, M. 590, 616
Dirksen, E. 431–2
Doar, J. 394
Doig, J.W. 507
Domitien, E. 553–4, 557, 563
Donaldson, L. 594, 597, 614
Dorfman, P.W. 588–90
Douglas, B. 396
Dreifuss, R. 554, 556
Droge, C. 597
Drucker, P. 506, 513, 545
Du Bois, W.E.B. xiii, 464, 472, 480
Du Deffand 227
Dukakis 76
Dunlop, A. 295
Durant 88
Durkheim 245
Dutton, J.E. 615
Duvalier 426

Eagly, A.H. 570
Ebenstein, W. 128
Einstein 60
Eisenhower, D.D. 5, 100, 434, 442, 451
E.L. 60–65
Eliot, T.S. 341, 461–3, 477
Elizabeth I 169
Ellis, R. 450
Ellison, R. 477
Elster, J. 214
Ely, J.H. 416
Emerson 104

Enfantin 127
Engels, F. 249, 358, 360
Epictetus 652
Erikson, E. 9, 12, 244, 253, 316
Erzberger 125
Eshkol, L. 563
Estes, J. 388
Eudoxus 656
Euripides 643–5, 653, 658–9
Evans, S.M. 379–80, 382, 392
Everett, J. 565, 567, 574

Fairclough, A. 345
Fanon, F. 369, 466–7, 473
Farley, J.A. 248
Farley, M. 573
Fay, B. 381
Fayol, H. 536
Feder 136
Ferguson, I.R.G. 545
Ferguson, M. 57
Ferragamo, W. 573
Feuerbach 249
Fiedler, F. 544
Finlay, F. 564, 566–8
Finnbógadottir, V. 553–4, 558–60, 564, 569, 571
Fiori, J.L. 358
Fishbein, M. 595
Fisher, A.B. 572
Flaubert 175
Follett, M.P. 196
Ford, H. 88
Ford, J.F. 37
Forman, J. 382, 418
Forrester, J. 118
Foster, W.F. 41, 49, 52
Foucault, M. xvii, 200, 210, 467, 476
Fowlkes, M.R. 508, 524–5
Frame, D.M. 407
Franck, G. 545
Frank, H. 148
Franke, R.H. 637
Fraser, N. 206
Frederick the Great 227
Freeman, E. 322
Freire, P. xxi
Freud, S. 244–5, 250, 537, 540, 542
Friedrichs, R. 15
Fritsch, T. 138
Fromm, E. 365–6, 372, 375

Gagliardi, P. 599
Gallagher, C. 476
Gandhi 10

Gandhi, I. 5, 240, 553–4, 558–9, 561, 565, 567–8
Gandhi, M. 64, 66–7, 85, 87, 89, 91, 93, 95, 97, 99, 101, 298, 314, 323, 420, 510, 516–17
García Márquez, G. 477
Gardner, H. xvi
Gardner, J. 37, 64, 309, 321, 507
Garrow, D.J. 345, 378
Gaventa, J. 377
Geertz, C. 476
Gehry, F. 477
Genovese, E. 6
Genovese, M.A. 551, 561, 568–9, 575
Gerstner, C.R. 619
Gerth, H. 141, 262, 507, 514
Gevirtz, D. 513
Giamatti, A.B. 514
Gilbert, D. 322
Gilbert, S. 277
Giles, O.C. 147, 158
Gilligan, C. 320, 507–8, 516, 523–4
Girvetz, H. 239
Glen, J. 382
Goebbels 129, 139–40, 150, 160
Goering 157
Golden, H. 338
Goldstein, H.W. 597
Golob, E.O. 381
Goodwin, R. 455
Goodwin, W. 396
Gorbachev, M. 28, 95, 97, 516, 570
Goya 184
Graham, A.K. 120
Graham, K. 573
Gramsci 467
Gray, B. 507
Green, P. 495
Greenblatt, S. 476
Greenleaf, R.K. xvi, xix, xx, 102, 297–8, 318–19
Gregor, M.J. 288
Grube, G. 654
Gruber, H. 71
Gundemark, U. 301
Gupta, S. 564
Gupta, V. 640
Gurian, W. 136
Gutek, B. 507
Gutmann, A. 645
Gutting, G. 381
Guzzo, R.A. 597

Habermas, J. 197, 199–200, 205, 211, 413, 416
Hadamovsky, E. 123, 125, 136, 141–2, 149
Hadot, P. 655–6
Hall, S. 470, 472–3

Hamilton 450
Hamilton, C.V. 382, 387
Hamlet 269–70
Handley-Isaksen, A. 509
Hanges, P. 590, 594, 599, 603, 634, 639
Hare, R.D. 552
Hare, R.M. 259–61, 270–71
Hargrove, E.C. 507
Harold, G. 389
Hauser, M. 614
Havel, V. 69
Haynes, U. 393–4
Hays, H.R. 270
Hecuba 643–4, 648, 659
Heenan, D. 302
Hegel xxi, 224, 231, 245, 249–50, 356, 412
Heidegger, M. 474
Heiden, K. 130, 141, 144, 147, 158, 161
Heifetz, R. xxii, 313
Held, D. 504
Helvetius 188
Henderson, J. 455
Hennig, M. 524
Henry VIII 543
Heraclitus 233, 245, 656
Herder, J.G. 228–9, 235
Hersey, P. 40, 315
Herzberg, F. 537, 540, 543, 545
Herzen, A. 234–5
Hess, R. 160
Hesse, H. 102, 297, 318
Hesselbein, F. 297, 302
HH 318
Hicks, D.A. xiii, xv
Hickson, D.J. 594, 596, 614
Hill, T. xix, xx
Himmler, H. 124–5, 140, 142, 147–8, 150, 154, 157–8, 163, 165
Hinings, C.R. 594
Hipparchus 656
Hirsch, F. 409
Hirschman, A.O. 378–9
Hitler, A. 7, 11, 73, 124–6, 129–31, 135–41, 143–5, 147–9, 151–5, 158, 161, 163, 170, 233, 297–8, 309, 313–14, 317–18, 324, 334–5
Hobbes, T. 197, 245, 414, 416
Hoehn, R. 143
Hoerderer 260, 278–9
Hofstadter, R. 464
Hofstede, G. xxiii, xxiv, 532, 594–5, 601–2, 612, 619, 637–8
Honecker 426
Honig, B. 215
Horkheimer 467

House, R.J. xxiv, 587–9, 594, 597, 599, 604, 611–12, 614, 637
Howard 184
Hrabowski, A. 392
Hubenka, L.J. 411
Hulett, J. 395
Hull, C. 248
Hume, D. 325, 475, 645
Hunt, J.G. 322–3
Hurston, Z.N. 477
Hutchins, R.M. 66, 68–9, 84, 86, 88, 90, 92, 94, 96, 98, 100
Huxley, J. 244

Iacocca, L. 42, 512, 521
Izraeli, D.N. 559

Jackson, J. 55, 387, 481
Jackson, J.L. 436
Jacques 173
James, C.L.R. 473
James, L.R. 607
James, W. 416
Janeway, E. 518
Jardin, A. 524
Jefferson, T. 246, 338, 341
Jenkins, E. 389–91
Jobs, S. 512
John the Baptist 117
John XXIII (Pope) 61, 63, 68, 85, 87, 89, 91, 93, 95, 97, 99, 101
Johnson, B.T. 570
Johnson, C. 389
Johnson, F. 436
Johnson, L.B. 3–5, 243, 317, 429–45, 447–9, 451–5, 519
Johnson, S. 404
Jones 23
Jones, C. 473, 492
Joseph II 194
Jove 176
Joyce, J. 462
Julius, N.H. 194
Jung, C. 244

Kamaraj 565
Kampelman, M. 75
Kant, I. xiii, xix, xx, 236, 280, 288–9, 291–2, 294–9, 301, 303, 324, 407, 416, 650–53
Katzenbach 435
Kearns, D. 432, 437, 443
Keeley, M. 298
Kellerman, B. 322
Kemp 412

Kendall, W. 212–13
Kennedy, B. 5
Kennedy, J.F. 5, 101, 429–30, 434, 442
Kennedy, J.P. 240–43, 248
Kerr, S. 521
Khandwalla, P.N. 611
Khrushchev, N. 5, 101
Kindlon, D. 657–8
King 392
King, M.L. Jr xx, xxi, 62, 64, 66, 85, 87, 89, 91, 93, 95, 97, 99, 101, 304, 329, 342–9, 392, 397, 430, 433, 435–6, 441, 443–4, 452, 480, 516
Kissinger, H. 296
Kitto, H.D.F. 77
Kluckhohn, F.R. 594, 603, 612
Koettgen, A. 141
Kogut, B. 638
Kohlberg, L. 9, 251, 253, 298, 307, 316, 320
Kohn, I. 136
Kohn, M. 136
Kohn-Bramstedt, E. 123–4, 140
Koopman, P. 603
Kopelman, R.E. 597
Kouzes, J.M. 507
Koyré, A. 153
Kravchenko, V. 124, 133, 161
Kristeller, P. 643
Kronus 643
Kruger, B. 477
Kuhn, T.S. 310–11, 415
Kuhnert, K.W. 307
Kumaratunga, C.B. 554–6, 558, 560–61
Kurtz 463
Kymlicka, W. 501

Lamb, C. 559
Langer, L.L. 381
Langer, S. 253
Lapierre, D. 517
Larwood, L. 507
Lasswell 414
Laurent, A. 547
Lawrence, D.H. 168
Lawrence, P.R. 597
Lazerges, A. 566–7
Le Corbusier 477
Le Maire 194
Le Vaux 187
Leavitt, H.J. 509
Lee, S. 477
Lefebvre 467
Lefton, R.E. 520
Lenin 61, 129, 144, 155, 157, 169–70, 233, 235
Lennon, J. 409

Leo 102–3, 105, 297, 318
Leopardi 177
Lessing, D. 477
Lesueur, E. 139
Leung, K. 608
Lévi-Strauss 467
Lewis, A. 382
Lewis, C.J. 307
Lewis, D.L. 345
Lewis, J.L. 16–17
Liberia-Peters, M. 553–4, 558, 571
Likert, R. 543–4
Lincoln, A. 68, 167, 313, 337, 343
Lindahl, G. 301
Lipman-Blumen, J. xxiii, 508–12, 514, 518–19, 523–4
Liuzzo, V. 389
Lloyd George, D. 168
Lochmer, L. 129
Locke, J. 212, 416
Loisel, G. 187
Lombardo, M.M. 597
Lone Ranger 513
Lord, R. 594, 597, 619
Lorsch, J.W. 597
Lowell, E.L. 595
Luce, H. 463
Luckmann, T. 23
Ludendorff 148
Lukács, G. 359–60, 483
Lukes, S. 504
Lumpkin, G.T. 611
Luthans, F. 597
Luther, M. 337

MacDonald, D. 464
Machiavelli, N. xviii, xix, 73, 225–8, 235, 245, 263, 267, 274–6, 278, 296, 407, 410–11, 417, 536, 543
MacIntyre, A. 306, 380–81, 396
Macpherson, C.B. 205, 418
Maczynski 637
Madison, J. xiii, 247, 298
Madsen, R. 506
Magnuson, W. 435
Maher, K.J. 594, 597
Malcolm X 473
Malen, B. 552, 573
Malhotra, I. 567
Malinowski, B. 246
Mandela, W. 517
Mansbridge, J.J. xviii, 414
Mansfield, M. 435
Mao, T. 233, 324, 361, 549

Marcos, F. 426, 556, 558, 564, 570
Marcuse, H. 367, 467, 474
Mariategui, J.C. 480
Marsalis, W. 480
Marshall, G. 61, 68, 84, 86, 88, 90, 92, 94, 96, 98, 100
Marx, K. 206, 214, 224, 245, 249–50, 357–60, 364, 482
Maslow, A. 9, 12, 253, 316, 537, 540, 542
Maverick, M. 453
Maxwell, N. 383
McAdam, D. 348, 379–80
McCarthy, J. 100, 453–4
McClelland, D. 18, 511, 537, 540, 542, 594–5, 601–3, 637–8
McFarland, L.J. 588
McGill, R. 338
McGregor, D. 543–4
McMillan, J. 594
Mead, M. 61, 68–9, 79, 84, 86, 88, 90, 92, 94, 96, 98, 100, 464
Means 172
Meir, G. 553–4, 557, 559, 563–4, 567–8, 570
Melinda 390
Memmi, A. 369
Mendelsohn, J. 389
Mendes, C. 368
Menippus 656
Mercer, K. 471
Meredith, J. 434
Merleau-Ponty, M. 271
Meshach 334
Mill, J.S. 421
Miller 302
Miller, D. 597
Miller, J.B. 507–8, 516, 523–4
Mills, C.W. 262, 464, 507, 514
Minerva 417
Misumi, J. 630
Mitterrand, F. 566
Moloch 234
Momigliano, A. 228
Monnet, J. 65, 67, 69, 72, 75, 85, 87, 89, 91, 93, 95, 97, 99, 101
Montaigne 407
Montesquieu 417
Montrose, L. 476
Moore, G.E. 325
Moorer, M.L.H. 383, 386, 390, 395–6
Moraes, D. 565
More, T. 536, 543
Morris, A.D. 348, 379–80, 382
Morrison, T. 472, 477
Morse, W. 435

Mouton, J.S. 543-4
Muhammad, E. 336
Murray, J. 435
Mussolini, B. 170, 175-6
Myrdal, G. 253

Nadler, D.A. 597
Nagel, J.H. 209
Nagel, T. 259-60
Nanus, B. 314, 324
Napoleon 167, 169-70
Nash, C. 381
Neal, O. 391-2
Nebuchadnezzar 334
Neesse, G. 144, 149, 152
Nehru, J. 565
Neumann, F. 147
Neustadt, R. 35
Newman, W.H. 597
Newton, L. 299
Niebuhr, R. 332
Nietzsche, F. xiii, xvii, 166
Nilus, S.A. 138
Nixon, E.D. 345
Nixon, H.C. 389
Nixon, R. 5
Noblit, G.W. 552
Norell, R.J. 377, 398
Noriega 36
Norrell, R.J. 345
Nozick, R. 197, 270, 409, 416
Numa 274
Nussbaum, M.C. xxiv, 643, 647

O'Brian, J. 277
O'Brien, B. 109, 111, 118, 120
O'Connell, M.K. 619
O'Connell, M.S. 619
O'Neill, J. 271, 563
Oakeshott, M. 406
Oates, S.B. 345
Offe, C. 211
Ogawa, R.T. 552, 573
Okin, S M 494
Opfell, O.S. 556, 558-62, 565-72
Oppenheimer, J.R. 61, 63, 69, 84, 86, 88, 90, 92, 94, 96, 98, 100
Ortega 426

Pareto 245
Parker, C. 477
Parks, R. 345
Parsons, T. 244, 525
Pascal-Trouillot, E. 554, 556-8, 563, 569

Pastin, M. 306
Pateman, C. 201, 490
Paton, H.J. 288
Patterson, O. 468
Patton 28
Paul (the Apostle) 330, 337
Pavarotti, L. 477
Perón, E. 569
Perón, I. 553-4, 557, 561-3, 569
Perón, J. 561
Perrow, C. 379
Peter the Great 221
Peterson, M. 630
Pfeffer, J. 295, 507
Phillips, A. xxii
Piaget, J. 9, 244, 316
Picasso, P. 477
Pierson, C. 504
Pillay 302
Pindell, H. 477
Pinson, K.S. 136
Pintasilgo, M. de Lourdes 553-4, 558, 560, 563, 569, 571
Piranese 189
Planinc, M. 553-4, 560-61
Plato xiii, xvii, xix, 222, 229, 238-9, 407, 416, 474, 536, 645, 653
Pol Pot 233
Polsby, N. 377
Porras, J. 295
Posner, B.Z. 507
Prabhu Ahmedabad, R.K. 420
Price, T.L. xiii, xv
Price, T.S. 391
Prince, H. 322
Pritchett 341
Proust 659
Prunskiene, K.-D. 554, 556, 558, 560-61, 563, 570
Puranam, P. 614
Puryear, M. 477
Putnam, R.D. 450, 453, 603
Pynchon, T. 477
Pyrrho 656
Pythagoras 656

Rachels, J. 306
Racine 227
Raeder, E. 153
Rahman, M. 565
Rahman, Z. 561, 565
Rajak, T. 651
Rathenau 125
Rawls, J. 13, 407, 413, 416, 423

Reagan, R. 76, 468, 512, 556
Reck-Malleczewen, F.P. 129
Reeb, J.J. 436–7
Reed, R. 383
Reichheld, F. 295
Rentsch, J.R. 594
Rhodes, C. 170
Rice, E. 395
Rice, T. 387
Riesman, D. 125
Robinson, J.A. 345, 377
Robinson, M. 554, 556, 558, 560, 563–9, 571–2
Robinson, P. 381
Roddick, A. 302, 573
Roehm, E. 136, 148, 151, 158
Rohan 128
Rokeach, M. 9, 12, 252–3, 316, 325, 611–12
Rollin, H. 139
Romulus 274
Roosevelt, E. 62–3, 85, 87, 89, 91, 93, 95, 97, 99, 101
Roosevelt, F.D. 3, 10–11, 16–17, 240–43, 246, 248–9, 252, 440, 452, 512
Roosevelt, T. 512
Rorty, R. 475–6
Rosenberg 158
Rosengarten, T. 383
Rosner, J. 318
Ross, D. 272
Rost, J. xv, 306, 308–9, 311–13, 316, 320–21
Roth 412
Rousseau, J.-J. xiii, xviii, 221, 291, 414, 417–18, 645, 647–8
Rowe, E. 454
Rubenstein, F.D. 523
Ruckelshaus 450
Ruiz-Quintanilla, S.A. 590
Ruskin, J. 411
Russell, B. xvii
Russell, R. 431

Saint-Germain, M.A. 563, 567
Salamon, L.M. 387
Salter, J.R. 345
Sandelands, L.E. 615
Sartine 194
Sartre, J.-P. 231, 260, 278, 467
Saunders, B. 391–2, 395
Schattschneider, E.E. 247
Schein, E.H. 597
Schelling, T.C. 454
Schleicher 148
Schneider, B. 597
Schrag, C.O. 381

Schulke, F. 346
Schumpeter, J. 489
Schwartz, M. 383
Schwitter 594
Scott, J. 207, 380, 396–7
Seneca 227, 652, 655, 658
Senen, S. 588
Senge, P. xvi, 297
Senghor, L.S. 69
Sergiovanni, T. 321
Servan, J. 194
Shadrach 334
Shakespeare, W. 174, 269, 477
Shaw, G.B. 76
Shaw, J.B. 618
Sheehy 566
Shuttlesworth 331
Siculus, Diodorus 175
Simmel, G. 154–5, 158, 245–6, 482
Simon, E. 109, 120
Simonton, D.K. 71, 593
Simpson, E.L. 251
Singer, M.G. 293
Singer, P. 645
Singh, H. 638
Sipe, W.P. 594, 599
Sisyphus 104
Six, F.A. 125
Skinner, B.F. 420
Sloan, A. 61, 69, 84, 86, 88, 90, 92, 94, 96, 98, 100
Smircich, L. 308–9
Smith 23
Smith, A. 645–7, 649, 656
Smith, D.B. 597
Smith, L. 338
Smith, P.B. 592, 630
Smith, W.C. 594
Socrates 222–3, 331, 334–5, 656
Solomon, R. 297
Sophocles 227, 231
Sorabji, R. 651
Sorel, G. 250
Souvarine, B. 129, 141, 151–2, 156–7
Spengler 229
Spinoza 645
Spitz, E. 213
Springsteen, B. 409
Stalin 123–4, 127, 129–31, 137, 141–2, 144, 151–3, 155–7, 161, 463
Stalker, G.M. 597
Stallings 338
Stanton, E.C. xiii
Starr, M.K. 506

Stata, R. 120
Staw, B.M. 615
Steidlmeier, P. 307
Stein, A. 138
Stephen 462
Stevens, O.J. 547
Stewart, T.A. 302
Stogdill, R.M. 48, 308, 310, 315, 321–2
Strauss, L. 404
Streicher 158
Strodtbeck, F.L. 594, 603, 612
Stromberg, A. 507
Suchocka, H. 554, 556, 558, 569, 571
Sukarno 5
Sullivan, W. 306, 321, 381, 506
Suu Kyi, A.S. 554–5, 573–4
Swidler, A. 506

Takaki, R. 480
Tayeb, M.H. 630
Taylor, F.W. xxiv
Taylor, G.R. 511
Tempest, R. 573
Terry, B. 383
Thatcher, M. 66, 85, 87, 89, 91, 93, 95, 97, 99, 101, 553–4, 557–61, 567–8
Thierry, H. 603
Thomas, M.M. 480
Thompson, K.R. 597
Thompson, M. 657
Thompson, S. 561, 563, 569
Thor xvii, 177
Thoreau, H.D. xix, xx, 512
Tichy, N. 507
Tillich, P. 334
Tipton, S.M. 506
Tito 10
Tocqueville see de Tocqueville
Todorov 467
Tolstoy 173, 220–22, 237
Trevelyan, R.C. 177
Triandis, H.C. 588, 595, 609, 612, 618
Trice, H.M. 597
Trilling, L. 464–5
Trotsky 129, 134, 141–2, 151, 233
Truman, H.S. 5, 323
Tushman, M.L. 597
Tyler, P.E. 573

U Aung San 574
Ueberroth, P. 42
Uncle Tom 280–85, 287, 390, 392–3
Urmson, J.O. 269

Valéry, P. 462
Van Beethoven see Beethoven
VanderHorst, N. 511
Vann, R.R. 381
Vaughn, S. 477
Vico, G. xviii, 226–9, 235
Vieira Pinto, A. 376
Vinnicombe, S. 570
Voegelin, E. 127–8
Voltaire 227, 418
Von Hayek, F.A. 127
Von Martin, A. 141
Voznesensky, N. 124
Vroom, V. 540
Vulcan xvii, 177

Wajed, H. 565
Walesa, L. 571
Walker, D. xiii
Wallace 339
Wallace, G. 430, 433, 437, 441–3, 454
Walzer, M. xix, 197, 199, 211, 423, 494, 501
Warnock, G.J. 269
Washington, G. 304, 343, 450, 512
Washington, J.M. 348
Wayne, J. 28, 512, 587
Weber xix
Weber, J. 307
Weber, M. 141, 199, 210, 245, 254–5, 262, 275–6, 278, 482, 514, 536, 547
Weir, S.J. 557
Weisman, S.R. 564
Weizmann, C. 135
Welch, J. 296
West, C. xxii
Wheatley, M.J. 297
Whitman, J. 651
Whitten, B. 389
Wildavsky, A. 450
Wilde, O. 494
Wilderom, C. 603, 640
Wilkins, R. 431–2, 444, 454
Williams, B. 259
Williams, E. 388
Willkie, W. 241–2
Wilson 10
Wilson, W. 4
Wittgenstein, L. 475
Wolf, G. 607
Wolff, K.H. 154
Wolin, S. 197–9, 331
Wollstonecraft, M. xiii
Wonder, S. 477
Woolf, V. xiii

Wren, J.T. xiii, xv
Wright, N.S. 587
Wright, O. 109–10
Wright, W. 109–10

Yankelovich, D. 109
Yeats, W.B. 416

Young, I. 214, 492, 498–500, 505
Yukl, G. 324, 592, 597

Zeus 415, 643–4, 648
Zia 556, 564
Zia, K. 554, 556, 558, 560–62, 565, 568, 571
Zinn, H. 346